P9-AOT-262

j
An
ud
'ot
w
ls
an
Cl
rc
or
an
W.
se
a
O
a
c
c

t
v

# THE LIFE AND TIMES
## OF
# ST. AMBROSE

OXFORD
UNIVERSITY PRESS
AMEN HOUSE, E.C. 4
London  Edinburgh  Glasgow
New York Toronto Melbourne
Capetown  Bombay  Calcutta
Madras Shanghai
HUMPHREY MILFORD
PUBLISHER TO THE
UNIVERSITY

ST. AMBROSE

*From a mosaic in the Chapel of S. Satiro
in the Church of S. Ambrogio, Milan*

# THE LIFE AND TIMES
## OF
# ST. AMBROSE

BY

## F. HOMES DUDDEN, D.D.

CHAPLAIN TO THE KING
MASTER OF PEMBROKE COLLEGE, OXFORD
CANON OF GLOUCESTER
HON. FELLOW OF LINCOLN COLLEGE, OXFORD

## VOLUME I

## OXFORD
## AT THE CLARENDON PRESS
1935

UNIVERSITY OF
ALBERTA LIBRARY

BR1720
A5D84
v.1

PRINCETON
THEOLOGICAL SEMINARY
LIBRARY

H

# UXORI
## DILECTISSIMAE

1 /08 / /// /

# PREFACE

IN writing this book I have had a twofold object in view.
First, I have endeavoured to give a complete account, in the
light of the results of the latest historical research, of Ambrose's
life and work and teaching. It is surprising that this task has
not already been accomplished by an English scholar. Ambrose
was a personage of outstanding importance in the history of the
Church, and it might have been anticipated that an adequate
biography of him in the English language would long ago have
been forthcoming. But the works on the subject which have
been produced in this country are slight, superficial, and popular in character; while those more solid and scholarly mono-
graphs of foreign historians and theologians which have appeared
since the publication of Th. Förster's biography in 1884 have,
for the most part, aimed rather at elucidating particular aspects
of Ambrose's activity and thought than at providing a comprehensive study of his large and many-sided personality. In
attempting to supply this omission in recent ecclesiastical literature, I venture to hope that I have done something which may
be of service to those who are interested in the investigation of
the early developments of Western Christendom.

Secondly, it has been my aim to indicate and describe some
of the more remarkable features of the history, life, and thought
of the West in Ambrose's time, i.e. in the second half of the
fourth century. The period is one of extraordinary interest and
importance; yet, except among historical experts, very little
beyond the bare outline of its main events is generally known
about it. I have therefore thought it worth while to endeavour
to present, with some elaboration of detail, a picture of this
period, with Ambrose as its central and representative figure.

I desire to express my grateful thanks to Dom André Wilmart,
O.S.B., who with great kindness has spared time from his
learned researches to read my work in proof. I am also much
indebted to my niece, Joanna Dakin, who has given me invaluable help both in correcting the proofs and in compiling the

Index.  Finally, I must pay a thankful tribute to my wife, without whose constant patience and encouragement this book would never have been written.

F. H. D.

PEMBROKE COLLEGE, OXFORD
   *September,* 1935

# CONTENTS

## VOLUME I

## VOLUME II

# AMBROSE'S CHILDHOOD AND EDUCATION

ONE of the most important cities of the Western Empire, towards the middle of the fourth century, was the ancient Roman colony Augusta Treverorum, the modern Trier or Trèves. The poet Ausonius, in his catalogue of famous cities, has placed it sixth in order;[1] and to this high rank Trier appears to have been fairly entitled, not only on account of its size and beauty, but also as a residence of successive emperors and as the political capital of the Roman territory west of the Alps. Here Constantine frequently stayed in his earlier period, adorning the city with noble buildings, and delighting its inhabitants with the often-repeated spectacle of multitudes of captives torn limb from limb by wild beasts in the amphitheatre. From this place the sons of Constantine, and afterwards Valentinian and Gratian, dated numbers of their edicts. And here, later still, the usurper Maximus—'Trevericus imperator'[2]—held his Court.

Trier was pleasantly situated on a stretch of level ground on the right bank of the river Moselle. It was surrounded by gentle hills, the fertile slopes of which were covered with rose-gardens and vineyards, and dotted with farm-houses and luxurious villas. The city itself was rich and stately. A stranger would have gazed with admiration on the Circus—such a one as Rome herself might envy—on the Hall of Justice with its massive and extraordinarily lofty walls, on the Forum, the Baths, the spacious Amphitheatre. Especially he would have marvelled at the mighty pile of the Black Gate—that stupendous structure of un-cemented blocks of sandstone, with its two entrances, its flanks four stories high, and its decorative rows of Tuscan columns. Though not far distant from the frontier, the city was protected against barbarian attack by strong fortifications and an ample garrison, and its cheerful and prosperous inhabitants pursued their business and amusements undisturbed by war's alarms. Evil days, indeed, were coming when Trier was to be delivered up repeatedly to fire and sword; but in the middle of the fourth

---

[1] Ausonius, *Clarae Urbes*, iv.
[2] Gregor. Turon. *Mirac.* ii. 4; *Vitae Patrum*, 2. 1.

century the pervading atmosphere was one of secure tranquillity
and careless gaiety. Still—so the poet fancied—the grey-eyed
naiads sported in the pellucid waters of the Moselle, and wanton
fauns chased mountain-nymphs over the vine-clad hills.[1]

In this metropolis of the further West Ambrose was born—
probably about the beginning of the year A.D. 339.[2] He belonged to a distinguished Roman family,[3] which had given
consuls and praefects to the Empire, and at least one martyr—
a virgin named Soteris—to the Church.[4] His father, Aurelius
Ambrosius, had attained the highest rank in the civil hierarchy,
and at the time of his son's birth held the great and 'illustrious'
office of Praetorian Praefect of the Gauls.[5] From his palace at
Trier he administered a region roughly equivalent to the modern
countries of France, Spain, Portugal, part of Germany, and
Britain, together with the islands of Sardinia, Corsica, and
Sicily. Throughout this enormous area he acted as the representative of the sovereign—promulgating the imperial laws,
levying the imperial taxes, supervising and exercising discipline

[1] Auson. *Mosella*, 169–88.

[2] The date depends mainly on the interpretation of a passage in a letter written
by Ambrose to Severus, Bishop of Naples, in which he mentions that he is in his
fifty-fourth year, and refers to the disturbed condition of affairs in his neighbourhood; 'we, exposed to the outbreaks of barbarians (*barbaricis motibus*) and the
storms of war, are being tossed on a sea of troubles' (*Ep*. 59. 3). If the allusion is
to the invasion of Italy by Maximus in A.D. 387, Ambrose must have been born
in A.D. 334 (or possibly 333); if, on the other hand, the occupation of Italy by
Eugenius in A.D. 393 is referred to, the birth must be dated A.D. 340. But the arguments adduced in support of each of these two theories are by no means convincing,
and I am disposed to accept the conclusion of Jean-Rémy Palanque, who holds that
the passage in *Ep*. 59 refers to a barbarian outbreak in the spring of A.D. 392, which
caused great alarm in Milan (see below, chapter xvii, p. 415), and who accordingly
places Ambrose's birth in the beginning of A.D. 339. (*Saint Ambroise et l'Empire
Romain*, pp. 480–2, 542, 543.)

[3] The family may have been of Hellenic extraction (as is suggested by the names
Ambrose, Uranius Satyrus, Soteris); but, if it originally came to Italy from the
East, it had almost certainly been Roman for many generations. The name
Aurelius Ambrosius implies a connexion with the Aurelii. Certainly there appears
to have been a connexion between Ambrose's family and that of Quintus Aurelius
Symmachus, the orator. Ambrose refers to L. Avianius Symmachus, father of the
orator, as 'parens' of his brother Satyrus (*De Excessu Satyri*, i. 32); while Q. Aurelius
Symmachus, writing to his brother Celsinus Titianus, speaks of the same Satyrus as
'frater communis' (*Epp*. i. 63). Ambrose himself is most probably the person
addressed by Symmachus, *Epp*. iii. 30–7.

[4] Ambros. *Exhortatio Virginitatis*, 82; *De Virginibus*, iii. 38.

[5] Paulinus, *Vita Sancti Ambrosii*, 3. Nothing is known about the elder Ambrose
beyond what is here recorded. His praefecture may be placed between the dates
September A.D. 337 and April A.D. 340 (J.-R. Palanque, op. cit., p. 4).

over the provincial governors, hearing appeals from the lower courts, and providing for the upkeep of the great roads and the efficiency of the postal service. Military matters—apart from the supply of pay, food, and equipment for the troops—were outside of his jurisdiction; yet so exalted was his rank that even the chiefs of the army were accustomed respectfully to kneel in his presence.

There were already two children in the Praetorian Praefect's family. The elder was Marcellina, a girl of unusual force of character, who early developed an inclination for the life of religious asceticism.[1] The younger was a boy, Uranius Satyrus.[2] He seems to have been constitutionally delicate, and, as is often the case with persons in feeble health, was excessively shy and reserved. Between him and Ambrose there sprang up later on a fraternal affection of extraordinary warmth and intensity.

Of the early life of Ambrose very little is known. A single anecdote is recorded of his infancy. One day, when he was sleeping in his cradle in the open court of the Praefect's house, a swarm of bees alighted suddenly on his face, and began to crawl in and out of his mouth. The nurse, in alarm, would have driven the insects away; but the father, who fortunately chanced to be at hand, forbade her to disturb them—'waiting', says the biographer, 'to see what would be the end of the marvel.' After a while the swarm, with no harm done, took flight, and the Praefect, drawing a breath of relief, exclaimed, 'If that child lives, he will be something great.'[3]

When next we hear of Ambrose, the Praetorian Praefect is dead, and his widow and family have left the city on the Moselle and settled down in Rome.[4] Here, on the Festival of the Epiphany, 6th of January A.D. 353,[5] Marcellina solemnly dedicated herself to a life of virginity and received the veil from the hands of Pope Liberius. The ceremony took place in the Basilica of St. Peter and was witnessed by a great congregation. Though

[1] L. Biraghi, *Vie de la vierge romaine-milanaise sainte Marcelline, sœur de saint Ambroise* (tr. A. Corail), Toulouse, 1867.

[2] On Satyrus—younger than Marcellina, but older than Ambrose (Ambros. *De Excessu Sat.* i. 54)—see below, chapter vii.

[3] Paulinus, *Vita Ambros.* 3. For parallels to the story of the bees, see H. Delehaye, *The Legends of the Saints*, p. 34.

[4] Paulinus, *Vita Ambros.* 4. The name of Ambrose's mother is nowhere recorded.

[5] On the date see M. Ihm, *Studia Ambrosiana*, p. 54; J.-R. Palanque, op. cit., p. 483.

the bishops of Rome were not accustomed at this period to
preach publicly in the church,[1] Liberius, to show his sense of the
importance of the occasion, delivered a short address.[2]

Since convents of virgins were as yet unknown in Rome,
Marcellina, after her profession, continued to reside in her
mother's house.[3] The two ladies, together with another consecrated virgin, who lived with them, devoted themselves with
ardour to the practice of the ascetic life. They were among the
earliest members of that famous group of patrician women, who,
disgusted by the follies and vices of contemporary society, withdrew into seclusion, turned their houses into hermitages, and
gave themselves up to study, devotional exercises, and good
works.[4] Such a home, perhaps, hardly provided the ideal atmosphere for the nurture of a spirited lad. Yet Ambrose, though
reared in the company of priests and holy women, was neither
effeminate nor priggish. He was fond of playing boyish pranks.
He had observed, for example, that the ladies of his family were
accustomed to kiss the hands of the Pope and other high
ecclesiastics who came to visit them. He amused himself with
mimicking the gestures of the great churchmen, offering his own
hand for the salute, and laughingly exclaiming, when he met
with a refusal, 'You ought to do the same to me, for I am going
to be a bishop.'[5]

Meanwhile his schooling had begun. At this time a very high
value was attached to a liberal education. Innumerable elementary schools were scattered throughout the Empire, and in almost all the important cities there were academies for the
instruction of more advanced students. The emperors, partly
for political reasons and partly out of genuine enthusiasm for
learning, took a deep interest in the schools. Not only did they
spend money generously for the extension of higher education;
they further sought in various ways to improve the existing

[1] Sozomen. *H. E.* vii. 19.
[2] Summarized by Ambrose, *De Virginibus*, iii. 1–14.
[3] A tradition (to which, however, no importance can be attached) locates this
house near the Tiber and the Theatre of Marcellus, on the site of the convent of
Sant' Ambrogio della Massima.
[4] Specially prominent among these were Lea, Paula, and Marcella: see the
memoirs of them written by Jerome, *Epp.* 23, 108, and 127.
[5] Paulinus, *Vita Ambros.* 4; cf. ibid. 9. Ambrose alludes to an incident of his
boyhood, *In ps. 40 enarr.* 24. One of his friends at this early period is known to us
by name—Priscus (Ambros. *Epp.* 86, 88).

system, legislating with the twofold aim of promoting efficiency in the teachers and of regulating the studies of the scholars. The old Roman nobility also were enthusiastic admirers of literary culture and co-operated heartily with the emperors in their educational efforts.

Ambrose received the usual education of a Roman gentleman of the period.[1] This was divided into three main parts. First came the training in the elementary school, secondly that in the school of the grammaticus, and finally that in the school of the rhetor.

(i) When he was about seven years of age,[2] the boy was emancipated from the authority of his Greek nurse, and placed under the care of a *paedagogus*.[3] Escorted by his governor, he attended an elementary school, and was there initiated into the traditional routine—'those first irksome lessons in reading, writing and arithmetic', 'the odious sing-song of "One and one are two" ',[4] the moral maxims copied out and got by heart,[5] the recitation after the master of passages from the poets[6] with proper attention to accentuation and expression,[7] and, most trying of all, the rudiments of Greek,[8] in which tongue persons of culture were expected to be proficient. Very early in the morning he would wend his way to the school-room—generally a sort of verandah, shut off from the street by heavy curtains[9]— where, with an interval for breakfast, he spent some six hours of the day.[10] The time dragged heavily enough. The dingy chamber with its wall-maps[11] and dusty busts of poets—the writing-tablets, calculating-boards, and other paraphernalia—the little scholars wriggling on the hard wooden benches or standing in a group round the surly old man who occupied the master's chair[12] —all these details composed a scene which few young Romans found attractive. To sensitive children, indeed, owing to the

---

[1] Paulinus, *Vita Ambros.* 5 'edoctus liberalibus disciplinis'.

[2] Ambros. *Ep.* 44. 13. Cf. Boethius, *De Discipl. Schol.* i. pr. 'septennis infantia ducitur ad imbuendum'. But Paulinus of Pella began his education at five (*Eucharist.* 72), and Ausonius took charge of children 'lactantibus annis' (*Ad. Nep. Auson. Protrepticon*, 67). [3] Ambros. *Hexaemeron*, vi. 38.

[4] Augustin. *Confess.* i. 13. [5] Hieron. *Ep.* 107. 8. [6] Macrobius, *Sat.* i. 24. 5.

[7] Ausonius, *Protrept.* 47–50; Augustin. *De Ordine*, ii. 40.

[8] Augustin. *Confess.* i. 13, 14; Auson. *Profess.* viii. 14–17.

[9] Augustin. *Confess.* i. 13. [10] Auson. *Ep.* xviii. 10.

[11] Eumenius, *Pro Instaur. Scholis Orat.* 20.

[12] Prudentius, *Peristephanon*, ix. 21–2.

truculent methods commonly adopted by the teachers, school must have been a veritable purgatory. For, in spite of the contention of a few educational authorities that it was better to encourage the young with praise and prizes than to coerce them with stripes,[1] the Romans in general favoured the view that it was not possible to instil knowledge into youthful minds without liberal use of the rod. Hence the masters took care to arm themselves with various kinds of corrective instruments, and the hissing strokes of the cane or birch and the shrill cries of the child victims were the invariable accompaniments of the labours of the class-room.[2]

(ii) From the elementary school Ambrose passed in due time to the school of the grammarian. The term 'grammar' here denotes the critical study of the principal masterpieces—more especially the poetical masterpieces—of Greek and Latin literature.[3] The grammarians lectured on the poets, and more occasionally on the orators—history seems as a general rule to have been dealt with only incidentally[4]—in very much the same manner as our own University professors used to lecture before the new methods were introduced. They analysed the construction of sentences, emended the text, gave outlines of the subject-matter, criticized the style and diction, expounded mythological and historical allusions, and discoursed at large, and sometimes very profoundly, on any points of interest which

[1] Hieron. *Epp.* 107. 4; 128. 1; compare Salvian, *De Gubern. Dei* (ed. C. Halm), vi. 92.

[2] Auson. *Protrept.* 24–34; Augustin. *Confess.* i. 9; *De Civ. Dei*, xxii. 22; *De Discipl. Christ.* 12; Prudent. *Cathem.* Praef. 7, 8 'aetas prima crepantibus flevit sub ferulis'. The phrase 'manum ferulae subducere' was used as a synonym for attending school (Hieron. *Contra Rufin.* i. 17; *Ep.* 57. 12).

[3] 'Ars grammatica praecipue consistit in intellectu poetarum' (Sergius, iv, p. 486, ed. Keil). The usual custom was to begin with the Greek poets and proceed to the Latin; first Homer, afterwards Virgil (Auson. *Protrept.* 45 ff.; Paulinus of Pella, *Eucharist.* 72 ff.; Hieron. *Ep.* 107. 9; the same rule is indicated in Petronius, *Sat.* 5). But though Homer was read first, deeper impression was made by Virgil: see Augustin. *De Civ. Dei.* i. 3. At this period and through the Middle Ages, the *Aeneid* was by far the most popular school-book.

[4] Ausonius, indeed, prescribes for his grandson certain periods of Roman history (*Protrept.* 61–5), and mentions 'history' among the accomplishments of the professors of Bordeaux (*Profess.* xx. 8; xxi. 26; xxvi. 3); and Augustine writes 'huic disciplinae [sc. grammaticae] accessit historia, non tam ipsis historicis quam grammaticis laboriosa' (*De Ordine*, ii. 37). Yet history—if it be distinguished from the mythology—appears to have been a subordinate subject. Ambrose in his writings seldom alludes to Roman history; see, however, *In ps. 45 enarr.* 21; *De Officiis*, iii. 91; *Ep.* 18. 7 and 35.

might crop up in connexion with the book which they were interpreting. All this implied considerable erudition; and the grammarians were frequently men of encyclopaedic learning,[1] gifted, moreover, with extraordinary powers of memory.[2] Some of them were specialists. Ausonius has left an amusing little poem addressed to an assistant teacher of Bordeaux, who specialized exclusively in antiquarian research. This Victorius buried himself in long-forgotten books and never read anything that was not obscure. In the ancient pontifical lore, or in the enactments of prehistoric kings and legislators, he was profoundly learned; but in anything so modern as the speeches of Cicero or the poetry of Virgil he disdained to interest himself.[3]

It was in the school of the grammarian that Ambrose laid the foundations of that knowledge of classical literature, without which no fourth-century gentleman was considered complete. Which authors were read by him at this stage of his career it is, of course, impossible to determine. In his writings, however, we are afforded indications of the extent of his later acquaintance with the classics. His favourites were undoubtedly Virgil, Cicero, and Sallust. With Virgil, the idol of all literary people of the period, he was most thoroughly familiar, though he never refers to the poet by name and only three times quotes him literally;[4] he had also extensive and intimate knowledge of the works of Cicero.[5] Sallust—a popular author in the schools of the fourth century on account of his moral reflections and the crisp brevity

[1] Auson. *Profess.* xx. 9, 10.

[2] Auson. *Profess.* i. 21–30; xv. 13; xxii. 1; *Parent.* iii. 18. The *Cento Nuptialis* of this poet is proof of his own remarkable memory. Some of his sets of verses (e.g. (*De xii Caesaribus*, and many in his *Eclogarium*) appear to have been composed with the object of assisting the memory of the young student.

[3] Auson. *Profess.* xxii.

[4] M. Ihm, *Stud. Ambros.* pp. 83–94. Ambrose literally quotes Virgil only in three passages (*De Abraham*, i. 82, ii. 4; *In ps. 43 enarr.* 17); generally he paraphrases the words of the poet, abandoning the metrical form and interpolating expressions of his own. Yet his constant allusions to Virgil are easily recognizable.

[5] Apart from the *De Officiis*, which he closely imitated, Ambrose appears to have been acquainted with the following works of Cicero: *De Republica, De Finibus, De Natura Deorum, Academica, Tusculan Disputations, De Oratore, De Amicitia, De Senectute* ; the orations *Pro S. Roscio Amerino, In Verrem, Pro Caecina, Pro Murena, Pro Archia, Pro Sestio, In L. Pisonem, Pro Caelio, Pro Plancio, Pro Milone* ; *Epistolae ad Fam.* and *ad Quintum Fratrem* ; and the Ciceronian translations of Plato's *Timaeus* and Xenophon's *Oeconomicus*. For refs. see the Prefaces and Indices in the Vienna edition of Ambrose's Works, also M. Ihm, op. cit., p. 82.

of his style—he had evidently studied with some care.[1] He had
certainly read the *Prata* of Suetonius and probably the *De
Clementia* of Seneca;[2] and he seems in one place to be imitating
the *Epithalamium* of Gallienus (preserved by Trebellius Pollio).[3]
The occurrence in his writings of certain expressions and allusions may imply acquaintance with the works (or some of them)
of Plautus, Terence, Horace, Ovid, Lucan, Livy, Tacitus, Quintilian, and Valerius Maximus;[4] on the other hand, such seeming
imitations or reminiscences may have been originally derived,
not from perusal of the works in question, but from the lecture-
notes of the grammarians or from phrase-books compiled for the
use of students of rhetoric.[5] Of the Greek classics Ambrose knew
Homer[6] (whose popularity in the schools was second only to
that of Virgil), Plato[7] (the one philosopher still seriously studied
in the West), and parts at least of Xenophon.[8] Once in his own
writings he quotes Sophocles, and once Euripides; but these
quotations he apparently borrowed from Philo.[9]

The schools of pagan literature had a deep-reaching influence.
They affected not merely the literary style of those who were
bred in them, but also their feeling and habit of thought. The
Church realized the danger, and tried to counteract it. Efforts
were even made to produce a Christian literature which might
serve as a substitute for the classics. But the pagan works of
genius continued to attract both young and old with irresistible
fascination. Even Jerome, who heard in a dream a voice reproaching him with being 'a Ciceronian, not a Christian',[10] and

---

[1] M. Ihm, op. cit., pp. 64–6.

[2] K. Schenkl, *C.S.E.L.* xxxii, Ambrosii Opp. part i, Praef. xvi, xvii (on Suetonius):
as regards Seneca, cf. Ambros. *Hexaem.* v. 67, 68 with Seneca, *De Clementia*, i. 19. 2.

[3] M. Ihm, op. cit., p. 83.

[4] See for refs. the Prefaces and Indices in the Vienna edition of Ambrose, also
M. Ihm, op. cit., p. 82.

[5] Such compilations as that published later by Arusianus Messius (Ambros.
*De Fuga*, 16) with the title *Quadriga, vel exempla elocutionum ex Virgilio, Sallustio,
Terentio, Cicerone digesta per litteras*, and dedicated to the brothers Olybrius and
Probinus (coss. A.D. 395).

[6] Ambrose occasionally quotes Homer (*De Abraham*, ii. 68; *De Noe*, 4, 57; *De
Poenitentia*, ii. 32), and elsewhere shows that he has his poems in mind (e.g. *De
Fide*, iii. 4; *Expos. ev. Luc.* iv. 2, vii. 15; *De Tobia*, 16; *De Excessu Sat.* ii. 127; *In ps.
43 enarr.* 78; *De Noe*, 31).                              [7] See below, p. 13, n. 6.

[8] Ambros. *Hexaem.* v. 30, vi. 58, 72; *Expos. ev. Luc.* i. 43; *De Noe*, 24 (cf. K. Schenkl,
*C.S.E.L.* xxxii, Ambrosii Opp. part i, Praef. xv); *De Abraham*, i. 2; *De Elia*, 59.

[9] Ambros. *Ep.* 37. 28; *De Abraham*, i. 91; cf. M. Ihm, op. cit., p. 80.

[10] Hieron. *Ep.* 22. 30.

who permitted himself to exclaim, 'What has Horace to do with the Psalter, or Virgil with the Gospel, or Cicero with the Apostle?'[1]—even Jerome, though for conscience' sake he gave up the classics for fifteen years,[2] could not bring himself to abandon them permanently, and actually defended the use of profane literature in a celebrated letter to the Roman rhetorician Magnus.[3]

Ambrose himself in later years took a liberal view of the value of this literary education. Though he allowed himself to speak slightingly of both rhetoric and dialectic, he never uttered a single word in disparagement of 'grammar'. Nor did he scruple to introduce classical allusions into his writings. The Arians, indeed, accused him of levity on account of his use of pagan myths for purposes of illustration. But he defended himself on the plea that figures of poetic invention were to be found even in the Bible, and that, if an apostle might quote Aratus, it could hardly be wrong for a bishop to make references to Homer or Virgil.[4]

(iii) At the age of fourteen or fifteen Ambrose quitted the school of the grammarian and entered that of the rhetor. The training to which he was here subjected consisted partly of instruction in the theory of oratory and oratorical composition, and partly of exercises in the practical application of the rules laid down. The rhetoricians lectured on the text-books— especially those of Cicero and Quintilian—and on the best oratorical models.[5] The pupils, on their side, were practised first in writing exercises on given themes with special attention to arrangement and style, and afterwards in declamation. Of these scholastic declamations there were two kinds—*suasoriae* and *controversiae*. The former, which were easier inasmuch as they did not demand technical knowledge, were deliberative speeches of legendary or historical characters in crucial situations. The latter, which were reserved for more advanced pupils, were legal arguments in supposed civil or criminal trials. The students prepared their declamations with care, sometimes

---

[1] Hieron. *Ep.* 22. 29.      [2] Id. *Comm. in Gal.* iii, Praef.      [3] Id. *Ep.* 70.

[4] Ambros. *De Fide*, iii. 3, 4; cf. *Expos. ev. Luc.* vi. 108. He held that though the ancient fables lacked the note of 'seriousness', they often 'with poetic wit' enforced sound moral lessons, *De Virginitate*, 116.

[5] Hieron. *Comm. in Gal.* iii. Praef. 'si quis eloquentiam quaerit vel declamationibus delectatur, habet in utraque lingua Demosthenem et Tullium, Polemonem et Quintilianum'.

C

attending the law courts meanwhile with a view to picking up useful hints.[1] When their speeches were ready, they recited them, not without trepidation, in the presence of the teacher and class, who criticized the performance.[2]

In the fourth century rhetoric dominated education, just as logic did in the Middle Ages, and literature during the Renaissance. All other studies were more or less valued in proportion as they contributed to the production of an accomplished orator. The reasons for this are plain enough. Rhetoric was at this time the avenue to wealth and power. In the Imperial Civil Service there were innumerable lucrative posts which might be obtained by clever speakers; indeed there was literally no position of dignity to which an able man with a facile tongue might not aspire.[3] Moreover, rhetoric appealed to the depraved taste of the period. The pompous diction, the artificial flowers of speech, the contorted mannerisms—all the flash and flourish of contemporary declamation[4]—were naturally applauded by an age which delighted in freakish monuments interesting only for their size or for the value and rarity of their material, in dresses strangely spangled with sacred emblems and shapes of animals, in poems composed entirely of fragments of Virgil or consisting of lines of different lengths so arranged as to represent figures—in short, in everything that was pretentious and extravagant and bizarre.

---

[1] Hieron. *Comm. in Gal.* i. 2, 11; cf. Augustin. *Confess.* vi. 9.

[2] Hieron. *Apol. adv. Rufin.* i. 30. A good performance was applauded (Augustin. *Confess.* i. 17); if a blunder were made, the hearers uttered a shout of correction (Hieron. *Ep.* 66. 9).

[3] Palladius, a Greek rhetorician and friend of Symmachus, became Master of the Offices; Ausonius, rhetorician of Bordeaux, rose to be Praetorian Praefect of Gaul and Consul; the rhetorician Eugenius was made Emperor. There was some ground for the boast of Ennodius; 'qui nostris servit studiis mox imperat orbi.'

[4] The characteristic faults of Latin rhetoric at this period are well illustrated by the 'rich and florid luxuriance' (Macrobius, *Sat.* v. 1. 7) of Symmachus, by the tasteless and perverse ingenuity of Pacatus, and by the fantastic extravagance of Ausonius' *Thanksgiving for the Consulship*. The style of the rhetoricians is excessively elaborated, the prose often degenerating into a kind of poetry; fanciful images and unusual turns of phrase abound; in the effort after originality and distinction the sentences are not infrequently so tortured as to be scarcely intelligible. At this time the Gallican school of rhetoric was in great renown (Auson. *Mosell.* 383; Hieron. *Contra Vigilant.* 1; *Ep.* 125. 6), and furnished professors to Rome and Constantinople (Auson. *Profess.* i. 3–10; *Parent.* iii. 15, 16). Symmachus himself was trained by a Gallican professor (Symm. *Epp.* ix. 88). Rhetoric also flourished in Africa, especially at Carthage.

It is easy to indicate the defects of this rhetorical education. The habit of declaiming on trivial, unreal, or hackneyed themes was fatal to simplicity, sincerity, and good style. The speaker could not hope to attract attention by his matter: his success depended entirely on the manner in which he presented it. To keep his hearers awake, he was obliged to stuff his speech with startling epigrams, smart antitheses, and quaint conceits. Sense was sacrificed to sound, force to brilliance, and the art of saying true things to the art of making the false appear to be the true.[1]

Yet it must not be forgotten that the great Christian orators of this age of magnificent preachers were educated in the schools of rhetoric, and several of them were themselves at one time teachers of the art. These men, as a rule, did not hesitate to admit that they had benefited by the training. They were divided, however, on the question of the extent to which rhetoric might legitimately be employed in Church instruction. Some, like Augustine, thought it no harm that a minister of the Gospel should have a cultivated style.[2] Others, like Jerome, regarded rhetoric as detrimental.[3] Ambrose, in his maturity, was disposed to take the hostile side. He condemned the 'vain persons' who parade their eloquence amid roars of applause: how infinitely superior is 'the apostolic man who, holding fast the true faith, does not seek after ornamental diction and brilliant arguments and decorative periods for expressing his ideas'.[4] 'Away with the finery and paint of words, which weaken the force of what is said!'[5] A Christian teacher ought to place himself on the level of his audience, and, however learned or eloquent he may be, should make a point of using simple, plain, and familiar speech.[6]

(iv) While the ordinary course of Roman education was thus divided into three main parts—the elements, literature, and rhetoric[7]—there were also certain supplementary studies on which a boy of ability might bestow attention. For example, a

---

[1] Prudentius, *Cathem.* Praef. 8, 9 'Mox docuit toga (i.e. the school of rhetoric) infectum vitiis falsa loqui'.

[2] Augustin. *De Doctr. Christ.* iv. 3.

[3] Hieron. *Dial. contr. Lucifer.* 11; *Comm. in Jonam*, c. 3; *Comm. in Gal.* iii, Praef. Elsewhere, however, Jerome recognized that eloquence and learning might be useful, *Epp.* 52. 9; 53. 3; 58. 11.

[4] Ambros. *Expos. ev. Luc.* vii. 218; viii. 13. Cf. Paulinus, *Vita. Ambros.* 7.

[5] Ambros. *Expos. ev. Luc.* viii. 70.

[6] Id. *De Isaac*, 57. Cf. *Expos. ev. Luc.* ii. 42 'negligere verba debemus, spectare mysteria'.  [7] Apuleius, *Flor.* iv. 20

course in mathematics was sometimes taken by a pupil before
entering the school of rhetoric.  Again, a course in philosophy
was frequently included in the training received in the rhetoric
school.  Finally, towards the end of his educational career, a
youth who proposed to take the law as his profession received
special instruction in the technicalities of jurisprudence.

(a) The mathematical course comprised the study of the
theory of numbers (as opposed to the practical art of calculation), geometry, traditional astronomy, and mathematical geo-
graphy.  Whether Ambrose, as a boy, engaged in these studies
we do not know; certainly, as a man, he had a very poor opinion
of them.

'We ought not to occupy the mind with unnecessary, involved
or doubtful matters.  But what is so full of obscurity as to discuss
the questions of astronomy and geometry, to measure the depths
of space, to shut up the heavens and the sea within the limits of
numbers, to neglect the things which bring salvation and follow
after errors?'[1]

'We do not discuss with futile care the cubes of geometry, or the
tetrad of philosophy—which, they say, is the oath of the Pythagoreans
—or the ever-virgin numbers of the hebdomad; nor do we draw
with our measuring-rod a diagram of the world, or investigate the
heaven described in a figure on sand, or shut up the universe within
the narrow bounds of our calculating-tables; but we open the true
mysteries.'[2]

'Why should I inquire what is the measure of the circumference
of the earth, which the geometricians have estimated at 22,000 miles?
It is better to know the characteristics of the different lands than their
extent.  For how is it possible for us to ascertain the extent, or make
due allowance in our calculations for the sea and the regions inhabited by barbarians and the tracts of submerged and marshy
territory where no foot of man has ever trod?  Moses in the Holy
Scriptures described the things which bear on our eternal hope.
But he did not think it his duty to tell us how much of the air is
occupied by the shadow of the earth when the sun leaves us at the
close of day to illuminate the lower parts of the heavens, or how the
moon is eclipsed when it passes into the region of the earth's shadow.
These matters do not concern us.'[3]

(b) As regards philosophy, the teaching consisted chiefly of

[1] Ambros. De Officiis, i. 122.              [2] Id. De Abraham, ii. 80.
[3] Id. Hexaem. vi. 7, 8: cf. Hexaem. i. 22; vi. 67; Expos. ps. cxviii. 12, 20; De
Excessu Sat. ii. 86.

instruction in dialectic, the art of reasoning correctly.[1]  In addition to this the professors interpreted to their pupils (though in a scrappy and superficial manner) the characteristic doctrines of the various philosophical sects, and further imparted to them a certain amount of miscellaneous information concerning natural phenomena.  The course thus comprised the study of logic, of the chief philosophical systems, and of 'natural science'.

In the West, however—although there was a Faculty of Philosophy in the Roman University—this branch of learning was generally neglected.  The genius of the Romans did not take kindly to a subject which—apart from the logical discipline which it offered to budding rhetoricians—did not appear to be of obvious utility.  Business men despised it.[2]  Statesmen suspected it of fostering revolutionary ideas.  The Christian leaders regarded it with severe disfavour.[3]  Thus the number of the students continually declined.  'The philosophers sit desolate in their schools.  They who dispute with such fluency are daily forsaken by their fellows.  Not philosophers but fishermen, not logicians but tax-gatherers, now find credence.'[4]  'How few there are who now read Aristotle!  How few who know the books, or even the name, of Plato!  Here and there, in retired corners, old men who have nothing better to do, recall them to mind.  But our rustics and fishermen are the talk of all, and the whole world echoes with their words.'[5]

Ambrose may have taken the course in philosophy.  He had certainly read a considerable amount of Plato,[6] who was the

---

[1] Jerome mentions some of the text-books used by the logicians, *Ep.* 50. 1; cf. Augustin. *Confess.* iv. 16.

[2] Petron. *Sat.* 71: 'He began in a small way, and left thirty millions, and never listened to a philosopher' (Trimalchio's epitaph).

[3] See, for instance, Tertullian, *De Praescr. Haer.* 7 (a famous passage beginning, 'What has Athens to do with Jerusalem?'); Hieron. *Comm. in Tit.* iii. 9; *Adv. Helv.* 2; *Dial. contr. Lucifer.* 11. A more benign view was taken by Augustine, *De Doctr. Christ.* ii. 60 (cf. ibid. ii. 28, 48, 53, 55).

[4] Ambros. *De Fide*, i. 84.     [5] Hieron. *Comm. in Gal.* iii, Praef.

[6] Ambrose appears to be acquainted with the following works of Plato: Republic (*De Officiis*, i. 43; *De Abraham*, i. 2; *De Paradiso*, 14; *De Bono Mortis*, 45), Symposium (*De Bono Mortis*, 19, 21; *De Isaac*, 78; *De Fuga*, 51), Phaedrus (*De Abraham*, ii. 54; *De Isaac*, 65–7; *De Virginitate*, 111), Gorgias (*De Excessu Sat.* ii. 35; *Expos. ps. cxviii*, 18. 3), Timaeus (*Hexaem.* iii. 13; *De Abraham*, ii. 54), Phaedo (*De Bono Mortis*, 31, 42, 51), Apology (*Expos. ps. cxviii*, 16. 11; *De Excessu Sat.* i. 72), Meno (*Expos. ps. cxviii*, 18. 4), Laws (*Ep.* 34. 1). He further seems to have attempted a confutation of some of Plato's opinions in a lost work *De Sacramento Regenerationis sive de Philosophia* (see below, chapter xxii).

favourite philosopher at this epoch;[1] but his references to this author suggest that his reading had been hasty and unthorough. He seems further to have made himself acquainted with certain of the writings of Epicurus[2] and the Epicurean teachers Hermarchus and Philodemus,[3] and with the work of the Athenian philosopher Secundus in reply to various philosophical questions raised by the Emperor Hadrian.[4] He exhibits some general knowledge of the teachings of Aristotle,[5] though whether he had read any of the books of Aristotle must be considered doubtful. Most of his (obviously limited) information on the doctrines of the various philosophical schools was unquestionably derived from Cicero. In addition, he appears to have made use of some unknown philosophical manual or compendium.[6]

Ambrose's view of these studies was in the main unfavourable. He had a rooted dislike of dialectic, which he regarded, unfairly enough, as essentially destructive in character. 'Philosophers are agreed that dialectical disputation has no power to establish anything, but aims only at destruction. It was not by dialectic that it pleased God to save His people.'[7] 'The glory of the dialecticians is to appear to refute the truth with words.'[8] Both pagans and heretics had 'dyed their impiety in the vats of philosophy'.[9] The Arians, in particular, had 'left the Apostle to follow Aristotle'.[10] 'Away with arguments, where faith is required; let

---

[1] Called by Ambrose the 'prince of philosophers' and 'father of philosophy' (*De Abraham*, i. 2; ii. 37; cf. *Ep.* 34. 1 'patricia prosapia Platonis'). Augustine reverenced Plato (*De Civitate Dei*, viii. 4 ff.). Some of the Bordeaux professors were renowned for their knowledge of 'dogma Platonicum' (Auson. *Profess.* xxvi. 5).

[2] K. Schenkl, *C.S.E.L.* xxxii, Ambrosii Opp. part i, Praef. xxxii, xxxiii.

[3] Ambros. *Ep.* 63. 13, 19.        [4] K. Schenkl, loc. cit., Praef. xv, xxv.

[5] Ambros. *De Officiis*, i. 48, 50; ii. 4; *Ep.* 34. 1; *Hexaem.* i. 1, 3; *De Noe*, 92; *De Abraham*, ii. 70; *Expos. ps. cxviii*, 11. 19.

[6] This was probably the source of Ambrose's remarks on the various opinions of philosophers concerning the essence or quality of the soul (*De Noe*, 92: cf. Tertullian, *De anima*, 5; Macrob. *Comm. in Somn. Scip.* i. 14. 19 and 20), on the two parts of the soul (*De Abraham*, i. 4), on the three (*Expos. ev. Luc.* vii. 139) or four (*De Abraham*, ii. 54; *De Virginitate*, 113–14) affections of the soul, on the four characteristics of a good man (*De Abraham*, ii. 29), on the three things which constitute blessedness (ibid. ii. 68), on the threefold division of wisdom (*Expos. ev. Luc.* Prol. 2), on the three parts of justice (ibid. v. 76), and perhaps also on certain Stoic dogmas (*De Abraham*, ii. 37, 38; *Ep.* 37; *De Jacob* passim). He may further have used some collection of moral or philosophical maxims (*De Abraham*, i. 4; ii. 5; *Hexaem.* vi. 39; *Expos. ps. cxviii*, 2. 13).

[7] Ambros. *De Fide*, i. 42.

[8] Id. *De Incarn.* 89.                    [9] Id. *De Fide*, i. 85.

[10] Id. *Expos. ps. cxviii*, 22. 10. So Jerome says that Arianism 'draws its streams of

dialectic hold her peace in the very midst of her schools.'[1] 'I do not require reason from Christ; if I am convinced by reason, I reject faith.'[2] This strong hostility to dialectic, remarkable in one who in his controversial writings proved himself a competent dialectician, gave rise to the legend that Ambrose added a suffrage to the litanies, 'From the logic of Aristotle good Lord deliver us!'[3]

On the other hand, in respect of the content of philosophy, while Ambrose regarded metaphysical speculation with characteristic Roman indifference, he evinced a lively interest in the ethical teachings of the ancients. He was prepared to admit that a great deal of this ethical material was valuable. But that he might not be under the necessity of attributing merit to pagan thinkers, he availed himself of the daring hypothesis that all that is best in their teaching was plagiarized from the Sacred Scriptures. Thus (in Ambrose's opinion) the maxims of the sages, 'Follow God' and 'Know thyself', originated with Moses:[4] Pythagoras, who was of Jewish descent, drew from the Scriptures his famous injunction ' not to follow the beaten track', and imitated David in imposing on his disciples a rule of silence:[5] Socrates read and borrowed from sacred writings:[6] Plato went to Egypt and there became acquainted with the Scriptures,[7] from which he derived many of his finest ideas:[8] Sophocles repeated Job and David:[9] Aristotle, in his doctrine of blessedness, did but express 'in high tragic style' what the Scriptures declare in simple speech:[10] the Stoics were similarly indebted to the Scriptures for important elements of their teaching:[11] Cato reproduced the substance of Moses' prohibition of usury.[12] In a word, 'the things admired by the heathen in the books of philosophy' were 'transferred thither from our writings'—too often,

arguments from Aristotle's fountains' (*Dial. contr. Lucifer.* 11): cf. Epiphanius, *Adv. Haer.* ii. 69.              [1] Ambros. *De Fide,* i. 84.

[2] Id. *De Excessu Sat.* ii. 89. Compare *Hexaem.* i. 22 'fidei simplicitas argumentis omnibus antecellit'; *De Spiritu,* iii. 64 'scripto nitor, non argumento'; *De Fide,* i. 78 'iubemur credere magis quam discutere'.

[3] See Migne's note on Ambros. *De Fide,* i. 41.

[4] Ambros. *De Abraham,* i. 4; ii. 5; *Hexaem.* vi. 39; *Expos. ps. cxviii,* 2. 13.

[5] Id. *Ep.* 28. 1; *De Officiis,* i. 31; *Expos. ps. cxviii,* 2. 5.

[6] Id. *De Noe,* 24; *De Bono Mortis,* 51.     [7] Id. *De Noe,* 24; *Expos. ps. cxviii,* 18. 4.

[8] Id. *De Officiis,* i. 43, 44; *De Abraham,* ii. 54; *Expos. ps. cxviii,* 18. 3, 4; *De Paradiso,* 14; *De Bono Mortis,* 19, 21, 51; *De Fuga,* 51.

[9] Id. *Ep.* 37. 28.                [10] Id. *De Abraham,* ii. 70.

[11] Id. *De Officiis,* i. 132, 133, 179; ii. 6; *De Abraham,* ii. 37.

[12] Id. *De Tobia,* 46.

however, spoiled by an intermixture of 'superfluous and useless matter'.[1]

It has been stated that under the term 'philosophy' was included some general knowledge of natural phenomena. A brief summary of Ambrose's 'scientific' beliefs—though there was little enough of real science about them—may be of interest, as illustrating the views that were prevalent among educated persons in this period.[2] The world is spherical,[3] and is constituted of the four elements[4] (the idea of a fifth or aethereal element being a delusion[5]). The earth is poised in the void,[6] and round it revolves the globe of heaven.[7] It is heated by an 'interior fire' (the existence of which is demonstrated by the sparks struck from flints), but the heat is tempered by seas and rivers.[8] The sun, which looks as though it were only about a cubit in diameter, is in reality an immense body, as is proved by the fact that it illumines and warms such

---

[1] Ambros. *De Bono Mortis*, 45; cf. *Ep.* 37. 28. Ambrose is fanatical in his refusal to allow merit to pagan thinkers. When he cannot trace or invent a direct connexion between their words and those of the Scriptures, he affirms that, at any rate, the principles expressed had been already illustrated by Scriptural characters (*De Officiis*, i. 94, iii. 2). Even the persons praised by philosophers—Damon and Pythias (*De Officiis*, iii. 80, 81, 83; *De Virginibus*, ii. 34, 35), Pylades and Orestes (*De Officiis*, i. 204–6), Leaena (*De Virginibus*, i. 17, 19), Spurina (*Exhort. Virginitatis*, 83), the Greeks who scorned to make war unfairly (*De Officiis*, iii. 86–7)—were surpassed by the heroes of Scripture and Christian history.

[2] The main sources from which Ambrose derived his information on natural phenomena appear to have been (*a*) Virgil and the poets, (*b*) Basil's *Hexaemeron*, which he imitated very closely in his own work with this title, (*c*) the *Prata* of Suetonius (A. Reifferscheid, *C. Suetonii Tranquilli praeter Caesarum libros reliquiae*, 1860); on his indebtedness to this work see K. Schenkl, *C.S.E.L.* xxxii, Ambrosii Opp. part i, Praef. xvi, xvii, xviii. His remarks on instinct in the creatures (*Hexaem.* vi. 16, 23, 26) seem to have been based in part on Philo's *Alexander seu de ratione brutorum* (Euseb. *H.E.* ii. 18); his description of the phoenix (*Hexaem.* v. 79; *De Excessu Sat.* ii. 59; *Expos. ps. cxviii*, 19. 13) is derived from the Latin translation of the First Epistle of Clement c. 25; in his comments on the songs of birds (*Hexaem.* v. 39) he had in mind *Anth. Lat.* 762 R; his account of the topaz (*Expos. ps. cxviii*, 16. 41, 42) is taken from the *Lithognomon* of Xenocrates (ibid. 41); some observations on the constitution of the world (*Hexaem.* i. 1–3, 22) appear to be derived from the *Philosophumena* of Hippolytus (K. Schenkl, loc. cit. Praef. xiv). Strangely enough, Ambrose does not seem to have used Pliny's *Natural History*. Although he deals with subjects treated by Pliny, his language shows no sign of dependence on that author.

[3] Ambros. *Hexaem.* i. 10.　　　　[4] Ibid. i. 20.

[5] Ibid. i. 23. 24.　　　　[6] Ibid. i. 22; ii. 11.

[7] Ibid. ii. 9; *Expos. ps. cxviii*, 12. 20. On the derivation of the word *caelum* (taken from Suetonius) *Hexaem.* ii. 15.

[8] Ibid ii. 12.

vast tracts of earth and air.[1] It is naturally, and not accidentally, hot.[2] Light is distinguished from the sun, and is prior in the order of creation to the sun.[3] The sun's rays draw up moisture from the sea, which, being cooled in the shadow of the clouds, falls back on the earth as rain.[4] The moon influences the tides and also the brains of animals.[5] The eclipses of the moon are caused by the earth's shadow.[6] On still nights, when there is a full moon, the dew falls more abundantly.[7] The doctrine of the harmony of the spheres, though not entirely inconsistent with natural possibility, is not Scriptural and so remains open to question.[8]

In the vegetable kingdom, each tree and herb received its peculiar form at its creation,[9] the infinite diversities of bark, foliage, and fruit being deliberately designed for particular purposes.[10] Ambrose recognizes the distinction of sex in trees, and is acquainted with the methods of grafting.[11] As regards the characteristics of fishes, birds, and reptiles he possesses a certain amount of more or less correct information. Thus he knows something about the mode of respiration in fishes and insects,[12] the ways in which fishes spawn,[13] the migrations of fishes and birds,[14] and the habits of bees.[15] Yet he entertains and gravely repeats many extraordinary fancies. He believes the old tales about the phoenix,[16] about the swan's dying song,[17] and about the eagle holding up her young towards the sun and casting away those that turn their eyes from its rays—the rejected eaglets, he adds, are brought up by the coot.[18] The crab, when it feeds on an oyster, prevents the latter from closing its shell by thrusting in a pebble.[19] The little sucking-fish can hold motionless a great ship running under full sail.[20] Vultures do not pair.[21] Storks,

---

[1] Ambros. *Hexaem.* iv. 25–7.     [2] Ibid. ii. 14; cf. iv. 9.
[3] Ibid. iv. 1, 8.     [4] Ibid. iii. 22.
[5] Ibid. iv. 29, 30.     [6] Ibid. vi. 8.
[7] Ibid. iv. 29; but there is nothing in the popular superstition that a new moon brings rain, iv. 30.
[8] Ibid. ii. 6, 7; *De Abraham*, ii. 54; *De Isaac*, 63; *In ps. i enarr.* 2.
[9] Id. *Hexaem.* iii. 34–6.     [10] Ibid. iii. 59, 60, 65.
[11] Ibid. iii. 55, 56.     [12] Ibid. v. 10, 11, 76.
[13] Ibid. v. 7–9.     [14] Ibid. v. 29, 30, 48.
[15] Ibid. v. 67–72.
[16] *Ibid.* v. 79; *De Excessu Sat.* ii. 59; *Expos. ps. cxviii.* 19, 13; see above, p. 16, note 2.
[17] Id. *Hexaem.* v. 39.     [18] Ibid. v. 60, 61; cf. *Expos. ps. cxviii.* 19, 13.
[19] Id. *Hexaem.* v. 22.     [20] Ibid. v. 31. Cf. Cassiodorus *Var.* i. 35.
[21] Id. *Hexaem.* v. 64, 65. Ambrose uses this as an argument for the Virgin Birth.

when they migrate, are guided by crows.[1] During the fourteen
days when the kingfisher broods the sea is free from storms.[2]
Starlings feed on hemlock and quails on hellebore.[3] The turtle-
dove covers its nest with leaves of the leek to keep away wolves.[4]
The cicada sings loudest at midday, because at that time the
air is purer.[5] The viper at pairing season goes to the water's
edge and mates with the lamprey.[6] A serpent dies if blackberry
leaves are thrown upon it or if it tastes the spittle of a fasting
man ('you see what virtue there is in fasting!').[7] Snakes cure
blindness by eating fennel; tortoises eat snakes, and, if poisoned,
take marjoram as an antidote.[8]

With the habits of the better known animals Ambrose is fairly
acquainted. He makes some sound remarks on the instinct,
often surpassing the sagacity of human reason, which teaches
the creatures to foretell the weather, cure their ailments, and
nurture their young.[9] In his opinion a dog has not only instinct
but reason, and can frame a syllogism and draw a conclusion as
correctly as any logician in the schools.[10] He tells a good story
of a sagacious dog at Antioch that was instrumental in bringing
his master's murderer to justice,[11] and also refers to the familiar
tale of the elephant that avenged itself on an unfriendly trades-
man by imbibing a vast quantity of water and discharging it
into his shop.[12] Again, however, he commits himself to a variety
of fantastic statements. If a wolf sees a man, before it is itself
seen, it strikes him dumb; if a man sees it first, it is unable to
run.[13] The lion is terrified of a white cock, and cures itself, when
it is ill, by eating a monkey.[14] The she-bear heals her wounds by
bringing them into contact with the plant called mullein.[15] The
leopard cures its sickness by drinking the blood of a wild roe.[16]
Some interesting details are given respecting the methods by
which elephants—'those mountains in motion'—were killed[17]
and live tiger-cubs captured. As regards the latter, Ambrose
says that as soon as the hunters have taken the cubs, they ride off
at full speed. If they are pursued by the tigress, they throw down

---

[1] Ambros. *Hexaem.* v. 53.        [2] Ibid. v. 40.                    [3] Ibid. iii. 39.
[4] Ibid. vi. 29.        [5] Ibid. v. 76.        [6] Ibid. v. 18.        [7] Ibid. iii. 37, vi. 28.
[8] Ibid. vi. 19.        [9] Ibid. vi. 16 ff.; cf. v. 30, 31.                    [10] Ibid. vi. 23.
[11] Ibid. vi. 24. Ambrose took this from the *Prata* of Suetonius.
[12] Id. *De Elia*, 65.                              [13] Id. *Hexaem.* vi. 26; *Expos. ps. cxviii*, 10. 24.
[14] Id. *Hexaem.* vi. 26.                        [15] Ibid. vi. 19.        [16] Ibid. vi. 26.
[17] Ibid. vi. 32; on the elephant generally, vi. 31–5.

a sphere of glass. The animal, seeing her own reflection, imagines that it is the cub, and stops to examine it. If she resumes the pursuit, the trick is repeated; and so at last the horsemen get away with their booty.[1]

The human body excels the bodies of all animals in comeliness and grace.[2] It is an image of the world in miniature,[3] and, like the world, is constituted of the four elements.[4] Ambrose is aware that the brain is the centre of the nervous system and the heart of the arterial,[5] and that the pulse is the index of sickness or health.[6] He gives an account of the action of the heart,[7] describes the process whereby food is assimilated,[8] notices the sympathetic connexion between the brain and the stomach,[9] and enlarges on the physiological effects of intemperance.[10]

Ambrose appears to have known something of medicine, though he emphasizes the fact that he is only an amateur, and not a professional physician.[11] He considers that health is best preserved by a careful diet, and that herbs provide the most efficacious medicines.[12] He attests the value of mandragora juice as a soporific and of opium as an anaesthetic; and thinks that violent desire may be mitigated by hemlock.[13] Garlic has medicinal properties, but is not suitable for ordinary food.[14] He mentions the drug theriac, compounded of dried adders and other constituents;[15] speaks of *collyria* (eye-salves) and other remedies

[1] Ambros. *Hexaem.* vi. 21. Cf. Claudian, *De Raptu Proserp.* iii. 263–8.
[2] Id. *Hexaem.* vi. 54; cf. *De Noe*, 18 ff.      [3] Id. *Hexaem.* vi. 55.
[4] Id. *De Fide*, ii. 12; *De Virginibus*, iii. 21; *De Abraham*, ii. 64; *De Isaac*, 59.
[5] Id. *Hexaem.* vi. 61.      [6] Ibid. vi. 73.
[7] Id. *De Noe*, 14.
[8] Ibid. 27, 28; *Hexaem.* vi. 71.      [9] Id. *De Noe*, 23.
[10] Ibid. 29. Cf. *De Elia*, 59, 60.
[11] Id. *Hexaem.* vi. 70. He lays it down that 'principium medicinae est causas languoris incidere, ne diutius ea quae nocent ad incrementum aegritudinis ministrentur' (*De Noe*, 59), and holds that, in the case of internal ulcers and cancers, the knife should be freely applied, notwithstanding the unwillingness of patients to undergo surgical operations (*Expos. ps. cxviii*, 8. 26; 9. 16). While he advises that physicians should be sent for in time of sickness (ibid. 19. 2), and admits that their treatment may be beneficial (*De Virginibus*, iii. 24), he rebukes Christians who, on the plea of doctor's orders, neglect fasting, nocturnal devotions, and other religious exercises (*Expos. ps. cxviii*, 22. 23), and also those who, when they are ill, call in the doctor first of all, and only afterwards, when human efforts have failed, pray to God for healing (*De Cain*, i. 40). He notes that the leading doctors themselves undertook the care of the wealthier patients, leaving the poor to their apprentices (*In ps. 36 enarr.* 3).
[12] Id. *Hexaem.* iii. 57; cf. ibid. iii. 28.      [13] Ibid. iii. 39.
[14] Ibid. vi. 28.      [15] Id. *De Paradiso*, 59; *In ps. 37 enarr.* 8.

for diseases of the eye;[1] and refers to a curious remedy for jaundice.[2] One recipe is offered for keeping off mosquitoes—they will not come near a man who has smeared himself with an ointment made of wormwood boiled in oil.[3]

(c) Finally, it is fairly certain that, towards the end of the period of his education, Ambrose devoted himself to the intensive study of jurisprudence. The scheme of study in this subject was very defective, and at a later time was severely criticized by Justinian. Nevertheless, in the fourth century, the Roman school of jurisprudence had a world-wide reputation, and attracted young men from all parts of the Empire.[4] It is inconceivable that Ambrose, residing as he did in Rome, and aspiring to practice at the Bar, should have neglected to attend the courses of the celebrated Roman jurists.

Such was the general plan of Ambrose's education. The atmosphere in which he moved was intellectually stimulating. The learning and talent of the world tended to concentrate in Rome. Grammarians tramped the streets, like the mendicant friars of the Middle Ages, or swarmed in the booksellers' shops, where they were eager to debate literary questions with all comers. Rhetoricians, perfumed, beringed, and crowned with flowers, gave free exhibitions of their artistic dexterity. Poets recited 'polished verses' to literary assemblies in the Forum of Trajan. In the handsome halls of the Athenaeum some of the greatest teachers of the period were giving public lectures. Donatus expounded Virgil;[5] Minervius of Bordeaux, described by Ausonius as scarcely inferior to Quintilian in oratorical skill and as superior to Demosthenes in action, was instructing the aristocratic youth in rhetoric;[6] C. Marius Victorinus, grammarian, rhetorician, and philosopher, was at the very height of a reputation which was so great as to gain for him the honour

---

[1] Ambros. *Expos. ps. cxviii*, 3. 22.

[2] Ibid. 10. 23. Jerome also mentions some strange remedies for various ailments —among them, snakeskin boiled in oil as a cure for ear-ache and peacock's dung for gout (*Adv. Jovin.* ii. 6).                              [3] Id. *Hexaem.* iii. 37.

[4] Augustin. *Confess.* vi. 8; Rutil. Namatian. *De Reditu*, i. 209, 210; *Vita S. Germani*, Bolland. Jul. vii, p. 202 'ut in eum perfectio litterarum plena conflueret, post auditoria Gallicana intra urbem Romam iuris scientiam plenitudini perfectionis adiecit'; Cassiod. *Var.* x. 7. The great legal universities at this period were Rome, Constantinople, and Berytus.

[5] Hieron. *Chron.* A.D. 358: *Adv. Rufin.* i. 16.

[6] Auson. *Profess.* i; Hieron. *Chron.* A.D. 358.

of a bronze statue in Trajan's Forum.[1] The city, moreover, was rich in libraries. Twenty-eight great public libraries, stocked with innumerable papyrus-rolls, were open for the use of serious students. In addition to these, private libraries were to be found in almost all houses of importance. The books themselves were reasonably cheap. *Éditions de luxe* on purple vellum, with gold and silver lettering and illuminated borders,[2] naturally fetched a high price in the market; but a treatise or poem, in a neat purple or yellow cover, could generally be purchased for about the equivalent of a shilling.

At Rome the students were under the supervision of the civil authorities, and, if hopelessly idle or refractory, might be punished by stripes or expulsion. But the discipline was lax, and doubtless many a youth, like Jerome,[3] succumbed to the temptations of the gay metropolis. It may be conjectured, however, that the influence of a pious home saved Ambrose from serious lapse. At any rate, he drops no hint of any grave irregularities in his early period.

[1] Hieron. *Chron.* A.D. 358; *Comm. in Gal.* Praef. 'Victorinum, qui Romae me puero rhetoricam docuit'; *De Vir. Illustr.* 101; Augustin. *Confess.* viii. 2.

[2] Hieron. *Epp.* 22. 32; 107. 12.

[3] Ibid. 7. 4; 14. 6; 48. 20.

## CHAPTER II

# ROME AND ROMAN SOCIETY

IN the spring of A.D. 357, when Ambrose was pursuing his studies at the University, the Emperor Constantius visited Rome.[1] Being anxious to impress the people, he entered the city in state. Through streets lined with soldiers and crowded with spectators,[2] an imposing procession slowly advanced. First came a throng of generals and high officials, clad in gorgeous uniforms, and surrounded with dragon-shaped standards, which seemed to hiss and coil as the breeze inflated their silken bodies. Next marched detachments of troops—infantry with crested helmets, shields painted with emblems, and long spears, and mounted guards encased from head to foot in impenetrable scale-armour. After these, preceded by more of the great purple dragon-standards, came a gigantic car, bedizened with gold and jewels, and drawn by milk-white horses. High aloft on this glittering chariot—so high that people were obliged to throw back their heads to look at him—sat the 'divine' Augustus. Over a white-sleeved tunic, girt with a crimson scarf, he wore a robe of Tyrian purple embroidered with golden crosses; in his right hand he grasped the sceptre; his legs and feet were vested with purple hose and scarlet slippers. Though short in stature and bow-legged, Constantius bore himself with dignity. Amid the thunders of applause he kept an absolutely impassive face, his goggle eyes staring straight before him and his head held stiffly erect as though it were in a vice. Even when the car jolted him he did not nod; and during the whole of the tedious journey under the blazing sun, he never stirred so much as a finger, even to wipe away the perspiration which gathered in beads upon his forehead and trickled down his scrupulously shaved and painted cheeks.

In Rome the Emperor spent much of his time in viewing the

---

[1] For a description of this visit see Ammianus Marcellinus, xvi. 10. 1–17; and for the Emperor's personal appearance ibid. xxi. 16. 19.

[2] Ambrose speaks of the crowds which were wont to gather to see the Emperor, and mentions that criminals, prostitutes, and disreputable persons were kept out of the way by the police, 'ne turpissimorum visus offendat vultus regii claritatem' (*Expos. ps. cxviii*, 8. 19).

sights of what was then, even more than now, the chief show-city of the world. Attended by a train of courtiers and soldiers, he would start early in the morning from his lodging on the Palatine, and ramble for hours through the different quarters of the city, often extending his excursions even into the more distant suburbs. Everything that he saw astonished and delighted him. With unbounded admiration he gazed on the ancient Forum, with the historic temples and basilicas that clustered thickly round it; on the shimmering tangle of gilded roofs and marble columns which crowned the Capitol;[1] on the thermae, 'as huge as provinces', some of which in their enormous central buildings and dependent halls could accommodate literally hundreds of persons without inconvenient crowding;[2] on the cupola of the Pantheon, sheathed with gilt-bronze tiles; on the gigantic pile of the Flavian Amphitheatre—'the most expressive monument of the world-subduing, warlike, and cruel character of the Roman people'; on the Theatre of Pompey, which would by itself have been sufficient to confer upon its founder the title of 'the Great';[3] and on the incomparable Circus Maximus.[4] When he first set eyes on any of these structures, he was overcome with amazement, and would vow that nothing else that Rome might show could equal it. Yet, as he continued his exploration, fresh marvels were ever revealed. The climax was reached, however,

[1] Claudian. *De VI Cons. Honor.* 42–52. Cf. Cassiodorus, *Var.* vii. 6 'Capitolia celsa conscendere hoc est humana ingenia superata vidisse'.

[2] The Baths of Caracalla, for instance, contained 1,600 marble stools for bathers; those of Diocletian nearly twice as many. There were in Rome 11 great thermae and 856 balinea. Since the admission fee was extremely small (Ambros. *Expos. ev. Luc.* vii. 158 ('quadrantem in balneis dari solere reminiscimur') the amenities of the baths could be enjoyed even by the poor. The bathers were usually stark naked (Augustin. *Confess.* ii. 3), though some of the more modest wore bathing-drawers (Ambros. *De Officiis,* i. 79). The ancient Roman custom which forbade a father to bathe in company with his son after the latter had attained the age of puberty (Ambros. loc. cit.) was obsolete in the fourth century. In some of the baths, at any rate, men and women bathed together (Ammian. xxviii. 4, 9: Hieron. *Adv. Jovin.* ii. 36: cf. Clem. Alex. *Paedag.* iii. 5; Cyprian, *De Virg. Habitu,* 19). While respectable Christians avoided 'lavacra mixta', they did not scruple to frequent well-conducted bathing establishments. Even Tertullian considered bathing necessary for health (*Apol.* 42), and Augustine, after his mother's death, repaired to the bath in the hope of assuaging his grief (*Confess.* ix. 12). Apart from the actual bathing, the baths were places where people forgathered for conversation and to witness displays of boxing, wrestling, and other sports.

[3] Cassiod. *Var.* iv. 51.

[4] Id. *Var.* iii. 51. To the ornaments of the Circus Constantius added an obelisk, described by Ammian. xvii. 4.

when, traversing the series of the imperial fora, he arrived at the Forum of Trajan—a place 'without parallel in the world for beauty and admired even by the gods themselves'.[1] Surveying this scene, the Emperor stood for some moments transfixed; then, recognizing the futility of attempting any similar masterpiece, he despairingly exclaimed that all that he could imitate was the gilded bronze charger in the middle of the square, on which the figure of Trajan was seated. To this the Persian refugee, Prince Hormisdas, answered, pointing to the grand surrounding buildings, 'If your charger, Sire, is to be properly housed, first build for him, if you can, a stable such as this!'

In his admiration of Rome Constantius was by no means singular. The gorgeous splendour of the city, 'loveliest Queen of the world',[2] made a profound impression on all observers. 'The grand and glorious city of Rome', cries the orator Themistius, 'is a thing immeasurable; she lies before us as an ocean of beauty, baffling all description.'[3] To Ausonius she is 'golden Rome, first among cities, the home of the gods'.[4] Claudian, again, pays his tribute to a city 'than which there is nothing more sublime beneath the heavens. No eye can take in her vastness, no heart can feel all her beauty, no tongue can sing all her praise'.[5] Many similar eulogies might be quoted. Even as late as the sixth century, after Rome had suffered violence from barbarian spoilers, Cassiodorus writes that 'Rome is one great wonder',[6] and the African Fulgentius enthusiastically exclaims, 'If earthly Rome glows before us with such splendour, what must the beauty of the heavenly Jerusalem be!'[7]

At the period with which we are dealing Rome was still at the height of her glory. The seven hills with their valleys were covered by a labyrinth of marvellous buildings, intercepted with delightful parks and pleasure-grounds. One who looked down from the garden-crowned summit of the Janiculus, or some similar point of vantage, would contemplate a unique panorama—of stately piazzas and porticoes filled with an in-

---

[1] Ammian. xvi. 10. 15. Compare Cassiod. *Var.* vii. 6 'Traiani Forum vel sub assiduitate videre miraculum est'.
[2] Rutilius Namatianus, *De Reditu Suo*, i. 47.
[3] Themist. *Orat.* 13.
[4] Auson. *Clarae Urbes*, i; cf. Prudentius, *Contr. Symmach.* ii. 1113 'aurea Roma'.
[5] Claudian. *De II Cons. Stilich.* 131–3.    [6] Cassiod. *Var.* vii. 15.
[7] *Vita Fulgentii*, c. 13. (Migne, *P.L.* lxv. 130–1.)

finite number of statues,[1] of temples with gilded roofs and walls encased in marble, of vast secular basilicas rising several stories high upon ranges of perfectly proportioned columns, of magnificent theatres, baths, and circuses, of stupendous aqueducts,[2] of luxurious private palaces embosomed in shady plantations, wherein birds twittered.[3] The spectacle was one which could not easily be forgotten. Yet the architectural perfection of the city was marred by serious blemishes. In striking contrast with the beauty and symmetry of the fora and open spaces, the streets for the most part were tortuous and preposterously narrow. Indeed the less important thoroughfares were merely dark and fetid alleys, winding irregularly between lofty and unsightly blocks of flats.[4] These slum-dwellings, hastily constructed by speculating builders out of very frail materials, were chronically in a ramshackle condition. Collapses of houses and destructive fires were of constant occurrence.

The population of Rome at this time has been variously estimated, but we can hardly be wrong in computing it at about 2,000,000. Business and pleasure drew multitudes of aliens to the banks of the Tiber, so that Rome seemed to be indeed (in the phrase of Athenaeus) 'an epitome of the world'. On fine afternoons, when the business of the day was over, the streets and squares were thronged with motley crowds of people of every nationality, occupation, and condition. Here might be seen rhetoricians from Gaul, State official from Constantinople,

[1] Ambrose testifies that 'the baths, the colonnades, the streets are filled with images', *Ep.* 18. 31. Cf. Cassiodor. *Var.* vii. 15. Among the multitude at Rome were 2 colossi, 22 great equestrian statues, 80 gilded and 74 ivory images of the gods, and 3,785 bronze statues of emperors and generals; but these were only a fraction of the total number. Prudentius pleads for the preservation of these 'noblest ornaments of our fatherland' (*Contr. Symm.* i. 502–6).

[2] On the aqueducts see Cassiod. *Var.* vii. 6. The plentiful and refreshing waters, carried to Rome by these channels, and there bubbling up in hundreds of fountains, pouring down in waterfalls, and spread out in great reservoirs, are celebrated by Rutilius, *De Reditu*, i. 97–106.

[3] Rutilius Namat. *De Reditu*, i. 111, 112. The palaces themselves were often of enormous size. Olympiodorus ap. Photius, *Bibliothec.* cod. 80, ed. Bekker, p. 63: 'the larger palaces contain everything that is to be found in a moderate-sized town—a hippodrome, fora, squares, temples, fountains and several baths': cf. Ammian. xxii. 4. 5.

[4] Ambrose refers to the height of such buildings and the danger of collapse *Hexaem.* vi. 33. For a fanciful allusion to the many stories of these *insulae*, see Tertullian, *Adv. Valent.* 7. The projecting balconies, which were a common feature were removed by order of the City Praefect in A.D. 368, Ammian. xxvii. 9. 10.

blue-mantled physicians from Alexandria, charioteers from Sicily, Jew merchants from Africa, huge grey-eyed and yellow-haired Germans enlisted in the imperial service, Egyptian priests with shaven heads and sweeping linen vestments, Indian or Persian princes conspicuous in towering mitres, half-naked slaves from Cappadocia and Syria and Numidia. The scene at such an hour was extremely gay and animated. Aristo-cratic beaux, with little moustaches and long locks elaborately curled, lounged in the apothecaries' shops, discussing the latest Roman scandal or making bets upon the races. Senators, escorted by clients, were carried in swaying palanquins by liveried bearers. Spruce clergymen, elegantly perfumed and attired, minced on tiptoe through the streets, that no speck of dirt might dim the polish of their dainty leather shoes.[1] Ladies of quality passed in gilded and painted litters, surrounded by eunuchs, and preceded and followed by gangs of slaves.[2] Wild-looking monks with beards like goats, artisans in short-sleeved tunics of undyed wool, philosophers distinguished by their *pallia*,[3] petty magistrates strutting with ridiculously important airs, prostitutes in lilac shawls,[4] guides showing the sights to provincial tourists,[5] 'vulgar rich' wearing layer upon layer of gauzy cloaks over tunics embroidered with figures of animals,[6] black-robed nuns (or females who pretended to be such) 'look-ing like owls' in enormous hoods[7]—all these mingled and jostled in picturesque confusion. In corners, out of the traffic, pedlars, jugglers, ballad-singers, mountebanks with performing apes[8] invited the attention of the multitudes; while, wherever the crowd was densest, the Government spies crept in and out with open ears, and the deft metropolitan pickpockets plied their craft.

Yet Rome was no longer the chief political and governmental centre of the Empire. Owing partly to the distance of the city

[1] Hieron. *Ep.* 22. 28.

[2] Ammian. xiv. 6. 17; Hieron. *Epp.* 22. 16, 32; 54. 13.

[3] For the philosopher's cloak cf. Ambros. *De Virginitate*, 48 'pallium, id est, insigne philosophiae tuae'; Ammian. xiv. 9. 5; Symmach. *Epp.* i. 29; ii. 61; Cod. Theod. xiii. 3. 7.

[4] Hieron. *Ep.* 22.13.  [5] Ambros. *Hexaem.* vi. 2.

[6] Ammian. xiv. 6. 9.  [7] Hieron. *Ep.* 22. 27.

[8] For apes fantastically attired see Apuleius, *Metam.* xi. 8; Claudian. *In Eutrop.* i. 303–7. A wall-painting at Pompeii shows a boy with a whip teaching a clothed ape to dance.

from the vulnerable points on the Rhine and Danube frontiers, and partly to the incurably republican temper of the Roman people, which was naturally far from agreeable to despotic rulers,[1] the emperors had long ceased to inhabit the immense imperial residences on the Palatine. Indeed, during the fourth century, Rome only four times had the privilege of sheltering an emperor within her walls. The venerable capital had been superseded—in the East by Constantinople, in the West by Milan and Trier.

Nevertheless, the ancient forms of government were still maintained. The Senate still met for the transaction of business, debated public matters, sometimes with unseemly heat,[2] promulgated decrees (which were graven, as of old, on marble), and forwarded resolutions and petitions to the Emperor. The sovereign, on his side, treated the Senate with ceremonious consideration; sometimes sent it a dispatch,[3] and very occasionally went through the form of asking its advice.[4] But it was all a solemn farce. Except during an interregnum, or when pretenders usurped the purple, the acts of this once all-powerful corporation were of no political importance. So again, the old classical offices—the consulship, the praetorship, the quaestorship—still survived, but their glory, like that of the Senate, had irrevocably departed. The consul, for example, though now nominated by the Emperor,[5] was still installed with the time-honoured ceremonies. Still, as of old, he went in procession to the Circus to open the games[6] and to manumit slaves provided for the purpose.[7] Draped in a purple toga spangled with golden stars, over a tunic embroidered with palm-leaves, and grasping an ivory staff surmounted by an eagle, he rode in a lofty, laurel-

---

[1] The insolence of the Roman mob, which did not spare even the sovereign, is noted by Tertullian, De Spect. 16 (cf. Ad Nat. i. 17) and extenuated by Cassiodorus, Var. i. 27. Constantius, when in Rome, did not find it objectionable, Ammian. xvi. 10. 13.

[2] Symmach. Epp. vi. 22.

[3] To receive such a dispatch the Senate was summoned in hot haste, sometimes even before dawn, Symmach. Epp. i. 13. To be chosen to read it aloud to the assembled fathers was reckoned a high honour, ibid. i. 95.

[4] Symmach. Epp. iv. 5; Claudian. De I Cons. Stilich. i. 325–32.

[5] Auson. Grat. Act. 43.

[6] For a description of the various games given by a new consul see Claudian, De Mall. Theod. Cons. 279–332; and on the immense expense incurred Ambros. De Officiis, ii. 109; Claudian, De II Cons. Stilich. 223 ff.; Cassiod. Var. ii. 2; vi. 1, 10.

[7] Ammian. xxii. 7. 2; Claudian, De IV Cons. Honor. 611–18.

wreathed car drawn by four white horses.[1] A phalanx of senators and white-robed clients accompanied him as escort. When he entered the Circus the assembled thousands rose, waved handkerchiefs and cheered. It was the proudest moment of his life.[2] But after he had started the races by dropping a napkin from his state-box,[3] after he had freed the expectant slaves, after the diptychs bearing his likeness had been made and distributed,[4] the consul had practically nothing to do, except recline on his beautiful curule chair and enjoy, during the remainder of his term of office, the undisturbed contemplation of his own magnificence.

Of Roman society at this period two main sections must be distinguished. On the one hand, in the pages of Ammianus and Jerome we find some clever, satiric sketches of a frivolous, fast, fantastic set, constituted of both pagans and Christians,[5] and comprehending, it seems, the majority of the inhabitants of the city. On the other hand, in the writings of Symmachus and Macrobius we are introduced to a select aristocratic pagan circle, of literary refinement, zealous piety, and unimpeachable respectability; along with which, for the present purpose, may be reckoned a small but increasing Christian group, recruited from serious persons of all social ranks, and characterized by a strongly marked propensity for asceticism.

(i) Of the men and women belonging to the first of these two worlds we are given some piquant descriptions. Here, for instance, is a noble lord holding his crowded morning reception. If you chance to be a distinguished stranger, visiting Rome, he

---

[1] For the consular robes see Claudian. *In Prob. et Olyb. Cons.* 177 ff.; *De IV Cons. Honor.* 584 ff.; Ambros. *In ps. i enarr.* 46 'nitentes auro triumphales palmatae'. The 'palmata' sent to Ausonius by Gratian was embroidered with a figure of the Emperor Constantius (Auson. *Grat. Act.* 53). On the staff with eagle, Prudent. *Peristeph.* x. 146–50; Claudian, *De I Cons. Stilich.* ii. 362–3; *In Prob. et Olyb. Cons.* 205: on the car with its white horses, Claudian, *De II Cons. Stilich.* 20, 21.

[2] The consulship was regarded as the highest of all honours (Cod. Theod. vi. 6. 1). The *Thanksgivings* of Mamertinus and Ausonius, and the congratulatory poems of Claudian, show how greatly it was prized. Pacatus refers to it as the greatest distinction that the Emperor could bestow on his friends (*Paneg.* 16). John Lydus enlarges on the sublime dignity of the office, and mentions the expense which it entailed (*De Magistrat.* ii. 8).

[3] Tertullian, *De Spect.* 16; Cassiod. *Var.* iii. 51.

[4] Claudian, *De II Cons. Stilich.* 345 ff.

[5] Augustin. *Serm.* 62. 17 observes that many Christians of his time were still half heathen; their bodies were in the Church, but not their hearts.

will welcome you (though he has never set eyes on you before) as though he had been pining for your arrival, will ask you so many questions that in desperation you tell any number of lies, and at last will dismiss you with such delightful affability that you regret that you did not settle years ago in so hospitable a city. But if, encouraged by these civilities, you call again next day, you will find yourself utterly forgotten, and will be kept waiting for hours in ante-rooms while the great gentleman is wondering who on earth you are, and whence you come, and what you want.[1] Or here is a sketch of a Roman 'blood'. He is a notable judge of horse-flesh, a patron of jockeys, and a connoisseur of pretty slave-girls. He fancies himself as a whip, and drives a gig in dashing style. At night he roves the streets with a gang of roistering fellows, seeking gallant adventures and playing off practical jokes on strangers.[2] Of a widely different type is the curled and scented fop, too languid to endure even the slightest fatigues of ordinary life. If this pampered person rouses himself to make a little excursion into the country, he is as proud as though he had equalled the marches of Caesar and Alexander; or if, on a summer day, he ventures on a short voyage in his commodious pleasure-barge, and in spite of the golden fans a fly alights on his silken robe or a tiny ray of sunshine pierces through a hole in his parasol, he laments plaintively that he was not born amid the darkness of the Cimmerians.[3] Another repulsive figure is that of the gastronomist, wallowing amid 'whirlpools of banquets'. All lands and seas are ransacked to furnish him with delicacies. He knows all that is to be known about 'Apician and Lurconian condiments',[4] and can tell at first taste from what lake or sea the oysters have been gathered and what province the game comes from. Meals absorb his whole attention. When he gives one of his prodigious dinners he can talk of nothing but the quality of the viands; he will even send for scales to weigh the fish and birds and dormice which are brought

[1] Ammian. xiv. 6. 12–13.
[2] Id. xiv. 6. 16; xxviii. 4. 9, 11; Augustin. *Confess.* iii. 3; cf. Apuleius, *Metam.* ii. 18.
[3] Ammian. xxviii. 4. 18. Ambrose also is acquainted with the effeminate dandy who uses perfumes (*Expos. ev. Luc.* vi. 27), curls his hair like a woman (*Ep.* 69. 6) and wears clothing of silk, because forsooth woollen garments are too heavy (*Expos. ev. Luc.* v. 107; cf. Claudian. *In Eutrop.* ii. 337, 338).
[4] Tertullian's phrase, *De Anima*, 33.

to table, while his secretaries stand by with note-books to record the figures.[1] Next follows the society beauty. Her cheeks are smeared with white lead and rouge; her eyelids are darkened with black powder; her hair, dyed a reddish tint, is frizzed out low on the forehead and piled high on the top of the head in the shape of a gigantic helmet. To make herself look taller she wears a long straight tunic which trails upon the ground: her neck, her arms, her fingers, her ears are loaded with jewels. In compliance with the ridiculous fashion of the period she clips her words and speaks with an affected lisp. Her salon is always crowded with chattering girls and greedy parasites, who are per-petually egging her on to every species of extravagance: 'Dear creature, make the most of your advantages, and live while life is yours', or 'Surely you are not going to hoard up money for your children!' Her temper is extremely capricious, and, to stimulate her wit, she is apt to drink more honey-flavoured wine than is quite good for her.[2] Finally here is a portrait—sketched evidently from the life—of a very un-evangelical clergyman. He is known by the nickname of 'the City News-carrier'.

'He rises and goes forth with the sun; he has the order of his visits duly arranged; he takes the shortest road, and, troublesome old man that he is, pushes his way almost into the bedrooms of ladies yet asleep. If he sees a cushion that takes his fancy, or a pretty table-cloth, or an attractive piece of furniture, he praises it, admires it, handles it, complains that he possesses nothing like it, and so begs—or rather, extorts—it from the owner; for all the women are afraid of giving offence to the City News-carrier. He has two enemies whom he abhors—one is continence, the other fasting. What he likes is a savoury luncheon, and his pet weakness is a plump young

[1] Ammian. xiv. 6. 14–16; xxviii. 4. 13; Hieron. Ep. 52. 6; Claudian. In Eutrop. ii. 327–34. Macrobius, indeed, insists that the entertainments of his time were less luxurious than those of former days—peahen's eggs which once fetched 3s. 6d. apiece were no longer on the market (Sat. iii. 13. 2); the dish called porcus Tro-ianus, pig stuffed with other meats, was no longer served (ibid. iii. 13. 13); the fattening of hares and snails for food had ceased (ibid. iii. 13. 14–15); the very meaning of many of the dishes named in the old sumptuary laws was forgotten (ibid. iii. 17. 12). But Macrobius is inclined to exaggerate the improvement in the manners of his contemporaries.

[2] Hieron. Epp. 22. 29; 38. 3; 45. 5; 54. 7; 107. 5; 117. 7; 127. 3; 130. 7, 18. Ambrose likewise calls attention to the use of cosmetics (Hexaem. vi. 47; De Cain, i. 14; De Virginibus, i. 28, 29), the habit of curling the hair (De Virginitate, 71; Exhort. Virginit. 64) and the partiality for expensive dresses and jewellery (De Virginibus, i. 29; De Virginitate, 68; De Viduis, 28; Expos. ev. Luc. viii. 76; De Nabuthe, 26; De Abraham, i. 89).

crane which is vulgarly called 'pipizo'. He has a rude and forward tongue, always ready to bandy abuse. Go where you will, he is the first man you set eyes on; whatever news you hear, he has either put in circulation or exaggerated the report. He is never tired of buying new horses, and those he gets are so sleek and spirited that one would imagine him to be own brother to the Thracian king.'[1]

The 'smart set' depicted by Ammianus and Jerome was morally degenerate. Its members appear to have been incapable of friendship,[2] and even of family affection. Jerome speaks of girls who hated their parents and deserted them to live with strangers;[3] and Ambrose appears to be referring to an incident which had actually occurred at Milan when he describes a lady, beautifully dressed and covered with jewels, entering a place of worship and contemptuously passing her pauper mother who was soliciting alms at the church door.[4] Gross forms of sensuality were practised without restraint and without disguise.[5] Nor was even this the worst. In the time of the Emperor Valentinian the First there was an appalling outbreak of crime among the upper classes in Rome. Very many people of exalted station were found guilty of murders, poisonings, and adulteries. So grave were the crimes and so numerous were the persons implicated that the Emperor, to facilitate the judicial investigation, ordered that torture should be applied even to those who, by reason of their rank, were ordinarily exempt.[6]

The intellectual tone of this society was also low. Although these people had not a particle of religious belief, they were insanely superstitious, and would not dine out or take a bath or

[1] Hieron. *Ep.* 22. 28. Compare the unpleasant portrait of the deacon Sabinianus, ibid. 147. 8. The luxury of the higher clergy in Rome is attested not only by Jerome (see especially *Ep.* 52), but also by Ammianus, xxvii. 3. 14. Vettius Agorius Praetextatus used to say in jest to Pope Damasus, 'Make me Bishop of Rome, and I will turn Christian at once!' (Hieron. *Contr. Joan. Hieros.* 8.) Damasus himself was nicknamed 'the ear-scratcher of the ladies' (*auriscalpius matronarum*).

[2] Ammian. xxviii. 4. 21.

[3] Hieron. *Ep.* 125. 6; cf. *Ep.* 117.

[4] Ambros. *Expos. ev. Luc.* viii. 76. He alleges that many refuse to maintain their parents, though the laws prescribe punishment for the neglect of this duty, *Hexaem.* v. 55.

[5] Salvian later inveighs against the horrible licentiousness prevalent in all parts of the Roman world; see, e.g., *De Gubernatione Dei* (ed. C. Halm), vii. 14 ff., 26 ff., 56, 57, 62–80, 83–8.

[6] Ammian. xxviii. 1. 11.

manicure their finger-nails until they had consulted an almanac and assured themselves that the signs were favourable.[1] Learning they hated as they hated poison. Their libraries were shut up as closely as their family vaults. If ever they attempted to read even the lightest literature, they would yawn, rub their foreheads, and nearly faint with boredom.[2] They were, in fact, egregiously stupid. The only things they really cared for were music[3]—of the gay theatrical kind—racing, dining, and playing at dice. A skilful dice-player, even though of humblest origin, commanded universal homage.[4]

The one serious occupation of these degenerate Romans was the pursuit of wealth. Men were frantically eager to get rich, or, if rich already to get richer. Avarice was their ruling passion.[5] Even the most trifling gains were rapaciously sought after. The Romans were terrified of illness; yet, though they might feel extremely unwell, they would travel as far as Spoleto to attend a wedding, merely for the sake of receiving the presents which were distributed among the guests on such occasions.[6] The

---

[1] Ammian. xxviii. 4. 24; cf. the rule stated by Ausonius, 'ungues Mercurio, barbam Jove, Cypride crines'; Ambros. *Ep.* 23. 4; *Hexaem.* iv. 34. Augustine speaks of the careful selection of auspicious days for marrying, sowing, breeding cattle, &c. (*De Civitate Dei*, v. 7; cf. *Enchir.* 79), and Prudentius remarks that the astrologers make the very stones and timbers of the houses subject to fate, as though it mattered under what star the ash was cut down from which the roof-beams were fashioned (*Contr. Symmach.* ii. 449–57). Arborius, grandfather of Ausonius, was an expert on astrology, and left among his papers a sealed horoscope of his grandson (Auson. *Parent.* iv. 17–22). Jovius, to whom Paulinus of Nola wrote his *Ep.* 16, was a believer in astrology. Augustine studied the art and mentions others who did so (*Confess.* iv. 3; vii. 6). He admits that the predictions of the astrologers sometimes came true, but attributes this either to chance or to the intervention of demons (*Confess.* iv. 3; *De Civitate Dei*, v. 7; *De Gen. ad Litt.* xii. 46). Ambrose acutely criticizes the pretensions of the astrologers, *Hexaem.* iv. 12–19.

[2] Ammian, xiv. 6. 18; xxviii. 4. 14; Hieron. *Ep.* 43. 2.

[3] Ammianus, xiv. 6. 18 mentions the singers and musicians that crowded the houses of the wealthy—the flutes, hydraulic organs, lyres as big as wagons, and ponderous machinery for theatrical exhibitions. Even people of moderate means were expected to provide some sort of musical entertainment when they gave a dinner-party.

[4] Ammian. xxviii. 4. 21.

[5] On the avarice of the rich, see further below, pp. 465, 466. The prevalence of this vice in the fifth century is attested by Salvian, *Ad Ecclesiam*, passim. Cf. also Mommsen's description of Roman society at an earlier date: 'For gold the statesman sold his country, and the citizen his freedom; an officer's commission and the ballot-balls of the jury could equally be had for money; and high-born dames sold themselves as readily as the lowest street girl.'

[6] Ammian. xiv. 6. 24.

disgusting art of legacy-hunting was very widely practised. 'It is incredible', says Ammianus, 'with what a variety of polite attentions men without children are courted at Rome.'[1] Such persons, if they were wealthy, were everlastingly besieged by 'professional ghouls-in-waiting', who used every device to persuade them to make wills in their favour.[2] In this discreditable industry the Christian clergy were conspicuously proficient. To any wealthy and childless old person they were unremitting in their civilities. If he fell ill they would watch beside his bed, and with their own hands perform the meanest and most revolting offices. With trembling voices they would question the physician as to the prospect of his recovery: when a favourable reply was given, they would feign to be in ecstasies, while inwardly they were raging because the preposterous old creature seemed determined on living as long as Methuselah.[3] The scandal, indeed, reached such a pitch that in A.D. 370 a law was promulgated rendering bequests to the clergy by widows and virgins invalid; and it is significant that even such sturdy defenders of the rights of the Church as Ambrose and Jerome were constrained to confess that the enactment was needed.[4]

No description of the Roman pleasure-world would be complete without some reference to the city-mob, at this time perhaps more licentious and degraded than in any other period of Roman history. Since the days of Julius Caesar the populace had been fed at the expense of the State. In the fourth century bread-rations were regularly distributed; to which allowances of oil, wine, and bacon were added.[5] The dole was sufficient to sustain life in a southern climate, and the recipients were accordingly relieved from the necessity of work. Thus Rome was burdened with a multitude of able-bodied paupers, who neither sought nor desired employment, but spent their days and nights soaking and gambling in the wineshops or loafing around the stews and stables in the neighbourhood of the Circus.

[1] Ammian. xiv. 6. 22. Ambrose refers to the legacy-hunters (*Expos. ps. cxviii*, 9. 21; cf. 8. 54), and says, 'Let those who are nearing their end use their own judgement, and freely make their wills as they think best, since they will not have a chance of altering them later. It is not honourable to divert the savings which are due to, or have been accumulated for, others' (*De Officiis*, iii. 58).

[2] Ammian. xxviii. 4. 22; cf. ibid. 26.

[3] Hieron. *Ep.* 52. 6.

[4] Cod. Theod. xvi. 2. 20; Ambros. *Ep.* 18. 14–15; Hieron. *Ep.* 52. 6.

[5] Cod. Theod. xiv. 24. 1.

For the sake of the public peace it was important that this *canaille* should be kept in good humour. Generous provision was accordingly made for its amusement by means of theatrical performances, gladiatorial and wild-beast shows, and races in the Circus.

The theatrical exhibitions comprised broad farces, musical recitations, dramatic ballets, and pantomimic dances. The mimes, which represented farcical scenes from low life, were adored by the rabble, who delighted in the rough horse-play, the ribald jokes, and the grotesquely indecent dances which were characteristic of these performances.[1] More refined play-goers were entertained with musical recitals from the tragedies rendered by skilled soloists,[2] with dramatic ballets representing mythological subjects (e.g. the Judgement of Paris or the Adventures of Dionysus),[3] and with the picture-dances of the pantomimes. These dances were amazingly clever. Sensational episodes, adapted from mythological or tragic literature, were enacted without speech—solely by means of rhythmic gesticulation—by a single masked performer, who represented several characters, male and female, in rapid succession. The motions of the actor's hands and body were accompanied by *cantica* sung by a chorus.[4] As a rule the exhibitions were enchantingly seductive and abnormally improper.[5]

[1] In Jerome's time mimes were still written (*Ep.* 54. 15) and acted (*Ep.* 52. 2). There were generally coarse parodies of vulgar scenes and persons. The two chief performers were the 'archimimus', dressed in a sort of harlequin costume, and the 'stupidus' or booby, with shaven head, who was the recipient of much buffeting and abuse. The object of the performance was to provoke a laugh (Joan. Lydus, *De Magistrat.* i. 40), and the actors sought to attain this end by indecent jokes (Macrob. *Sat.* ii. 1. 9) and grossly obscene actions. (Lactantius, *Inst. Div.* i. 20, vi. 20; Cyprian, *Ad Donat.* 8; cf. [Cyprian] *De Spect.* 6.)

[2] Ambros. *De Elia*, 35. Occasionally the old tragedies and comedies appear to have been acted in full (Donatus, *Andr.* iv. 3 'sive haec (persona feminea) personatis viris agitur, ut apud veteres, sive per mulierem, ut nunc videmus'; Ambros. *De Officiis*, i. 206; Augustin. *De Civit. Dei*, ii. 8).

[3] For a description of such a ballet see Apuleius, *Metam.* x. 29–34.

[4] Cassiod. *Var.* iv. 51 (a *locus classicus* on the pantomime).

[5] Prudentius, *Peristeph.* x. 221 ff. Ambrose complains of theatrical music and dancing as morally enervating (*Hexaem.* iii. 5; *De Poenit.* ii. 42; *Ep.* 58, 5; *Expos. ev. Luc*, vi. 8, vii. 237), and denies that a person 'theatralibus ludibriis occupatus' can be truly religious (*Expos. ps. cxviii.* 16. 17). Augustine ascribes the invention of stage performances to devils, and maintains that they are morally more dangerous than the Circus itself (*De Civitate Dei*, i. 32). Cassiodorus also notes the tendency to licence of theatrical entertainments (*Var.* vii. 10). On the corrupting influence of the pantomime dances see Zosimus, i. 6.

If the lustful propensities of the people were stimulated by the theatre, its tigerish instincts were gratified by the sanguinary spectacles of the arena. The Romans, as of old, loved the sight and smell of blood; their supreme delight was to watch the gladiators slaughtering one another.[1] The strange fascination of these 'awful holocausts of human life' is illustrated by the story of Augustine's friend, Alypius. When he was studying law in Rome he was forcibly compelled by some fellow students to accompany them to the Colosseum. Being a Christian he determined not to gaze on the unhallowed spectacle, and sat for some while with eyes closed. A sudden shout, however, occasioned by the fall of one of the combatants, startled him to look, and his soul, says Augustine, received a wound more fatal than that inflicted on the body of the prostrate gladiator. His eyes started out of his head to glut themselves with the sight of blood; he was excited to madness by the crimson flow; and thenceforward he became one of the most regular and enthusiastic frequenters of the amphitheatre.[2] Hardly less thrilling than the combats of the gladiators were the beast-baitings or *venationes*. For a single one of these as many wild animals were often collected as would suffice to stock half the Zoological Gardens of modern Europe. Lions, tigers, bears, leopards, elephants, hippopotami, ostriches, crocodiles, and other creatures were snared by intrepid hunters and imported into Italy by firms of wild beast merchants.[3] In the amphitheatre they were used in

---

[1] Lactantius, *Inst. Div.* vi. 20. Ammianus says of the Caesar Gallus that 'he would rejoice as if he had made some great gain to see half a dozen gladiators killing one another', xiv. 7. 3. The gladiators were either prisoners of war (Symmach. *Epp.* ii. 46), condemned criminals (Valentinian forbade Christians to be condemned to the gladiatorial school as a punishment for crime, Cod. Theod. ix. 40. 8), or free volunteers. There were four gladiatorial *ludi* in Rome. Here the gladiators were fed on nourishing diet (Cyprian. *Ad Donat.* 7) and taught the various forms of fighting by skilled *magistri*. The words of command used by the instructors (*dictata*) were sometimes shouted by the people to the antagonists in the arena (Hieron. *Ep.* 48, 12). Generally the gladiators fought in pairs. When one was struck, the spectators cried *habet* (Prudent. *Psychom.* 49–54). Those who wished a vanquished gladiator to be killed turned their thumbs towards their breast; those who wished him to be spared turned their thumbs downwards (Prudent. *Contr. Symm.* ii. 1096–8). Prudentius pleaded for the abolition of the combats (ibid. ii. 1113–31), and Honorius prohibited them in A.D. 404, after the heroic intervention of the monk Telemachus (Theodoret. *H.E.* v. 26). But Augustine, some ten years later, speaks of gladiators as still existing (*De Civitate Dei*, iii. 14).

[2] Augustin. *Confess.* vi. 8.

[3] Claudian indicates the number and variety of the animals provided for the

three ways. Sometimes they were incited to fight one another—
a rhinoceros, for instance, being pitted against an elephant, or
a bear against a bull. Sometimes they were baited by armed
*venatores* with the assistance of sporting hounds.[1] Sometimes
they were turned loose on condemned criminals, who were
either inadequately armed, or entirely unarmed, or bound so
that they could neither fight nor flee.[2] Elaborate stage contrivances and artistic scenery enhanced the interest of these
ghastly executions.

But the favourite amusement in Rome, as in most of the great
cities of the Empire, was afforded by the Circus. The passion
for racing was extraordinarily strong even among the upper
classes; with the common people it was a mania. To them the
Circus Maximus was 'their temple, their home, their place of
assembly—in short, their whole hope and desire'.[3] All day long
they would hang about the stables, quarrelling over the points
of the Spanish and Cappadocian racers and making bets on the
charioteers. On the night before the contest few were calm
enough to sleep, and with the first streak of morning light there
was a headlong rush for the hippodrome. Men fought like beasts
in the terrible crush; women and children fell shrieking and
were trampled on; tunics were torn and sandals lost; but still
the crowds swept on. Along the marble tiers of the Circus
thousands of people, in gala attire, waited in a fever of im-
patience. At the signal of the dropped napkin the eight
chariots, representing the four racing colours—Blue, Green,
White, and Red—dashed from the barriers and commenced the
first of the seven-lap races. The drivers, wearing sleeveless
tunics and close-fitting caps, bent forward in their rocking cars

greater spectacles (*De II Cons. Stilich.* 237–369; *De Mall. Theod. Cons.* 291–310).
Ambrose refers to the hunters who captured them (*Expos. ps. cxviii*, 8. 42); Symmachus to the merchants who arranged for the supply of those that were needed
(*Epp.* v. 22). A duty of 2½ per cent. was paid—not, however, by senators—on
imported beasts (Symmach. *Epp.* v. 62, 65). Often, however, the animals hardly
survived the fatigues of the journey (ibid. ii. 76).

[1] Cassiodorus, *Var.* v. 42, gives an obscure description of the various methods of
fighting the beasts, ending with the words, 'Alas for the pitiable error of mankind!
If we had any insight into what is right, we should sacrifice as much wealth for
the preservation of human life as we now lavish on its destruction'. Prudentius
(*Hamart.* 370–5) denounces the brutality of these spectacles.

[2] In earlier times Christians were often martyred in this way, Tertullian. *Apol.*
12, 40; *De Pudicit.* 22; *Passio SS. Perpet. et Felicit.* 6.

[3] Ammian. xxviii. 4. 28.

and lashed their teams to their utmost speed. As, again and again, they swung round the conical pillars which marked the two ends of the course, the vast assembly, agonized with excitement, sprang up and stamped, clapped their hands, and howled encouragement to the favourites.

'The Green charioteer flashes by; half of the people is in despair. The Blue gets a lead; the greater part of the city is in misery. They cheer frantically, when they have gained nothing; they are cut to the heart, though they have suffered no loss; they plunge into these empty contests with as much eagerness, as if the welfare of the State itself depended on the issue.'[1]

Terrible accidents often occurred, for the charioteers used every device, whether fair or foul, to win. But the spectacle of an overthrown driver battered to death by the hoofs of his horses, or crushed under the wheels of his opponent's car, did but add a new thrill to the enjoyment of the on-lookers. Throughout the day (except for an interval at noon)[2] they watched their favourite sport with passionate absorption: at sundown, the races being ended, they streamed reluctantly from the exits— hoarse, grimed with dust, and exhausted by their emotions, but still wrangling about the merits of rival favourites. Christian teachers fulminated against the 'vanity' of these spectacles,[3] but without effect. Many people used to stay away from church in order to attend them;[4] others would rush precipitately from the sacred services when they heard that the races had begun.[5]

Although the rabble was pampered with food and amusements, its temper could not be relied on. With very slight excuse —if there was a temporary shortage of wine,[6] for example, or

---

[1] Cassiod. *Var.* iii. 51. The noise of the Circus, the intense excitement and passionate rivalry are constantly mentioned; see, e.g., Tertullian. *De Spect.* 16, 23; Lactantius, *Inst. Div.* vi. 20; Ambros. *In ps. 39 enarr.* 4 'circensium plena furoris studia'; *Hexaem.* v. 34 'cum e carceribus mittuntur quadrigae, quanto studio spectantium et amore certatur'; Auson. *Idyll.* xvii. 10, 11 'furiosi iurgia Circi'; Prudent. *Hamart.* 362 'vesania fervida Circi'. Rutilius, returning from Rome, heard the roar of the Circus shouts long after the city itself had faded from view, *De Reditu,* i. 201–4.

[2] The show was divided into an *antemeridianum* and a *pomeridianum spectaculum,* Augustin. *Confess.* viii. 6.

[3] Ambros. *De Fuga,* 4; *Hexaem.* v. 34; *Expos. ps. cxviii,* 5. 28; *In ps. 39 enarr.* 4.

[4] Ambros. *Expos. ps. cxviii,* 16. 45.

[5] Salvian. *De Gubern. Dei,* vi. 36–8.

[6] Ammian. xiv. 6. 1; xv. 7. 3.

if the African corn-ships were delayed in reaching Ostia[1]—it
would take to rioting. On such occasions the properties, and
even the lives, of the highest personages were imperilled. Ter-
tullus, who was Praefect of Rome in Constantius' reign, was
once assaulted by a furious mob, and saved himself only by the
dramatic device of offering to deliver his two young sons into
its power.[2] The house of L. Avianius Symmachus on the other
side of the Tiber was burned by the angry rabble.[3] Another
praefect, Lampadius, was obliged to retire from the city, while
the populace endeavoured to set fire to his house.[4] The contest
between Damasus and Ursinus for the Papacy in the autumn of
A.D. 366 occasioned a sanguinary tumult. The party of Ursinus
seized and fortified the Basilica of Liberius on the Esquiline.
The opposition mob of Damasus attacked the building with
hatchets and firebrands, and eventually broke down the doors.
A furious battle ensued. When order was at last restored no
fewer than a hundred and thirty-seven bodies were found dead
upon the floor.[5]

(ii) From this insufferable society, with its repulsive levity and
lubricity, one turns with relief to the contemplation of the better
elements, both pagan and Christian, of the fourth-century
Roman world.

The virtues and excellences of superior pagan society are
admirably represented by certain distinguished aristocrats, who,
born within a few years of Ambrose, flourished towards the end
of the century, and concerning whose lives and characters we
have a considerable amount of information. Foremost among
these was the devout and erudite nobleman, Vettius Agorius
Praetextatus—statesman, philosopher, antiquary, and chief
defender of the failing cause of paganism. A man of profound
piety and unrivalled knowledge of pagan rites, he loved to
accumulate priestly offices and titles, and made a point of being
initiated into all the principal heathen mysteries.[6] His marked

---

[1] Ammian. xix. 10. 1; xxvi. 3. 6; Symmach. *Epp.* ii. 6; vi. 14, 18. Rome depended on Africa for her grain-supply, Constantinople on Egypt (Claudian. *De Bell.
Gildon.* 49–65).
[2] Ammian. xix. 10. 1–3.                                    [3] Id. xxvii. 3. 4.
[4] Id. xxvii. 3. 8–9. This Lampadius was so vain that he was annoyed if he
were not praised even when he spat, as though he did it more cleverly than any one
else, ibid. 5.
[5] Id. xxvii. 3. 11–13.
[6] Praetextatus was born before A.D. 330; served as Proconsul of Achaia, Praefect

ability and unblemished integrity made him universally respected.[1] Another leading noble, of whom we shall hear more
later, was a kinsman of Ambrose—Quintus Aurelius Symmachus.[2]
Symmachus was a good example of the 'pagan gentleman and
official'. He had a strong sense of duty, a still stronger sense of
deportment, and no sense at all of humour. He was a patron
of literature, an indefatigable writer of the dullest epistles in
the Latin language, an orator whose moderate talents were
immoderately admired by his contemporaries, and withal an
honourable, pious, pompous, and intensely narrow-minded
man. Yet another grand seigneur was the brilliant and versatile
Virius Nicomachus Flavianus,[3] a cousin of Symmachus. One of
the most accomplished men of his day, he cultivated a refined
taste for all the elegances of life, and a manner which is reputed to have been exceptionally gracious and charming. Yet
he could also bestir himself vigorously when occasion called for
action, and he is still remembered for his energetic championship
of paganism, in the cause of which eventually he laid down
his life. To the same coterie belonged the pontiff, Publilius
Caeionius Albinus.[4] Although a pillar of the pagan party,
Albinus was amiably tolerant in matters of religion. His wife
and daughter were Christians, and his son-in-law became a convert to Christianity; but religious differences did not disturb the

of Rome, Praetorian Praefect of Italy; was designated for the consulship, A.D. 385,
but died in A.D. 384. He was an enthusiastic devotee of the pagan religion. His
inscription describes him as 'augur, priest of Vesta, priest of the Sun, quindecemvir,
curial of Hercules, devoted to Liber and the Eleusinian deities, hierophant, neo-
corus, cleansed by the rite of the taurobolium, pater patrum' (*C.I.L.* vi. 1779). Cf.
Macrobius, *Sat.* i. 17. 1 'sacrorum omnium praesulem esse te, Vetti Praetextate,
divina voluerunt'; *ibid.* i. 24. 1. See O. Seeck, *Symmachus*, pp. lxxxv–lxxxviii.
 [1] Symmachus praises him as a model of public and private virtue, *Relat.* x; cf.
Ammian. xxvii. 9. 8–10. All Rome was moved by his death (Hieron. *Ep.* 23. 3).
 [2] Symmachus was born in A.D. 340, and died soon after Feb. A.D. 402. His career
is summarized in his inscription: 'Quintus Aurelius Symmachus, vir clarissimus,
Quaestor, Praetor, Pontifex Major, Governor of Lucania and Bruttii, Count of
the third order, Proconsul of Africa, Praefect of the City, Consul of his year, a most
eloquent orator' (*C.I.L.* vi. 1699). Prosper, *De Promiss. Dei*, iii. 38, 41, describes
him as 'mirabili eloquio et scientia praeditus, tamen paganus'. All that is known
about him may be found in the exhaustive Introduction to Seeck's edition of his
works, pp. xxxix–lxxiii.
 [3] *C.I.L.* vi. 1782, 1783. He was born about A.D. 334. Macrobius testifies to his
noble character and profound knowledge (especially of augural science), *Sat.* i. 5.
13; cf. Sozomen. *H.E.* vii. 22. See O. Seeck, op. cit. cxii–cxix.
 [4] He was born about A.D. 340; for an account of him see O. Seeck, op. cit.
pp. clxxviii, clxxix.

happy harmony of the family. Jerome has left us a pretty picture of the kindly and broad-minded pontiff, holding his little Christian granddaughter on his knee and listening delightedly while she sang to him a baby hymn in praise of Christ.[1] Finally, in connexion with this group of pagan worthies mention may be made of that magnificent, but not very estimable, patrician, Sextus Petronius Probus.[2] Nominally Probus was a Christian, but he was only baptized on his death-bed. Certainly he was no saint. Love of money and lust of power were his dominating passions, and he was not burdened with many scruples as to the means which he used to gratify them. Though he did not belong to the inner circle of Symmachus and Praetextatus, his affinities lay rather with the pagan senatorial aristocracy than with the Christian party in Rome.

The members of this high society belonged, for the most part, to illustrious families, and were immensely proud of their noble birth.[3] Many of them were also extremely wealthy. A senatorial income sometimes reached the figure of £180,000 a year. Symmachus was considered a man of only modest fortune, yet his income amounted to £60,000 a year. He had three palaces at Rome, fifteen country seats in different parts of Italy, and large properties in Samnium, Apulia, Sicily, and Mauretania.[4] Probus, again, was fabulously rich and owned estates in all parts of the Empire—'whether justly or unjustly acquired', says Ammianus, 'it is not for a humble individual like myself to

---

[1] Hieron. *Ep.* 107. 1.

[2] Probus was born about A.D. 334, and filled more important offices than any man of his time. He was Proconsul of Africa A.D. 357–8, Praetorian Praefect of Italy A.D. 368–76, Consul A.D. 371, Praetorian Praefect of Gaul A.D. 380, Praetorian Praefect of Italy A.D. 383–4 and A.D. 387; he died before the end of A.D. 394 (*C.I.L.* vi. 1751, 1753, 1756; cf. O. Seeck, op. cit. pp. cii–civ). Ausonius (*Ep.* 16) and Claudian (*In Prob. et Olybr. Cons.* 31 ff.) lavish compliments upon him, but Ammianus (xxvii. 11. 1–7; xxix. 6. 9–11; xxx. 5. 4–10) characterizes him in caustic terms. His sarcophagus may still be seen in St. Peter's at Rome. On his admirable wife, Anicia Faltonia Proba, see Hieron. *Ep.* 130. 7; Claudian, op. cit. 194–202; *C.I.L.* vi. 1754, 1755.

[3] Family pride was characteristic of the Roman nobility of this period; see Hieron. *Ep.* 108. 3, 4; Ambros. *Expos. ps. cxviii*, 20. 17 (cf. his description of the great gentleman 'avis atavisque nobilis, et maiorum honestatus infulis, prosapiae veteris clarus insignibus', *Hexaem.* iii. 30). Even *nouveaux riches* pretended to be of ancient and distinguished lineage, Ammian. xxviii. 4. 7; Auson. *Epig.* xxvi *in divitem quendam.* The *imagines* or portrait-masks in coloured wax of the ancestors of a noble family are alluded to by Ambrose, *In ps. 38 enarr.* 24.

[4] O. Seeck, op. cit., pp. xlv, xlvi.

decide'.[1] These affluent nobles, however, did not succumb to the temptation to abandon themselves to a life of mere dissipation or inglorious ease. They were active in public affairs, and devoted themselves generously to the service of the State. It was, indeed, their great delight to occupy positions of responsibility. 'He pined, when out of office, like a fish out of water', the historian writes of Probus.[2] Yet few showed striking gifts as statesmen or administrators. Conservative to the backbone, they lived and moved and had their being in the past, and had apparently neither the power nor the wish to understand the forces and ideas of their own age.

When not engaged in governing provinces, Symmachus and his friends led a stately, spectacular life in their sumptuous palaces on the Caelian or the Aventine or in the region of the Circus Flaminius. Their days were spent in a trivial round of conventional social observances. They held morning receptions of their clients; paid innumerable ceremonial visits;[3] attended such social functions as the wedding of a friend, the sealing of a will, or a declamation by some new rhetorician; and entertained one another with stiff and solemn dinner-parties. Always the most scrupulous attention was paid to etiquette. To omit to return a call was accounted a heinous offence, and a new praetor or consul felt himself grievously affronted if a distinguished acquaintance neglected to take part in the ceremonies of his inauguration.

When the autumn heats rendered the city unendurable, or a popular riot occasioned alarm, the great people would send for their travelling-coaches and withdraw for a while to their country seats.[4] Perhaps Formiae would attract them with its delicious climate and lovely bay, or Tibur with its sunny terraces, or 'cool' Praeneste famous for its rose-gardens, or Laurentum with its fine sea-views and extensive boar-forests, or fashionable Baiae, 'the Brighton of Rome'. In their beautiful

---

[1] Ammian. xxvii. 11. 1. So Ausonius describes the estates of his friend Paulinus as 'regna', and says that, if sold, they would pass into the hands of 'a hundred masters' (*Ep.* 24. 115, 116).

[2] Ammian. xxvii. 11. 3.

[3] Hieron. *Ep.* 43. 2: 'I am ashamed of the time we daily waste in paying and receiving visits'; cf. ibid. 46. 11.

[4] A charming picture of a great Roman country house at this period is found in *Vita sanctae Melaniae iunioris*, c. 18 (published in *Analect. Bolland.* vol. viii, 1889).

and luxurious villas, where everything was so admirably
designed to minister comfort and satisfy artistic taste, they
occupied themselves agreeably—hunting,[1] ball-playing, breeding cattle, improving the culture of their fields, decorating their
saloons with marbles or mosaics, dispensing hospitality to troops
of guests, and sedulously nursing their health about which they
exhibited perpetual anxiety.[2] If they wearied of one mansion
they would move on to another, where similar gardens and
colonnades, similar libraries and baths, similar apartments
arranged to suit the varying temperature of the seasons, and
similar occupations and amusements awaited them. It is
evident that they were not insensible to the reposeful charm of
country life.[3] Yet their tastes were predominantly urban, and
they could not long settle in any place, however pleasant or
salubrious, that was far away from Rome.

The society of Symmachus was fastidiously decorous. With
sublime self-complacency these well-bred people blessed themselves on their emancipation from the grosser forms of self-
indulgence which had been prevalent among their ancestors.[4]
In their highly respectable company the 'slavish gluttony' of the
famous epicures of former days was providentially unknown.[5]
The extravagant items of the old menus astonished and dis-

[1] An interesting description of the manners of a hunting squire is given by
Maximus of Turin, *Serm.* 25: 'All day long he spends in the hunt; now urging his
thralls to measureless clamour, now signing them to keep perfect silence. He is
full of good humour if he has had a good bag, but furious if by chance he has "lost"
(as he says) the game which he never had. He carries on the business with such
zeal that you might suppose that the Lenten fast was commanded on purpose that
he might go coursing. . . . There are many who, when they return from the chase,
take more care of their hounds than of their men, making the former lie down by
them, sleep near them, and have their meals in their presence, while they care not
a jot whether their slaves are dying of hunger or not. Nay, what is worse, unless
the hound's food has been carefully prepared, the servant is punished on the hound's
account. Thus in many mansions you see sleek, well-fed hounds running about,
while the servants walk pale and tottering.' Hunting was commended as a suitable sport for young men (Symmach. *Epp.* v. 68).

[2] Symmachus, for instance, was perpetually fussing about his health or that of
members of his family; see *Epp.* i. 20, 85; ii. 22, 48; iii. 38; iv. 54; v. 33, 96; vi. 4,
15, 16, 28, 29, 41, 45, 47, 48, 54, 55, 58, 59, 64, 65, 73; vii. 71. The chief enemy of
the Roman nobles appears to have been gout (Symmach. *Epp.* vii. 73; viii. 18;
ix. 127, 128). Ammianus, xiv. 6. 23, notes the prevalence of diseases in Rome, and
the elaborate precautions taken against infection.

[3] Symmach. *Epp.* ii. 26; iii. 23; v. 78; vii. 15, 18, 31.

[4] Macrob. *Sat.* iii. 14. 2; cf. iii. 13. 16; 17. 12.

[5] Ibid. iii. 13. 1–3; 15. 1–9; 16. 7–9, 11.

gusted them, and they did not even know the meaning of
many of the fantastic delicacies mentioned in the old sumptuary
laws.[1] No fourth-century man of quality could ever so far forget
himself as to associate familiarly with common persons, as
Cicero used to associate with Roscius;[2] still less could he exhibit
himself (as some old nobles had been known to do) reeling
intoxicated in the Forum or sitting on the Bench so overcome
by liquor as hardly to be able to keep his eyes open.[3] Neither he
nor his elegant wife nor his exquisitely mannered daughters
could conceivably so far unbend from their frigid dignity as to
dance.[4] At his 'abundant but admirably regulated' dinners,[5]
with their 'reasonable succession of dishes',[6] no indecent panto-
mine or ballet-dancer was introduced to amuse the guests;[7]
instead there was conversation, which might be sprightly and
entertaining, but must in any case be strictly unexceptionable
in moral tone.[8]

The great ambition of these grandees was to maintain the
prestige of themselves and their order.[9] Thus it was considered
a point of honour to discharge with lavish magnificence the one
remaining function of the old City offices—the provision of
spectacles for the people.[10] Many, indeed, ruined themselves in
their extravagant attempts to out-do their predecessors in the
splendour of such exhibitions.[11] The letters of Symmachus concerning the spectacles which he provided on his son's behalf
give some idea of the immense trouble that was taken and the
enormous expense that was incurred.[12] The praetorian games of
the younger Symmachus cost his father about £80,000.

Most of the nobles were zealous pagans. They were anxiously
concerned about the maintenance of the traditional rites—the
performance of the sacrifices, the celebration of the festivals,
the observation of prodigies which required expiation.[13] They

---

[1] Ibid. iii. 13. 10–13; 17. 11–12.   [2] Ibid. iii. 14. 11–12.   [3] Ibid. iii. 16. 14–16.
[4] Ibid. iii. 14. 4–8.   [5] Ibid. i. 2. 12.   [6] Ibid. ii. 1. 1.
[7] Ibid. ii. 1. 7; iii. 14. 4.   [8] Ibid. i. 1. 2–4; ii. 1. 5–9.
[9] Symmachus honestly believed that the great senatorial families constituted
'the better part of the human race' (*Epp.* i. 52); Prudentius characterized them as
'the fairest lights of the world' (*Contr. Symmach.* i. 545-6).
[10] Symmach. *Epp.* iv. 60.   [11] Ambros. *De Officiis*, ii. 109.
[12] Symmach. *Epp.* ii. 46, 76–8, 81; iv. 8, 58–60, 63; v. 20–2, 56, 59, 62, 65;
vi. 42, 43; vii. 76; ix. 12, 117, 119, 132. Cf. Claudian's account of the splendid
*ludi* provided by Flavius Mallius Theodorus (*De Fl. Mall. Theod. Cons.* 279 ff.).
[13] Symmach. *Epp.* i. 49; ii. 34, 53; vi. 40.

attended the Chapters of the Pontifical College—though some even of the most orthodox pagans, in order to ingratiate themselves with the Christian Court, were inclined to invent excuses for the evasion of this duty.[1] Symmachus himself stood firmly for the most rigid conservatism in religious matters. To him all old customs were sacred. When the Vestals decided to honour their patron Praetextatus by erecting a statue of him in their hall, Symmachus protested against the innovation;[2] he was shocked that a Vestal should desire release from her vow before she had completed her full term of service;[3] he was even so bigoted as to demand that the archaic punishment should be inflicted on one of the sacred sisterhood who was proved to have been frail.[4] By him and all his circle the great new religious movement, which was already triumphing in every part of the Roman world, was contemptuously ignored. It is significant that in the conversations of the *Saturnalia* of Macrobius, although religion is largely dealt with, not one solitary reference to Christianity occurs.

One attractive feature of this society is its enthusiasm for literature and every kind of learning. It is pleasant to see Symmachus 'renewing his youth' as he superintends his son's initiation into the study of the Greek classics.[5] But Symmachus and his friends did more than supervise the education of their children. They were themselves not contemptible scholars. Praetextatus, for example, translated Aristotle's *Analytics*, and was a skilful emendator of Greek and Latin texts.[6] Flavian, again, was a learned historian, translated Philostratus' *Life of Apollonius of Tyana*, and compiled a work on philosophy which was still read in the Middle Ages.[7] They and the rest were never so happy as

[1] Symmach. *Epp.* i. 46, 47, 49, 51; ii. 36, 53.
[2] Ibid. ii. 36. The statue with its inscription was found in 1883, when the Atrium of Vesta was excavated. [3] Ibid. ix. 108.
[4] Ibid. ix. 147. A lapsed Vestal was scourged, attired as a corpse, and carried with funeral ceremony to the Campus Sceleratus, near the Colline Gate, where she was buried alive in an underground vault.
[5] Ibid. iv. 20: cf. the interest taken by Macrobius in the education of his son (*Sat.* Praef. 1, 2) and by Ausonius in that of his grandson (*Ad nepotem Ausonium Protrepticon de studio puerili*).
[6] *C.I.L.* vi. 1779 d; O. Seeck, *Symmachus*, p. lxxxvii.
[7] *C.I.L.* vi. 1782, 1783; O. Seeck, op. cit. p. cxv. Attached to the circle were Servius, the great commentator on Virgil, Sallust, who emended the text of Apuleius (Hildebrand, *Apuleius*, Prol. p. lxi), Eustathius the philosopher (Macrob. *Sat.* i. 5. 13; vii. 1. 8), and others.

when engaged in the discussion of some literary, philosophical, or antiquarian subject, which afforded them an opportunity of displaying their erudition.[1] If they were unable to meet for conversation, they indited elaborate letters in the fashionable euphuistic style, or circulated verses and other literary trifles for criticism. Their admiration for each other was unbounded. Symmachus considered—or affected to consider—the poetry of his friend Ausonius to be equal to that of Virgil; Ausonius, not to be surpassed in politeness, declared that the oratory of his friend Symmachus combined the excellences of Isocrates, Demosthenes, and Cicero.[2] It was all very amiable but manifestly absurd. For, with the exception of Ausonius, not one of these dilettanti possessed a spark of original genius. They were mere stylists—pedantic imitators of classic models—with whom it was an acknowledged principle that 'the fruit of reading is to emulate what you find good in others, and by dexterous borrowing to turn to your own use whatever is most admirable in their utterances.'[3]

It is evident that these 'Romans of the old school' were not deficient in fine qualities. Perhaps they were rather selfish—too exclusively engrossed in themselves and their order, too unconcerned for the suffering masses outside the charmed circle of rank and wealth, too indifferent even to the supreme interests of the State. But, at any rate, we observe in them warm family affection, generous capacity for friendship, and considerable kindliness towards servants and dependants.[4] Their minds were cultivated; their lives were decent; and they seem

---

[1] The fictitious conversations in the *Saturnalia* of Macrobius illustrate the topics debated and the manner in which they were handled. The subjects include Virgilian criticism (*Sat.* i. 24; iii–vi *passim*; cf. D. Comparetti, *Vergil in the Middle Ages*, pp. 63–9), antiquities (*Sat.* i. 6 ff.; 12 ff.), the philosophy of religion (ibid. i. 17–23), etymology (ibid. i. 12. 8; 15. 4–20; vi. 9. 1–7), witticisms of famous persons (ibid. ii. 2 ff.), Roman manners and social customs (ibid. iii. 13–15. 17), subjects and methods of conversation at the dinner-table (*ibid.* vii. 1–3), and 'science', i.e. the consideration of such questions as whether a simple or varied diet is better for the digestion, why women get drunk rarely and old men easily, why spinning round makes one dizzy, what causes people to blush, and why honey is best when fresh and wine when old (ibid. vii. 4–16). It is noteworthy that the subject of politics is avoided.

[2] Symmach. *Epp.* i. 14; Auson. *Ep.* 17.

[3] Macrob. *Sat.* vi. 1. 2.

[4] For generous sentiments concerning slaves see Macrob. *Sat.* i. 11 (cf. Seneca, *Ep.* 47). Symmachus, however, had a poor opinion of slaves (*Epp.* vi. 8; ix. 140).

honestly to have tried to do their duty as they understood it. With their moral respectability, their devout yet tolerant piety, their passionate delight in literature, their consummate breeding and perfect manners, they certainly represented fourth-century pagan society at its highest.

Again, just as there were sounder elements in the pagan society of Rome than might be inferred from Ammianus, so also there were sounder elements in the Christian society of the city than Jerome's bitter diatribes would lead us to imagine. In the latter part of the century the increasing company of sincere and devoted Christians attracted considerable attention. Many wealthy and aristocratic women about this time withdrew from fashionable society, and dedicated themselves to works of piety and charity. Marcella was the leader of one group, Lea of another. Paula, before she migrated to the East, was the centre of a distinguished ascetic circle.[1] Fabiola devoted her wealth to the establishment of a great hospice in Portus Romanus and to the endowment of monasteries in Rome and in the islands off the coast.[2] Among the men, perhaps the most conspicuous was the senator Pammachius—the chief of the Christian party in Rome, who at one time, though a layman, was seriously thought of for the Papacy. After the premature death of his wife, he had adopted a life of strict asceticism. A large portion of his fortune was spent in helping Fabiola to found her hospice, and his princely palace on the Caelian was converted into the Chuch of the martyrs St. John and St. Paul. He himself, while renouncing the splendours appropriate to his rank, continued conscientiously to discharge public duties. He regularly attended the debates of the Senate; but even in the Senate-House he wore the black habiliments of a monk, and on his way thither he was escorted, not by the usual retinue of obsequious clients, but by a grateful throng of indigent people whom he had generously befriended.[3] In view of such examples one who knew something of the degradation of the mass of Rome's population was yet emboldened to declare, 'Thou, Rome, wouldest have no need to

[1] See above, p. 4, n. 4.
[2] For the history of Fabiola see Hieron. *Ep.* 77.
[3] Hieron. *Ep.* 66; cf. 49, 4; Paulin. Nolan. *Ep.* 13. For an account of the hospice at Portus built by Pammachius and Fabiola, see De Rossi, *Bullett. archeol. crist.* 1866, p. 99 'Lo xenodochio di Pammachio in Porto'; and for the Caelian building, P. Germano, *La casa celimontana dei SS. martiri Giovanni e Paolo*, Rome, 1889.

dread the judgements with which the Babylon of the Apocalypse is threatened, if thy senators ever devoted themselves to such services of charity.'[1]

In the beginning of this chapter I mentioned a few of the classical edifices which astonished the Emperor Constantius in the spring of A.D. 357. I will end by referring briefly to certain features of Christian Rome which would have attracted the attention of a foreign pilgrim[2] in the closing years of the fourth century.

As the stranger explored the city and its environs, he would observe a great number of buildings connected with Christian worship—oblong basilicas, circular baptisteries, oratories, and mortuary chapels. The greater basilicas naturally would first claim his consideration. At first sight of one of these, however, he would probably experience some disappointment; for the plain brick church, with its long straight body and sloping roofs, must have seemed dull and insignificant—especially when compared with the external loveliness of the pagan temples. Without pausing, therefore, to bestow more than a cursory glance on the exterior of the building, the pilgrim would push his way, through vociferous crowds of beggars,[3] to the stately gateway which opened into the *atrium*. Here he would find himself in a flagged square, surrounded by a colonnade, with a fountain or vase containing water (*cantharus*) in its centre. On the further side of the square rose the lofty front of the church, pierced by three (or occasionally by five) entrances. Immediately before the entrances there was a covered walk or porch, the left corner of which was in some cases walled in, so as to form a sacristy.

After dipping his hands in the fountain[4]—a symbol of inward purification—and devoutly kissing the threshold or door-posts

---

[1] Paulin. Nolan. *Ep.* 13. 15. For the comparison of Rome with the mystic Babylon, see also Hieron. *Ep.* 46. 11.

[2] Prudentius describes the throngs of pilgrims visiting the tombs of the martyrs in Rome, *Peristeph.* xi. 195–212; xii. 1–4, 57–66.

[3] The approaches to churches were the favourite resort of beggars, to whom the faithful, on their way to worship, distributed alms; see Hieron. *Ep.* 22. 32; Ambros. *Expos. ev. Luc.* viii. 76; Chrysost. *De Poenit. Hom.* 3. 2. On special occasions the poor were entertained at banquets, in, or in front of, the *atria* (Paulin. Nolan. *Ep.* 13. 11; 34. 2).

[4] Eusebius, *H.E.* x. 4; Paulin. Nolan. *Ep.* 32. 15. The custom is perhaps referred to by Tertullian, *De Orat.* 13: 'What is the sense of entering on prayer with hands, indeed, washed, but with unclean spirit?'

of the church,[1] the pilgrim would pass through the richly
ornamented central door, with its heavy embroidered curtains,
and enter the basilica. Just within, at the commencement of the
nave and stretching across its entire width, was the *narthex*—
a space fenced off by a lattice and intended for the accommodation of catechumens and penitents. This enclosure was guarded
by vigilant door-keepers, whose duty it was to prevent unauthorized persons from penetrating further into the interior during
the celebration of the Sacred Mysteries.

Beyond the *narthex* stretched the nave, with aisles on either
side. The aisles were separated from the nave by lines of
columns, whose capitals supported arches or a marble entablature with decorative frieze and cornice. A softened light was
admitted through the perforated marble windows of the cleres-
tory. The columns were of marble; the walls were faced with
marble slabs and adorned with pictures in mosaic; the broad
floor, unencumbered by benches, was covered with marble or
coloured mosaic. Over all was a flat wooden ceiling, ornamented with panels and lavishly gilded, from which metal
chandeliers depended.

Towards the further end of the nave was the square choir or
chancel, occupied by the inferior clergy and choristers. It was
enclosed by a marble balustrade; and on each side of it was an
*ambo* or lectern, from which the lessons were read.

The transept—where one existed—was separated from the
nave by a lofty triumphal arch, resplendent with mosaics,
which spanned the space between the last two columns. Immediately behind this arch the arms of the transept opened out
to right and left. Though broad, they were not generally prolonged, and projected but slightly beyond the main lines of the
building.

In the centre of the transept, near the triumphal arch, stood
the altar—a square marble slab, supported by pillars, and
generally raised on steps. If the church contained the body of a
saint, it rested in a vault immediately below the altar. Over the
altar was a marble or metal canopy, upheld by four columns.

Across the basilica, between the altar and the choir, there
was frequently set a light barrier, called the *pergula*, consisting of

---

[1] Prudentius, *Peristeph.* ii. 519–20; Paulin. Nolan. *Poem.* xviii. 250. On the custom of kissing sacred spots and objects see Prudent. *Peristeph.* v. 556; ix. 100; xi. 193.

a row of delicate columns connected at the top by an entablature and below by a balustrade. This structure served to mark off the hallowed space about the altar from the body of the church. Ornamental in itself, it was further embellished by a profusion of valuable objects—crowns, monograms, crosses, chalices, candelabra, inscribed tablets, and other gifts and votive offerings[1]—which were suspended from the columns or rested on the balustrade.

Beyond the altar, at the extreme end of the church, was the semicircular apse. Its wall was sheeted with marble, and its shell-shaped vault was incrusted with mosaics, usually depicting the glorified Saviour and saints on a golden background. Round the base of the semicircle ran a marble bench for the use of the higher clergy; against the wall in the centre, approached by a flight of steps, was the elevated episcopal throne.

The splendour of such an interior could hardly fail to make an impression even on the most stolid observer. At the solemn night vigils especially, the scene must have been dazzling. Innumerable lights blazed in the chandeliers which depended from the ceiling, and in candlesticks and candelabra in the vicinity of the altar.[2] The marble columns, the polished walls,

---

[1] The custom of presenting offerings in acknowledgement of deliverance from peril or sickness, or of some special answer to prayer, was prevalent among both pagans and Christians. Large numbers of such offerings made by heathen have been discovered near famous temples. They include tablets with inscriptions, figures of deities, lamps intended to burn before the statue of a god, imitations of members of the human body. Similar offerings were made by Christians in the churches. Some of them, belonging to the fourth and fifth centuries, are still preserved. They are generally inscribed with the name of the donor, followed by the formula 'votum solvit'. Theodoret, speaking of the offerings at the tombs of martyrs, mentions models of eyes, arms, legs, and other parts of the human body, made of gold, silver, or wood, as well as gifts (presumably tablets) attesting the cures wrought by the martyrs (*Graec. Affect. Curat.*, viii; Migne, *P.G.* lxxxiii, p. 1032).

[2] Many writers notice the brilliant illumination of the basilicas. Paulinus of Nola mentions the lights depending from the roof (*Poem.* xxvii. 389 ff.) and massed in the neighbourhood of the altar (*Poem.* xiv. 99). Prudentius says that those hanging from the panelled ceiling resembled a host of stars of which heaven seemed to have been robbed (*Cathem.* v. 141–8). For the maintenance of the lights special endowments were provided by Constantine and other founders or benefactors of churches. At this period lights were not placed on the altar itself, but were accumulated in its vicinity. Lamps and candles were burned also at the tombs of martyrs and in their honour—a custom attacked by Vigilantius and defended by Jerome (*Contr. Vigilant.* 4, 7). On this it may be observed that the burning of lights in honour of the gods was a feature of paganism frequently ridiculed by earlier Christian writers (Tertullian, *Apol.* 35, 46; *De Idol.* 15; Lactant. *Inst. Div.* vi. 2).

the gorgeous mosaics on the triumphal arch and apse, flashed and sparkled as if on fire. Huge curtains of rich material were stretched over the entrances, and between the columns of the nave, and across the terminal arches of the aisles. The whole interior scintillated with light and colour; and when, at the time of service, it was filled with throngs of worshippers clad in the picturesque vesture of antiquity—the men and women separated by movable wooden screens, the consecrated virgins in their own enclosure, distinguished persons in places specially reserved—the spectacle must have been one of extraordinary magnificence.

Of the Roman basilicas three at least would inevitably be visited by our pilgrim. He would probably hasten first to the papal cathedral—the venerable Basilica of the Saviour, built by Constantine the Great close to the palace once owned by the Laterani in the second region, and generally known as the Constantinian or Lateran Basilica.[1] This famous sanctuary —described in the Middle Ages as 'the mother and head of all the churches of the city and of the world'—exhibited features of special interest. While, in accordance with early custom, the other Roman basilicas possessed but one altar, the Lateran had in addition seven silver altar-tables, which were disposed near the high altar, and were probably used for the reception of the oblations of the people. Over the great altar Constantine had placed a superb canopy of beaten silver; and in front of it he had set two magnificent candelabra, one of silver and the other of gold. Between the altar and the apse he had further erected four bronze-gilt Corinthian pillars, which at the present day are still standing near the side altar of the Blessed Sacrament. The apse was decorated with a mosaic bust of Christ, which in later centuries was believed to be the earliest portrait of the Saviour publicly displayed in Rome. The nave was covered with a marvellous gilded ceiling; and it was possibly to this adornment that the building owed its name of 'the Golden Basilica'. Hard by the church was the spacious Episcopium Lateranense, which since A.D. 311 had been the official residence of the popes.

Leaving the Lateran, the pilgrim would probably proceed through the city, along the route which became traditional in the Middle Ages, to the Vatican region beyond the Tiber. Here

[1] On this church see Rohault de Fleury, *Le Latran au moyen-âge*, 1877.

in a sparsely inhabited district of gardens and olive-yards, inter-
sected by high roads bordered with sepulchral monuments,
stood the Basilica of St. Peter, Prince of the Apostles.[1] According to tradition the saint had suffered martyrdom by crucifixion
in the Circus of Nero, and had been buried at a spot close at
hand on the Via Cornelia.[2] The basilica, erected by Constantine over the site of the entombment, was built on the northern
side of the Neronian Circus and largely out of its materials. It
was a church of imposing dimensions. The entrances, which
were at the east—this was a usual orientation at Rome in the
case of the Constantinian and more ancient churches—were
approached through a large square *atrium*, with a *cantharus* in the
centre. The interior showed a nave and four aisles, crossed at
the end by a transept, beyond which curved the semicircular
apse. What constituted the chief distinction of the church,
however, was the Tomb of the Fisherman.[3] The small subterranean mortuary-chamber had been overlaid by Constantine
with an 'immovable' covering of bronze. Above the chamber a
little shrine or 'ark', glittering with gold, had been erected.
From the floor of this 'ark' a hollow shaft descended into the
chamber underneath, and through this channel small objects,
such as handkerchiefs, could be let down and blessed by
touching the hallowed vault. Above the 'ark' was the altar of
the basilica—a silver table edged with gold and precious stones.
Before the 'ark' hung a golden candelabrum adorned with fifty
figures of dolphins, and at the four corners of the shrine were
placed four brazen candlesticks covered with silver medallions.
The mosaic on the triumphal arch depicted Constantine presenting a model of the basilica to Christ and St. Peter. The inscription ran—'Since, under Thy guidance, the world has risen
triumphant to the skies, the victor Constantine has raised this
hall to Thee.'

The last of the three principal Roman basilicas stood on the
left bank of the Tiber, on the high road to Ostia. It was a very
small three-aisled church, built by Constantine over the Tomb

---

[1] R. Lanciani, *Pagan and Christian Rome*, pp. 126 ff.; H. Grisar, *History of Rome
and the Popes in the Middle Ages*, i, pp. 277 ff.

[2] The earliest authority for St. Peter's crucifixion at Rome is Tertullian, *Scor-
piace*, 15; *De Praescr. Haeret.* 36. That he was crucified head downwards is first
attested by Origen, quoted by Eusebius, *H.E.* iii. 1.

[3] Gregory of Tours, *De Glor. Mart.* 28, furnishes some interesting details.

of the Apostle Paul.[1] Here, as at the Vatican, the sepulchral chamber was covered by an 'ark', above which stood the altar under its stately canopy. But this early Constantinian edifice was about to disappear. In the year A.D. 386 the Emperors Theodosius, Valentinian II, and Arcadius directed the Praefect of Rome to submit to the Senate and people a scheme for the complete reconstruction of the church. To carry out the design, it was necessary to reverse the orientation of the basilica; but the Tomb of the Apostle was not disturbed, and the new altar still occupied the ancient site. The beautiful new building,[2] the work of the architect Cyriades, was dedicated by Pope Siricius in November A.D. 390, and continued in existence till the disastrous fire of July 1823.

There were other historic churches which a pilgrim would hardly fail to visit. Among these may be mentioned the Sessorian Basilica (S. Croce in Gerusalemme), wherein was deposited a portion of the True Cross discovered by Helena; the small but renowned Basilica of the Roman martyr Lawrence, erected by Constantine above the saint's grave in the Cemetery of Cyriaca —a shrine more frequented than any in Rome excepting the churches of SS. Peter and Paul;[3] the venerated Basilica of the Roman martyr Agnes on the Via Nomentana;[4] the large and beautiful Basilica of St. Valentine, built by Pope Julius I behind the first milestone on the Flaminian Road, adjoining the cemetery of the martyr;[5] and the new Basilica Liberii (S. Maria Maggiore), which Pope Liberius had founded on the Esquiline near the Macellum of Livia, and the nave of which (according

---

[1] See P. Belloni, *Sulla grandezza e disposizione della primitiva basilica ostiense*, 1835.

[2] See the description of Prudentius, *Peristeph.* xii. 45–54.

[3] St. Lawrence, in the estimation of the Romans, ranked next after the two Apostles. Ambrose gives some particulars concerning his martyrdom (*De Officiis,* i. 204–6; ii. 140, 141) and mentions vows made to him by pious people (*De Excessu Sat.* i. 17; *Exhort. Virginitatis,* 15). Prudentius describes his martyrdom and attests the veneration with which he was regarded (*Peristeph.* ii). See also Augustin. *Serm.* 302–5. But the genuine acts of the martyrdom were lost in Augustine's time.

[4] On St. Agnes see Ambros. *De Officiis,* i. 203; *De Virginibus,* i. 5–9; Prudentius, *Peristeph.* xiv. A sermon and a poem on St. Agnes, and an undoubtedly spurious *Passion,* are printed in the Appendix to Ambrose's Works (Migne) vol. iv, pp. 701–5, 735–42, 1210–11. See further P. Franchi de Cavalieri, *Santa Agnese nella tradizione e nella leggenda,* Roma, 1899.

[5] O. Marucchi, *Il cimitero e la basilica di S. Valentino,* Roma, 1890. We know little more of St. Valentine than that he suffered martyrdom under the Emperor Claudius II (Gothicus).

to the view of many modern critics) the same Pope had adorned with the famous series of exquisite mosaics.

Finally, the pilgrim would not quit Rome without inspecting some of the catacombs—those vast subterranean cemeteries outside the walls, wherein so many of the early Roman martyrs were interred. In the latter part of the fourth century burial on the surface was coming into fashion:[1] yet the catacombs were still visited by crowds of people, consisting partly of sight-seers, eager to view those strange constructions which were commonly reckoned among the 'marvels' of Rome,[2] and partly of devout persons who came to do honour to the martyrs whose remains were buried there.[3]

'When I was a boy at Rome', writes Jerome, 'and was being educated in liberal studies, I was accustomed, with others of like age and mind, to visit on Sundays the sepulchres of the apostles and martyrs. And often did I enter the crypts, deep dug in the earth, with their walls on either side lined with the bodies of the dead, where everything is so dark that it almost seems as if the psalmist's words were fulfilled, *Let them go down quick into hell.* Here and there the light, not entering in through windows, but filtering down from above through shafts, relieves the horror of the darkness. But again, as one cautiously moves forward, the black night closes round, and there comes to the mind the line of Virgil, *Horror ubique animos, simul ipsa silentia terrent.*'[4]

We may imagine our pilgrim mingling with the throng of

[1] The dated inscriptions prove that a change was taking place from underground to surface burial. Taking these as a basis of calculation, we can state roughly that between A.D. 338 and 360 one-third of the corpses buried, between A.D. 364 and 369 one-half, between A.D. 373 and 400 two-thirds, were interred outside the catacombs. After A.D. 410 the use of the subterranean cemeteries as places of burial appears to have ceased. Henceforward the dead were laid in graveyards situated above or near the catacombs, and still outside the city walls. Intramural burial at Rome did not become common till the sixth century.

[2] An inscription found at Thebes and published in *Archives des missions scientifiques,* 1866, ii, p. 484, thus refers to the Roman catacombs and the crypts of Egypt: 'Antonius Theodorus, intendant of Egypt and Phoenicia, who has spent many years in the Queen-city of Rome, has seen the marvels both there and here.'

[3] Hieron. *Comm. in Gal.* ii, Praef. 'Ubi alibi tanto studio et frequentia ad ecclesias et ad martyrum sepulcra concurritur?' Prudentius, in his description of the subterranean tomb of St. Hippolytus (*Peristeph.* xi. 153 ff.), speaks of the dim crypt into which one descended by many winding stairs, of the gathering darkness, of the occasional apertures cut in the roof to let in air and light, and of the crowds of Roman and foreign pilgrims hastening in the early morning to invoke the assistance of the saint and receive the sacrament at his altar: compare ibid. xii. 1–2, 57 ff.　　　　[4] Hieron. *Comm. in Ezech.* c. 40, v. 5.

tourists and worshippers. Near the entrance to the catacomb, if it chanced to be the anniversary of a local martyr, he might witness the curious spectacle of a funerary feast in progress. For the pagan custom of holding banquets in honour of the dead[1] had been adopted by Christians, especially in Italy and Africa, and associated with the martyrs' commemorations. Sometimes these meals took place in a hall belonging to the cemetery, sometimes in, or in front of, the forecourt of the basilica built above a martyr's tomb. The provision of food for such celebrations was a popular form of charity. Pious persons were in the habit of going from cemetery to cemetery with baskets of victuals and flasks of wine, which they distributed among the poor.[2] The observance was productive of serious scandals. 'Many,' writes Augustine, 'drink most luxuriously over the dead, and, when they make a feast for the departed, bury themselves over the buried and place their gluttony and drunkenness to the score of religion.'[3] 'Drunkenness,' says the author of the treatise *De Duplici Martyrio*, 'is so common in our Africa that it is scarcely deemed a crime. Do we not see Christians compelled by Christians to be drunk at the memorials of the martyrs?'[4] Ambrose forbade these feasts in Milan[5]—though not with immediate success, since, even after his prohibition, he still had reason to complain of those 'who bring cups to the sepulchres of the martyrs, and there drink till evening, imagining forsooth that otherwise their prayers cannot be heard'.[6] Augustine eventually procured their abolition in Africa.[7] At Rome, however, the objectionable custom lingered on, and we have the testimony of Augustine that 'cases of drunkenness are daily reported at the Basilica of St. Peter'.[8]

[1] According to pagan custom (at least in the case of great funerals) a feast was held on the day of the funeral, either near the tomb or in the house of the deceased. On the ninth day after there was also a *novendialis cena*, and sometimes the anniversary was similarly commemorated. Besides these private celebrations the pagans observed a festival of All Souls (Feralia) on 21 February, which was preceded by the Parentalia, 13–21 February. Among other ceremonies commemorative meals were eaten near the tombs of the departed: see Macrob. *Sat*. i. 4. 14; Tertullian. *De Test. An.* 4; *De Res. Carn.* 1; *De Spect.* 13.
[2] Augustin. *Confess.* vi. 2; cf. *De Civit. Dei*, viii. 27.
[3] Id. *De Mor. Eccl.* i. 75; cf. *Contr. Faust.* xx. 21.
[4] *De Dupl. Mart.* 25 (Hartel's *Cyprian*, Appendix, p. 236).
[5] Augustin. *Confess.* vi. 2.                                    [6] Ambros. *De Elia*, 62.
[7] Augustin. *Epp.* 22. 3–6, and 29; Third Council of Carthage, can. 30.
[8] Augustin. *Epp.* 29. 10.

Entering the catacomb, and descending a flight of steps, the pilgrim would find himself in a bewildering network of passages and sepulchral chambers. The long and extremely narrow galleries, crossing one another in all directions, were lined with *loculi*. These were low, shelf-like cavities, excavated in the walls, and just large enough to accommodate bodies placed lengthwise. Commencing a few inches above the level of the floor, they rose tier upon tier, on each side of the gallery, to the number of six or eight ranges. Each *loculus* usually contained but a single body; some, however, were dug more deeply, so as to be capable of receiving two, three, or four bodies, lying side by side. After the introduction of the corpse, the *loculus* was hermetically closed with a marble slab, or with tiles very carefully cemented. Opening out of the galleries, rather like bedrooms opening out of the passages of a monster hotel, were numerous vaulted sepulchral chambers or *cubicula*, containing, in addition to the usual *loculi*, artistically ornamented sarcophagi and altar-tombs, placed in arched or rectangular recesses which had been hollowed out of the tufa. Into the galleries and chambers light and air were admitted at intervals by means of shafts, called *luminaria*, communicating with the surface. Further illumination was supplied by lamps, suspended from the roof or standing in niches or on brackets.

This complex system of corridors and chambers constituted the first story of the catacomb. At lower levels there were similar systems. Steep and narrow staircases connected the different stories of the vast necropolis.

Through the mysterious ramifications of this subterranean labyrinth the pilgrim, lamp in hand, would make his way. Sometimes he would pause to admire the mural paintings with which many of the chambers were decorated. Sometimes he would stoop to examine a delicately executed bas-relief adorning the front of some early sarcophagus. Or with curiosity he would scan the inscriptions on the *loculi*. One slab bears simply a name daubed in red or black pigment; a second displays in addition one or other of the Christian symbols—the palm-branch, the fish, the anchor of eternal hope; a third reports that the deceased had in his lifetime purchased this double tomb for himself and his wife; a fourth attests that somebody, long dead and doubtless forgotten, 'in the place of coolness, light and peace reposes'; others refer to the powers of the saints —'May Valentine refresh thee', 'May the lord Hippolytus refresh thee', 'May the glory of St. Valentine be granted thee'. In one of the *cubicula*, perhaps, would be found a group of people praying before the shrine of a martyr. The atmosphere is stifling. The eyes are dazzled with the glare of many lamps. A priest is reciting prayers, to which the small congregation, kneeling on the tessellated pavement, makes responses. Meanwhile, just outside the entrance of the chamber, a wealthy Roman is driving a bargain with one of the cemetery-architects[1] for the purchase of a burial-site in close proximity to the martyr's resting-place.[2]

Such was that strange, picturesque, pagan-Christian confusion that was Rome, wherein Ambrose passed his boyhood and youth. In the next chapter I shall resume the history of his career.

[1] A large number of inscriptions, belonging to the latter part of the fourth century and the first quarter of the fifth, preserve record of such transactions. The *fossores* appear to have established a sort of right of property in the catacombs and sold burial-sites, often at immoderate prices.

[2] Burial near the remains of a saint or martyr was esteemed a high privilege: see the inscription of Damasus in the vault of the popes in the Cemetery of Callistus: 'Here lie together in great numbers the holy bodies you are seeking. These tombs contain their remains, but their souls are in the heavenly kingdom. . . . I confess that I wished to find my last resting-place here, but I did not dare to vex the holy ashes of the pious.' Augustine in his treatise *De cura gerenda pro mortuis* discusses a question raised by Paulinus of Nola, viz. whether burial in proximity to saints and martyrs does really benefit the deceased. He considers that it is advantageous, inasmuch as the surviving relatives are thereby reminded to commend their departed friends to the protection and intercession of the martyrs near whom they are interred (*De cura*, 6, 7).

## CHAPTER III

# AMBROSE MADE BISHOP

WHEN Ambrose was a student at Rome, education was still mainly in the hands of pagans. Even before the notorious measure of Julian (A.D. 362), which forbade Christians to teach grammar, rhetoric, and philosophy,[1] it was considered unseemly that Christians should lecture on the literature of paganism and observe pagan festivals, as was the custom in the schools.[2] The paucity of monumental inscriptions and literary notices referring to Christian teachers is a proof that their numbers were few. Under these circumstances Christian parents were accustomed to send their sons to some clergyman or ascetic, that, in addition to the school education, they might receive instruction in the elements of the Christian religion. In Ambrose's case this appears to have been done. The preceptor chosen for him was (perhaps, though by no means certainly) the presbyter Simplician—a distinguished scholar who had travelled widely and was reputed to be profoundly versed in philosophy and theology.[3] Ambrose, in one of his letters, speaks warmly of 'the long-standing friendliness, and, what is more, the tender fatherly love' shown by Simplician towards himself;[4] and, when he was compelled to accept the burden of the episcopal office, he begged his old tutor to come to him and prepare him for baptism and ordination.[5]

[1] Ammianus, xxii. 10. 7, condemns the measure as 'inclemens, obruendum perenni silentio'. As a result of it, many Christian teachers resigned their chairs (Orosius, *Hist.* vii. 30), including Prohaeresius at Athens and Victorinus in Rome.
[2] The objections are stated by Tertullian, *De Idol.* 10.
[3] Ambros. *Ep.* 65. 1. Simplician was born early in the fourth century, resided in Rome between A.D. 350 and 360, removed to Milan in A.D. 373, and succeeded Ambrose as Bishop of Milan in A.D. 397. Four letters addressed to him by Ambrose (*Epp.* 37, 38, 65, 67) are extant. He was a friend of the great Victorinus, who was influenced by him to make a public profession of Christianity (Augustin. *Confess.* viii. 2); and afterwards of Augustine, on whom, at a critical period, he made a profound impression (ibid. viii. 1, 2, 5), and who later addressed to him his two books *De Diversis Quaestionibus*. It was Simplician who reported to Augustine the saying of 'a certain Platonist'—that the opening verses of the Fourth Gospel ought to be written in letters of gold and displayed in the most conspicuous places in all churches (Augustin. *De Civit. Dei*, x. 29). [4] Ambros. *Ep.* 37. 2.
[5] Augustine is probably alluding to this preparation when he calls Simplician Ambrose's 'father in receiving Divine grace, whom Ambrose loved truly as a father', *Confess.* viii. 2.

Thenceforward Simplician took up his residence in Milan, where he ultimately succeeded Ambrose on the episcopal throne.[1]

Under the guidance of this divine, Ambrose studied the Holy Scriptures and was initiated into the rudiments of the Christian faith. Since, however, he was designed for a secular career, his religious education did not at this period go deep. After he became bishop he experienced considerable embarrassment by reason of his ignorance of theology. He complained that he was called upon to teach what he had not learned, and was thus under the necessity of learning and teaching at the same time.[2]

Neither Ambrose nor his brother Satyrus, though brought up in a pious household, had yet been baptised. Such delay, however, was not unusual. In the fourth century, while it was held permissible to bring young children to the font, adult baptism was the prevailing practice. Further, even in the case of adults, an unquestioning belief in the efficacy of the sacrament to cleanse the recipient from all previous sin, combined with an extreme view of the heinousness of post-baptismal lapse, frequently led to an indefinite postponement of the rite.[3] Of Ambrose's contemporaries, Basil, Gregory of Nazianzus, Augustine, and Chrysostom—all of them sons of pious mothers—were not baptized until they were grown up: Jerome at the time of his baptism was about twenty years of age, Rufinus of Aquileia about twenty-six, and Paulinus of Nola about thirty. The Church, however, was coming to realize that such postponement was objectionable, and Christian parents were urged to bring their children to the laver without unnecessary delay.[4]

After completing their education, Ambrose and Satyrus quitted Rome—possibly in the year A.D. 365—and went to Sirmium as advocates attached to the Court of the Italian Praefecture.[5] At this period the legal profession was followed by very many young men of talent who were ambitious of obtaining appointments in the Imperial Civil Service. Yet the lawyers, as a body,

---

[1] Paulinus, *Vita Ambros.* 46.       [2] Ambros. *De Officiis,* i. 4.
[3] See Augustin. *Confess.* i. 11.
[4] Ambrose himself advocated baptism in infancy (*De Abraham,* ii. 81, 84); and rebuked unbaptized adults who kept putting off the rite (*De Elia,* 84, 85; *Expos. ev. Luc.* vii. 221).
[5] Paulinus, *Vita Ambros.* 5; on the place (Sirmium) and the date (that of the inauguration of a new Praetorian Praefect, Vulcatius Rufinus), see J.-R. Palanque, op. cit., pp. 13, 483.

had a bad reputation. Ammianus, with pungent humour, has delineated some leading types of this 'violent and outrageously greedy' class.[1] First we are shown the plausible mischief-maker, ravenous for plunder, who unwearyingly dances attendance on the rich—more particularly on well-to-do widows and orphans—with the definite object of inducing them to quarrel with their relatives and carry their quarrels into the courts. Next is described the shady jurisconsult, with portentously solemn countenance, who specializes in the study of obsolete statutes and long-forgotten precedents. He boasts that, by means of this curious learning he can draw up a plea which will secure a man's acquittal, even though he is known to have murdered his mother. But his fees for this valuable service are unconscionable. Another legal personage is the dishonest advocate. His only aim is to pocket money; so he cultivates the art of involving a suit in such a tangle of technicalities that no settlement can be reached until years have elapsed and his miserable client has been sucked completely dry. Lastly, there is the idle, good-for-nothing young barrister—an impudent puppy who has 'run away from school too young', and is so ignorant that if the name of some ancient author be mentioned he fancies it to be the designation of a foreign fish or eatable. When he ought to be studying his brief, he is at the theatre or about the streets; and until he actually comes into court, he hardly troubles himself even to inquire his client's name. Then, however, knowing nothing whatsoever of the case and having no arguments to offer, he rises and 'barks out'[2] a torrent of scurrilous abuse—for which not unfrequently he is afterwards brought to trial himself. No doubt there is an element of caricature in the lively sketches of the historian;[3] yet the principal heads of his accusation against the gentlemen of the robe[4] can be confirmed from other sources.

[1] Ammian. xxx. 4. 8–19.

[2] Prudentius, *Hamart.* 402 'inde canina foro latrat facundia toto'. For the phrase 'canina facundia' compare Hieron. *Epp.* 125. 16; 134. 1.

[3] See also Jerome's sarcastic description of the mannerisms of a barrister; 'Had he been unwilling, who could have been proved innocent? And, if he had once begun to reckon the points of the case upon his fingers, and to spread his syllogistic nets, what criminal would his pleading have failed to save? Had he but stamped his foot, or fixed his eyes, or knitted his brow, or waved his hand, or twirled his beard, he would at once have thrown dust in the eyes of the jury' (*Ep.* 50. 2).

[4] The ceremonial toga was worn by advocates when pleading in the courts, Joan. Lydus, *De Magistrat.* iii. 8.

At Sirmium Ambrose and Satyrus practised in the Court of the Praetorian Praefect of Italy—an old man of distinguished family and honourable career, named Vulcatius Rufinus—and speedily attracted attention by the brilliance of their oratory.[1] In A.D. 368 Rufinus died, and a new Praefect was appointed. This was that very magnificent personage, Sextus Petronius Probus,[2] who was at this time only about thirty-four years of age. For his early advancement to so high a dignity Probus appears to have been indebted, not so much to his talent for administration—which, to say the least, was mediocre—as to his enormous wealth. He was certainly rich enough to buy anything he wanted. It may be true, as the gossips alleged, that his vast fortune had been acquired by questionable methods; but at any rate he spent it royally.

'He did not hide his riches in caves of night or doom his wealth to darkness: more bountiful than the rain, he was wont to enrich innumerable throngs of men. As stream the clouds across the heaven, so one might behold his gifts streaming over the earth. His house was filled to overflowing with men of every nation; poor they entered, rich they went away. His lavish hand surpassed the rivers of Spain, pouring out a flood of golden gifts.'[3]

The fame of this most sumptuous and generous of men extended far and wide—even beyond the confines of the Empire.[4] About the year A.D. 391 two Persian nobles arrived in Italy. Their object in making the journey was twofold—to converse with Ambrose at Milan, and to visit Rome and feast their eyes on the grandeur of Petronius Probus.[5]

Personally Probus was a poor creature—suspicious, vindictive, cowardly, always ailing and always in excessive fidget about his health. But he was a staunch friend, who could be relied on to push the fortunes of those in whom he was sincerely interested.[6] Probably he was already acquainted with Ambrose and Satyrus, and was therefore predisposed to show them kindness; certainly he was impressed by their exceptional ability. Thus, after his arrival at Sirmium, he promoted the brothers—

---

[1] Paulinus, *Vita Ambros.* 5; Ambros. *De Excessu Sat.* i. 49.
[2] Ammian. xxvii. 11. 1. On Probus see above, p. 40, n. 2.
[3] Claudian, *In Prob. et Olybr. Cons.* 42–9.
[4] Ibid. 31–8.
[5] Paulinus, *Vita Ambros.* 25; on the date J.-R. Palanque, op. cit., p. 539.
[6] On the character of Probus, see Ammian. xxvii, c. 11.

or, at any rate, Ambrose, for nothing is explicitly stated about Satyrus—to be members of the Praefect's Judicial Committee.[1] Shortly afterwards—perhaps about the year A.D. 370[2]—Satyrus was given a provincial governorship[3] (the locality is not recorded), and Ambrose was nominated 'Consular', or Governor, of the province of Aemilia-Liguria.[4] On the eve of setting out to take up his new appointment Ambrose waited on his noble patron, to bid him farewell. The Praefect received him graciously, and at the close of the interview dismissed him with the words: 'Go; conduct yourself, not as a judge, but as a bishop.'[5]

Ambrose had now become a person of consequence. A provincial governor was technically a member of the Roman Senate, and was enrolled in the third order of the official aristocracy, with the right to style himself 'Worshipful' (*clarissimus*). He was primarily responsible for public order in his province, where he was also judge of first instance in civil and criminal matters. Every morning he sat within the chancel of his praetorium and listened to the pleadings of the advocates; with the assistance of assessors he then formulated his decisions, which were handed in writing to the litigants.[6] Within his province it was his duty to see that the imposts were duly collected, to supervise the conduct of the lesser officials, and generally to control affairs; but he was himself subordinate to the Vicar of the diocese and to the Praetorian Praefect. Twice a year he was bound to forward a report of his administration to the latter, who had power to punish governors guilty of negligence or misdemeanour. On the other hand, the governor possessed the right, in special circumstances, of going direct to the Emperor for advice, without having recourse to either of the officials immediately superior to him.

[1] Paulinus, *Vita Ambros.* 5.

[2] This date, though conjectural, seems to be more probable than that usually given (A.D. 372–3), inasmuch as it allows reasonable time (which the later date does not) for the growth of Ambrose's popularity in Milan before his unexpected election to the bishopric.

[3] Ambros. *De Excessu Sat.* i. 58.

[4] Paulinus, *Vita Ambros.* 5. The name 'Consular' was an official title, at this time borne by the governors of some thirty-six provinces.

[5] Paulinus, *Vita Ambros.* 8.

[6] Ambrose, having himself acted in a judicial capacity, understood the qualities requisite for a good judge, *De Cain*, ii. 38; *Expos. ps. cxviii*, 20. 36, 37, 39. Sometimes he seems to refer to his own judicial experiences, e.g. *Expos. ps. cxviii*, 8. 25; *De Paradiso*, 56; *De Tobia*, 36.

The Consular of Aemilia-Liguria had his head-quarters at Milan, 'the first great stage on the roads from Rome to Gaul, the Illyrian provinces, and Constantinople', and the most important city of Italy after Rome itself. His lot was cast in a pleasant place. The city was planted in the midst of a fertile plain, bounded on one side by the 'blue' waters of the River Adda, and on the other side by the 'beautiful' Ticino, its low banks lined with woods and marshy thickets.[1] Some twenty-eight miles to the north lay Como with its lovely lake and mountains,[2] and about an equal distance southwards the Po swirled its rapid stream between belts of poplars near Pavia. Under the walls of the city flowed the little river Olona. The sunny, well-watered plain, with its rich pastures and fruitful orchards, presented the appearance of an ever-green garden.

Since the beginning of the century, when Maximian fixed his residence there, Milan had been the principal seat of the Imperial Government in the West.[3] It was in every way worthy of its dignity as capital.[4] Its handsome public buildings included a Circus, 'the people's joy', where chariot-races and other sports were regularly held, an exceptionally fine theatre, many temples, an imperial palace, a mint, and luxuriously equipped baths built by Maximian. In the streets and open spaces fresh water bubbled up from innumerable fountains, while extensive arcades, lavishly decorated with works of art, afforded agreeable protection alike from the sun and from the north wind. A double range of massive walls, surrounded by a moat and bordered within by dwelling-houses, enclosed the area of the metropolis. In the suburbs, beyond the walls, a succession of palaces, mausoleums, and other edifices stretched far into the country.[5]

---

[1] Claudian. De VI Cons. Honor. 194–6.

[2] Cassiod. Var. xi. 14.

[3] So it continued till A.D. 404, when Honorius, through fear of the barbarians, transferred his Court to Ravenna.

[4] See the description of Ausonius, Clarae Urbes, v.

[5] Of all this ancient splendour hardly anything now remains. The edifices have vanished along with the gay and garrulous population that formerly lived among them. Only a few battered fragments survive. In the Via Ticinese there is a row of sixteen Corinthian columns—remains of the peristyle of some structure (possibly the thermae of Maximian) which once occupied the site of the present church of San Lorenzo. Among the lime-trees on the piazza near the church of Sant' Ambrogio stands a single antique column, which seems also to be a relic of some classic building; and over a door leading into the belfry of the church is a charming

Concerning the Christian buildings existing in Milan before the episcopate of Ambrose we have little reliable information. There were apparently two cathedral basilicas. One of them, the more ancient, went by the name of the Old Basilica;[1] it was dedicated to St. Thecla, and was demolished in the sixteenth century to enlarge the Piazza del Duomo. The other, in Ambrose's time, had been recently erected, and was known as 'the New Basilica within the Walls';[2] it occupied the site of the present cathedral. Near by was the ancient baptistery,[3] where Augustine, Adeodatus, and Alypius were to receive baptism. These three buildings were in close proximity to each other. Ambrose mentions three other churches already existing in his day—the Naboriana, dedicated to SS. Felix and Nabor,[4] which according to tradition was once the house of a rich Christian named Philip, and stood on a site afterwards occupied by the Church of St. Francis; the Basilica Faustae,[5] represented by the Chapel of San Vittore in Ciel d'Oro, or San Satiro, annexed to the Church of Sant' Ambrogio; and the Portiana or Basilica of Portius,[6] where Bishop Myrocles was buried, and which stood where now stands the Church of San Vittore al Corpo.

Although the ecclesiastical history of Milan appears to date from the beginning of the third century, hardly anything is known of it during the first hundred years.[7] By far the most momentous religious event in connexion with the city was the

bas-relief of the vintage, which may once have decorated a pagan temple. Remains of an ancient bridge and of the ancient walls have been discovered. These poor remnants, however, together with various inscriptions and architectural fragments now preserved in the Museum, comprise practically all that is left of a city once so fine that, in the opinion of Ausonius, it had no cause to fear comparison even with Rome (*Clar. Urb.* v. 11).

[1] Ambros. *Ep.* 20. 10.

[2] Ibid. 1 'basilica nova, hoc est, intramurana, quae maior est'. 'Ecclesia maior' signifies cathedral church: cf. *Ep.* 63. 68 'cum raperentur de ecclesia maiore'.

[3] Ambrose. *Ep.* 20. 4.

[4] Id. *Ep.* 22. 2; Paulinus, *Vita Ambros.* 14. It was called originally Basilica Philippi, subsequently Naboriana.

[5] Ambros. *Ep.* 22. 2.   [6] Id. *Ep.* 20. 1.

[7] The tradition that St. Barnabas, after having preached the Gospel in Rome, became Founder and first Bishop of the Church of Milan, is pure invention. The tradition took material form in a monument—the little church called S. Barnabà al Fonte, which was rebuilt by Cardinal Frederico Borromeo in 1623 and pulled down about the middle of the last century. The earliest well-authenticated Bishop of Milan is Myrocles (Ambros. *Serm. contr. Auxent.* 18), who was certainly in occupation of the see in A.D. 314, when he attended a Council at Arles. Some martyrs appear to have shed lustre on the Church. Before the time of Ambrose the names

publication in A.D. 313 of the celebrated edict of Constantine and Licinius granting liberty of worship to Christians. It is true that this edict was no more than an Act of Toleration. It gave the Church no special privilege, but merely accorded to it the religious freedom which was already enjoyed by foreign pagan cults. Yet the recognition of the Church as a lawful society was a first step—and a singularly important one—towards the ultimate adoption of Christianity as the official religion of the Roman Empire.

In the period with which we are dealing the Bishop of Milan was the sole metropolitan of northern Italy. His jurisdiction, though not strictly organized, was effective over the whole of the political diocese of Italia Annonaria, that is, over the whole of the northern part of the peninsula as far as Pisa and Ravenna.[1] In the beginning of the fifth century, indeed, Aquileia was detached from Milan, and became the metropolis of the north-eastern Italian sees. A little later the south-eastern portion of the old unwieldy province was placed under the metropolitan authority of the Bishop of Ravenna. In the fourth century, however, these divisions had not been made, and the Church of the chief capital of the Western Emperors possessed (even before the time of Ambrose's episcopate) extraordinary prestige and influence.[2]

The throne of this illustrious Church, when Ambrose first became acquainted with it, was occupied by an uncommonly astute and energetic prelate named Auxentius. A Cappadocian by birth and an Arian by conviction, he had early attached himself to the circle of Court clergy that surrounded the Emperor Constantius; and when, in A.D. 355, Dionysius, the orthodox Bishop of Milan, was sent into exile,[3] he was nominated by the Emperor to the vacant see. Like so many of the Arian leaders, Auxentius was an adroit diplomatist, and by his moderation and tact he

---

of St. Sebastian, who was a native of Milan though he suffered in Rome (Ambros. *Expos. ps. cxviii*, 20. 44), and SS. Felix, Nabor, and Victor (id. *Expos. ev. Luc.* vii. 178 'martyres nostri') were remembered and venerated. But the memory of the rest seems to have died out, until revived by Ambrose's 'discoveries' (see chapter xii of this work).

[1] The province included Aemilia, Liguria, Venetia, the two Rhaetias, the Cottian Alps, and part at least of Tuscia.

[2] The title of Archbishop does not appear to be applied to the Bishops of Milan before the time of Charlemagne.

[3] Ambrose refers to the banishment of Dionysius and his death in exile, *Serm. contr. Auxent.* 18; *Ep.* 63. 68–70.

soon made himself acceptable to the mass of the citizens. The strict Catholics, however, were not conciliated. With the encouragement and help of such doughty champions of orthodoxy as Hilary of Poitiers,[1] Eusebius of Vercelli, Evagrius of Antioch,[2] and Philaster of Brescia[3]—who visited Milan at various times and with pious zeal did all they could to stir up trouble for the bishop—the more rigid upholders of the faith of Nicaea consolidated themselves into an opposition and held assemblies for worship outside the churches of the city. Notwithstanding this schism, however, Auxentius kept his ground. Indeed, there is some reason to believe that he left an abiding mark on the usages of the Milanese Church. In Ambrose's time the worship and discipline at Milan exhibited certain peculiarities of a definitely Oriental character. That Ambrose himself, a Roman by birth and a Roman in feeling, was responsible for the original introduction of these elements is hardly credible. But if, as appears to be the case, they were already in existence at the time of his consecration, there is something to be said for the theory which would connect them with Auxentius, who was himself an Eastern and whose sympathies were with the Eastern Churches rather than with those of the West. It is certainly not inconceivable that this able Cappadocian, in the course of

[1] The unsuccessful campaign against Auxentius which Hilary conducted at Milan in A.D. 364 is described in his fiery polemic *Contra Auxentium*, wherein the faithful are urged not to let their affection for the churches of their city and their natural desire to worship therein seduce them into holding communion with Antichrist. Hilary was accompanied and assisted by Eusebius of Vercelli, whose devotion to and sufferings for the orthodox faith are alluded to by Ambrose, *Ep.* 63. 2, 66–71.

[2] The exertions of Evagrius at Milan, by means of which 'Auxentius, that curse of the Church, was buried, so to speak, before he was dead', are warmly praised by Jerome, *Ep.* 1. 15. But we have no details concerning his activities.

[3] Gaudentius of Brescia writes concerning Philaster, that 'filled with the Holy Ghost, he fought with such valiant vigour of faith, not only against heathen and Jews, but also against all heresies, and especially against the Arian perfidy which was raging at that time, that he even suffered flogging with whips, and used thereafter to bear in his body the marks of our Lord Jesus Christ. For in the city of Milan he was formerly a worthy pastor of the Lord's flock; he opposed the Arian Auxentius, before the blessed Ambrose was elected. He stayed also for a long time at Rome, and converted many to the faith both in public and in private disputations. Travelling through villages and country towns in all directions, this faithful disciple of Christ preached unceasingly the word of God' (*Serm.* xxi). Evidently Philaster, at some date before the autumn of A.D. 373, visited Milan and ministered as pastor to the separate Catholic community, and on account of his violent attacks on Auxentius was beaten and turned out of the city.

his long episcopate, should have introduced into his Church certain Oriental features; nor is it unlikely that Ambrose, who was broad minded in such matters, should afterwards have refrained from disturbing established customs which, though originally imported by a heretic, had in themselves no doctrinal significance.[1]

It was probably in October, A.D. 373, that Auxentius died.[2] As his predecessor in the see, the exiled Dionysius, was by this time also dead, it was necessary to elect a new bishop. The reigning Emperor, Valentinian the First, was in residence at Trier, and the people of Milan, free from the restraint of the imperial presence, broke into vehement contention. The Catholics were determined to capture the bishopric; the Arians were equally determined to retain it. A meeting for the election was held in the cathedral, and it was feared that, in the excited state of public feeling, acts of violence might be committed. Accordingly Ambrose, in his official capacity as Governor of the province, went in person to the church and spoke some soothing words to the people. Suddenly a voice (a child's voice, it is said) rang out: 'Ambrose Bishop!' The whole congregation instantly took up the cry. Arians and Catholics forgot their differences, and, as though carried away by a supernatural impulse, began to shout in unison, 'Ambrose Bishop! Ambrose Bishop!'[3]

But Ambrose had no wish to be bishop.[4] He was not an ecclesiastic; he had not even been baptized: except as regards his character, he was not in any way qualified to undertake so grave a responsibility. He may also have been influenced by more worldly considerations. Although the episcopal dignity was coveted by ambitious men, yet even so exalted a position as that of Bishop of Milan may well have seemed a poor ex-

---

[1] L. Duchesne, *Christian Worship*, pp. 93, 94. But a distinction must be drawn between such usages and the Creed itself. It has been suggested that Auxentius imported into Milan a Creed based on the Creed of Cappadocia with certain Arian additions of his own (F. J. Badcock, *The History of the Creeds*, pp. 48–50), and that Ambrose, refusing to tolerate the Arian character of the Creed which he found in use, imported in his turn the Creed of the Church of Rome—'the Creed of the Apostles which the Roman Church has always kept and preserved inviolate' (*Ep.* 42. 5; see Badcock, op. cit., pp. 80–5).

[2] See below, p. 68, n. 5.

[3] Paulinus, *Vita Ambros.* 6; Rufinus, *H.E.* ii. 11; cf. Socrates, *H.E.* iv. 30; Sozomen. *H.E.* vi. 24; Theodoret. *H.E.* iv. 6, 7 (very unreliable).

[4] Ambros. *De Officiis*, i. 2 'officium docendi quod nobis refugientibus imposuit sacerdotii necessitudo'; *Ep.* 63. 65.

change for the brilliant Government appointment which Ambrose, now fairly started on the road of official promotion, had every reason to anticipate.

As soon as he realized that the people were in earnest, Ambrose had recourse to some singular devices for evading the honour thrust upon him.[1] Pushing his way through the noisy crowd, he quitted the cathedral and proceeded to his court of justice. There, contrary to his usual custom, he ordered torture to be applied to some persons under arrest,[2] apparently hoping to disgust his admirers by a show of cruelty. But the multitude, which had followed him into the court, cried out, 'Your sin be on us!' Much disturbed, he then went home and gave out that he meant to retire from the world and devote himself henceforth to solitary meditation.[3] This expedient also failing, he endeavoured to shake public confidence in the integrity of his character, and actually caused some common street girls to be brought openly to his lodging. But the people saw through the ruse, and only cried the more, 'Your sin be on us!' Ambrose now became really alarmed, and decided to flee to Pavia. He left Milan secretly at midnight; but the night was dark, and he took a wrong road. After driving for some hours, he found, when the day broke, that he had only passed round the city to the Roman Gate. Then the people, with a view to preventing any future attempt at escape, took their Governor into custody. He was conducted to his residence and kept under strict surveillance, while a courier was despatched to Trier, to inform the Emperor of what had occurred and request him to ratify the strange election.[4]

[1] Paulinus, *Vita Ambros.* 7.

[2] Torture was used to extort confessions from persons suspected of treason or very heinous crimes; for instances see Ammian. xiv. 5. 1, 9; xv. 3. 10; xvi. 8. 6; xviii. 3. 5; xix. 12. 9, 12, 13; xxi. 16. 10; xxvi. 10. 9, 13; xxviii. 1. 11; xxix. cc. 1 and 2 *passim*. Some horrible details of the judicial torture of a woman accused of adultery are given by Jerome, *Ep.* 1. 3–6. The most common forms of torture were the 'eculeus' or rack (Ammian. xiv. 5. 9; Ambros. *De Cain*, ii. 27), flogging with whips loaded with lead, the application to the body of red-hot plates (Hieron. *Vita Pauli*, 3), laceration with 'unci' (Ammian. xiv. 5. 9; xxvi. 10. 13 'lateribus fodicatis'; Prudent. *Peristeph.* v. 173–4); see the enumeration Ambros. *Expos. ps. cxviii*, 12. 30; 15. 18; Prudent. *Peristeph.* x. 108–20.

[3] Paulinus, *Vita Ambros.* 7 'philosophiam profiteri voluit'.

[4] Paulinus, *Vita Ambros.* 8. The intervention of the Emperor in episcopal election was not normal at this period. In this case, however, his consent was necessary because the person elected happened to be a high civil official; also because the

Valentinian, delighted by the surprising unanimity with which this contentious business had been concluded, and gratified that the popular choice had fallen on one whom he himself had appointed to a high post in the imperial service, assented willingly to the petition.[1] But in the meantime, while the Emperor's reply was still awaited, Ambrose managed to elude the vigilance of his guards and concealed himself on the country estate of a friend named Leontius. Thus, when the letters of confirmation at length arrived, the bishop-elect had disappeared. The Vicar of Italy, however, immediately issued a proclamation, threatening with severe punishment any person who, knowing the place of concealment, failed to give information. Leontius was frightened, and betrayed the secret. Thereupon the deserter was arrested and brought back to Milan.[2]

Then at last Ambrose yielded, 'recognizing', says the biographer, 'the Divine Will concerning him'. It appears that Valentinian had sent him a message, promising that, if he would accept the bishopric, he should not be molested by the Arians.[3] Relying on this assurance Ambrose reluctantly consented to do what was required; he stipulated, however, that the bishop who was to baptize him should be a Catholic. This condition was conceded. But when he sought further to get his consecration postponed, that he might not violate the Nicene canon which forbade the ordination of neophytes, he met with a definite refusal. The whole affair of the election seemed so evidently providential, that the consecrating bishops agreed that in his case the ordinary rule of the Church might to some extent be set aside.[4] Accordingly he was baptized on the 24th of November; then, on the following six days, he was apparently made to pass formally through the successive grades of the ministry; and finally on the eighth day after his baptism, that is, on Sunday, the 1st of December, A.D. 373, he was consecrated bishop.[5]

see of Milan, the capital of Italy, was of quite exceptional importance. Theodoret's account of Valentinian's personal interview with the bishops on the subject of the election (H.E. iv. 6, 7) is pure invention; but it serves to illustrate the historical fact that Valentinian as a general rule deliberately abstained from interfering in Church affairs.

[1] Rufinus, H.E. ii. 11; Paulinus, Vita Ambros. 8.
[2] Paulinus, Vita Ambros. 9. The name of the Vicar was Italicus, Cod. Theod. xiii. 1. 10 (Feb. A.D. 374).
[3] Ambros. Ep. 21. 7.                                                    [4] Ibid. 63. 65.
[5] Paulinus, Vita Ambros. 9. It is not without great hesitation that I abandon

The consecration was performed by the bishops of the province, the principal consecrator being the Bishop of Aquileia. While the prayer of consecration was said, an open Book of the Gospels was held over the head of the bishop-elect, and all the bishops present laid their hands upon him.[1]

Thus, 'from the tribunal of the magistrate and the fillets of secular office'[2] Ambrose passed in the space of one week to the throne of the bishop. His first duty, after being put in occupation of his see, was to dispatch letters to his episcopal brethren in both West and East, notifying them of his consecration and giving a brief account of his faith. Among the rest he wrote to the great Basil of Caesarea; and he used this opportunity to request that the remains of his orthodox predecessor, Bishop Dionysius, who had died in Cappadocia and was there venerated as a martyr, might be restored to Milan. The request is significant of the attitude which he proposed to adopt in respect of the burning Nicene-Arian controversy. The reply of Basil, the staunch defender of Catholicism in the East, is interesting. He first expressed his thankfulness to God for having raised up for the care of the Church's flock 'a man from the imperial city, experienced in government, exalted in character, in lineage, in

the traditional date of Ambrose's consecration (7 December, A.D. 374), which until recently has been accepted by all authorities since Tillemont. I think, however, that it has now been shown by H. von Campenhausen (*Ambrosius von Mailand*, 1929) and J.-R. Palanque (*Saint Ambroise*, 1933) that this date cannot be correct, and that for A.D. 374 must be substituted the year which is indicated in the *Chronicle* of Jerome, i.e. A.D. 373. As regards the day and month, von Campenhausen would assign the consecration to 7 December, A.D. 373; this, however, was a Saturday, and it was the general (though not invariable) rule of the Church that consecrations should be celebrated on Sunday. Palanque argues ingeniously in favour of Sunday, 1 December, A.D. 373; and, on the whole, his conclusion appears the more acceptable: see his careful statement on this highly perplexed and obscure question, op. cit., pp. 484–7. If this date be adopted, it follows that Ambrose's baptism, which was a week earlier than his consecration, must have taken place on 24 November, A.D. 373. Further, after allowance has been made for the delay occasioned by Ambrose's efforts to avoid the episcopal dignity and by the necessity of obtaining the imperial consent, it seems reasonable to place the death of Auxentius and the election of Ambrose by popular acclamation in October, A.D. 373. (Ambrose's reference to the anniversary of his consecration in *Expos. ev. Luc.* viii. 73 'pulchre mihi hodie legitur legis exordium, quando mei natalis est sacerdotii' does not assist us to determine the date, since the date of this section of the Commentary on St. Luke is unknown; nor is any help afforded by his words in *Ep.* 4. 2, 3).

[1] Ambros. *Ep.* 4. 6 refers to the imposition of hands and 'the benediction in the name of the Lord Jesus' as constituting the essence of the rite.

[2] Ambros. *De Officiis*, i. 4; cf. *De Poenit.* ii. 67, 72.

station, in eloquence, in all that this world admires'. He urged
Ambrose to fight the good fight against 'the Arian madness',
and to write frequently to himself. He then went on to commend his zeal concerning the relics of Dionysius. The brethren
who had been commissioned to arrange for the translation had
negotiated with such tact that they had persuaded the guardians of the holy body to relinquish it. The deceased prelate
had been buried in a coffin by himself, with no other body beside
him, and his tomb had been honoured as the resting-place of a
martyr. Those who had buried him had now reverently dis-
interred the remains, and, weeping as sons bereft of a father,
had committed them to the care of Ambrose's messengers. Basil
guarantees the genuineness of the relics. 'Let no one dispute.
Let no one doubt. Here you have the unconquered athlete.
These bones, which shared with the blessed soul in the conflict,
are known to the Lord. These bones He will crown, together
with that soul, in the righteous day of His requital.'[1]

In this manner, at the age of thirty-four, Ambrose entered on
an episcopate which lasted for rather more than twenty-three
years.

## NOTE

*Some points of interest in connexion with Ambrose's elevation*

IN the curious story of Ambrose's elevation to the episcopate certain
details demand brief comment.

(i) In the first place, it may be noted that Ambrose was chosen
by acclamation of the people. The biographer, in his account of the
proceedings, makes mention of the people only: and to the people
Ambrose himself attributes his elevation. 'You are my fathers', he
says in one of his sermons, 'who made me a bishop.'[2] Doubtless, in
his case, the choice of the laity was approved by the majority of the
Milanese clergy; but it was the call of the people that was the chief
factor in the election. This was in accordance with prevailing
Western custom. The people demanded a certain person for their
bishop, the clergy concurred, and the neighbouring bishops examined and, according to the case, approved the nomination and gave
effect to it by consecrating. When the parties were divided, the will
of the people usually prevailed over the wishes both of the local
clergy (as in the case of Cyprian) and of the visiting bishops (as in

[1] Basil. *Ep.* 197.
[2] Ambros. *Expos. ev. Luc.* viii. 73 'vos mihi estis parentes, qui sacerdotium detulistis'.

the case of Martin of Tours). The laity, in short, still played the leading part in episcopal elections.[1] At Rome, however, in the middle of the fourth century, the influence of the clergy was becoming predominant, as is shown by the story of the intrigues connected with the elections of Felix and Damasus; and a little later Pope Siricius speaks of a deacon being promoted to be presbyter or bishop, if he be elected and chosen by the clergy and the people—the clergy, it should be remarked, being mentioned first.[2]

(ii) A second point of interest is the compulsion brought to bear on Ambrose. Such violence was not uncommon at this time. (a) We meet with instances of persons constrained against their will to receive ordination as presbyters. Augustine is said to have been seized by the people, who brought him to the bishop and insisted that he should be ordained presbyter, while he shed abundant tears at the force that was put upon him.[3] Jerome records the ineffectual struggles of his friend Nepotian to avoid the presbyterate.[4] Jerome's brother, Paulinian, ran away from his bishop to avoid ordination. Epiphanius, however, whom he visited upon some business, caused him to be seized during Mass by the deacons, who gagged him that he might not adjure the bishop in the name of Christ to spare him. Epiphanius then ordained him deacon, and later, apparently in the course of the same service, after gagging him a second time, ordained him presbyter.[5] (b) Similarly, compulsion was not infrequently used to compel the unwilling to receive episcopal consecration. Cornelius, made Bishop of Rome in A.D. 251, 'suffered violence so as to receive the episcopate by compulsion'.[6] Cyprian, being demanded as bishop, concealed himself, and when his house was besieged by a tumultuous crowd, wished to escape by a lattice.[7] Eusebius, Basil's predecessor at Caesarea, was unwilling to accept the bishopric and the bishops were equally unwilling to consecrate him; so military force was employed to overcome the reluctance of both.[8] Martin of Tours was lured from his monastery by a stratagem, and conducted by the people, 'as though under guard', to his consecration.[9] It is

---

[1] Ambrose emphasizes the 'obsecratio' or 'postulatio' of the people, when he refers to the elections of Acholius of Thessalonica (Ep. 15. 12 'obsecratus a populis, electus a sacerdotibus') and Eusebius of Vercelli (Ep. 63. 2). Jerome also bears witness to the action of the people in episcopal elections (Comm. in Ezech. x, c. 33 'speculator ecclesiae, vel episcopus, vel presbyter, quia a populo electus est'); and points out that the popular choice was not always right, good men being sometimes passed over in favour of inferior but more attractive candidates (Adv. Jovin. i. 34).

[2] Siricius, Ep. 1. 10.
[3] Possidius, Vita Augustini, 4.
[4] Hieron. Ep. 60. 10.
[5] Epiphan. ap. Hieron. Ep. 51. 1.
[6] Cyprian, Ep. 55. 8.
[7] Pontius, Vita Cypriani, 5.
[8] Gregor. Nazianzen. Orat. xviii. 33.
[9] Sulpicius Severus, Vita Martini, 9.

rather surprising that Ambrose, who so bitterly complained of the
pressure put upon himself, had afterwards no scruple in applying
similar pressure to others. When, on the death of Philaster, the see
of Brescia fell vacant, and the citizens bound themselves by an oath
that they would have no other for their bishop than a certain
Gaudentius, who was absent on pilgrimage in the East, Ambrose
and the Western prelates not only wrote in the most urgent terms to
Gaudentius himself, but seem even to have requested the bishops of
the East to exclude him from communion until he should consent to
receive consecration.[1]

(iii) The third point of interest in connexion with Ambrose's consecration is the violation of the second Nicene canon which prohibited ecclesiastical promotion without adequate probation. This
canon, indeed, made no explicit reference to a gradual ascent
through the various ecclesiastical degrees; yet such an ascent, ana-
logous to the system of gradual promotion to the high civil and
military offices of the Empire, was unquestionably the ideal of the
Church.[2] The ideal, however, was imperfectly realized. We often
find, for instance, that laymen were ordained directly to the presbyterate, without passing through any preliminary stages: Origen,
Augustine, Jerome, and Paulinus of Nola afford illustrations.
Similarly, laymen were occasionally elevated immediately to the
episcopate. When Pope Anteros died in A.D. 236, a layman named
Fabian, who had come to Rome from the country, mingled with the
crowd which had gathered in the church to elect a new bishop. It is
said that a dove flew down and alighted on his head; whereupon all
shouted, 'He is worthy', and at once placed him on the episcopal
throne.[3] In A.D. 319 Philogonius, a married layman and eminent
advocate, who had won universal esteem by his championship of the
poor and oppressed, was suddenly consecrated Bishop of Antioch.[4]

---

[1] Gaudentius, *Serm.* xvi.

[2] Cyprian notes as one of the merits of Cornelius of Rome that 'he was not one
who came to the episcopate hastily, but, being promoted through all the ecclesiastical offices . . . he ascended by all the steps of religion to the lofty summit of the
priesthood' (*Ep.* 55. 8). Gregory of Nazianzus commends Basil on similar grounds,
and refers to the army rule that a man must first serve as a common soldier and
captain before he can be promoted to be general (*Orat.* xliii *in laud. Basil.* 26, 27).
Jerome complacently records that Nepotian was promoted to the presbyterate
'per solitos gradus' (*Ep.* 60. 10). The 10th of the canons ascribed to the Council
of Sardica (A.D. 347) directed that no one should be consecrated bishop until he
had served as reader, deacon, and presbyter, and that no one should be hastily
ordained to any of these offices (Labbe, *Concilia*, ii, p. 635).

[3] Eusebius, *H.E.* vi. 29. 'He is worthy' was the common acclamation at the election of a bishop; cf. Philostorgius, ix. 10; *De Dignitate Sacerdotali*, 5; Gregor. Turon.
*Hist. Franc.* ii. 13.

[4] Chrysost. *Hom. de sancto Philogonio*, 2 (Migne, *P.G.* xlviii, p. 751).

In A.D. 362 Eusebius, a layman and at the time of his election only a catechumen, was made Bishop of Caesarea.[1] In A.D. 381 Nectarius, an unbaptized layman with an unedifying past, was nominated by Theodosius to the bishopric of Constantinople,[2] and we find Ambrose referring with satisfaction to his consecration as justifying his own.[3] About A.D. 409, again, Synesius, a sporting country gentleman and philosopher, married and still unbaptized, was made Bishop of Ptolemais.[4] Further evidence as to the prevalence of such irregularities is furnished by the patristic writers. Gregory of Nazianzus, for example, complains that premature promotions were only too common in his time. Men come to the episcopate, he says, from the army, from the navy, from the plough, from the forge; though they have undergone no probation, they are deemed at once fit for sees.[5] Jerome likewise laments that the 'clear and unmistakable' command of 1 Timothy iii. 6, that novices should not be made bishops, was recklessly disregarded. 'One who was yesterday a catechumen is to-day a bishop; one who was yesterday in the amphitheatre is to-day in the church; one who spent the evening in the circus stands in the morning at the altar; one who a little while ago was a patron of actors is now a dedicator of virgins.'[6]

In mitigation of the irregularity of Ambrose's consecration, two things may be said. First, the extraordinary circumstances of his election not unnaturally suggested the idea that he was providentially designated to preside over the Church of Milan.[7] And the Divine Will, clearly indicated, overrode, as a matter of course, ecclesiastical prescription. In the second place, there is some evidence that Ambrose was not consecrated bishop quite immediately, but passed rapidly through the inferior offices. 'After his baptism', writes the biographer, 'he is reported to have filled all the ecclesiastical offices, and on the eighth day he was consecrated bishop.'[8] If this 'report' be true, it may be conjectured that the procedure was as follows. On

---

[1] Gregor. Nazianzen. *Orat.* xviii. 33.   [2] Sozomen. *H.E.* vii. 8.
[3] Ambros. *Ep.* 63. 65.
[4] His scruples about accepting the dignity are set forth in a letter (*Ep.* 105) to his brother Evoptius (Migne, *P.G.* lxvi, pp. 1481 ff.).
[5] Gregor. Nazianzen. *Carm.* ii. 12 *de seipso et de episcopis* 155–80, 375–81.
[6] Hieron. *Ep.* 69. 9.
[7] Paulinus, *Vita Ambros.* 9, 'cum intelligeret circa se Dei voluntatem'. In this case the Divine Will was indicated by the surprising unanimity of the popular demand; Rufinus *H.E.* ii. 11 'Dei ait esse, quod discordantem populi fidem et animos dissidentes conversio subita in unum consensum atque unam sententiam revocaverit'. So Ambrose writes concerning the election of Eusebius of Vercelli, 'merito creditum quod divino esset electus iudicio, quem omnes postulavissent' (*Ep.* 63. 2).
[8] Paulinus, loc. cit.

Sunday, the 24th of November, Ambrose was baptized and confirmed; on Monday, the 25th of November, he was made doorkeeper; on Tuesday, the 26th of November, reader; on Wednesday, the 27th of November, exorcist; on Thursday, the 28th of November, acolyte-subdeacon; on Friday, the 29th of November, deacon; on Saturday, the 30th of November, presbyter; and on Sunday, the 1st of December, bishop. Such a passage through the various grades was of course, purely formal; yet it shows that the ideal of gradual promotion was—so far as was possible under the circumstances—respected.

## CHAPTER IV

# THE WESTERN EMPEROR AND THE WESTERN EMPIRE

## 1. *The Emperor Valentinian the First*

THE Emperor Constantius, whose state entry into Rome in the year A.D. 357 was probably witnessed by Ambrose, was succeeded in A.D. 361 by that 'belated son of a great bygone age', Julian called the Apostate. He, having received a mortal wound during the calamitous Persian campaign, was in turn succeeded by the convivial and Christian Jovian. But after a reign of only eight months Jovian died suddenly in the night of the 16–17th of February, A.D. 364, at Dadastana, an obscure town on the borders of Galatia and Bithynia. He had over-eaten himself at supper, and had then retired to sleep in a damp bed-chamber where a charcoal fire was burning; but whether his death was caused by the excessively copious repast or by the fumes of the charcoal is uncertain. For ten days the Empire was without a ruler. Meanwhile the army, slowly returning home after its fearful experiences in Persia, advanced to Nicaea, the capital of Bithynia; there, under pressure of the emergency, the military and civil authorities proceeded to elect an Emperor. Their choice fell on a capable officer named Valentinian, then Colonel of the Second Regiment of Imperial Guards.[1] He was proclaimed on the 27th of February, A.D. 364.

Valentinian—the son of a Pannonian peasant (Gratian the Ropeseller) who by sheer ability had risen from the ranks to be general of the Roman forces in Africa and afterwards in Britain[2] —had spent most of his life in the army. Julian, when Caesar, had noticed him, and later, as Emperor, had given him advancement. An unfortunate incident, however, brought him into temporary disfavour. Valentinian was a Christian; yet it was

---

[1] Ammian. xxvi. 1. 5. On Valentinian I see Ammianus, Bks. xxvi–xxx; Zosimus, iii. 36–iv. 17; Aurelius Victor, *Epit.* 45; cf. the ecclesiastical historians, Socrates, *H.E.* iv, cc. 1, 2, 10, 29–31; Sozomen. *H.E.* vi, cc. 6, 10, 24, 36; Theodoret. *H.E.* iii. 16; iv. 6, 7; Philostorgius, viii. 8; also W. Heering, *Kaiser Valentinian I.*, Magdeburg, 1927.

[2] Ammian. xxx. 7. 2–3.

part of his official duty to attend the Emperor when he went to sacrifice in pagan temples. One day Julian visited a temple in Antioch. At the entrance a priest was stationed, who, according to custom, sprinkled the party with lustral water. Some drops fell on the uniform of Valentinian; and the Christian officer so far forgot himself as to insult the priest, impetuously tearing off that portion of his military cloak which had been touched by the 'defiling' fluid.[1] For this offence he was deprived of his commission and ordered into exile. In the Persian war, however, his military talents were needed, and he was recalled to the imperial standards.

Valentinian, at the time of his accession, was a tall, muscular, well-built man of forty-two, with flaxen hair, ruddy complexion, and steel-blue eyes, very stern and piercing.[2] A soldier first and foremost, he was nevertheless not entirely unversed in the arts of peace. At any rate, he was able to write tolerable Latin, and could speak, when necessary, with rough yet vigorous eloquence. He was a keen observer of men and things, and possessed— an invaluable quality in a sovereign—an amazingly retentive memory.[3] Morally he was, in many respects, superior to his contemporaries. Accustomed from his youth to the discipline of the camp, he had no patience with the laxities of Roman society. As Emperor, he endeavoured to correct the public morals with the aid of the strictest magistrates and the most efficient executioners.[4] His rigour was unmitigated; never was he known to grant a reprieve to any person sentenced to death.[5] 'Authority must always be enforced with severity' was one of his maxims.[6]

Yet he himself had grave faults. He was afflicted with a diabolical temper, which, in his later years at any rate, he seldom attempted to control. The most trivial provocation threw him into a paroxysm of fury. Then his features became distorted, his voice and colour changed, and for the moment he appeared to be no better than a madman.[7] Moreover he

---

[1] Sozomen. *H.E.* vi. 6; Theodoret. *H.E.* iii. 16; cf. Zosimus, iv. 2. Ambrose, with some exaggeration, speaks of Valentinian's 'confession' (*Ep.* 21. 3 'cuius fides confessionis constantia comprobata est') and says 'militiam sub Iuliano et tribunatus honores fidei amore contempsit' (*De Obitu Val.* 55).

[2] Ammian. xxx. 9. 6.    [3] Ibid. xxx. 9. 4; Aurelius Victor, *Epit.* 45.

[4] Ammian. xxx. 8. 13; 9. 2.    [5] Ibid. xxx. 8. 3.

[6] Ibid. xxx. 8. 10.    [7] Ibid. xxvii. 7. 4; xxix. 3. 2.

was shockingly cruel. This horrible and revolting trait, which excited astonished comment even in a cruel age, is illustrated by many anecdotes. On one occasion, at a hunting-party, a page let loose a Spartan hound too soon, because the animal, in its efforts to escape the leash, had bitten him. For this trifling act of carelessness, the youth, by the Emperor's order, was beaten to death with clubs and buried the same day.[1] Another time, an able provincial governor named Africanus, being anxious to obtain promotion, persuaded the Master of the Horse to present a petition to the Emperor. Valentinian replied with a savage jest. 'Away with you, Count!' he said. 'Off with the head of the man who desires to be off from his province!'[2] In cages close to his bed-chamber he kept two fierce she-bears, which were named respectively 'Innocence' and 'Golden Darling'. The keepers had strict orders not to allow these monsters to grow tame; and it was rumoured that from time to time ghastly scenes were enacted in the interior of the palace in which condemned criminals and the ravenous bears played the leading parts. Eventually, after witnessing the dismemberment of many bodies, the Emperor commanded that his pet 'Innocence' should be let loose into the forest, as having fairly earned her freedom.[3]

When Valentinian was proclaimed at Nicaea, the ceremony was interrupted by shouts of the troops, 'Name at once another Emperor'. For the moment he excused himself from complying with this request; but the wishes of the army could not be disregarded. On the 28th of March, A.D. 364, being then at Constantinople, in the suburb of the Hebdomon, he created his brother Valens full and co-ordinate partner in the Empire.

The choice can hardly have been popular. Never was a more impossible person adorned with the diadem and purple. A swarthy, squinting, pot-bellied, bandy-legged little man, uncultivated in mind and boorish in manners, Valens had Valentinian's vices without his virtues. Like his brother, he was

---

[1] Ammian. xxix. 3. 3.

[2] Ibid. xxix. 3. 6. For other stories of Valentinian's cruelty, see Ammian. xxvii. 7. 5–7; xxix. 3. 4–8. The ferocity of the Emperor was imitated by his ministers, e.g. Maximin (ibid. xxviii. 1. 10–41).

[3] Ammian. xxix. 3. 9. Perhaps, like Nero, Valentinian used to watch realistic representations of the mime *Laureolus*, wherein a live criminal was exposed upon a cross to be mangled by a bear.

passionate and cruel; unlike him, he was feeble and vacillating,
destitute of taste and judgement, alternately foolhardy and
cowardly.[1] Yet his very lack of qualities recommended him;
for under no conceivable circumstances could he ever become
the rival of the senior Emperor. He was, in fact, quite content
merely to act on his instructions, 'attending to his wishes as if
he had been his orderly'.[2] This was the kind of colleague that
Valentinian wanted. And it must be admitted that, so long as
he himself lived, this queer imperial partnership worked well
enough.

The proclamation of Valens was followed by a partition of
the Empire between the two rulers. Valentinian kept the
Western half, comprising Italy, Africa, Illyricum, Gaul, Spain,
and Britain: the Eastern portion was assigned to Valens. The
troops, the generals, the officials of the Civil Service and the
Court were also divided in accordance with the new arrangement. When the details of this delicate business had been finally
adjusted, the imperial brothers travelled together as far as Sirmium. There they separated—Valens returning to Constantinople and Valentinian proceeding to Milan.[3]

It is not necessary to follow minutely the career of Valentinian
during the years A.D. 364–74. The great work which entirely
preoccupied him was the restoration of the western defences
of the Empire. Most of his time was spent in Gaul. We hear of
him, now at Paris, now at Rheims, now at Amiens or Trier or
Mainz, indefatigably engaged in the prosecution of his tremendous task of holding the encroaching swarms of barbarians at
bay. The main result of his arduous labours was the recovery
of the Rhine frontier. The Roman bank was swept clear of
barbarians, and the entire course of the river was fortified with
a chain of muniments. Castles and watch-towers, which had
fallen into decay, were restored, and new ones were built at
measured distances; embankments and palisades were constructed at critical points; the frontier camps were adequately
garrisoned, and the strength of the flotilla on the waterways was
increased. Fortresses were even erected on the further side of

---

[1] Ammian. xxix. 1. 11, 18–20; xxxi. 14. 5–7. Aurelius Victor, *Epit.* 46, describes
Valens as 'valde timidus'. But the impartial Ammianus allows that, as a ruler, he
exhibited some respectable qualities, xxxi. 14. 2–4.

[2] Ammian. xxvi. 4. 3.

[3] Ibid. xxvi. 5. 1–4; Zosimus, iv. 3.

the river in the very territory of the enemy.[1]  The completion
of this work of defence, in the midst of incessant fighting and in
face of an infinite number of almost insuperable difficulties, was
a notable achievement.  It constitutes Valentinian's chief title
to honour.

One event during this decade seems to demand more detailed
record—the elevation to the purple of the child Gratian, the
pupil of Ausonius and afterwards the well-beloved protégé of
Ambrose.  In the year A.D. 367 Valentinian was overtaken by
a serious illness, and, his life being despaired of, the question of
his successor was discussed by the Court.  Contrary to expectation the Emperor recovered; and, in order to ensure that, if any
fatal mischance should at any time happen to himself, the diadem should not be removed from his family, he determined
without delay to confer the rank of Augustus on Gratian, his
eight-year-old[2] son by his first wife Severa.  The ceremony took
place at Amiens on the 24th of August, A.D. 367.  In an open
space outside the walls a lofty platform was erected.  In front
of it the ensigns and eagles were planted, and around it the
legions, whose sentiments concerning the business had already
been privately ascertained, were drawn up in an immense circle.
Presently Valentinian, accompanied by his generals and the
civil dignitaries of Gaul, ascended the tribunal.  When the
trumpets had blared for silence, the Emperor, taking his handsome boy by the hand, presented him to the army with a few
suitable words.  Almost before he had finished speaking, a roar
of acclamation went up from the legionaries, and every man
clashed his arms to signify his approval.  Valentinian invested
his son with the imperial insignia, kissed him, and addressed
him thus: 'You have now, my Gratian, the imperial robes,
granted to you in an auspicious hour by the will of myself and
our comrades.  Gird yourself, therefore, to take your share of
the burden of affairs that weighs on your father and your uncle.
Prepare to pass fearlessly with the soldiers over the frost-bound
Danube and Rhine, to take your stand beside your warriors, to
shed your blood and give your life willingly for your subjects,

---

[1] Ammian. xxviii. 2. 1; xxx. 7. 6.  But the historian considers that Valentinian's
passion for building forts was sometimes excessive, xxix. 6. 2.

[2] Born, according to Idatius, on the 18th of April, A.D. 359.  On this date see
T. Hodgkin's note, *Italy and her Invaders*, i, p. 187.

to think nothing unworthy of your regard which may contribute
to the preservation of the Roman Empire. This advice is enough
for the present; later I will not fail to give you more.' Then,
turning to the attentive troops, he added: 'To your loyalty,
defenders of the State, I recommend your boy-emperor, and
I beg and entreat you to protect him with unswerving devotion.'
At these words Eupraxius the Moor, who held the office of
Imperial Remembrancer, gave the signal for the cheers, shouting, 'The family of Gratian deserves this'; and from the ranks
came the thunderous reply, 'Gratianus Augustus! Gratianus
Augustus! Prosperity to the Emperor Gratian!' So the ceremony ended. The soldiers, marched back to their quarters
and afforded the usual gratifications, were enthusiastic in their
praise of both the Emperors, but especially of the child, whose
bright eyes and attractive countenance had won all hearts.[1]

In the autumn of A.D. 374 the Quadi and Sarmatians invaded
Pannonia. For this outbreak there was some excuse. It appears
that Valentinian, anxious to protect the Danube frontier, had
ordered the construction of a fortress within the territory of the
Quadi on the left bank of the river. The barbarians, indignant
at the encroachment, sent an embassy, headed by Gabinius
their king, to remonstrate with the young Duke of Valeria, who
was superintending the operations. The treacherous Roman
received the chief with friendly words and entertained him at a
banquet, but caused him, on his departure, to be foully murdered. Such an outrage not unnaturally roused the barbarians
to fury. A great host of Quadi and Sarmatians immediately
threw themselves across the river and spread havoc through
Pannonia.[2] Mounted on swift ponies, armed with long, bone-
tipped lances, and wearing instead of breastplates linen tunics
sewn with overlapping scales of polished horn,[3] they struck
terror into the provincials, to whom they seemed like an army
of fabulous monsters.

---

[1] Ammian. xxvii, c. 6; Zosimus, iv. 12. The date (24 August A.D. 367) is given
by Idatius (cf. Socrates, *H.E.* iv. 11). Ammianus notes that Valentinian departed
from precedent in creating his brother and son, not Caesars, but Augusti, xxvii.
6. 16.
[2] Ammian. xxix. 6. 1–18; Zosimus, iv. 16. Ambrose, *De Excessu Sat.* i. 30–2,
appears to refer to this invasion of Quadi and Sarmatians in A.D. 374–5 (O. Seeck,
*Symmachus*, p. xlix; G. Rauschen, *Jahrbücher der christlichen Kirche*, p. 476).
[3] Ammian. xvii. 12. 2.

The Romans appear to have been stupefied by the suddenness of the incursion. Unfortunately many of the troops usually stationed in Moesia and Pannonia had recently been withdrawn; the remainder, fearing to risk an engagement in the open, shut themselves up in the walled towns. At Sirmium, Ambrose's patron, the valetudinarian Petronius Probus, cut a pitiable figure. This was his first experience of war, and so panic-stricken was he that he scarcely dared to lift up his eyes from the ground. His one anxiety was to save himself, and he actually gave orders that his swiftest horses should be got ready to carry him from the city under cover of night. When, however, it was represented to him that if he executed this design nothing could possibly save Sirmium, and that the fall of so important a stronghold would inevitably involve the ruin of his own fortunes, he pulled himself together, and, after his first alarm had a little subsided, even displayed some amount of energy. He cleared out the fosses of the city, repaired the neglected fortifications, and strengthened the garrison with a contingent of archers. By these measures he was able to repulse the barbarians, who passed into Valeria, and eventually, hearing of reverses which had befallen some of their allies and being further disquieted by rumours of the approach of imperial troops from Gaul, turned homewards and made overtures for peace.[1]

In the late spring of A.D. 375 Valentinian himself appeared upon the scene. His arrival caused consternation to the Roman officials. Every one trembled lest his own incompetence or misconduct should be exposed and punished. But no formal inquiry was held. Even the wretch who murdered Gabinius seems to have got off without rebuke. Only on Probus, whose disgraceful misgovernment was accidentally brought to the Emperor's notice, were the vials of imperial wrath outpoured. In the closet of the dreadful Augustus the reprehensible Praefect was bullied and threatened till he was brought to the point of mental and physical collapse; yet, though the scandal of his administration was patent, he was not dismissed from office.[2]

---

[1] Ammian. xxix. 6. 9–16.

[2] Ibid. xxx. 5. 1–10. Ammianus draws an appalling picture of the desperate condition of Illyricum under the government of Probus. Taxes and exactions of all kinds were multiplied to such a degree that many wealthy provincials fled from their homes; others, having been stripped of everything by the revenue officials,

During June, July, and August Valentinian remained at Carnuntum, a frontier town in the north of Pannonia. In the autumn he crossed the Danube, and laid waste the territories of the Quadi with fire and sword. When the winter approached he recrossed the river, and took up his quarters at Bregetio (Szöny), intending to complete the subjugation of the barbarians in the following spring.[1]

But now all kinds of sinister portents were observed. Comets, foreboding misfortune, flashed across the heavens. At Sirmium a thunderbolt fell, setting fire to the palace, the senate-house, and the forum. At Sabaria an owl, uttering the most dismal hootings, settled on the roof of the imperial baths, and refused to be dislodged by the stones and arrows aimed at her by the soldiers. The Emperor himself suffered from unaccountable depression. His sleep was disturbed by fearful dreams. One night he had a vision of his absent wife, sitting with grief-stricken look and dishevelled hair, and clad in the attire of a mourner.[2] The following day—it proved to be his last—he emerged from his chamber, morose and haggard, and ordered his charger to be saddled, that he might refresh himself with a gallop in the open air. As he was mounting, the horse suddenly reared, and the hand of the equerry, who was holding it, was brought into violent contact with the imperial person. In an outburst of senseless rage, Valentinian ordered the offending member to be cut off.[3]

A few hours later ambassadors arrived from the Quadi, offering, if peace were granted, to comply with all conditions and

were thrown into prison because they had no more to give, and there languished in perpetual confinement; others, to escape the incessant persecution, committed suicide. Every one knew about these scandals except Valentinian—'it seemed as though his ears had been stopped with wax'. His attention, however, was drawn to them by the courageous philosopher Iphicles (loc. cit.).

[1] Ammian. xxx. 5. 11, 13–15.
[2] Ibid. xxx. 5. 16–18. The importance attached to prodigies and portents, even by enlightened persons, is shown by the frequent references made to them by Ammianus (xviii. 3. 1; xix. 12. 19, 20; xxi. 15. 2; xxiii. 5. 8 ff.; xxv. 10. 1, 2, 11; xxvii. 3. 1, 2; xxviii. 1. 42; see also his remarks on the intimations of the future vouchsafed by the Deity, xxi. 1. 8–14). Ambrose says that the death of Theodosius was heralded by earthquake, rain, and extraordinary darkening of the sky (*De Obitu Theod.* 1). Even the most trivial omens were seriously regarded. A man would go back to bed, if he happened to sneeze when putting on his shoes; he would re-enter his house, if he stumbled when going out; and he was convinced that some misfortune was about to befall him, if mice gnawed his clothes (Augustin. *De Doctr. Chr.* ii. 31).
[3] Ammian. xxx. 5. 19.

furnish recruits for the imperial armies. They were ushered into the audience-chamber, where sat the Emperor, pallid and glowering. Bowing to the very ground, the ambassadors began to make humble excuses for the conduct of their people. They urged, however, that the erection of a Roman fortress in their territory was an unjust and inopportune act, and that it was only to be expected that the sight of such a work would inflame the fierce temper of the tribesmen. At this remonstrance Valentinian lost all self-control. He upbraided the envoys in extravagant terms, exclaiming frantically that their nation had been guilty of the grossest, the blackest ingratitude. Suddenly his voice choked, his face became purple, and a stream of blood gushed from his mouth. The Emperor was stricken with apoplexy. He was carried by chamberlains into the private apartments, where he lay on his bed fighting for breath, but still in possession of his faculties. It was some time before a surgeon could be found to bleed him; and even when at length the operation was performed, it failed to bring him any relief. Soon it was whispered in the palace that he was dying, and the generals and Court officials were hurriedly summoned. The final scene was horrible. Gasping for breath, grinding his teeth, twisting his limbs into frightful contortions, Valentinian writhed in an agony which no remedies seemed to alleviate.[1] At last all was over. On the 17th of November, A.D. 375, the heralds shouted the death of the Augustus through the streets.

As a man Valentinian was unattractive and even forbidding, but he was a meritorious ruler. His great work, as has been said, was the securing of the frontiers, and to this he devoted himself with a self-sacrificing patriotism that was worthy of the best traditions of Rome. No personal interests, however absorbing, were ever allowed to interfere with the paramount duty of maintaining the defences of the Roman world.[2] In other ways

---

[1] Ammian. xxx, c. 6; Zosimus, iv. 17; Aurelius Victor, *Epit.* 45; Socrates, *H.E.* iv. 31; Sozomen. *H.E.* vi. 36.

[2] Ammianus, xxix. 4. 1, says that not even the most prejudiced critic of Valentinian would deny him the merit of solicitude for the State. One instance of his patriotic conduct may be mentioned. In the autumn of A.D. 365, when on his way to Paris, he learned on the same day that the Alemanni had crossed the Rhine, and that a relative of Julian named Procopius had risen in revolt against Valens. His first impulse was to hasten to the assistance of his brother; but his councillors urged the need of his presence in Gaul, and deputations from the principal cities implored him not to abandon them to the barbarians. Thus pressed, Valentinian sacrificed

he was solicitous to promote the welfare of his subjects. He restored provincial towns, and settled colonies of captives on lands which were passing out of cultivation;[1] he did what was possible to reduce the exorbitant taxation;[2] and he made strenuous efforts to secure uncorrupt administration.[3] Unhappily his attempts at reform were perpetually thwarted by the inveterate dishonesty of the officials—dishonesty which the Emperor, through fear lest the degradation of highly placed delinquents might diminish the respect of the people for the Government, was culpably negligent to restrain.[4] In spite of all shortcomings, however, the magnanimous self-devotion of this rugged, hard-working soldier to the service of the State made a profound impression on the popular mind, so that long afterwards, when men wished to praise the Ostrogothic prince Theodoric, they were accustomed to compare him with the two best sovereigns of earlier times—Trajan and Valentinian.[5]

In religious matters Valentinian, unlike Constantius and Julian, adopted a policy of non-interference. 'He tolerated all the various cults', writes the admiring Ammianus, 'and never troubled any one, or issued orders that any particular divinity should be worshipped. He did not promulgate threatening edicts to bend the necks of his subjects to adore what he did, but left the different forms of worship without alteration as he found them.'[6] Thus, on the one hand, the pagans were allowed to practise their religion unmolested. It is true that, for moral and political reasons, severe measures were taken against magicians;[7] but the ordinary ceremonies and observances of pagan worship

his inclination to his duty. His final conclusion was worthy of one of the heroic Romans of ancient times: 'Procopius is the enemy only of my brother and myself, but the Alemanni are the enemies of the whole Roman world' (Ammian. xxvi. 5. 7–13).

[1] Ammian. xxx. 9. 1; xxviii. 5. 15.

[2] Ibid. xxx. 9. 1; but contrast Zosimus, iv. 3.          [3] Ibid. xxx. 8. 13.

[4] Ibid. xxx. 5. 3; 9. 1.          [5] Anon. Valesii, 60.

[6] Ammian. xxx. 9. 5; cf. Cod. Theod. ix. 16. 9: 'Testes sunt leges a me in exordio imperii mei datae, quibus unicuique quod animo imbibisset, colendi libera facultas tributa est.' On Valentinian's religious policy see V. Sesan, *Kirche und Staat im römisch-byzantinischen Reiche seit Konstantin dem grossen*, i, pp. 306 ff.; W. Heering, *Kaiser Valentinian I*, pp. 60 ff.

[7] Cod. Theod. ix. 16. 8. Magical rites were held objectionable, (*a*) partly because they were believed to be associated with immoralities (Ammian. xxviii. 1. 14, 50), and (*b*) partly on political grounds, as being used for making inquiries concerning the life of the sovereign (Ammian. xxix, c. 1).

were not interfered with. The temple ministers were not disturbed in the enjoyment of their pensions and privileges, and the heathen altar of Victory remained in the Senate-house where Julian had restored it.[1] Valentinian did indeed enact a law prohibiting nocturnal sacrifice to the genius of the domestic hearth—a practice which was thought to be politically dangerous —but when Praetextatus, the Proconsul of Achaia, represented that 'life would be unlivable for the Greeks, if they were to be prevented from celebrating after the traditional fashion the most holy rites which knit together the human race', he permitted the measure to remain in abeyance.[2] On the other hand, the various Christian bodies were accorded similar liberty. Although he was himself a Catholic, Valentinian tolerated all the sects,[3] and deliberately refrained from taking part in ecclesiastical disputes, except when the maintenance of public order required him to do so.[4] He held that the settlement of questions of dogma and ecclesiastical policy should be left entirely to the bishops,[5] and even promulgated a law whereby ecclesiastical jurisdiction was made independent of civil.[6] But this curiously modern attitude of neutrality with regard to religion was not one which was likely to be acceptable to Ambrose. It is significant that the latter, who was so lavish in praise of other rulers, had hardly anything to say in commendation of Valentinian—a Catholic who had countenanced the errors of pagans and heretics, who had taken an Arian as his second wife, and who had supported

[1] Symmach. *Relat.* 3. 20. Ambrose tries to explain away this tolerant policy by suggesting that the Emperor was unaware that the pagan rites were still being solemnized (*Ep.* 17. 16). Elsewhere, while he praises Valentinian's faith, he implicitly censures his action in leaving the 'privileges of the temples' intact (*De Obitu Valent.* 55).

[2] Cod. Theod. ix. 16. 7; Zosimus, iv. 3.

[3] Socrates, *H.E.* iv. 1; Sozomen. *H.E.* vi. 6. Only the Manichaeans were persecuted. By a law of A.D. 372 (Cod. Theod. xvi. 5. 3) the teachers of this sect were subjected to heavy pecuniary penalties, and the places of assembly were confiscated. This severity, however, was due to the belief that the Manichaeans were addicted to immorality and practised magic.

[4] As, for instance, in the case of the disturbances occasioned by the rivalry of Damasus and Ursinus at Rome. The letter to the Pneumatomachi of Asia published by Theodoret (*H.E.* iv. 8) is apocryphal.

[5] Sozomen. *H.E.* vi. 21. Theodoret's account of Valentinian's interview with the bishops after the death of Auxentius (*H.E.* iv. 6, 7) is certainly unhistorical; but it could hardly have been invented apart from the known fact of the Emperor's reluctance to interfere in matters purely ecclesiastical.

[6] Ambros. *Ep.* 21. 2; cf. ibid. 5. The law referred to is not extant.

against the attacks of the orthodox the notorious heretic Auxentius.[1]

When Valentinian expired at Bregetio, the other Emperors were far away—Gratian at Trier, and Valens at Antioch. In their absence the army on the Danube determined to raise a nominee of its own to the purple. But, through the skilful management of a loyal general, Merobaudes, the diadem was still retained in Valentinian's family. The late Emperor some while before his death—perhaps about the year A.D. 368—had divorced Severa, the mother of Gratian, and had married a beautiful, heretical, and very *difficile* Sicilian lady, named Justina.[2] By her he had three daughters—Justa, Grata, and Galla—and one son called Valentinian. It was this child, then about four years old,[3] that the generals, under the influence of Merobaudes, decided to place upon the throne. At the moment he chanced to be staying, with his mother and sisters, at the Villa Murocincta, some hundred miles distant from Bregetio. Thence he was hastily fetched in a litter, and on the sixth day after his father's death he was presented to the assembled troops and acclaimed Augustus.[4]

Gratian received the news of his half-brother's elevation with complacency. It was arranged that the Empire should be again divided. Valens retained the East; Gratian took Gaul, Spain, and Britain as his share; Italy, Illyricum, and Africa were allotted to Valentinian.[5] For the moment, however, owing to the extreme youth of the youngest Emperor, no actual partition of the Western Empire took place. Gratian administered his brother's territories as regent.

[1] Almost the only act of Valentinian which is warmly commended by Ambrose is his refusal to apostatize under Julian, *Ep.* 21. 3; *De Obitu Valent.* 55. The interview between Ambrose and Valentinian reported by Theodoret (*H.E.* iv. 7) has no historical foundation. For other allusions to Valentinian, see Ambros. *Epp.* 17. 16; 21. 2, 5, and 7.
[2] Justina is said to have been the widow of the usurper Magnentius (Zosimus, iv. 19, 43). She was already married to Valentinian I in A.D. 369, since Ammianus, referring to that year, speaks of her brother as a kinsman of the Emperor (xxviii. 2. 10). No credit can be given to the fable of Socrates (*H.E.* iv. 31) that Valentinian married Justina without repudiating Severa, and issued a law permitting a man to have two lawful wives at the same time. Severa was divorced between A.D. 367 and 369, ostensibly on account of an act of injustice (*Chron. Pasch.* i, p. 559, ed. Bonn). She survived her husband, since, subsequently to his death, Gratian is spoken of as acting 'matris consilio' (Ammian. xxviii. 1. 57).
[3] Ammian. xxx. 10. 4; Philostorg. ix. 16; Zosimus, iv. 19.
[4] Ammian. xxx. 10. 4–6.
[5] Zosimus, iv. 19.

This was the political situation soon after the beginning of Ambrose's episcopate. The Roman Empire was in the hands of three—the first a timorous, middle-aged man with the mind and manners of a peasant, the second a charming but inexperienced boy of sixteen, and the third a child of four under the control of an unwise mother. With such rulers, at a time of peculiar danger and difficulty, it may well have seemed that nothing could save the State from complete disaster.

## 2. *The Organization and General Condition of the Western Empire*

(*a*) Since the days of Diocletian and Constantine the government of the Roman world had been undisguisedly despotic. At the head of the State was the Emperor—no longer merely the foremost Roman citizen, but absolute autocrat, 'Lord of the whole world', the sole ultimate source of all law and all authority. His powers were practically unbounded. No person or class had any rights against him. No constitutional restraints in any way hampered his freedom of action. His ministers were simply servants, appointed or discharged according to his pleasure. He could dictate laws, impose taxes, dispense consulates and crucifixions, without taking advice from or rendering account to any one. His governmental omnipotence was symbolized outwardly by the amazing pomps and vanities with which he was surrounded. His palace was thronged by hordes of eunuch chamberlains[1] and other attendants; body-guards, armed with long spears and brightly painted oval shields, protected his person; the greatest dignitaries, when they approached him, bowed profoundly, while humbler persons bent the knee and kissed the hem of his purple robe. On state occasions, when he gave audience, he wore a diadem enriched with a double row of magnificent pearls,[2] and sat on a gold and ivory throne,

---

[1] From the third century onwards eunuchs were customarily employed as confidential servants in the imperial household. The highest of these was the Grand Chamberlain, who in the time of Theodosius the Great was actually a member of the Privy Council. Ammianus gives a bad account of the Court eunuchs, who are said to have been generally greedy, ill mannered, ill natured, and arrogant (xvi. 7. 8) and to have abused their opportunities to prejudice the mind of their master against honourable men (xviii. 4. 4). He speaks respectfully, however, of Eutherius, Grand Chamberlain of Constantius (xvi. 7. 4–7). Perhaps the most loathsome Court eunuch during this period was Eutropius, on whom see below, chapter xix.

[2] From the time of Constantine (Aurelius Victor, *Epit.* 41), the diadem was worn by the emperors at state functions. Julian had a specially magnificent one

beneath a canopy of silver. The descendant of the Caesars, when not actually on campaign, affected the oriental seclusion and splendour of a sultan.[1] He was officially recognized as a kind of divinity.[2] His person was 'sacred', and the same term was applied to everything connected with him—to his mind, his countenance, his acts, his expenditure, his letters, his bedchamber. He did not hesitate to refer to himself as 'My Eternity'.[3] Even to doubt the correctness of his judgement was 'sacrilege'.[4]

Yet there were elements of weakness in the Emperor's position. For one thing, being elevated to so sublime a height, he was unable to come into direct and personal contact with affairs, and was consequently compelled to rely on his ministers for information. Thus he was liable to become the dupe of a corrupt official clique. Again, the crown was not hereditary, and its wearer was not protected by that sentiment of loyalty which is engendered in subjects who have been governed for generations by one ruling house. Most of the emperors of the period were chosen by the army and accepted by the people; but the army might become dissatisfied and elect some one else, and the mob was nothing if not fickle. Hence, amid all his superlative grandeur, the divinized Augustus was never secure. The ferocious cruelty exhibited by rulers like Constantius and Valens towards those who were suspected of disaffection[5] is not astonishing under the circumstances. No one knew better than the Emperor that any agitation, not ruthlessly crushed, might speedily issue in a revolution, which would be likely to deprive him both of his sceptre and of his life.

Below the Emperor came the civil and military hierarchies. About this time the Western Empire (with which alone we are concerned) was divided into two great praefectures (of Italy and of the Gauls), which were in turn subdivided into six dio-

adorned with precious stones (Ammian. xxi. i. 4). The pearls in the diadem are mentioned by Claudian, De Nupt. Honor. et Mar. 167–8.   [1] Pacatus, Panegyr. 21.
[2] Pacatus does not scruple to address Theodosius as a divinity, ibid. 6, 18, 19. Ausonius, Grat. Act. 5, says, with reference to Gratian, 'ades enim locis omnibus, nec iam miramur licentiam poetarum, qui omnia deo plena dixerunt'.
[3] Cod. Theod. xii. 1. 160; cf. Symmach. Relat. 6 'aeternitas vestra'.
[4] Cod. Theod. i. 6. 9; cf. ibid. ix. 29. 3.
[5] Ammian. xiv, c. 5; xxi. 16. 8–11 (Constantius); xxvi. 10. 9–14; xxix, cc. 1, 2; xxxi. 14. 5, 6 (Valens). Ammianus admits that very searching investigation is necessary where there is the slightest suspicion of treasonable plots, but censures cruelty in punishment, xix. 12. 17, 18; xxix. 1. 18.

ceses (three for each praefecture), and yet again into some
fifty-nine provinces. In these divisions, as a rule, two orders of
officials—one civil and one military—existed side by side; for
it was the policy of the emperors, since Diocletian, to keep the
civil and military services distinct. Each of these orders was
a hierarchy, consisting of functionaries of graded rank. Officials of the first class bore the title of Illustrious (*illustres*),
those of the second class had the style of Honourable (*specta-
biles*), while those of the third class were designated Worshipful
(*clarissimi*).

(i) At the head of the civil aristocracy was a group of eight
great ministers, dignified with the coveted title of Illustrious.
These were the Praetorian Praefect of Italy, the Praetorian
Praefect of the Gauls, the Praefect of Rome, the Master of the
Offices, the Quaestor, the Chancellor of the Exchequer (*Comes
Sacrarum Largitionum*), the Controller of the Privy Purse (*Comes
Rerum Privatarum*), and the Grand Chamberlain (*Praepositus Sacri
Cubiculi*). Each of the Praetorian Praefects administered an
immense area, with an authority resembling that of a modern
viceroy. The Praefect of Rome was President of the Roman
Senate, and had jurisdiction over the City and district within a
hundred miles thereof.[1] The Master of the Offices was the most
important executive officer at the centre of government.[2] He
had control of the four great Imperial Bureaux—the *Scrinium
ab epistolis* or Secretariat of the Empire,[3] the *Scrinium a libellis* or
Office of Petitions and Legal Inquiries, the *Scrinium a memoria*

---

[1] The Praefect of Rome had the oversight of the various administrative departments within the urban area. He was ultimately responsible for the public security,
for the food and water supply, for the preservation of public buildings and objects
of art, for the repair of the aqueducts, cloacae, and river banks, for the regulation
of the markets, for the census, for the levy of taxes—in short, for everything connected with the administration of the City and its environs. He wore a purple-
bordered toga, drove through the streets of Rome in a silver chariot, and had the
right to display the imperial portraits. For an account of his functions and privileges
see Cassiod. *Var.* vi. 4.

[2] See Cassiod. *Var.* vi. 6. If we can imagine one man exercising functions, some of
which are in Britain discharged by the Secretary for Foreign Affairs, some by the
Home Secretary, some by the Private Secretary to the King, some by the War
Office, and some by the Commissioner of Police, we shall get some notion of the
various activities of the Master of the Offices. Owing to his close relations with the
sovereign, he was frequently his confidant, and not seldom his master.

[3] This Department dealt with all communications touching foreign affairs and
with the general correspondence of the Government, except that relating to
petitions and legal business, which belonged to the *Scrinium a libellis*.

or Record Office,[1] and the *Scrinium dispositionum* or Office for the Emperor's engagements and travel-arrangements. To him, moreover, was entrusted the general direction of the huge Secret Service of the Empire (*schola agentum in rebus*),[2] of a corps of Imperial Guards (*scholae scutariorum et gentilium*), of military commanders on the frontiers, of functionaries concerned with Court ceremonial, and of the arsenals. The Quaestor was the highest legal officer of the Crown. His main work was to advise on legal questions, to give final revision to the laws which were presented for the Emperor's signature, and to draft in suitable terms the imperial answers to petitions.[3] The Chancellor of the Exchequer was ultimately responsible for the elaborate arrangements connected with the supply and expenditure of the public revenue; he further controlled the treasuries, the mints, the mines, the linen and woollen factories and the purple-dye works, and exercised general supervision over the foreign trade of the Empire.[4] The Controller of the Privy Purse administered the Crown demesnes, which through forfeitures and confiscations were continually becoming more enormous.[5] Finally, the Grand Chamberlain had authority over the vast multitude of servants employed about the palace and the Emperor's person, including the thirty brilliantly armed officers called *silentiarii*, who kept order in the imperial chambers.

The two Praetorian Praefects, the Praefect of Rome, the

[1] It was actually more than a Record Office, since it not only recorded documents, but issued them. It assisted the other offices in giving final form to imperial announcements, and sent them out. It was also responsible for diplomas of appointment and the various official permits. In the fourth century it had absorbed many of the duties formerly discharged by the *Scrinia ab epistolis* and *a libellis*, and its head, the Magister Memoriae, was far more influential than the presidents of the other bureaux.

[2] The business of the *agentes in rebus* was to watch the conduct of officials, to receive denunciations, and to act generally as imperial spies. As they were scattered through the provinces in great numbers, nothing escaped their observation. They served also as imperial couriers, and were sometimes employed to collect special contributions to the Exchequer. Reference is made to them by Ambrose, *Ep.* 20. 7; *De Officiis*, ii. 150. Unfortunately the spies were often as corrupt as the officials whom they were set to watch. Their exactions are alluded to in a remark of Julian, reported by Ammianus, xvi. 5. 11 'rapere non accipere sciunt agentes in rebus'.

[3] Symmachus describes this officer as 'the disposer of petitions and constructor of laws' (*Epp.* i. 23); Claudian says that he 'issued edicts to the world and answers to suppliants' (*De Mall. Theod. Cons.* 33–7). The chief requirements for the office were a thorough knowledge of the law and the gift of dignified legal expression (Cassiod. *Var.* v. 4; vi. 5).

[4] Cassiod. *Var.* vi. 7.                    [5] Ibid. vi. 8.

Master of the Offices, the Quaestor, the two finance ministers, and (from the time of the Emperor Theodosius) the Grand Chamberlain were *ex officio* members of the *Consistorium* or Privy Council.[1] Five military officers of the highest rank were also *ex officio* members of that body. The Consistory was both a Council of State for advising the Emperor on imperial questions and a Supreme Court of Judicature. It met at times fixed by the Emperor, and in his presence. The sessions, however, were not secret; any one with the rank of Honourable might attend and listen to the proceedings.

Below the 'Illustrious' personages came the 'Honourables'. These included the Vicars in charge of Dioceses, the Presidents of the four Imperial Bureaux, the Chief of the Notaries (*Primicerius notariorum*), and certain important officers of the palace. To the third class, the 'Worshipful', belonged all members of the Roman Senate, the Governors of provinces, and various highly placed civil servants.

Such was the civil aristocracy of the Empire. It was a hierarchy of salaried officials. Each member of it earned his rank as a reward for the industry and capacity which he had displayed in the earlier stages of his public career. Promotion followed a regular course, and it was rare for a man to receive high preferment without having first passed through the inferior grades of the service. The emperors, with whom all such appointments rested, were very circumspect in this matter; of Constantius, for instance, it is said that 'he weighed out dignities as if with scales', never advancing to high office any one who had not been tested by years of service in subordinate posts.[2] In general, the lower officials were under the control of the higher; yet the relationship of subordination was not mechanically rigid. For instance, not only the praefects, but also the vicars of dioceses, and even the provincial governors, were in touch with the Emperor, and could, on certain occasions, have recourse to him directly.

(ii) In the army, as in the civil service, we meet with a hierarchy.[3] At the top were five officers who were entitled Illus-

[1] The name *Consistorium* first occurs in an inscription of the year A.D. 353 (C.I.L. vi. 1739). Ambrose refers to this body, *Epp.* 17. 10; 21. 1, 17; 24. 2, 3; *Serm. contr. Auxent.* 3.
[2] Ammian. xxi. 16. 3.
[3] On the organization of the army see Mommsen's article, 'Das römische

trious. These were the Master of the Infantry in the Presence, the Master of the Cavalry in the Presence, the Master of the Horse for the Gauls, the Count of the Domestic Infantry, and the Count of the Domestic Cavalry. Of these officers the first two commanded the troops nearest to the imperial residence, and the last two the household troops. Below the illustrious five, there was a varying number of Counts with the style of Honourable, whose rank corresponded roughly with that of the vicars of the civil dioceses. There were also military Dukes, quartered for the most part in the frontier provinces, who were generally subordinate to the Counts, though like the latter they were entitled Honourable.

The army itself was divided into three main bodies—the frontier troops, the *comitatenses* and the *palatini*. (*a*) The first body consisted of *riparienses*, who garrisoned the frontier camps, and *limitanei*, who were not merely soldiers but also cultivators of lands on the border, which they held on military tenure. These troops on the outskirts of the Empire were accounted inferior to the forces of the interior; they drew less pay, and were obliged to serve for a longer term, namely twenty-four years. (*b*) The second body, the *comitatenses*, consisted of the regular forces quartered in the interior of the Empire. They could be moved about as occasion required, and concentrated at any point where additional military strength was needed. Connected with the *comitatenses*, but of a lower rank, were the *pseudo-comitatenses*— detachments drawn from the frontier troops and united temporarily with the regular field army of the interior. (*c*) The third body, the *palatini*, consisted of troops which were stationed in the neighbourhood of the capital, and which accompanied the Emperor whenever he took the field in person. Connected with them were the very important *auxilia palatina*, composed mainly of Gauls and Germans.

In addition to these three principal divisions we must reckon the *domestici* or household troops. Highly privileged, splendidly

Militärwesen seit Diocletian', in *Hermes*, vol. xxiv, 1889, pp. 195 ff. During the fourth century the cavalry was continually increasing in importance, because it could be more easily transferred from the interior to threatened points on the frontier, and was also better adapted for countering the tactics of mounted barbarians. Further, increasing reliance was placed on missile weapons—especially on the arrows of mounted archers. In Italy there were famous manufactories of bows at Pavia and of arrows at Concordia.

accoutred, and generously paid, these troops may be described as Imperial Guards. They served in close proximity to the Emperor, and were admired and envied as the *élite* of the army. There existed also another corps of Imperial Guards consisting of *scholae scutariorum* (who were Romans) and *scholae gentilium* (who were barbarians). By a curious arrangement this corps was detached from the general army organization and was under the command of the Master of the Offices.

The condition of the army was far from satisfactory. While the wealthy aristocratic proprietors and the well-to-do members of municipal corporations were not allowed to serve, lest the finances of the Empire should suffer, among the mass of the people the old military spirit had utterly died out. The number of men in the legion seems to have steadily diminished. Recruiting became more and more difficult; even among the sons of veterans self-mutilation to avoid service was common.[1] Military discipline, moreover, the main foundation of the ancient superiority of the Roman troops, had grievously decayed. The soldier of the period was far more a terror to the provincials on whom he was quartered than to the barbarians whom he was meant to fight. Rapacious and violent, he was also soft and luxurious. The catches of the theatre were more to his taste than the battle-cry; and instead of bivouacking in the open with a stone for his pillow he expected to be billeted in marble chambers furnished with feather-beds.[2] The officers set a scandalous example. They were mostly intent on making their fortunes, partly at the expense of the provincials, whom they mulcted, and partly at the expense of their own men, whom they unblushingly defrauded of pay and rations.[3] Finally, the military administration, in striking contrast with the civil, was astoundingly chaotic. Legions were broken up into detachments which were dispersed in different stations; commands were so divided that it was almost impossible to ascertain exactly for what troops any individual commander was responsible; every conceivable kind of blunder in organization and management was common. The whole military machine was in complete disorder.

---

[1] Cod. Theod. vii. 13. 4, 5; Ammian. xv. 12. 3. Ambrose notices the common dislike of military service, *Hexaem.* v. 52.

[2] Ammian. xxii. 4. 6, 7; cf. ibid. xxiii. 5. 21; Zosimus, ii. 34.    [3] Zosimus, iv. 27.

(b) Passing now to a survey of the general condition of the Western Empire, we might not unreasonably expect to discover indications of great prosperity. The Empire of the West was still a unity. That vast area, which is now divided into many kingdoms, was still one integral whole in the lifetime of Valentinian; and even in the last quarter of the century the partition thereof was more formal than real. Over all its huge extent the Roman language was current, Roman culture flourished, and Roman law prevailed.[1] A magnificent system of narrow but solidly constructed roads, with inns (mansiones) and intermediate post-houses (mutationes), linked up the extremities with the great cities in the interior, while an adequate service of ships connected the principal ports. Hence social and commercial intercourse was easy.[2] Moreover—except on the frontiers, where there was incessant fighting—the inhabitants of the provinces enjoyed, as a rule, the blessings of peace. There were occasional local disturbances, of course; but at any rate there were no 'European wars', no internecine clashings of rival kingdoms. Nor were other conditions of prosperity lacking. The administration, if scientifically conducted, ought not to have been expensive. No doubt the cost of running the Government machine was heavy; but, after all, there was only one Government to be maintained in an area which to-day supports a number of different Governments, a number of different armies, poten-

---

[1] Prudentius describes the unification of nations under the rule of Rome, Contra Symmach. ii. 601–17. Cf. Orosius, Hist. v. 2 'ubique patria, ubique lex, et religio mea est'; Rutil. Namat. De Reditu, i. 63–6.

[2] Some principal commodities may be mentioned. Purple fabrics were conveyed from the Government dye-works on the Syrian coast; linen wares from Scythopolis, Tyre, Berytus, and Byblus; furs from Cappadocia; woollen goods from Miletus and Laodicea; cloth garments from Phrygia and Spain; parchment from Pergamus; arms and armour from Hadrianople, Thessalonica, Antioch, and Damascus; chased iron from Cibyra; diaphanous textiles from Cos; flax from Elis; carpets from Sardes; pottery from Attica and Samos; glass from Sidon; cabinet furniture from Thessaly. Egypt and Africa were the granaries respectively of the Eastern and the Western Empire. Bacon and cheese were imported from Dardania; oil from the province of Africa; dates from Phoenicia; raisins and figs from Rhodes; oil, bacon, and mules from Spain. Numidia supplied cattle, Spain and Cappadocia horses, Hierapolis in Syria wild beasts for the spectacles. The fishing-trade of Epirus was famous. Other commodities were brought by the merchants from more distant regions—silk from China; sapphires and tortoise-shell from Ceylon; aloes, cloves, and sandalwood from the Gangetic Gulf; rare woods, spices, and pepper from the Malabar coast; pearls from India, Persia, and Britain; myrrh and frankincense from Arabia Felix; black slaves, ivory, and cinnamon from Barbaria; emeralds from Aethiopia; amber and furs from the Baltic and Far North.

tially hostile to one another, and a number of different groups of 'unproductive and mischievous politicians'. In addition, the emperors devoted a generous proportion of the Crown revenues to the service of the State, while the nobles were frequently liberal in assisting the provincial towns. We further observe that extraordinary educational facilities were afforded, and that the highest offices in the State were ungrudgingly thrown open to men of industry and talent.

In spite of all this, however, the condition of the Western Empire in the time of Ambrose was deplorable. In the provinces large tracts of land had ceased to be cultivated,[1] public buildings had fallen into a state of dilapidation,[2] the great highways were not kept in proper repair,[3] and the postal service was disorganized.[4] Banditti swarmed everywhere.[5] Trade, for various reasons, languished; prices fluctuated wildly notwithstanding imperial attempts to stabilize them.[6] The poverty of the people was appalling. Men and women died of starvation, and parents, being unable to support their children, sold them into slavery.[7] Public spirit was extinct. The middle class, cruelly harassed and burdened, did not even make a pretence of patriotism; the wealthy aristocrats still repeated with becoming unction the old patriotic platitudes, but their actions hardly matched their fine professions.[8] To the majority of the subjects of the Empire life was horrible and hopeless. The idea gained

[1] Symmachus refers to the desolate aspect of the deserted countryside (*Epp.* v. 12). Cf. Lactantius, *De Mort. Persecut.* 7.

[2] Constantine complained of the neglected condition of public buildings (Cod. Theod. xv. 1. 2); Gratian and Theodosius ordered the authorities to repair ancient buildings before erecting new ones (ibid. xv. 1. 21); and Honorius forbade the alienation of municipal funds allocated to the restoration of public edifices (ibid. xv. 1. 48). But legislation did not stop the decay. For the efforts made to preserve the buildings of Rome see especially the edict of Majorian in A.D. 458 (Gregorovius, *Rome in the Middle Ages*, i, pp. 224, 225).

[3] Cod. Theod. xv. 3. 4.

[4] Ibid. viii. 5. 53–65.

[5] Brigands are frequently mentioned by Ambrose, e.g. *De Officiis*, i. 242; ii. 77; *Expos. ps. cxviii*, 8. 25; 15. 7; 19. 7; *Expos. ev. Luc.* vi. 48; *Hexaem.* vi. 59; *In ps. 36 enarr.* 15; *De Interpell. Job*, iv. 21. Cf. Ammian. xxviii. 2, 10; Ausonius, *Ep.* iv. 22–7; Symmach. *Epp.* ii. 22; and the anecdote related by Jerome, *Vita S. Hilarion.* 12. In A.D. 391 the right of carrying arms was granted to civilians that they might protect themselves against brigands, Cod. Theod. ix. 14. 2.

[6] Lactantius, *De Mort. Persecut.* 7.

[7] Ambros. *De Nabuthe*, 21.

[8] See, e.g., the unpatriotic resistance of the senators to the levy of recruits from their estates at the time of the Gildonic war, Symmach. *Epp.* vi. 62, 64.

ground that Roman civilization was afflicted with incurable decay and that the end of all things was approaching.

Six causes of weakness may particularly be specified. (i) The first was *the decline of the population*. The vitality of a state depends ultimately on the people; and all over the Empire the free population was dwindling. Owing to exorbitant taxation and acute economic distress, legitimate wedlock was widely abandoned in favour of inexpensive temporary unions with slave concubines.[1] Children were not wanted. The practice of exposing infants was prevalent among the poor, and the use of drugs to ensure sterility was common among the well-to-do.[2]

(ii) A second cause of weakness was *the infiltration of barbarians into the Empire*. As the native population declined, an ever-increasing multitude of barbarians took its place. Barbarians cultivated Roman soil as *coloni*.[3] Barbarians served, either voluntarily or by compulsion, in the Roman armies.[4] Barbarians laboured as slaves on the Roman agricultural estates and performed domestic duties in the Roman palaces. Barbarians even occupied the highest offices.[5] The careers of such men as Merobaudes the Frank, Bauto the Frank, Arbogast the Frank, Richomer the Frank, and Stilicho the Vandal show that there was no station of honour, short of the imperial throne itself, which was inaccessible to barbarians. But this wholesale importa-

---

[1] Ambros. *De Abraham*, i. 19 'discant homines coniugia non spernere, nec sibi sociare impares'. Cf. Pseudo-Ambros. *Serm.* 52. 9 (Migne, Ambrosii Opp. iv, p. 711); Paulinus of Pella, *Eucharist.* 166.

[2] Ambros. *Hexaem.* v. 58.

[3] We read, for example, of Bastarnae allowed to settle in Thrace (Zosimus, i. 71), of Carpi in Pannonia (Ammian. xxviii. 1. 5), of Salian Franks in the region between the Scheldt and the Meuse (ibid. xvii. 8. 3, 4), of Alemanni in the valley of the Po (ibid. xxviii. 5. 15), of Taifali in the neighbourhood of Modena, Parma, and Reggio (ibid. xxxi. 9. 4). The story of the admission of the Goths by Valens will be related in chapter vii of this work.

[4] Warlike tribes, when subdued, were forced to pay a tribute of their youth to the armies of the Empire (Ammian. xvii. 13. 3; xix. 11. 7; xxviii. 5. 4; xxx. 6. 1; Zosimus, iv. 12). Others received grants of land on condition of rendering military service. Moreover, barbarian contingents, under the command of their own chiefs, were encouraged to serve voluntarily on agreed terms with the imperial forces. The Roman armies of the fourth century comprised great numbers of barbarians (see, e.g., Zosimus, ii. 15; iv. 56–8). The tendency to compose the cavalry of barbarians is noticeable.

[5] The consulship itself was not excepted: Dagalaephus, Merobaudes, Richomer, Bauto, and Stilicho were consuls. The Emperors Gratian and Theodosius particularly favoured barbarians, even admitting them to intimate friendship, Zosimus, iv. 35, 56.

tion of barbarians was a serious danger to the Empire.[1]  For although the majority of these foreigners had no hatred of Rome,
although they professed admiration and reverence for the Roman
polity and civilization,[2] they never became completely Roman-
ized.  The wolves might masquerade as sheep-dogs, but at heart
they were still wolves—one in sympathy, as in blood, with the
savage packs beyond the border that were hungrily waiting for
an opportunity to break into the Roman fold.

(iii) A third cause of weakness was the *merciless system of
taxation*, whereby the middle-class country taxpayer was being
literally crushed out of existence. The principal source of revenue
was the land-tax, which pressed so hardly on the smaller proprietors that multitudes of them, finding it impossible to make
their holdings pay, abandoned them altogether.  In such cases
the deserted lands were still taxed, the amount payable being
divided up among the neighbouring proprietors in proportion
to their means.  Thus the possessor of a flourishing farm was
compelled to pay, not only the tax on his own land, but also
a proportion of the tax on the deserted or barren land in his
district.[3]  As a consequence it was extremely difficult to make
a profit even on a good holding.  More and more land was
deserted, while those proprietors who still retained their farms
became more and more embarrassed.  Besides the land-tax,
there was a poll-tax on all able-bodied adult labourers (male
and female) employed on country estates; cattle and animals
useful to the farmer, such as dogs, were similarly taxed.[4]

In addition to these taxes various imposts were levied, those
for the military commissariat and the maintenance of the postal
service being the most burdensome.  Merchants paid port and
frontier duties (*vectigalia*).  Traders in towns were subject to a
tax called *collatio lustralis* or *chrysargyron*, which was collected
every fourth year.[5]  The decurions of municipalities, on every
plausible occasion of public rejoicing (e.g. on the accession of
an emperor or on each fifth anniversary of his accession), were
obliged to present to the sovereign a substantial congratulatory

[1] See the warning given by Synesius in his *Oratio de regno* (Migne, *P.G.* lxvi.
1053–1108).
[2] See, e.g., the sentiments of Ataulph in Orosius, *Hist.* vii. 43.
[3] Cod. Theod. xi. 1. 10; xiii. 11. 12.
[4] Cod. Theod. xi. 20. 6.
[5] Zosimus, ii. 38; Evagrius, iii. 39.

'gift', known as *aurum coronarium*.[1]  Wealthy senators, in addition
to a special land-tax,[2] were required on signal occasions to offer a
subscription designated *aurum oblaticium*, and also, when nominated to the ancient City offices (consulship, praetorship, and
quaestorship) to provide games for the people.

The taxes were oppressive in themselves, but they were rendered wellnigh intolerable by the methods employed in their
assessment and collection.  This was particularly the case in
respect of the taxes levied on the small country proprietors.
Every fifteenth year a reallotment of taxes took place; it was
based on an actual survey, which too often was carried out in
a very arbitrary and cruel manner.  Lactantius, indeed, com-
pares the coming of the imperial surveyors to an invasion by a
hostile army ruthlessly intent on plunder.  Even when at last,
amid scenes of desolation and mourning, the first inquisitors had
finished their work and taken their departure, a fresh company
soon arrived, whose business was to review the returns of their
predecessors, and who, to justify their mission, generally increased and sometimes even doubled the original assessment.[3]
Then again, while the imperial authorities prescribed the total
amount to be paid by a district, they did not apportion that
amount among the individual proprietors, nor did they collect
it.  These odious duties devolved on the decurions, or members
of the local senate, who were as a body responsible for raising
the total amount required, and who were obliged to make good
any deficiency out of their own resources.  As the smaller proprietors, unable to meet their financial obligations, went bank-
rupt in increasing numbers, the task of the decurions became
continually more difficult, and many of them, in the desperate
endeavour to save themselves from ruin, appear to have treated
their poorer neighbours harshly and unjustly.[4]  On the top of
all this came the audacious dishonesties of the various officials
appointed to receive the tributes in kind, or to keep the revenue
accounts, or to enforce payments, or to discover and call up
arrears.  Incredible frauds were regularly practised.  False
weights and measures were used; accounts were shamelessly
cooked; receipts were withheld or given designedly in invalid
form; very old receipts, which had long been lost, were suddenly

[1]  Cod. Theod. xii. 13. 1–4.                [2]  Zosimus, ii. 38.
[3]  Lactantius, *De Mort. Persecut.* 23.       [4]  Salvian, *De Gubern. Dei*, v. 18.

and unreasonably demanded; and payments were extorted with shocking violence and brutality.

From this financial system, as unscientific as it was inhumane, two notable consequences resulted. First, the middle class of small proprietors—the very 'sinews of the commonwealth'— wasted away and disappeared. Some farmers, abandoning their excessively burdened farms, took to brigandage for a living.[1] Others resorted to private patronage, voluntarily surrendering their bits of land to the neighbouring senatorial landowners, for whom, in return for protection, they were prepared to work on certain terms.[2] Some actually transferred themselves to districts under barbarian sway, deeming the rule of some half-savage chief preferable to the tyranny of the officials of the Roman Treasury.[3] Secondly, the aristocratic capitalists, taking advantage of the unique opportunities for accumulating property which the circumstances of the time afforded, became dangerously rich and powerful. Their estates, continually augmented by small accretions, grew ever larger and larger. Supplying their own wants, and constituted as separate districts for the purposes of police, taxation, and conscription, they indeed resembled principalities. It was inevitable that their owners should be unhealthily influential. With their vast domains, their immense revenues, their armies of slaves, serfs, and clients, they were able at pleasure to paralyse the imperial administration and to set the imperial laws at defiance.[4]

(iv) Another cause of weakness was *the rigid caste-régime* whereby multitudes of the subjects of the Empire were reduced to a condition of hereditary bondage. All callings and crafts connected with the vital needs of the State had become compulsory and hereditary services. A man who was engaged in such an employment might not change it; his sons also were obliged by law to follow their father's occupation. The sons of bakers had to bake bread; the sons of miners had to work the mines; the

---

[1] Cf. Ambros. *De Interpell. Job*, iv. 21.
[2] Salvian, *De Gubern. Dei*, v. 38–45.
[3] Ibid. v. 21–3, 26, 36–8; Orosius, *Hist.* vii. 41.
[4] The bailiffs of the great landlords were notorious for their lawless conduct. They sheltered deserters from the army (Cod. Theod. vii. 18. 5, 12), fugitive curials (ibid. xii. 1. 179), and brigands (ibid. ix. 29. 2), and were guilty of many wrong and illegal practices (ibid. i. 7. 7). 'Tanquam soluti legibus vivunt', says Symmachus (*Epp.* ix. 6).

sons of shippers were compelled to maintain vessels for the Government. It was the same with the millers, the cattle-breeders and butchers, the purveyors of wine and oil, the weavers, the dyers, the shoemakers, the armourers, the mint-men, the police, the muleteers of the postal service, the men who fed the furnaces in the public baths; in short, with all whose labour was essential for Government purposes. In the case of every such person, freedom to choose a trade, to select a place of abode, to marry outside his guild, to dispose of property at pleasure, was rigorously restricted and even virtually abolished. The boundaries between class and class, between occupation and occupation, had become fixed and almost impassable. Millions of nominally free citizens—the lower-grade officials, the members of the great commercial and industrial corporations—were in a condition approximating to hereditary slavery.

How grievous was this slavery is best seen in the case of the curials. The curials—who at this time were practically identical with the decurions or actual members of the provincial senates[1]—managed the affairs of their municipalities, administering the finances, providing for the upkeep of roads, bridges, and public buildings, acting as petty justices, and discharging the various functions of local government. In addition to these duties, they were made responsible for the individual apportionment and the collection of the imperial taxes levied on their localities. For these arduous services they received no salaries.

In the fourth century the financial burdens had become so overwhelming that the curials, who formerly esteemed it an honour to hold office in their native towns, now sought every means of evading the ruinous distinction. Some endeavoured by bribery to get themselves enrolled on the lists of the Roman Senate;[2] others fled into the civil service or the army;[3] others sought refuge in the Church; others hid themselves on the estates

[1] The decurions were the actual members of the city senates; the curials were strictly the body of well-to-do local landholders who possessed more than 25 *jugera* (Cod. Theod. xii. 1. 33), out of which the decurions were selected. Since, however, at this period practically all curials were made to serve as senators, the terms 'curial' and 'decurion' can be used interchangeably.

[2] Cod. Theod. xii. 1. 180, 183.

[3] Ibid. xii. 1. 22, 50, 147.

of the great proprietors,[1] where they lived in a condition of
dependence almost amounting to serfdom. Thus the number
of curials, exercising their functions, decreased alarmingly.
There was a real danger that the smaller municipalities would
be entirely deserted by the local officers.[2]

In the interest of the imperial financial system, which was
seriously menaced by this 'flight of the curials', drastic measures
were taken. The curial became, in effect, a hereditary Government serf. He could not divest himself of his position—at any
rate until he had over a long period of years laboriously passed
through all the grades of municipal office. If, before that, he
made his escape into one of the privileged professions—even
into the ranks of the Christian clergy[3]—he was liable to be
dragged back. If he desired to quit his town for business or
travel, he was obliged to get permission from the governor of
the province; if he absented himself for five years, his property
was confiscated; if he wished to transfer his residence permanently to another place, he was bound either to provide a substitute to perform his curial duties, or else to resign to his curia a
considerable portion of his fortune. Since his property was
security for the discharge of his financial obligations to the State,
he could not dispose of it at pleasure. He could not sell his land,
or the slaves who cultivated it, without the governor's permission. If he had no children, he could bequeath by will no more
than a quarter of his estate, the remainder passing to the municipal treasury. If he had sons, he could leave them everything,
but the sons inherited their father's curial obligations.

It is unnecessary to enlarge on the unhappy effects of this
caste-system. Liberty, in a real sense, had ceased to exist. The
subjects of the Empire—and precisely those subjects who

[1] Cod. Theod. xii. 1. 76, 146, 179.

[2] In a law of A.D. 326 (Cod. Theod. xii. 1. 13) the phrase occurs, 'quoniam curias
desolari cognovimus'. Once, when for some offence Valentinian I ordered the
execution of three magistrates in each of certain towns, the Praetorian Praefect of
Gaul said: 'What is to be done if the town does not possess so many as three curials?
Are we to suspend the executions till there be a sufficient number to be executed?'
(Ammian. xxvii. 7. 7).

[3] Ambrose speaks of some who, 'having filled the office of priest or deacon for
thirty years or more, are now, to their bitter grief, dragged away from their sacred
functions and sent back to the municipal senate' (Ep. 40. 29). Elsewhere he complains that 'if a priest seeks the privilege of exemption from curial burdens, he must
relinquish his family estate and all his other property' (Ep. 18. 13; cf. Cod. Theod.
xii. 1. 59).

rendered the most important services to the Empire—were in
a condition of virtual slavery. Inevitably they developed the
qualities of slaves, hating the tasks which they were forced to
perform, and loathing the Government which forced them to
perform them. Any revolution of affairs, however mischievous,
was welcome, which gave them hope of release from their
intolerable situation.

(v) To the causes of weakness already enumerated yet another
must be added—*the venality and rapacity of the officials of the Government.* The official hierarchy, indeed, was corrupt from top to
bottom—from the Praetorian Praefect who regarded his exalted
office as a grand opportunity for organized robbery,[1] to the
petty agent of the Treasury busily making a little fortune by
paltry pilferings and peculations. No doubt the corruption was
more gross among the minor functionaries; but even the highest
were badly tainted. Most of them were out for loot.[2] The few
who were honest themselves found it wellnigh impossible not
to connive at the malpractices of dishonest colleagues.

The provincials, who suffered from the depredations of these
miscreants, had practically no redress. It is true that they could
send deputations to the Emperor to represent their grievances.
But they gained little by this privilege. It was only with infinite
difficulty that the deputation could reach the Court; and even
when it arrived, it was generally terrorized into silence, or else
found that the Emperor had been prejudiced against it.[3] In fact,
it was almost impossible to bring a criminal official to justice; and
the provincials as a rule thought it better to endure their wrongs

[1] Salvian, *De Gubern. Dei*, iv. 21 'quid aliud quorundam quos taceo praefectura
quam praeda?' Cf. v. 25; vii. 91, 92.

[2] Paulinus speaks of the voracious avarice of men in influential positions: 'omnia
pretio distrahebantur. Quae res primo omne malum invexit Italiae, et exinde
omnia verguntur in peius' (*Vita Ambros.* 41). Salvian writes that 'the life of merchants is all fraud and perjury, that of the curials is nothing but injustice, that of the
administrative officials is devoted to collusion, while the career of the soldiers is a
career of rapine' (*De Gubern. Dei*, iii. 50). So Maximus of Turin, 'If you regard the
military profession cupidity is the whole reason for entering the service. If you look
at the host of civilian officials, you will find men not led by honourable feelings to
the fulfilment of their duties, but making a business of government for the sake of
gain. Almost all of them are intent on profits and dividends' (*Hom.* 82). Cf. Cod.
Theod. i. 7. 1 'cessent iam nunc rapaces officialium manus; cessent, inquam; nam
si moniti non cessaverint, gladiis praecidentur'.

[3] The story of the embassy from Leptis, related by Ammianus, xxviii, c. 6,
throws a lurid light on the common fate of such deputations.

than to expose themselves to the vengeance of the infuriated bureaucracy.[1]

(vi) The last main cause of weakness that need here be noticed was *the corruption of Roman justice.* It was a grave defect of the imperial system that in the administration of justice a distinction was recognized between the upper or 'more honourable' and the lower classes, the latter being subject to processes and punishments from which the former were exempt. It was, perhaps, an even graver defect that the dispensation of justice was in the hands of the administrative officials. The Governor of a province was judge of first instance in all civil and criminal matters within the provincial area; the Vicar of the diocese and the Praetorian Praefect were judges of appeal. Thus the ordinary subject had no protection against wrongs inflicted by officials, since the judge who tried the case was himself a member of the official gang.

The officials being what they were, it is not surprising that impartial judges were extremely scarce. The laws were good enough, but they were administered disgracefully. Rich people exerted their influence, with little attempt at concealment and with almost invariable success, to procure judicial decisions in favour of themselves or of their protégés.[2] It was useless for a

---

[1] It is true that the emperors did everything they could to secure good administration. (*a*) Edicts were issued, threatening corrupt officials and their staffs with very severe punishments. These, however, produced no effect. (*b*) *Agentes in rebus* were commissioned to watch the conduct of officials and receive complaints. Unfortunately the spies became themselves as corrupt as those whom they kept under observation. (*c*) Each municipality was allowed to choose a protector or *defensor civitatis*, whose duty was to defend the townsfolk and rustics against the insolence and injustice of officials, especially in respect of financial exactions (Cod. Theod. i. 11. 2). This contrivance also failed. The 'father of the people' succumbed to the corrupting influences by which he was surrounded, and not only omitted to defend his 'children', but took to oppressing them on his own account. Thus the well-meant attempts to check the malpractices of officials came to nothing.

[2] Symmachus did not hesitate to write to his friends about cases which were to come before them (*Epp.* ii. 41, 87; iv. 68). Ambrose congratulates Titianus on the removal of Rufinus from the post of Master of the Offices, where he was exercising an unfavourable influence on a family suit in which Titianus was engaged (*Ep.* 52). Augustine relates the story of the resistance of Alypius to the bribes and threats of a wealthy senator who wished to bring about a miscarriage of justice, and remarks that such unusual integrity on the bench excited surprise (*Confess.* vi. 10). How hopeless it was even for a man of good position to contend at law with opponents who were powerful enough to influence the judges is shown in the case of an army treasurer named Antoninus, who, in despair of obtaining justice, admitted an unjust claim, discharged it with public money, and finally, to avoid punishment, fled to the Persians (Ammian. xviii. 5. 1–3).

poor man to bring an action against a wealthy one. To take
proceedings against an official of rank was positively dangerous.
In Valentinian's time a person of standing named Diodorus was
put to death because he ventured in a perfectly constitutional
manner to set the law in motion against the Count of Italy;
three apparitors of the Vicar of Italy, who had served the summons on the Count, were also executed.[1]

It is true that some measures were taken to restrain the more
flagrant abuses in the administration of justice. It was ordered,
for instance, that all causes should be heard in open court,[2] and
that no one should be admitted to an interview with a judge after
his court had closed at midday.[3] But the corruption was in-
eradicable. Ammianus tells us how, in the time of Constantius,
'rich men relying on the protection of those in office bought
acquittals at immense prices, while poor men, who had little
or no means of purchasing favourable verdicts, were condemned
out of hand';[4] how, under Julian, 'it was extremely hard for
any one who was accused by any magistrate to get justice';[5] and
how, under Valens, the judges were only too willing 'to sell the
interests of smaller men to the military officers or to powerful
persons in the palace, gaining wealth and promotion for themselves by their complacency'.[6]

While the emperors in normal times were generally in favour
of judicial reform,[7] they did not scruple on occasion—when they
were alarmed for their personal safety or had reason to believe
that the public security was imperilled—to sanction the grossest
violations of the fundamental principles of justice. For example,
when Maximin was commissioned by Valentinian to suppress
an outbreak of crime in Rome, he did not even pretend to
observe the correct procedure of the courts. Anonymous denunciations, deposited under cover of night in the loop of a cord
which hung from a window of the praetorium, were received

---

[1] Ammian. xxvii. 7. 5. Ammianus says that, if any one petitioned Valentinian
that he might not be tried by a judge who was his personal enemy, the Emperor
invariably refused the reasonable request, xxvii. 7. 8.

[2] Cod. Theod. i. 7. 2.

[3] Ibid. i. 7. 6.

[4] Ammian. xv. 2. 9; cf. xv. 13. 2; xvi. 6. 1–3.

[5] Ibid. xxii. 9. 12.                                        [6] Ibid. xxx. 4. 2.

[7] Yet of Valens it is said that, while he desired to preserve the appearance of a
just administration of justice, 'he allowed no judicial decision to be given which
was contrary to his personal wishes' (Ammian. xxxi. 14. 6).

as evidence. Persons under sentence were offered free pardons if they would make depositions implicating men of rank. The accused were roused in the middle of the night, and, before they had time to collect their faculties, were hustled into court, where their slaves were tortured to furnish evidence against them. 'No one can be proved innocent, unless I choose', the truculent inquisitor was fond of saying.[1] Similar illegalities were practised in the East during the investigation of what was believed to be a treasonable plot against Valens. Secret informations were received. Officers would suddenly come and search people's houses, and, when sealing the properties, would stealthily slip in some incriminating document which they had brought with them. Multitudes of suspected persons were condemned unheard. 'Men were everywhere slaughtered like sheep', writes Ammianus, 'while the question was still being argued whether they had actually committed any offence at all.'[2]

It is evident that the law-courts afforded neither protection to the innocent nor satisfaction to the injured. The poor and humble could get no justice. Even members of the privileged senatorial class, if once accused of grave offences against the State, were seldom granted a fair trial.[3] It would be difficult

---

[1] Ammian. xxviii, c. 1.          [2] Ibid. xxix, cc. 1, 2.

[3] The rich were always at the mercy of the spite or cupidity of informers, who infested all places, and accumulated fortunes by the simple process of accusing wealthy men of treason. So readily were such accusations believed, and so grave consequently was the peril to the accused, that even innocent people were willing to pay large sums in return for a guarantee that no information should be laid against them. Julian, who in his early years had suffered at the hands of delators, disliked them and refused to listen to their reports (Ammian. xxii. 9. 9–11); but other emperors encouraged them—especially Constantius (ibid. xiv. 5. 1–5; xv. 3. 3; xix. 12. 5) and Valens (xxix. 1. 19; xxxi. 14. 6). During the reign of Constantius two informers were specially notorious. One was a Spaniard named Paulus, nicknamed 'the Chain' on account of his skill in involving his victims in artfully forged and unbreakable chains of calumny (ibid. xiv. 5. 6–9; xv. 3. 4; xix, c. 12; xxii. 3. 11). The other was a Persian named Mercurius, nicknamed 'the Count of Dreams'. If any one at a social gathering chanced to mention something he had dreamed, Mercurius would discover in it a treasonable meaning and report accordingly to the Emperor. At last, when many had lost their fortunes or lives simply through dreaming things which they had no business to dream, people were afraid of admitting that they ever dreamed at all, and, if a stranger were within earshot, would loudly protest that they were martyrs to insomnia (ibid. xv. 3. 5, 6). Ammianus describes the methods of the informers employed by Gallus at Antioch. 'A body of obscure men, such as by reason of their condition were little likely to excite suspicion, were sent through all the districts of Antioch, to collect

to imagine a more pernicious state of things. The administration of justice in the least civilized kingdom of modern Europe seems ideal in comparison with the system which obtained during the fourth century in the Roman Empire. Thus the Roman world was already in decay. The population was steadily dwindling. Hundreds of thousands of acres formerly cultivated had returned to waste. The middle class, crushed by overwhelming financial burdens and degraded by the caste-system to a condition resembling serfdom, was ruined and fast disappearing. The bureaucracy, from top to bottom, was incorrigibly corrupt. The army, packed with barbarians, was in a state of chaos. Justice was in abeyance; political freedom was non-existent. In short, the fabric of the Empire, though still imposing in appearance, was rotten to the core. A series of shocks from without could hardly fail to bring about a complete and final and irremediable collapse.

reports and bring news of whatever they might hear. These, going about and concealing their object, hung about the circles of *honorati*, and also, in the disguise of beggars, obtained admission to the houses of the rich. When they returned, they were secretly admitted into the palace by a back door, and then reported all the things which they had heard. They all conspired together to invent many false-hoods, to exaggerate for the worse what was true, and to suppress any praises of Gallus that had come to their ears, although such praises were really uttered by some, not sincerely but through fear. And sometimes it happened that the secret which a man whispered in his wife's ear in his most private apartment, when no confidential servant was by, was reported the next day to the prince. Hence the very walls of the innermost chambers, which seemed to be the only hearers of the secret words, were regarded with suspicion' (xiv. 1. 6, 7). The activities of the odious tribe are neatly summarized by Sidonius—'inferre calumnias, deferre personas, afferre minas, auferre substantias' (*Epp.* v. 7).

## CHAPTER V

# AMBROSE'S LIFE AND WORK AT MILAN

AFTER his consecration Ambrose settled his private affairs, that he might henceforth devote himself without distraction to his episcopal duties. Paulinus asserts that he gave away all his 'gold and silver' to the Church or to the poor, and made over his estates to the Church, reserving merely a suitable provision for his sister.[1] This can hardly be quite correct, however, since, some years after his consecration, he certainly possessed private property.[2] Possibly he made a donation of his acquired property to the Church, but retained his inherited property under his own control, though he devoted the bulk of the income to charitable objects. Such a course would be in harmony with his own regulations for his clergy, whom he permitted to keep at least part of their patrimony,[3] and whom he further advised to make regular contributions to charities rather than give away their entire fortune at once.[4] Such property as he reserved he committed to the charge of his brother Satyrus, who now resigned his governorship and took up his abode in the episcopal house at Milan.[5]

## 1. His Private Life

Of Ambrose's manner of life we learn something from his writings. His habits were simple and even austere. They were shaped by the conviction that a bishop should be distinguished from the common herd by 'nobility' (not of rank, indeed, but) of character,[6] and should therefore surpass all others in the practice of the Christian virtues.[7] 'Nothing vulgar, nothing popular, nothing in common with the ambitions and customs and manners of the rude multitude, is expected in priests. The

---

[1] Paulinus, *Vita Ambros.* 38.
[2] Ambros. *Ep.* 20. 8; *Serm. contr. Auxent.* 5; *De Excessu Sat.* i. 24.
[3] Id. *De Officiis*, i. 152. Some of the Milanese clergy owned estates (ibid. i. 184; *Ep.* 81. 2); those who had no private means received stipends from the Church (*De Officiis*, i. 184).
[4] Id. *De Officiis*, i. 149.
[5] Id. *De Excessu Sat.* i. 20, 40. Marcellina continued to occupy the family mansion in Rome, Paulinus, *Vita Ambros.* 9.
[6] Id. *Ep.* 63. 49; *Exhort. Virginit.* 82.     [7] Id. *Ep.* 63. 59, 64.

dignity of the priesthood demands a sober and elevated calmness, a serious life, a special gravity.'[1]

Much of his time was spent in prayer. From a very early period religious people were accustomed to observe the third, sixth, and ninth hours as stated times of devotion.[2] In the third century two other solemn times of prayer were added—the early morning and the end of the day.[3] In the fourth century six hours were observed at Bethlehem and elsewhere, prayers being offered at dawn, at the third, sixth, and ninth hours, in the evening and also in the night.[4] Sometimes—in order to conform to the psalmist's rule, *Seven times a day do I praise thee* —the number was increased to seven by doubling the nightprayers.[5] In his instructions to virgins Ambrose recommended this sevenfold offering of prayer, and we can hardly be wrong in supposing that this was his own practice.

'Certainly solemn prayers are to be offered with giving of thanks, when we rise from sleep, when we go forth, when we prepare to take food, when we have taken it, at the hour of incense, and when we go to bed. Moreover, in your bedchamber itself I would have you join psalms in frequent interchange with the Lord's Prayer, either when you wake up or before sleep bedews your body. . . . We ought also specially to repeat the Creed daily before light, as a seal upon our hearts, and to recur to it in thought whenever we are in fear of anything.'[6]

It may be noted that Ambrose laid very special stress on the duty of prayer in the night;[7] he even urged that 'the greater part of the night' ought to be devoted to prayer and reading.[8] His own 'great assiduity in prayer by day and by night', and his 'many vigils', are particularly mentioned by his biographer.[9]

Next after prayer, Ambrose valued the discipline of fasting.[10]

[1] Ambros. *Ep.* 28. 2.
[2] Hieron. *Comm. in Dan.* vi. 10: 'There are three times in which the knees are to be bent to God. Ecclesiastical tradition understands the third, sixth, and ninth hours.' Cf. Tertullian, *De Jeiun.* 10.
[3] Cyprian, *De Orat. Dom.* 35.
[4] Hieron. *Epp.* 107. 9; 108. 20; 130. 15.          [5] Hieron. *Ep.* 22. 37.
[6] Ambros. *De Virginibus*, iii. 18–20; cf. *Expos. ev. Luc.* vii. 88.
[7] Id. *Expos. ps. cxviii*, 8. 45–52; cf. ibid. 7. 31; 19. 18, 22, and 30; *Expos. ev. Luc.* vii. 87, 88; *De Abraham*, i. 84.
[8] Id. *Expos. ps. cxviii.* 7. 32.          [9] Paulinus, *Vita Ambros.* 38.
[10] The treatise *De Elia et Jeiunio* is a glorification of fasting. In commending the practice Ambrose neglects no argument. He urges that fasting is economical (*De Elia*, 22), preserves beauty (ibid. 30) and health (ibid. 22), and stimulates the

He strongly urged his people to practise fasting, especially in Lent,[1] and he himself was scrupulous in this observance. At Milan, all Wednesdays and Fridays were, of course, kept as fasts;[2] though on these days the fast did not extend beyond the ninth hour, that is, about three o'clock in the afternoon.[3] In Lent, however, all days, except Saturdays and Sundays, were observed as fasts,[4] and during this season the fast lasted until evening.[5] In keeping Saturday as a festival, the Church of Milan followed the custom of the Eastern Churches, and differed from the usage of Rome. To satisfy his mother's doubts, Augustine once questioned Ambrose on the subject of this peculiarity. Ambrose treated it simply as a matter of the ordinance of this or that Church, and said that when he himself was at Milan he observed the Sabbath festally, but when he was at Rome he conformed to the usage of the Roman Church and fasted.[6] Of course the Milanese rule about Saturday did not apply to Easter Eve, which was kept as a fast in all the Churches. During Pentecost—the season between Easter and Whitsunday—there was no fasting. Ambrose says that according to ecclesiastical tradition this whole period should be kept as part of Easter; the fifty days are each like a Sunday, and while they last the Church does not fast.[7]

appetite (ibid. 32). In the moral sphere it is the enemy of vice (ibid. 4), the nurse of chastity and all virtues (ibid. 22), a chief means whereby we may triumph over the flesh and the devil (ibid. 1. 79). It cancels the dire effects of the Fall and re-opens the way to Paradise (ibid. 7. 9), and enables us to live, though still in the body, the life of angels (ibid. 3. 4). It is also the price that must be paid for the privilege of partaking of the Eucharist (ibid. 33). Fasting is as old as the world (ibid. 6); it was the first commandment given by God to our first parents (ibid. 7). 'The fast is the refreshment of the soul, the food of the mind, the life of angels, the end of guilt, the destruction of transgressions, the remedy of salvation, the root of grace, the foundation of chastity. By this stair we draw near to God more quickly' (ibid. 4). See also, in praise of fasting, Ep. 63. 15–31.

[1] Id. De Elia, 1. 79; cf. De Virginibus, iii. 17.

[2] These Wednesday and Friday fasts were called Stations (Tertullian, De Jeiun. 14). The author of a sermon wrongly attributed to Ambrose thus explains the term: 'Our fasts are our encampments which protect us from the devil's attack; they are called stations, because standing and staying in them we repel our plotting foes' (Serm. 21. 1. Migne, Ambrosii Opp. iv, p. 644).

[3] For the hour see Prudentius, Peristeph. vi. 54, 55; Cathem. viii. 9–16. Cf. Tertullian. De Jeiun. 13 'stationum semiieiunia'.

[4] Ambros. De Elia, 34.          [5] Id. Expos. ps. cxviii, 8. 48.

[6] Augustin. Ep. 36 ad Casulanum, 32.

[7] Ambros. Expos. ev. Luc. viii. 25; cf. Apol. David, 42 'vacant ieiunia, laus dicitur Deo, alleluia cantatur'.

During the fasting hours—i.e. on stational days till the afternoon, in Lent till evening—no food at all was taken. When the
fast of each day ended, however, there seems to have been no
restriction on the kind of food that might be eaten. But in Lent,
at any rate, religious people were accustomed in various ways to
abridge and simplify the evening meal. Some abstained from
meat and wine; others refused also fowl and fish; the very strict
limited themselves to bread and water.[1] Ambrose recommended
that during Lent some special austerity should be practised in
the matter of diet.[2] He also advised that the money saved by
abstinence on fasting-days should be bestowed upon the poor.[3]

In addition to the fasts prescribed by the Church, ascetic
persons were in the habit of undertaking voluntary fasts. Ambrose's sister, Marcellina, used to deprive herself of food for
lengthy periods, extending over several days and nights.[4] Other
pious women were accustomed all the year round to abstain
from food until the evening meal.[5] This was Ambrose's own
practice. Except on Saturdays, Sundays, and the festivals of
celebrated martyrs, he took no food until late in the day.[6]

His ordinary diet was simple. Though he was not a vegetarian,[7] he thought that flesh food inflamed the passions and
should therefore be eaten sparingly.[8] Wine in strict moderation
might sharpen the wit and conduce to health;[9] yet, having regard to the horrible evils resulting from its intemperate use,[10]
he held that it had better be avoided by those who were
physically able to do without it.[11] 'To drink wine is lawful, but
to drink much of it is not expedient.'[12] Of elaborate and expensive entertainments he disapproved;[13] hospitality, however, he
deemed a duty, the neglect of which not even poverty could excuse.[14] He himself kept open table for all comers—not only for

---

[1] Socrates, *H.E.* v. 22.                          [2] Ambros. *De Virginibus*, iii. 17.
[3] Id. *De Nabuthe*, 19. Cf. ibid. 45; Pseudo-Ambros. *Serm.* 25. 6; 29. 4.
[4] Ambros. *De Virginibus*, iii. 15.                  [5] Id. *De Instit. Virgin.* 31.
[6] Paulinus, *Vita Ambros.* 38; cf. Ambros. *De Viduis*, 38.
[7] Ambros. *De Noe*, 89, 90.
[8] Id. *Ep.* 63. 26; *De Virginibus*, i. 53; *De Poenit.* i. 76.
[9] Id. *Hexaem.* iii. 72; *De Noe*, 111.
[10] Id. *De Abraham*, i. 57, 58; *De Elia*, 10–12.
[11] Id. *Ep.* 63. 27. The clergy especially should abstain from wine, *De Officiis*, i.
246.
[12] Id. *De Viduis*, 68.                          [13] Id. *De Officiis*, ii. 109.
[14] On the duty of hospitality, see *De Officiis*, i. 167, ii. 103–7; *Expos. ev. Luc.* vi. 66;
*Hexaem.* v. 54; *Ep.* 63. 105; *De Abraham* i. 32–5.

poor people and strangers, but also for persons of the highest rank.[1] Count Arbogast, at one period, used frequently to dine with him, and Polybius, Proconsul of Africa, stayed with him for some days.[2] But he rarely or never dined out. 'Dinner-parties at other people's houses', he said, 'take up one's time, and also encourage the taste for feasting. Moreover, stories of the world and its pleasures are often told. One cannot shut one's ears, and to forbid the tales would be thought arrogant. One's glass, too, is filled time after time against one's will. It is better to refuse once for all in one's own house than to keep on refusing in another's.'[3]

As in his diet, so also in his attire, Ambrose cultivated simplicity. He considered fine clothes unsuitable for the clergy. A man in Holy Orders has no business to array himself in the costly white robes affected by fashionable people; he should dress decently and as befits his station, but his apparel should be of ordinary quality and sober hue.[4] In the fourth century the dress of clergymen was not different from that of laymen of the same social rank.[5] Thus Ambrose's everyday attire was the same as that worn by senators and persons of position when not engaged in ceremonial or official functions.[6] It consisted essentially of two garments—a white or light-coloured linen tunic reaching to the ankles, which was the original of the ecclesiastical alb, and over it a brown or violet woollen *paenula* or *planeta*, which was the original of the chasuble. The *paenula* was a large heavy cloak, closed all round so as to fall over the arms and having merely a slit for the head to pass through.[7] Besides these two essential garments there might be a third—a dalmatic

---

[1] Sulpicius, *Dial.* i. 25 'consules et praefectos pascere ferebatur'.
[2] Paulinus, *Vita Ambros.* 30; Ambros. *Ep.* 87. 1.
[3] Ambros. *De Officiis*, i. 86.
[4] Ibid. i. 83. Cf. Jerome's advice to Nepotian on the subject of dress, *Ep.* 52. 9.
[5] Ambrose and his brother Satyrus, who was a layman, were often mistaken for one another when they went abroad, *De Excessu Sat.* i. 38. There was nothing in point of costume to distinguish the bishop from the retired official.
[6] The toga was still the dress of ceremony; but it had been discarded from ordinary wear—partly, no doubt on account of the difficulty of fixing the folds in the correct lines and keeping the elaborate arrangement in place (Tertullian, *De Pall.* 5).
[7] In the early fifth-century mosaic of Ambrose in the Chapel of San Vittore in Ciel d'Oro (see below, p. 114), he is represented wearing a *paenula*. So, in the picture described by John the Deacon, Pope Gregory the Great and his father Gordianus, who was a layman, were each dressed in a chestnut-coloured *planeta* over a dalmatic (Joan. Diac. *Vita S. Gregor.* iv. 83, 84).

or large-sleeved over-tunic, made of linen, silk, or wool, and worn immediately over the under-tunic.[1] Even when discharging liturgical functions a fourth-century ecclesiastic still wore lay costume. It appears, however, that the garments used for the ministry of the altar were reserved exclusively for that use and did not form part of the wardrobe of everyday life.[2]

In accordance with the fashion of the period, Ambrose held daily 'audiences', which were attended by crowds of people of all classes and conditions. Sometimes he was visited by strangers from far-distant countries. Once, for example, two noble and learned Persians came, primed with many questions, and, with the assistance of an interpreter, conversed with him from six o'clock in the morning till nine at night.[3] Ambrose considered that a bishop ought to be easily approachable by any one who needed advice;[4] so the doors of his house were always open, and visitors were allowed to enter unannounced. Often, however, the throng of callers was so great that late comers were unable to get within sound of his voice.[5]

When the long reception was over, Ambrose devoted himself to study. But not even then did he seclude himself. He used to read in a corner of the cloister surrounding the open court of his house, and people still came in and waited at a respectful distance for an opportunity of addressing him. Augustine often watched him as he pored over his books, and was struck by his habit of reading silently—'his eyes scanned the page and his mind penetrated the meaning, but his voice and tongue were silent'. Augustine conjectured that he adopted this practice to save his voice, or else because he feared that, if he were to read aloud some perplexing passage, a bystander might interrupt him with a request for an explanation.[6]

---

[1] On the day of his martyrdom Cyprian wore a dalmatic over the under-tunic, *Acta procons.* 5.

[2] Hieron. *Comm. in Ezech*, xiii. c. 44. v. 17. Nepotian left as a legacy to Jerome 'tunicam qua utebar in ministerio Christi', id. *Ep.* 60. 13.

[3] Paulinus, *Vita Ambros.* 25.

[4] Ambros. *De Officiis*, ii. 61.

[5] Augustin. *Confess.* vi. 3.

[6] Ibid. vi. 3. It may be remarked that, as in reading Ambrose dispensed with the services of a reader, so for writing—unless he happened to be ill—he seldom employed an amanuensis (Paulin. *Vita Ambros.* 38). He found that he was better able to express his thoughts if he wrote with his own hand; also, since he preferred to write at night, he was loath to deprive his secretary of rest (Ambros. *Ep.* 47. 1, 2).

It was probably at this period of his life that Ambrose (under the guidance of his old friend and tutor Simplician, now resident at Milan)[1] became acquainted with the works of various Jewish and Christian writers, to some of whom he shows himself extensively indebted in his own compositions. Of these authors his favourites undoubtedly were Philo,[2] Origen,[3] and Basil;[4] but he also shows knowledge of various works of Josephus,[5] Eusebius,[6] Hippolytus,[7]

[1] Augustin. *Confess.* viii. 2.

[2] See Th. Förster, *Ambrosius, Bischof von Mailand*, pp. 102–12; M. Ihm, 'Philon und Ambrosius', *Neue Jahrb. für Philol. und Pädag.* 1890, cxli, pp. 282–8; and K. Schenkl's Preface to *C.S.E.L.* xxxii, Ambrosii Opp. part i, pp. xv, xxi, xxii, xxiii, xxiv, xxv, xxvi, xxvii, xxviii, xxx. Ambrose appears to be acquainted with the following works of Philo: *De Mundi Opificio, Sacr. Legum Allegoriae, De Cherubim, De Sacrificio Abelis et Caini, Quod deterius potiori insidiari soleat, De Posteritate Caini, De Gigantibus, De Agricultura Noe, De Plantatione Noe, Quod Deus sit immutabilis, De Abrahamo, De Migratione Abrah., De congress. quaerendae eruditionis gratia, Quis rerum divin. haeres sit, De Profugis, De Mutatione Nominum, De Somniis, De Vita Moysis, De Praemiis et Poenis, Quaestiones in Genesin, De Providentia, De Incorruptibilitate Mundi, Quod omnis probus liber*, and *De ratione brutorum*. So numerous are the reminiscences of Philo scattered through Ambrose's writings (especially *De Paradiso, De Cain, De Noe, De Abraham, De Fuga*) that successful attempts have been made to reconstruct from the latter the corrupt Philonic text.

[3] See Th. Förster, op. cit., pp. 112–17. Ambrose appears to have read Origen's *Commentary on Genesis*, of which only fragments are extant (Hieron. *Ep.* 84. 7), also his *Homilies on Genesis*, his *Homilies on Psalms 36–8*, his *Commentary on Psalm 1*, and one at any rate, (the 13th) of his *Homilies on Numbers*; he had also studied very closely Origen's *Homilies on St. Luke* (K. Schenkl, *C.S.E.L.* xxxii, Ambrosii Opp. part iv, Praef. xiii, xiv) and his *Commentary on the Song of Songs* (K. Schenkl, *C.S.E.L.* xxxii, Ambrosii Opp. part i, Praef. xxx, xxxi). Ambrose's dependence on Origen is noted by Jerome, *Epp.* 84. 7; 112. 20; *Apol. adv. Rufin.* ii. 14.

[4] Th. Förster, op. cit., pp. 117–23; J. B. Kellner, *Der heilige Ambrosius als Erklärer des alten Testaments*, pp. 93 ff. Ambrose was familiar with Basil's *Homilies on the Hexaemeron*, on which he modelled his own work (K. Schenkl, *C.S.E.L.* xxxii, Ambrosii Opp. part i, Praef. xiii); with his *Homilies on Psalms 1 and 14*; with the following homilies: *In illud Attende tibi ipsi, De Paradiso, De Jeiunio i, In Ebriosos, Exhortator. ad sanctum Baptisma, In Luc. xii 18, In Divites* (K. Schenkl, *C.S.E.L.* xxxii, Ambrosii Opp. part ii, Praef. xix, xx); and with the treatise *De Spiritu Sancto*.

[5] Ambrose was acquainted with the *Antiquities* (M. Ihm, *Studia Ambrosiana*, pp. 66, 67), with the *Jewish War* (of which, either before or early in his episcopate, he published a Latin condensation; see below, chapter xxii), and with the work (wrongly ascribed to Josephus by Eusebius, *H.E.* iii. 10) *IV Maccabees* or *On the Supremacy of Reason* (K. Schenkl, *C.S.E.L.* xxxii, Ambrosii Opp. part ii, Praef. xv).

[6] Ambrose was certainly acquainted with the *Ecclesiastical History* and with the work, preserved only in fragments, *On the Discrepancies of the Gospels* (K. Schenkl, *C.S.E.L.* xxxii, Ambrosii Opp. part iv, Praef. v, xiv, with references to Eusebius in the Index). He does not, however, appear to have read Eusebius' *Commentary on St. Luke*.

[7] Jerome asserts (*Ep.* 84. 7) that Ambrose availed himself of the lost *Hexaemeron* of Hippolytus; and he seems also to have used his *Philosophumena* (K. Schenkl, *C.S.E.L.* xxxii, Ambrosii Opp. part i, Praef. xiv).

Didymus,[1] and Athanasius,[2] and he had read a Latin version
of the First Epistle of Clement.[3] Further, in order to qualify
himself to refute erroneous views, he seems to have studied
certain heretical books—the voluminous *Syllogisms* of Apelles,[4]
and publications emanating from the Apollinarian[5] and
Novatianist[6] schools.

We may get some idea of the external appearance of Ambrose
from the remarkable mosaic in the Chapel of San Vittore in Ciel
d'Oro, or San Satiro, which opens out from the south aisle of the
Church of Sant'Ambrogio. On each side-wall of this chapel are
three standing saints—St. Ambrose between St. Gervasius and
St. Protasius on one wall, St. Maternus between St. Nabor and
St. Felix on the other. The mosaic of Ambrose (with which
alone we are concerned) is almost certainly a work of the early
fifth century, and may well be regarded as a true portrait of
the Bishop, as he appeared a little while before his death in A.D.
397.[7] According to this representation, Ambrose was of short
stature[8] and rather delicate appearance.[9] His face was elon-
gated, his forehead high, his nose long and straight, his lips thick;
his eyes were large, and one of the eyebrows was perceptibly
higher than the other. He had short hair and beard[10]—perhaps
light brown in colour—and wore a drooping moustache. His
general expression was grave and even a little melancholy. It is
impossible to attribute to him physical beauty, but the attraction
which he exercised on many—on Monnica and Augustine,

[1] The treatise of Didymus, *De Spiritu Sancto*, known to us only in Jerome's translation, was used extensively by Ambrose; cf. Hieron. *Liber Didymi de Spiritu Sancto*,
Praef. ad Paulinianum; Rufin. *Apol.* ii. 23 ff.
[2] Ambrose had evidently read Athanasius' *Letter to Epictetus* (cf. Ambros. *De
Incarn.* 36, 46 ff., 77), probably also the *Orations against the Arians*.
[3] K. Schenkl, *C.S.E.L.* xxxii, Ambrosii Opp. part i, Praef. p. xvii.
[4] K. Schenkl, loc. cit., p. xxi.
[5] Ambros. *De Incarn.* 51.
[6] In his *De Poenitentia* Ambrose seems to have in mind some recent publication
of the Novatianists.
[7] See A. Ratti, *Il più antico ritratto di S. Ambrogio* (in *Ambrosiana*, Milan, 1897).
[8] This is confirmed by the evidence of his bones, which were carefully examined
in 1871; A. Ratti, op. cit., p. 71.
[9] We know that he suffered from illnesses (*De Excessu Sat.* i. 36; *Epp.* 15. 10; 51.
5) and that his voice was 'easily weakened' (Augustin. *Confess.* vi. 3); also that he
'macerated' his body with constant fasts and mortifications (Paulin. *Vita Ambros.*
38).
[10] On the beard, see A. Ratti, op. cit., pp. 72, 73. Fair hair (*capilli flavi*) is
ascribed to him by a late tradition, ibid., pp. 68–70.

for example—proves that he possessed the indefinable quality of charm.

From his frequent commendation of the virtue of silence,[1] it might possibly be inferred that Ambrose was inclined to taciturnity. Certainly he held that jesting was unseemly for clergymen.[2] Yet he was not without a sense of humour; he seldom let slip an opportunity of playing on words or making a pun.[3]

## 2. His Work as Bishop

The work of the chief pastor of a great city such as Milan was both arduous and varied. Among the activities in which, as bishop, Ambrose was called upon to engage, the following may be mentioned.

(a) First, he had heavy duties in connexion with *the administration of Baptism and Penance*. He took infinite pains to give adequate instruction to catechumens; and Paulinus affirms that, in connexion with the baptismal rite, he by himself laboured more than the five succeeding bishops of Milan did together.[4]

In the exercise of penitential discipline he was equally conscientious. 'Whenever any one confessed his sins to him with a view to doing penance, he so wept as to make the penitent weep also, for he seemed to share the fallen one's fall. But the misdeeds which were confessed he never mentioned to any one except God, with whom he interceded. Thus he left a good example to the bishops who came after him, that they should be intercessors with God rather than accusers before men.'[5] The confession here referred to is the private confession made to the bishop, who then determined whether public penance must be undertaken. The decision, of course, depended on the degree of heinousness of the sins confessed. A distinction was drawn between lighter and graver offences.[6] In the case of the

---

[1] Ambros. *De Officiis*, i. 5–22, 31–5; *De Virginitate*, 80, 81; *De Instit. Virginis*, 4, 5; *Exhort. Virginitatis*, 86–9.

[2] Ambros. *De Officiis*, i. 102, 103.

[3] For examples see *Epp.* 3. 2; 30. 15; 54. 1; 60. 1; 63. 107; 82. 12; 88. 1; *De Excessu Sat.* i. 10; *Serm. contr. Auxent.* 33; *De Tobia*, 13, 14, 15, 16, 17, 29, 34, 36, 38, 40.

[4] Paulinus, *Vita Ambros.* 38. On the baptismal rite at Milan, see below, chapter xiii. It was mainly, no doubt, on account of the pre-baptismal instruction that Ambrose would not absent himself from Milan in Lent, *Ep.* 2. 27.

[5] Paulinus, op. cit. 39. Ambrose himself prayed for the gift of compassionate sympathy with sinners, *De Poenit*, ii. 73.   [6] Ambros. *De Poenit.* i. 10, ii. 95.

former Ambrose deprecated harsh measures, holding that trans-
gressors were more easily reclaimed by gentleness than by
severity.[1] But in the case of the latter—since pardon for very
great sins could be obtained only through the intercession of the
Church[2]—the guilty were suspended from communion and
ordered to do penance.

This penance consisted partly of public humiliation and
partly of private mortification.[3] First, the delinquent was required to make public acknowledgement of his transgression,
and, with tears and prostrations, implore the intercession of the
faithful.[4] 'I have known some', writes Ambrose, 'who have
furrowed their cheeks with continuous tears, who have laid
their bodies in the dust for all to trample on, and who, with
faces emaciated and pallid with perpetual fasting, have presented the appearance of living ghosts.'[5] Secondly, in addition
to this public humiliation, the penitent was required to practise
rigorous austerities. He dressed in squalid attire, fasted almost
continually, restricted the time allotted to sleep, abstained from
wine, from the use of the bath, and from the pleasures of marriage, and absented himself from public festivities and private
entertainments.[6] While the penance lasted, he lived a life
resembling that of a professed ascetic.

The duration of public penance was determined by the
bishop, who was under obligation not to readmit a penitent
to communion too easily or too speedily.[7] In extreme cases an
offender might be condemned to do penance for life.[8] Ordinarily,

---

[1] Ambros. De Poenit. i. 1–4.

[2] Ibid. i. 80, 81; ii. 91, 92; Expos. ev. Luc. v. 11.

[3] The three or four stages of penitential discipline which were customary in some
parts, at any rate, of the East do not appear to have been observed in Latin
countries (F. X. Funk, Theol. Quartalschrift. 1886, pp. 373 ff.). See generally
A. Lagarde, 'La Pénitence dans les Églises d'Italie au cours des iv<sup>e</sup> et v<sup>e</sup> siècles'
in Revue d'histoire des religions, Paris, xcii, 1925, pp. 108 ff.

[4] Ambros. De Poenit. i. 90; ii. 91: In ps. 37. enarr. 51. Cf. Jerome's description of the
penance of Fabiola, Ep. 77. 4.

[5] Ambros. De Poenit. i. 91.

[6] On the austerities practised by penitents, see Cyprian, De Lapsis, 35; Pacian,
Par. ad. Poenit. 19.

[7] Ambros. Expos. ps. cxviii, 8. 26; De Poenit. i. 78, 79; ii. 87. At Milan, although
penitents were excluded from communion, they seem to have been permitted to be
present at Mass; see Ambros. Ep. 51. 13, 15; Paulinus, Vita Ambros. 24, and the
remarks of P. Lejay, 'Ambrosien Rit', in Dict. d'Archéologie chrétienne et de Liturgie
(Paris, 1906).

[8] [Niceta Remes.] De Lapsu Virginis, 38.

however, he was readmitted to Christian privileges when the bishop was convinced of the genuineness of his repentance, and when the congregation had petitioned for his forgiveness. The day usually chosen for the solemn reconciliation of penitents was the Thursday in Holy Week.[1]

(b) Another of Ambrose's episcopal duties was *the superintendence of the charities of the Church*. Although the details of this business were entrusted to the deacons,[2] yet the ultimate responsibility naturally rested with the bishop, who was also directly consulted on special cases. These charities included the relief of the poor, the care of the sick and of convicts, the entertainment of strangers, the payment of debts incurred by honest men who through no fault of their own were unable to meet their liabilities, the maintenance and education of orphans, the assignment of dowries to impecunious girls, and the provision of graves for the pauper dead.[3] With regard to the bestowal of relief, Ambrose laid down some very sensible regulations. He cautioned his almoners against the artfulness of knaves who often pretended to be in distress that they might squeeze money out of the Church;[4] and especially warned them not to be taken in by the plausible tales of the professional beggars.

'Nowhere is the greed of the beggars greater than it is here. They come, though they are strong and healthy; they come for no reason but that they are on the tramp. Not content with a little, they ask for more. They parade their rags, that they may entice you to comply with their demands. They try to persuade you to increase your alms by telling you lies about their noble birth. Many pretend that they have debts. They protest with tears that they have been stripped of everything by robbers. Do not believe it unless the misfortune be proved or the sufferer be personally known to you.'[5]

On the other hand, people who were really in dire necessity should be assisted without too curious scrutiny into their character and deserts.[6] Even the excommunicated ought to be relieved when in destitution.[7] The old and infirm, who were no longer able to earn a living, should receive special consideration; also men of good family, who had fallen on evil days and were

---

[1] Ambros. *Ep.* 20. 26; *Hexaem.* v. 90.
[2] Id. *De Officiis*, i. 252, ii. 140.
[3] Ibid., i. 148; ii. 71, 72, 77, 103, 109, 111, 142; *De Tobia* 5.
[4] Id. *De Officiis*, i. 149.                [5] Ibid. ii. 76, 77.
[6] Id. *De Nabuthe*, 40.                      [7] Id. *De Officiis*, ii. 77.

ashamed to beg.[1] Concerning these last detailed reports were
to be submitted to the bishop.[2] In the dispensation of relief due
measure must be observed between extravagance and parsi-
mony. 'When men see a really good almoner, they are ready
enough to give him something to distribute when he goes his
rounds. But they will not give a penny to an extravagant
almoner or to one who is too niggardly; since the first wastes
the fruits of their labour in unnecessary outlay, while the second
hoards it in his money-bags.'[3]

In Ambrose's opinion, 'the highest kind of liberality' was the
redemption of captives, especially those who had been carried
off by barbarians.[4] After the disaster of Hadrianople in the
year A.D. 378, when the Goths ravaged Illyricum to the foot of
the Julian Alps, great multitudes of men and women—'more
than the population of a province'—were taken prisoners. To
redeem them, Ambrose did not hesitate to break up and sell the
plate of the Church. His action was severely criticized by the
Arians, who were eager to embrace an opportunity of bringing
a Catholic prelate into discredit. But Ambrose was not to be
frightened by the cry of 'Sacrilege!'

'It is far better', he said, 'to preserve souls for the Lord than to
preserve gold. For He who sent forth the apostles without gold, also
gathered together the churches without gold. The Church has gold
—not, however, that she may store it up, but that she may spend it in
helping those who are in necessity. If we were to save up our gold
and silver, surely the Lord would be likely to say, "Why have so many
captives been offered for sale in the market? Why have so many,
who were not redeemed, been slain? It would have been better to
preserve living vessels than metal ones." And what reply could we
make to Him? Should we plead that we feared that God's temple
would be left without adornment? He would answer, "The sacraments need not gold. They are not bought with gold, and therefore
gold is not required to beautify them. The adornment of the sacraments is the redemption of captives." Yes, those are verily precious
vessels which redeem souls from death. That is the true treasure of the
Lord which effects what His Blood effected. Then do we recognize the
cup of the Lord's Blood when we see it effecting a twofold redemption—when the chalice redeems from the enemy those whom the
Blood has redeemed from sin. How beautiful that it should be said,

---

[1] Ambros. *De Officiis* i. 158.                [2] Ibid. ii. 69.
[3] Ibid. ii. 78.                                 [4] Ibid. ii. 70, 71.

when troops of captives are redeemed by the Church, "These Christ has redeemed"! Behold the gold that is approved! behold the gold that is profitable! behold the gold of Christ which saves men from death! behold the gold with which modesty is ransomed and chastity preserved! This great company of captives is more glorious than the splendour of cups. It is right that the gold of the Redeemer should contribute to the work of delivering those in peril.'[1]

(c) Another important function of a fourth-century bishop was *the defence of the oppressed*. At a time when the weak received no adequate protection from the State, great numbers of people, when threatened with injury, put themselves under the protection of the Church. Widows and orphans, for example, who were specially liable to be robbed by unscrupulous neighbours, were accustomed to use the Church as a kind of bank and entrust their property to its keeping.[2] Even when this precaution had been taken, nefarious attempts were sometimes made, by persons who had interest with the Government or at Court, to appropriate such deposits. A typical case occurred in the time of the Younger Valentinian—perhaps early in the year A.D. 386, when Valentinian was at Pavia.[3] A widow had committed some valuable property to the custody of the Church in that city. The property, however, was coveted by an influential person, who procured from the Emperor an order authorizing him to lay hands on it. This order was read to the clergy. It had been issued by the Master of the Offices, and was in correct form; an imperial messenger was in attendance to carry it out. The clergy, having been assured by the local notables that resistance was out of the question, weakly agreed to surrender the deposit. The Bishop of Pavia, however, consulted Ambrose, and by his advice took possession of the chamber where the property was, and boldly refused to allow its removal. Thereupon a new order was issued; but the intrepid prelate continued to set the imperial authority at defiance and even sent a message to the Emperor threatening him with Divine vengeance if he should persist

[1] Ambros. *De Officiis*, ii. 136–9. In this connexion Ambrose tells the well-known story of St. Lawrence, ii. 140. Augustine also broke up and sold the plate of his Church for the redemption of captives (Possid. *Vita Augustini*, 24).

[2] Ambros. *De Officiis*, ii. 144, 149.

[3] Valentinian was at Pavia on 15 February of this year (Cod. Theod. xii. 12. 11). J.-R. Palanque, however, places the incident in A.D. 388, and connects it with the usurpation of Maximus (*Saint Ambroise et l'Empire Romain*, p. 526).

in his sacrilegious purpose. Notwithstanding this threat, yet
another attempt at seizure was made. But when the officers
came to take away the deposit by force, it was nowhere to be
found; for the bishop, foreseeing what was likely to happen, had
prudently restored it to the rightful owner.[1]

Closely connected with the episcopal duty of defending the
oppressed was the duty or privilege of interceding for the condemned. 'If any be a bishop', wrote Ambrose, 'let him rescue
by his intercession and influence the man who is being haled to
death.'[2] Although he recognized that great discretion was
needed in the exercise of this function,[3] he held that in cases
of life and death, when the circumstances afforded grounds
for remission or mitigation of punishment, a bishop could not
properly refuse to intervene.[4] He himself was frequently
active in intercession. In Gratian's reign a pagan noble was
sentenced to death for having spoken disrespectfully of the
Emperor. Ambrose immediately hastened to the palace to
plead for mercy. Gratian, however, was watching games in his
private circus, and the guards at the gates refused the visitor
admission. Ambrose wasted no time in argument, but, pretending to retire, he unobtrusively joined a group of ostlers and
*bestiarii* and in their company entered the building through a
side door. He then made his way to the pavilion of the Emperor,
from whom he extracted a free pardon for the criminal.[5]
Another time, during the reign of the same Emperor, he called
at the residence of Macedonius, Master of the Offices, to intercede for some offender, but found that by the Master's order
the doors were closed against him. Angry at the slight, he is
said to have uttered words which were literally fulfilled later on
when the fallen minister fled for sanctuary to a church: 'The
day will come when you in your turn will go to the Church,
but will not be able to enter.'[6] Again, after the victory of Theodosius over Eugenius, he exerted himself vigorously to obtain
mercy for some of the usurper's adherents who had taken refuge

[1] Ambros. *De Officiis*, ii. 150, 151.
[2] Id. *Expos. ps. cxviii*, 8. 41.
[3] Id. *De Officiis*, ii. 102.                              [4] Ibid. iii. 59.
[5] Sozomen. *H.E.* vii. 25.
[6] Paulinus, *Vita Ambros*. 37. For another case of intercession made by Ambrose
on behalf of an official threatened with severe (but not capital) punishment, see
*Ep.* 54. 1.

in a church.[1] It may be remarked that Ambrose had a strong objection to capital punishment. He was once asked by a magistrate named Studius whether it was permissible for a Christian judge to pass the death-sentence. He replied that it was certainly lawful, and that magistrates who had so acted ought not to be excluded from communion, though they would do well if they were to abstain temporarily from communicating: nevertheless capital punishment was a mistake. Christian magistrates should incline to leniency and afford the guilty opportunities of repenting and submitting to penance.[2] 'When we put a criminal to death', he writes elsewhere, 'we punish the person rather than the crime; but when we cause a criminal to forsake his crime, then the person is set free while the crime is avenged.'[3]

(d) Yet another episcopal function was that of *hearing and determining civil causes*.[4] The corruption and chicanery of the secular courts had brought it about that great numbers of causes were carried before the ecclesiastical tribunals, where the moral integrity of the judge could be relied on and where the procedure was cheaper, simpler, and more expeditious. Indeed to conscientious bishops this legal business was fast becoming a grievous burden.[5] In Ambrose's view, however, a bishop might not decline to arbitrate in really important causes, wherein the laws of God or the interests of the Church were involved,

[1] Ambros. *Ep.* 62. 3; Paulinus, op. cit., 31. Among famous instances of intercession the following may be recalled—that of Leontius on behalf of Symmachus (Socrates, *H.E.* v. 14), that of Martin of Tours on behalf of the Priscillianists (see below, chapter ix), that of Flavian on behalf of the people of Antioch (see below, chapter xiv), and that of Augustine on behalf of the Circumcellions (Augustin. *Epp.* 134 and 139).

[2] Ambros. *Ep.* 25. The secular power punishes, the spiritual power forgives (*De Cain*, ii. 15); but the rules of Roman law are inferior to the authority of the Scriptural saints (*De Officiis*, iii. 67). Judges ought, at any rate, to take time before ordering the infliction of capital punishment (*De Cain*, ii. 38). Yet Ambrose does not condemn magistrates for carrying out the law, provided that they do so impartially (*Expos. ps. cxviii*, 20. 37); he recognizes that mercy to a criminal may in certain circumstances occasion disorder (*De Officiis*, ii. 102) and be unjust to the criminal's victim and others (*Expos. ps. cxviii*, 8. 25). Nor does he condemn the ordinary legal procedure; even judicial torture he mentions without a hint of disapproval (*De Cain*, ii. 27; *De Elia*, 63).

[3] Id. *Ep.* 26. 20.

[4] This privilege was granted to bishops by a law of Constantine (Sozomen. *H.E.* i. 9), alluded to by Ambrose (*Ep.* 82. 1).

[5] Possidius says that Augustine often spent all the morning, and sometimes the whole day, hearing causes (*Vita Augustini*, 19).

though he might legitimately refuse to do so in mere sordid
disputes about property.[1] He himself was prepared, at the
request of the litigants, to give judgement even in pecuniary
actions. His conciliatory methods may be illustrated by the
following example. A certain bishop, named Marcellus, made
a grant of land to a widowed sister, on the condition that at her
death she should bequeath it to the Church of which he was
bishop. Marcellus, however, had a cantankerous brother,
Laetus, who, feeling aggrieved by the transaction, applied in the
Praefect's Court to get it annulled. After the suit had dragged
on for some while and heavy expense had been incurred, counsel
on both sides agreed to refer it to Ambrose for arbitration. Ambrose settled it by a compromise. He gave as his award that
Laetus should have the land on condition of paying annually to
his sister, during her lifetime, a stipulated quantity of corn, oil,
and wine; after the lady's death, he was to retain possession of
the estate, without obligation to make any further payments
either to Bishop Marcellus or to his Church. By this judgement
Ambrose claimed that he had satisfied all the parties—Laetus,
because he was given the land, the sister, because she was
guaranteed a fixed income for life, and Marcellus, because the
dissension in his family was now happily composed, and because
the award embodied a compromise which he had himself suggested. The only loser was the Church; but the Church was rich in
things eternal and could afford to dispense with temporal gains.[2]

(e) Finally, the bishop was responsible for *the discipline of his
clergy*. At Milan the ecclesiastical hierarchy consisted of presbyters, deacons, subdeacons, exorcists, readers, and doorkeepers.[3]
Towards these ministers the bishop's relation was that of a father
to his sons;[4] he was accordingly bound to keep them in good
discipline, taking care to avoid the extremes of laxity and harshness.[5] Ambrose appears to have been specially vigilant in the
oversight of his spiritual family, and issued minute instructions
on the proprieties of clerical behaviour. Some of the points
which he makes are interesting. In respect of conversation

[1] Ambros. *De Officiis*, ii. 125; cf. iii. 59.
[2] Ambros. *Ep*. 82. For a discussion of this case see F. Martroye, 'Une Sentence
arbitrale de S. Ambroise', in *Revue Historique de Droit Français et Étranger*, 1929,
pp. 300–11.
[3] See Note at the end of this chapter.
[4] Ambros. *De Officiis*, i. 24; ii. 134, 155.                        [5] Ibid. ii. 120.

(Ambrose insists) a clergyman must never indulge in scandalous gossip or indelicate talk;[1] even innocent jokes had better be avoided.[2] He ought, however, to cultivate affability and courtesy, 'so as to make himself agreeable to his friends, to his fellow citizens, and, if possible, to all men'.[3] If he has occasion to speak on controversial topics, he must do so good-humouredly, in a manner which will not cause irritation.[4] Yet, though suave, he must be sincere; to flatter or accept flattery is highly indecorous.[5] As regards conduct, a cleric should exercise the greatest circumspection. He would be wise to refuse all invitations to dine out;[6] he must also refrain from entering on lawsuits and from engaging in trade.[7] Particularly he must keep clear of discreditable methods of making money—legacy-hunting, for example. 'Even in the case of men who are not ministers of religion to angle for inheritances is reckoned unbecoming.'[8] Towards the secular authorities a cleric should comport himself with extreme discretion, scrupulously avoiding provocative utterances which might furnish the heathen with an excuse for persecution.[9] Young clergymen must not visit virgins and widows, except in the company of the bishop or of a senior presbyter; instead of wasting their time in paying calls and compliments they ought to devote themselves to reading.[10] They are further advised to associate with older men of approved virtue, who, even if they are rather dull companions, are at any rate prudent counsellors and responsible guides.[11] To gad about abroad is unbecoming for a cleric. If he is sent by the bishop on some mission, of course he must go; but he should return and resume his duties with as little delay as possible.[12]

Even to comparatively trifling details of clerical behaviour Ambrose attached considerable importance. He recognized that 'bodily attitudes express states of mind',[13] and took sharp notice of them accordingly. He was extremely irritated by the slow and pompous movements of certain of his clergy, who stalked about, like tragic actors, with monstrous stiffness and solemnity; nor could he tolerate the type of man who is everlastingly in a hurry.[14] Uncouth gestures and affected mannerisms

---

[1] Ambros. De Officiis, i. 76.    [2] Ibid. i. 102, 103.    [3] Ibid. i. 225; ii. 29.
[4] Ibid. i. 99.        [5] Ibid. ii. 96; cf. i. 208.        [6] Ibid. i. 86.
[7] Ibid. i. 184.        [8] Ibid. iii. 58.        [9] Ibid. i. 207.
[10] Ibid. i. 87, 88.        [11] Ibid. i. 211; ii. 97.        [12] Id. Ep. 85. 2.
[13] Id. De Officiis, i. 71.        [14] Ibid. i. 73, 74.

alike excited his displeasure. He refused to admit one person into the ranks of the clergy simply on the ground that he was offended by his bearing; another, who was already a cleric, he forbade ever to walk in front of him, because he found his gait insufferable.[1] In respect of the manner of speaking he was equally particular. He detested a strident tone, a provincial accent, a stagey articulation; nor would he put up with the languid drawl which was assumed by some of the clergy, in the mistaken belief that it made their utterances more impressive. He required that those about him should speak naturally and simply, with reasonable vigour, and with clear and correct pronunciation.[2]

In dispensing promotions Ambrose endeavoured to be strictly just.[3] His action in these affairs was determined by three principles—first, that merit, as well as seniority, should be taken into account;[4] secondly, that negligent clerics should under no circumstances be promoted, but should rather be deprived of the offices which they held;[5] and thirdly, that each individual should be assigned the office—whether it were that of reader or of exorcist or of minister of the altar—for which he was temperamentally best fitted, 'since the duty which suits a man, and which is in line with his natural bent, is always discharged with greater grace'.[6]

On certain questions relating to the marriage of the clergy Ambrose took an austere line. He insisted, for instance, on the strict observance of the rule—which seems at this time to have prevailed universally in the West and generally in the East— that married men who received ordination as bishops, presbyters, or deacons, should not, after their ordination, be at liberty to cohabit with their wives or beget children. The reason given for this decision is that those ministers who are immediately concerned with the offering of the Holy Sacrifice ought to continue permanently in a state of physical purity. 'You must have a pure body for celebrating the sacraments.'[7] On another

---

[1] Ambros. *De Officiis*, i. 72; cf. his severity to the fanciful deacon Gerontius, Sozomen. *H.E.* viii. 6.
[2] Ambros. *De Officiis*, i. 67, 84, 104.   [3] Ibid. ii. 121.
[4] Id. *Expos. ps. cxviii*, 2. 18.   [5] Ibid. 2. 22, 23.
[6] Id. *De Officiis*, i. 215.
[7] Ibid. i. 248; cf. *De Viduis*, 65; *Ep.* 63. 62. Towards the end of the fourth century the rule of continence was accepted as binding married bishops, presbyters, and

question, affecting the ordination of married persons, Ambrose expressed himself strongly. It was the rule both in the East and in the West that a man who had been twice married could not be ordained. In enforcing this rule, however, the Eastern Church did not take into account any marriage which had been entered upon before baptism. Thus, if a man had been only once married since his baptism, he was regarded in the East as eligible for ordination, notwithstanding any other marriage which he might previously have contracted as a heathen or catechumen.[1] Ambrose, however, maintained the view—which was afterwards adopted by the Church of the West—that two marriages, irrespective of the question whether they were contracted before or after baptism, constituted an impediment to ordination.

'As regards marriage, the law is not to marry again. Many indeed wonder why two marriages, of which the first and perhaps even the second was contracted before baptism, should debar a man from election and ordination to clerical office, seeing that even grave sins are not usually an impediment, if they have been remitted by the Sacrament of the Laver. We ought to understand, however, that while sin can be removed by baptism, law cannot be abolished. In marriage there is no sin, but there is law. Hence in baptism all sin is put away, but the law respecting marriage is not set aside.'[2]

Ambrose's solicitude for his clergy is shown by the trouble he took in their instruction. For their benefit he composed the

deacons, not only in Milan and Rome, but also in other churches of Italy (Ambros. *Exhort. Virginit.* 24). It was observed generally in Gaul, Spain, and Africa; also in Thessaly, Macedonia, and Achaia (Socrates, *H.E.* v. 22). Ambrose says that many refrained from taking Holy Orders 'because in the uncertain age of youth continence seemed too difficult' (*De Officiis*, i. 217). On the other hand, notwithstanding Jerome's assertion that in the Orient the rule of continence for the higher orders was general (*Contr. Vigilant.* 2), it seems that in some parts of the East the clergy were allowed to use their discretion in this particular (Socrates, loc. cit). For the story of the protest of Paphnutius against the proposal to impose the discipline of continence on bishops, presbyters, and deacons who had married before their ordination, see Socrates, *H.E.* i. 11; Sozomen. *H.E.* i. 23.

[1] The Eastern interpretation of the rule is defended by Jerome, *Ep.* 69; cf. *Comm. in Tit.* i. 6.

[2] Ambros. *De Officiis*, i. 247; cf. *Ep.* 63. 63. Ambrose states (*Ep.* 63. 64) that the Fathers of Nicaea had decreed that no one who had contracted a second marriage should be admitted to any clerical office. Since, however, no such regulation is found among the Nicene Canons, it may be assumed that he possessed an inaccurate copy, in which a canon of some other Council had been interpolated. Augustine accepts Ambrose's view as to the ineligibility of the twice-married (whether before or after baptism) for Holy Orders (*De Bono Conjug.* 21).

important series of addresses which were afterwards gathered up in that very famous treatise, *Concerning the Duties of the Clergy.*[1] Moreover, apart from his public lectures, he was always ready to advise them individually and privately. He encouraged them to apply to him in their intellectual and spiritual difficulties, and several of his letters are answers (frequently lengthy and elaborate) to questions propounded by clerical correspondents.[2]

### 3. *His Duties as Metropolitan*

In addition to the government of his own Church, Ambrose, as sole metropolitan of northern Italy, had the general superintendence of the dioceses of the province. Thus we find him discharging the various duties of the office of metropolitan— convoking ordinary or extraordinary provincial councils,[3] hearing appeals,[4] issuing directions as to the proper day for observing Easter,[5] and consecrating bishops to vacant sees.[6] As regards

[1] On the *De Officiis*, see below, p. 502, note 2; pp. 694-5.

[2] To one clergyman, named Horontianus, who had been brought up from childhood among the clergy of Milan and had been ordained presbyter by Ambrose (*Ep.* 70. 25), he sent a series of expository letters (*Epp.* 34–6, 43, 44, 70, 71, 77, 78). Among the questions propounded to the bishop by Horontianus were, Is the soul constituted of a heavenly substance? (*Ep.* 34), What spirit is it that *maketh intercession for us with groanings that cannot be uttered*? (*Ep.* 36), Why was man, the highest of God's creations, created last? (*Ep.* 43). Another series of expository letters was addressed to Irenaeus, who may have been a cleric of Milan (M. Ihm, *Studia Ambrosian.* p. 46, note 251; see, however, J.-R. Palanque, 'Deux correspondants de S. Ambroise: Orontien et Irénée', in *Revue des Études Latines*, Paris, xi, 1933, pp. 153–63), and who had no scruple in making demands on Ambrose's time and patience (*Epp.* 26–31, 33, 64, 69, 73, 76). In this correspondence we find, among other matters, a discussion of the Pythagorean maxim 'not to follow the beaten track' (*Ep.* 28), a meditation on Christ as the Chief Good of Man and the True Source of Happiness (*Ep.* 29), a solution of the question, Why does not God rain manna in our own days? (*Ep.* 64), an explanation of the severity of the Mosaic law against those who disguised their sex (*Ep.* 69), and a summary of the Epistle to the Ephesians (*Ep.* 76). In another letter Ambrose endeavoured to comfort some of his clergy who were in despondency (*Ep.* 81). Four letters—the first of exceptional interest—containing dissertations on philosophical and Scriptural themes were written to, and in response to requests of, Simplician (*Epp.* 37, 38, 65, 67). [The Romulus, to whom the expository *Epp.* 66, 68 are addressed, was not a clergyman, but a distinguished layman, Flavius Pisidius Romulus, who was Consular of Aemilia-Liguria in A.D. 385.]

[3] For references to synods at Milan, see Ambros. *Epp.* 13; 14; 21. 17 and 18; 42; 51. 6.

[4] Id. *Epp.* 5 and 6.                                   [5] Id. *Ep.* 23.

[6] Among the bishops consecrated by Ambrose were Felix of Como (Ambros. *Ep.* 4. 1 and 6), Gaudentius of Brescia (Gaudent. *Serm.* xvi), Vigilius of Trent

the consecrations, it was customary for the metropolitan to go in person to the Church where a vacancy had occurred, and there preside over the election and the subsequent ceremony of consecration. Ambrose generally followed this course. After the death of Philaster of Brescia, for instance, he went himself to Brescia, officiated at the consecration of the new bishop, Gaudentius, and preached a sermon.[1] He was not able, however, to leave Milan for long; hence, in the case of difficult and protracted elections, he was accustomed to transact the preliminary business by correspondence. The Church of Vercelli gave him a good deal of trouble. After the death of Bishop Limenius, the clergy and people could not agree in the choice of a new pastor, and in consequence the see continued for a long while vacant. In some quarters Ambrose was blamed because he did not exercise his authority to put an end to the disorder and compel the electors to proceed to an election. He was reluctant to force matters; but he wrote a voluminous letter to the Church of Vercelli, exhorting its members to compose their quarrels and unite in choosing some worthy man to be their bishop.[2] Unfortunately the admonition produced no result; and in the end Ambrose was compelled to go in person to the place and settle the dispute.

His vigilant care for the welfare of the dioceses of the province may be illustrated by his instructions to the bishops Constantius and Vigilius. He requested the former—who was perhaps the Bishop of Claterna—to pay frequent visits to the neighbouring Church of Imola, which at the time happened to be without a bishop, and take measures to protect the faithful from being infected with the heresy of some Arian refugees who had settled there.[3] Similarly, Vigilius (who should probably be identified with Vigilius, Bishop of Trent) was urged to do everything in his power to discourage intermarriage between Christians and pagans in his diocese.[4] Vigilius appears to have carried out this precept with less tact than zeal; at any rate he incurred the

(Ambros. *Ep.* 19. 1), Anemius of Sirmium (Paulin. *Vita Ambros.* 11), Constantius of (?) Claterna (Ambros. *Ep.* 2. 1), Chromatius of Aquileia (to whom probably *Ep.* 50 was addressed), and Honoratus of Vercelli (M. Ihm, *Studia Ambrosian.* p. 56).
[1] Gaudent. Brix. *Serm.* xvi.
[2] Ambros. *Ep.* 63.
[3] Id. *Ep.* 2. 27–9.
[4] Id. *Ep.* 19.

bitter hatred of the pagans, and eventually suffered at their hands a martyr's death.[1]

With several of the provincial bishops Ambrose maintained a friendly correspondence. To one he sent graceful thanks for a present of fine mushrooms and promised to pray for him on the anniversary of his consecration;[2] to another he furnished by request a dissertation on certain difficulties in the story of Balaam;[3] to a third he forwarded some sound advice on the subject of preaching and also an essay on the rite of circumcision;[4] to a fourth he transmitted, in reply to an inquiry, an explanation of the half-shekel of redemption (Exodus xxx. 12, 13) and an answer to the common objection that the Holy Scriptures were not written according to the rules of art;[5] to a fifth he addressed a mystical interpretation of Paradise.[6] This last—Sabinus, Bishop of Piacenza—was Ambrose's chief episcopal correspondent.[7] He seems to have been a man of cultivated literary taste, and Ambrose was glad to submit to him some of his own compositions for criticism. 'Apart from that besetting carelessness which clouds my mind', he wrote, 'every one is apt to be deceived about his own writings and to overlook their faults. Just as a father is pleased with his own children even when they are ugly, so an author is proud of his own productions even when they are ungraceful. Be so good, then, as to give my work your keen attention. Read all the discourses carefully. Criticize them minutely. See if they exhibit, not merely rhetorical elegance, but a sound faith and a sober confession. Put a mark against any word of doubtful import. The book is a bad one which needs an interpreter and does not speak clearly for itself.'[8] Paulinus informs us that Ambrose used to weep very bitterly whenever he heard news of the death of a good bishop; and, when his atten-

[1] On Vigilius, who is of considerable importance in the history of the christianization of the Rhaetian Alps district, see *Acta Sanctorum* (Bolland) June v. 165–8: his episcopate is dated A.D. 385–405 (G. Rauschen, op. cit., p. 221, note 6).

[2] Ambros. *Epp.* 3 and 4.

[3] Id. *Ep.* 50. This letter was intended to be the first of a series (*Ep.* 50. 16).

[4] Id. *Ep.* 2. 5 ff.; *Ep.* 72.

[5] Id. *Epp.* 7 and 8. The Justus to whom these letters were addressed appears to have been a bishop (*Ep.* 7. 1 'frater'), but there is no reason to identify him (as do Tillemont and G. Rauschen, op. cit., p. 106) with Justus of Lyons.

[6] Id. *Ep.* 45.

[7] Letters 45–9, 58, and (probably) 32 were addressed to him: see J.-R. Palanque, *S. Ambroise et l'Empire Romain*, pp. 471, 472.

[8] Id. *Ep.* 48. 2 and 3. For Ambrose's appreciation of fair criticism, see *Ep.* 46. 2.

dants tried to console him, would say that he wept 'because the deceased had died before himself', or, 'because it was difficult to find a man worthy to hold the exalted office of bishop'.[1]

## NOTE

### The Orders of Ministers in the Time of Ambrose

At Milan the following orders of ministers are known to have existed in Ambrose's time—doorkeepers, readers, exorcists, subdeacons, deacons, and presbyters.

(i) Lowest in rank was the *Doorkeeper*. This officer is not mentioned by Ambrose; but Augustine informs us that, when Monnica brought her gifts for the poor to the 'memorials of the saints' in Milan, she was repulsed by an *ostiarius*.[2] The duties of the doorkeeper resembled those of the modern verger. He attended to the cleaning of the church, kept order among the worshippers, and prevented the intrusion of unauthorized persons during the celebration of the Sacred Mysteries.

(ii) Next above the doorkeeper was the *Reader*.[3] Those who aspired to enter the ministry, if they were not yet adult, began their career as readers.[4] Thus many of the clerics belonging to this order were very young—often, indeed, little more than children.[5] Their function was to recite the lessons and intone the psalms.[6] In Ambrose's time, however, the reading of the Gospel in the Mass seems to have been reserved, in the West, to the deacons.[7]

[1] Paulinus, *Vita Ambros.* 40.      [2] Augustin. *Confess.* vi. 2.

[3] Tertullian is the first writer to mention readers as a distinct order in the Church (*De Praescr.* 41). Cyprian witnesses to the existence of this order in the Church of Carthage (*Epp.* 23, 29, 38, 39), Cornelius in the Church of Rome (Eusebius, *H.E.* vi. 43), and Ambrose in the Church of Milan (*Ep.* 20. 13; *De Excessu Sat.* i. 61). Ambrose may allude to the low rank of readers in the hierarchy when, commenting on the reading of Isaiah by our Lord in the synagogue at Nazareth, he says, 'Jesus so humbled Himself to every kind of service, that he did not disdain even the office of reader' (*Expos. ev. Luc.* iv. 45). Ambrosiaster, however, appears to rank readers above exorcists (*Comm. in Ephes.* iv. 11).

[4] Siricius, *Ep.* 1. 13 'quicunque se ecclesiae vovit obsequiis a sua infantia, ante pubertatis annos baptizari et lectorum debet ministerio sociari'.

[5] Ambros. *De Excessu Sat.* i. 61 'per vocem lectoris parvuli'. Cf. Paulinus Nolan. *Poem.* xv. 108 'primis lector servivit in annis'. Such youthful readers seem to have been brought up among the clergy. Ambrose writes to the presbyter Horontianus, 'tu, fili, qui a primo flore pueritiae es haeres ecclesiae, quae te suscepit et tenet' (*Ep.* 70. 25); and speaks of himself as 'non in ecclesiae nutritus sinu, non edomitus a puero' (*De Poenit.* ii. 72).

[6] Ambros. *De Officiis*, i. 215 'alius distinguendae lectioni aptior, alius psalmo gratior'.

[7] Cyprian connects the Gospel with the reader (*Epp.* 38, 39); but in the fourth century, in the West, the reading of the Gospel seems to have been the function of

(iii) After the reader came the *Exorcist*.[1] Adults, entering the ministry, frequently commenced as exorcists.[2] Their duty was to exorcize catechumens who were preparing for baptism,[3] and to minister to energumens or frenzied persons.[4] Many of these energumens abode permanently, or for long periods, within the precincts of the churches, where they were daily visited by the exorcists; others were brought for treatment on special occasions. Thus, on the eve of the dedication of the Ambrosian Basilica with the newly discovered relics of SS. Gervasius and Protasius, there was an all-night vigil in the Basilica of Fausta, with 'imposition of hands' on possessed persons.[5] It is true that the treatment of such sufferers was not strictly confined to the exorcists. Ambrose himself was credited with remarkable powers for the expulsion of demons.[6] The exorcists, however, were the regular ministers. The ceremony of exorcism appears to have consisted mainly of the recitation of a formula of adjuration in the name of Christ, accompanied by an imposition of hands. The spurious *Exorcism of St. Ambrose*, printed by the Benedictine editors in the Appendix to Ambrose's *Works*, may perhaps illustrate the kind of formula that was used at an earlier period.[7]

(iv) The three higher orders of ministers were distinguished from the three inferior orders by the circumstance that they were attached to the service of the altar. First came the *Subdeacons*, who performed certain minor functions in connexion with the altar, and also did duty as the personal and secretarial staff of the bishop. At Rome and Carthage, and in some other large communities, the subdiaconate was subdivided into subdeacons and acolytes.[8] This subdivision, however, was not universal at this period; and the evidence suggests that as yet no distinct order of acolytes existed at Milan. Ambrose, in his writings, makes no reference to acolytes. Also, if the statement of Paulinus about Ambrose be correct that 'after his baptism he fulfilled all the ecclesiastical offices and on the eighth day was conse-

---

the deacon (cf. Hieron. *Ep.* 147. 6 'evangelium Christi, quasi diaconus, lectitabas'). In the East the custom varied, the Gospel being read in some Churches by deacons, in others by presbyters, in others—on great festivals—by bishops (Sozomen. *H.E.* vii. 19).

[1] Ambrose refers to this order, *De Officiis*, i. 215; *Expos. ev. Luc.* vii. 29.

[2] Martin of Tours is an example (Sulpicius, *Vita Martini*, 5).

[3] L. Duchesne, *Christian Worship*, pp. 344, 349, 350.

[4] See the Fourth Council of Carthage, canons 7, 90, 92.

[5] Ambros. *Ep.* 22. 2.

[6] Paulinus, *Vita Ambrosii*, 43; cf. ibid. 21.

[7] *Ambrosii Opera*, iv, p. 1019; M. Magistretti, *La Liturgia della Chiesa Milanese nel Secolo iv*, p. 36. The effects of exorcism on the patient were often extremely startling: see Cyprian, *Quod idola dii non sint*, 7; *Ad Demetrian.* 15.

[8] Eusebius, *H.E.* vi. 43; Cyprian, *Ep.* 78.

crated bishop',[1] and if further it be rightly assumed that on the first day he was made doorkeeper and on the two following reader and exorcist, then only one day is left before that on which he was ordained deacon; and on this day he must certainly have been made subdeacon.

(v) The chief function of the *Deacons*, according to Ambrose, was to tend the sanctuary,[2] and assist at the altar during the celebration of the Sacred Mysteries.[3] They read the Gospel, and also administered the chalice to communicants.[4] At baptisms also certain duties were assigned to them.[5] In addition to their functions in connexion with the sacraments, they acted, under the direction of the bishop, as relieving officers of the Church.[6] We do not know how many deacons were at this time attached to the Church of Milan. But, while there is no reason to suppose that their number was limited to seven as at Rome, it is probable that here as elsewhere the deacons were few in comparison with the presbyters. This numerical paucity naturally enhanced the deacons' importance, and in many quarters led to ambitious attempts on the part of the deacons to exalt themselves at the expense of the presbyteral order.[7]

(vi) The *Presbyters* constituted the Council of the bishop, which advised and assisted him in the government of the Church. Like the bishop, they were *sacerdotes*,[8] and consequently entitled to celebrate the rites of Christian worship. They attended the bishop when he functioned in his cathedral, and were sent by him to minister as his

---

[1] Paulinus, *Vita Ambrosii*, 9. Paulinus himself, who lived under the care of Castus the deacon (ibid. 42), was probably a subdeacon.

[2] Ambros. *De Officiis*, i. 255 'eligitur levita qui sacrarium custodiat'; cf. ibid. i. 215 'alius sacrario oportunior'.

[3] Ibid. i. 248.

[4] Ibid. i. 204; cf. Cyprian, *De Lapsis*, 25.

[5] Id. *De Mysteriis*, 6, 8; cf. *De Sacramentis*, i. 4.

[6] Id. *De Officiis*, i. 252; ii. 140: cf. Hieron. *Ep.* 146. 1 'mensarum et viduarum minister'.

[7] On the presumption of deacons, see Council of Arles, A.D. 314, canon 18; Council of Nicaea, canon 18; Hieron. *Ep.* 146; Ambrosiaster, *Quaest. Vet. et Nov. Test.* 101.

[8] Though Ambrose not unfrequently refers to the presbyter as *sacerdos* (*De Mysteriis*, 6; *De Officiis*, i. 152; ii. 69), he more often employs that term to designate the bishop. This was the traditional usage. In Cyprian's letters, for instance, 'the word *sacerdos* is never distinctly applied to a presbyter, though once or twice the whole clerical body is spoken of as *sacerdotes et ministri*' (E. W. Benson, *Cyprian*, p. 33). From Ambrose's time, however, presbyters begin to be called *sacerdotes*. So Jerome (*Epp.* 52. 7; 108. 28; *Adv. Jovin.* ii. 28) and Ambrosiaster (*Comm. in Ephes.* iv. 11); who both assert a fundamental parity of order between presbyter and bishop (see especially Ambrosiaster *Comm. in 1 Tim.* iii. 8, and cf. Hieron. *Ep.* 146. 1; *Comm. in Tit.* i. 5). Optatus strangely considers that not only presbyters, but even deacons, are in some degree sharers in the priesthood (*De Schism. Donat.* i. 13).

representatives in other churches of the diocese.[1] On the bishop's invitation they sometimes preached.[2] The fact that Ambrose gave instruction to his clergy on the subject of preaching[3] suggests that at Milan presbyters of mature age were occasionally requested, in the absence of the bishop, to discharge this duty. The presbyters further assisted the bishop at baptisms—the foot-washing, for instance, though begun by the bishop was completed by the presbyters.[4] Poor presbyters were supported by the Church.[5] 'Give to the presbyter', writes Ambrose, 'the earthly goods which you have in abundance, that you may receive from him the spiritual goods which you lack. He receives from you not as a pauper, but as one who will repay you with larger measure.'[6]

---

[1] Ambros. *Ep.* 20. 22.

[2] Since the sermon was part of the Eucharistic service, it was held to be the duty of him who presided at that service (Justin. *Apol.* i. 67), i.e. of the bishop. Ambrose enlarges on the duty of teaching which his episcopal office laid upon him (*De Officiis*, i. 2–4). The bishop could, if he chose, appoint a deputy; but the deputy was chosen from those to whom could be also deputed the right of celebrating the Eucharist, i.e. the presbyters. Deacons did not preach (Ambrosiaster, *Comm. in Ephes.* iv. 11: the case of Aetius was exceptional, Philostorgius, iii. 17). In the East it was usual for a presbyter to preach in the presence of the bishop, who himself preached after him; in the West presbyters did not preach in the presence of the bishop—a bad custom, in Jerome's opinion (*Ep.* 52. 7). Valerius of Hippo, however, being himself a Greek, adopted the Eastern usage and authorized Augustine, when a presbyter, to preach before him; and this example, though criticized at first, was afterwards followed (Possidius, *Vita Augustini*, 5). The presbyters appear to have preached only in the cathedral or bishop's church. In the sixth century, the Second Council of Vaison, canon 2, gave them the right to preach in country parishes.

[3] Ambros. *De Officiis*, i. 101.                    [4] *De Sacramentis*, iii. 4.

[5] Ambros. *De Officiis*, 1. 184.                    [6] Id. *Expos. ev. Luc.* viii. 79.

CHAPTER VI

# WOMEN IN THE FOURTH CENTURY AND AMBROSE'S WORK AMONG THEM

ONE of the most interesting features of the century with which we are dealing is the growing importance of women in the life of society. Both in law and in fact the position of women had materially improved. The State now accorded them an ampler measure of protection against unjust or cruel treatment: the Church held them in high honour and even allowed them to minister as deaconesses. In the secular world we find women playing prominent parts. Of the great ladies, who through their husbands, brothers, or sons exercised influence on public affairs, it is sufficient to mention Constantia, sister of Constantine and patroness of Arius; Eusebia, the second wife and good genius of Constantius; the gentle and saintly Flaccilla, first wife of Theodosius; Justina, mother of Valentinian II and bitter enemy of Ambrose; and Serena, the brilliant wife of Stilicho. In the ecclesiastical world, again, we encounter many women of remarkable ability and force of character. Such were Macrina, sister of Basil, whose singular piety was matched by her splendid intellectual endowment; Marcellina, the strong-minded sister of Ambrose; Melania, the friend of Rufinus; Paula, with her fine capacity for business, who 'had the care of' Jerome and found it a difficult task; Augustine's mother Monnica, whose intelligence and good sense were such that her son declared, 'we fairly forgot her sex and thought that some great man was in our circle'; Anthusa, the mother of Chrysostom, concerning whom Libanius exclaimed, 'Good heavens! what women these Christians have!'; and the sagacious and spirited Olympias, whose friendship cheered Chrysostom in persecution and exile.

In this chapter I propose (1) to give a brief account (with special reference to Ambrose's writings) of the ordinary life of upper-class women in the fourth century, and (2) to describe Ambrose's influence on and work among them.[1]

---

[1] It may be worth while to summarize Ambrose's views about women. Although he sometimes speaks as though he considered that women were not naturally

## 1. The Life of Women in the Fourth Century

A girl born of well-to-do parents escaped the danger of being exposed or cast away, which was still too often the fate of female children of the poor.[1] Almost immediately after her birth she was handed over to a wet-nurse, since Roman ladies seldom took the trouble to nurse their babies.[2] During the first few months of her existence she was immoderately coddled, being smothered in baby-clothes and confined in stuffy nurseries, where no breath of fresh air was allowed to enter.[3]

When she emerged from babyhood into childhood she was given toys—especially dolls—to play with,[4] and was amused with fairy-tales.[5] She had her set of letters made of light box- or cedar-wood,[6] and was taught to write in copy-books[7] and to ply the needle.[8] In old-fashioned families she was further instructed in the old-fashioned accomplishment of spinning.[9]

inferior to men (*De Viduis*, 44, 51), yet he generally describes the male sex as the 'stronger' (*De Instit. Virginis*, 25), 'better' (*Ep.* 69. 4), and 'principal' sex (*In ps. 1 enarr.* 14). Hence he thought it 'becoming' that woman should be 'subject' to man (*De Instit. Virginis*, 32), and that man should govern her (*Hexaem.* v. 18). Husbands, however, though they have a right to govern, must not tyrannize (ibid. v. 19); for wives, though subject, are not slaves (*Ep.* 63. 107). If woman, however, is subordinate, she is also necessary to man, who cannot come to his perfection without her (*De Instit. Virginis*, 22). The two sexes, in fact, though characterized by essential differences (*Ep.* 69. 2 and 5), are complementary. Men are more suited for public, women for domestic, duties (*De Paradiso*, 50; *De Noe*, 43). Women should, therefore, keep at home, and be seen and heard by strangers as little as possible (*De Abraham*, i. 42; *De Elia*, 66). Ambrose had a higher opinion of women than many of his contemporaries. While others were never weary of inveighing against woman as the cause of man's fall (*De Instit. Virginis*, 16), he argued that Eve's guilt was less heinous than Adam's, since (*a*) Eve was weaker than Adam and therefore more liable to fall; (*b*) was exposed to greater temptation (*De Instit. Virginis*, 25); (*c*) and atoned for her sin by frank confession (ibid. 27) and by working out her punishment (ibid. 29). By her assiduous prayers and fasts woman has set man an example of repentance and amendment (ibid. 31). Finally, Eve's fault was cancelled by Mary, who, as the Virgin Mother of the Saviour, has restored and exalted her sex (ibid. 33).

[1] Ambros. *Hexaem.* v. 58, 61. On the exposure of infants see Lactantius *Inst. Div.* vi. 20; Tertullian *Apol.* 9; Minucius Felix, *Oct.* 30. Often exposed children were taken up by vile persons, who used them for immoral purposes (Justin Martyr, *Apol.* i. 27).

[2] Ambros. *Hexaem.* v. 58; *De Abraham*, i. 63; *Ep.* 63. 108.

[3] Id. *Hexaem.* v. 42.          [4] Hieron. *Ep.* 128. 1; Lactantius, *Inst. Div.* ii. 4.

[5] Tertullian, *Adv. Valent.* 20; Arnobius, *Adv. Gent.* v. 14.

[6] Ambros. *Hexaem.* iii. 53; *Expos. ps. cxviii*, 22. 38; cf. ibid. 14. 1.

[7] Hieron. *Ep.* 107. 4.          [8] Ambros. *De Virginibus*, i. 7.

[9] Hieron. *Ep.* 107. 10. Ausonius refers to the skill in spinning of some of his female relations, *Parent.* ii. 4; xvi. 4: cf. Symmachus, *Epp.* vi. 67.

Next came her literary and artistic education. If she belonged to a Christian household, the Bible was her first study. Very early—as soon as she was able to learn at all—she began to learn the Psalter by heart,[1] and later was made to read other portions of the Scriptures.[2] In secular literature her education followed the same lines as that of a boy.[3] Special attention was given to the study of the Greek and Latin poets. Claudian commends Maria, the bride of Honorius, for having kept up her studies in classical literature under her mother's guidance; among the authors read by her Homer and Sappho are specially mentioned.[4] In addition to literature, a young girl was usually taught to sing, to play on the guitar and other instruments, and to dance. It is true that these elegant accomplishments were regarded with disapproval in the stricter Christian circles.[5] Ambrose, however, was disposed to tolerate them. In church, at any rate, he liked to hear girls singing the psalms, and even thought that the apostolic precept about women keeping silence in church might be set aside in their favour, because they sang so well.[6] About dancing he was less certain. He admitted that it was a 'not incongruous' amusement for children,[7] yet considered it dangerous to modesty.[8] 'A modest and chaste mother ought to teach her daughter religion, not dancing.'[9]

Up to the time of her marriage a girl lived in strict seclusion. Even among pagans this was the custom, and Christian parents were still more careful to keep their daughters in retirement. Jerome, who was an authority on the method of bringing up young ladies, laid down the following regulations: a girl must never appear in public, even in church, except in her mother's company; she must not take her meals at her parents' table; she must not attend weddings, dinner-parties, or similar festivities; she must never look at a young man or associate with any

---

[1] Ambros. *In ps. 1 enarr.* 9.
[2] Jerome (*Ep.* 107. 12) prescribes the order in which the sacred books should be read by a little girl.
[3] Girls of the middle class attended school with boys (Ausonius, *Protrept.* 33); though some Christian educationists, e.g. Jerome (*Ep.* 128. 3a), disapproved of this mingling of the sexes. Aristocratic girls were usually educated at home.
[4] Claudian, *De Nupt. Honor. et Mariae*, 229 ff.
[5] Hieron. *Ep.* 107. 8: 'let her be deaf to the sound of the organ, and not know even the uses of the pipe, the lyre and the guitar'.
[6] Ambros. *In ps. 1 enarr.* 9.        [7] Id. *Expos. ev. Luc.* vi. 5.
[8] Id. *De Virginibus*, iii. 25, 27.        [9] Ibid. iii. 31.

lively, gaily dressed young woman, but must spend her whole
time with a governess of mature age and austere virtue; if she
bathed—an operation seldom necessary for a full-grown maid—
it must not be in the society of married women or in the presence of eunuchs: her diet must be of the simplest kind, and she
must always rise hungry from table.[1]

When she had completed her twelfth year a girl was considered
marriageable, though as a rule she was not actually married until
she was about fourteen. As she was still so young, her parents
selected her husband for her. Ambrose entirely approved of
this procedure. He quotes two lines of Euripides to the effect
that a father will look after his daughter's marriage, for it is
not her business to have an opinion on such a matter; and adds
that even a young widow ought to commit to her parents the
choice of her second husband.[2] But though a girl was not free
to choose her mate, she had the right of refusing the suitor
selected by her parents, nor could she be compelled to marry at
all, if she were disinclined to do so.

In arranging a daughter's marriage, parents were apt to be
unduly influenced by worldly considerations. They were distracted by fears lest a poor man should beguile their girl, or a
rich man flout her, or a man of good family despise her.[3] Often,
for the sake of a distinguished alliance, they would settle a
considerable part of their property on their daughter, and not
infrequently they suffered grievously at the hands of a greedy
son-in-law.[4] In Ambrose's opinion those marriages turn out best
where the fortune and social position of the two parties are
approximately equal.[5]

Two impediments to marriage are insisted on by Ambrose.
The first is that of consanguinity. One of his letters is addressed
to a certain Paternus—perhaps Aemilius Florus Paternus, Pro-

[1] For these details, see Hieron. *Epp.* 107 and 128. Compare the strictness with
which Monnica was brought up by her old nurse (Augustin. *Confess.* ix. 8).
[2] Ambros. *De Abraham*, i. 91. Even a man was not supposed to marry without
the consent of his parents. In *Ep.* 83 Ambrose commends a certain Sisinnius for
having forgiven his son who had dared to marry without his permission. He admits
that Sisinnius had reason for anger, since a father has a right to exercise his judgement concerning the girl who is to become his daughter.
[3] Ambros. *De Virginibus*, i. 56.
[4] Ibid. i. 33.
[5] Id. *De Abraham*, i. 6. In a wife the thing most to be desired is worth of character,
*De Abraham*, i. 85; *Expos. ev. Luc.* viii. 70; *De Instit. Virginis* 30; *In ps. 37 enarr.* 27.

consul of Africa in A.D. 393, and Chancellor of the Exchequer in A.D. 396—who was set on promoting a marriage between his son and his daughter's daughter. Ambrose denounced the proposed union as contrary to Divine and human law, and also as calculated to limit the extension of Paternus' family.[1] In the same letter he referred to a law of Theodosius, whereby marriages of first cousins were forbidden under stringent penalties.[2] The second impediment on which Ambrose, as a Christian bishop, naturally laid stress, is difference of religious faith. The law of the Empire disallowed marriages of Christians with Jews; the Catholic Church further disallowed marriages with pagans or heretics. The latter prohibition, however, appears to have been widely ignored[3]—often with very unhappy consequences.[4] Hence Ambrose found it necessary to warn his people against such unions. 'How can two be united in love, if they be divided in faith? Beware, Christian, of giving your daughter to a pagan or a Jew. Beware of taking to yourself as wife a pagan woman, or a Jewess, or a heretic, or any one at all who is not of your own faith.'[5] The only unions blessed by God are those between men and women who have received Christian baptism, who hold the same religious beliefs, and who can join together in prayer to the Author of their wedded happiness.[6] Ambrose conceded, indeed, that a Christian might contract a marriage with a pagan, provided that the latter was prepared to adopt the Christian faith;[7] but he cautioned Christian parents against the deceitfulness of pagan suitors, who often made a

[1] Ambros. *Ep.* 60, written either in A.D. 393 (J.-R. Palanque, op. cit., p. 546) or in 396 (G. Rauschen, op. cit., pp. 401, 402); cf. *Ep.* 84. Marriage with a niece was forbidden by a law of Constantius, A.D. 339 (Cod. Theod. iii. 12. 1).

[2] Ambros. *Ep.* 60, 8; cf. Augustin. *De Civitate Dei*, xv. 16. The law of Theodosius is not extant. It is referred to, however, by Honorius and Arcadius, who at first confirmed the prohibition of the marriage of first cousins, though with mitigation of the penalties originally imposed (Cod. Theod. iii. 10. 1; iii. 12. 3), but afterwards allowed such marriages to take place—by imperial dispensation in the Western Empire, and without any restriction in the Eastern.

[3] Both Cyprian (*De Laps.* 6) and Jerome (*Adv. Jovin.* i. 10) speak of frequent marriages between Christians and pagans. Augustine, himself the offspring of a Christian mother and a pagan father, says that in his time union with an unbeliever had ceased to be regarded as a sin (*De Fide et Operibus*, 35).

[4] See Tertullian's famous description of the trials of a Christian woman married to a pagan husband, *Ad Uxor.* ii. 4–6.

[5] Ambros. *De Abraham*, i. 84; cf. *Expos. ev. Luc.* viii. 3.

[6] Id. *De Abraham*, i. 84; *Ep.* 19. 7.

[7] Id. *De Abraham*, i. 86.

pretence of conversion in order to obtain Christian girls who would otherwise have been withheld from them.[1]

When a husband had been chosen, the formal betrothal took place at the house of the girl's father, in the presence of friends of both parties. The suitor presented the customary presents called *arrhae*—consisting of jewels, rich dresses, and an espousal ring, 'the sign of sincere fidelity and the expression of good faith'.[2] The instrument of marriage-settlement was read, and attested by ten witnesses.[3] The hands of the couple were then joined and a kiss of betrothal was exchanged.[4] The contract thus made could not be broken by either party without discredit.[5] But the betrothal, unlike the modern 'engagement', did not initiate free communication between the pair. Until they were actually married, they were kept rigorously apart and had practically no opportunities of getting to know each other.[6]

Next the wedding-day arrived. The houses of both bride and bridegroom were perfumed with incense and decorated with myrtle-branches and carpets.[7] The bride was attired for the marriage ceremony by her mother.[8] She was dressed in the *stola*, the Roman married woman's robe, which though no longer fashionable for ordinary wear was still used as 'the nuptial garment' and recognized as the 'badge of marriage';[9] her hair was braided, sprinkled with gold-dust,[10] and crowned with flowers.[11] The wedding ceremony was performed in the church, and comprehended the following elements: (*a*) the public declaration, in the presence of witnesses, of the consent of each party, which declaration was regarded as the essence of the marriage;[12] (*b*) the celebration of the Eucharist, whereat

---

[1] Ambros. *Expos. ps. cxviii*, 20, 48.
[2] Id. *Expos. ev. Luc.* vii. 231. For an allusion to the ring, jewels, and garments presented at betrothals, see the speech of St. Agnes to the son of the Roman praefect in the Acts of St. Agnes, erroneously ascribed to Ambrose (Migne, Ambrosii Opp. iv, p. 736).
[3] [Niceta Remes.] *De Lapsu Virginis*, 20.
[4] Ambros. *Expos. ps. cxviii*, 1. 16; cf. Tertullian, *De Virgin. Veland.* 11.
[5] Siricius, *Ep.* 1. 4.
[6] See the passage of Seneca quoted by Jerome, *Adv. Jovin.* i. 47: 'Horses, cattle, slaves, even pots and pans, are examined and tested before purchase; only a wife is never shown, for fear that she may fail to give satisfaction before she is married.'
[7] Claudian. *De Nupt. Honor. et Mariae*, 208–12.    [8] Id. *De VI Cons. Honor.* 523–8.
[9] Ambros. *Expos. ev. Luc.* vii. 231; ix. 39; cf. *De Virginibus*, iii. 34.
[10] Id. *De Instit. Virginis*, 108.    [11] Id. *De Virginibus*, i. 8.
[12] Id. *De Instit. Virginis*, 41; *Expos. ev. Luc.* ii. 5.

the bride and bridegroom made their offering and communicated;[1] (c) the veiling of the bride and the solemn benediction.[2]
After the service the bride returned to her father's house,
whence, as evening drew on, she was conducted in gay procession, with flaring torches,[3] to her future home. Here the keys
were formally delivered to her.[4] Then followed a banquet,
accompanied by music, dancing,[5] and sallies of wit,[6] often of
highly questionable propriety. The proceedings ended with a
distribution of presents to the guests.[7]

If we were to accept literally the statements of ascetic Christian writers, we should be forced to conclude that the young
wife's lot was far from happy. Ambrose, for instance, draws
an extremely sombre picture of the disadvantages of matrimony.
He represents marriage as a bondage, an indignity, a burden,
a perpetually galling yoke;[8] his favourite word for it is 'slavery'.[9]
'Even a good marriage', he says, 'is slavery; what, then, must
a bad one be?'[10] He is eloquent on the inconveniences which a
wife has to put up with. To make herself attractive to her
husband she must take no end of trouble—making up her face,
drenching her body in perfumes, and squandering money on
jewels and smart clothes.[11] Then the husband, of whom before
marriage she knew practically nothing, may turn out very undesirable—'rough, or treacherous, or boorish, or unsteady, or a
tippler'.[12] Many husbands treated their wives with harshness

---

[1] Tertullian, *Ad Uxor.* ii. 8 'confirmat oblatio'.

[2] Ambros. *Ep.* 19. 7. Ambrose derives the word 'nuptials' from *obnubere* (*De Abraham*, i. 93). The veil was used at marriages by both pagans and Christians. But (a) the pagan nuptial veil or *flammeum* was yellow or flame-coloured, while the Christian veil, though still called *flammeum* (*De Virginibus*, i. 65; *De Instit. Virginis*, 108) was purple and white (*De Instit. Virginis*, 109 'purpureo Dominici cruoris redimita velamine'); (b) the pagan bride was brought to her husband already veiled, while the Christian bride was veiled by the priest in the course of the marriage service (*Ep.* 19. 7; cf. *Exhort. Virginitatis*, 34; Siricius, *Ep.* 7. 3: 'those marriages at which we assist with the veil'). After her marriage a woman was accustomed to wear her veil when she appeared in public (*De Poenit.* i. 69).

[3] Id. *De Viduis*, 87. The door-posts of the bridegroom's house were wreathed with garlands, and the nuptial chamber, containing the great bed resting on gilded supports, was filled with roses, *De Virginibus*, ii. 40, 41.

[4] Id. *Expos. ps. cxviii*, i. 16.

[5] Id. *Expos. ev. Luc.* vi. 9; *De Virginibus*, iii. 25.

[6] Id. *Ep.* 19. 15.

[7] Ammian. xiv. 6. 24.

[8] Ambros. *Exhort. Virginitatis*, 21, 24, 31, 34; *De Virginitate*, 31, 33; *De Viduis*, 81.

[9] Id. *Exhort. Virginitatis*, 19–24; *De Virginibus*, i. 27, 56.

[10] Id. *De Viduis*, 69.     [11] Id. *De Virginibus*, i. 28, 29.     [12] Id. *Hexaem.* v. 18.

and even brutality;[1] many insulted and pained them by openly keeping mistresses.[2] Besides all this there was the worry of bearing and bringing up children.[3] 'These troubles are real enough even when everything goes prosperously. Of adverse happenings I dare not speak, lest the hearts even of the holiest parents tremble.'[4]

But there is much exaggeration in such accounts. As a matter of fact the 'slavery' to which the young wife was subjected does not seem to have been very dreadful. She was certainly expected to obey her husband; but, in view of her youth and inexperience, this was not unreasonable. In general, a married girl, especially if she were wealthy, enjoyed a large measure of independence. In her home she could do pretty much as she liked. A host of eunuchs, footmen, and waiting-maids was at her beck and call; a steward looked after her jewels and favourite slaves; a pro-curator or business manager administered her estates under her direction. She was free to go abroad as she pleased—to pay visits, to witness spectacles, to attend dinner-parties. If her husband was sometimes unfaithful, she, on her side, did not hesi-tate to amuse herself with flirtations. Probably the husbands had quite as much to put up with from their wives, as the wives had from their husbands.[5]

The change which marriage effected in the life of an upper-class girl was startling. We may get some idea of it, if we imagine an innocent child taken straight from the school-room, and plunged without any preparation into the loosest and liveliest circles of modern fast society. Yet the temp-tations which would beset a twentieth-century girl thus cir-cumstanced are as nothing compared with those to which an attractive young wife in the fourth century was exposed. The whole social atmosphere was saturated with sensuality. Gallants pestered her with attentions. Eunuchs and maids, ex-perienced in amorous affairs, used every artifice to undermine

---

[1] Ambros. *Hexaem.* v. 19; *Expos. ev. Luc.* i. 44. Cf. Augustin. *Confess.* ix. 9; Hieron. *Ep.* 77. 3.

[2] Ambros. *De Abraham,* i. 26, 65; ii. 78. Cf. *Serm.* 52. 8 (Migne, Ambrosii Opp. iv, p. 711).

[3] Ambros. *De Virginitate,* 32.

[4] Id. *De Virginibus,* i. 26. Of the daily worries of a young married woman a lively description is given by Jerome, *Adv. Helvid.* 22.

[5] See the amusing passage on the sufferings of husbands quoted by Jerome, *Adv. Jovin.* i. 47.

her virtue. She could go nowhere without finding something to violate her natural feelings of modesty. At the theatre she witnessed realistic representations of indescribable abominations. At private dinner-parties the very plate on the table was engraved with shocking incidents of classical mythology.[1] In the Circus, where men and women sat together, she was frequently the subject of undesirable addresses.[2] Not even in the churches was she safe. The all-night vigils occasioned many scandals, and Jerome goes so far as to say that for a young woman it was almost more perilous to show herself in a place of worship than to walk abroad.[3] It is not surprising that in such surroundings women often lost their balance. Many permitted themselves indiscretions. There seems also to have been much laxity in the matter of divorce. Tertullian had formerly complained that the ladies married only in order to get divorces;[4] and Ambrose hints that in his day they were hardly less addicted to matrimonial experiments.[5]

It may be observed that Roman law was much more severe on unchastity in a wife than on unchastity in a husband. The wife who took a lover (whether married or unmarried) was stigmatized as an adulteress. But a husband might err with any number of unmarried females without being liable to the charge of adultery. In the eyes of the law he was an adulterer only if he had relations with a married woman not his wife.[6] The unfairness of the legal view is obvious, and many Christian teachers urged that the same standard ought to be applied without discrimination to both men and women.[7] 'Let no one plume himself on human laws', wrote Ambrose. 'Every act of debauchery is adultery, nor is that permitted to a man which is not permitted to a woman. The same chastity which is required of a wife is required also of a husband.'[8] Ambrose held, indeed, that adultery in the limited legal sense was a more heinous offence,[9] as being contrary not only to the Divine law but also to the

---

[1] Hieron. *Ep.* 27. 2.      [2] Tertullian, *De Spect.* 25.
[3] Hieron. *Ep.* 130. 19.      [4] Tertullian, *Apol.* 6.
[5] Ambros. *Hexaem.* v. 18.
[6] Papinian's definition is 'Adulterium in nuptam committitur, stuprum vero in virginem viduamve' (Dig. 48. 5. 6. 1). Ambrose uses the term in the strict legal sense, *Hexaem.* v. 19; *De Abraham*, i. 8; ii. 78.
[7] See, e.g., Lactantius, *Inst. Div.* vi. 23; Hieron. *Ep.* 77. 3.
[8] Ambros. *De Abraham*, i. 25.      [9] Ibid. i. 59.

law of nature;[1] nevertheless he insisted that for a Christian husband every species of incontinence is inexcusable.[2] 'Men believe
that it is allowable to stray, if only they abstain from technical
adultery; they think mere fornication agreeable to the law of
nature. Yet, outside of marriage, it is not lawful either for a
man or for a woman to take a companion.'[3]

In respect of remarriage after divorce, the accepted Christian
view was that a woman who divorced her husband was not free,
while he lived, to marry again.[4] In some quarters, however, it was
held that a husband who had divorced an adulterous wife might
contract a new marriage during her lifetime.[5] Even Augustine,
though disapproving of such remarriage on the part of the husband, concedes that it is only a venial error, since the teaching
of Holy Scripture on the subject is not clear.[6] Nevertheless the
general sense of the Church was against remarriage whether of
a husband or of a wife, so long as the other party was living.

Of the occupations of women during this period something
has already been said. The average woman, no doubt, was
mainly taken up with her husband, her children, her house, her
toilet, and her amusements. There were many, however, who,
not content with the common round of social and domestic
duties, sought an outlet for their energies in pursuits which until
recently had been regarded as inappropriate for females. Some
of these ladies were mere eccentrics, who delighted in scanda-
lizing old-fashioned people by shingling their hair, dressing
like men, and defying the conventions.[7] These, however, must
not be confounded with the intelligent and 'advanced' women,
who actively interested themselves in literature and science, in
philanthropy and religious work.

Of those who distinguished themselves in intellectual pursuits a few instances may be mentioned. Serena, the wife of
Stilicho, was an enthusiastic student of Greek and Latin literature.[8] Paula, Jerome's friend, was a fine Greek scholar, and

[1] Ambros. *Hexaem.* v. 19; *De Abraham*, i. 8.
[2] Id. *De Abraham*, i. 23.                                    [3] Ibid. ii. 78.
[4] See, e.g., Hieron. *Epp.* 55. 3; 77. 3.
[5] Lactantius, *Inst. Div.* vi. 23; Epiphanius, *Haer.* 59. 4; Ambrosiaster, *Comm. on
1 Cor.* vii. 10, 11.
[6] Augustin. *De Fide et Oper.* 19.
[7] Conc. Gangr. cc. 13, 17; Hieron. *Ep.* 22. 27. Ambrose wrote a letter (*Ep.* 69)
concerning those who wore the dress of the opposite sex.
[8] Claudian, *Laus Serenae*, 146–58.

learnt Hebrew in order that she might be able to sing the Psalms in that tongue.[1] Blaesilla, Paula's daughter, was even more accomplished than her mother; Jerome says that she rivalled Origen himself in her knowledge of languages.[2] Monnica, mother of Augustine, was profoundly versed in the Sacred Scriptures.[3] Two erudite ladies of Gaul named Hedibia and Algasia applied to Jerome for a solution of various difficulties which they had encountered in their Scriptural studies.[4] Proba, the wife of a Praefect of Rome, constructed a Christian poem out of lines taken entirely or in part from Virgil.[5] Towards the end of the third century Porphyry married a widow named Marcella, who attracted him by her remarkable talent for philosophy;[6] at the beginning of the fifth century Hypatia was lecturing on Platonism at Alexandria.[7] An aunt of the poet Ausonius, despising the ordinary activities of women, devoted herself to the study of medicine.[8] Similarly Nicarete of Constantinople, one of the ladies of Chrysostom's circle, enjoyed a high reputation for skill in the physician's art. With her own hands she used to compound the drugs which she dispensed gratis to the poor, and her admirers claimed that she succeeded in curing many patients who had been abandoned as hopeless by the medical faculty.[9]

It was religion, however, that made the strongest appeal to the women of the fourth century. Those who were pagans were peculiarly attracted by the exotic Oriental cults—especially by those of Syria and Egypt. There were doubtless many devotees of the type of Fabia Aconia Paulina, the pious wife of Praetextatus, who emulated her husband's enthusiasm for all the varieties of multiform paganism, and travelled far and wide, with indefagitable zeal, to be initiated into new mysteries. On the whole, however, the women of this period appear to have been more deeply influenced by Christianity than by paganism; and certainly in the Church they found abundant scope for their activities. Some of them—e.g. Melania, Paula, Silvia of Aquitaine—became pilgrims and travellers, seeking new life in

---

[1] Hieron. *Ep.* 108. 27.   [2] Id. *Ep.* 39. 1.
[3] Augustin. *De Ordine*, i. 32.   [4] Hieron. *Epp.* 120, 121.
[5] Proba, *Cento*, ed. K. Schenkl, Poetae Christiani minores, part i, *C.S.E.L.* xvi.
[6] Porphyr. *Ad Marcell.* 1–3.
[7] Socrates, *H.E.* vii. 15.
[8] Ausonius, *Parent.* vi.   [9] Sozomen. *H.E.* viii. 23.

daring adventure amid new scenes and new societies.[1]  Others as deaconesses undertook ministerial duties—especially that of assisting at the baptism of female catechumens.[2]  Others (who were not less than sixty years of age,[3] who had been once married, and who had no children or grandchildren capable of supporting them[4]) were enrolled in the order of 'widows' and maintained by the Church.[5]  They devoted themselves to prayer and fasting, and to various kinds of charitable work among indigent, sick, distressed, and tempted women.  Finally there were many who adopted a life of religious celibacy and austerity as consecrated virgins.

## 2. Ambrose and the Profession of Virginity

The fourth century was pre-eminently the age of Christian asceticism.[6]  In the life of seclusion and self-discipline vast multitudes were finding a refuge from the horrible corruption of contemporary society, an opportunity for the undistracted cultivation of the inner life, and an outlet for that spiritual passion which could not be content with anything short of the fulfilment of the so-called 'counsels of perfection'.  Of asceticism the characteristic expression was monachism.  This originated in Egypt, where it developed into two main types —Antonian monachism (eremitical or semi-eremitical) and Pachomian monachism (cenobitical, though not so fully cenobitical as the form afterwards instituted by Basil).  By the close of the century the monks in Egypt numbered many thousands. Meanwhile the movement had spread to Palestine, Asia Minor

---

[1] T. R. Glover, *Life and Letters in the Fourth Century*, pp. 125–47.

[2] Epiphan. *Haer.* 79. 3.

[3] This apostolic rule with regard to age seems to have been generally observed in Ambrose's time, *Exhort. Virginitatis*, 25 'adhuc immaturam viduitatis stipendiis'; cf. *De Viduis*, 9.

[4] Ambrosiaster, *Comm. in 1 Tim.* v. 3, 5.

[5] Ibid. v. 5, 9; Hieron. *Ep.* 123. 6.

[6] Enthusiasm for the ascetic life was not, however, by any means universal. At the funeral of Blaesilla in Rome there was a popular demonstration against the monks (Hieron. *Ep.* 39. 5).  The ladies and clergy of the city were constantly carping at them (ibid. 54. 5) and the rabble called them insulting names (ibid. 38. 5; 54. 5).  The word 'monk' was for long a term of reproach among the Romans (ibid. 127. 8).  In Gaul, Martin of Tours, by reason of his ascetic ways, incurred the dislike of many of the bishops (Sulpicius, *Vita S. Martini*, 27). In Spain, also, the ecclesiastical authorities were generally unfriendly to asceticism (see below, chapter ix).  In Africa the pale faces and sombre garb of the monks were jeered at in the streets (Salvian, *De Gubern. Dei*, viii. 21, 22).

(under the influence of Basil, 'the real father of Greek monachism'), and other parts of the East. Jerome asserts, though doubtless with exaggeration, that 'from India, from Persia, from Ethiopia, we daily welcome monks in crowds'.[1] In the early part of the century—perhaps even before the visit to Rome of Athanasius and his Egyptian monks—monachism appeared in the West, and there also became widely propagated. In Gaul it was warmly encouraged by Martin of Tours, who, before he became bishop, established the monastery of Ligugé near Poitiers, and after his consecration planted a colony of eighty monks just outside his episcopal city, at Marmoutier. Other monasteries sprang up in the vicinity of Tours and Rouen and in the north-western parts of Gaul, and when Martin died he was escorted to his grave by two thousand monks. In Spain the beginnings of monasticism are obscure; but the sixth canon of the Council of Zaragossa (A.D. 380), forbidding clerics to become monks, indicates that the movement had already made some progress on Spanish territory at that date. In northern Italy monachism took early root. At Vercelli Bishop Eusebius (d. A.D. 371) introduced an innovation when he caused his clergy to live together in community according to monastic rule;[2] at Milan, outside the walls, Ambrose founded a large monastery 'full of good brothers';[3] at Aquileia there was a monastery of which Rufinus and Jerome were at one time inmates;[4] and similar institutions appear to have existed in Ravenna, Pavia, and other North Italian cities. In Rome, before the century ended, many monastic communities had been established.[5] Augustine visited several of these 'homes of saints, where in the midst of brethren who live together in Christian charity, piety, and freedom there presides one distinguished for gravity, prudence, and ecclesiastical learning'.[6] The little islands off the coast literally swarmed with monks and hermits, whose psalm-singing, Ambrose tells us, blended harmoniously with the gentle plash of the surrounding waters.[7]

---

[1] Hieron. *Ep.* 107. 2.      [2] Ambros. *Ep.* 63. 66, 71, 82.
[3] Augustin. *Confess.* viii. 6; cf. *De Mor. Eccl.* i. 70; Paulinus, *Vita Ambros.* 49.
[4] Rufin. *Apol.* i. 4.
[5] Hieron. *Ep.* 127. 8; cf. ibid. 77. 6.
[6] Augustin. *De Mor. Eccl.* i. 70.
[7] Ambros. *Hexaem.* iii. 23. Jerome (*Ep.* 3. 4) describes the life of his friend Bonosus who was living as a hermit on a barren island in the Adriatic. The pagan

Lastly, in Africa, during the episcopate of Augustine and under his influence, both monastic communities of clerics (similar to that instituted at Vercelli by Eusebius) and also monasteries of the normal type became widely prevalent.

In this great movement women shared. In the middle of the third century, before any monasteries for men had been founded, congregations of women appear already to have existed; for, when Antony withdrew from the world, he placed his sister in a 'house of virgins', of which she afterwards became the superior. In the course of the fourth century convents of women rapidly multiplied. Pachomius founded two—one, under his sister, at Tabennisi, the other near Panopolis (Akhmīn)—and after his death many others arose in all parts of monastic Egypt. In Palestine, again, there were numerous nunneries; specially famous were those organized by the Roman ladies Paula, Eustochium, and the Melanias. In Pontus, Emmelia and Macrina, the mother and the sister of Basil, resided in a community of holy women at Annesi on the bank of the Iris; and in Constantinople and the larger Eastern cities similar establishments existed. Ambrose, indeed, states that at Alexandria and throughout the whole of the East, as well as in Africa, great numbers of virgins were annually consecrated.[1] (Not all such virgins, however, lived in organized communities; in Africa, at any rate, it is doubtful whether regular nunneries existed before Augustine's time, though several sprang up under his patronage.[2]) In Rome, towards the close of the century, many convents of nuns were prosperously settled;[3] and we have record of others in other Italian cities. At Bologna, for instance, where the bishop, Eusebius, was an enthusiastic advocate of virginity, there was a sisterhood of twenty virgins, living together under rule and supporting themselves by their own labour.[4] A similar community was established at Verona.[5]

As has been pointed out, not all consecrated virgins were

poet Rutilius makes a bitter attack on the monks who had settled on the islands of Capraria and Gorgona (De Reditu Suo, i. 439 ff., 515 ff.).

[1] Ambros. De Virginitate, 36.
[2] Augustine's famous Letter 211 was written for the guidance of a nunnery.
[3] Hieron. Ep. 127. 8.
[4] Ambros. De Virginibus, i. 60. On Eusebius see De Virginitate, 129 'piscator ecclesiae Bononiensis aptus ad hoc piscandi genus'.
[5] Id. Ep. 5. 19.

segregated in nunneries. There were many who, though dedicated to virginity, resided with their parents, or in houses of
their own, or even—though this was condemned as an abuse
—in the lodgings of the clergy.[1] At Milan, in Ambrose's time,
no convent of women appears to have existed, and Milanese
girls who took the vow of virginity usually continued to live
with their parents.[2]

At this period religious celibacy was extravagantly admired.[3]
It was regarded as 'the chief asceticism', the supreme and consummate achievement of the Christ-imitating life. Of this view
Ambrose was an enthusiastic exponent. To him virginity was
a 'principal virtue'—a virtue not merely in accordance with
natural law, but 'transcending the course of nature'.[4] It was
also peculiarly a Christian virtue, being seldom met with among
the Old Testament saints,[5] and not in a true sense found
at all among the heathen, since even the Vestals, though constrained to live in celibacy for a limited period, could not be
reckoned as true virgins.[6] Its Author was the Immaculate Son
of God, who, virgin Himself, was born on earth of a virgin and
took the virgin Church as His bride;[7] its most illustrious human
example was the Virgin Mary.[8] Ambrose ecstatically describes

---

[1] Hieron. *Ep.* 22. 14; cf. Cyprian, *Ep.* 4.

[2] Ambros. *De Virginibus*, i. 32 'non emigratione destituat'; *De Instit. Virginis*, 1
'istam semper tecum habebis'. Ambrose's sister Marcellina, after taking the veil,
lived at Rome with her mother and a female companion. The virgin daughters
of Juliana of Florence seem likewise to have lived with their mother (*Exhort. Virginitatis*, 54, 55). Indicia of Verona lived in a private house, though there was a
nunnery in the city (*Ep.* 5).

[3] This admiration of virginity is illustrated by the curious composition of the
Lycian bishop Methodius (died *c.* A.D. 311) entitled *The Banquet* or *On Virginity*. The
work is modelled on Plato's *Symposium*, and as there the praises of love are celebrated, so here the praises of virginity are proclaimed. The scene is laid in the
gardens of Arete, where ten virgin guests are entertained at a banquet. Each in
turn pronounces a panegyric on virginity, and at the end a hymn is intoned to the
Bridegroom Christ. The conclusion arrived at is that virginity is incomparably
the highest state—indeed, the perfect Christian life itself.

[4] Ambros. *De Virginibus*, i. 10, 11.

[5] Ibid. i. 12.

[6] Id. *De Virginitate*, 13; *De Virginibus*, i. 15; *Ep.* 18. 11 and 12.

[7] Id. *De Virginibus*, i. 21, 22; *Ep.* 63. 33 and 36.

[8] Id. *De Virginibus*, ii. 6, 15; *De Instit. Virginis*, 35, 44, 45. Other eminent examples
of virginity cited by Ambrose are Thecla (*De Virginibus*, ii. 19, 20; *De Virginitate*,
40; *Ep.* 63. 34), Agnes (*De Virginibus*, i. 5–9), an unnamed virgin 'of Antioch' who
was consigned to outrage and delivered by a soldier (ibid. ii. 22–33), Pelagia of
Antioch (ibid. iii. 33–6), and Soteris (*De Virginibus*, iii. 38; *Exhort. Virginitatis*, 82).

it as the present practice of the innocent life of Adam and Eve in Paradise,[1] of the glorious life of the saints after the resurrection,[2] of the life of heaven,[3] of the life of the angels,[4] since it is chastity that has made even the angels what they are.[5] So meritorious is virginity, that it is even capable of atoning for the sins of others. 'The virgin is an offering for her mother, and by her daily sacrifice the Divine Power is appeased.'[6] 'Let one virgin redeem her parents, another her brothers.'[7]

Holding such views, Ambrose naturally considered it the duty of a bishop 'to sow the seeds of chastity and stir up zeal for virginity'.[8] He accordingly addressed himself with ardour to the congenial work of persuading young women to adopt the celibate life. His impassioned preaching on the subject caused a widespread sensation. Pious females flocked to Milan, not only from Piacenza, Bologna, and other cities of Italy, but even from the distant parts of Mauretania, to receive the veil from his hand.[9] In his own episcopal city, however, his exhortations had little effect. 'I am daily singing the praises of virginity', he complained, 'but I have no success. It is very strange. I preach here, and persuade those who are elsewhere. Under the circumstances I think that I had better preach elsewhere that I may persuade you.'[10] This comparative failure was due less to disinclination for celibacy on the part of the girls than to the opposition of their parents. These certainly did all they could to frustrate Ambrose's efforts. Mothers used to lock up their young daughters within doors, that they might not fall under the spell of the bishop's eloquence in the cathedral.[11] Fathers threatened to disinherit their girls, if they insisted on taking the veil in contravention of their wishes. Ambrose thought that such

---

[1] Ambros. *Exhort. Virginitatis*, 36; *De Instit. Virginis*, 104.
[2] Id. *De Virginibus*, i. 52; *De Virginitate*, 27.
[3] Id. *De Virginibus*, i. 11, 13, 20.
[4] Id. *De Virginitate*, 27; *De Instit. Virginis*, 104; *Exhort. Virginitatis*, 19; *Expos. ps. cxviii*, 4. 8; *Ep.* 6. 19.
[5] Id. *De Virginibus*, i. 52.
[6] Ibid. i. 32.
[7] Ibid. ii. 16; cf. *Exhort. Virginitatis*, 26 'vestra integritas meos solvat errores': [Niceta Remes.] *De Lapsu Virginis*, 16 'hostiam vivam Domino, propitiatricem videlicet delictorum'.
[8] Ambros. *De Virginitate*, 26.
[9] Id. *De Virginibus*, i. 57, 59.
[10] Ibid. i. 57; cf. his confession of failure *De Virginitate*, 25.
[11] Id. *De Virginibus*, i. 58.

threats were not seriously meant;[1] but in some cases, at any rate, they seem to have been actually carried out.[2]

When parents were quite intractable, Ambrose did not scruple to declare that they should be disobeyed. He held that 'religion is to be preferred above the duties of affection'.[3] 'Great are the obligations of affection, but those of religion are greater still.'[4] 'Religion is to be preferred above friendship, piety above kinship.'[5] 'Conquer your affection first, my daughter. If you conquer your home, you conquer the world.'[6] Such teaching was inflammatory to excitable young women, and many were emboldened to defy their relatives and friends. One girl of good family, being pressed to marry, fled for refuge to the altar of the church. Seizing the bishop's hand, she placed it on her head, and implored him to recite the prayer that was customary at consecrations. When he hesitated, she impulsively placed her head beneath the altar, crying, 'What better veil can cover me than the altar which hallows the veils themselves? There can be no more fitting veil than that on which Christ is daily consecrated.' One of her relations, who had followed her to the church, remonstrated with her roughly. 'If your father were alive', he said, 'would he allow you to remain unmarried?' 'Perhaps for this very reason he died', she answered, 'that no one might be able to hinder my purpose.' Shortly afterwards this kinsman met with a sudden death; and the other members of the family were so scared by the event that they encouraged the girl to take the veil, and even permitted her to retain her full share of her father's property.[7]

Owing to his vehement advocacy of virginity Ambrose was exposed to some bitter attacks.[8] An outcry was raised that the welfare of the world was jeopardized by this teaching, that young people were hindered from marrying, that the birth-rate was declining. But he was unmoved by the clamour. History proved (he replied) that the world had suffered more ills from

---

[1] Ambros. *De Virginibus*, i. 62, 63.      [2] Hieron. *Ep.* 130. 6.

[3] Ambros. *Expos. ev. Luc.* vii. 146. This doctrine was common among the ascetic teachers of this period; see, e.g., Jerome's praise of Melania's heartless conduct towards her children, *Ep.* 39. 4, and Paulinus of Nola, *Ep.* 25. 7 'volo, inquit, vos sine sollicitudine esse, hoc est, ut nihil praeter Deum et salutem nostram cogitemus. Nam uxor et filii, quanquam et ipsa divinitus nobis pignora data sint, tamen gravissima curarum onera sunt.'

[4] Id. *De Viduis*, 6.                                 [5] Id. *Ep.* 66. 7.

[6] Id. *De Virginibus*, i. 63.     [7] Ibid. i. 65, 66.     [8] Id. *De Virginitate*, 11, 24.

marriage than from virginity; eligible young men were not in such straits that they could find none except consecrated virgins to be their brides; the fall in the birth-rate had no connexion with the spread of religious celibacy, as was demonstrated by the fact that in Africa and the East, where the greatest number of virgins was annually consecrated, the population had actually increased.[1]

The writings of Ambrose furnish us with some interesting particulars concerning the practice of religious celibacy in the latter part of the fourth century.

It was not uncommon for pious parents to dedicate their children to a life of virginity from their birth.[2] When the children so dedicated reached the age of puberty, they were expected —though not compelled[3]—to fulfil the vows which had been made on their behalf. As yet, however, there was no general prescription as to the age at which virgins might be formally veiled. Ambrose was censured because he was accustomed to consecrate them very young. But he replied to his critics, 'I do not deny that a bishop should be careful not to veil a young girl rashly. Certainly he ought to take maturity into account; but let it be the maturity of faith and modesty. Every age is meet for God. The Holy Innocents were not too young to die for Christ, and even young girls are not too young to embrace a life of continence for His sake. Children followed Christ in the desert, and may not girls of age to marry follow Him into the Kingdom?'[4] The phrase 'of age to marry' suggests that Ambrose took the view that a girl might properly receive the veil on the completion of her twelfth year.

Since the virgin was regarded as 'the bride of Christ',[5] it was not unnatural that the ceremonies connected with the solemn profession of virginity should present analogies with those of marriage. Just as the bride wore the *stola* as emblem of the

---

[1] Id. *De Virginitate*, 35–8.

[2] A wealthy Florentine lady named Juliana vowed her three daughters to virginity, and also her son, whom (as she believed) she had conceived with the help of St. Lawrence (Ambros. *Exhort. Virginitatis*, 51, 52; cf. ibid. 15). Paula, the daughter of Toxotius and Laeta, was 'dedicated to Christ before her birth and vowed to His service before her conception' (Hieron. *Epp.* 107. 3; 108. 26). Asella was similarly dedicated before her birth and consecrated a virgin when she was little more than ten years old (id. *Ep.* 24. 2). Cf. Hieron. *Ep.* 128. 2.

[3] Ambros. *Exhort. Virginitatis*, 17.

[4] Id. *De Virginitate*, 39, 40.          [5] Id. *De Virginibus*, i. 36, 37.

wedded state, so the virgin assumed a dark-coloured dress as an outward token of her vocation;[1] just as the bride received from the priest the bridal veil, so the virgin received from the bishop the *flammeum Christi*,[2] which henceforth she always wore when she appeared in public;[3] and just as the marriage was witnessed by friends of the contracting parties, so the consecration was witnessed by the congregation of the faithful, which, by its shouted 'Amen', gave endorsement, as it were, to the spiritual marriage-settlement.[4]

The consecration, at which the bishop himself was the officiating minister, was solemnized with much pomp on one of the great festivals—in the case of Marcellina on the Feast of the Epiphany;[5] more usually, however, at Easter,[6] when it was attended by the newly baptized wearing their white robes and carrying lighted tapers.[7] The bishop delivered an address to the virgin,[8] and offered a solemn prayer.[9] The girl then publicly pledged herself to a life of chastity.[10] Next the bishop took the veil, which had been lying on the altar,[11] and placed it over her head, with the words, 'I wish to present you as a chaste virgin to Christ.'[12] A benediction was then recited,[13] to which the congregation responded 'Amen'.[14] At some point in the service Psalm xlv was chanted,[15] and possibly some hymns in praise of virginity were sung.[16]

After their consecration, virgins were under the special care of the bishop, who visited them at intervals, explained the Scriptures to them, and instructed them concerning their duties.[17] In the church they occupied a place of honour, shut off from that assigned to the women of the congregation by a screen inscribed with appropriate texts.[18] Devout matrons, before

---

[1] Ambros. *De Virginibus*, iii. 1; cf. Hieron. *Epp.* 24. 3; 128. 2.
[2] Hieron. *Ep.* 147. 6.       [3] Ambros. *De Abraham*, i. 93.
[4] [Niceta Remes.] *De Lapsu Virginis*, 20.
[5] Ambros. *De Virginibus*, iii. 1.       [6] Id. *Exhort. Virginitatis*, 42.
[7] [Niceta Remes.] *De Lapsu Virginis*, 19.
[8] For two examples of such addresses, see Ambros. *De Virginibus*, iii. 1–14; *De Instit. Virginis*, 16–103.
[9] See, for example, Ambros. *De Instit. Virginis*, 104–14.
[10] [Niceta Remes.] *De Lapsu Virginis*, 19.
[11] Ambros. *De Virginibus*, i. 65.
[12] Hieron. *Ep.* 130. 2.       [13] Ambros. *Ep.* 5. 1.
[14] [Niceta Remes.] *De Lapsu Virginis*, 20.       [15] Ibid. 19.
[16] Ibid. 20 'multis super castitatem praeconiis'.
[17] Ibid. 28, 29.       [18] Ibid. 24.

leaving the church, were accustomed to approach this enclosure and request from the sacred virgins the favour of the kiss of peace.[1]

For the direction of the life of virgins Ambrose issued detailed precepts. Starting from the principle that virginity is a question less of physical chastity than of purity of mind[2]—'it is preferable, if one is forced to choose, to have a virgin mind than a virgin body'[3]—he framed his rules with the primary object of safeguarding the mind from contaminating influences. The regulations may be summarized briefly as follows:—

(a) *Seclusion*. A virgin must live in the strictest privacy.[4] She ought not to show herself in the forum or the streets;[5] neither ought she to be in and out of other people's houses,[6] since in ladies' drawing-rooms there is too much idle tittle-tattle, in which it is unseemly for her to join.[7] Society visits, dinner-parties, and all lighter festivities should be avoided.[8] A young virgin had better not go too often even to church.[9] In her own home she ought to spend much of her time alone, content with the companionship of good books and good thoughts.[10] It is specially her duty to cultivate the art of holding her tongue becomingly.[11] Not only must she refrain from oaths, abuse, excuses, arguments about religion, babble about the Mysteries;[12] she ought not to talk at all, beyond what is absolutely necessary. 'Even to speak what is good is generally a fault in a virgin.'[13] Above all, silence must be kept in church, where only too frequently the lessons were drowned, and the very Canon of the Mass was interrupted, by chatter, laughter, coughing, and other unseemly noises.[14] In Ambrose's opinion, unrestrained cheerfulness and immoderate laughter were indecorous in a virgin.[15]

---

[1] [Niceta Remes.] *De Lapsu Virginis*, 24.
[2] Ambros. *De Viduis*, 26; *De Virginitate*, 15; *Ep.* 5. 6.    [3] Id. *De Virginibus*, ii. 24.
[4] Id. *Ep.* 5. 16 'quid praestantius (praesertim in virgine, cuius praecipuum opus verecundia) quam secretum? quid tutius secreto, et ad omnes actus expeditius?'; *Exhort. Virginitatis*, 71 'gymnasium pudoris secretum est'; *De Viduis*, 57.
[5] *De Virginitate*, 83; cf. ibid. 46.                [6] Id. *Expos. ev. Luc.* ii. 21.
[7] Id. *Exhort. Virginitatis*, 72.            [8] Id. *De Virginibus*, iii. 8, 9, 25.
[9] Id. *Exhort. Virginitatis*, 71.            [10] Id. *De Virginibus*, ii. 10.
[11] Id. *De Virginibus*, iii. 9; *De Virginitate*, 80; *De Instit. Virginis*, 5.
[12] Id. *Exhort. Virginitatis*, 74, 85, 89; *De Virginitate*, 102; *De Instit. Virginis*, 4.
[13] Id. *Exhort. Virginitatis*, 86.
[14] Id. *De Virginibus*, iii. 11, 13; cf. *In ps. 1 enarr.* 9 'quantum laboratur in ecclesia ut fiat silentium, cum lectiones leguntur! Si unus loquatur, obstrepunt universi.'
[15] Id. *Exhort. Virginitatis*, 75, 76.

(b) *Attire.* The two external signs of the profession of virginity were the dark-coloured habit and the white linen veil. In this costume it was not altogether easy to look attractive. Yet some of the more flighty virgins, with the aid of their paint-and-powder boxes, used to display countenances more blooming and decorative than Ambrose considered suitable.[1] He told them that 'a virgin's adornment is absence of adornment'.[2] Hair crimped with curling-irons and artistically arranged was an offence;[3] it ought to be neatly bound up in a chignon.[4] The use of black powder, to darken the eyebrows and eyelashes, was forbidden, together with other like contrivances for the enhancement of feminine beauty.[5] Yet it may be noted as characteristic of Ambrose's moderation that, while he condemned vanity in virgins, he abstained from recommending that personal slovenliness and squalor which, as exhibited by some devoted ladies, evoked the enthusiastic admiration of Jerome.[6]

(c) *Devotions.* The virgin is ordered to occupy herself with regular devotional exercises; no explicit injunctions are given with regard to any kind of active work. In particular, she must be instant in prayer. Before praying, she should prepare herself, that she may not offend God in her petitions;[7] while praying, she should be careful to observe the correct order. First should come praise of God, then supplication for the overthrow of the devil and all his works, then petition for blessings needed, and lastly giving of thanks.[8] Offices, consisting mainly of psalms interspersed with frequent repetitions of the Lord's Prayer, were to be said seven times in the course of the twenty-four hours.[9] Every morning before daylight the virgin should recite the Creed, and during the day she should frequently reflect upon

---

[1] Ambros. *Exhort. Virginitatis,* 81.          [2] Id. *De Virginibus,* i. 54.
[3] Id. *De Virginitate,* 71; cf. *Exhort. Virginitatis,* 64.
[4] Id. *De Instit. Virginis,* 109. At this period, except in the convents of Egypt and Syria (Hieron. *Ep.* 147. 5)—where sanitary precautions were specially necessary—a virgin's hair was not usually cut. The Council of Gangra, c. 17, forbade women to cut their hair under pretext of religion; and Ambrose's allusions clearly indicate that ordinarily the hair was retained by virgins. Sometimes, however, the cutting of the hair was part of the punishment of those condemned to penance (Niceta Remes. *De Lapsu Virginis,* 35).
[5] Ambros. *De Virginitate,* 79.
[6] Hieron. *Epp.* 23. 2; 24. 5; 108. 15 and 19.
[7] Ambros. *Exhort. Virginitatis,* 70.
[8] Ambros. *De Instit. Virginis,* 8, 9: cf. *De Sacramentis,* vi. 22.
[9] Ambros. *De Virginibus,* iii. 18, 19.

it.[1] She ought further to employ herself in psalm-singing,[2] in the study of the Scriptures,[3] and in nightly meditation in her chamber.[4] 'Learn to be in the world, yet above the world; even if you carry about a body, let the bird within you soar.'[5]

(d) *Abstinence.* It was the duty of a virgin to practise abstinence, not merely in respect of meat and drink, but also in respect of all carnal luxury and worldly pomp, which is 'more intoxicating than wine itself'.[6] Heating foods should be taken very sparingly;[7] and wine, unless prescribed for health, had better be avoided.[8] Not even considerations of health excuse neglect of fasting.[9] Ambrose thought it sufficient, however, to fast for single days; continuous fasting for many days seemed to him (more particularly in the case of the older virgins) inexpedient.[10]

If a virgin's character were defamed, she could publicly in the church demand the punishment of her calumniators. Then the bishop, in co-operation with her relatives, took the matter up, and made every effort to track the slander to its source.[11] If there seemed reason for suspecting a virgin of immorality, the bishop investigated the charges, and could, if necessary, order the girl to be medically examined. The procedure is illustrated by a notorious case in Ambrose's time.[12] Indicia was a consecrated virgin of Verona, who did not, however, reside in the nunnery in that city, but occupied a private house. Some years after her consecration she was delated to Syagrius, Bishop of Verona, as having been engaged in a criminal intrigue. The real author of the charge—though he took care not to put himself forward—was her brother-in-law Maximus, who hated her on account of some litigation which had taken place between

[1] Ambros. *De Virginibus*, iii. 20.
[2] Id. *De Instit. Virginis*, 103; *De Virginitate*, 69.
[3] Id. *Exhort. Virginitatis*, 56.
[4] Id. *De Virginitate*, 68; *Exhort. Virginitatis*, 58.
[5] Id. *De Virginitate*, 108.
[6] Id. *De Virginibus*, i. 53; *Exhort. Virginitatis*, 81.
[7] Id. *De Virginibus*, iii. 8.    [8] Ibid. iii. 5; cf. *De Viduis*, 40.
[9] Id. *Exhort. Virginitatis*, 79.    [10] Id. *De Virginibus*, iii. 15–17.
[11] [Niceta Remes.] *De Lapsu Virginis*, 25.
[12] On the affair of Indicia, see Ambros. *Epp.* 5 and 6: F. Martroye, 'L'Affaire Indicia: une sentence de saint Ambroise', in *Mélanges Fournier*, Paris, 1929, pp. 503 ff. There are no reliable indications of date (M. Ihm, *Studia Ambrosiana*, p. 40). It seems likely, however, that Ambrose's firm action in this case was taken in the later, rather than in the earlier, years of his episcopate.

them. Making skilful use of Indicia's unpopularity with the ladies of Verona (who had been offended by her neglect to call on them), this man succeeded in setting the scandalous report in circulation. The bishop was forced to take action; but he did not behave well. He heard the case without assessors, and, although no satisfactory evidence was produced by the accusers, condemned the virgin to undergo medical examination. Thereupon Indicia's friends, indignant at these irregularities, requested Ambrose, who was Syagrius' metropolitan, to intervene. With the assistance of certain 'brethren and fellow bishops', Ambrose held a fresh trial. It was then shown that the evidence offered at the former trial was both second-hand and inconsistent, that the witnesses were corrupt, and that all the probabilities were in favour of the innocence of the accused, whose good character was vouched for by Ambrose's own sister. Ambrose, therefore, acquitted the virgin, censured Syagrius, and excommunicated Maximus and the lying witnesses. In his comments on the case he expressed emphatic disapproval of the practice of subjecting virgins to medical examination. He allowed, indeed, that such inspection was very occasionally justifiable; as when a virgin, confronted with a mass of circumstantial evidence, could find no other means of establishing her innocence. Except as a last resort, however, he objected to the method as degrading to the girl, and further as inconclusive in respect of the proof which it was supposed to afford.[1]

Concerning the punishment of virgins proved guilty of very grave offences, detailed information is furnished in a discourse entitled *De Lapsu Virginis*, which was formerly ascribed to Ambrose, but which should probably be attributed to Niceta of Remesiana.[2] A young lady of good family, named Susanna, against the wishes of her parents, and on the pretence of having been the recipient of Divine revelations, made solemn profession of virginity and entered a convent. Here she became entangled in a love affair, and gave birth to a child, whom she secretly destroyed. In spite of her precautions, however, the crime became known, and an information was lodged against her. The bishop tried her, and found her guilty. She was then conducted to the church, where, in the presence of a great congregation, the

[1] Ambros. *Epp.* 5. 5–9, 14; 6. 1 and 19.
[2] On *De Lapsu Virginis*, see below, chapter xxii.

episcopal judge addressed to her a vehement, and even savage, rebuke. After expatiating on the heinousness of her sin, he sentenced her to the severest form of penance. She was to abandon all care for this life, and regard herself as one dead; she was to cut off her hair and wear mourning; she was to scourge herself, to fast, to weep, to disfigure her beauty with dust and ashes; she was to meditate day and night on the awfulness of her fall, and recite daily, with tears and groans, the fifty-first psalm and such other portions of Scripture as seemed appropriate to her desperate case.[1] The penance was to be continued throughout the whole remainder of her life, for so outrageous a sinner could never receive pardon in this world.[2] If, however, she persevered in it to the end, she might venture to hope, not certainly for glory, but for remission of punishment, in the world to come.[3]

The case of a virgin who lapsed into immorality must be distinguished from that of one who broke her vow of celibacy and contracted a marriage. Of this latter offence some persons took a harsher, and others a milder, view.[4] Ambrose was attacked by some of his detractors on the ground that he forbade such marriages. He retorted with some heat that he was not ashamed to confess a crime of which John the Baptist had been guilty; for John had suffered martyrdom because he dared to say to Herod, *It is not lawful for thee to have her*.[5] This allusion to John's rebuke of Herod might imply that Ambrose viewed the marriage of a consecrated virgin as adultery. But although he certainly condemned such a marriage as highly offensive and irregular, he never explicitly pronounced it adulterous. Much more severe is the judgement of the author of *De Lapsu Virginis*.

'Some one will say, *It is better to marry than to burn*. This saying refers to a girl who has made no promise of virginity and has not been veiled. But she who has betrothed herself to Christ and has received the consecrated veil is now married, is now joined to an immortal Husband. And if she now wishes to marry according to the common

---

[1] [Niceta Remes.] *De Lapsu Virginis*, 35, 43 ff.
[2] Ibid. 38.                                                    [3] Ibid. 36.
[4] Jerome stigmatizes the marriage of a consecrated virgin as 'incest', meriting 'damnation' (*Adv. Jovin.* i. 13). Cyprian, although he describes a profligate virgin as an adulteress against Christ (*Ep.* 4. 3), yet distinctly states that virgins who cannot persevere in their profession had better marry (ibid. 4. 2). Augustine views the marriage of a virgin as highly reprehensible, but still as a true marriage (*De Bono Viduit.* 12–14).
[5] Ambros. *De Virginitate*, 11.

law of marriage, she commits adultery and is made the handmaid of death.'[1]

On one occasion Ambrose was requested by his sister Marcellina to state his opinion concerning virgins who committed suicide to avoid violation.[2] He did not, however, express himself very clearly. On the one hand, he told the story of the suicide of St. Pelagia of Antioch and of her mother and sisters in a manner which suggests that, if he did not actually commend, he certainly did not condemn their act.[3] On the other hand, he spoke with unqualified admiration of another Antiochene virgin, who, being sentenced to violation in a brothel, on account of her refusal to sacrifice, prepared to undergo the penalty, without anticipating it by suicide.[4] In relating the incident, he said, 'A virgin of Christ may be dishonoured, but she cannot be polluted. Everywhere she is the virgin of God and the temple of God. Places of infamy do not stain chastity; on the contrary, chastity abolishes the infamy of the place.'[5]

Closely connected with the class of virgins was the class of widows. These persons must be distinguished from the poor and elderly 'Church widows' already mentioned, who undertook definite duties in return for maintenance out of the ecclesiastical funds.[6] They were simply married women, of any age and social standing, who, having lost their husbands by death, determined on religious grounds to continue in the state of widowhood.

The old Roman admiration of the faithful widow, combined with the new Christian enthusiasm for continence, had created a prejudice against second marriages. Some heretical sects, indeed, forbade such marriages altogether. Even the Catholic Church, while permitting a second marriage, was disposed to regard it as a regrettable impropriety.[7] Thus it became increasingly the custom for women, whose husbands had died, to

---

[1] *De Lapsu Virginis*, 21.

[2] Ambros. *De Virginibus*, iii. 32. Augustine discussed this question, and, with some hesitation, pronounced against suicide (*De Civitate Dei*, i. 16–26). Eusebius extolled as martyrs those women who killed themselves to escape the lust of their persecutors (*H.E.* viii. 12, 14).

[3] Ambros. *De Virginibus*, iii. 33–6; cf. *Ep.* 37. 36.

[4] Id. *De Virginibus*, ii. 22–33. On the question whether this anonymous virgin 'at Antioch' should be identified with Theodora of Alexandria (*Acta Sanctorum*, 28 April, p. 572) see Migne's note on *De Virginibus*, ii. 22.

[5] Ibid. ii. 26.    [6] See above, p. 144.

[7] Ambros. *De Viduis*, 12, 68; Ambrosiaster, *Comm. in I Cor.* vii. 40.

dedicate themselves to perpetual widowhood. They do not appear to have made any public profession in the church; but, like the virgins, they adopted the dark-coloured costume[1] and lived under ascetic discipline.[2] The high estimation in which this religious widowhood was held, and the arguments which were used to induce widows to persevere therein, are illustrated in *De Viduis*—a treatise composed by Ambrose, after receiving information that a widow in his diocese, old enough to be the mother of marriageable and married daughters, was contemplating a second marriage.[3]

Although Ambrose quotes several pre-Christian examples of pious widowhood—especially Anna, who 'shows us what widows ought to be'[4]—he maintains that 'the grace of widowhood, like the grace of virginity, did not flourish in perfection before the coming of Christ'.[5] For true widowhood does not consist simply in abstinence from remarriage, but involves the practice of all the virtues that are appropriate to the widowed state.[6] As such, it is not easy of achievement; and accordingly is not commanded, but only counselled.[7] Nevertheless, it is unseemly for a widow to marry again, unless she have very cogent reasons for so doing. But the reasons commonly advanced are manifestly frivolous. The plea of defencelessness, for instance, will not hold; for, although a widow has no husband to defend her, she generally has kinsfolk, and even if she have no kinsfolk, she can rely on the protection of the apostles and martyrs.[8] Nor can desire for children be accepted as a valid excuse; for, if a widow have children already, she ought to be content and refrain from taking a step which may injure their prospects, while, if she have none, she is a fool to attempt again what she has hitherto failed to achieve.[9] 'But you want to marry', Ambrose cries. 'Very well; it is permitted. The simple desire is not a crime. But do not concoct reasons to justify your act.'[10]

---

[1] Ambros. *De Viduis*, 59 'suasimus, fateor, ut vestem mutares'; Hieron. *Epp.* 38. 3; 39. 3.

[2] The descriptions which Jerome gives of the widows Blaesilla (*Ep.* 38), Paula (*Ep.* 108), and Marcella (*Ep.* 127), the rules which he lays down for the guidance of Furia (*Ep.* 54), together with his letters of appeal to Salvina (*Ep.* 79) and Ageruchia (*Ep.* 123), furnish indications of the kind of discipline which might be practised by pious widows.          [3] On *De Viduis*, see below, chapter xxii.

[4] Ambros. *De Viduis*, 21.                [5] Id. *Expos. ev. Luc.* iii. 18.

[6] Id. *De Viduis*, 3, 11.                    [7] Ibid. 68, 72, 82.

[8] Ibid. 52 ff., 67.          [9] Ibid. 86-8.          [10] Ibid. 58.

It should be observed that, with all his ardent advocacy of continence, Ambrose was careful to avoid Manichaean disparagement of marriage. 'Some one may say, Do you advise against marriage? Nay, I advise it, and I condemn those who advise against it. I am accustomed to speak of the marriages of Sarah, Rebecca, Rachel, and other women of ancient times as instances of singular virtues. For whoever condemns wedlock, condemns also children, and condemns the fellowship of the human race carried on by successive generations.'[1] Apart from its other merits, marriage is commendable because it brings into the world those who will consecrate themselves to virginity.[2] Good and useful though it is, however, marriage is represented as definitely inferior to celibacy.[3] The former is a remedy for human weakness, the latter is glorious and wins praise;[4] the former is permitted, the latter is recommended;[5] the former is the right of all, the latter is the grace of the few.[6] In short, 'marriage is honourable, but celibacy is more honourable. That which is good need not be avoided, but that which is better should be chosen.'[7]

Pure marriage, widowhood, virginity—these are the three degrees of the virtue of chastity. In the Church, Ambrose says, there is room for all three; yet they are not to be accounted of equal excellence. 'We are taught that chastity has three forms —one that of married life, a second that of widowhood, and a third that of virginity. We do not so extol one form as to exclude the others. In this, indeed, the Church is rich, in that it has those whom it can rank before others, but none whom it rejects. We have therefore so extolled virginity as not to reject widowhood, and we so revere widowhood as to reserve its own honour for marriage. It is not our precepts, but the Divine testimonies, that teach this.'[8]

---

[1] Ambros. *De Virginibus*, i. 34.
[2] Ibid. i. 35; cf. Hieron. *Ep.* 22. 20.
[3] Ambros. *De Virginitate*, 31.
[4] Id. *De Virginibus*, i. 24; *De Virginitate*, 29.
[5] Id. *De Viduis*, 72, 75, 78–80; *De Virginibus*, i. 23; *Exhort. Virginitatis*, 17.
[6] Id. *De Virginibus*, i. 35; *Exhort. Virginitatis*, 18.          [7] Id. *De Viduis*, 72.
[8] Ambros. *De Viduis*, 23; cf. the three ways to the one goal, *Ep.* 63. 40, and the three products of the one field, *De Virginitate*, 34; *De Viduis*, 83. Mary, Anna, and Susanna are examples of the three types, *De Viduis*, 24. On the degrees of chastity, see also Hieron, *Ep.* 48. 11; *Adv. Jovin.* i. 3 (thirtyfold, sixtyfold, hundredfold).

## CHAPTER VII

## THE GOTHIC WAR. THE DEATH OF SATYRUS

WHILE Ambrose was declaiming on the blessedness of celibacy, to the edification of young ladies and the aggravation of ambitious mothers, momentous events were taking place in the Eastern Empire.

As sovereign of the East, the grotesque Valens had turned out better than was anticipated. He seems honestly to have tried to do his duty by his subjects. In imitation of the policy of his capable brother, Valentinian, he restored the frontier defences, lightened the burden of taxation, and adorned the provincial cities with magnificent public buildings. The impartial historian goes so far as to admit that the East never fared better than under his government.[1] Yet—owing partly to religious fanaticism,[2] partly to an intense timidity which in times of peril goaded him to wild and tyrannical excesses, and partly to sheer stupidity—Valens made some grave mistakes, which his people could neither forget nor forgive. Thus, as time went on, he became increasingly unpopular. Vague rumours of an impending change began to be circulated. It was whispered that the soldiers were dissatisfied, that the intellectuals were plotting something, that a *coup* was being prepared. Attempts were made on the Emperor's life.

About the year A.D. 372[3] this widespread disaffection had crystallized into a conspiracy, in which many influential pagans were implicated. The conspiracy was associated with the name of a certain Theodorus—a young man of distinguished family, amiable character, and marked ability, who had risen to a high position among the imperial notaries and was thought likely to rise still higher. Theodorus was not one of the original movers of the conspiracy, but became involved in it under the following

[1] Ammianus Marcellinus, xxxi. 14. 2.

[2] In his religious policy Valens did not see fit to follow the line taken by Valentinian. Like the Emperor Constantius, he was a bigoted Arian, and disposed to persecute the orthodox. Yet his anti-Catholic activities have probably been exaggerated by the ecclesiastical historians: see Gibbon, *Decline and Fall* (ed. Bury), iii, pp. 26–8; T. Hodgkin, *Italy and her Invaders*, i, p. 206.

[3] So Clinton; Tillemont, for some reason which is not clear, fixes the affair of Theodorus in A.D. 374.

circumstances. A sort of spiritualistic séance was held, apparently at Antioch, the object of which was to ascertain the name
of the person who was destined to succeed Valens. In a house,
which had previously been purified with Arabian perfumes, a
small consecrated tripod of laurel-wood was set up. On it was
placed a circular dish, made of different metals, round the rim
of which, at carefully measured intervals, were engraved the
letters of the alphabet. Next entered a person wearing garments and slippers of linen, and carrying in his hand 'twigs of
an auspicious tree'. After propitiating the god of divination with
magic songs, he shook gently over the dish a fine flaxen thread,
to which was attached a consecrated ring. As the thread was
agitated, the ring danced to and fro, touching now one and now
another of the letters engraved round the edge of the dish. In
this way, letter by letter, were spelt out words, which, put
together, formed hexameter verses, answering the questions of
the bystanders. Some of these verses foretold that those who
participated in the séance would speedily suffer death for their
audacious attempt to pry into the future, and further hinted
obscurely at some fearful retribution which would overtake their
judges, including the Emperor himself. 'Your blood shall not
be unavenged ; against them also wrathful Tisiphone makes
ready dire destruction, when they ward off battle in the plains
of Mimas.' Somebody inquired, 'Who will be the successor of
the present Emperor?' The dancing ring spelt out the letters
THEOD—thereupon an impatient observer exclaimed, 'It means
Theodorus'; and, without waiting for the name to be completed,
all present agreed that Theodorus was indicated as the future
ruler of the Eastern Empire.[1]

[1] The account of the séance given by Ammianus (xxix. 1. 29–33) is confirmed
by Zosimus (iv. 13), Socrates (*H.E.* iv. 19), and Sozomen (*H.E.* vi. 35). Zonaras
has a different description of the method of divination. He says that the twenty-
four letters of the alphabet were written on the ground, and by each one was placed
a grain of wheat or barley: then, after some magical ceremonies, a cock was loosed,
which picked up successively the grains lying on the letters THEOD. It may be
noted that the ancient world was familiar with phenomena curiously resembling
those of modern spiritualism. At séances the spirit or demon communicated in
various ways. Sometimes he gave messages by means of contrivances similar to
that described in the text; sometimes he spoke through the mouth of an entranced
medium (Eusebius, *Praep. Evang.* v. 8) either in his own character or in that of the
spirit of some dead person (Augustin. *De Civ. Dei*, x. 11); sometimes he showed himself in immaterial or even in material form (Proclus, *Ad Tim.* 142). That many of
the communications really came from spirits even Christian critics were disposed

Theodorus himself was not present at the séance, but he was soon made acquainted with what had taken place. His first impulse was to report the affair to the Emperor ; but from this course he was dissuaded by a friend, who represented that if fate had destined him to wear the purple, the destiny would be fulfilled in spite of everything that he could do to hinder it. For the moment, therefore, he held his tongue; and there can be little doubt that, when his first alarm had subsided and he had grown accustomed to the brilliant prospects which the oracle seemed to predict for him, he abandoned his honourable scruples and threw in his lot with the conspirators.

Not long afterwards, however, the secret was betrayed. Valens, being informed that many nobles, officials, and literary men were plotting against him, was wellnigh beside himself with fear and fury—'like a wild beast in the amphitheatre', says Ammianus. Then commenced a reign of terror.[1] So many persons were arrested that the public jails could not contain them; private houses were commandeered and crammed to suffocation with prisoners. The trials went on continuously day and night, and the procedure was so summary that many found themselves condemned before they had had time to realize that they were accused. Vast multitudes, after suffering excruciating tortures, were handed over to the executioners and 'slaughtered like sheep'. It was vain to seek safety by flight. All over the East the imperial officials were on the alert, and any one against whom there was the least shadow of suspicion was sent off in chains to Antioch. Professors of occult science were in special jeopardy. People actually took to burning their libraries, for fear lest some book might be discovered therein which might cause them to be suspected of unhealthy knowledge of the magical art. The too-ambitious Theodorus was, of course, put to death; and it is said that many innocent men who were so unfortunate as to possess names beginning with the fatal letters designated by the oracle—Theodotus, Theodosius, Theodulus, and the like—were also executed.[2] The terror continued— victim upon victim, corpse upon corpse—for nearly two years.

to believe; yet some of the mediums were proved to be charlatans and confessed under torture the frauds they had practised.

[1] Ammian. xxix. 1. 5 ff.; Zosimus, iv. 13–15.
[2] Socrates, H.E. iv. 19; Sozomen. H.E. vi. 35.

'At that time', writes Ammianus, 'we all crept about as though in Cimmerian darkness; a sword of Damocles hung suspended by a hair over our heads.'[1]

A few years after these agitations had subsided the Emperor found himself confronted with a European crisis of unprecedented magnitude. The occasion of this new trouble was the triumphant advance of the terrible Huns. From the Asiatic steppes, soon after the year A.D. 370, these hideous Mongolian hordes had burst into Europe, and flung themselves with irresistible force on the nations that lay in their path. A more repulsive race of men it would be impossible to imagine. With shapeless, hairless faces, horribly scarred with branding-irons, with swollen lips, flattened noses, and black beady eyes, the skinny, squat-shaped, swarthy warriors presented the appearance of uncouth two-legged animals rather than of human beings. Their habits were brutish and disgusting. They lived on roots and nearly raw meat, and never changed their clothes until from age and filth they dropped to pieces. All their time was spent on horseback; they were believed to eat, drink, deliberate, and even sleep without dismounting. Their favourite occupation was fighting; and herein, by reason of their swarming numbers, their ferocious courage, the rapidity of their evolutions, and the unerring skill with which they overwhelmed the enemy with deadly showers of bone-tipped arrows, they were extraordinarily formidable.[2] Penetrating Europe, these unspeakable savages overcame all attempts to resist their progress. First, they subjugated the fierce, sword-worshipping Alani, who occupied the region between the Volga and the Don; next, they conquered the mighty empire of the Ostrogoths, extending from the Don to the Dniester; then they attacked the Visigoths. The principal Visigothic chief, Athanaric, mustered his forces on the bank of the Dniester; but, being out-manœuvred by the Huns, he abandoned all thought of resistance in the open field, and retired with a portion of his army to the impenetrable fastnessess of the Transylvanian highlands. The mass of his people, however, refused to follow him. Putting themselves under the leadership of two influential chieftains, Fritigern and Alavio, they withdrew, with all possible speed, in the direction of the

[1] Ammian. xxix. 2. 4.
[2] On the Huns see Ammian. xxxi. 2. 1–11; Jordanes, *De Rebus Geticis*, 24.

Danube. In the year A.D. 376 a vast multitude of Visigoths—numbering, it is said, 200,000 men of fighting age, besides old men, women, and children—gathered on the northern margin of the river, and with outstretched hands and piteous cries besought permission to take refuge on Roman territory.[1]

Valens was by no means unwilling to accede to this request. His vanity was flattered by the humble petition of so powerful a people, and his avarice was pleased by the prospect of acquiring without expense (and without relinquishment of the huge sums annually paid by the provincials for the hire of military substitutes) large reinforcements for his army. Moreover, there were many precedents for the settlement of barbarians on Roman soil. No doubt there was some danger in admitting so great a number. Yet the Goths were friendly; most of them, including Fritigern, were Christians;[2] and, since they brought their families with them, they had the strongest of reasons for cultivating peaceable relations with the Romans. If only they had been handled tactfully all might have been well. Unfortunately, in a business which demanded the most delicate and statesmanly management, Valens and his ministers blundered.

The first mistake was made in framing the conditions of reception. If the Goths' request were granted at all, it ought to have been granted graciously. Valens, however, with inexcusable stupidity, imposed conditions which were not only harsh, but positively insulting. He insisted that the Goths should surrender their sons below military age as hostages, and should further deliver up their weapons. This first blunder was followed by another. If the ignominious conditions were imposed, they should have been rigorously enforced. This, however, was not done. The hostages, whose fine physique excited surprise and admiration, were taken and distributed through the cities of the East; but the vital stipulation with regard to the arms was not insisted on. The truth is that the Roman officers allowed themselves to be bribed. The favour of a beautiful girl or fair-skinned boy, the timely gift of some linen fabric or of a valuable fringed carpet, was sufficient to ensure that the search for weapons would be perfunctory.

---

[1] Ammian. xxxi. 2. 12–4. 1; Jordanes, *De Rebus Geticis*, 24, 25; Eunapius, *Excerpt. de Legat.* 6 (ed. Bonn, p. 48); Zosimus, iv. 20.
[2] Socrates, *H.E.* iv. 33.

The work of transportation was carried out under the superintendence of two rascally Roman generals, Lupicinus Count of Thrace and Maximus Duke of Moesia. For many successive days and nights a fleet of ships, rafts, and canoes plied backwards and forwards across the Danube, conveying the vast multitude to the Roman bank. Although it was found impossible to compute the numbers accurately, it seems likely that nearly a million persons of both sexes were brought over. Arrived on Roman soil, they covered all the country round 'like the rain of ashes from an eruption of Mount Etna'.

But now a horrible situation arose. No preparations had been made for the provisioning of this great host, and almost immediately the supply of food failed. Lupicinus and Maximus profited handsomely by the famine. They sold bread and meat to the Goths at outrageously extortionate prices. They even killed all the dogs in the neighbourhood and sold their carcasses for food, demanding a slave as the price of each dead dog. So lucrative was this traffic that they were loath to bring it to an end, and invented excuses for detaining the barbarians on the Danube bank. Thus passed the winter of A.D. 376–7. The starving Goths were despoiled of all their possessions—even of their sons and daughters, whom they bartered into slavery for bread; but they retained their arms.[1]

At last the barbarians, who had hitherto borne their sufferings with exemplary patience, began to vent their resentment in sinister murmurs. Lupicinus, in alarm, at once took measures for their dispersion in the interior, and ordered Fritigern to march slowly in the direction of Marcianople (Shumla), the capital of Lower Moesia. His instructions were punctiliously obeyed. At Marcianople, however, an incident occurred which converted the irritated but still submissive Goths into open enemies. Fritigern and Alavio were invited by Lupicinus to a banquet, and not suspecting any treachery entered the city with a small retinue. The rest of the barbarians were denied admission, though they pleaded that, as loyal subjects of the Emperor, they ought to be allowed to purchase provisions in

---

[1] On the events connected with the transportation of the Goths, see Ammian. xxxi. 4. 5–11; 5. 1; Jordanes, *De Rebus Geticis*, 26; Eunapius, *Excerpt. de Legat-* 6 (ed. Bonn); Zosimus, iv. 20. On the subsequent massacre of the hostages, Ammian. xxxi. 16. 8; Zosimus, iv. 26.

the well-stocked market. A brawl ensued between them and the Roman soldiers at the gates, wherein some of the latter were killed and stripped of their armour. News of the affray was whispered to Lupicinus, as, drowsy and half-drunk, he lingered over the banquet watching the performance of some comedians. He instantly gave orders for the massacre of the guard of honour which had accompanied the Gothic leaders; and, a few minutes afterwards, the company assembled in the dining-hall heard shrieks of men being butchered in a distant part of the palace. Fritigern realized his danger. With great presence of mind, he rose from the table and courteously asked permission to retire, exclaiming that 'a quarrel had evidently arisen which might have grave results, if it were not immediately pacified by his personal intervention'. Then, before any one could hinder him, he and his suite rushed with drawn swords from the apartment, and, leaping on their chargers, returned at a gallop to their camp. Alavio, however, seems to have perished in the palace, for we hear of him no more.

Then at length the Goths rose in open rebellion. After engaging and routing the forces of Lupicinus nine miles from Marcianople, Fritigern crossed the Balkans, and laid siege to Hadrianople. Realizing, however, that he could effect nothing against a fortified town, he broke up his camp with the words, 'I do not war with stone walls', and turning westward, spread havoc through the fertile plains of Thrace. As he pushed on, he was joined by multitudes of his fellow countrymen who had been sold as slaves, and also by many workmen from the imperial gold-mines, who rendered invaluable service by guiding him to the secret magazines of corn and other hiding-places wherein the Romans had concealed themselves and their treasures. This was in the summer of A.D. 377.[1]

The news of this outbreak caused consternation in the Eastern Empire. At Antioch, for some time past, men's spirits had been oppressed with all kinds of evil portents—the howlings of wolves, the melancholy cries of night-birds, strange glooms which obscured the sunrise, and apparitions of murdered persons screaming verses of fearful import. It was afterwards remem-

---

[1] Ammian. xxxi. 5. 2–9; 6. 1–8; Jordanes, *De Rebus Geticis*, 26. The frightful sufferings of the provincials at the hands of the barbarians are graphically described by Ammianus, xxxi. 6. 7 and 8.

bered, as a presage of the Emperor's fate, that when any of the common people felt himself aggrieved, he would voice his indignation in a slang expression of the day, 'May Valens be burnt alive!' The call of the criers, too, who went every morning through the streets, shouting to the people, 'Bring fuel for Valens' (i.e. for heating the splendid baths which the Emperor had erected), was recognized later as a baleful omen.[1] How far the Emperor himself was affected by the general uneasiness we do not know. At any rate, he made up his mind to take the field in person against the enemy, and in April, A.D. 378, left Antioch for Constantinople, which he reached on the 30th of May.

Meanwhile the generals of Valens, with the assistance of Western reinforcements, had won some successes against the barbarians and at one time had even driven the main body of them back beyond the line of the Balkans. But, owing to the arrival of hordes of Huns and Alans from the Danube, they were unable to maintain their advantage. Further help was promised from the West. This, however, was delayed, because in February, A.D. 378, the Alemanni—more particularly the tribe of the Lentienses, which dwelt near the Lake of Constance—encouraged by the news that a large contingent of Roman troops was being sent from Gaul to the East, burst across the Rhine in considerable force. Gratian achieved a brilliant victory over them at Argentaria (Horburg, near Colmar), and, crossing the river, pursued the flying remnant into the very heart of their native mountains and eventually compelled them to surrender.[2] After this triumph, he marched with all speed to the assistance of his uncle.

At the end of June Valens led out his army from Melanthias, a few miles distant from Constantinople. Not long after the start, a distressing prodigy was encountered. By the roadside was found the body of a man, who appeared to have been barbarously scourged from head to foot. He lay without motion and seemingly dead; only his wide, anguished eyes glared on the soldiers who approached him. They asked him many questions, but received no answer; then, thinking the matter uncanny, they showed the creature to the Emperor. Suddenly, as they

[1] Ammian. xxxi. 1. 2 and 3.
[2] On Gratian's victory over the Alemanni, see Ammian. xxxi. 10. 2–17.

stood round wondering, the body vanished. Those who were skilled in the interpretation of portents declared that the apparition symbolized the future condition of the State, which, after suffering blow upon blow, would linger awhile like a half-dead man, until at last, through the wickedness of its rulers and ministers, it would perish utterly.[1]

The Emperor pitched his camp outside the walls of Hadrianople. Fritigern, who had concentrated his forces at Cabyle, in the north-east corner of Thrace, moved slowly southward, with the object of cutting off Valens' communications with his capital. Thus the Roman and Gothic armies were within a few miles of one another. Valens now had to make a momentous decision. Either he might engage the enemy at once, or else he might take up a strong position at Hadrianople and wait for the reinforcements which were coming from the West. The latter course was strongly urged by many of the generals, and a letter arrived from Gratian himself, announcing his approach and advising his uncle to take no action till he could join him. On the other hand, the experienced general Sebastian, elated by a success which he had recently achieved against the enemy, gave his counsel against postponement; and Valens, who seems to have underestimated the numbers of the Goths, and who had set his heart on greeting his brilliant nephew with the tidings of a victory no less glorious than that of Argentaria, decided to adopt this recommendation.[2]

While preparations were being made for an advance, an embassy from Fritigern, consisting of 'a presbyter of the Christian worship' and some other persons of humble rank, arrived in the camp. The presbyter bore a letter, in which the Gothic chief offered to make a perpetual peace with the Empire, provided that the province of Thrace were ceded to his countrymen for a habitation. Having delivered this document, the ambassador is said to have produced a second communication of a very confidential character, wherein Fritigern confessed that his followers were not yet disposed to agree to terms of peace which would be satisfactory to the Romans, and advised the Emperor to lead out his army against them, and by a demonstration of superior force terrorize them into a more reasonable frame of mind. It is unlikely that the open proposal was seriously meant; it is still

[1] Zosimus, iv. 21.        [2] Ammian. xxxi. 11. 5–12. 7.

more unlikely that the secret message—if any such message were really delivered—was sent in good faith. Valens, at any rate, considered the affair suspicious, and the strange ambassador, with his mean attendants, was curtly dismissed.[1]

At dawn on the 9th of August, A.D. 378, the Emperor set forward with his army, leaving the military chest and the imperial insignia at Hadrianople. The day promised to be very hot. The legionaries marched with extreme difficulty, stumbling painfully over the stretches of rough and broken ground which divided them from the barbarians. It was not till about noon that they sighted (probably near the modern Demeranlija) the Gothic *carrago* or wagon-encampment.[2] The heat was now intense. Amid considerable confusion, the generals halted the troops and marshalled them in battle-order. Then followed a long wait. Fritigern was anxious to gain time: partly because the main body of his cavalry was absent, though, in response to an urgent summons, it was making all haste to join him; and partly because he realized that delay was prejudicial to the Romans who, hungry and tired after their exhausting march, were suffering intolerably from the heat both of the sun and of the plain, which the barbarians had fired. Accordingly he engaged the Emperor with artfully protracted negotiations. The legionaries, sweltering in full armour, grew wearier and wearier. At last some light-armed troops ventured on their own responsibility to attack the enemy. At the same moment the barbarian cavalry, which Fritigern had been so anxiously expecting, swept down 'like a thunderbolt' from the hills, and their charge, combined with the onset of the whole Gothic host, threw the imperial forces into disorder.[3]

The course of the battle is obscure. It appears that the left wing of the Roman cavalry pushed forward as far as the Gothic *carrago*, but, being unsupported, was beaten down. Far behind, the Roman infantry was attacked by the Goths with irresistible ferocity. So terrific was the impact that the com-

---

[1] Ammian. xxxi. 12. 8 and 9.

[2] The Goths, when on the march, carried with them a train of wagons for the accommodation of their wives and children. Their slaves were accustomed to walk and ride on the wagons by turns (Zosimus, iv. 25). When a halt was made, the wagons were drawn up in a huge circle, in the midst of which the troops encamped. This encampment was called *carrago* (Ammian. xxxi. 7. 5 and 7).

[3] Ammian. xxxi. 12. 10–17.

panies were driven inwards, and jammed together in one suffocating mass of flesh and iron. The men were almost helpless. Unable, for lack of space, to use their spears, they despairingly drew their swords and slashed and prodded at the breasts and stomachs of their foes. Surrounded on all sides by swarms of barbarians, blinded by clouds of dust, exposed to a hail of missiles which could not fail to hit the mark, they fought heroically but hopelessly. The ground was saturated with blood and piled with corpses. In the end a few thousands forced their way out from the place of carnage and scattered in headlong flight.[1]

When the rout became general, Valens, nearly crazed by the horrors that encompassed him, spurred his charger over the heaps of dead to a spot where two regiments of the Palatine Guards—the Lancearii and Mattiarii—were still holding out against the pressure of the barbarians. A general, who was with them, shouted, 'All is lost, unless the auxiliaries can be brought to the rescue of the Emperor.' Hearing the words, a certain Count Victor dashed away to fetch up the Batavian reserve, which should have been in the vicinity. But the Batavians had disappeared, and Victor, realizing that nothing more could be done, himself galloped from the field. What happened to Valens was never known. It was rumoured, indeed, that he fled at twilight in the midst of a crowd of common soldiers, and, being wounded by an arrow, sank down amid the slain and shortly afterwards expired. No one, however, seems actually to have seen the purple chlamys and gold-crested helmet of the Emperor, nor was his body ever discovered. According to another report Valens did not die immediately. After receiving his wound, he was carried—so it was said—by some guards and eunuchs into a two-storied wooden cottage. While they were attending to his injury, a company of Goths appeared before the hovel, and, although unaware that the Emperor was within, demanded admittance. Finding the door barred against them, and being further assailed by a shower of arrows from the roof, the barbarians heaped logs and straw against the wooden walls and set the place on fire. All within perished in the flames, except one young guardsman, who, leaping from an upper

[1] Ammian. xxxi. 13. 1–7. See Judeich, 'Die Schlacht bei Adrianopel am 9 August, 378', in *Deutsche Zeitschrift für Geschichtswissenschaft*, 1891, vol. vi, pp. 1–21.

window and being taken prisoner, revealed to the mortified Goths
how narrowly they had missed the glory of capturing the person
of the Roman Emperor.[1]

The catastrophe was appalling. More than two-thirds of the
imperial army perished, including many officers of the highest
rank. Ammianus describes it as a second Cannae.[2] But when
we take into account, not merely the actual losses sustained, but
also the melancholy fact that the Roman State had by this time
lost power of recovering from its reverses, we must regard the
disaster of Cannae as almost trifling in comparison with the
crushing humiliation of Hadrianople. It may be added that in
this battle the oracle warning Valens that he would meet his doom
'on the plains of Mimas' was curiously fulfilled. The Emperor
himself had thought that a mountain in Asia Minor, anciently
known as Mount Mimas, was referred to, and in consequence had
'shuddered at the very name of Asia'. After his death, however,
there was discovered, on the plain where the battle had raged,
a monument with a Greek inscription, recording that a noble
of old time, named Mimas, was buried there.[3]

After achieving their signal triumph, the Goths made an unsuccessful attempt to storm Hadrianople, hoping to lay hands
on the treasure which Valens had deposited within its walls.[4]
Being foiled in this endeavour, they passed southward to the
neighbourhood of Constantinople. Here again, however, they
were repulsed by a body of Saracen auxiliaries ; and thenceforward they wisely reverted to their former policy of leaving
fortified cities alone.[5] In the open country they were irresistible,
and they wandered without hindrance, and apparently also
without definite purpose, through Thrace, Moesia, and Illyricum, up to the very foot of the Julian Alps, plundering, burning,
and slaughtering as they went. The provincials suffered terribly.
Multitudes were massacred; multitudes were carried into slavery; noble matrons and sacred virgins were ravished; bishops

[1] Ammian. xxxi. 13. 8–16. On the two accounts of the death of Valens see
G. Rauschen, op. cit., pp. 22, 23 with references; cf. Claudian. *De Bell. Get.* 610 'ab-
sumptique igne Valentis exuvias'. Idatius says simply, 'ex ea die Valens Augustus
nusquam apparuit.'

[2] Ammian. xxxi. 13. 19.      [3] Ibid. xxxi. 14, 8 and 9.      [4] Ibid. xxxi. c. 15.

[5] Ibid. xxxi. 16, 4–7. Ammianus notices the horror inspired in the barbarians
by the proceedings of one of the long-haired and almost naked Saracen warriors,
who with wild screams threw himself on a Goth, stabbed his throat with a dagger,
and greedily sucked his blood.

were taken captive, priests and deacons butchered at the altars, and churches demolished or turned into stables.[1] Panic-stricken refugees, fleeing precipitately before the enemy, made their appearance in Italy.[2] The miseries of the time were aggravated by famine and by a pestilence which attacked both men and cattle; and Ambrose, in a sermon probably preached towards the end of the year, announced his conviction that all this was the last agony preceding the end of the world.[3]

Gratian, after receiving the news of the defeat at Hadrianople, had withdrawn to Sirmium. He now did the very best thing that could have been done under the circumstances. He summoned to his aid the one man capable of rescuing the Empire from its desperate plight—the vigorous and efficient Theodosius.

Theodosius, like Trajan, from whom he is said to have been descended, was a Spaniard. He was born about A.D. 345[4] at Cauca (the modern Coca)—a small town situated on a tributary of the Douro, some thirty miles from Segovia. His father, who also bore the name of Theodosius, had been one of the ablest of Valentinian's generals, who in Britain, Germany, and Africa had rendered eminent services to the Empire.[5] In A.D. 376, however, he was beheaded at Carthage, apparently by order of the Empress Justina. What charges were brought against him we do not know, but he seems to have been guiltless of any crime.[6] After this execution the younger Theodosius, who had already given proof of high military capacity as Duke of Moesia, deemed it prudent to resign his command and retire into the safe obscurity of private life. He accordingly betook himself to his estate at Cauca, where, for over two years, he lived the life of a country gentleman, busying himself with social duties in the little town and amusing his leisure with farming.[7] Amid these rural interests and occupations there came to him the startling

---

[1] See Hieron. *Ep.* 60. 16 (written some eighteen years later); Ambros. *De Fide*, ii. 139–41; *De Noe*, 1, 2; *De Officiis*, ii. 70. To ransom the prisoners Ambrose spent all his available funds, and even melted down and sold the plate of the Church; see above, pp. 118, 119.

[2] Ambros. *Ep.* 2. 28.     [3] Id. *Expos. ev. Luc.* x. 10: see the whole passage 10–14.

[4] The date is uncertain ; see G. Rauschen, op. cit., p. 430.

[5] On the elder Theodosius, see Ammian. xxvii, c. 8; xxviii, c. 3; xxix, c. 5; Pacatus, *Panegyricus Theodosio Aug. dictus*, 5: Claudian. *De III Cons. Honor.* 51–60; *De IV Cons. Honor.* 24–40.

[6] Orosius, *Hist.* vii. 33 'instimulante et obrepente invidia iussus interfici'.

[7] Pacatus, *Panegyr.* 9.

news of the *débâcle* at Hadrianople; and this was speedily followed by Gratian's message of recall. On his return to the Imperial Court he was given an important command, and conducted a short but successful campaign against some roving bands of Sarmatians, who appear to have invaded Pannonia.[1] Then Gratian, who had conceived the highest opinion of his abilities, invited him to become his colleague in the government of the Empire. He seems to have been genuinely reluctant to undertake the responsibility;[2] he yielded, however, to pressure, and was proclaimed Augustus at Sirmium on the 19th day of January in the year A.D. 379.

The new Emperor, at the time of his accession, was about thirty-three years old. In appearance he is reputed to have borne a close resemblance to Trajan. Men admired his strong, straight limbs, his handsome though florid countenance, his stately carriage. He had precisely the figure which the purple adorns, and the Court orator Themistius did but voice the popular sentiment when he applied to him the words of Homer: 'Never have mine eyes beheld so comely, so majestic a man.' In disposition he was frank, debonair, and generous to a fault; but, though capable of energetic action on occasion, he was constitutionally indolent. He loved pomp and splendour, and spent money with reckless profusion on gorgeous spectacles and entertainments; personally, however, he was abstemious. Owing to the regularity of his habits and the attention which he gave to diet and exercise, he enjoyed throughout the greater part of his life the best of health. Of literary attainments he could not boast, though he was interested in the study of history; but he had a strong understanding, and by means of free and unceremonious converse with those who approached him, he kept himself well informed on all contemporary affairs. In religion he was a typical Spaniard—fanatically orthodox. There is one other feature of his character which ought specially to be noticed. He was choleric to an extreme degree, and so violent in his tempestuous rages that at such times even his wife and children dared not come into his presence. In these moods he was capable of issuing monstrous orders; yet, when his furious passion had cooled and his natural reasonableness reasserted

[1] Theodoret. *H.E.* v. 5; Themistius, *Orat.* xiv. 182 c ; Pacatus, *Panegyr.* 10.
[2] Pacatus, *Panegyr.* 11; Claudian. *De IV Cons. Honor.* 47, 48.

itself, he was not ashamed to modify or cancel them. Finally, it is alleged of him by one authority that, after his elevation to supreme power, his character, so far from degenerating, improved—which is certainly a singular trait in a sovereign of the Roman Empire.[1]

Theodosius received from Gratian the whole Eastern Empire, formerly ruled by Valens, with the important addition of Eastern Illyricum, that is, of the two Dioceses of Dacia and Macedonia.[2] He established his head-quarters at Thessalonica, and proceeded to prosecute a guerrilla warfare against the Goths —not hazarding his fortunes in one great pitched battle, but falling on detachments of the barbarians whenever he found them in a position of disadvantage. These tactics were highly successful. The Goths suffered many reverses and lost their former confidence. They were further discouraged by a devastating pestilence, which broke out, Ambrose informs us, in answer to the prayers of the holy Acholius, Bishop of Thessalonica.[3]

Unfortunately, in the February of A.D. 380 Theodosius himself fell seriously ill at Thessalonica—perhaps of the same epidemic which in the previous summer had brought discomfiture on the enemy. Being still unbaptized, and believing that his end was near, he summoned Acholius to his bedside and requested him to administer the baptismal rite.[4] Though he did not die, he was laid aside for many months; and the barbarians were not slow to take advantage of his absence from the scene of action. The Visigoths invaded Epirus, Thessaly, and Achaia; a host of Ostrogoths devastated Pannonia. Gratian, however, sent effective help to his sick colleague, and, coming himself from Gaul, negotiated, with the concurrence of Theodosius, a truce with the barbarians.[5] In September the two Emperors met in conference at Sirmium; then Gratian returned to the West, and Theodosius,

[1] On Theodosius, see especially Aurelius Victor, *Epitome*, 48; Pacatus, *Panegyricus Theodosio Aug. dictus*; Themistius, *Orat.* xiv, xv; Ambros. *De Obitu Theodosii Oratio* and *Ep.* 51. 4; Jordanes, *De Rebus Geticis*, 27; Zosimus, iv. 24, 27–29; Claudian. *Laus Seren.* 134–8; *De IV Cons. Honor.* 41 ff. Consult also generally A. Güldenpenning and J. Ifland, *Der Kaiser Theodosius der Grosse* (Halle, 1878); and G. Rauschen, *Jahrbücher der christlichen Kirche unter dem Kaiser Theodosius dem Grossen* (Freiburg, 1897).
[2] Sozomen. *H.E.* vii. 4.                              [3] Ambros. *Ep.* 15. 5–8.
[4] Sozomen. *H.E.* vii. 4. Socrates, *H.E.* v. 6, mistakenly places the Emperor's illness in November.
[5] Prosper, *Chron.* A.D. 380 'procurante Gratiano, eo quod Theodosius aegrotaret, pax firmatur cum Gothis'.

whose health by this time was completely re-established, proceeded to Constantinople, which he entered in triumph on the
24th of November, A.D. 380.

The end of the war was now in sight. The prospects of peace
were advanced by the death of the gallant Fritigern, which seems
to have occurred in the year A.D. 380, and also by the submission
of the grand old Gothic chief, Athanaric. Having been expelled
by Ostrogothic invaders from his refuge in Transylvania, he
crossed the Danube and surrendered to the Romans. On the
11th of January, A.D. 381, he was graciously welcomed by Theodosius a few miles from Constantinople, and escorted into the
city with royal honours. The barbarian was astounded by the
splendour of his surroundings. 'As he entered the capital, he
exclaimed in amazement, "Lo, now do I behold what I never
could believe when I was told of it—the glory of this mighty
city!" Then, casting his eyes this way and that, and viewing
the fine situation of the city, the concourse of ships, the magnificent walls, the crowds of people of all nations (like waters from
many jets mingling in a single fountain), the troops drawn up
in military order along his route, he cried, "Truly a god upon
earth is this Emperor, and whoever lifts a hand against him is
guilty of his own blood." ' The exciting entertainment, however,
was too much for the aged king. He died a fortnight after his
state entry. Theodosius gave him a superb funeral, and personally accompanied his body to the grave.[1] Such magnanimity
astonished and gratified the Goths, and contributed much to
dispose them towards a permanent reconciliation.

At last, on the 3rd of October, A.D. 382, a final treaty was
concluded.[2] Although the details are not indicated, we gather
that the Goths were recognized as *foederati*[3] of the Empire
and were assigned settlements within the imperial territories—
chiefly (it seems likely) in Lower Moesia. Here they were
permitted to establish themselves, inhabiting their own villages,

---

[1] Jordanes, *De Rebus Geticis*, 28; Zosimus, iv. 34; Ambros. *De Spiritu*, i. 17; cf.
Ammian. xxvii. 5. 10. The dates of Athanaric's entry into Constantinople and
death are supplied by Idatius and confirmed by Marcellinus.

[2] Idatius 'ipso anno (A.D. 382) universa gens Gothorum cum rege suo in Roma-
niam se tradiderunt die v Non. Oct.'; cf. Marcellinus 'mense Octobri'.

[3] Whether the actual word *foederati* was at this time applied to the Goths is
uncertain. The earliest extant text in which the term is so used is Cod. Theod.
vii. 13. 16, A.D. 406.

cultivating their own lands, preserving their own ancestral usages, and governed by their own chiefs under the suzerainty of the Emperor. They were probably also exempt from imperial taxation. In return for these privileges they were required to furnish bodies of troops, led by officers of their own, for the service of the Empire. Such an arrangement, whereby compact masses of barbarians were settled permanently on Roman soil, retaining still their native language, their racial customs, and their domestic government, was obviously fraught with peril. For the moment, however, the treaty of A.D. 382 appears to have worked well. In the following year Themistius described, in sonorous periods, its beneficent effects. Already, he said, the desolated provinces were beginning to recover. The roads were again open; the fields were once more cultivated; villas and farm-buildings were rising again from their ashes. A delightful tranquillity pervaded the scene of the late sad disturbances. The dreaded enemies, now transformed into loyal friends, were sowing and ploughing the land which they had formerly laid waste, and paying their joyous devotions, no longer to Mars, but to Ceres and Bacchus. Daily they became more reasonable and gentle; and daily they grew more grateful to the wise and clement Emperor, who had forgiven them their past misdeeds and elevated them to the honourable position of allies of the Empire. Thus the wounds inflicted by long years of war were healing, and the Roman State, like a living creature, was reviving to new happiness after its protracted and bitter sorrow.[1]

I must here turn back to notice an event which caused acute distress to Ambrose. This was the death, in the early part (perhaps February) of the year A.D. 375, of his beloved elder brother, Uranius Satyrus.[2]

[1] Themistius, *Orat.* xvi.
[2] Adopting the view of O. Seeck (*Symmachus*, p. xlix), G. Rauschen (*Jahrbücher der chr. Kirche*, pp. 475, 476) and J.-R. Palanque (*Saint Ambroise*, pp. 488–93) place the death of Satyrus in the year A.D. 375. The date depends mainly on the interpretation of the passage *De Excessu Sat.* i. 30–2. The barbarian peril there referred to should probably be identified, not with the outbreak of the Goths in the latter part of A.D. 378, but with that of the Quadi and Sarmatians in A.D. 374–5 (Ammian. xxix. c. 6), whereby Northern Italy may well have seemed menaced (*De Excessu Sat.* i. 31), though Ambrose uses exaggerated language in describing the situation (ibid. i. 30). This date explains the perplexing reference to Symmachus as

The two brothers, who both physically and temperamentally were curiously alike,[1] had all their lives been inseparable companions.[2] Together they had passed their boyhood, together they had pursued their studies at the Roman University, and together they had practised as advocates at Sirmium.[3] Then Satyrus went off for a while to a provincial governorship.[4] After Ambrose's consecration, however, he resigned his post and settled down with his brother at Milan, where he superintended the episcopal household, administered the family estates, and relieved Ambrose of much of the temporal business of his see.[5] Once more, as in the old days, the two became inseparable. They shared everything—not only their property, but their thoughts and feelings, their cares and pleasures, even their very sickness and health.[6] There was nothing, indeed, which they had not in common, except the secrets which were communicated to each in confidence by friends.[7]

Satyrus appears to have been an amiable person. During the period of his governorship his benevolence, impartiality, and integrity had endeared him to the provincials,[8] and at Milan he was extraordinarily popular with all classes.[9] The outstanding feature of his character was a child-like 'innocence' or 'simplicity'.[10] He was very affectionate—though he shrank from

'parens' of Satyrus (ibid. i. 32), for the person alluded to would be, not Symmachus the orator (who was younger than Satyrus) but his father, the venerable L. Avianius Symmachus, who resided at Rome and died in A.D. 376. This date also harmonizes with the statement that Prosper's misbehaviour took place near the beginnning of Ambrose's episcopate (ibid. i. 24); further, on the assumption that Ambrose was consecrated in A.D. 373, it allows several months for Satyrus's residence in Milan (ibid. i. 20, 40, 62) before his voyage to Africa. It seems probable, therefore, that Satyrus sailed for Africa in October, A.D. 374, just before the incursion of the Quadi and Sarmatians. Having transacted his business, he started for home precipitately in the winter (ibid. i. 50), and, after a delay in Sicily occasioned by illness (ibid. i. 17), reached Milan via Rome, and died soon afterwards (ibid. i. 17, 24). Since the period of his absence, which was shortened as much as possible (ibid. i. 26), can hardly have lasted longer than three months, we must place his return to Milan in January, A.D. 375, and his death (at latest) in February. The day of the death given in the Roman Martyrology—17 September —though accepted by Rauschen, is evidently wrong.

[1] Ambros. De Excessu Satyri, i. 37–9.          [2] Ibid. i. 6, 21, 22.
[3] Ibid. i. 49.                                       [4] Ibid. i. 25.
[5] Ibid. i. 20, 40, 62. It was not until after the death of Satyrus, in the later part of his episcopate, that Ambrose took his clergy to live with him in his house under ascetic rule, after the fashion set by Bishop Eusebius of Vercelli (Ep. 63, 66).
[6] Ibid. i. 7, 21–3, 79.          [7] Ibid. i. 39.          [8] Ibid. i. 58.
[9] Ibid. i. 5, 28.                               [10] Ibid. i. 51; cf. i. 23.

demonstrations of affection—deeply religious, and singularly pure-minded; loose and improper talk particularly offended him.[1] In any disputes which arose—between Ambrose and his strong-willed sister, for example—he was invariably the peacemaker.[2] Almost his only fault was an excess of sensitiveness. Even in the company of men he was shy; and if he suddenly encountered a woman, although she might be old enough to be the mother of a family, he was ready to sink to the ground with bashfulness.[3] His relatives frequently urged him to marry; but he resolutely declined to do so, partly because he could not bring himself to separate from his brother, and partly because he had fallen in love with that ideal of religious celibacy which fascinated so many devout spirits at this period.[4]

With all his gentleness and guilelessness, Satyrus exhibited rare capacity in the conduct of practical affairs.[5] He was a first-rate man of business, and not at all the kind of innocent that could easily be victimized by 'financial hawks'.[6] Now it happened, in the year A.D. 374, that one of these 'hawks'—a rogue named Prosper, who lived in Africa—fancying that a bishop could be cheated with impunity, took advantage of Ambrose's elevation to the episcopate to filch some property belonging to him.[7] Indignant at this robbery, Satyrus determined to go in person to Africa, and force the fellow to disgorge. Although Ambrose earnestly endeavoured to persuade him to arrange the matter through an agent,[8] he set off in the autumn. On the voyage he was shipwrecked; and his proceedings in the hour of danger are interesting.

'He had not been initiated in the more perfect Mysteries. When the ship in which he travelled struck a reef and was being broken in pieces by the waves, beating upon it on every side, he was afraid, not indeed of dying, but of dying without the Mystery. He accordingly went to some of his fellow voyagers, whom he knew to be initiated, and begged them to give him that Divine Sacrament of the Faithful. And this he did, not that he might gaze on the Secret Thing with curious eyes, but that he might obtain a support for his faith. For he caused It to be bound up in a napkin, and twisted the napkin round his neck, and so flung himself into the sea. Nor did he try to help himself to keep afloat by clinging to any plank, loosened from the

---

[1] Ambros. *De Excessu Sat.* i. 37, 43, 52.     [2] Ibid. i. 41.     [3] Ibid. i. 52.
[4] Ibid. i. 53, 59.          [5] Ibid. i. 23.          [6] Ibid. i. 55.
[7] Ibid. i. 24.               [8] Ibid. i. 26.

framework of the ship, seeing that he had sought the succours which faith alone provides.'[1]

Satyrus was a good swimmer, and got safe to land. After attending to the rescue of his servants, he sought for a church, wherein he might give thanks for his deliverance.[2] He desired also to be baptized and receive the Eucharist; 'for, having found the Heavenly Mystery wrapped in a napkin such a protection, he knew not what blessing he might not expect, if he were to receive It with his mouth and absorb It into his innermost being'.[3] Eager though he was, however, he proceeded with caution. He requested the bishop of the place to come to him, and inquired whether, in matters of faith, he 'agreed with the Catholic bishops, that is, with the Church of Rome'. Unfortunately the bishop was a follower of Lucifer of Cagliari, who, though orthodox in faith, had withdrawn from communion with the Catholics. This did not satisfy Satyrus, who 'held that there could be no true faith in schism'.[4] He accordingly sought baptism elsewhere.[5]

Having arranged the business which had brought him to Africa, on terms satisfactory to Ambrose and generous to Prosper,[6] Satyrus was impatient to return. Braving the cold of the winter,[7] he set sail in an old and leaky vessel,[8] wherein nevertheless he reached Sicily[9] without mishap. Here, however,

[1] Ambros. *De Excessu Sat.* i. 43. The narrative shows that the practice of taking the consecrated Bread from church and preserving it at home or carrying it about as a protection against danger was not extinct. See Tertullian, *Ad Uxor.* ii. 5; *De Orat.* 19. Cyprian tells a story of a woman who kept 'the Holy Thing of the Lord' in her chest (*De Laps.* 26). The author of *De Spectaculis* speaks of a man hastening from the church to the Circus, carrying the Eucharist with him (*De Spect.* 5 in Hartel's *Cyprian*, Appendix, p. 8). Jerome refers to persons who take the Sacrament in their own homes, when, for a certain reason, they cannot do so in church (*Ep.* 48. 15). In A.D. 380 the Council of Zaragossa c. 3 anathematized those who received the Eucharist in church, but did not consume it there; and in A.D. 400 the same practice was prohibited by the Council of Toledo c. 14. It appears that those who participated in the sacraments of the pagan cults sometimes carried home the consecrated elements (Zeno Veronens. *Tract.* i. 5. 9).

[2] Ambros. *De Excessu Sat.* i. 27, 44.

[3] Ibid. i. 46.

[4] Ibid. i. 47. The name of the place to which Satyrus escaped from shipwreck is not mentioned. The reference to the Luciferian schism might suggest that the ship was wrecked off the island of Sardinia. But it is not unlikely that the schism may have extended to the coast of Africa. On the Luciferian schism see G. Krüger, *Lucifer, Bischof von Calaris, und das Schisma der Luciferianer*, Leipzig, 1886.

[5] Ambros. *De Excessu Sat.* i. 48.          [6] Ibid. i. 24, 62.

[7] Ibid. i. 50.          [8] Ibid. i. 26.          [9] Ibid. i. 17.

he was delayed by an illness—brought on, no doubt, by fatigue and exposure. But he made a vow to St. Lawrence, and obtained that his life might be sufficiently prolonged to enable him to reach home.[1] Though still in a weak state, he pushed on to Rome, where he dutifully paid his respects to his venerable kinsman, L. Avianius Symmachus. The city was full of rumours of a threatened invasion of Quadi and Sarmatians, and Symmachus urged his young friend to remain where he was, and not venture into the imperilled region of northern Italy. But Satyrus insisted that he must without delay join Ambrose and share his danger.[2] He reached Milan, probably in January. His health, however, was shattered, and soon after his return— in February, at latest—he died[3] in Ambrose's arms.[4] He did not make a will, but left his property (which was considerable)[5] at the disposal of his brother and sister, only requesting that a suitable proportion thereof should be given to the poor.[6]

The ritual customary in connexion with a death may briefly be indicated. First, the nearest relative bestowed the last kiss on the dying person—the idea being to catch the final breath[7]— and reverently closed the eyes of the dead.[8] Psalms were chanted by those who were present.[9] The corpse was then washed, prepared with perfumes and fragrant ointments,[10] and arrayed in garments of white linen[11] or else in robes appropriate to the person's social or official rank.[12] It was placed on a wooden bier,[13] and covered with a pall of rich material.[14] This done, the body was sometimes removed immediately to the church,[15] where it

---

[1] Ambros. *De Excessu Sat.* i. 16, 17.     [2] Ibid. i. 32.
[3] Ibid. i. 17, 24.     [4] Ibid. i. 19.
[5] Ibid. i. 56.     [6] Ibid. i. 59.
[7] Ibid. i. 19.     [8] Ibid. i. 36.
[9] Augustin. *Confess.* ix. 12; Hieron. *Ep.* 108. 29. In devout Christian households the chanting of psalms was substituted for the 'conclamation' (Ammian. xxx. 10. 1; Ambros. *De Obitu Theodosii,* 3), i.e. calling the name of the deceased, with the object of awakening him if he were not really dead.
[10] Ambros. *Expos. ev. Luc.* ii. 44; Augustin. *Confess.* ix. 13; Prudentius, *Cathem.* x. 51, 52.
[11] Prudentius, *Cathem.* x. 49, 50.
[12] Emperors were dressed in the purple, magistrates in their robes of ceremony, rich people sometimes in garments of silk or cloth of gold. Jerome protested against the practice of vesting the dead in costly attire, *Vita Pauli,* 17.
[13] Ambros. *Expos. ev. Luc.* v. 90.
[14] Hieron. *Ep.* 39. 1.
[15] Paulinus, *Vita Ambrosii,* 48; Hieron. *Ep.* 108. 29; Gregor. Turon. *De Glor. Confess.* 104.

remained until the funeral. More usually, however, it lay in state in the house. After an interval of a few days[1] the burial took place. It was attended, not only by the men, but also by the women of the family,[2] who sometimes displayed extravagant grief.[3] The bier was carried by the nearest relatives.[4] In cases where public feeling was deeply stirred, great multitudes of people escorted it in token of respect.[5] The procession made its way to the cemetery church, where the funeral Eucharist was celebrated.[6] After the reading of the Gospel—at the place in the service where the sermon was ordinarily introduced[7]— a funeral oration was sometimes delivered. A famous example of this type of discourse is Ambrose's oration *On the Death of his brother Satyrus*.

The scene, on this ocasion, was exceedingly impressive. The church was packed with a vast congregation, for the most part dissolved in tears.[8] In the midst, upon his bier, lay the dead man, with face uncovered.[9] Ambrose, who found difficulty in controlling his emotion, fixed his eyes on that lifeless countenance, and thus began his sermon. 'We have brought hither, dearest brethren, my sacrifice, a sacrifice undefiled, a sacrifice well pleasing to God—my lord and brother Satyrus.' After thanking God for having given him such a brother, he protested his conviction that Satyrus, though dead, was not really lost to him. 'Why should I weep for thee, my most loving brother? Thou wert taken from me only that thou mightest belong to all. For I have not lost, but only changed the form of, my inter-

[1] Servius (on *Aeneid*, v. 64) states that it was customary for the body to lie in state for seven days. But the period varied. Ambrose died on the night of Good Friday and was buried on Easter Day (Paulinus, *Vita Ambros*. 48). Paula lay in the church for three days (Hieron. *Ep*. 108. 29).

[2] The funeral of Satyrus was attended by Marcellina, that of Valentinian II by his sisters (Ambros. *De Obitu Val*. 38–42), that of Blaesilla by Paula (Hieron. *Ep*. 39. 5), that of Paula by Eustochium (ibid. 108. 29).

[3] Ambros. *De Excessu Sat*. ii. 12 (cf. ibid. i. 76).

[4] Ambrose helped to carry that of Satyrus, ibid. i. 36.

[5] Paulinus, *Vita Ambros*. 48: Hieron. *Epp*. 77. 11; 108. 29. The funeral of Satyrus was celebrated with public mourning in Milan (Ambros. *De Excessu Sat*. i. 5).

[6] Ambros. *De Obitu Val*. 56; Augustin. *Confess*. ix. 12; Possidius, *Vita Augustini*, 31.

[7] In *De Excessu Sat*. i. 61 Ambrose refers to the psalm which had been intoned between the lessons; and in *De Obitu Val*. 56 he indicates that the oration preceded the Missa Fidelium.

[8] Ambros. *De Excessu Sat*. i. 5, 28.

[9] Ibid. i. 14, 78. Paula's face, at her funeral, was also exposed, Hieron. *Ep*. 108, 29.

course with thee. Formerly we were inseparable in our bodily companionship, now we are undivided in affection. For thou remainest with me—yea, and ever wilt remain.'[1] He told the story of the last months of Satyrus' life and pronounced a panegyric on his many virtues; then he again declared his conviction that this beloved brother was not lost in death. Though his words are not free from obscurity, they seem to suggest a belief that Satyrus was truly present, not merely as a haunting memory, but personally, as a living though disembodied spirit, with power to minister comfort and render assistance to his friends.

'Thou art present, I say, and art always before me; and with my whole mind and soul do I embrace thee, gaze on thee, speak to thee, kiss thee, grasp thee, whether in the quiet of the night or in the light of day, when thou dost vouchsafe to visit me and console my sorrow. And now the very nights, which in thy lifetime seemed irksome, because they denied us the power of looking on each other, and sleep itself, once hated as an interruption of our intercourse, have begun to be sweet, because they have restored thee to me. . . . Thus recently, when evening drew on, and I was complaining that thou didst not visit me in my rest, thou wert in truth all the time wholly and inseparably present with me; so that, as I lay with limbs bathed in sleep, but with mind awake for thee, thou didst live to me, and I said, "What is death, my brother?" For indeed thou wert not separated from me for a single moment; nay, thou art so present with me everywhere, that the enjoyment of each other, which we could not have always in this life, is now everywhere and always ours. . . . Therefore I hold thee, my brother, and neither death nor time shall tear thee from me. Tears themselves are sweet, and weeping itself is pleasant, for by these the ardent longing of the mind is assuaged and affection is soothed and quieted. For I cannot be without thee, or ever forget thee, or remember thee without tears. O bitter days, which show that our union is broken! O nights of tears, which reveal the loss of the gentle partner of my rest, of my inseparable companion! What agonies would you cause me, were it not that the image of my ever-present brother comes to me, were it not that the visions of my mind bring vividly before me him whom in the body I may look upon no more!'[2]

He implored the spirit of Satyrus to visit him often and lighten

[1] Ambros. *De Excessu Sat.* i. 6.
[2] Ibid. i. 72–4. Cf. his words concerning Valentinian, *De Obitu Val.* 41.

his sorrow,[1] and to hasten by his intercession the day when he should be called to rejoin him in the other world.[2] He also begged his help for Marcellina. 'Comfort her, thou who canst approach her soul and penetrate her mind. Let her perceive thy presence, let her feel that thou art not dead; that, being assured of thy merit and having experienced thy consolation, she may learn not to mourn for thee immoderately, since thou thyself didst warn her that thou wert not to be mourned for.'[3]

Having concluded his oration and offered a short prayer commending the 'blameless soul' to God,[4] Ambrose, in the presence of the people, uttered the last solemn *Vale*, and bestowed on the corpse the final kiss of peace.[5] The body was then consigned to a sepulchre in the Basilica Faustae, close to the tomb of the martyr St. Victor. The practice, which was still in vogue, of scattering flowers upon the tomb does not seem to have been approved by Ambrose;[6] but it is likely that he followed the usage, which was coming into fashion among Christian mourners, of making a distribution of alms to the poor.[7]

It was customary to commemorate the dead on the anniversary of the death;[8] sometimes also on stated days—the third and the thirtieth, or the seventh and the fortieth[9]—after the funeral. The Eucharist was celebrated, with intercession for the departed;[10] and in some cases, on one of these days, a commemorative oration was pronounced. On the seventh day after the funeral of Satyrus[11] a memorial service was held, and Ambrose delivered his second address on the death of his brother. In this discourse, which he had very carefully prepared and written out,[12] he dealt at considerable length with the subject of Death

---

[1] Id. *De Excessu Sat.* i. 75.

[2] Ibid. i. 79; ii. 135.     [3] Ibid. i. 77.

[4] Ibid. i. 80. Cf. the two prayers (*De Obitu Val.* 52–5, 80) introduced into the funeral oration on Valentinian II.

[5] Ibid. i. 78. The bestowal of the kiss of peace on the dead was forbidden by the Council of Auxerre, A.D. 578, c. 12.

[6] Id. *De Obitu Val.* 56.     [7] Hieron. *Ep.* 66. 5.

[8] Ambros. *De Excessu Sat.* ii. 5. Cf. Tertullian, *De Coron. Milit.* 3 'oblationes pro defunctis, pro natalitiis, annua die facimus'.

[9] Ambros. *De Obitu Theodos.* 3.

[10] For the offering of intercession for the departed, see Tertullian, *De Monogam.* 10; *De Coron. Milit.* 3; *De Exhort. Cast.* 11; Cyprian (ed. Hartel), *Epp.* 1. 2; 12. 2; 39. 3; Epiphan. *Haeres.* 75. 8; Ambros. *Ep.* 39. 4; Augustin. *Confess.* ix. 13; *De cura pro mort.* 6; *Enchirid.* 110.

[11] Ambros. *De Excessu Sat.* ii. 2.     [12] Ibid. ii. 42.

and Resurrection. His argument briefly is that death is not an evil and ought not to be lamented: first, because it is the law of nature and the common lot of all men,[1] secondly, because it brings release from the miseries of this life,[2] and thirdly, because of the sure and certain hope of the resurrection of the body and the life of the world to come.[3]

The epitaph of Satyrus, composed by Ambrose, runs as follows:

> Uranio Satyro supremum frater honorem
> Martyris ad laevam detulit Ambrosius.
> Haec meriti merces ut sacri sanguinis umor
> Finitimas penetrans adluat exuvias.'[4]

---

[1] Ambros. *De Excessu Sat.* ii. 7 ff.                     [2] Ibid. ii. 18 ff.

[3] Ibid. ii. 50 ff. For the details of Ambrose's teaching concerning Death and Resurrection, see below, chapter xxi, section 11.

[4] *C.I.L.* v, p. 617, n. 5; cf. De Rossi, *Bullet. Christ.* i (1863), p. 5.

## CHAPTER VIII

# AMBROSE'S ACTION AGAINST ARIANISM. HIS RELATIONS WITH THE EASTERN CHURCH

THE fourth century was an era of great intellectual activity, which, in the sphere of religion, expressed itself in endless formulations and counter-formulations of theological doctrine. Innumerable heresies flourished,[1] imperilling with their bewildering subtleties the faith even of the elect. To elaborate, to discuss, to defend or criticize such opinions was a fascinating occupation. Learned men devoted their leisure to collecting rare and recondite heresies, and cataloguing them in prodigious manuscripts. People of fashion gossiped about them, and in their salons the latest theory of the Deity was debated with hardly less zest than the newest topic of the turf or the most recent scandal of the green-room. Even the vulgar herd was interested. At Constantinople, at any rate, the very slaves and mechanics were expert theologians, and their hair-splitting distinctions in the matter of dogma delayed the business of the bazaars. 'If you ask a man for change', says a writer of the period, 'he will give you a piece of philosophy concerning the Begotten and the Unbegotten; if you inquire the price of a loaf, he replies, "The Father is greater and the Son inferior"; or if you ask whether the bath is ready, the answer you receive is that the Son was made out of nothing.'[2]

In the West, no doubt, the public interest in theological questions was neither so keen nor so widely diffused as in the East. Yet in the principal Western cities there was certainly a good deal of independent thinking on religious topics. At Rome there were many nonconformist societies; and in Milan—a rendezvous for strangers from every quarter of the world—all kinds of eccentric opinions circulated. Ambrose in his writings refers to many such opinions—some of them the tenets of

---

[1] Ambros. *De Incarnatione*, 35 'dies me citius defecerit quam nomina haereticorum diversarumque sectarum'.

[2] Gregor. Nyssen. *Orat. de deitate Filii et Spiritus Sancti* (Migne, *P.G.* xlvi, p. 557).

B b

decaying sects (e.g. the Marcionites[1] and Valentinians,[2] or the Sabellians[3]), others the propaganda of more flourishing denominations. Among the latter were Manichaeans,[4] who, in spite of persecution by the Government, were numerous in Italy; Novatianists, calling themselves 'The Pure', who challenged the Church's right to grant absolution to grievous sinners;[5] Eunomians or ultra-Arians, who maintained that the Son of God is a creature and essentially 'unlike' the Father;[6] compromising Arians, who were accustomed to describe the Son as 'like to the Father', and discreetly refrained from explaining wherein precisely the likeness consists;[7] Macedonians, nicknamed 'Contenders against the Spirit', who denied the proper Deity of the Holy Ghost; Photinians, who regarded the Person of Christ as essentially human;[8] and Apollinarians, who taught that in Christ the Logos took the place of the rational human mind, and some of whom further contended (though without the authority of their master) that the flesh of the Lord was not really formed from the Virgin but was pre-existent and of a celestial substance.[9] It is evident that even in the West all manner of fantastic speculations were in the air.

At the time of Ambrose's accession to the episcopate the most prominent opponents of the Catholic Church were the Arians, who with varying degrees of explicitness denied the true Divinity of the Son and of the Holy Spirit. Already, however, through-

---

[1] Referred to by Ambrose, *De Fide*, ii. 44; iii. 57; v. 105, 162; *De Incarn*. 8; *Ep*. 72. 10; *Hexaem*. i. 30; *De Paradiso*, 28; *Expos. ps. cxviii*, 13. 4; *Expos. ev. Luc*. viii. 13; *De Officiis*, i. 117.

[2] The Valentinians appear to have been at this time less numerous than the Marcionites. Ambrose refers to them, *De Fide*, ii. 44; v. 105; *De Incarn*. 8; *Hexaem*. i. 30; *Expos. ev. Luc*. viii. 41; *Epp*. 40 and 41.

[3] Referred to by Ambrose, *De Fide*, i. 6, 57; ii. 33, 80, 86, 118; iii. 12, 58, 126; v. 19, 104, 162; *De Spiritu*, i. 136; ii. 135, 142; iii. 117; *De Incarn*. 8; *De Paradiso*, 58; *Expos. ev. Luc*. i. 13; viii. 9, 13, 41; x. 21: *Expos. ps. cxviii*, 4. 25; *Ep*. 48. 4.

[4] Referred to by Ambrose, *De Fide*, i. 57; ii. 44; iii. 57; v. 104, 105; *De Incarn*. 8; *Hexaem*. i. 30; iii. 32; *Ep*. 72. 10; *Expos. ev. Luc*. viii. 13; *De Officiis*, i. 117.

[5] See Ambros. *De Poenitentia*, passim.

[6] These were not numerous in the West. Ambrose refers to them, *De Fide*, i. 44, 45, 57; *De Incarn*. 7; *Hexaem*. ii. 20; iii. 32; *De Officiis*, i. 117.

[7] It was with this form of Arianism that Ambrose was mainly concerned.

[8] Referred to by Ambrose, *De Fide*, i. 6, 57; ii. 117; iii. 58; iv. 29; v. 104; *De Spiritu*, i. 164; ii. 117; iii. 117, 129; *Hexaem*. iii. 32; *De Paradiso*, 58; *Expos. ev. Luc*. i. 13; v. 4; viii. 13; *De Obitu Theod*. 49; *Ep*. 48. 5.

[9] The Apollinarian doctrines are confuted by Ambrose in *De Incarnatione*; see also his references in *De Spiritu*, iii. 76–9; *Epp*. 14. 4; 46. 1 ff.; 48. 5.

out the greater part of the West this heresy had been eradicated. After the death of the martinet Emperor Constantius, who had badgered the Western bishops into signing the ambiguous formula of Rimini,[1] there had been a remarkable reaction. Gaul and Spain showed edifying alacrity in returning to the faith of Nicaea.[2] Southern Italy was solidly Catholic. In Northern Italy special efforts were made to extirpate the lingering remnants of the heresy. Eusebius of Vercelli, Hilary of Poitiers, and Philaster of Brescia toured through the northern provinces, restoring the orthodox faith.[3] When finally that foxy old Arian, Auxentius, died at Milan, the ultimate triumph of orthodoxy in this region was assured. 'After the death of Auxentius,' Jerome writes, 'when Ambrose was established at Milan, all Italy was converted to the right faith.'[4]

In Pannonia, however, and the Latin provinces near the Danube Arianism was still fairly strongly entrenched. Here the veteran Arian leaders, Ursacius Bishop of Singidunum (Belgrade) and Valens of Mursa, had shown considerable adroitness in managing the local episcopate; and here Germinius, Bishop of the very important see of Sirmium (Mitrovitz), staunchly upheld, though in its least offensive form, the Arian tradition. There is evidence that in these parts the orthodox were subjected to a certain amount of persecution. When Martin of Tours visited his home in Sabaria, and with impolitic vehemence denounced the 'perfidy' of the ecclesiastical authorities, he was publicly scourged and compelled to depart.[5] At Sirmium, in A.D. 366, three Catholic stalwarts—Heraclian, Firmian, and Aurelian—were thrown into prison. We have an interesting record of an interview which took place between them and the bishop. Germinius sat in his chair, surrounded by his clergy; the city magistrates and some of the general public were present.

---

[1] Ambrose, as a loyal upholder of the doctrine of Nicaea, expressed abhorrence of the Council of Rimini, which he inaccurately describes as having determined that 'Christ is a creature' (Ep. 21. 13 and 14; Serm. contr. Auxent. 25). He recognized, indeed, the orthodoxy of the first confession which the majority of the bishops at Rimini sent to Constantius, but 'what began well ended badly', since the Catholics, under imperial pressure, betrayed the faith (De Fide, i. 122; Ep. 21. 15; Expos. ev. Luc. v. 71).

[2] Id. Ep. 21.14.                    [3] See above, p. 65 with notes.

[4] Hieron. Chron. A.D. 378; cf. Ambros. De Fide, ii. 142 'Italia aliquando tentata, mutata nunquam'.

[5] Sulpicius, Vita Martini, 6.

Germinius began by flattering Heraclian. 'You have a good heart', said he, 'and are born of a decent family, and I have known you from a baby. Come, join our Church.' Being irritated, however, by the obstinacy of the prisoner, he ordered him to be struck on the mouth. He charged the people, if they should meet Heraclian anywhere, to blow out against him, as against a putrid corpse, because he was already spiritually dead. The priests and deacons shouted that the prisoners should be forced to anathematize Hilary of Poitiers and Eusebius of Vercelli. When they refused to do so, a cry was raised that they ought to be indicted before the Governor of Pannonia and have their heads taken off, because they were dividing the people into two parties and inciting them to riot. Germinius, however, had recovered his temper. 'No, no, my brothers', he cried; 'they do not understand what they are saying. If bishops have been led astray, how much more simple fellows like those before us here.'[1] Ambrose himself was in residence at Sirmium at this time, as an advocate in the Praetorian Praefect's Court, and it is not unlikely that he was present at the discussion.

This, then, was the situation in the early years of Ambrose's episcopate. In all parts of the West, except in the Danubian provinces, Arianism was dying out. The Emperor Valentinian I, though he had deliberately refrained from according official support to any particular religious party, had been himself a Catholic and had made Catholicism the religion of his Court at Trier. His son and successor, Gratian, who after his father's death became the senior Emperor in the West, was also a Catholic.[2] Thus there was reason to hope that the triumphs already won by orthodoxy over heresy would be consolidated. Danger threatened, however, from two quarters. In the first place, many of the barbarian soldiers serving in the Western armies, and in some cases holding important commands, were Arians. Secondly, Justina, the Arian mother of the child Emperor Valentinian II, clung to Arianism as a manageable and accommodating form of State religion, and did everything in her power to foster it in her son's Court at Sirmium.

---

[1] *Altercatio Heracliani laici cum Germinio episcopo Sirmiensi*, publ. by C. P. Caspari, *Kirchenhistorische Anecdota* (Christiania, 1883), i. pp. 131–47.

[2] Gratian's orthodoxy is effusively commended by Ambrose, *De Fide*, i. 2; ii. 139, 142, 143; *De Spiritu*, i. 19.

The part taken by Ambrose in effecting the complete and final overthrow of Arianism in the Western Empire must now be indicated.

In the spring of the year A.D. 378 the Emperor Gratian, on the eve of marching eastward to the help of Valens against the Goths, requested Ambrose, who had already acquired a reputation as defender and restorer of orthodoxy in his once Arian episcopal city, to write for him a treatise on the true faith.[1] This appears to have been the first direct contact between the young Emperor at Trier and the great Bishop of Milan.[2] At his father's Court Gratian had been brought up in the orthodox belief; but, though Ausonius was his tutor in literature, he does not seem to have received special theological instruction from any one.[3] He must have realized that, in any discussion of religious matters, he would certainly be no match for the learned and keen-witted Arian divines whom he would be likely to meet at the Courts of his brother and uncle, and therefore decided to apply to Ambrose for a little preparatory 'coaching' on the principal Catholic points and arguments.

Ambrose did not respond to the imperial demand immediately. Not long afterwards, however—perhaps in July at Sirmium—he had a personal interview with Gratian, who pressed him to comply with his request.[4] Accordingly, after his return to Milan, he put together 'hastily and summarily, and in rough rather than exact form',[5] two books[6]—the first two of his extant work *Concerning the Faith*—which, though admittedly inadequate as a comprehensive treatment of the subject, seemed sufficient for the Emperor's instruction at a time when his attention was absorbed by the operations of war.[7] They were probably composed in August–September, A.D. 378,[8] and

[1] Ambros. *De Fide*, i. 3.
[2] They may possibly have met in the summer of A.D. 376, when Gratian paid a hasty visit to Rome; but there is no evidence for this hypothesis.
[3] Ambros. *De Fide*, i. 2.
[4] Ibid. iii. 1. We know nothing more of this interview.
[5] Ibid. ii. 129.    [6] Ibid. iii. 1; *Ep.* i. 7.    [7] Id. *De Fide*, ii. 136.
[8] The prediction of victory over the barbarians (*De Fide*, i. 3; ii. 136–42) does not necessitate the conclusion that the work was written before the catastrophe of Hadrianople. Ambrose's point is that, just as the heresy of Valens had brought disaster on the Empire (ibid. ii. 139), so the faith of Gratian would bring good fortune. His description of the devastation of the various provinces by the barbarians (ibid. ii. 139–41) is strictly correct if applied to the great Gothic invasion after Hadrianople. Further the designation of Gratian as 'totius orbis Augustus'

were received by the youthful 'master of the whole world' with approbation.[1]

The months which followed were anxious ones for Ambrose. Bodies of refugees from beyond the Alps, fleeing before the Goths, crossed over into Italy. As many of them were Arians, Ambrose was under some concern lest they should infect the native population with their heretical opinions. He gave directions that the strangers should be carefully watched, and not allowed to mix too freely with the faithful. 'Let them remember what their perfidy has brought upon them; let them be quiet and follow the truth faith.' Those who expressed a desire to be received into the Catholic Church were to be dealt with kindly, but too much credence should not be given to their glib professions.[2]

In Milan itself there was trouble. The local Arians, emboldened, perhaps, by the augmentation of their numbers by Illyrian refugees, and taking advantage of the disturbances of the time, had the audacity to occupy a Catholic basilica. A complaint was, of course, laid before Gratian at Sirmium. But the Emperor, whatever his personal feelings may have been, felt unable to resist the strong counter-representations of the Arians by whom he was at the moment surrounded. He did not, indeed, allow the heretics at Milan to retain the church, but neither did he restore it to the Catholics; he sent an order to the Vicar of Italy that the building should be sequestrated.[3]

Further, it was probably about this time that Ambrose was annoyed by the activities of a certain Arian bishop named Julian Valens—not the celebrated Valens of Mursa, but a younger man —who had formerly been intruded by the Arians into the Pannonian see of Pettau. He was an odd and scandalous prelate. He had pro-Gothic sympathies, and when the barbarians invaded Pannonia after the victory of Hadrianople, he betrayed his episcopal city into their hands. He was impudent enough

(ibid. i. 1) accurately expresses the position of the young emperor after Hadrianople, but could hardly have been used if Valens had been still alive. I think, therefore, that the work must have been completed after the news of the catastrophe of 9 August and of the subsequent movements of the barbarians had been received in Milan—probably in September, A.D. 378.

[1] Ambros. *Ep.* i. 7.

[2] Ibid. 2. 27–9. This letter was written before Lent (*Ep.* 2, 27) in A.D. 379.

[3] Id. *De Spiritu,* i. 21. This took place, it seems likely, early in A.D. 379.

even to show himself in public, wearing a necklace and bracelets after the Gothic fashion. But the people of Pettau, furious at the pillage of their city, hounded the traitor out of the place. Thereupon he betook himself to Milan, where he gathered together an Arian congregation, for which he illegally ordained ministers.[1] The man was perhaps a little mad, and, if he had been by himself, would not have been taken very seriously. He was assisted, however, by the secret counsels of a much more capable person—the turbulent antipope Ursinus, who bore a grudge against Ambrose for having sided with his rival Damasus and gladly embraced an opportunity of paying off old scores.[2] All this Arian activity in his own city must have caused much embarrassment and distress to Ambrose. He himself was bitterly attacked by the heretics for having sold his Church plate for the redemption of captives taken by the barbarians.[3]

But in the course of the year A.D. 379 the situation improved. In the summer of this year, Gratian, having committed the care of the East to Theodosius, set out on his return journey to Gaul. He was at Aquileia early in July,[4] and thence passed to Milan, where he stayed until after the beginning of August.[5] Here he again met Ambrose, and there can be no question that he was profoundly impressed by the personality of the bishop. Of this we have two proofs. First—perhaps at the end of July—he spontaneously and of his own motion restored the sequestrated basilica to the Catholics. This act—the first definite rebuff to the Arians which Gratian had permitted himself—caused great delight to Ambrose, who did not hesitate to attribute the imperial change of attitude to the direct inspiration of the Holy Spirit.[6] Secondly, Gratian revoked an edict of toleration which he had issued at Sirmium, whereby (in the hope of restoring peace to the Eastern Churches) he had granted liberty of worship to all except Manichaeans, Photinians, and Eunomians (or extreme Arians); he now decreed that all heresies must for ever cease.[7] Such a

---

[1] Ambros. *Ep.* 10. 9 and 10.      [2] Id. *Ep.* 11. 3.
[3] Id. *De Officiis*, ii. 70, 136.
[4] Cod. Theod. xiii. 1. 11.      [5] Ibid. xvi. 5. 5.
[6] Ambros. *De Spiritu*, i. 19–21. Perhaps Ambrose was alluding to the restoration of the basilica and its effect on his heretical adversaries in Milan in *Ep.* 1. 2, when he wrote 'reddidisti mihi quietem ecclesiae, perfidorum ora, atque utinam et corda, clausisti'.
[7] Socrates, *H.E.* v. 2; Sozomen. *H.E.* vii. 1; Theodoret. *H.E.* v. 2; Cod. Theod. xvi. 5. 5.

sudden and total abandonment of the policy of religious neutrality, which he had inherited from his father and which he had himself hitherto scrupulously observed, seems almost inexplicable, unless it be attributed to the powerful influence of Ambrose.

Gratian resumed his journey, and by the middle of September was again at Trier.[1] The deep impression made on him by the Bishop of Milan, who had induced him to cast the weight of his imperial authority decisively on the side of Catholic orthodoxy, did not wear off. As he meditated by the banks of the Moselle on the complicated political-religious problems which confronted him, he grew ever more conscious of his need of a continuance of such experienced guidance. As a result of these reflections, he wrote—probably in January, A.D. 380[2]—an autograph letter to Ambrose, inviting him to join him at Trier. The short letter—the only one of Gratian which we possess—runs as follows:

'I greatly long to enjoy the bodily presence of him whom I ever bear in mind, and with whom I am present in spirit. Therefore hasten to me, religious priest of God, to teach me the doctrine of the true faith. It is not that I am eager for controversy, or that I wish to apprehend God in words rather than with my mind; but I would have my heart opened more fully to receive the abiding revelation of His Godhead. For He will teach me, whom I deny not, whom I confess to be my God and my Lord, not cavilling at the fact that He took upon Himself a created nature like my own. I confess that I can add nothing to the glory of Christ. But by glorifying the Son I would fain commend myself to the Father also; for in God I can apprehend no jealousy. I will not imagine that His Godhead can be exalted by my poor words of praise. Weak and frail, I glorify Him according to my powers, not according to His Divine Majesty. I request you to send me a copy of the same treatise which you gave me some while ago, enlarging it with an orthodox dissertation on the Holy Spirit. Prove, both by Scripture and by reason, that He is God. God keep you for many years, my father and servant of the Eternal God whom we worship, even Jesus Christ.'[3]

[1] Cod. Theod. xiii. 3. 12.

[2] Most authorities place this letter of Gratian and Ambrose's reply in A.D. 379, before the Emperor's stay in Milan in July–August of that year. But J.-R. Palanque has shown convincingly that the contents of the documents are best explained on the assumption that they were written, not before, but after the meeting of Gratian and Ambrose in Milan in A.D. 379 (op. cit., pp. 67 ff., 501, 502).

[3] *Gratiani Epistola*, prefixed to Ambrose's Letters. The letter was written by the Emperor with his own hand (Ambros. *Ep.* i. 3).

The invitation to Trier must have been embarrassing to Ambrose, who, even for the sake of forming the religious opinions of the young sovereign, could hardly have been willing, at so critical a time, to absent himself from Milan for an indefinite period. Circumstances, however, extricated him from his difficulty. In February Gratian, having been informed of the illness of Theodosius at Thessalonica and of a fresh outbreak of the Goths,[1] left Trier in haste, and, returning to Italy, established himself at Aquileia in the middle of March. To this place and at this date Ambrose forwarded his reply to the imperial letter.[2] There was now no need to excuse himself from visiting Trier; he had to apologize, however, for not having gone to meet the Emperor at some point on his journey to Aquileia. He pleaded that his failure to do this was due partly to modesty and partly to the pressure of 'episcopal duties' (doubtless those in connexion with Lent); certainly not to lack of affection. He had daily been informed of Gratian's route, and had been with him continually in thought and prayer.[3] He expressed, in terms of courtier-like flattery, his admiration of the Emperor's letter ('I have never read, I have never heard, anything so good'),[4] forwarded the two books asked for, but demanded time for the composition of a new work on the Holy Spirit.[5] Finally he promised that he would come himself speedily;[5] and it is likely that he did actually visit Gratian at Aquileia immediately after Easter in A.D. 380.[6]

In this year Ambrose was busy preaching against the Arians. The two books which he had written for Gratian had been severely criticized,[7] and Palladius of Ratiaria had even published a refutation of them.[8] In face of the cavils of the heretics, he felt himself obliged to enter on a more elaborate defence of the Catholic position. It was probably at the end of the year that he completed his famous treatise *Concerning the Faith*.[9] The work consists of the two *libelli* sent to Gratian supplemented by three new books compiled out of sermons preached to the people

---

[1] See above, p. 174.          [2] Ambros. *Ep.* 1.          [3] Id. *Ep.* 1. 1.
[4] Id. *Ep.* 1. 4. Yet in this very flattering letter he protests, 'nihil hic adulationis est, quam tu non requiris, ego alienam nostro duco officio' (ibid. 2).
[5] Id. *Ep.* 1. 7.          [6] J.-R. Palanque, op. cit., p. 71.
[7] Id. *De Fide*, iii. 2.
[8] J. Zeiller, *Les Origines chrétiennes dans les provinces danubiennes de l'Empire romain*, Paris, 1918, pp. 489–90.
[9] On *De Fide* see below, chapter xxii.

during the preceding months. It was directed, not against any particular form of Arianism, but against Arianism in general.[1] Of this heresy Ambrose certainly had the worst opinion. It seemed to him to have 'collected poisons from every heresy'.[2] Its adherents were 'not so much men as beings outwardly human, but inwardly filled with the madness of beasts'.[3] They had no right to call themselves Christians.[4] They resembled the Jews, but were worse than the Jews;[5] they resembled the pagans, but were worse than the pagans;[6] they were more blasphemous than Antichrist[7] and more insolent in unbelief than the devil himself.[8]

In confuting the Arian doctrines Ambrose based himself frankly on authority. He had a profound distrust of the dialectic in which the Arian controversialists excelled.[9] Hence, instead of attempting to philosophize about the mysteries of the faith, he was content to confront his opponents with a massive array of Scriptural testimonies.[10] 'I would not, holy Emperor, have you rely on argument and our disputation; let us inquire of the Scriptures, let us inquire of the apostles, of the prophets, of Christ.'[11] By the 'oracles of the Lord' the faith is established.[12] True, the Arians also appealed to the Scriptures; but in their interpretation of the sacred writings they erred in two ways— they took expressions, obviously metaphorical, in the superficial literal sense, and founded arguments upon them;[13] and they laid exaggerated stress on isolated phrases or sentences which seemed to favour their contentions, without investigating their meaning in the light of the contexts. With reference to the latter error, Ambrose insisted, quite in the manner of a modern commentator, that the true meaning of a text of Scripture can be ascertained only by careful and critical examination of the whole passage in which it occurs.[14] He was convinced that if the favourite proof-texts of the Arians were thus judiciously investigated, they would be found to support, not the Arian but the

---

[1] Ambros. *De Fide*, i. 44–6.  
[2] Ibid. ii. 135.  
[3] Ibid. ii. 15.  
[4] Id. *De Spiritu*, iii. 131.  
[5] Id. *De Fide*, ii. 130; iii. 38; cf. *Serm. contr. Auxent.* 31.  
[6] Id. *De Fide*, i. 85; v. 119.  
[7] Ibid. ii. 135.  
[8] Ibid. iii. 32; v. 230.  
[9] See above, pp. 14, 15.  
[10] Ambros. *De Fide*, i. 4.  
[11] Ibid. i. 43.  
[12] Ibid. ii. 12.  
[13] Ibid. i. 66, 67; iii. 37; v. 95; cf. *De Spiritu*, iii. 17, 18.  
[14] Ibid. ii. 16, 42; iv. 143; v. 49, 93, 115, 120, 160.

Catholic propositions—the true Godhead of the Son, and His consubstantiality, co-equality, and co-eternity with the Father.[1]

In spite of certain obvious defects (more especially in arrangement) Ambrose's *De Fide* is a powerful piece of polemic and a really valuable contribution to constructive theology. It may be admitted that the author is less than fair to his opponents. Being utterly out of sympathy with them, he fails to appreciate the reasons which led them to their conclusions, and even misapprehends the import of the conclusions themselves. He also brings against them rash accusations, e.g. of tampering with the sacred text.[2] His own views, however, are stated vigorously and incisively; his arguments are usually well drawn; and his method of confuting his adversaries by demonstrating the absurdities logically involved in their position is singularly effective. One need not dissent from the word used by Prosper, when he said that Ambrose wrote on behalf of the Catholic faith 'sublimely'.[3]

In the autumn of A.D. 380 Gratian, after inspecting the Danube frontier, returned to Gaul. It was perhaps about this time—i.e. in the later part of A.D. 380, though the date cannot be fixed with certainty[4]—that the incident of the Sirmium election occurred, whereby Ambrose was brought into conflict with the Arian Empress Justina. Germinius, the artful old Bishop of Sirmium, who had so cleverly and successfully maintained the cause of moderate Arianism, had died; and the Empress was naturally anxious to secure the see for a man of the same religious views. The matter was indeed of vital importance. Sirmium was the capital of Western Illyricum, the seat of Valentinian's Court, and the chief centre from which Arianism was industriously propagated through the Danubian provinces. If the heresy was to continue to flourish in this area, it was essential that the successor of Germinius should be, like him, a

---

[1] On Ambrose's Christological teaching, see below, chapter xxi.
[2] Ambros. *De Fide*, ii. 135; v. 193; cf. *De Spiritu*, ii. 46; iii. 59.
[3] Prosper, *Chron.* A.D. 380.
[4] Most of the authorities place the consecration of Anemius in A.D. 380; though J. Zeiller, *Les Origines chrétiennes dans les provinces danubiennes de l'Empire romain*, pp. 308 ff. would date it some four years earlier. In any case Anemius must have been consecrated before the Council of Aquileia in A.D. 381, which he attended as Bishop of Sirmium.

convinced and energetic Arian. In Sirmium itself, however, there was a strong Catholic party, which, notwithstanding the machinations of the Empress and her Arian Court, was determined to carry the election of a good Catholic, named Anemius. The situation was not unlike that at Milan at the time of the death of Auxentius. Ambrose realized that the fate of orthodoxy in the whole region of the Danubian provinces was at stake, and, in great anxiety, went himself to Sirmium to superintend the election and consecration. He found the city in commotion. The women especially, whose sympathies were with the Empress, were extremely excited. In the cathedral a large crowd gathered. It was rumoured that mischief was intended—that Ambrose was to be seized and ejected from the basilica, and that a nominee of the Court was then to be elected and consecrated by some heretical bishops who were in attendance. Ambrose, however, paid no attention to this report. He proceeded to the church and took his place in the *tribunal*. At the same moment an Arian female, one of the sacred virgins, dashed up the steps and laid hold of his robes. She endeavoured to drag the bishop to the part of the church reserved for women, where some of her companions were waiting to give him a beating and throw him out. The congregation was in tumult; but Ambrose remained calm. He said sternly to the virago, 'Though I am unworthy of the greatness of the priesthood, it ill becomes you or your profession to lay hands upon a priest, be he who he may. You ought to fear the judgement of God, lest some evil happen to you.' Awed by his voice and manner, she relaxed her hold and slunk away, and the proceedings were not further interrupted. Curiously enough, the woman died on the following day; and Ambrose himself, whom she had so grossly insulted, officiated at her funeral. The event made a salutary impression on the Arians, who dared not afterwards persist in their opposition to the new bishop. Thus, by the establishment of a vigorous and enthusiastic Catholic in the influential see of Sirmium, a very important step was taken towards the ultimate suppression of heresy throughout the region of the Lower Danube. Ambrose, however, by his intervention in this affair, had provoked the malevolent resentment of Justina, of which he was destined to have unpleasant experience later on.[1]

---

[1] Paulinus, *Vita Ambros.* 11.

The spring of the following year, A.D. 381,[1] was marked by another valuable treatise from Ambrose's pen. As has been stated, the Emperor Gratian had requested him to write something on the Holy Spirit, and Ambrose in reply had demanded time for consideration. For some months he had kept the subject in mind, and in A.D. 380 he had attended a Council held by Damasus at Rome, in which the orthodox faith concerning the Holy Spirit was discussed, and the heresy of the Macedonians, the 'Contenders against the Spirit', was anathematized.[2] At last, probably in April, A.D. 381, he published a work in three books, *Concerning the Holy Spirit*.[3] It was an attack on the Macedonians, who, whether or not they adopted the Arian view with regard to the Second Person of the Trinity, were at any rate Arian in their doctrine of the Holy Spirit, whom they affirmed to be a creature, inferior both to the Father and to the Son, the chief of ministering spirits.[4] In maintaining against these heretics the true Divinity of the Holy Ghost, Ambrose borrowed extensively from Greek authorities—especially Didymus and Basil. The result did not please Jerome, who wrote, with evident relish, a slashing criticism of the book. He compared the author (though he did not name him) to a daw tricked out in other birds' plumage, and rudely accused him of having translated good Greek into bad Latin: the book itself he characterized as 'flaccid and spiritless, sleek and pretty, decorated with purple patches, but defective in its logic, and lacking that restrained and manly force which compels the assent of the reader even against his will'.[5] Jerome's criticism, however, is extravagantly severe. If Ambrose borrowed largely from the writings of the Greeks, he at any rate did so with discrimination, selecting his materials carefully, altering the order and arrangement, and

---

[1] On the date of *De Spiritu*, see below, chapter xxii.

[2] Vigilius, *Constit. pro damnatione trium capit.* 26.

[3] A written treatise, not (as *De Fide*, iii–v) composed of sermons.

[4] The Macedonians were called after Macedonius, the semi-Arian bishop of Constantinople, who taught that the Holy Spirit 'had no claim to the Divine honours which were attributed to the Son, being but a minister and a servant, as the holy angels may without offence be called' (Sozomen. *H.E.* iv. 27; cf. Socrates, *H.E.* ii. 45).

[5] Rufinus, *Apol. adv. Hieron.* ii. 23–5. Jerome had little admiration for Ambrose's literary activities. Cf. his biting notice, *De Vir. Illustr.* 124, 'Ambrose, Bishop of Milan, is writing to the present day. Of whom, since he is alive, I will reserve my judgement, lest I be blamed either for flattery or for speaking the truth.'

adding a good deal of his own. Nor can his performance fairly be condemned as feeble. The logic is, perhaps, less cogent than that of Didymus, and the exposition is marred by redundancies and other blemishes. Yet the treatise furnishes a clear, straightforward statement of the Catholic doctrine of the Holy Spirit, and is peculiarly important as the first attempt made in the West to deal systematically and exhaustively with this great topic.[1]

At Easter, in this year A.D. 381, Gratian returned to Milan, and henceforth made this city, instead of Trier, his principal place of residence. It was some time after the transference of the Court to Italy that an event took place which resulted ultimately in the publication of another notable treatise, *On the Sacrament of the Lord's Incarnation.*[2] Two Arian chamberlains of the Emperor took exception to certain expressions which Ambrose had used in a sermon on the Incarnation, and challenged him to answer them publicly on the following day in the Portian Basilica. The Bishop accepted the challenge and kept the appointment. The courtiers, however, instead of presenting themselves at the church, went out driving in a travelling-carriage, and meeting with an accident were killed.[3] Meanwhile Ambrose, knowing nothing of the death of his challengers, imagined that they were purposely delaying their arrival, with the object of confusing him by a sudden entrance in the middle of his discourse.[4] That he might not keep the congregation waiting, he began to preach; but that the chamberlains might have a chance of hearing his reply, he did not attack his main subject at once. He expounded the Bible story of the sacrifice of Cain and Abel, which had just been read as the 'prophetic lesson' in the Mass, and showed that God's words to Cain were applicable to all heretics.[5] Then, finding that the chamberlains did not appear, he commenced his real sermon, which consisted in part of a refutation of the Arians who denied our Lord's proper Divinity,[6] and in part of a refutation of the Docetae and Apollinarians, who denied His true Humanity.[7] Afterwards, when he put his discourse into form for publication, he added some extra

---

[1] For Ambrose's teaching on the Holy Spirit, see below, chapter xxi, section 3.
[2] On the date of this work, see below, chapter xxii.
[3] Paulinus, *Vita Ambros.* 18.
[4] Ambros. *De Incarn.* 1.
[5] Ibid. 2–12.
[6] Ibid. 13 ff.
[7] Ibid. 46–78.

paragraphs, designed to answer an objection emanating from the Arian bishop Palladius, which had been referred to him by Gratian. The objection was, 'How can the Unbegotten and the Begotten be of one Nature and Substance?'[1]

Hitherto Ambrose had achieved several isolated victories over the Arians; the time had now arrived to consolidate his conquests. His aim was to strike a blow which would effectively crush the lingering remnants of the heresy in Northern Italy and Illyricum. This object, with Gratian's assistance, he did actually accomplish by means of the Council of Aquileia.[2]

The origin of this Council was as follows. In the later months of A.D. 378 Gratian had received an appeal from two Danubian bishops, Palladius of Ratiaria (Artcher in Bulgaria) and Secundianus of Singidunum (Belgrade), who, being notorious Arians, were threatened with deprivation of their sees. These prelates requested the Emperor to convoke an Oecumenical Council for the elucidation of points in dispute between themselves and their Catholic adversaries—hoping, no doubt, to secure acceptance for their views by means of the votes of the Arianizing bishops of the East. Gratian granted the petition; but the troubles of the time caused the matter to be deferred. In September, A.D. 380, however, Palladius had an interview with the Emperor at Sirmium,[3] and it was arranged that a 'General and Full Council' should assemble at Aquileia for a

---

[1] Ambros. *De Incarn.* 79 ff.; cf. F. Kauffmann, *Aus der Schule des Wulfila* (Strassburg, 1899), p. xxxviii.

[2] For the Acts of the Council see Labbe, *Conc.* ii. 979 ff. They are also printed in the Benedictine ed. of Ambrose's Letters, between letters 8 and 9. The Acts are found in a work ascribed to Vigilius of Thapsus; and P. F. Chifflet (*Vindic. Opp. Vigilii*, p. 37) suggested that they were fabricated by Vigilius. But it is inconceivable that Vigilius should have been rash enough to attempt to pass off a forgery or part forgery as the Acts of a Council, the genuine records of which must have been circulated, and were doubtless still preserved in the *scrinia* of the Western Churches. Chifflet's view has been refuted by Tillemont (*Mém.* x, p. 738, n. 15) and Fuchs (*Biblioth. der Kirchenvers.* ii, p. 433). Notwithstanding the suspicion of J. Langen (*Geschichte der röm. Kirche*, i, p. 510), the Acts must be accepted as genuine. The existing text, however, is both corrupt and defective. After section 64 there appears to be a lacuna; and the abrupt termination suggests that the concluding portion of the record (containing the latter part of the examination of Secundianus, and the decision of the bishops concerning him and Attalus) has been lost. If the Acts are genuine, there seems to be no valid reason for doubting the genuineness of the letters written on behalf of the Council (G. Rauschen, op. cit., pp. 481, 482). That the writer was Ambrose is unproved, but probable. On the Council, see also the *Dissertatio Maximini contra Ambrosium* in F. Kauffmann, *Aus der Schule des Wulfila.*

[3] *Gesta Concil. Aquil.* 10.

discussion on controverted questions of dogma. This was not at all acceptable to Ambrose. Although he wished for a Council, to complete the work of suppressing heresy in Italy and Illyricum, he was far from wishing for the sort of Council that Palladius desired. He saw the danger of a theological discussion in which Eastern bishops participated. What he wanted was, not a debate on matters of faith, but a trial of heretics, conducted by Western judges whose verdict on unorthodox persons and views could safely be relied on. He accordingly represented to Gratian that it was unnecessary to order a multitude of bishops to come at great inconvenience and expense from the most distant parts of the Roman world to Aquileia, for the purpose of settling a comparatively simple affair;[1] it would be enough if the bishops of the Praefecture of Italy were convoked, the rest being permitted to attend or not as they thought fit.[2] By such argument he persuaded the Emperor to modify his original plan. Eventually some thirty-two bishops assembled at Aquileia. Most of them came from Upper Italy and the Diocese of Pannonia; the bishops of Gaul and Africa were represented; no one arrived from Rome, nor yet from Spain and Britain. The Eastern bishops did not take advantage of the 'permission' to attend; but the presbyter Evagrius who signed the Acts may perhaps be identified with Evagrius of Antioch. All at the Council, except Palladius and Secundianus, were orthodox in faith. Valerian, Bishop of Aquileia, was the nominal president, but it was Ambrose who really directed the business. He had got exactly the sort of Council he wanted, and the game was now in his own hands.

After Easter (28 March, A.D. 381), during the month of April, the bishops slowly assembled at Aquileia. While they were waiting for late comers, they held some preliminary discussions with Palladius and Secundianus, in the course of which, since no records were taken, the heretics gave frank expression to their 'sacrilegious' opinions.[3] At last, after a week or two had been wasted in desultory and inconclusive conversations, Palladius

---

[1] *Gesta Concil. Aquil.* 4; cf. Ambros. *Ep.* 10. 2 and 3. Yet the fiction that the Council was Oecumenical was not dropped; see *Ep.* 13. 4.

[2] *Gesta. Concil. Aquil.* 3. 7, 8; cf. Ambros. *Ep.* 10. 1. It should be noted that the sees of Palladius and Secundianus belonged ecclesiastically to the West (*Gesta Concil. Aquil.* 7; Ambros. *Epp.* 11. 1; 12. 3).

[3] *Gesta. Concil. Aquil.* 2.

himself suggested that the Council should sit formally in three days' time.[1] Accordingly on a certain day, probably in May, A.D. 381,[2] the bishops assembled at daybreak[3] in the small sacristy of the cathedral.[4] When Palladius entered, he said, 'We come as Christians to Christians.'[5] The bishops' seats were arranged in a circle, in the midst of which was a throne supporting an open copy of the Gospels; copies of the Pauline Epistles and of the other Scriptures were at hand for reference.[6] Shorthand-writers were in attendance to take a report of the proceedings.[7]

First of all, the imperial rescript, addressed to the Praetorian Praefect of Italy, in virtue of which the Council was held, was read by a deacon.[8] Then Ambrose proposed that a notoriously heretical document—a letter of Arius to Alexander of Alexandria, containing a clear and unambiguous exposition of his doctrine—should be used as a test, Palladius being invited to indicate his agreement or disagreement with the propositions therein set forth.[9] The letter was read. Ambrose next addressed himself to the examination of Palladius. Here the ex-magistrate was in his element. He skilfully turned the Council into a heresy-trial, and himself played the double part of public prosecutor and principal judge.

Palladius saw his danger, and immediately interposed an objection to the constitution of the Council. The Emperor, he said quite truly, had promised an Oecumenical Council, whereas this was simply a packed Italian-Illyrian synod; he claimed the right to reserve his defence for a future Council in which

[1] Ambros. *Ep.* 10. 4: *Gesta Concil. Aquil.* 10, 12, 42.

[2] The *Gesta Concil. Aquil.* 1 give as the date of the plenary sitting of the Council 3 September A.D. 381 ('iii non. Sept.' being the true reading). But the evident ignorance of the Fathers of Aquileia (shown both in the *Gesta* and in Ambros. *Ep.* 12) of the Council of Constantinople (May–July A.D. 381) is incomprehensible if this date be right; while the statement in *Ep.* 13. 4 that the Fathers of Constantinople were aware (in June) that Maximus the Cynic had appealed to the Council of Aquileia is sheer nonsense if the latter Council did not sit till September. I therefore follow J.-R. Palanque in abandoning the traditional date, and placing the arrival of the bishops and the preliminary discussions at Aquileia in April, A.D. 381; the plenary session of the Council and *Epp.* 9. 10 and 11 in May; *Ep.* 12, the arrival of Maximus, and the conclusion of the Council in June; and *Epp.* 13 and 14 in the autumn (op. cit., pp. 504–6).

[3] Ambros. *Ep.* 10. 5.

[4] *Gesta Concil. Aquil.* 1; cf. *Dissert. Maximin.* 89.          [5] *Gesta Concil. Aquil.* 12.

[6] Ibid. 5.          [7] Ibid. 2, 34.          [8] Ibid. 3, 4.          [9] Ibid. 5.

the Eastern episcopate should be represented.[1] Ambrose retorted that the Eastern bishops had been given formal permission to attend, but it was not customary for the Easterns to take part in Western Councils.[2] He urged Palladius to withdraw his objection and express his opinion candidly on the heretical statements in Arius's letter.[3] Arius had asserted that the Father is alone eternal, alone without beginning, alone true, alone immortal, alone wise, alone good, alone mighty, Judge of all.[4] These statements were taken in order, and Palladius was pressed to condemn them or else defend them from the Scriptures. But no plain, unequivocal answers could be extracted from him. He fenced and quibbled; complained that the records were not being taken fairly;[5] and protested again and again that he reserved his defence for a 'full Council'.[6] It was impossible to bring him to the point. For example, when asked if the Son of God is 'very God', he replied, 'Since the Apostle says that Christ is God over all, can any one deny that He is very Son of God?' Ambrose refused to accept this answer; would Palladius admit that the Son of God is 'very Lord'? He responded, 'When I call Him very Son, what more is needed?' Eusebius of Bologna said, 'According to the faith of all and the Catholic profession, Christ is very God; do you assent to that?' Palladius repeated, 'He is very Son of God.' Eusebius pointed out that Christian men are also sons of God, though only by adoption, and asked, 'Do you confess that the very Son of God is very Lord essentially and according to His Divine Generation?' 'I call Him very Son of God, only-begotten', snapped Palladius. Eusebius then inquired, 'Do you think that it is contrary to the Scriptures to designate Christ very God?' Palladius was at first silent; but, being urged to reply, he at last confessed his faith in Christ's 'true Divinity'. The answer was obviously evasive, and again he was pressed with the question, 'Is Christ very God according to the faith of all and the catholic profession? Or, in your opinion, is he not very God?' But he would say no more than 'He is the Power of our God'.[7]

So the interrogation went on through the long hours of the

---

[1] *Gesta Concil. Aquil.* 6.                    [2] Ibid. 7, 8.                    [3] Ibid. 9, 11.
[4] Ibid. 17, 27, 28, 31, 33; cf. Ambros. *Ep.* 10. 5; *Dissert. Maximin.* 100–8.
[5] Ibid. 34, 43, 46; cf. *Dissert. Maximin.* 19, 21, 97.
[6] Ibid. 12, 29, 32, 43, 48, 52, 54.                    [7] Ibid. 17–21.

morning. Palladius declared more than once that he 'did not follow Arius', that he 'knew nothing of Arius'; but he refused to condemn the statements in Arius's letter, nor would he assent to the counter-statements proposed to him by the Council. The discussion became heated. At one time, irritated beyond endurance by the equivocation of the accused, Ambrose burst out, 'Anathema to him who will not explain his faith freely', and the bishops echoed, 'Anathema.'[1] At another time, when they were dealing with the question of the Son's equality with the Father, one of the bishops exclaimed, 'The blasphemies of Arius are much lighter than those of Palladius.' Palladius sprang up in uncontrollable agitation, and seemed about to rush from the church. The bishop called out, 'Palladius has risen because he sees that he is to be convicted by the clear testimonies of the Scriptures—indeed, he has already been convicted!' The heretic thereupon flung himself back into his chair, vociferating, 'The Father is greater.' He then propounded an Arian view of the Son's relation to the Father.[2] At a later stage he made a personal attack on Ambrose. 'I charge you with impiety', he cried; 'I refuse to have you as my judge; you are a wicked man.' Sabinus of Piacenza asked, 'With what impieties do you reproach our brother and fellow bishop, Ambrose? State them.' Palladius said, 'I have told you already I will answer in a full Council and with arbiters present.' Ambrose said angrily, 'I am perfectly willing to be confuted and convicted in an assembly of my brethren. State what I have said impiously. But you think me impious because I affirm what is pious.' Valerian of Aquileia said, 'Do not press Palladius so much; he cannot confess our truths with sincerity. He knows that he is guilty of two heresies; for he was ordained by the Photinians and condemned with them, and now he is going to be condemned more fully as an Arian.' 'Prove it', cried Palladius. 'You have reproached me with impiety', Ambrose retorted; 'prove that.' He added, 'Condemn the impiety of Arius.' Palladius gave no answer, and Eusebius said, 'He who does not condemn Arius is like him, and may rightly be called a heretic.' There were murmurs from all the bishops, 'Anathema to Palladius.'[3]

Towards the end of his examination Palladius demanded an

---

[1] *Gesta Concil. Aquil.* 26.
[2] Ibid. 38 ff.; cf. Ambros. *Ep.* 10. 6 and 7.          [3] Ibid. 48–50.

adjournment of the Council over the following Sunday, that each side might appoint some laymen of rank to act as arbitrators, and might also bring its own reporters to take down the questions and answers. 'Bishops ought to judge laymen', said Ambrose severely, 'not laymen bishops.' 'Let there be umpires and reporters on both sides', Palladius insisted. Ambrose glanced round the indignant assembly; very adroitly he seized the opportunity of terminating a discussion which threatened to drag on endlessly.

'Although Palladius has been convicted of many impieties', he said, 'yet we should blush that a person who claims to be a bishop should appear to have been condemned by laymen; and on this very ground and in this very point he deserves condemnation, because he wishes to submit to the judgement of laymen. In consideration of what we have to-day heard Palladius confessing and of what he has refused to condemn, I pronounce him unworthy of the episcopal office, and hold that he ought to be deprived thereof, in order that a Catholic may be consecrated in his room.'

All the bishops shouted, 'Anathema to Palladius!' Ambrose reminded them that the Emperor had committed to them the decision of the case, and invited them to condemn the heretic. 'We all condemn him', they clamoured. 'Let him be accounted anathema!'[1] Then the individual prelates, one after the other, gave their verdicts. Valerian, the president of the Council, voted first. When he declared his opinion that Palladius, by refusing to condemn the blasphemies of Arius, had proved himself an Arian, and ought as such to be cut off from the fellowship of bishops, the heretic exclaimed with a sneer, 'You have begun to play; play on! Without an Eastern Council we do not answer you.'[2] Anemius of Sirmium next pronounced his judgement, and the rest followed in order.[3] Thus the case of Palladius was disposed of.

The Council then proceeded to deal with Secundianus. Hitherto this bishop had preserved an impenetrable silence. During the latter part of the examination of Palladius he had withdrawn, but now returned to the Council. The question was put to him, 'Do you say that our Lord Jesus Christ, the Son of God, is or is not very God?' But he would admit no more

---

[1] *Gesta Concil. Aquil.* 47, 51–3.     [2] Ibid. 54.
[3] Ibid. 55–64. The sentences of twenty-five of the bishops are given in the *Gesta.*

than 'He is very Son of God, very only-begotten Son of God'.
'Is the very Son of God also very God?' demanded Ambrose.
Secundianus objected that the expression was not found in the
Scriptures: 'that He is very God is not written'. Again and
again he was asked, 'Is the Son of God very God?' But in the
end all that could be got from him was 'I say that He was
begotten of the Father; I say to all that He was very begotten'.[1]
He also was condemned and deposed from the episcopate; and
a presbyter of Pettau, named Attalus—a disciple of Julian
Valens—was deposed from the priesthood.[2] These were the
only heretics present and sentenced; for the rule of the Church
was not to condemn persons in absence and unheard.[3] The sitting of the Council terminated at one o'clock.[4]

After this business had been concluded, the bishops did not
immediately quit Aquileia. First it was necessary to draw up
a letter, addressed formally to the three Emperors but really
meant only for Gratian, wherein an attempt was made to justify
the revised constitution of the Council, a summary of the proceedings was given, and a request was made that the sentence
of deposition passed on the heretics might be executed by the
secular arm; the authority of the State was also invoked to expel
Julian Valens from Milan and to suppress the meetings of some
Photinians within the walls of Sirmium.[5] The letter, with its
very discreet and cautious phrasing, was almost certainly composed by Ambrose. While they were waiting for the reply to
this document, the bishops, under Ambrose's direction, occupied themselves with other matters—the malicious activities of
the antipope Ursinus,[6] the dissensions in the Eastern Church[7]—
and finally separated (it seems likely) in June after authorizing
Ambrose with the bishops of Upper Italy to continue certain
negotiations with Theodosius touching the Oriental sees.

The Council of Aquileia marks the victory of Catholicism
over Arianism, so far as the Western Empire was concerned.
In one of the conciliar documents it is stated that practically all

---

[1] *Gesta Concil. Aquil.* 65–75; cf. 28. Only the beginning of the examination has
been preserved.
[2] Ambros. *Ep.* 10. 9; cf. *Gesta Concil. Aquil.* 44.
[3] Ambros. *Ep.* 14. 4 and 5.                                    [4] Id. *Ep.* 10. 5.
[5] Id. *Ep.* 10. That the requests of the Council were granted is evident from the
thanks expressed in *Ep.* 12. 1 and 2.
[6] Id. *Ep.* 11.                                                   [7] Id. *Ep.* 12.

the Western bishops now held the faith of Nicaea;[1] in another, that in two corners only of the West, where Palladius and Secundianus had their sees, were murmurs raised against the faith, whereas elsewhere 'through all territories and districts and village departments as far as the Ocean, the communion of the faithful remains one and unpolluted'.[2] Again, in a letter written from Milan in the autumn of A.D. 381 it is alleged that Italy, Gaul, and Africa were peacefully settled in orthodoxy.[3] Even the Danubian provinces, where Arianism had so obstinately maintained its ground, became gradually reconverted to the Catholic faith. Those few bishops who still remained Arian, warned by the fate of Palladius and Secundianus, henceforth prudently kept themselves and their opinions in the background; and as they died off, their places were occupied by Catholics. Ultimately the heresy was compelled to seek a home among the newly converted barbarians outside the Roman boundaries. Thus, within a decade of his elevation to the episcopate, Ambrose had the satisfaction of witnessing the restoration of Nicene orthodoxy in practically all parts of the Western Empire. Only Justina, with her supple courtiers and barbarian mercenaries, still clung desperately to a creed which all sensible people recognized to be effete and lifeless.

Meanwhile in the East also Catholicism was gradually being re-established. On the 24th of November, A.D. 380, Theodosius entered Constantinople in state. Two days afterwards, on the 26th of November, all the churches in the city were taken from the Arians and handed over to the Catholics.[4] On the 10th of January, A.D. 381, was issued the famous edict, beginning, 'Let the heretics have no place for celebrating their mysteries, no opportunity for exhibiting their demented obstinacy'—whereby all who did not accept the Nicene faith were forbidden to approach the thresholds of the churches, or to hold their illegal assemblies within the cities.[5] In May of the same year the great Council of Constantinople met, and continued its sittings till July.[6] It reaffirmed the faith of the Nicene Fathers,

---

[1] Ambros. *Ep.* 10. 3.        [2] Ibid. 12, 3.        [3] Ibid. 14. 3.
[4] Socrates, *H.E.* v. 7; Sozomen. *H.E.* vii. 5: cf. Ambros. *Ep.* 12. 1 and 3.
[5] Cod. Theod. xvi. 5. 6.
[6] G. Rauschen, op. cit. p. 95.

and anathematized the principal heresies.[1] The overthrow of Arianism in the Eastern Empire was henceforth merely a question of time.

The East, however, had religious troubles of its own, wherein Ambrose and the Western bishops—not very tactfully, it must be owned—endeavoured at this time to intervene. Thus in June, A.D. 381, the Council of Aquileia—partly in consequence of letters received from Antioch,[2] partly, perhaps, at the instigation of the presbyter Evagrius, who seems to have attended the Council as the representative of Bishop Paulinus—saw fit to draw up a document calling the attention of the Emperors, and especially of Theodosius, to the scandal of the Antiochene Schism.[3]

Certainly the condition of the Church at Antioch was one which was calculated to cause distress to pious people. In the beginning of A.D. 381 there were in this city (besides an Arian prelate named Dorotheus) two Catholic bishops—Meletius, a charming saint, 'honey-like in name and honey-like in conduct', who, although he had originally been consecrated to the see as a sympathizer with the Arians, had adopted the Catholic position and was recognized as their bishop by the great majority of the Catholics of Antioch; and Paulinus, the shepherd of a small community of uncompromising Nicenes, who could not bring themselves to overlook the Arian antecedents of Meletius. On the subject of the respective claims of these two bishops the Christian world was divided. The Church of Alexandria, the bishops of Egypt, and the Westerns (who took their cue from Alexandria)[4] supported Paulinus; the rest of the bishops of the East, together with the vast majority of the inhabitants of Antioch, ranged themselves on the side of Meletius.

Some negotiations appear to have taken place between the rival pastors, though nothing definite is known about them. We can hardly believe that Meletius actually suggested to Paulinus that they should sit together, with the Book of the Gospels on a throne between them. It is not unlikely, however, that an understanding was reached that, if either of the two died, he

Canon 1.      [2] Ambros. Ep. 12. 4.
[3] Id. Ep. 12. On this schism consult F. Cavallera, Le Schisme d'Antioche (Paris, 1905). The Council referred also to religious troubles at Alexandria which needed adjustment, Ep. 12. 4.
[4] Ibid. 12. 6.

should have no successor, but that the survivor should be recognized by both parties as the legitimate occupant of the see.[1] If this sensible compact was made, it was not adhered to. About the middle of the year Meletius expired suddenly at the Council of Constantinople. Most of the members of the Council were his partisans, and bitterly resented the coldness with which he had been treated by Alexandria and the Westerns. They were determined not to give a triumph to the latter by recognizing Paulinus. In vain was it represented to them that, whatever their personal feelings might be, they were in duty bound to embrace this opportunity of putting an end to the unedifying schism. They refused to listen to counsels of peace. The younger men chattered like a flock of jays and were as furious as a swarm of wasps; the older ones made no attempt to control them.[2] In the end the violence of anti-Western sentiment prevailed. After the close of the Council, the presbyter Flavian was consecrated at Antioch in the place of Meletius, though (according, at least, to a current report) he had formerly bound himself by an oath not to allow himself to be put forward as a candidate for the bishopric.[3]

When the Western bishops at Aquileia wrote their letter on the subject of the schism, they had not heard of the Council of Constantinople or of Meletius' death. They urged that an agreement with regard to the succession should be enforced in case of the decease of either Meletius or Paulinus; and meanwhile requested that 'a Council of all Catholic bishops' might be held at Alexandria to explore the possibilities of reunion between the rival parties. The bishops made it clear that they were firm supporters of Paulinus, but indicated their willingness to receive his opponents into communion, if the latter showed themselves conciliatory and proved to be orthodox in faith.[4]

Hardly had this letter been dispatched, when there presented himself to the astonished eyes of the Fathers of Aquileia[5] an extraordinary personage, who positively claimed recognition as the legitimate bishop of Constantinople. This was Maximus the Cynic—most impudent and disreputable of ecclesiastical

---

[1] Socrates, *H.E.* v. 5; Sozomen. *H.E.* vii. 3; Theodoret. *H.E.* v. 3.
[2] Gregor. Nazianzen. *Carm.* xi *de vita sua*, 1680–9.
[3] Socrates, *H.E.* v. 5; Sozomen. *H.E.* vii. 3, 11.
[4] Ambros. *Ep.* 12. 4–6; cf. *Ep.* 13. 2.                    [5] Ibid. 13. 4.

adventurers.[1] His career had been eventful and exciting. A vagabond of Alexandria, who strangely combined the Cynic philosophy with the seemingly earnest profession of Nicene Christianity, he had more than once been in difficulties with the police and had been banished for a time to an oasis in the Egyptian desert. Emerging from exile, he cleverly explained these troubles—and he still bore the scars of the scourgings inflicted on him for his misdeeds—as persecutions which he had endured on account of his zeal for the Catholic faith. Thus he imposed upon simple people. He even attracted the furtive attention of the Alexandrine bishop, Peter. The latter was by no means simple and probably saw through the man; but he was ambitiously intent on securing for Alexandria a primacy over the Eastern Churches, and thought that he might use Maximus as an instrument for bringing his most formidable rival, the powerful Church of Constantinople, very completely under his influence. Accordingly a plot was hatched. In the year A.D. 379 Maximus appeared in Constantinople, where (the Great Church being still in the possession of the Arians) Bishop Gregory of Nazianzus was ministering to the Catholic flock in the Chapel of the Resurrection (Anastasia). With his white robe, his philosopher's staff, and his enormous crop of ringleted, yellow-dyed hair, the Cynic had scarcely the appearance of a confessor of the faith. As such, however, he was accepted by the guileless Gregory, who gave him his entire confidence, welcomed him to his 'house and board', and even took the curious step of reciting publicly in the church a mellifluous panegyric on this most perfect philosopher-martyr,[2] who was present in person at the performance. Meanwhile the sly recipient of these gratifying attentions was maturing his plans for supplanting his benefactor. One night, in the following year, A.D. 380, when Gregory was confined to his room by illness and his clergy were asleep, some Egyptian bishops, armed with a secret commission from Peter of Alexandria, and escorted by a gang of sailors from the Alexandrine corn-ships, arrived at the Anastasia. The door was opened to them by a presbyter who was in the plot.

---

[1] On Maximus, see Gregor. Nazianzen. *Carm.* xi *de vita sua*, 807–1029; *Orat.* xxv; Hieron. *De Viris Illustr.* 127.

[2] Gregor. Nazianzen. *Orat.* xxv *in laudem Heronis philosophi.* On the title see Hieron. *De Vir. Illustr.* 117.

They seated Maximus in the episcopal chair and proceeded to consecrate him Bishop of Constantinople. His hair, however, was much longer than was deemed suitable for a bishop;[1] so they started to shear those curling locks which the devout ladies of the capital had so ardently admired, but which were now discovered to be no more than the artistic handiwork of the wig-maker. The ceremony was still in progress when the dawn broke. Some of the clergy appeared in the church; then a crowd of people gathered. There was an uproar, and the police were sent for. The Egyptians, carrying Maximus with them, retreated in disorder to a neighbouring 'hovel of a flute-player', where they completed the consecration, and 'fashioned' the dandy philosopher 'into a pastor'.

The Catholics of Constantinople were furious at this outrage, and the farcical new bishop, together with his consecrators, found it advisable to disappear from the scene. Maximus posted off to Thessalonica, hoping to obtain recognition from Theodosius; but the Emperor, who had already heard the story of the affair and was very far from pleased by it, 'spurned him like a dog'. He then returned to Alexandria, expecting that at any rate Bishop Peter would champion his claim. But the artful old intriguer was in a difficult position. His little plan for capturing the Constantinopolitan see had failed; the Emperor was seriously annoyed; moreover Pope Damasus (having received a full report from the Bishop of Thessalonica) condemned the whole business as a gross violation of ecclesiastical discipline and expressed his opinion of the 'long-haired' claimant and his 'idolatrous garb' in terms the reverse of complimentary.[2] Peter

---

[1] At this period, however, there was no tonsure. Ambrose speaks of hair as 'veneranda in sacerdotibus' (*Hexaem.* vi. 56), and, alluding to the custom of shaving the head and eyebrows adopted by the priests of Isis, clearly implies that it was not the habit of Christian priests to shave the head (*Ep.* 58. 3). While he disapproved of long hair as effeminate in men, he admitted the convenience of wearing it somewhat longer in winter than in summer (*De Noe*, 21). Jerome lays it down that the clergy should neither have their heads closely shaven like the priests of Isis, nor let their hair grow to extravagant length like barbarians, but should keep their hair just long enough to cover the skin (*Comm. in Ezech.* xliv. 20; cf. Gregory the Great, *Reg. Past.* ii. 7). This regulation, that the hair should be of moderate length, seems to have been generally observed; cf. Prudentius' description of Cyprian, *Peristeph.* xiii. 30, 'deflua caesaries compescitur ad breves capillos'. Some monks, however, wore their hair extravagantly long (Hieron. *Ep.* 22. 28): Hilarion's hair was cut only once a year, on Easter Day (id. *Vita Hilarion.* 10).

[2] Damasus, *Epp.* 5, 6 (Migne, *P.L.* xiii. 365–70); written early in A.D. 381.

concluded that it would be wise to drop his protégé. But Maximus was not the kind of person who could easily be dropped. He coolly threatened that, unless he were given the throne of Constantinople, he would have that of Alexandria, and stirred up the mob to riot against the Bishop in the streets. Finally the Praefect intervened, and drove the ruffian out of Egypt.

In the summer of A.D. 381 the Council of Constantinople considered the affair of Maximus and decreed that he neither was nor ever had been a bishop, and that all episcopal acts done by him, especially his ordinations, were null and void.[1] Further, when, towards the close of June, Gregory of Nazianzus, the Bishop of Constantinople, preached his impressive farewell sermon[2] and resigned his see, the Council concurred in the imperial nomination of Nectarius to the vacant post. It was certainly an odd appointment. Nectarius was an elderly layman of good family, accommodating temper, patriarchal appearance, and extremely courtly manners, who held the office of Praetor of Constantinople. In his youth he had sown a fine crop of wild oats; but years had brought him gravity, and his early peccadilloes were almost forgotten. One day, about the time of Gregory's resignation, when every one was talking and speculating about the election of his successor, this nobleman, who was a native of Tarsus, went to pay his respects to Diodorus, the bishop of that city, who had come to Constantinople for the Council. The ascetic and learned prelate was struck by the venerable appearance of his visitor—he had just the air of an archbishop—and for this and apparently for no weightier reason arranged that his name should be added to one of the lists of candidates for the bishopric. In due course this list was submitted to Theodosius. The Emperor read it through; stopped at the name of Nectarius, and seemed lost in thought; read the list again; and finally, to the stupefaction of the bishops, announced his intention of nominating Nectarius. There was then brought to light a fact of which nobody appeared to have been hitherto aware—that the sacerdotal-looking senator had not even been baptized. The Emperor, however, was unmoved by this circumstance; possibly he hoped that Nectarius would be a second Ambrose. At any rate he stuck to his choice, and the Council, after offering some respectful remonstrances, yielded to his wishes. Nectarius

[1] Canon 4; cf. Sozomen. *H.E.* vii. 9.          [2] Gregor. Nazianzen. *Orat.* xlii.

was baptized, and, while still wearing the white robes of baptism, was consecrated Bishop of Constantinople. He did not turn out to be a second Ambrose; yet, all things considered, he made a tolerably good bishop.[1]

Meanwhile the irrepressible Maximus, undaunted by adverse fortune, had betaken himself to Aquileia, where Ambrose and the Western bishops were still in Council. He produced letters once written to him by Peter as proof that he was in communion with the Church of Alexandria, gave a plausible explanation of the shady proceedings in connexion with his consecration, and successfully hoodwinked the whole assembly. Without waiting to consult the bishops of the East or even the Roman Pope, who had correctly taken the measure of the slippery Cynic, they impetuously received him into communion, and requested Theodosius to take such action as might be calculated to secure him his rights in the Eastern capital—rights which, in their view, were superior on canonical grounds to those claimed and exercised by Gregory of Nazianzus.[2]

Soon after this the Council of Aquileia broke up, having given authority to Ambrose to continue, in collaboration with the bishops of Upper Italy, the negotiations with Theodosius. In the autumn of A.D. 381 these bishops proceeded to act on their commission. During the interval since Aquileia they had been informed of what had been done in the Council of Constantinople, and found it little to their liking. The Antiochene compact had been set aside, and Flavian had been chosen to succeed Meletius. The claims of Maximus to the see of Constantinople had been dismissed, and the episcopal throne had been given to Nectarius—a man who, according to a false report which had reached Italy, had been immediately excommunicated by those who had ordained him. No attention whatsoever had been paid to Western opinion. The bishops considered that they had a grievance. They wrote, therefore, to Theodosius in a distinctly peevish tone. They complained that they had not been treated with courtesy by the bishops of the East, who had settled everything out of hand, without making the slightest effort to ascertain the views of their Western colleagues. In consequence they were themselves in a very embarrassing

---

[1] Sozomen. *H.E.* vii. 8, 10; cf. Socrates, *H.E.* v. 8.
[2] Ambros. *Ep.* 13. 3 and 4.

situation; for, having already recognized Paulinus and Maximus, how could they extend recognition to Flavian and Nectarius? Thus the communion between East and West was interrupted. There seemed to be only one way out of the impasse, and that was the convocation of a General Council for the consideration of these thorny questions. This Council should be held, not (as had formerly been suggested) at Alexandria, but at Rome, which was recognized even in the East as the premier see in Christendom; surely the Easterns would not disdain the assistance of 'the Bishop of Rome and the neighbouring bishops and the bishops of Italy' in the regulation of their affairs. The writers added that in thus approaching Theodosius, they were acting on the 'advice' of 'the Most Blessed Prince and Brother of Your Piety', the Emperor Gratian.[1]

In his reply, now lost, Theodosius took some trouble to enlighten his correspondents, both as to the character of Maximus and as to the regularity of Nectarius's consecration. But, good Catholic though he was, he was not by any means prepared to submit to the dictation of bishops. He refused to approve the proposal concerning a General Council at Rome, and appears to have made some rather tart observations on the subject of Western interference.[2]

Ambrose and his colleagues, on their side, were not in the best of tempers. They were satisfied, indeed—they could hardly be otherwise—concerning the preposterous claim of Maximus. But they still considered that they ought to have a share in the settlement of the dispute at Antioch. Once more, therefore, they addressed a letter to Theodosius—whose 'holy mind' must have been growing weary of these constant solicitations—reiterating their request for a General Council at Rome. For the holding of such a Council they urged, not only the importance of arranging the differences between themselves and the Easterns on the Antiochene question, but also another and new reason. It was desirable, they said, that an inquiry should be held into the opinions of Bishop Apollinaris, and that

---

[1] Id. *Ep.* 13. Gratian's 'advice' may have been dictated by Ambrose; yet it is possible that the young Emperor had himself been cajoled by Maximus, who had presented to him at Milan a bulky work which he had composed against the Arians (Hieron. *De Vir. Illustr.* 127).

[2] The general tenor of this lost letter may be gathered from the bishops' reply (Ambros. *Ep.* 14).

Apollinaris should appear in person and be given a hearing, and, if found guilty of heresy, deposed from the episcopate.[1] This new argument is astonishing. The North Italian bishops not only disdained to notice the condemnation of Apollinarianism by the Council of Constantinople, but also calmly ignored the fact that the person and doctrine of this heretic had already been condemned in Rome.[2]

However exasperated Theodosius may have been by the importunity of the Westerns, he judged it expedient to make a concession. He accordingly ordered the Eastern bishops to assemble in Council—not, however, in far-distant Rome, but in Constantinople, where they would be under his own imperial observation. This Council met in the summer of A.D. 382. Letters had come from Gratian, and also from the Western bishops, inviting their attendance at a Council to be held in Rome.[3] But the Eastern prelates were not inveigled. They wrote an exquisitely polite, but stingingly sarcastic, epistle to their Western colleagues. They thanked them for the extraordinary interest which now at last they were displaying in Eastern affairs; it was the more gratifying since, during the recent terrible Arian persecution in the East, the Westerns had refrained from demonstrative sympathy. They wished that they were provided with the wings of a dove, for then they would gladly have flown to the side of their loving brethren; not being furnished with these conveniences, or otherwise prepared for so long a journey, they felt it their duty to stay at home and attend to the business of their own Churches. They had pleasure, however, in sending three delegates, who would certify their ardent desire for peace and unity as well as their zeal for the true faith. They added a (really important) confession of their belief, and a curt vindication of the legitimacy of the consecrations of 'the most reverend and dear-to-God' prelates,

---

[1] Ambros. *Ep.* 14.

[2] Ambrose himself had indirectly refuted this heresy in a digression in his treatise *De Spiritu* (iii. 76–9); he dealt more fully with it in *De Incarnatione*, though he abstained from referring to Apollinaris by name. It was probably later that an Apollinarian teacher 'of very light character', having been condemned at Piacenza, sought an interview with Ambrose at Milan. He cavilled against a passage in *De Fide* (v. 102), and advanced some wrong interpretations of Scriptural texts; but Ambrose refuted him publicly and informed the Bishop of Piacenza that the heretic was 'preparing for flight' (Ambros. *Ep.* 46).

[3] Sozomen. *H.E.* vii. 11.

Nectarius and Flavian. The Westerns would doubtless rejoice to learn that these appointments had been made in so strictly canonical a manner. They concluded with the pious hope that East and West would henceforth be united in sound faith and Christian love, to the exclusion of all private partisanships and partialities.[1] Ambrose and his friends cannot have derived much satisfaction from this provokingly clever document.

The Council of Rome took place under the presidency of Pope Damasus about the same time, i.e. in the summer of the year A.D. 382. The curiosity of the Romans was gratified by the spectacle of quite a number of famous personages. Among the more notable of the Westerns were Ambrose of Milan, Valerian of Aquileia, Anemius of Sirmium, and Acholius of Thessalonica (who counted as a Western ecclesiastically). From the East, besides the three delegates from the Council of Constantinople, came Paulinus of Antioch, Epiphanius of Salamis, and the violent and vitriolic Jerome. The aristocratic Roman ladies were charmed to converse with these eminent men, and vied with one another in showing them hospitality. Epiphanius stayed with Paula; Paulinus, too, was entertained by her, though he lodged elsewhere.[2] Jerome, of course, was the lion —a very terrifying, though adored, one—in the salons of all devout virgins and widows. Ambrose put up at the house of his sister Marcellina;[3] but, soon after his arrival, he fell ill, and was for some while confined to his room. Here he was visited by Bishop Acholius, whom he had not previously met; and the two holy men enjoyed a consoling interview, shedding floods of tears together over the evils of the age.[4] As for the Council, it did nothing remarkable. The Apollinarian heresy was condemned. Paulinus was recognized as the legitimate bishop of Antioch, the election of Flavian being treated as void. The case of Nectarius does not appear to have been dealt with. Theodosius, however, sent commissaries to make representations on

---

[1] Theodoret. *H.E.* v. 9.    [2] Hieron. *Ep.* 108. 6.
[3] Paulinus, *Vita Ambros.* 9. It was, perhaps, during this visit to Rome that the incident related, *ibid.* 10, occurred.
[4] Ambros. *Ep.* 15. 10. Although the expression 'eo [*sc.* Acholio] veniente ad Italiam' might suggest that the visit of Acholius was to Milan (Upper Italy) rather than to Rome, and should therefore be assigned to another date, I am inclined to adopt the view commonly accepted that the interview referred to took place in Rome in A.D. 382.

his behalf, with the result that the Pope was induced to forward letters of communion to Constantinople.

It must be admitted that in his dealings with the Eastern Church Ambrose failed to exhibit his usual statesmanly sagacity. Whether any intervention on his part in the ecclesiastical politics of the East was either necessary or desirable, is open to question. The most that can be said in favour of such intervention is that the Schism of Antioch, at any rate, was a matter which seriously concerned the whole of Christendom. But apart from the general question of the propriety of taking any action in respect of Eastern affairs, it can hardly be denied that the action which Ambrose took was in all points injudicious. Determined at any cost to support Paulinus and his little group of irreconcilables, he refused communion to the saintly and well-beloved Meletius, and to Flavian who was consecrated as his successor with the approval of a great Council. He permitted himself to be gulled by that outrageous impostor Maximus, questioned the right of Gregory of Nazianzus to the Constantinopolitan see, and rejected Nectarius partly on the ground of an incredible rumour concerning his excommunication by his consecrators. Finally he struggled to obtain a fresh investigation of the teaching of Apollinaris, which had already been condemned, not only by the Easterns, but also by the Pope himself. In all this Ambrose and the bishops under his influence displayed a strange lack of understanding of Eastern persons and opinions. Nor, in the end, with all their fussy agitation, did they succeed in effecting anything. The Eastern bishops, though perfectly civil, made it clear that they had every intention of retaining in their own hands the management of their own business; and the Eastern Emperor showed no less plainly that he was prepared to back them up in their independent attitude. It is not unlikely that Ambrose recognized that his well-meant but officious attempt to put things right had been a blunder. At any rate it was some while before he ventured to meddle further in the affairs of the Eastern Church.[1]

[1] See the account of the Council of Capua, below, chapter xvi.

## CHAPTER IX

# THE USURPATION OF MAXIMUS AND THE TRAGEDY OF PRISCILLIAN

IN the year A.D. 383 the Emperor Gratian was foully murdered. This prince, whom we have seen waging war on the barbarians and applying to Ambrose for religious instruction, was in many respects a highly estimable young man.[1] 'He was faithful in the Lord', writes Ambrose, 'dutiful and gentle and pure in heart. He was also chaste in body, and never associated familiarly with any woman except his wife.'[2] 'In food', declares Ausonius, 'no priest could be more abstinent; in the use of wine no grey-beard could be more sparing. The altar of Vesta was not more holy, the bed of the pontifex not more chaste, the couch of the flamen not more unsullied, than the private apartment of the Emperor.'[3] It is true that, concerning his morals, some slanderous tales were afterwards set in circulation by his murderers;[4] also, the spiteful gossip, Philostorgius, 'forged many calumnies' about him.[5] But this was mere malignant scandal. The leading historian of the period warmly eulogized the sterling goodness of the young Emperor's disposition, which he regarded as not inferior to that of the best of the rulers who preceded him.[6]

Nature had endowed Gratian with a sprightly intellect,[7] which his tutor Ausonius had taken infinite trouble to cultivate. He was well read in literature,[8] and could express his sentiments in the Consistory with the art and eloquence of a professional rhetorician.[9] He had also a talent for scribbling verses. Often, when on campaign, he would 'lay aside the swift, singing arrows to take up the reeds of the Muses', sitting late into the night in his tent, while he laboured to recount some tale of ancient wars

---

[1] On Gratian see Ausonius, *Gratiarum actio pro consulatu*; Themistius, *Orat.* xiii; Ammian. xxvii. 6. 15; xxxi. 10. 18 and 19; Aurelius Victor, *Epitome*, 47. On the usurpation of Maximus, see C. Jullian, *Histoire de la Gaule*, vii, pp. 290 ff.; and on Gratian's death, G. Rauschen, op. cit., pp. 482–4.

[2] Ambros. *De Obitu Valent.* 74.

[3] Auson. *Grat. Act.* 66.          [4] Ambros. *In ps. 61 enarr.* 21.

[5] Philostorgius, x. 5. He compared him with Nero.

[6] Ammian. xxvii. 6. 15; xxxi. 10. 18.     [7] Auson. *Grat. Act.* 40 'mens aurea'.

[8] Aurelius Victor. *Epit.* 47. 4.          [9] Auson. *Grat. Act.* 67, 68.

in heroic verse. Ausonius, whose pride in his pupil knew no bounds, congratulates Achilles on having found in Gratian a Latin Homer.[1] In the science of war, again, he had proved himself remarkably competent. His victory over the Alemanni at Argentaria was a really considerable achievement, and he brought vigorous and effective help to Theodosius against the Goths.

Unfortunately these excellent qualities were counterbalanced by one grave defect. Gratian was bored with the business of government. Living amid crises which would have taxed to the utmost the statesmanship of a Marcus Aurelius, the healthy, athletic young sovereign could think and talk of nothing but sport.[2] Certainly he was highly proficient in all out-door games and exercises. He excelled in running, wrestling, jumping, and throwing the javelin; as for riding, the very sight of him on horseback enabled Ausonius to understand the descriptions in the poets of the exquisite horsemanship of the Numidians.[3] His favourite pastime, however, was shooting wild beasts with bow and arrows. Regardless of State affairs, he would spend his time, day after day, in his extensive beast-preserves, slaughtering innumerable animals[4] with a skill that seemed almost supernatural.[5] Some years after his death, Ambrose alluded in a sermon to his prowess on this sport, adapting the familiar words of David's lament over Jonathan: 'The arrow of Gratian turned not back.'[6]

This wholesome, vivacious, high-mettled young man—poet, athlete, and crack shot—would have been a pleasing figure in private life; but as the ruler of a great empire he was not a success. His subjects, left at the mercy of unscrupulous officials and smarting under grievances for which they could obtain no remedy,[7] resented the negligence of a monarch, who refused to

[1] Auson. *Epigram.* i.
[2] Ammian. xxxi. 10. 19; Aurelius Victor. *Epit.* 47. 4. Eunapius, *Excerpt. de Sent.* 48 (ed. Bonn, p. 84), observes that 'being young and having been bred from childhood in the purple, he had never learnt what it is to rule and what to be ruled'.
[3] Auson. *Grat. Act.* 64, 65.                              [4] Ammian. xxxi. 10. 19.
[5] Auson. *Epigram.* ii. 10. He could kill a lion with a single arrow, ibid. vi.
[6] Ambros. *De Obitu Valent.* 79.
[7] It is true that he did spasmodically investigate the grievances of individuals (Auson. *Grat. Act.* 71). He also pitied the oppressed provincials, and on one occasion even remitted all arrears of taxation and caused the registers to be burnt (ibid. 73, 74; Themist. *Orat.* xiii. 175 c.). But such acts of grace did not atone for his confirmed inattention to business.

give serious attention to the duties of his high office, and seemed to be interested in nothing but the number of creatures which he killed. This decline of his early popularity would not, perhaps, have mattered much, if the army had continued loyal. But the army also was dissatisfied. Gratian, it is true, did all he could to conciliate the troops. After a battle it was his custom to go in person round the tents, inquiring after the men's welfare, examining their wounds, urging them to take nourishment, and encouraging them with cheery words; during the long marches, also, he considerately befriended the tired legionaries, directing that one man's baggage should be conveyed by the Court mules, lending a horse to another, or sending his own attendants to replace missing camp-followers. Many a poverty-stricken soldier was supplied with money or uniform at the Emperor's personal expense.[1] But the army could not forgive his partiality for barbarian mercenaries. He had a small bodyguard of tall, yellow-haired Alani, to whom he was foolishly devoted. He loaded them with favours, condescended to associate with them on terms of intimacy, and even paid them the extravagant compliment of arraying his imperial person in their barbarian attire.[2] This tactless conduct cost him his life.

In the year A.D. 383 the discontent of the soldiery came to a head. The army in Britain revolted. The leader was a Spanish officer, Magnus Maximus, who claimed kinship with Theodosius[3] and had formerly been his comrade in arms in Britain.[4] He was an energetic and honourable man—'well worthy of the purple if he had not broken his plighted faith to obtain it'.[5] His temper, however, was 'fierce',[6] and he seems to have cherished feelings of bitterness towards Gratian, who had conferred on Theodosius the highest honours but had failed to show adequate appreciation of his own merits.[7] Determined to avenge the slight, Maximus set himself to undermine the loyalty of the troops. Soon a mutiny was organized. At the

[1] Auson. *Grat. Act.* 77.
[2] Zosimus, iv. 35; Aurelius Victor. *Epit.* 47. 6. It may be noted that, at the end of the fourth century and the beginning of the fifth, there was a rage for barbarian fashions, which had to be forbidden by law, Cod. Theod. xiv. 2. 3, 4.
[3] Pacatus, *Panegyr. Theodosio Aug. dict.* 24. But Pacatus attributes to him a very humble origin, ibid. 31.
[4] Zosimus, iv. 35.
[5] Orosius, *Hist.* vii. 34; cf. Sulpicius, *Dial.* ii. 6.
[6] Sulpicius, *Vita Martini*, 20.                    [7] Zosimus, iv. 35.

220 THE USURPATION OF MAXIMUS AND

last moment, indeed, he drew back, or made a feint of doing so; but the soldiers were now effectually roused, and, in spite of his real or pretended reluctance, constrained him to assume the purple.[1]

From Richborough[2] Maximus crossed the Channel, and, landing at the mouth of the Rhine, marched at top speed to the neighbourhood of Paris. Here Gratian, who had hastened from Verona into Gaul on the first news of the rebellion, was encamped. The Emperor had a considerable army, and was attended by two loyal and competent generals—the veteran Merobaudes and Count Vallio. He made a grave mistake, however, in that he did not immediately engage the rebels. For five days the armies skirmished; then the Emperor's Moorish cavalry, raising a shout of 'Maximus Augustus', deserted in a body to the enemy, and the rest of the troops prepared to follow. Seeing his forces melting away, Gratian put himself at the head of a company of three hundred horsemen and fled headlong towards the Alps.[3] His one hope now was to make his escape into Italy and take refuge behind the impregnable fortifications of Milan.

The young Emperor's plight was indeed pitiable. All the cities of Gaul, which lay on his route, closed their gates at his approach.[4] All his former friends—even those who were under obligation to his family—avoided him. He was unable to obtain even the barest necessaries. Behind him Andragathius, Maximus' Master of the Horse, with a body of picked men mounted on the swiftest and strongest chargers, followed hotly in pursuit. In these appalling circumstances the fallen monarch found support and consolation in religion. His trust in Providence was unshaken, and he calmed his fears with the reflection that, though his enemies might destroy his body, they could not hurt his immortal soul.[5]

At Lyons, by a bridge over the Rhone, the fugitive was overtaken. His capture is said to have been effected by a stratagem. A closed litter appeared on the opposite bank of the river, and

---

[1] Maximus afterwards professed that he had been made Emperor against his will (Sulpicius, Vita Martini, 20), and Sulpicius seems disposed to believe this (Dial. ii. 6). Cf. Orosius, Hist. vii. 34 'invitus propemodum ab exercitu imperator creatus'.
[2] Auson. Clarae Urbes, vii. 9 'Rutupinum latronem'.
[3] Zosimus, iv. 35; cf. Pacatus, Panegyr. 23.
[4] Hieron. Ep. 60. 15.          [5] Ambros. In ps. 61 enarr. 17.

Gratian was told that it contained his newly wedded wife, the Empress Laeta. But when he hastened across to welcome her, there sprang forth from the litter, not his amiable young consort, but the grim-visaged Andragathius, who made him prisoner.[1] He was conducted into Lyons, where his purple chlamys was taken from him, and he was ordered to dress in a plain white toga. For a while he was kept in the strictest confinement: presently it was decided that he had lived long enough. The imperial purple was restored, and he was bidden to a banquet. At first, suspecting treachery, he declined the invitation; but when Andragathius took an oath on the Gospel that no evil should befall him, he consented to attend. During the feast, however, he was assassinated, apparently by the host himself.[2] With his last breath he is said to have gasped out a name—'Ambrose!'[3]

Thus perished, on the 25th of August, A.D. 383, the charming but too irresponsible Gratian, being then in the twenty-fifth year of his age, and having reigned sixteen years.[4] Maximus subsequently protested that he had given no order for the murder.[5] Yet he rewarded the murderer;[6] and refused to allow the corpse to be sent to Italy for burial.[7] Towards the adherents of Gratian, however, he did not act harshly. The leading loyalists, of course, could not be permitted to escape. The gallant general Merobaudes was compelled to commit suicide; Vallio was hanged in his own house; and Macedonius, the Master of the Offices, was killed as he was fleeing for sanctuary to a church.[8] But there was no general proscription.[9]

[1] Socrates, *H.E.* v. 11; Sozomen. *H.E.* vii. 13. These historians suppose that Gratian was killed on the spot; but this is a mistake. Laeta was his second wife; on her see Zosimus, v. 39. He left no children (Theodoret. *H.E.* v. 12).

[2] These details are gathered from Ambros. *In ps. 61 enarr.* 23–5; cf. *In ps. 40 enarr.* 23.     [3] Ambros. *De Obitu Valent.* 79.

[4] It was perhaps with reference to Gratian's death that Ambrose wrote (*Ep.* 29. 18): 'He who has tasted of the Fountain of living water, what else can he desire? what kingdoms? what powers? what riches? perceiving how miserable even in this world is the condition of kings, how mutable the imperial state, how short the span of this life, what slavery sovereigns themselves endure, seeing that they live not according to their own will but by the will of others.' But the allusion may be to Valentinian II.

[5] Ambros. *Ep.* 24. 10.     [6] Id. *In ps. 61 enarr.* 24.

[7] Ibid. 26; *Ep.* 24. 10.

[8] Pacatus, *Panegyr.* 28; Ambros. *Ep.* 24. 11; Paulinus, *Vita Ambros.* 37. Prosper *Chron.* A.D. 384 mistakenly speaks of Merobaudes as a traitor.

[9] Cf. Maximus' own statement, Sulpicius, *Vita Martini*, 20.

Towards Valentinian—now the sole legitimate Emperor of the West—Maximus does not appear to have cherished animosity. He did not desire to deprive him of life or even of the diadem. Had this been his object, he could, with his immensely superior forces, have achieved it without difficulty; instead, he spontaneously made an offer of peace.[1] What he seems to have purposed was that the boy Emperor should come to him at Trier—the Gallican capital wherein he intended to reside—and there remain under his own 'paternal' tutelage and surveillance.[2] Thus, without any violent measures and simply by keeping his twelve-year-old colleague completely under his control, he himself would become, what Gratian had actually been, supreme master of the whole Western Empire. The simple and ingenious plan, however, was not at the time understood by Valentinian's ministers.

Meanwhile, on receipt of the news of Gratian's death, Justina and Valentinian transferred their Court from Sirmium to Milan. Here great anxiety prevailed. It was feared that Maximus would invade Italy; and Count Bauto the Frank,[3] who played the part of Protector of the young Emperor, immediately dispatched troops to secure the passes of the Alps. Justina herself, who ever since the episode of the Sirmium election had detested Ambrose, suppressed her feelings, and condescended to request his help. She brought her son and presented him to the Bishop; at the same time she invited him to undertake a diplomatic mission to the Court of Trier, and endeavour to negotiate a peace.[4] Such a request, made to a Christian ecclesiastic, was unprecedented. But Justina and her advisers were right in their view that they could find no ambassador more likely to make a favourable impression on the fanatically orthodox Maximus than the great prelate whose reputation as a champion of ortho-

[1] Ambros. *Ep.* 24. 6.                               [2] Ibid. 24. 7.

[3] Bauto was a Frank (Zosimus, iv. 33; Ambros. *Ep.* 24. 8) and probably a pagan (see on this point O. Seeck, *Geschichte des Untergangs der antiken Welt*, v, pp. 511, 512). Under Gratian he had risen to be Magister Militum (Zosimus, iv. 33, 53). As Protector of Valentinian he was so powerful that he seemed to rule the kingdom (Ambros. *Ep.* 24. 4). He was Consul with Arcadius in A.D. 385, and Augustine composed a panegyric in his honour (Augustin. *Confess.* vi. 6; *Contr. Litt. Petil.* iii. 30). His daughter, Eudoxia, married Arcadius (Philostorgius, xi. 6, and below, chapter xix). He appears to have died not long before the murder of Valentinian (Zosimus, iv. 53)—perhaps about A.D. 391.

[4] Ambros. *De Obitu Valent.* 28.

doxy had spread far and wide throughout the West. Ambrose, on his side, was not unwilling to render this service. Apart from his patriotic regard for the welfare of the State and his loyalty to the legitimate sovereign, he probably hoped that by a successful accomplishment of his difficult mission, he would establish a claim on the gratitude of the Imperial Government which would be advantageous to the Church, and perhaps even acquire such influence with the Emperor himself as would counteract in some measure that of the Arian Empress Mother.

In the autumn—perhaps in October—of A.D. 383[1] Ambrose started for Trier. In the hope of propitiating the usurper, he carried with him into Gaul the latter's brother, Marcellinus, who had been arrested at Milan and might have been held as a hostage.[2] When he arrived in the neighbourhood of Mainz, he met Count Victor, the son of Maximus, who was travelling as envoy to Milan, to offer peace and also to urge Valentinian to come in person to Trier.[3] Ambrose was both relieved and troubled by this interview. He had received the comforting information that Maximus was prepared to make peace; but he had learned also that the usurper attached very great importance to the coming of Valentinian to Gaul—a proposal which could not possibly be accepted by the Court at Milan. He realized that he must proceed with the utmost circumspection, if his mission were not to end in failure.

In the palace at Trier Ambrose was received, not, as his episcopal rank demanded, in the private apartments of the Emperor, but publicly in the Consistory. He was determined, however, to be conciliatory, and did not (as on a later occasion) make a protest.[4] He explained briefly that he had been sent by Valentinian to treat for peace. Maximus answered gruffly, 'Valentinian should come to me himself, as a son to a father.' Ambrose pointed out that it was unreasonable to expect that a young boy with his widowed mother should cross the Alps in winter; in any case he himself had not been commissioned to discuss such a visit, but only to negotiate for peace. Maximus replied, 'Let us wait and see what answer Victor will bring back.'[5]

---

[1] Before the winter, Ambros. *Ep.* 24. 7.
[2] Ibid. 24. 9.  [3] Ibid. 24. 6.
[4] Ibid. 21. 20; 24. 3.  [5] Ibid. 24. 7.

Ambrose remained in Gaul for some weeks. At last Count Victor arrived and made his report—that while Valentinian was ready to make peace, he was not prepared (at any rate, for the present) to come in person to Trier. It is true that Ambrose, in his account of these events, seems to state that Valentinian sent back an unqualified refusal of the pressing invitation of Maximus.[1] But this can hardly be correct. Would the Government at Milan, fearful of an invasion, have dared so rashly to provoke the anger of the usurper? Would Maximus, if so uncompromising a reply had been sent, have concluded a peace? And how, on this hypothesis, could he have complained later on that he had been 'cajoled' by Ambrose and Bauto,[2] that he had been 'circumvented' by Ambrose[3] and 'withheld' from Italy by his representations?[4] It seems evident that the answer sent by Bauto on behalf of the Emperor was ambiguous, as had been the reply made to Maximus at Trier by Ambrose himself—'it was impossible for Valentinian to attempt so long a journey while the winter lasted'. Such an answer would imply that he might come at a more convenient season, and would give Maximus some ground for his later complaint that he had been tricked by false promises. For the moment the usurper appears to have been satisfied with the equivocal response, and accorded peace on condition that he should be acknowledged as legitimate Emperor. Ambrose then, having successfully discharged his mission, left Trier for Italy. At Valence he met envoys of Valentinian who were conveying to Maximus a formal reply to the invitation delivered by Victor.[5] He reached Milan probably in January, A.D. 384. In the same year (A.D. 384) Theodosius, after long hesitation and with obvious reluctance, consented to recognize the usurper as ruler of the Roman territories west of Italy and the Alps.[6]

In ecclesiastical history Maximus has a sinister reputation as the first Christian emperor who inflicted the death penalty on heretics. The 'heretics' who thus suffered from his 'fierceness' were the Priscillianists.[7]

---

[1] Ambros. *Ep.* 24. 7.　　[2] Ibid. 24. 4.　　[3] Ibid. 24. 7.　　[4] Ibid. 20. 23.
[5] Ibid. 24. 7.　　　　　　　　[6] Zosimus, iv. 37; Pacatus, *Panegyr.* 30.
[7] On Priscillian and the Priscillianist movement see especially Sulpicius Severus, *Chron.* ii. 46–51; *Dial.* iii. 11–13; the writings of Priscillian edited, together with the *Commonitorium* of Orosius, by G. Schepss in vol. xviii of the Vienna Corpus; the

Some years before the usurpation of Maximus an ascetic movement of a peculiar character had been started in Spain. Its leader was a rich, well-born, and profoundly learned scholar named Priscillian. He was a restless, excitable man, endowed with brilliant gifts of wit and eloquence, but too much addicted to unprofitable studies.[1] He interested himself in Manichaean and Gnostic literature, prosecuted researches in astrology,[2] and was a diligent reader of apocryphal writings.[3] Yet, though somewhat puffed up with his intellectual attainments, Priscillian bore a stainless character, and was, indeed, a person of sincere and austere piety.[4] Shocked by the laxity which prevailed in Spanish ecclesiastical circles, he determined to initiate a religious reformation on ascetic lines.

The society which he founded was undeniably eccentric. Its members aspired to a perfection beyond that attained by ordinary members of the Church,[5] from whom they accordingly tended to separate. They were rigidly ascetic. They practised continence, subsisted on a vegetarian diet, and (perhaps) fasted on Sundays.[6] Lent and the three weeks before Epiphany they observed with special strictness, absenting themselves from public worship and shutting themselves up at home or in hermitages among the mountains. It was their custom to hold meetings by night in private dwellings, whereat apocryphal

Councils of Zaragossa (A.D. 380) and Toledo (A.D. 400); the letter of Maximus to Pope Siricius (Labbe, *Conc.* ii. 1030); Pacatus, *Panegyr.* 29; Hieron. *De Vir. Illustr.* 121–3; *Epp.* 75, 133; *Comm. in Isaiam,* lxiv. 4, 5; Philastrius, *De Haer.* 84; Augustin. *De Haer.* 70; *Reply* to Orosius (Migne, *P.L.* xlii, pp. 669 ff.); and *De Mendacio.* Among modern authorities the following may be consulted: G. Schepss, *Priscillian, ein neuaufgefundener lat. Schriftsteller des IV. Jahrhunderts* (1886); id. 'Pro Priscilliano' in *Wiener Studien* (1893), pp. 128–47; F. Paret, *Priscillian, ein Reformator des IV. Jahrhunderts* (1891); P. Dierich, *Die Quellen zur Geschichte des Priscillianismus* (1897); K. Künstle, *Antipriscilliana* (1905); E. C. Babut, *Priscillien et le priscillianisme* (1909); A. Puech, 'Les Origines du priscillianisme et l'orthodoxie de Priscillien', in *Bulletin d'anc. littérature et d'archéologie chrétiennes* (Paris, 1912), pp. 81 ff., 161 ff.

[1] Sulpicius, *Chron.* ii. 46.
[2] Hieron. *Ep.* 133. 4; cf. Augustin. *De Haer.* 70.
[3] He attempted to justify these studies in his (imperfect) *De Fide et de Apocryphis* (*Tract.* iii ed. Schepss, pp. 44 ff.).
[4] Sulpicius, *Chron.* ii. 46.
[5] Hieron. *Ep.* 133. 3.
[6] Since Sunday fasting was known to be a Manichaean custom (Ambros. *Ep.* 23. 11), and since Priscillian publicly and comprehensively repudiated the opinions and practices of the Manichaeans (*Tract.* ii, ed. Schepss, p. 39), it seems doubtful whether the observance (condemned by the Council of Zaragossa, c. 2) was followed by Priscillian and his immediate disciples.

books were read and instruction was given by unlicensed teachers; to these conventicles women were admitted. When they came to the church they allowed the Eucharist to be given to them, but they were never seen to communicate.[1] Finally, they preserved a mysterious silence about their practices and doctrines. Lying itself was considered preferable to divulgement of these secrets.[2]

A society of this kind could hardly fail to incur suspicion. It was rumoured that Priscillian was propagating Manichaean and Gnostic errors, and the innocence of those midnight assemblies in lonely villas was questioned. Nevertheless the movement spread. It was strongest in the provinces of Lusitania and Galicia, but it rapidly extended through the greater part of Spain. Even among the bishops it found support; two especially, Instantius and Salvian, became enthusiastic allies of Priscillian. Others, however, were alarmed, and at last Hyginus, the venerable Bishop of Cordova, formally denounced the movement to Ydacius, Bishop of Merida and Metropolitan of Lusitania. The latter, a fiery bigot, took up the matter with excessive zeal. His measures against the Priscillianists were so violent that moderate men were scandalized; and Hyginus himself, disgusted by the severity with which the new ascetics were being treated, took their part and admitted them to communion.[3] Nothing, however, could stop Ydacius. Not content with inflaming the Spanish episcopate, he sent a memorandum to Pope Damasus, charging Priscillian and his associates with immoral practices. In his reply the Pope suggested that a Council should be held to investigate the matter, but recommended that the accused should not be condemned in absence or unheard.[4]

In the autumn of A.D. 380 a Council was held at Zaragossa. It was attended by ten Spanish and two Gallican bishops. Priscillian and his friends, however, did not appear. In their absence the Council condemned certain irregularities—admission of women to conventicles, retreats in Lent and before

---

[1] I have assumed that the canons of the Council of Zaragossa furnish reliable evidence as to the practices of the early Priscillianists, with the possible exception of Sunday fasting (referred to in the last note).

[2] 'Jura, periura, secretum prodere noli', is said to have been a maxim of the Priscillianists (Augustin. De Haer. 70).

[3] Sulpicius, Chron. ii. 46, 47.

[4] Priscillian, Tract. ii, ed. Schepss, p. 35.

Epiphany, sermons by unlicensed preachers, reservation of the Eucharist—of which the Priscillianists were supposed to be, and probably really were, guilty.[1] But the Priscillianist leaders were not condemned by name, nor were charges of heresy or immorality formally alleged or proved against them.[2]

Having thus escaped direct condemnation by the Council, the Priscillianists were emboldened to strengthen their position. Instantius and Salvian consecrated Priscillian (though only a layman) as bishop of the little town of Avila, in the province of Tarragona.[3] Priscillian, moreover, addressed to his brother bishops, 'most blessed priests', a remarkable *Apology*, in which he strongly protested the soundness of his faith and the purity of his morals, condemned all heresies (particularly that of Manes), and earnestly appealed to be absolved from the evil suspicions raised against him by his enemies.[4] The document, though written in an obscure and fantastic style, made a good impression; and Priscillian, encouraged by the sympathy which he received, actually ventured to carry the war into the very camp of his principal adversary. He went in person to Merida, to accuse Ydacius of grave misconduct. He got nothing by his journey, however, except a severe beating at the hands of an infuriated mob.[5]

In the course of the year A.D. 381 Ydacius invoked the help of Gratian's Government against Priscillian and his adherents. He artfully described them as Manichaeans (i.e. members of a proscripted sect), who had been condemned and deposed by a Spanish Council; and requested the authorities to take action against them. The demand was strictly in accordance with law and custom; and the Imperial Government, having received the report of the Metropolitan, followed the ordinary procedure[6]—

---

[1] Hefele, *Hist. of the Councils*, ii, pp. 292, 293. Apparently there was also some discussion concerning the use of apocryphal writings, Ydacius maintaining the thesis 'damnanda damnentur, superflua non legantur' (Priscillian, *Tract.* ii, ed. Schepss, p. 42).

[2] Priscillian, *Tract.* ii, ed. Schepss, p. 35 (cf. pp. 39, 42). Sulpicius, *Chron.* ii. 47 says that Instantius and Salvian, bishops, and Helpidius and Priscillian, laymen, were condemned; but this is a mistake.

[3] Sulpicius, *Chron.* ii. 47.

[4] Priscillian, *Tract.* i, ed. Schepss, pp. 2 ff.

[5] Ibid. ii, ed. Schepss, pp. 39, 40.

[6] There is no evidence for the theory that the rescript was obtained through the influence of Ambrose, nor is it at all likely that he intervened actively at this stage.

though perhaps a little too precipitately—and forwarded a rescript expelling 'pseudo-bishops and Manichaeans' from the Churches.[1] Though the Priscillianists were not mentioned by name, it was evident that the instrument would be enforced against them. The situation was critical. Only one course seemed open, if they were to escape destruction. They must go themselves to Rome and plead their cause before the Pope.

Furnished with letters testimonial from their clergy and flocks, Priscillian, Instantius, and Salvian set forth on their long journey. Their road lay through Aquitaine, where they met with a magnificent welcome from the people. When they came to Bordeaux, they were warned off by the bishop;[2] but they stayed for a while in the vicinity, on the country estate of a wealthy widow named Eucrocia. This lady and her daughter Procula became ardent disciples of Priscillian, and later, with some other women, accompanied him to Rome. The circumstance gave occasion for malicious gossip. It was alleged, quite unwarrantably, that Procula was Priscillian's mistress.[3]

Followed by a train of adoring females, the Priscillianist bishops proceeded to Milan. They were courteously received by the Quaestor; Ambrose, however, whose mind had been prejudiced by the misrepresentations of Ydacius, coldly declined to have any dealings with them. They accordingly pushed on to Rome,[4] which they reached in the last weeks of A.D. 381. Here, however, a bitter disappointment was awaiting them—Pope Damasus refused them audience. No doubt he had been told that they had already been condemned by the Council of Zaragossa; perhaps he thought that the facts of this Spanish affair could not profitably be investigated out of Spain; at any rate he would neither see nor hear them.[5] In vain did Priscillian

---

[1] Priscillian, *Tract.* ii, ed. Schepss, p. 40; Sulpicius, *Chron.* ii. 47.

[2] The bishop's name was Delphinus. One of Ambrose's letters (*Ep.* 87) is addressed to him.

[3] Sulpicius, *Chron.* ii. 48. Priscillian had the power of attracting women, who flocked to him 'in crowds' (ibid. 46).

[4] Priscillian, *Tract.* ii, ed. Schepss, p. 41.

[5] Sulpicius, *Chron.* ii. 48. The action of Damasus was very unfortunate, for Priscillian had a right to request him to hear his case. The famous rescript of Gratian to Aquilinus (A.D. 378) provided that all bishops of the Western Empire, who considered themselves unfairly condemned by their own metropolitans or by local episcopal judges, might appeal to the Bishop of Rome (see *Rescriptum Gratiani Aug. ad Aquilinum Vicarium Urbis*, Labbe, *Conc.* ii. 1003–5).

forward to him an impassioned *Appeal*,[1] in which he rapidly reviewed the events of the controversy, protested his innocence in respect of all charges, and entreated the Pope (who 'holds the highest rank and is first among all')[2] to convoke a Council of Spanish bishops (including Ydacius) in Rome, and afford him an opportunity of re-establishing his reputation.[3] Damasus remained obdurate.

Greatly disheartened by their failure, Priscillian and Instantius—Salvian had died in Rome—retraced their steps to Milan. Both Damasus and Ambrose had taken sides against them, without condescending even to hear what they could urge in their own defence. It was only too evident that they could expect no redress of their grievances from the Church. The one hope now was to obtain protection from the State. They, therefore, addressed themselves to Macedonius, Gratian's Master of the Offices. He was a cynical man of the world, with the looseness of principle and extravagant greed of money which characterized the typical fourth-century official; he was also on bad terms with Ambrose, whose occasional intervention in State affairs he seems to have resented.[4] By means of a judicious bribe the venal minister was soon persuaded that the rescript concerning 'pseudo-bishops and Manichaeans' had been issued too hastily and without proper investigation of the facts. The order was accordingly cancelled, and the Priscillianists, completely exculpated and rehabilitated, were given permission to resume possession of their sees (A.D. 382).[5]

The triumphant return of Priscillian to Spain portended trouble for the party of Ydacius. The most prominent member of that party was a blatant and blasphemous bully, Ithacius Clarus, Bishop of Sossuba (Ossonoba). 'He was an audacious, chattering, shameless, extravagant man, devoted to gluttony and a slave to his belly.' He had savagely persecuted the Priscillianists because they stood for the principle of asceticism, and asceticism in any form was to him an abomination. Indeed, 'to such a pitch of folly did he go that he charged all men, no matter how holy, who loved reading or were addicted to strenuous fasting, with being associates or disciples of Priscillian'.[6] Against this coarse *bon-vivant*, of whom even his friends

---

[1] Priscillian, *Tract.* ii, ed. Schepss, pp. 34 ff.    [2] Ibid., p. 42.    [3] Ibid., pp. 42, 43.
[4] Paulinus, *Vita Ambros.* 37.       [5] Sulpicius, *Chron.* ii. 48.       [6] Ibid. ii. 50.

could say nothing good, Priscillian instituted proceedings, accusing him of being a disturber of the public peace. It was a test case, and both sides made use of all the influence they possessed with high officials of the Government. The Priscillianists, however, had the advantage of the support of the powerful Macedonius, and felt confident that they would win. Their view of the situation was shared by Ithacius. He discreetly disappeared.[1]

Suddenly, however, in the summer of A.D. 383, the complexion of affairs was changed by the successful revolt of Maximus and the fall of Gratian and his ministers. The new Emperor was not disposed to favour the protégés of the late Government; he was also anxious to conciliate the good opinion of the Spanish Catholics, many of whom had been greatly shocked by Gratian's murder; moreover he was himself an orthodox Spaniard and had the orthodox Spaniard's detestation of everything that savoured of heresy. With his accession, therefore, the drooping spirits of the anti-Priscillianist party revived. Ithacius emerged from his hiding-place. Maximus at Trier listened to his denunciation, and ordered that the leading Priscillianists should be sent to Bordeaux, there to be tried by a synod of bishops.[2]

The Council met probably in the autumn of A.D. 384. Ithacius acted as accuser, and presented a document in which the charges were elaborately set forth.[3] The case of Instantius was taken first. His carefully prepared defence did not favourably impress the judges, and he was deposed from the episcopate. Then came Priscillian's turn. Realizing that he had no chance of obtaining an acquittal from this tribunal, he appealed to the Emperor. The Council offered no objection.[4]

The Priscillianists were conducted to Trier, and many of the Council followed. Among the rest came that renowned bishop, missionary, and wonder-worker, Martin of Tours.[5] He had

---

[1] Sulpicius, *Chron.* ii. 49.     [2] Ibid.     [3] Isidor. *De Vir. Illustr.* 15.

[4] Sulpicius, *Chron.* ii. 49. It is clear that the charge of heresy was not pressed, and that Priscillian was accused of criminal offences, which could properly be dealt with by the secular authorities. Strangely enough, Priscillian, in the 46th of the *Pauline Canons*, had maintained that 'ecclesiastici non debeant ob suam defensionem publica adire iudicia sed tantum ecclesiastica' (ed. Schepss, p. 129).

[5] On Martin of Tours, see J. H. Reinkens, *Martin von Tours*; J. Rabory, *Vie de S. Martin, apôtre des Gaules*; also J. G. Bulliot and F. Thiollier, *La Mission et le culte de S. Martin d'après les légendes et les monuments populaires*. Sulpicius Severus and Gregory of Tours are the two most important early authorities.

been present at the Council of Bordeaux, and was evidently uneasy about the course which the affair was taking. At Trier he implored Ithacius to drop the prosecution; but the only result of his expostulation was that Ithacius had the audacity to charge the saint himself with heresy. Martin then applied to the Emperor. He entreated him to refrain from extreme measures against the prisoners. 'It is enough and more than enough that those who have been condemned as heretics by the verdict of the bishops should be expelled from their Churches; it is a new and unheard-of scandal that a secular judge should give sentence in an ecclesiastical cause.' His bold and dignified attitude, in striking contrast with the sycophancy of the other prelates, affected Maximus, who finally pledged his word that no blood should be shed. Martin then left the city. But, as soon as he was safely out of the way, the Ithacians set to work to convert the Emperor to their views. In a little while an inquiry was ordered. It was entrusted to Evodius, the Praetorian Praefect of Gaul—a harsh man, but incorruptibly just.[1]

Evodius tried Priscillian in two sittings, and convicted him of sorcery (*maleficium*).[2] Torture appears to have been used to obtain evidence;[3] and some of the Priscillianists, to save their own skins, gave information.[4] It is said that Priscillian himself confessed that he 'had studied obscene doctrines, had held conventicles of depraved women by night, and had been accustomed to pray naked'.[5] The habit of praying in a state of nudity may have been a form of ascetic discipline actually practised by Priscillian; but, though fantastic, it was not a crime. As for the other alleged confessions, they may possibly have been lies extorted by the agony of torture; more probably, however, they are malevolent misrepresentations of admissions made by the prisoner—namely, that he had studied Manichaean and Gnostic doctrines, and had held night-meetings to which women were admitted. Such statements could easily have been distorted. An unscrupulous antagonist like Ithacius (who is the ultimate authority for this confession) would not have hesitated to describe the occult researches as 'obscene' magic or to characterize the women who attended the conventicles as 'immoral'.

---

[1] Sulpicius, *Chron.* ii. 50; *Vita Martini*, 20.
[2] Id. *Chron.* ii. 50.        [3] Pacatus, *Panegyr.* 29.
[4] Sulpicius, *Chron.* ii. 51.       [5] Ibid. ii. 50.

Priscillian, having been found guilty, was remitted to prison, while Evodius made a report to the Emperor. Sorcery was a capital offence, and Maximus saw no reason for commutation of the penalty. The trial was formally resumed. Ithacius at this point withdrew from the case, that he might not conduct the prosecution up to the passing of the death sentence. His place was taken by an official of the Treasury. The subsequent proceedings did not last long. Priscillian, Eucrocia, and five others were sentenced to death and executed; Instantius, who had been condemned by the Council of Bordeaux, was banished to the Scilly Isles.[1] These events took place in A.D. 385. At the beginning of the following year a military Commission was appointed to go to Spain, with unlimited powers to hunt out and kill Priscillianists and confiscate their property.[2]

The executions caused a profound sensation. Ithacius and his accomplices, who were chiefly responsible for the tragedy, were exposed to a storm of popular indignation. Their conduct was even made the subject of inquiry by a synod; but, thanks to the influence of the Emperor, they were declared free from blame. One bishop, however, named Theognistus, had the courage to excommunicate them. Before the excitement had calmed down, early in the year A.D. 386, the formidable Martin reappeared in the neighbourhood of Trier. The Ithacians, who were gathered there for the election of a bishop, the see being vacant, were greatly alarmed. They did not know what Martin would do; but they had an uncomfortable suspicion that he might take the same line as Theognistus. They accordingly persuaded Maximus to forbid the saint to enter the city, unless he would promise to be at peace with his brethren. 'I will come with the peace of Christ,' was Martin's reply to the imperial message. He arrived late in the evening, and prayed for some while in the cathedral. The next day he went to the palace. He had heard that the Spanish Commission for the extirpation of Priscillianism had been appointed, and he was determined to stop it, if he could. For two days he bombarded the Emperor with entreaties and remonstrances. But Maximus, who hoped to replenish his exchequer by means of a proscription of Spanish heretics, put him off with evasive answers.[3]

---

[1] Sulpicius, *Chron.* ii. 51; Prosper, *Chron.* A.D. 385; Hieron. *De Viris Illustr.* 121–3.
[2] Sulpicius, *Dial.* iii. 11; cf. ibid. iii. 13.          [3] Ibid. iii. 11.

Meanwhile the fears of the Ithacians had been realized. Martin refused to hold communion with them. The bishops, in great agitation, besought the Emperor to do something. Could not Martin be indicted for heresy? He was posing as the avenger of Priscillian, and was clearly no better than a Priscillianist himself. But Maximus was not prepared to take a step which would certainly have set the whole of Gaul in commotion. Instead, he summoned Martin to a private conference, and endeavoured to mollify him by friendly argument. 'The heretics', he said, 'were condemned by regular process of law, and not at the suit of the bishops. Ithacius and his friends have done nothing worthy of excommunication; only a few days ago Ithacius was exonerated by a synod. No one has withdrawn from communion with them except Theognistus, and he did so from personal motives.' Martin, however, was not mollified. At last the Emperor lost his temper, rushed precipitately from the audience-chamber, and gave orders that the Commission should start for Spain without delay.[1]

Martin heard the news the same night. He instantly returned to the palace and made his submission. If the Spanish Commission were recalled, he undertook to communicate with the Ithacians. The Emperor agreed to these terms. On the morrow, Felix, 'a man of great sanctity, and clearly worthy of being made a bishop in happier times', was consecrated to the see of Trier. Martin attended the ceremony and communicated with Ithacius and the other prelates; but, in spite of great pressure, he refused to sign a document attesting the fact. The next day, in great sadness, he turned his back on Trier; and never afterwards could he be induced to show himself in any gathering of bishops.[2]

Theognistus and Martin were not the only bishops who were shocked by the execution of the Priscillianists. Pope Siricius, the successor of Damasus, appears to have asked for an explanation. Maximus sent him the minutes of the trial, and claimed credit for his prompt action against the infamous 'Manichaeans', whose abominable deeds he modestly blushed to mention.[3] But the Pope does not seem to have been satisfied; at any rate he refused to hold communion with the Ithacian party. Ambrose, again, though he had thought ill of Priscillian during his life, was horrified by the circumstances of his death. He also would have

<hr>

[1] Sulpicius, *Dial*. iii. 12.     [2] Ibid. iii. 13.     [3] Labbe, *Concil*. ii. 1030, 1031.

nothing to do with the Ithacians,[1] and plainly expressed his abhorrence of prelates who 'have begun to accuse criminals before public tribunals, some pressing the case even to the extremity of capital punishment, while others approve such accusations and bloody episcopal triumphs'.[2]

While Maximus reigned, the adherents of Priscillian suffered a measure of persecution. Ambrose describes how the aged Hyginus of Cordova—the same who first denounced Priscillian and afterwards became his friend—was hurried into exile in a dying condition, without being allowed even a change of clothing or a pillow whereon to rest his head.[3] But with the overthrow of the usurper in A.D. 388 the situation changed. The anti-Priscillianists were now attacked. Ithacius was deposed from the episcopate and banished to Naples; Ydacius, apprehending a similar sentence, resigned his see.[4]

The later developments of Priscillianism may be indicated in a few sentences. In Gaul the movement soon died out. For some while, however, there was discord among the bishops on the question of communion with Felix of Trier. No objection was made to Felix personally; but, since he had been consecrated by the Ithacians, he was banned by many, as representing the party hostile to asceticism. The matter seems to have been discussed in a Council at Milan in A.D. 390,[5] and the result was unfavourable to Felix. Both Ambrose and Pope Siricius refused to hold communion with him.[6] In the end he gave up his bishopric and retired into a monastery.

In Spain there was a reaction in favour of Priscillianism. The dead leader became the object of a cult. Men venerated him as a martyr, and whenever they desired to bind themselves by a particularly solemn oath, they would swear by his name.[7] The sect flourished especially in the province of Galicia, where a majority even of the bishops joined it, including the energetic metropolitan, Symposius of Astorga. Before long, however, a cleavage appeared within the party. While the less educated

---

[1] Ambros. *Ep.* 24. 12.
[2] Ibid. 26. 3. M. Ihm finds in this passage an allusion to the persecutors of Priscillian (*Stud. Ambrosian.* p. 46); see, however, G. Rauschen, *Jahrbücher der chr. Kirche*, p. 246.
[3] Ambros. *Ep.* 24. 12.    [4] Sulpicius, *Chron.* ii. 51.
[5] This Council is referred to by Ambrose, *Ep.* 51. 6.
[6] Council of Turin, c. 6.    [7] Sulpicius, *Chron.* ii. 51.

Priscillianists became increasingly unorthodox, an influential section, headed by Symposius, began to favour the idea of reunion with the Catholics. With this object in view, Symposius and his son, the presbyter Dictinius, went to Milan, to persuade Ambrose to act as mediator. Ambrose was not unwilling to help them; he insisted, however, as a condition of reconciliation, that they should condemn Priscillian and his doctrines, and also that Dictinius should receive no further ecclesiastical promotion. On their acceptance of these terms, both Ambrose and Siricius wrote to the Catholic bishops of Spain, recommending that the penitent Priscillianists should be restored to communion. Unfortunately, when Symposius returned to Astorga, he found it impossible to fulfil his compact. When he attempted to remove Priscillian's name from the catalogue of martyrs, he was violently opposed by the people, who further constrained him to consecrate Dictinius bishop.[1] This delayed, but did not prove fatal to, the negotiations for reunion. In the year A.D. 400 a Council was held at Toledo, at which Symposius, Dictinius, and the more moderate Priscillianists consented to renounce both verbally and in writing the books and doctrines of Priscillian, and to condemn their author.[2] Among the ignorant people of Galicia, however, Priscillianism lingered on into the second half of the sixth century.

Such is the history of the Priscillianist movement. But what view should be taken of Priscillian himself? Was he really guilty, as his enemies alleged, of heresy and immorality? The question is a difficult one. It may be granted that Manichaean-Gnostic opinions were really held by many of the later Priscillianists, who also tended to antinomianism in matters of conduct. This admission, however, proves nothing against Priscillian himself, who can hardly be held responsible for the intellectual and moral vagaries of his less enlightened followers. It is necessary, therefore, to review the evidence which bears directly on his personal opinions and practices.

(i) The evidence against him may be considered first. The principal authority on the early history of Priscillianism is Sulpicius Severus. But, for his information respecting Priscillian's

---

[1] See *Exemplar definitivum* attached to the Acts of the Council of Toledo, Labbe, ii. 1230.

[2] Ibid.; Idatius, *Chron.* A.D. 399.

teaching, Sulpicius relied on one source, which may unquestionably be identified with the lost document of accusation drawn up by Bishop Ithacius.[1] This source is tainted. Ithacius, as Sulpicius himself admits, was a man of bad character, who hated every form of asceticism and was eager to bring charges of heresy against any whose manner of life appeared to him inconveniently strict. The statements of a person who did not hesitate to calumniate even the saintly Martin of Tours are not to be trusted. Hence the information derived by Sulpicius from the Ithacian source—and outside of this source he seems to have gathered very little concerning the tenets of Priscillian—must be regarded with grave suspicion.[2]

Jerome, in his *De Viris Illustribus*, speaks doubtfully concerning Priscillian's personal implication in heresy;[3] elsewhere he assumes it.[4] Like Sulpicius, however, he seems to be dependent on Ithacius. There is no indication that he ever himself essayed any careful investigation of Priscillian's teaching.

Augustine describes Priscillian as an heresiarch.[5] But Augustine's information on the subject is derived from the *Commonitorium* of Orosius.[6] Orosius, a keen heresy-hunter, probably furnishes good evidence as to the perverse opinions held by some of the later Priscillianists. But it does not seem to have occurred to him to inquire how far these opinions could correctly be attributed to the original founder of the sect. If Gnostic influence may be detected in the obscure fragment quoted from one of Priscillian's epistles, as well as in what is reported con-

---

[1] Isidor. *De Viris Illustr.* 15, describes the work as 'librum sub Apologetici specie, in quo detestanda Priscilliani dogmata et maleficiorum eius artes libidinumque eius probra demonstrat, ostendens Marcum quemdam Memphiticum, magicae artis scientissimum, discipulum fuisse Manis et Priscilliani magistrum'.

[2] Sulpicius, though he does not explicitly state that he believes Priscillian guilty on the charges brought against him, evidently regards him as heretical. The heresy is represented as a species of immoral Gnosticism, but Sulpicius does not explain in what exactly it consisted. Following his Ithacian source, he says that it arose in Egypt, and was introduced into Spain by a certain Mark of Memphis, who converted to his views a noble lady named Agape and the rhetorician Helpidius, who in turn became the teachers of Priscillian (*Chron.* ii. 46).

[3] Hieron. *De Viris Illustr.* 121 'Priscillianus . . . usque hodie a nonnullis Gnosticae . . haereseos accusatur, defendentibus aliis non ita eum sensisse ut arguitur'.

[4] Id. *Ep.* 133. 3 and 4.

[5] Augustin. *De Haer.* 70 'Priscillianistae quos in Hispania Priscillianus instituit maxime Gnosticorum et Manichaeorum dogmata permixta sectantur'.

[6] Printed in the Vienna Corpus, vol. xviii, pp. 151 ff.

cerning his work entitled *Memoria Apostolorum*,[1] yet in view of Priscillian's own explicit and strong repudiation of Gnostic principles, this evidence is hardly sufficient to convict him conclusively of either Gnosticism or Manichaeism.

Finally, Priscillian was rejected by Damasus and Ambrose. But each of these bishops had been prejudiced against him by the representations of Ydacius,[2] and neither of them had complied with Priscillian's urgent request to be granted a hearing in his own defence. Under the circumstances their adverse judgement does not carry weight.

(ii) The evidence against Priscillian can hardly be regarded as convincing. We pass next to the evidence in his favour. This is mainly supplied by the eleven *Tractates*, written by Priscillian himself, which were discovered by G. Schepss in 1885, in a fifth- or sixth-century manuscript in the University Library at Würzburg, and were published by the same scholar, together with the *Pauline Canons* (statements on faith and morals drawn up by Priscillian and corrected by Bishop Peregrinus), in 1889. These documents, so far as they go, do not confirm the charges advanced either against Priscillian's doctrine or against his character.[3]

(*a*) As regards doctrine, the evidence of the *Tractates* seems to indicate that Priscillian was not either a Gnostic or a Manichaean. It is true that he was familiar with, and often made allusions to, Gnostic and Manichaean speculations. Yet there is no clear proof that he accepted or inculcated Gnostic or Manichaean principles. On the contrary, he comprehensively condemned these principles,[4] anathematizing various Gnostic sects[5] and (with peculiar vehemence) the Manichaeans. 'Anathema to him who condemns not Manes, his works, his doctrines, and his principles.'[6] 'And among them all we condemn the

---

[1] Orosius, *Common.* 2. Orosius (loc. cit.) maintains that Priscillian was worse than a Manichaean (cf. Augustin. *De Haer.* 70).

[2] Priscillian, *Tract.* ii, ed. Schepss, pp. 35, 41.

[3] 'But it is well to remember that this literature [i.e. the *Tractates*] is composed of three memoirs of self-justification, written for presentation to the ecclesiastical authorities, and of a few sermons preached to the faithful at Avila, at a time when the teaching of Priscillian was already looked upon with suspicion, and could scarcely have been exposed to the public. It is not in compositions of this kind that we can expect to find definite heresies' (Duchesne, *Early Hist. of the Church*, ii. p. 432). The *Canons* cannot be used as evidence of Priscillian's teaching, inasmuch as we have them only in the orthodox recension of Peregrinus (see G. Schepss' edition of Priscillian, p. 109).

[4] G. Schepss, pp. 14 ff.        [5] Ibid. pp. 23, 38.        [6] Ibid. p. 22.

Manichaeans, not heretics so much as idolaters and workers of wickedness, slaves of the sun and moon, hateful demons—we condemn them with all their founders, sects, morals, institutes, books, teachers, and disciples.'[1] There is no reason to suppose that these repudiations were not sincere. The creed which he sent to Pope Damasus commences, 'We believe in one God the Father Almighty, and in one Lord Jesus Christ.'[2] The insertion of the word 'one' is unusual in the West, and it is likely that Priscillian introduced it expressly to disavow the errors of the Manichaeans and the Gnostics, of whom the former postulated two Gods, and the latter, in addition, two Christs.

Was, then, Priscillian orthodox? Undoubtedly he professed to be so. He declared himself in complete agreement with the 'one faith'[3] of the Catholic world. As he had received that faith, so he held and taught it,[4] condemning all doctrines 'which seem to be against Christ'.[5] Yet the *Tractates* leave a distinct impression that Priscillian's teaching was not thoroughly in accordance with the Catholic tradition. There are manifest traces, for instance, of a dualism which is hardly orthodox; though it seems to be the dualism of a Christian preacher, preoccupied with the conflict between good and evil in the world rather than the 'two-principles' doctrine[6] of the Manichaean theorist. Again, his teaching concerning the Trinity (a word, it may be noted, which does not occur in the *Tractates*) has a strong flavour of Sabellianism—as when he speaks of one God 'invisible in the Father, visible in the Son, and united for the work of both as Holy Spirit'.[7] So in his

---

[1] G. Schepss, p. 39.     [2] Ibid. p. 36.     [3] Ibid. p. 5.     [4] Ibid. p. 36.

[5] Ibid. p. 3. Besides the Gnostics and Manichaeans, he anathematized the Docetae (ibid. pp. 21, 22), Patripassians (pp. 6, 38), Arians (pp. 23, 38), Novatians (pp. 7, 23, 39), Photinians (p. 38), and others. His own creed is explicitly stated (pp. 36, 37), and contains nothing to which objection can be taken. In his writings he strongly emphasized the unity of God (pp. 5, 7, 34, 35, 36, 37, 49), the Divinity of our Lord, whom he perpetually referred to as 'deus' (pp. 8, 9, 16, 23, 24, 27, 30, 33, 35, 39, 41, 66, 93), and the truth and reality of the Incarnation (pp. 7, 21, 24, 31, 59, 60). Christ's body was a real body, and in that body He was truly 'born of the Virgin Mary *ex Spiritu Sancto*' (p. 36), endured temptation (p. 61), and was crucified for us (p. 60)—'anathema is he who denies that Christ was fixed to the cross by nails, and drank the vinegar and the gall' (p. 22). He confessed his belief in 'the holy Church, the Holy Ghost' (p. 37), in 'one' baptism of salvation (pp. 5, 7, 39) wherein is remission of sins (pp. 32, 100), and in 'the resurrection of the flesh' (p. 37). The doctrine of *Filius innascibilis* attributed to him by Symposius and Comasius in their retractations (Labbe, *Conc.* ii. 1229) is not found in his own writings.     [6] Labbe, *Conc.* ii. 1229, recantation of Symposius.

[7] G. Schepss, p. 103. Cf. p. 37 'quia unus deus trina potestate venerabilis omnia

view of the Incarnation—particularly of the soul of Christ—he
approximates to Apollinarianism.[1] Some deviation from ortho-
doxy may also be detected in his doctrine of the human soul,
which he seems to have regarded as an emanation from the
Divine Substance.[2]

A careful study of the *Tractates* suggests that the teaching of
Priscillian was really in some respects unsound. Yet it hardly
justifies us in stigmatizing him as a heretic. He maintained no
heretical thesis. He did not consciously or deliberately depart
from the teaching of the Scriptures or of the Catholic Church.
It may well be argued that his utterances were judged by a
wrong standard. His critics made the mistake of regarding him
as an exact thinker, and of estimating his incoherent and fanciful
outpourings as though they were precise theological statements.
But he was not by any means an exact thinker. He was a mystic,
imaginative and emotional, afflicted moreover with an almost
incredibly bad and exaggerated style. His head was filled
with queer ideas which he had picked up in an extensive course
of Gnostic-Manichaean reading, and of which some, at least,
seemed to him capable of an orthodox interpretation. It is not
astonishing that such a one should have let fall things to which
objection might legitimately be taken. But that he purposely
sought to disseminate doctrines which he knew to be at variance
with the Catholic beliefs is unproven and seems improbable.

(*b*) As regards his conduct, it is hard to believe that Priscillian
was guilty of immorality. His impassioned denials of the accusations of misbehaviour have the ring of truth. He affirmed that
he and his followers 'having Christ' had 'decided to observe the
justice of the Lord unto sanctification';[3] that they had ever
loved and approved the Christian way of life and maintained
that 'lax morals and indecent principles of living' should be

et in omnibus Christus est'. A similar Sabellian tendency is found in a treatise on
the Trinity, discovered by C. H. Turner in a manuscript at Laon, which seems to
belong to the school of Priscillian and may possibly have been written by Priscillian
himself (*Revue Bénédict.* xxvi, p. 255).

[1] G. Schepss, p. 74.

[2] Ibid. pp. 70, 73, 80, 93, 98. Cf. Orosius ap. Schepss, p. 153; and the re-
tractation of Dictinius at the Council of Toledo (Labbe, *Concil.* ii. 1229 'Hoc in
me reprehendo, quod dixerim unam Dei et hominis esse naturam'). But the
question of the substance of the soul was debated even by Catholics. Ambrose wrote
a letter (*Ep.* 34) in answer to the question, 'Is the soul of heavenly substance?'

[3] G. Schepss, p. 9.

condemned.[1] He denounced the Nicolaitans and all others who persisted in 'sacrilegious deeds hateful to God';[2] and declared that the Manichaeans, on account of the foul practices ascribed to them, deserved to be, not only anathematized by the Church, but also punished by the State.[3] Even more convincing than these protestations is his urgent request for a public trial at Rome. He had no fear of the result of an impartial investigation. He was sure that, if an inquiry into his life and conduct were held, the verdict would be in his favour.[4] As for the confession which he is alleged to have made under examination before Evodius, it is almost certainly, in the form in which we have it, a distorted version of his admissions. That he was really addicted to vicious practices is most unlikely. The character of the man as delineated by Sulpicius, the grave doubts about his guilt which were evidently felt by Martin of Tours, and the earnest moral tone of his own writings, are alike inconsistent with such a supposition.

In conclusion it must be admitted that it was not without reason that Priscillian incurred suspicion. Although he 'was not either the inventor or the propagator of a dogmatic heresy', yet his familiarity with Gnostic and Manichaean ideas and phraseology imparted a peculiar, unconventional colouring to his teaching, which in certain points appears to have definitely diverged from the Catholic norms. Similarly, although he was not personally immoral—quite the contrary—he was indiscreet in admitting women to the private nocturnal meetings and in allowing them to accompany him on his travels. It is no wonder that to many Catholics this eccentric ascetic enthusiast, with his obscure and outlandish religious jargon[5] and his 'advanced' ideas concerning the relations of the sexes,[6] seemed a dangerous personage. The ecclesiastical authorities can hardly be blamed for taking action. Yet the action taken was unfortunate, and the final condemnation of Priscillian as an immoral Manichaean cannot be accounted as anything other than a deplorable mistake.

[1] G. Schepss, p. 35.  [2] Ibid. pp. 7, 23.  [3] Ibid. p. 22; cf. p. 24.  [4] Ibid. pp. 41–3.

[5] Priscillian's language sometimes seems to suggest the presence of veiled esoteric meanings (see e.g. Schepss, pp. 26, 102, &c.); but that he was really making allusions which would be understood only by initiates is not proven. The obscurities are probably sufficiently accounted for by his constitutional inability to speak plainly and to the point.

[6] See e.g. Schepss, p. 28, where Priscillian quotes Scriptural authority for his opinions.

## CHAPTER X

# AMBROSE AND THE PAGAN PARTY

IT was Ambrose's lot to play a prominent part in the last great conflict between Christianity and Paganism. But in order to appreciate the full significance of his intervention in this struggle, it is necessary to review briefly the character and condition of Western paganism at this period.[1]

## A

Four main types of pagan religion[2] may be distinguished. There was the ancient national religion, which flourished preeminently in Rome and was zealously supported by the Roman aristocracy. There was the crude, animistic religion, which still lingered in the country districts. There were the various mystery religions imported from the East. And there was Neoplatonism.

(i) The old Roman religious myths had long ceased to be literally credited by educated people. The slashing onslaughts made on them by Christian critics—Arnobius, Lactantius, and the rest—had almost completely lost their force. On this subject the cultivated Roman pagan was quite as sceptical as any Christian. The real faith of such a one can be summarized in a few words. He usually cherished a vague belief in one all-powerful, eternal, universal 'divinity', called by many different

---

[1] Among the most important sources of information on Western paganism in its decline are the writings of Symmachus and Macrobius; Firmicus Maternus, *De errore profanarum religionum* (ed. C. Halm), probably composed about A.D. 347; Prudentius, *Contra Symmachum* and *Peristephanon* x; the anonymous *Carmen adversus paganos* (about A.D. 394), discovered in the Paris MS. of Prudentius (Cod. Puteanus), published by L. Delisle (*Bibliothèque de l'École des Chartes*, series vi, 1867, iii. 297–303) and edited anew by Mommsen (*Hermes*, 1870, iv. 350–63): the contemporary *Carmen ad senatorem ex Christiana religione ad idolorum servitutem conversum* (ed. by Hartel in his *Cyprian*, Appendix, 302–5); and Maximus of Turin, *Tract. contra paganos*. Consult further G. Boissier, *La Fin du paganisme*; A. Beugnot, *Histoire de la destruction du paganisme en Occident*; V. Schultze, *Geschichte des Untergangs des griechisch-römischen Heidentums*; also F. Martroye, 'La Répression de la magie et le culte des Gentils au IVe siècle' in *Revue historique de droit français et étranger*, 4 ser. ix, 1930, pp. 669 ff.

[2] The term *religio paganorum*, applied to heathenism, first occurs in a law of A.D. 368 (Cod. Theod. xvi. 2. 18), and soon obtained wide currency; cf. Augustin. *Retract.* ii. 43 'deorum falsorum multorumque cultores, quos usitato nomine paganos vocamus'.

names;[1] he believed also in the existence of demons, and in the possibility of holding intercourse with, and in some measure controlling, them by means of elaborate magical ceremonies.

Yet the national religion was not discarded. Under the patronage of the ancient gods Rome had originally risen to greatness, and with the worship of these divinities the continued prosperity of Rome was by many held to be bound up.[2] The official religion had, in fact, become a form of patriotism—a kind of symbol of men's reverence for and loyalty to Rome herself. The Senate—a body remarkable both for its patriotic sentiment and for its obstinate conservatism—was the stronghold of this worship. In Ambrose's time the majority of the Senate was pagan.

The whole business of Roman paganism was still punctiliously carried on. The members of the Pontifical College still enjoyed their ancient privileges,[3] held their Chapters at stated intervals,[4] and superintended the observance of the ceremonies and festivals.[5] The nuns of Vesta, comfortably supported by State subsidies, still occupied their hallowed and pleasant abode at the foot of the Palatine Hill.[6] Occasionally they appeared in public, flaunting through the streets in luxurious litters surrounded by servants, or displaying their fillets and purple-bordered robes in the reserved seats of the amphitheatre.[7] The ivory doors of the

---

[1] The educated view is well set forth by Maximus of Madaura. 'The forum of Madaura is indeed filled with statues of the divinities; and I approve of the custom. But do not suppose that any one is so foolish as not to understand that there is only one supreme God, who has neither origin nor descent, the great and almighty Father of the whole of nature. His energies, diffused through the universe, we invoke under many names, since we are all ignorant of His real name. . . . Thus, by successively offering our supplications to His different members, we arrive at honouring Him in His entirety' (Augustin. *Ep.* 16. 1). Cf. Macrobius, *Sat.* i. 17. 1–6; also the description of Isis by Apuleius, *Metam.* xi. 5. Augustine discusses the view held by many pagans that all the deities are but parts or powers of Jupiter, the animating soul of the world (*De Civitate Dei*, iv. 11 and 31; vii. 6 ff.). So Themistius told the Emperor Valens that the pagans had three hundred ways of conceiving and honouring the deity, whose inscrutable majesty is the more glorified by such diversity of homage (Socrates, *H.E.* iv. 32).

[2] This view is combated by Augustine in the early books of *De Civitate Dei*, and by Prudentius. Expression is given to it by Zosimus, v. 41.

[3] Symmachus, *Relatio*, 3. 15.

[4] Id. *Epp.* i. 46, 47, 51; ii. 36.                                [5] Ibid. ii. 53.

[6] O. Marucchi, *Nuova descrizione della casa delle Vestali secondo il resultato dei più recenti scavi* (Rome, 1887).

[7] Ambros. *Ep.* 18. 11; Prudentius, *Contra Symmach.* ii. 1063–1112. Cf. Ambros. *De Virginibus*, i. 15.

temples still stood open. On the altars the customary sacrifices were regularly offered, and incense-smoke curled upwards in honour of the gods.[1] Many of the old festivals were kept up; on 15 February, for instance, the day of the Lupercalia, youths clad in skins still frolicked through the City, striking women with their sacred whips, the blows of which were credited with the power of inducing fertility.[2] The solemn expiations prescribed by the sacred code were still performed.[3] Prodigies and portents were still observed.[4] Finally, the serene and venerable forms of the Olympian deities, wrought in metal or chiselled in marble, everywhere presented themselves to view; the baths, the colonnades, the streets were filled with images.[5] In the Senate-House itself there was a gilded statue of Victory, bought originally from Tarentum. It represented a winged female figure, poised on bare foot, with flowing robe lightly covering her swelling breasts.[6] Before the statue stood an altar whereat the senators still burned incense and swore allegiance to the imperial laws.[7]

Such was the situation in respect of the Roman religion in the latter half of the fourth century. It was the State religion, maintained at the cost of the State, symbolizing the majesty of the State, and appealing strongly to the patriotic sentiment of all who gloried in Rome's greatness. The Roman gods had ceased to have any but a purely literary existence; but the Roman worship, so inextricably intertwined with the history of 'divine Rome', the 'mother of arts and arms', the conqueror and beneficent queen of the whole world,[8] lasted on.

(ii) In the country paganism of a more primitive type was strongly entrenched. The peasants adhered with invincible tenacity to their superstitious rites, and the landlords, even those who were themselves Christian, seldom ventured to interfere

---

[1] Ambros. *Ep.* 18. 7 and 31.
[2] This festival was prohibited by Pope Gelasius; see his tractate *Adversus Andromachum senatorem ceterosque Romanos qui Lupercalia secundum morem pristinum colenda constituebant* (Migne, *P.L.* lix, pp. 110 ff.).
[3] Symmachus, *Epp.* i. 49; cf. Zosimus, v. 41; Claudian, *In Eutrop.* i. 18–23.
[4] Symmachus, *Epp.* vi. 40. On the importance attached to prodigies and portents, see Claudian, *De Bell. Get.* 227 ff., and the references given above, p. 82, n. 2.
[5] Ambros. *Ep.* 18. 31.
[6] Prudentius, *Contr. Symmach.* ii. 27–38.
[7] Ambros. *Epp.* 17. 9 and 16; 18. 31 and 32.
[8] Claudian, *De Bell. Get.* 50 ff.; *De II Cons. Stilich.* 130 ff.; *De Bell. Gild.* 46 ff.; Rutil. Namat. *De Reditu*, i. 47 ff.

with them. In Italy heathenism flourished on the great agricultural estates;[1] in Gaul Martin of Tours found it rampant in
the rural districts;[2] in Spain people sacrificed and made offerings
to idols,[3] and Pacian of Barcelona wrote a work entitled *Cervulus*
against the pagan excesses customary at the celebration of the
new year;[4] in Africa, not only in the country, but also in the
towns, there was a considerable pagan population, which, on
the occasion of a pagan festivity, was apt to riot against the
Christians.[5] The deep-rooted superstition of the peasantry is
illustrated by the story of the murders of Anaunia in A.D. 397.
Vigilius, Bishop of Trent, was distinguished by his efforts to
evangelize the heathen of the Tyrol. A few miles from Trent lay
the heathen township of Anaunia, and thither Vigilius dispatched an elderly deacon named Sisinnius, with two younger
companions—Martyrius, a reader, and Alexander, a doorkeeper. At first all went well. A mission church was built, and
many of the people were converted. In May, however, it was
usual to hold a rustic festival, when the images of the local
deities were carried in procession round the fields, and prayers
and sacrifices were offered for plentiful crops. The whole
village took part in this ceremony, and even the new converts
were pressed to join. The missionaries were horrified and tried
to interfere; whereupon a savage attack was made on them by
the mob. Sisinnius, seriously injured, was carried into his cottage
by his two companions. At dawn on the following day a band
of peasants, armed with clubs and hatchets, pillaged and
smashed the church, and then broke into Sisinnius' house. The
wounded deacon, who was already dying, was murdered on the
spot; Martyrius was caught in the garden and so maltreated
that he speedily expired; Alexander was next taken and bound
alive between the two corpses. The three bodies, one living and
two dead, were then dragged to the village green and burned
on a pyre before the idol.[6]

[1] Zeno Veron. *Tract.* i. 15. 6; Maximus Taurin. *Serm.* 101, 102.
[2] Sulpicius, *Vita Martini*, 12–15.          [3] Concil. Eliberit. cc. 1, 3.
[4] Pacian, *Paraenesis ad poenitentiam*, c. 1; cf. Hieron. *De Viris Illustr.* 106. The
*Cervulus* is lost.
[5] The serious riot at Calamus in Numidia, in June A.D. 408, is a case in point
(Augustin. *Epp.* 90, 91, 103, 104).
[6] See the two letters written by Vigilius to Simplician of Milan and Chrysostom
(Migne, *P.L.* xiii. 549–58). The relics of the martyrs were brought to Milan; for a
miracle wrought in connexion with them, see Paulinus, *Vita Ambros.* 52.

(iii) But the most remarkable feature of Western paganism in this period is the prevalence of foreign cults, which, emigrating from the East, had established themselves in all the principal cities of the Western Empire. It is not difficult to account for this phenomenon. In large and constantly increasing numbers, Easterns had penetrated Western society. From Eastern lands had come soldiers to serve in the Western armies, slaves to cultivate Western estates, merchants to trade in Western marts, artists to embellish Western temples and palaces, professors to teach in Western universities, officials to occupy posts in the Western Civil Service. These had brought their religions with them. The attractive gods of the Orient, accompanying their Oriental worshippers, had invaded the Western countries and captivated the hearts of the Western populations.

(*a*) From Asia Minor had come the Great Mother of Pessinus, tower-crowned and drawn by lions, whose cult was the first Oriental religion adopted by the Romans.[1] The holidays of this Phrygian deity were regularly celebrated in Ambrose's time—especially the great March festival (15–27 March), when the legend of Cybele and Attis was developed into a kind of mystic drama. The felled pine, representing Attis dead, wreathed with woollen bands and violets, was ceremonially carried by the *dendrophori* to the temple on the Palatine; then came days of fasting and mourning for the god; on March the 24th his funeral was celebrated, and, amid the shrilling of flutes and the piercing cries of worshippers, the *galli* gashed and flagellated themselves and frenzied neophytes underwent castration; next followed a day called *Hilaria* (25 March), when the devotees abandoned themselves to rapturous rejoicing to commemorate the awakening of Attis from the sleep of death; finally on March the 27th, the last day of the festival, a splendid procession (of priests, wearing gorgeous costumes covered with amulets, and of barefooted members of fraternities, beating tambourines and chanting

---

[1] On the cult of Cybele, see G. Wissowa, *Religion und Kultus der Römer*, pp. 263 ff.; H. Graillot, *Le Culte de Cybèle mère des dieux à Rome et dans l'empire romain*; and H. Hepding, *Attis, seine Mythen und sein Kult*. Augustine attacked the cult with special vehemence (*De Civitate Dei*, ii. 4, 7; vi. 7, 8; vii. 24–6); cf. the anonymous *Carmen ad senatorem* 6–19 (Hartel's *Cyprian*, Appendix, p. 302). Julian has left an oration on the Mother of the Gods (*Or.* v); Proclus also wrote a philosophic commentary on the Cybele myth (Marinus, *Vita Procli*, 34). The Great Mother was specially worshipped by women, who were even admitted to the ranks of her clergy.

hymns of triumph) escorted the car of Cybele to the banks of the river Almo, where the silver image and sacred implements were solemnly purified in the waters.[1] This fanatical and sensual cult, with its violent transports, its vertiginous dances, its voluntary mutilations, its sacramental feasts of food and wine from the mystic tambourine and cymbal of Attis,[2] was immensely popular, and, next after the worship of Mithra, was perhaps the most dangerous rival of Christianity. The most impressive of its rites, the *taurobolium* or blood-bath, is described by the poet Prudentius.[3] It was performed usually in the early spring. A pit was dug, about twenty feet deep, into which the neophyte descended; then the opening was covered with planks, placed slightly apart and perforated. On this platform a steer, with gilded horns and garlanded neck, was stabbed by a priest with a sacred boar-spear, in such a manner that the blood gushed out abundantly and fell through the holes of the platform upon the person stationed below.

'Through the countless crevices the bloody dew descends; the neophyte entombed below takes up a position in which he may catch as many as possible of the falling drops on his head, his clothing and his body. He leans backward; he offers his cheeks, ears, lips and nostrils to the rain of blood; he bathes his eyes in the liquid; he even moistens his tongue with blood and swallows it. His whole body becomes soaked through and through with the dark gore.'

When the blood at length ceased to flow, the platform was removed, and the neophyte emerged, all dripping and drunk with blood, and received the homage of the on-lookers. He was believed to be 'regenerated to eternal life'.[4] The beneficial effects of the red baptism lasted for twenty years; at the end of this period the ceremony might be repeated.[5]

[1] This celebration is referred to by Ammianus, xxiii. 3. 7, and Ambrose, *Ep.* 18. 30. Augustine in his youth witnessed at Carthage the procession on the last day of the festival, and was shocked by the grossly indecent words and acts of those who participated in the carnival (*De Civitate Dei*, ii. 4; cf. vii. 26). In Gaul the car, with the image of the goddess, was taken, with songs and dances, through the fields and vineyards, to stimulate fertility (Gregor. Turon. *De Glor. Confess.* 77; cf. *Passio S. Symphoriani* in Ruinart, *Acta Sinc.* pp. 67 ff.).

[2] F. Cumont, *Oriental Religions*, p. 68: 'I have eaten from the tambourine; I have drunk from the cymbal; I have become a mystic of Attis.'

[3] Prudentius, *Peristephanon*, x. 1011–50. On this ceremony see F. Cumont, *Monuments relatifs aux mystères de Mithra*, i, pp. 334 ff. It was practised in the worship of Mithra as well as in that of Cybele.

[4] 'In aeternum renatus'; *C.I.L.* vi. 510.       [5] *C.I.L.* vi. 512.

(*b*) From Syria, in the dubious company of various Baals, came Atargatis, the Dea Syria, whose rites in many respects resembled those of the Great Mother of Pessinus.[1] Apuleius has given us a vivid picture of a wandering band of devotees of the goddess. We are shown a beastly old eunuch, his bald head fringed with grizzled curls; a crew of effeminate, painted young men, wearing turbans and robes of saffron crossed with purple stripes; and an ass, which carried the sacred image covered with a silken veil. When it came to a village or to some nobleman's country seat, the sorry procession halted. Then the fanatics, brandishing swords and axes and emitting discordant howls, would whirl round and round to the accompaniment of Syrian flutes, till their long ringlets stood out in a circle about their heads. Having thus worked themselves into delirium, they gashed their bare arms with knives and lashed their backs with knotted scourges. At the conclusion of the crazy performance, a collection was made among the spectators. These gains were supplemented by thefts, and by fees earned by uttering bogus predictions.[2] But the description of the proceedings of these debauched and fantastic vagabonds, with their image, their ass, their womanish attire, their flutes and castanets, gives no adequate idea of the worship of the Syrian Goddess, as it was carried on in Ambrose's day. Strangely enough, this cult, which was formerly notorious for the immorality of its practices and the puerility of its beliefs, had in course of time developed an austere moral discipline and an exceptionally advanced theology and eschatology.[3] Thus it appealed to earnest and thoughtful persons, who eagerly sought initiation into its mysteries, and, under the tuition of its erudite priests, devoted themselves to religious contemplation, philosophical speculation, and the rigorous practice of asceticism.

(*c*) From Egypt the cult of Isis 'of myriad names' passed by way of Alexandria into the West, penetrating to the shores of the Danube and the Rhine and even to far-distant Britain.[4] It was

---

[1] On Syrian religions in the West see G. Wissowa, op. cit., pp. 299 ff.

[2] Apuleius, *Metam.* viii. 24–8; ix. 8–10.

[3] F. Cumont, *Oriental Religions*, pp. 120 ff.

[4] On the Isis cult see G. Wissowa, op. cit., pp. 292 ff.; G. Lafaye, *Histoire du culte des divinités d'Alexandrie hors de l'Égypte.* See also Apuleius, *Metam.* xi, with K. H. E. de Jong, *De Apuleio Isiacorum mysteriorum teste* (1900). The goddess was worshipped as 'nature's mother, mistress of all the elements, the first-begotten offspring of the ages, mightiest of deities, queen of the dead, first of heaven's denizens, in

universally popular, partly by reason of its magnificent and suggestive ritual, and partly on account of the assurance which it offered of continued life beyond the grave. The ceremonies of Isis were calculated to attract. Very striking, for instance, were those in connexion with the festival of March the 5th, which was celebrated in all coast towns of any size to mark the reopening of navigation after the winter. Through the crowded streets a gay, many-coloured procession made its way. First marched a throng of persons in carnival attire, representing various callings and professions; next came white-robed and garlanded women, some scattering flowers and perfumes, others carrying mirrors, combs, and other articles pertaining to the goddess's toilet; these were followed by bearers of tapers and torches, choirs of singers intoning hymns, and the flute-players of Serapis; behind them a crowd of initiates, the women wearing gauzy veils, the men distinguished by the tonsure, rattled *sistra* of brass or silver; finally the priests, in long white linen vestments, bore the venerable symbols of the deities—the boat-shaped lamp, the 'altar of succour', the palm of gold, the pyx with the mysteries, and, greatest of all, the golden urn containing the sacred water of the Nile. Pausing frequently at altars erected at intervals along the route, where the holy objects were exposed to view, the procession advanced to the sea-shore. Here a ship, bedizened with gold and citrus-wood and richly painted with Egyptian hieroglyphics, was consecrated by the chief priest. Gifts and votive offerings were placed on board; the canvas, on which was inscribed in golden letters a prayer for prosperous navigation in the new year, was spread to the breeze; the cables were loosed, and, amid the acclamations of the multitude, the vessel went slowly out to sea.[1]

In the sanctuaries of Isis two offices—matins and vespers— were daily performed. The first took place at dawn.[2] A priest

whose aspect are blent the aspects of all gods and goddesses' (Apul. *Metam*. xi. 5). She was everything in one—'una quae est omnia' (*C.I.L.* x. 3800). For an interpretation of the Isis myth, see Plutarch, *De Isid. et Osir.*

[1] Apuleius, *Metam*. xi. 8–11, 16, 17. There was another great festival in November commemorating the quest and finding of Osiris, when priests and people abandoned themselves, first to a passion of grief for the death of the god, and then to exuberant rejoicing over his resurrection (Minucius Felix, *Oct.* 21; Lactantius, *Instit. Divin.* i. 21; Firmicus Maternus, *De Errore Profan. Relig.* 2; Augustin. *De Civitate Dei*, vi. 10).

[2] Apuleius, *Metam*. xi. 20 'templi matutinas apertiones'; ibid. xi. 22 'rituque solemni apertionis celebrato ministerio'.

drew apart the shining curtains which veiled the shrine, and, while litanies were recited, kindled fires upon the altars and offered libations of water, supposed to be of the Nile; finally, standing on the threshold, he awakened the deity, calling aloud the holy name in the Egyptian tongue.[1] Meanwhile female attendants completed the toilet of the statue, combing its hair and arraying it with sumptuous robes and jewels.[2] It was then displayed, with the other images, for the silent adoration of the faithful.[3] At two o'clock in the afternoon a vesper office was sung, in the course of which the urn of holy water (symbolizing the fructifying power of Osiris) was lifted up and venerated. At the termination of this service the temple was closed for the night.

The ceremonies of initiation were of a specially solemn character. The candidate for the mysteries took up his abode for an indefinite period within the precincts of the temple, devoting himself to fasting and prayer, attending the daily offices, and at night being often comforted by visions of the goddess. At length he received a divine sign that his time of probation was nearly ended. Having paid the initiation-fees, which were considerable, he was baptized in the sacred font, and stationed at the feet of the image of the goddess, where certain secret instructions were whispered to him. During the next ten days he ate no flesh and drank no wine. Then came the evening of supreme revelation. About sunset the neophyte was received by the congregation of initiates, who welcomed him and offered him gifts. A new linen robe was cast about him, and he was led into the inner sanctuary, where—so he was told—he must needs suffer voluntary death that he might attain to new life. What happened in that secret chamber was known to none, save the initiates of Isis. Probably a symbolic drama was enacted in semi-darkness. The neophyte, intensely excited, dazzled by rays of coloured light which came and went in the deep gloom, bewildered by weird music played by an invisible orchestra, intoxicated and half-suffocated with incense and perfumes, seems to have fallen into a hypnotic trance. One who underwent the experience describes it thus: 'I drew near to the confines of

---

[1] Apuleius, *Metam.* xi. 20; Porphyr. *De Abstin.* iv. 9; cf. Arnobius, *Adv. Gentes*, vii. 32. [2] Apuleius, *Metam.* xi. 9.

[3] Silent meditation before the image was a characteristic of the Egyptian worship; cf. Apuleius, *Metam.* xi. 17 'intuitans deae specimen pristinos casus meos recordabar'; ibid. xi. 24; Porphyr. *De Abstin.* iv. 6.

K k

death; I trod the threshold of Proserpine; I was swept through all the elements and returned to earth again. At midnight I saw the sun flashing with brilliant radiance. I drew near to the gods of heaven and the gods of hell,' and worshipped them face to face.' On the following morning the new initiate, clad in the 'cloak of Olympus' embroidered with figures of beast-deities, and wearing a crown of palm with leaves extended like rays, was placed on a wooden dais before the image of the goddess; the curtains were then swung back and the congregation was permitted to gaze on one who had been born to a superhuman life and become assimilated to the immortals.[1]

While the religion of Isis stimulated the imagination by its affecting ritual and vivid symbolism, it also satisfied, by the promise of a blessed immortality, one of the deepest and most persistent cravings of the human heart. No religion, except Christianity, had hitherto offered to mankind so definite an assurance of a life to come. The initiate who continued faithful in the observances of religion and showed himself worthy of the deity, was guaranteed prolongation of life 'beyond the space ordained by his fate', and enjoyment 'in the Elysian fields' of that beatific communion with the goddess of which, while yet on earth, he had been vouchsafed a foretaste.[2] The lotus, the emblem of immortality, everywhere appears on symbols of the cult. A motto inscribed on many tombs, 'May Osiris give thee the water of refreshment',[3] seems to have suggested the familiar phrase, 'the place of refreshment',[4] whereby Christians were wont to designate the abode of the departed.

(d) Finally, from Persia came the religion of Mithra[5]—'the purest and most elevated of all non-Biblical religions'. This cult, which was pre-eminently the religion of soldiers, was based on dualism. The world was conceived as the scene of a truceless conflict between the supreme deity and the deified principle of evil. Human life was a holy war, wherein the warriors of Mithra,

[1] Apuleius, *Metam.* xi. 19, 21–4. The initiation was gradual. The hero of Apuleius was obliged to undergo three initiations in order to obtain the whole revelation; ibid. xi. 28, 29.

[2] See the concluding words of the speech of Isis, ibid. xi. 6.

[3] *C.I.G.* 6562. For the idea cf. Rev. vii. 17; xxi. 6.

[4] 'Refrigerii sedes'.

[5] See F. Cumont, *Textes et monuments figurés relatifs aux mystères de Mithra*; id. *Les mystères de Mithra*; S. Reinach, *Cultes, mythes et religions*, ii, pp. 220 ff.; J. von Grill, *Die persische Mysterienreligion im römischen Reiche und das Christentum.*

aided by angels or celestial spirits, contended against the hosts of demons to bring about the triumph of righteousness. Those who fought this good fight were required to submit to discipline and to help one another. Thus Mithraism inculcated a remarkably pure and vigorous morality, exalted the virtues of obedience, loyalty, and good faith, and laid great stress upon fraternity. Further, the fighters, in view of the apparent triumph of evil in the world, needed the encouragement of a future hope. So Mithraism developed its interesting doctrines of the second coming of Mithra at the end of the world, of the resurrection of the dead, of the Great Judgement, of the committal of the wicked along with the spirit of evil to the fire, and of the ascent of the souls of the just through the seven planetary spheres to the region of eternal light.

The worship of Mithra was conducted in small, underground crypts,[1] brilliantly illuminated and adorned with symbolic figures. Along the sides of the sanctuary were stone benches for the accommodation of the initiates. The central aisle ended in an apse—apparently railed in—within which was set the familiar sculptured slab, with altars in front. The slab, on one side, displayed the scene of the slaying of the bull—the set piece in Mithraic art corresponding with the crucifix in Christian art; at the climax of the service the plaque turned on a pivot, exhibiting, on its other side, a representation of the banquet of reconciliation between Mithra and the Sun. In these chapels three offices—at dawn, at noon, and in the evening—were daily recited; and, for those who were initiated, sacraments were celebrated, which were supposed to impart immortality.

In many points this solar cult curiously resembled Christianity. The 'unconquered' Mithra himself was the 'Mediator' between the unknowable God and the human race, the Lord of light and truth, the Conqueror of death, the Protector and Saviour of souls. He was miraculously born, and conferred immense benefits on mankind by means of a sacrifice. His work

[1] There were several of these shrines in Rome. The most famous was that in the seventh district. This was probably the object of the attack of the City Praefect Gracchus, who in A.D. 377 broke into a Mithreum and destroyed the images which it contained, thereby qualifying himself for Christian baptism (Hieron. *Ep.* 107. 2; cf. Prudentius, *Contr. Symmach.* i. 562–6). In northern Italy, Milan and Aquileia were the chief seats of the cult. An allusion to the Mithraic crypts may perhaps be detected in Ambros. *In ps. 45 enarr.* 24.

ended, he retired to heaven, whence he was expected to descend at the end of the world, to separate the good souls from the bad and to give to the former the mystic drink which would immortalize them. His ceremonies included baptism for the washing away of sins, and a liturgical meal (commemorative of Mithra's last supper after the conclusion of his labours) of consecrated bread and mingled wine and water. All his initiates were brethren, owing one another fraternal love; the highest of them were termed 'fathers'. There were seven degrees of initiation,[1] of which the first three were merely preparatory and did not admit to full communion. When a man entered the third grade he was called 'soldier', was branded on the brow, and henceforth belonged to the Church Militant of the Invincible God. The real initiation was designated *sacramentum* (perhaps from the oath not to divulge the mysteries). Ideals of purity were inculcated, physical continence being specially commended. The seventh day of the week was sacred, and the 25th of December, the birthday of the Sun, was the great festival of the Mithraic year. The Christian Fathers were disposed to explain these startling resemblances as Satanic parodies of Christian things.

'The devil', wrote Tertullian,[2] 'baptizes some, his own believers and faithful ones, and promises remission of sins after immersion. And, if I still recollect rightly, Mithra there signs his soldiers on their foreheads, celebrates the oblation of bread, introduces a symbol of the resurrection, and wins a crown under the sword. Moreover he restricts his high priest to one marriage. The devil too has virgins and those who practise continence.'

On the other hand, some modern critics have supposed that Christianity borrowed certain features from Mithraism. It is possible that, in matters of detail, there was some imitation and adaptation on either side. Yet the main similarities are better accounted for as parallel developments. Both Mithraism and Christianity were mystery religions; each had the same general conceptions of blessing conferred on the race through a sacrifice, of a fellowship of the initiated, of salvation mediated through sacraments; and each tended almost inevitably to develop along similar lines.

[1] Hieron. *Ep.* 107. 2; Corax, Cryphius, Miles, Leo, Perses, Heliodromus, and Pater.

[2] Tertullian, *De Praescript. Haeret.* 40; cf. *De Corona*, 15. See also Justin Martyr, *Apol.* i. 66; *Trypho*, 78.

These were the principal Oriental cults which flourished in the West in the time of Ambrose. In them we discover the real religion of paganism. In striking contrast with the official Roman religion, the exotic cults from Asia Minor, Syria, Egypt, and Persia did actually and efficaciously minister to the essential needs of the soul. First, they satisfied the *emotions*. The old Roman religion—representing, as it did, a sort of legal contract between the deity and the worshipper, in accordance with which the former dispensed blessings in precise proportion to the observance of prescribed rites by the latter—was a cold, prosaic, formal business, and definitely discouraged religious enthusiasm as 'superstitious'. The Oriental religions, however, by music and art, by impressive and voluptuous ritual, by fasts and festivals in which the sentiments of joy and grief and hope and terror were granted unrestrained expression, both stimulated and provided an outlet for that religious sensibility which nowhere else on pagan soil received adequate recognition. Secondly, the Oriental religions satisfied the *intellect*. In the West faith and reason had become hopelessly divorced. Speculation on the problems of nature and human life was completely independent of conventional acceptance of the sacred tradition. Roman religion was, in fact, an unintelligible thing—a farrago of ridiculous and obsolete conceptions. It was otherwise, however, with the religions of the Orient. The priests of these cults were indefatigable students of contemporary science and philosophy, and the results of their learned researches, by means of subtle allegorization, were progressively incorporated in the religious dogma.[1] Thus, not only the simple-minded, but also people with enlightened views were able with sincerity to accept the archaic myths, so brilliantly interpreted by the sacred exegetes, and find them intellectually satisfying. Thirdly, the Oriental cults acted on the *conscience*. The old Roman religion failed to adapt itself to advancing morals, just as it failed to keep pace with advancing knowledge. It is true that it inculcated the antique virtues—temperance, courage, obedience to parents and magistrates, reverence for the laws, devotion to

---

[1] Augustin. *Ep.* 91. 5 'Illa omnia quae antiquitus de vita deorum moribusque conscripta sunt longe aliter sunt intelligenda atque interpretanda sapientibus. Ita vero in templis populis congregatis recitari huiuscemodi salubres interpretationes heri et nudiustertius audivimus'.

one's country; but the virtues which it emphasized were not so much personal as national and social. It required externally decorous conduct in the interest of public order; with the conscience and character and inward habit of the individual it was hardly at all concerned. On the other hand, the Oriental religions—though their legends and rites contained features which may well have appeared immoral to those who did not understand the symbolism—did in fact profoundly influence the moral life. They stimulated in the individual the desire for personal redemption through union with a Higher Power; they provided means of purification, which is the condition of such union; they further took measures to preserve the purified being from fresh defilement. Mystic banquets ministered spiritual nourishment to the initiate; fastings, confessions, and penances helped to keep him emancipated from the tyranny of the passions; a priesthood skilled in the direction of souls afforded him ghostly comfort and guidance. Finally the sure hope of blessed immortality encouraged the tempted man to overcome temptation and endeavour to win that celestial reward in comparison with which all earthly and material happiness seemed insipid and contemptible.

(iv) Even the briefest account of fourth-century paganism would be seriously defective if it did not contain some reference to Neoplatonism.[1] This system, compounded of Platonism and Orientalism, and developed successively by the Egyptian Plotinus, by his Syrian disciple Porphyry, by the Syrian Iamblichus, and (in the fifth century) by Proclus the Lycian, afforded powerful intellectual support to paganism in its last conflict with Christianity. As presented by Porphyry and later exponents, it was itself not merely a philosophy, but also a religion. Its basic theory may be thus outlined. The great First Cause, the Fount of all being and thinking, the supreme Good, is the One—the transcendent God, incomprehensible and indescribable, to be approached only in ecstasy. From this Absolute Unity issues or emanates pure Mind; from Mind proceeds Soul, which includes the World-Soul; from the World-Soul is engendered the universe

---

[1] See E. Vacherot, *Histoire critique de l'école d'Alexandrie*; E. Zeller, *Die Philosophie der Griechen*, iii; A. Richter, *Neuplatonische Studien*; A. E. Chaignet, *Hist. de la Psychologie des Grecs*, iv, v; C. Bigg, *Neoplatonism*; W. R. Inge, art. 'Neoplatonism' in Hastings' *Encycl. of Religion and Ethics*.

of sense, with all its graduated existences. Matter, however, is not exactly an emanation from the World-Soul, but is conceived rather as a passive principle on which rational form is imprinted, yet which is itself evil and the cause of evil. All individual souls are of celestial origin. But these, descending into bodies, forget more or less completely the source from which they spring, and become imprisoned and entombed in matter. What they need, therefore, for their salvation, is a way of return from the earthlies to the heavenlies—'to the most dear fatherland, where is the Father and where are all things'.[1] The way of return lies in the devoted practice of the various classes of virtues—not merely of the ordinary 'political' or social virtues, but also of the purifying virtues which aim at emancipating the soul from the dominion of the passions, and of the mystic or deifying virtues whereby the soul is trained to concentration on, assimilation to, and identification with, the divine. The supreme beatitude consists in ecstatic elevation to immediate knowledge of and union with God.

Neoplatonism provided paganism with intellectual justification. It found room in its system for all the gods and all the cults. The innumerable deities were identified with the series of potencies or emanations, issuing originally out of the essence of the Ineffable and Inscrutable One. The innumerable myths and legends were interpreted as symbolic expressions of the pure truths of a primitive divine revelation. The innumerable worships were recognized as different means to the same end—the beatific union of the worshipper with the Deity. By the Neoplatonists of the fourth and fifth centuries even magic and theurgy were sanctioned and defended. Thus, by ingenious exegesis, all the various heathen cults, with their various traditions and superstitions, were happily harmonized with one another, and given accommodation in a system which embodied the most advanced philosophical and spiritual ideas of the time. Neoplatonism, in short, effected a rational unification of paganism. The heathen religions ceased to be isolated. Thanks to the Neoplatonic expositors, they came to be regarded as but different parts of one great whole, different branches of one great tree, different sections or denominations of one great pagan Church.

It must be admitted that in Ambrose's time paganism showed

---

[1] Words of Plotinus quoted by Augustine, *De Civitate Dei*, ix. 17.

to great advantage. Yet the Christian leaders of the period, from their own point of view, were right when they urged that it ought not to be tolerated. These worships, in fact, were too attractive. Not only did they hinder men from adopting Christianity; they tempted those who were Christians already either to lapse altogether,[1] or at any rate to participate occasionally in the seductive heathen ceremonies.[2] There was, indeed, a real danger that, if Christianity did not succeed in ousting paganism, paganism would succeed in ousting Christianity. Hence we can understand the fervent energy with which Ambrose threw himself into the Christian-pagan struggle, the history of which must now briefly be related.

## B

From the time of Constantine to that of Gratian paganism equally with Christianity had been recognized by the State. It is true that the Emperor Constantius exhibited some unfriendliness towards the old religion. He ordered the abolition of the heathen sacrifices and the closing of the temples;[3] and removed the altar of Victory from the Roman Senate-House.[4] It is certain, however, that, at any rate in the West, the anti-pagan enactments were not strictly put in force. The Emperor realized that it would not be politic to push religious reform too far, and on his visit to Rome in A.D. 357 he prudently assumed an attitude of genial toleration.[5] Such reforms as he did carry out were abrogated by his successor. Julian reopened the temples, restored the sacrifices and the altars (including that of Victory), and loaded the sacred ministers with privileges and pensions.[6] Jovian, in his turn, while he reinstated the Church in the rights of which it had been deprived, took no repressive measures against paganism. And the same tolerant policy, as has been already pointed out,[7] was pursued by Valentinian. During the

---

[1] Ambrose, *Ep.* 17. 4, speaks of many Christians having lapsed. Cf. the *Carmen* addressed to a senator who had reverted to the worship of Cybele and Isis (Hartel's *Cyprian*, Appendix, 302–5); and the legislation against apostasy, Cod. Theod. xvi, tit. 7.

[2] Pseudo-Ambros. *Serm.* vii *de kalendis Januariis* (Ambrosii Opp. iv. 617, 618); Maximus Taurin. *Hom.* 16; Salvian, *De Gubern. Dei*, viii. 2.

[3] Cod. Theod. xvi. 10. 4; cf. Ambros. *Ep.* 17. 5.

[4] Symmachus, *Relatio* 3. 4 and 6 (ed. O. Seeck in *M.G.H.*); Ambros. *Ep.* 18. 32.

[5] Symmachus, *Relat.* 3. 7; cf. Ammian. xvi. 10.

[6] Sozomen. *H.E.* v. 3.                              [7] See above, pp. 84, 85.

whole of his reign the altar of Victory stood, as of yore, in the Senate-House at Rome, and incense was burnt thereon by the senators.[1]

After Valentinian's death, however, the situation changed. It was probably in the year of his accession to the government of the whole Western Empire—i.e. in A.D. 375—that Gratian startled the world by a gesture of definite hostility to paganism. From the time of Augustus all Roman emperors had assumed the style and dignity of Pontifex Maximus. On the accession of an emperor the sacerdotal robe was formally presented to him by the Pontifical College, and his name was enrolled in the catalogue of Chief Pontiffs. Even Christian rulers had complacently taken the honourable pagan title. Gratian, however, had scruples; when, according to precedent, the priestly vestment was offered him by the pontiffs, he refused it. The pontiffs were deeply offended, and the senior among them is said to have muttered, 'If the Emperor does not wish to be called Pontifex, yet very soon there will be a Pontifex, Maximus!'—a remark which was remembered, and, after the successful revolt of Maximus, was deemed prophetic.[2] No public remonstrance was made, however; for the use or disuse of an imperial title was obviously an affair of the Emperor's prerogative.

After this 'secularization of the purple' Gratian abstained for some years from further action against paganism. His attention, so far as religious matters were concerned, was absorbed by the struggle against Arianism in Upper Italy and the Danubian provinces. But by the end of A.D. 381 Arianism (outside Justina's circle) was virtually defeated in the Western Empire, and the Emperor's thoughts—no doubt under Ambrose's discreet direction, though Ambrose himself denied that he had explicitly suggested the particular measures taken[3]—turned once more to the question of paganism. As a sincere Christian he was disquieted by the flourishing condition of heathenism in Rome; and it was this Roman heathenism—the religion of the Senate and the Roman aristocracy, which insolently claimed to be the national religion—that he determined to

[1] Ambrose affirms that Valentinian himself was ignorant of these facts (*Ep.* 17. 16); but this statement, which occurs in a highly rhetorical passage, cannot be taken seriously.
[2] Zosimus, iv. 36. On the date, see G. Rauschen, op. cit., p. 120.
[3] Ambros. *Ep.* 57. 2.

attack. Towards the end of the year A.D. 382[1] he issued an important edict of disestablishment and disendowment.[2] It provided that the revenues hitherto allocated by the State for the maintenance of the heathen sacrifices and ceremonies should be confiscated, partly to the Imperial Treasury and partly to the Praefect's Exchequer;[3] that the subsidies hitherto paid to the Vestal Virgins and to the priests should be diverted to the service of the State Post;[4] that landed estates bequeathed to the Vestals and the priests should be appropriated by the Treasury (though other gifts and legacies were still permitted);[5] and that the exemptions from public burdens hitherto enjoyed by the pagan religious dignitaries should be abolished.[6] A second edict, published at the same time, ordained that the altar of Victory— the symbol of Rome's loyalty to her ancient religion—should be removed from the Senate-House.[7] By these two measures— though the pagans were allowed to retain their religious opinions and even to celebrate their religious rites at their own charges[8] —Roman paganism was disconnected from its official association with the State and deprived of the subvention customarily granted by the State for its support.

The Senate, being notified of the imperial proceeding, was extremely perturbed. In this body there was a pagan majority,[9] led by three distinguished nobles—Praetextatus, Symmachus, and Flavian. This party made prompt arrangements for the maintenance of the sacrifices and sacred rites by private subscription. Meanwhile a resolution was moved and carried in the Curia that a deputation, headed by Symmachus, should wait upon the Emperor and present to him a petition for the repeal of the

---

[1] For the year, see Ambros. *Ep.* 17. 10 (written in the summer of A.D. 384) 'ante biennium ferme'. In the summer of A.D. 382 (between May and November) Gratian was absent from Milan. In the same summer Ambrose attended the Council at Rome. It is not unlikely that he was scandalized by what he then saw of Roman paganism, and, when he again met the Emperor at Milan in the autumn, communicated to him his unfavourable impressions. This may well have decided Gratian to take drastic measures.

[2] Ibid. 17. 5 and 16.  [3] Ibid. 17. 3.  [4] Symmachus, *Relat.* 3. 15.

[5] Ibid. 3. 13; Ambros. *Ep.* 18. 16.

[6] Symmachus, *Relat.* 3. 11; Ambros. *Epp.* 17. 4; 18. 11.

[7] Symmachus, *Relat.* 3. 3 and 4; cf. Ambros. *Epp.* 17. 9; 18. 10 and 31.

[8] Ambros. *Ep.* 17. 7.

[9] Ambrose mistakenly affirms that the majority was Christian (*Epp.* 17. 9 and 10; 18. 31). If this had been so, the appeal to the Emperor could not have been carried. Ambrose's attempt to explain this point (*Ep.* 17. 11) is hardly satisfactory.

decrees. But an influential minority of Christian senators immediately drew up a counter-petition, wherein they protested that they had not consented to the deputation, and even threatened that, if its request were conceded, they would in future abstain from attending the meetings of the House. This document was forwarded by Pope Damasus to Ambrose for transmission to the Emperor.[1] Backed by a strong recommendation from the Bishop of Milan and by the representations of Christian officials in the palace, it produced the desired result. When the senatorial embassy reached the Court, it was refused an audience.[2]

It is not unlikely that the incident, related by Sozomen,[3] of Ambrose's intercession on behalf of a pagan noble condemned to death for having said that Gratian was unworthy of his imperial father, was connected with these events. The pagan aristocrat, indignant at the anti-pagan edicts, seems to have commented unfavourably on the contrast between Gratian's religious policy and that of the elder Valentinian. His incautious remarks were regarded as insulting to the Emperor's Majesty, and he was found guilty of high treason. Ambrose, however, realized that the execution of a pagan under such circumstances, though strictly the punishment for a political offence, would be interpreted as an instance of religious persecution. This could not fail to be detrimental to the cause which both he and Gratian had at heart. Hence his eagerness to procure a pardon for the offender, and the Emperor's willingness to grant it. It was the object of both to demonstrate that the recent legislation was directed only against pagan institutions and not against pagan persons.

But now the outraged gods seemed to bestir themselves to avenge the injuries inflicted on them. In the August of the following year, A.D. 383, Gratian was foully murdered; moreover in Egypt, Africa, Spain, and the central and southern parts of Italy the crops failed to such a degree that they did not suffice even for the needs of the provincials, still less for the supply of provisions for the capital.[4] In Rome a shortage of food was

---

[1] Ambros. *Ep.* 17. 10.     [2] Symmachus, *Relat.* 3. 1 and 20.
[3] Sozomen. *H.E.* vii. 25; cf. above, p. 120.
[4] Symmachus, *Relat.* 3. 15–17; *Epp.* ii. 6, 7, 52; iv. 74; Ambros. *Ep.* 18. 17–21. Symmachus exaggerates, Ambrose minimizes, the extent of the disaster (see Seeck's *Symmachus*, p. cxx). Prudentius, *Contr. Symmach.* ii. 913, takes the same line as Ambrose.

threatened. The mob became restive;[1] and the authorities, fearing a famine with its inevitable accompaniment of popular disturbance, took the extreme step of ordering all foreign residents to quit the City.[2] Innumerable aliens, many of whom had passed the greater part of their lives in Rome, were seen issuing from the gates, followed by their weeping wives and children. It was remarked as a scandal that, while professors of the liberal arts were ejected without a moment's breathing-space, three thousand ballet-girls, with their dancing-masters and choruses, were left unmolested, without a single question being put to them by the officials who organized the expulsion.[3]

With the death of Gratian the hopes of the pagan party revived. At the Court of Valentinian there was a strong pagan element. Bauto, the all-powerful prime minister of the Emperor, was probably an adherent of the old religion; Rumoridus, the distinguished general, was so undoubtedly.[4] By their influence and that of other courtiers of the same persuasion, the pagan stalwarts Praetextatus and Symmachus were, in A.D. 384, made respectively Praetorian Praefect of Italy and Praefect of the City. Moreover, in the same year Praetextatus obtained an imperial edict—obviously aimed at Christian despoilers of temples—by which the Praefect of Rome was authorized to search out and restore the materials which had been abstracted from public buildings and converted to private use.[5] All these circumstances encouraged Symmachus to believe that 'the bad reputation of recent times [i.e. the reign of Gratian] was being redeemed by pious Emperors' [i.e. Valentinian].[6]

The hour seemed favourable for making an attempt to procure the repeal of Gratian's anti-pagan legislation. The Senate, egged on by Symmachus, resolved to petition the Emperor[7] to restore the altar of Victory to the Senate-House, and the subsidies and immunities to the ministers of the old religion; and

---

[1] Symmachus, *Epp.* ii. 6.
[2] Ambros. *De Officiis*, iii. 49; Symmachus, *Epp.* ii. 7.
[3] Ammian. xiv. 6. 19.                                         [4] Ambros. *Ep.* 57. 3.
[5] Symmachus, *Relat.* 21. 5; cf. ibid. 3. The phrase of Symmachus in *Relat.* 3. 1 'subjecta legibus vitia' may be an allusion to this edict.
[6] Symmachus, *Relat.* 3. 1.
[7] Notwithstanding the mention of the three Emperors (Valentinian, Theodosius, and Arcadius) in the final copy of the Memorial (*Relat.* 3. 1), the document was clearly intended only for Valentinian (Ambros. *Ep.* 57. 2; cf. *Ep.* 17. 12). See Seeck, *Symmachus*, p. xvii.

a deputation was nominated to convey the petition to the Court.[1] This was in the summer of A.D. 384.[2] The petition was formulated by Symmachus himself in a Memorial,[3] which evoked universal admiration. Even Ambrose could not refrain from praising the 'golden tongue' and glittering eloquence of his learned rival;[4] while so determined an anti-pagan as the poet Prudentius expressed his hope that the superb composition of the great orator would live for ever and be honoured with the fame which so glorious a masterpiece deserved.[5]

Symmachus commenced his plea with the statement that he was approaching the Sovereign in a twofold capacity. As Praefect of the City, it was his duty to report the transactions of the Senate; as delegate of the senators and citizens of Rome, he was bound to present the petition which they had entrusted to him. But in either capacity his sole anxiety was to safeguard the honour and popularity of the Emperor.[6] Hence he ventured to appeal to him to preserve for his loyal subjects their venerable religious institutions.

'We ask for the restoration of that condition of religion under which the State has so long prospered. Let the Emperors of either sect and either opinion be reckoned up. Julian observed the rites of his ancestors; Valentinian the First did not abolish them. If the example of Julian does not constitute a precedent, let the connivance of Valentinian and Valens do so.'[7]

'Every one', he continued, 'has his own customs, every one his own rites. The Divine Mind has distributed to different cities different guardians and different worships. As to each man when he is born there is given a separate soul, so to each nation is given a genius which presides over its destiny. And here comes in the evidence of benefits received, which is the best proof to man of the existence of

---

[1] Paulinus, *Vita Ambros.* 26. Paulinus confuses this embassy with that of A.D. 391.

[2] Ambrose's two letters with reference to the petition (*Epp.* 17, 18) were written when Symmachus was Praefect of Rome, i.e. early summer A.D. 384–5 (*Ep.* 57. 2; cf. Symmachus, *Relat.* 3. 2), and before the death of Pope Damasus, 11 December, A.D. 384 (Ambros. *Ep.* 17. 10). More precisely, *Ep.* 18 was composed after the harvest of A.D. 384 (*Ep.* 18. 20). If we allow time for the conveyance of the petition to Milan, for the deliberation of the Consistory thereon, and for the composition of Ambrose's refutation, we must place the resolution of the Senate about the middle of the summer of the year A.D. 384.

[3] Symmachus, *Relat.* 3, edited by O. Seeck, *Symmachus*, pp. 280–3. On the text see Seeck's Introduction, pp. xvii ff.

[4] Ambros. *Ep.* 18. 2.

[5] Prudentius, *Contr. Symmach.* i. 649, 650; cf. ibid. i. 633–8; ii. Praef. 56–8.

[6] Symmachus, *Relat.* 3. 2.        [7] Ibid. 3. 3.

the gods. For, since our reason is wholly in the dark, whence can we better derive our knowledge of the divinities than from the record and evidence of prosperity enjoyed in their service?'

'Now if a long course of time gives sanction to religious customs, we ought to keep faith with so many centuries and follow our ancestors, who in their day prospered through following theirs. Imagine Rome herself standing before you and thus addressing you—"Excellent Emperor, Father of your country, respect the years which I have attained in the practice of these holy rites. Let me keep the ancient ceremonies, for I have no desire to change them. Let me live after my own fashion, for I am free. It is this worship which has subdued the world to my laws. It is these mysteries which repulsed Hannibal from the walls, the Gauls from the Capitol. Can it be that I have been preserved for this—to be censured after so many centuries? I am willing to consider any innovation that is thought needful; yet late and ignominious is the reformation of old age." We plead, then, for a respite for the gods of our fathers, the gods of our native land. It is right to believe that that which all men worship is The One. We look on the same stars; the same heaven is above us all; the same universe environs us. What matters it by what method each of us seeks the truth? We cannot by a single road arrive at so great a secret.'[1]

The orator dwelt at some length on the removal of the altar of Victory and on the withdrawal of the subsidies and privileges. As regards the former, he urged that the Emperor's relations with the barbarians were not so amicable as to justify him in rejecting the patronage of Victory. Why should he desert that kindly power which had blessed his arms with triumphs? And what a sinister omen was this—the putting away of Victory! But quite apart from omens, the ornaments of the Senate-House ought to be spared and its traditional procedure respected. 'Where shall we swear to obey the imperial laws and statutes? By what sanction shall the deceitful be deterred from false attestation? All places, indeed, are full of God, nor is any spot safe for the perjured; yet to feel that one is in the very presence of the Divine is of great avail for producing a fear of sin. That altar preserves the concord of all; that altar guarantees the good faith of each; and nothing gives more weight to the decisions of the Senate than the fact that all its decrees are issued, as it were, under the sanction of an oath.'[2] It was true that the

[1] Symmachus, *Relat.* 3. 8–10.
[2] Ibid. 3. 3–5. In this connexion it is worth noting that Victoria appears to have

Emperor Constantius had removed the altar; but his act had been an experiment, the failure of which should be a warning to his successors. In other respects Constantius had set a laudable example of reverence for Rome's time-honoured sanctities.

'He diminished none of the privileges of the sacred virgins, he filled the priestly offices with men of noble birth, he allowed the cost of the Roman ceremonies, and, following the rejoicing Senate through all the streets of the Eternal City, he beheld the shrines with unmoved countenance, read the names of the gods inscribed on their pediments, inquired about the origin of the temples and expressed admiration for their founders. Although he himself followed another religion, he preserved its own for the Empire.'[1]

With regard to the withdrawal of the subsidies, Symmachus's arguments are much the same as those which have again and again been advanced in later times against the disendowment of religious institutions by the State. The gain to the Treasury would be inconsiderable and could not compensate the Government for the odium which it would incur by the sacrilegious spoliation of the ministers of religion—the testamentary dispositions of pious benefactors should be respected—the religious functionaries deserved fair and even generous treatment, since through the instrumentality of their prayers the Empire itself had been divinely preserved and strengthened—the gods would punish wrongs inflicted on their servants; indeed, they had already shown their anger by the unparalleled scarcity of the previous year, which could not adequately be accounted for by purely natural causes.[2]

Finally Symmachus entreated the young Emperor not to allow himself to be deceived by the specious Christian argument that 'no grant of public funds ought to be made for the support of an alien religion'. It was not a question of a new grant. Long ago the supplies had been granted; the Emperor was only asked not to take back, by an arbitrary exercise of power, what had already been bestowed.

'May the unseen guardians of all the sects be propitious to Your Grace, and particularly may those who of old succoured your ancestors defend you and be worshipped by us! We ask for that

been particularly revered by the Symmachi. The orator's father, Lucius Aurelius Avianius Symmachus, Praefect of Rome in A.D. 364, set up a figure of Victory on or near the Valentinian Bridge; see H. Grisar, *Hist. of Rome and the Popes*, i, p. 155.

[1] Symmachus, *Relat.* 3. 6, 7.         [2] Ibid. 3. 11–17.

condition of religion which preserved the Empire to Your Majesty's father and blessed him with lawful heirs. That venerable father beholds from the starry height the tears of the priests, and feels himself censured by the abolition of a custom which he himself willingly observed. Correct also for your brother of blessed memory that which he did by the counsel of others; cover up the act by which he unwittingly offended the Senate. For it is certain that the deputation from the Senate was denied access to him, that the public opinion concerning his measures might not come to his knowledge. For the credit of former times you should not hesitate to annul that which was demonstrably not the doing of the Emperor.'[1]

This document was read in the Consistory and produced a profound impression. The councillors—not only the pagans but even some who were nominally Christian—recommended that the petition should receive favourable consideration.[2] The business, however, was adjourned; and, before a final decision was reached, Ambrose intervened. It appears that the pagans at Court, knowing that nothing but the most determined opposition was to be expected from the Bishop, had taken precautions to keep the senatorial deputation secret. After the reading of the Memorial in the Consistory, however, the affair could no longer be concealed. A report of what had happened speedily came to Ambrose's ear. The crisis was so sudden that he had no time to convoke a synod to draw up a formal protest; if the situation were to be saved, he had to act on his own responsibility and at once.[3] Accordingly, in great agitation, he addressed to 'the Most Blessed Prince and Most Christian Emperor, Valentinian', a stern, almost cruel, letter,[4] wherein he vehemently charged him, under threat of excommunication, not to countenance the worship of idols or assist it with endowments. For to restore the confiscated emoluments would be equivalent to granting a new endowment to paganism.[5] And what had the pagans done that they should be dealt with so indulgently? In the old days they had shed the blood of Christians and laid their churches in ruins; even so lately as the reign of Julian they had applauded the iniquitous law which deprived Christians of the right of teaching in the schools of literature.[6] Such people could not reasonably complain of oppressive treatment. Even

---

[1] Symmachus, *Relat.* 3. 18–20.  [2] Ambros. *Ep.* 17. 6 and 8.
[3] Ibid. 17. 10.  [4] Ibid. 17. Cf. *Epp.* 18. 1; 57. 2.
[5] Ibid. 17. 3; cf. *Ep.* 57. 2.  [6] Ibid. 17. 4.

if Constantius and Gratian had taken no measures against paganism, it would have been Valentinian's duty to make a beginning; as things were, he could not possibly repeal the pious ordinances of his predecessor.[1] Ambrose implored the young Emperor not to be misled by bad advisers—either by distinguished heathen, or by opportunists who called themselves Christians.[2] If a heathen monarch were to set up an idolatrous altar in the Senate-House and were to compel Christian senators to assemble there and participate in the idolatrous sacrifices, he would rightly be deemed a persecutor; what, then, would be thought of a Christian sovereign who perpetrated such atrocities?[3]

'I appeal to your faith, I appeal to your feelings, not to give your assent to this heathen petition, or be guilty of the sacrilege of appending your signature to any such assent. Refer the matter, I beg you, to the father of Your Piety, the Emperor Theodosius, whom you have been accustomed to consult on almost all questions of importance. Nothing is more important than religion, nothing is of higher moment than the faith. If this were a civil affair, the right of reply would be reserved for the opposing party; it is an affair of religion, and I, as bishop, make an appeal to you. Let a copy of the Memorial be handed to me, that I may answer it fully; and then let Your Grace's father be consulted on the whole business and vouchsafe an answer. Assuredly, if a decree adverse to us be issued, we bishops cannot patiently suffer it and take no notice. You, Sir, may come to the church, but either you will find no priest there, or you will find one who will resist you. What answer will you give to the priest, when he says to you, "The Church seeks not your offerings, because you have adorned with offerings the temples of the heathen. The altar of Christ rejects your gifts, because you have made an altar to idols— made it by your word, your hand, your signature, your act. The Lord Jesus refuses and rejects your service, because you have served idols; for He has said to you, *Ye cannot serve two masters.*" What will you answer to these words? That you fell into sin because you were only a boy? But no childhood is recognized in faith, for even little children in the face of their persecutors have fearlessly confessed Christ.'[4]

In a bold, rhetorical passage Ambrose conjured up before the

---

[1] Ambros. *Ep.* 17. 5.
[2] Ibid. 17. 6–8. In 6 Ambrose seems to refer to Symmachus, in 7 to Bauto, though no names are mentioned.
[3] Ibid. 17. 9.
[4] Ibid. 17. 12–15.

Emperor, first, the pathetic figure of the murdered Gratian bitterly reproaching his brother for meditating the repeal of those decrees of which he had been most proud and for which he had been most praised, and then the stern spirit of the elder Valentinian reproving his son for having so grossly misunderstood him as to imagine that he had knowingly connived at the superstition of the heathen. 'You see, then, Sir', he concluded, 'that if you decree what is now being asked for, you will be wronging, first God, and next your father and brother. I implore you to do that which you know will be profitable to your salvation in the sight of God.'[1]

The tone of this document, addressed by a great ecclesiastical statesman to a boy of thirteen, is admittedly unfortunate. It must be remembered, however, that Ambrose wrote in extreme hurry and under stress of painful excitement, and further that nothing less than a protest of the strongest character would have availed to counteract the pressure brought to bear on Valentinian by the Senate and the Court. At any rate, the letter achieved its purpose. Having heard it read in the Consistory, the young Emperor announced that he would follow the course advised by Ambrose, and the Council—even the two powerful pagan Counts, Bauto and Rumoridus—acquiesced in his decision.[2] The senatorial petition was accordingly dismissed.

Meanwhile Ambrose received a copy of the Memorial, and, with the text before him, proceeded to compose a detailed Refutation.[3] Though written in the form of a letter to Valentinian, the little work was not designed to influence the Emperor's action on the question of the pagan petition. That question was already settled. The senatorial deputation had been repulsed, and an abundant harvest had disproved its most telling argument.[4] Hence, though the Refutation, like the first letter of Ambrose to Valentinian, was read formally in the Consistory,[5] it was of no practical significance. It was not a

---

[1] Ambros. *Ep.* 17. 16 and 17.

[2] Ibid. 57. 3. I adopt Seeck's emendation, 'acquieverunt comites duo' for 'comiti suo'. In *Ep.* 18. 1 Ambrose seems to say that Valentinian, young in years but old in faith, had disapproved of the pagan petition, even before the receipt of his protest (*Ep.* 17); but this is merely a polite fiction, disproved by the intensely anxious tone of the protest itself.

[3] *Ep.* 18; cf. Paulinus, *Vita Ambros.* 26 'praeclarissimum libellum conscripsit'.

[4] Ambros. *Ep.* 18, 20.         [5] Ibid. 57. 3.

State paper, but a piece of Christian apologetic, intended to supply, for the edification of the general public, a reasoned answer to the contentions of the eloquent spokesman of paganism. We are bound to acknowledge, however, that in merit it is much inferior to Symmachus's Memorial. The rhetoric is exaggerated, the taste not always unexceptionable, the reasoning as a rule more clever than convincing. Yet the criticism of the three main points of the petitioners—that Rome desired the restoration of her ancient rites,[1] that stipends and privileges ought to be granted to the pagan ministers,[2] that the famine and the fate of Gratian were punishments for the anti-pagan legislation of A.D. 382[3]—is, on the whole, not ineffective. The Refutation, together with the Memorial and Ambrose's first letter to Valentinian, was published in a little book. Some years later this fell into the hands of the poet Prudentius, who (in the Second Part of his *Contra Symmachum*) translated the anti-pagan argument into verse with singular felicity.[4]

In the encounter with the pagans Ambrose had won a decisive triumph. The altar and statue of Victory remained hidden in the dusty obscurity of some lumber-room of the Senate-House. The priests and Vestals continued vainly to deplore their lost prosperity. Yet the pagan leaders, Praetextatus and Symmachus, retained the favour of the Emperor. The former was designated Consul for the ensuing year. The latter successfully escaped a trap which had been artfully laid for him by some Christian courtiers. As has been stated, he had been commissioned, as Praefect of the City, to conduct an inquiry into the misappropriation of ornaments of public buildings. His enemies now accused him of having abused the powers conferred on him to start a persecution against the Christians. They alleged that he had dragged Christian people to torture

[1] Ambros. *Ep.* 18. 4 ff.　　　　　　　　　　[2] Ibid. 18. 11 ff.

[3] Ibid. 18. 17 ff., 34 ff. Symmachus, it is true, had not dared openly to state the argument based on Gratian's death; but it had evidently been suggested, and was therefore answered by Ambrose.

[4] V. Both, *Des christlichen Dichters Prudentius Schrift gegen Symmachus*, 1882. Such passages as those in which Prudentius describes the true temple of God, which is the heart of man (*Contra Symmach.* ii. 244–55), or shows how the growth of the Roman Empire and the spread of Roman peace prepared the way for the triumph of Christ (ibid. ii. 582 ff.), or contrasts the two ways of religion (ibid. ii. 850 ff.), or appeals to Honorius to put an end to the gladiatorial games (ibid. ii. 1113 ff.), are incomparably finer than anything in Ambrose's *Refutation*.

even from the precincts of the churches, and had sent for bishops from far and near and thrown them into prison. The Emperor was persuaded to issue an edict, wherein he rebuked the Praefect in terms of unusual severity, withdrew the commission he had given him, and ordered that all who had been imprisoned on the charge of despoiling the temples should immediately be set at liberty. But those Christian courtiers were clumsy intriguers. For Symmachus, who had doubtless anticipated accusations of this kind, had acted with extraordinary caution, and at the date when the imperial censure was issued had not even commenced the inquiry into misappropriations. He had, therefore, no difficulty in proving his innocence. The affidavits of the officers of his staff, and a letter from Pope Damasus himself, certifying that no Christians had been imprisoned or otherwise ill-treated, completely exonerated him from blame and brought confusion on the Court faction.[1]

But towards the end of this year, A.D. 384, the pagan party suffered an irreparable loss in the death of their high-minded and capable chief, Praetextatus.[2] The event threw Rome into mourning. Even Jerome, who brutally announces to a correspondent that 'the consul-elect is now in Tartarus', bears witness to the sorrow that was felt throughout the city;[3] and Symmachus records that the people were so afflicted by the news of his decease that they actually abstained from attendance at the theatre.[4] Symmachus himself was overwhelmed with grief, and despairing of being able, without the support of his friend and colleague, to defeat the manœuvres of the Christians, asked permission of the Emperor to resign his office.[5] This request, however, was refused. He accordingly continued to administer the affairs of the city till the September of the following year, A.D. 385. But his adversaries lost no opportunity of harassing and annoying him, and he was unfeignedly thankful when the time came for him to retire.[6]

[1] For this incident see Symmachus, *Relat.* 21.
[2] G. Rauschen, op. cit. p. 177.
[3] Hieron. *Ep.* 23. 2 and 3; cf. 39. 3.
[4] Symmachus, *Relat.* 10. 2. The Senate asked leave of the Emperor to erect a statue in his honour (id. *Relat.* 12); and the Vestals, with the permission of the Pontifical College, set one up in their hall (id. *Epp.* ii. 36).
[5] Id. *Relat.* 10. 2 and 3.
[6] Early in October A.D. 385 Symmachus left Rome (*Epp.* ii. 48) and during the following month remained in seclusion on Campania (ibid. ii. 26). In spite of

The further history of the struggle between the old and the new religion will be narrated in a later chapter. It may be observed, however, that the most acute crisis in that struggle was unquestionably that of the year A.D. 384. In this year Christianity and paganism, the cult of demons,[1] came to grips, and for a moment it seemed doubtful which of the two would win the victory. The vigour of Ambrose saved the situation. Thanks mainly to his spirited action, the definitive triumph of Christianity as the State religion of the Western Empire was assured. One other point is worthy of notice. This momentous success was won, not by the Pope (who appears to have been incapable of offering effective resistance to heathenism even in his own episcopal city), but by the great Metropolitan of Northern Italy. Not Damasus but Ambrose, not Rome but Milan, determined the issue of the Christian-pagan controversy.

the attacks made on him he does not appear to have forfeited the favour of the Emperor; at any rate he was invited to Milan in A.D. 387 to assist in celebrating Valentinian's assumption of the consulship for the third time (ibid. iii. 52, 63). After his retirement he continued to be the leader of the Senate (Socrates, *H.E.* v. 14), and in A.D. 391 he was honoured with the consulship.

[1] Ambrose firmly believed that the heathen gods were not merely creations of the imagination, but real demonic existences (*De Incarn.* 83 'daemones, quorum simulacra Dei appellatione donantur'); hence his horror of pagan worship.

## CHAPTER XI

# THE PERSECUTION OF JUSTINA[1]

SINCE the death of Gratian, Valentinian II and his mother Justina had resided at Milan. The Empress, whose activities are the subject of this chapter, is a rather enigmatic figure. She is referred to in very unflattering terms by Ambrose, who does not hesitate to compare her with Jezebel and Herodias;[2] and Paulinus speaks of her intrigues, her rage, her fury.[3] But such expressions, used by Catholics with reference to the protectress of the execrated Arian heresy, must in some measure be discounted. Justina's character may not have been amiable; yet it is not necessary to assume that she was quite as black as she is painted. Perhaps only two things can be said of her with absolute certainty—she was an Arian in faith and she detested Ambrose.

The Empress's hatred of the Bishop was not based solely on religious grounds. She appears to have been an ambitious woman, bent on exercising supreme power by means of her influence over her son. To the realization of this ambition Ambrose threatened to be an obstacle. By his successful negotiation with Maximus he had laid Valentinian under an obligation, and his intervention in the affair of the senatorial petition proved that he had power to impose his will on the young and pliant Emperor. Suppose that this episcopal influence were to be still further increased; what would be the position of the Empress

---

[1] For the story of the 'persecution' see Ambrose, *Epistles* 20 and 21, and the *Sermon against Auxentius*; Augustin. *Confess.* ix. 7; Rufinus, *H.E.* ii. 15, 16; Paulinus, *Vita Ambros.* 12, 13, 20; cf. Socrates, *H.E.* v. 11; Sozomen. *H.E.* vii. 13; Theodoret. *H.E.* v. 13. Notwithstanding the arguments of O. Seeck (*Geschichte des Untergangs der antiken Welt*, v, pp. 201–2, 515) and J.-R. Palanque (*Saint Ambroise*, pp. 511–14), I interpret the Ambrosian documents as indicating that there were two separate 'persecutions'—the first in connexion with the claim to the Portian Basilica, before Easter, A.D. 385; the second in connexion with the law of 23 Jan. 386, probably in February and March, A.D. 386. That similar incidents occurred in connexion with each persecution is not incredible; nor can much stress be laid on the fact that Paulinus and the ecclesiastical historians speak of one crisis only, and not of two. See the discussion of G. Rauschen, *Jahrbücher der chr. Kirche*, pp. 488 ff.

[2] Ambros. *Ep.* 20. 18; cf. Rufinus, *H.E.* ii. 15 'illa Jezebel'. The reference to Herodias in *De Virginitate*, 11, may be pointed at Justina.

[3] Paulinus, *Vita Ambros.* 11, 12, 13, 15, 20.

Mother? Justina saw in Ambrose, not only an energetic enemy of her faith, but also a dangerous political rival.

Round the Empress gathered a party of opposition to the Bishop. It comprised a few pagans—we hear, for instance, of an expert in the forbidden art of magic, named Innocent, who was apparently in Justina's service[1]—some Gothic officers and members of the Imperial Household, who were Arians,[2] and a number of Court functionaries (e.g. Calligonus the Grand Chamberlain,[3] Euthymius,[4] and others) who were jealous of Ambrose and feared that he might supplant them in the good graces of the imperial boy whom they desired to keep under their own exclusive control. The object of the coalition was to discredit, and if possible procure the removal of, the too-powerful Bishop.

The point on which it was decided to do battle was the question of providing facilities for Arian worship in Milan. Justina was an Arian; some of the courtiers and officials, whether from honest conviction or for the sake of conciliating imperial favour, professed the same faith as the Empress; there was also quartered in the city a body of Gothic troops—perhaps sent by Theodosius for the protection of Valentinian—who were mostly Arians. Although there were practically no Arians among the townspeople,[5] who were solidly on the side of the Bishop, still the Arian courtiers, officials, and soldiers constituted a congregation of some dimensions. This congregation, however, had no church wherein to worship, all the Milanese basilicas being in the possession of the Catholics. Here was a grievance which Justina and the coalition determined to exploit.

It did not seem arbitrary to require that a single basilica should be given up to the Arians. According to the theory of the Roman Empire all places of public worship belonged to the Sovereign, who could dispose of them at pleasure.[6] Gratian, as we have seen, had acted on this theory and sequestrated a basilica;[7] no Catholic had protested. Theodosius had also acted on it, summarily confiscating Arian churches and handing them over to the Catholics; the proceeding had been applauded by

---

[1] Paulinus, *Vita Ambros.* 20.     [2] Ambros. *Ep.* 20. 12.     [3] Ibid. 20. 28.
[4] Paulinus, *Vita Ambros.* 12.     [5] Ambros. *Ep.* 20. 12.
[6] Ibid. 20. 8 'dicentibus imperatorem iure suo uti, eo quod in potestate eius essent omnia'; 19 'allegatur imperatori licere omnia, ipsius esse universa'.
[7] See above, p. 190.

the whole Catholic episcopate. But if the Emperor had a right to dispose of the property of one religious party, he had also the right to dispose of that of another. The quick intelligence of Justina grasped this point. The theory of the right of the Sovereign, which had already been used to justify the seizure of buildings belonging to heretics, could be employed to justify a similar seizure of buildings belonging to Catholics.

Outside the walls of Milan there was a Catholic church called Portiana or the Basilica of Portius (San Vittore al Corpo). This building Justina resolved to place at the disposal of her co-religionists.

Near the beginning of Lent, in the year A.D. 385, Ambrose was summoned to the imperial palace, where—no doubt with the object of overawing him—the illustrious members of the Emperor's Privy Council were already assembled. In their presence he was curtly ordered to give up the Portian Basilica. Of course, he refused. Argument was then resorted to; but, in a matter which concerned the vital interests of the Church, Ambrose was inflexible. While the discussion was proceeding in the council-chamber, the people, who had heard a rumour of what was going forward, rushed tumultuously to the palace, and a military Count with some light troops was sent out to disperse them. But the mob stood its ground, shouting, 'We are ready to die for the faith of Christ.' So great was the excitement, that at last Ambrose himself was requested to go to the gates and speak some soothing words. He accordingly addressed the people, pledging his word 'that no one should invade the basilica of the Church'. The crowd then became quiet. But the Palace clique made capital out of the incident, and by representing that the Bishop was responsible for the disturbance, prejudiced the Emperor's mind against him.[1]

For a few weeks the matter rested, but when Easter approached Justina renewed her attack. This time she was less moderate in her requirement. There were in Milan two adjacent cathedral basilicas—one, the ancient church, commonly called the Old Basilica; the other, of recent foundation, known as the New Basilica within the Walls. Justina, having failed in her attempt to get possession of the Portian Basilica in the suburbs, now actually had the audacity to demand the

---

[1] Ambros. *Serm. contr. Auxent.* 29.

surrender of the New Basilica within the Walls—the more important of the two main buildings of Ambrose's own cathedral church.[1] On the 4th of April, A.D. 385, which was the Friday before Palm Sunday, certain Counts of the Consistory waited upon the Bishop, and commanded him in the Emperor's name to hand over the New Basilica and restrain the people from making a disturbance. Ambrose replied tartly, 'A bishop cannot give up the temple of God.'[2]

The following day, Saturday, Ambrose reported his refusal to the congregation in the New Basilica, who received the announcement with applause. While this was going on the Praetorian Praefect of Italy appeared in the church. Ambrose's rebuff to the Consistorians had evidently shaken the Court, which now not only reduced its demand but condescended to urge it in a conciliatory manner. The Praefect uttered no threat, but endeavoured amicably to persuade the Bishop to give up at any rate the Portian Basilica, which, being only a suburban church, was not of such vital importance. Even this modified proposal, however, was unacceptable to the people, who uttered shouts of protest. The Praefect then withdrew, saying, 'I shall make a report to the Emperor.'[3]

On Palm Sunday, the 6th of April, Ambrose officiated in the New Basilica. The first part of the Mass—the Mass of the Catechumens—was duly solemnized, and the catechumens were dismissed. At this point in the service, in accordance with the custom observed at Milan on Palm Sunday, the Bishop went in procession to the baptistery, and there commenced 'the delivery of the Creed', that is, the exposition of the Creed to those who were preparing for baptism on Easter Eve. While thus engaged, he was informed that officers had been sent from the palace to the Portian Basilica, to make preparation for the appropriation of the building as imperial property. He was also told that the people were flocking thither in great numbers. Nevertheless he

---

[1] Ambros. *Ep.* 20. 1. This letter appears to have been written in haste, immediately after the events related, i.e. about Easter, A.D. 385. The account of what happened, particularly during the days between Palm Sunday and Maundy Thursday, is very confused. When Ambrose speaks of 'the basilica', it is often extremely difficult to understand to which of the three basilicas—the Portian, the Old, and the New—he is referring. The letter therefore requires a certain amount of interpretation, the correctness of which at all points cannot be guaranteed.

[2] Ibid. 20. 2.                                                    [3] Ibid. 20. 3.

continued his exposition, and, at its conclusion, returned to the
New Basilica and began to celebrate the Mass of the Faithful.
While he was offering, fresh tidings reached him that an excited
mob had laid violent hands on an Arian presbyter named
Castulus—probably one of the Court chaplains—whom they
had encountered in the street. He burst into tears, and, as he
made the oblation, prayed fervently that no blood might be
shed in the Church's quarrel, or at least that, if any one must
suffer, the victim might be himself. Meanwhile he dispatched
some of the presbyters and deacons who were assisting at the
celebration, to rescue Castulus from his perilous plight.[1]

The Court lost no time in exacting punishment for the rough
handling of the chaplain. On the Monday and Tuesday of Holy
Week—'during the sacred days of that last week wherein it was
usual to loose the bonds of debtors'[2]—the rich merchants of
Milan were thrown into prison and ordered pay within three
days a fine roughly equivalent to £8,000. To this requisition
the merchants replied, 'We will gladly pay that, and as much
again, if we may be allowed to retain our faith.' It seems that
the Government was uneasy concerning the loyalty of its own
servants. Stringent orders were issued that the minor officials of
the civil service—the clerks of the Record Office, the secret
police, the magistrates' officers—should keep close within doors,
that they might not become involved in any seditious outbreak.
At the same time persons of rank were threatened with severe
penalties, if they did not procure the surrender of the basilica.[3]

---

[1] Ambros. *Ep.* 20. 4 and 5.

[2] Ibid. 20. 6. Valentinian I enacted that in honour of Easter persons detained
in prison should be released, excepting such as were in custody on account of
the major crimes of sacrilege, treason, robbing of graves, poisoning, magic, rape,
adultery, and murder (Cod. Theod. ix. 38. 3 and 4). In A.D. 381 Valentinian II
and Theodosius made laws to much the same effect, though the number of excepted
crimes was increased, and relapsed criminals were excluded from indulgence (ibid.
ix. 38. 6 and 7). The same Emperors enacted that, if through accident the imperial
letters of pardon arrived too late, provincial governors should release on Easter
Day all prisoners who were not charged with any of the greater crimes (ibid.
ix. 38. 8). 'The imperial letters are sent forth', writes Chrysostom (*Hom. in ps.*
*cxlv.* 1), 'commanding all prisoners to be loosed from their bonds. For as our Lord,
when He was in Hades, set at liberty all who were under the power of death, so
His servants, contributing what they are able, in imitation of the mercy of the
Lord, loose men from visible bonds, though they have no power to loose them
from those that are spiritual.' See also Flavian's plea to Theodosius for pardon of
the rioters of Antioch, below, p. 367.

[3] Ambros. *Ep.* 20. 6 and 7.

It was, perhaps, on the Tuesday in Holy Week that new emissaries of the Court interviewed Ambrose in the Old Basilica, whither he had gone to celebrate the Sacred Mysteries. They urged him to deliver up the Portiana without delay. 'The Emperor', they added 'is acting strictly within his rights, for he has sovereign power over all things.' 'No!' said the Bishop. 'If the Emperor require of me that which is my own—my land, my money, anything of the sort that is mine—I will not refuse it, although all that I have belongs to the poor. But not even the Emperor has sovereign right over things that are God's. If my patrimony is demanded, take it; if my person, here I am; if you would hale me to prison or to death, I will go with pleasure. I will not shelter myself behind the throng of people. I will not lay hold of the altar and beg for my life; rather for the altar's sake I will gladly be a sacrifice.' He was horrified to learn that Gothic troops had been sent to occupy the Portian church, and shuddered at the possibility of bloodshed. Yet he remained firm in his refusal to obey the imperial mandate. Some Gothic officers were present, and he said to them angrily, 'Is it for this that you have taken up your abode within the Roman Empire—to disturb the public peace? Whither will you go next, if all Italy is ruined?' The ambassadors requested him to tranquillize the people; but he answered, 'All I can do is not to inflame them; God alone can pacify them. If the Emperor imagines that I have stirred them up, let him punish me or send me into exile.' The stormy interview then terminated. Ambrose spent the rest of that day in the Old Basilica; but in the evening he retired to his house, that the Government might have an opportunity of arresting him, if it desired to do so.[1]

On the following morning (Wednesday, the 9th of April) Ambrose left his lodging before dawn and went to the Portian Basilica. He found the church invested by Gothic soldiers. Some of these, however, were Catholics, whose sympathies were with the Bishop rather than with the Emperor. It was even rumoured that they had sent a message to the latter, offering to attend him if he would go in state to the assembly of the Catholics, and intimating that they themselves would in any case join the congregation over which Ambrose presided.[2] While the Mass was being celebrated, a number of these soldiers,

---

[1] Ambros. *Ep.* 20. 8–10.  [2] Ibid. 20. 11.

having heard that Ambrose had excommunicated them, rushed precipitately into the church to make their peace. Their appearance, however, caused a panic, especially among the women, who imagined that a general massacre was intended. But the guards called out, 'We have come to pray, and not to fight.' The congregation, relieved of its fears, broke into a singular kind of chant, repeating again and again, as though the Emperor were present in person, 'We petition you, Augustus; we do not fight, we do not fear, but we petition.'[1]

Meanwhile tumultuous scenes were being enacted in the New Basilica. Here a great crowd of people had assembled. They clamoured for the presence of the Bishop; they tore down the purple hangings about the Emperor's throne. The congregation in the Portiana begged Ambrose to transfer the whole assembly to the New Basilica. This seemed to him inexpedient, but he sent thither some presbyters. 'I trust in Christ', he said, 'that the Emperor himself will espouse our cause.'[2]

He began to preach on the Book of Job, a portion of which had just been read as the Prophetic Lesson in the Mass. He reminded his hearers how the devil had tempted Job through his possessions, through his children, and through his body.

'Me also he wished to deprive of the riches which I have in you, and desired to destroy your peace, which is my patrimony. He strove to snatch from me yourselves also—my good children, for whom I daily offer the Sacrifice; you he endeavoured to involve in the ruins of the public commotion. Already, then, I have experienced two of the temptations of Job. And perhaps it is because the Lord God knows me to be too weak, that He has not yet given the devil power over my body. Though I myself desire it, though I offer myself, perhaps He deems me still unequal to the conflict, and exercises me instead with divers labours.'

The temptation of Job by his wife carried Ambrose's thoughts to Justina, who was pressing him not merely to speak against, but to act against, God—yes, to deliver up God's altar. He expressed his opinion that the worst temptations come through women, and proceeded to compare the Empress with Eve, who caused Adam to be expelled from Paradise, with Jezebel, who so unmercifully persecuted Elijah, and with Herodias, who brought about the death of John the Baptist. 'Each man is persecuted by

---

[1] Ambros. *Ep.* 20. 13 and 14.        [2] Ibid. 20. 13, 20, and 22.

some woman or other; for me, in proportion as my merits are far less, the trials are heavier.' He alluded to his conversation with the messengers of the Court on the previous day.

'At length comes the command, "Deliver up the basilica." I reply, "It is not lawful for me to deliver it up, nor is it profitable for Your Majesty to receive it. You have no right to violate the house of a private man, and do you think that you can appropriate the house of God?" It is alleged that all things are lawful for the Emperor, that the whole world is his. I answer, "Do not deceive yourself, Sir, with the fancy that you have any imperial right over Divine things. Exalt not yourself, but, if you wish for a long reign, be subject to God. It is written, 'The things which are God's to God, and the things which are Caesar's to Caesar.' Palaces belong to the Emperor, churches to the Bishop. You can do what you please with secular buildings, but not with those which are sacred." Again, the Emperor is said to have declared, "I also ought to have *one* basilica." I answer, "*It is not lawful for thee to have her.* A church given up to heretics is no true bride of Christ, but an adulteress; and what has the Emperor to do with an adulteress?"'[1]

Yet even amid these troubles there was cause for thankfulness.

'You remember, brethren, the psalm that was read at Matins, and how we chanted in bitter grief, *O God, the heathen are come into thine inheritance.* And in truth the heathen came; nay, worse than heathen came. For Goths came, and men of divers nations. They came with arms and surrounded and occupied the basilica. In our ignorance of Thy Greatness we grieved for this; but we knew nothing and were mistaken. The heathen came, but in very truth they came *into thine inheritance*; for they who came as heathen have been made Christians, they who came to invade Thine inheritance have been made co-heirs of God. I have those as my defenders whom I looked upon as enemies; I have those whom I accounted adversaries as my allies. And whose work is this but Thine, Lord Jesus? Thou sawest armed men coming to Thy temple; on the one hand the people wailing and thronging together, that they might not seem to give up God's basilica, on the other hand, the soldiers ordered to use force. But Thou, O Lord, didst come between, and make the twain one. Thou didst restrain the armed men, saying, If ye run to arms, if those shut up in My temple are troubled, *what profit is there in my blood?* Thanks, then, be to Thee, O Christ. No ambassador, no messenger, but Thou, O Lord, hast delivered Thy people; *Thou hast put off my sackcloth and girded me with gladness.*'[2]

[1] Ambros. *Ep.* 20. 15–19.          [2] Ibid. 20. 20 and 21.

Scarcely had Ambrose finished his sermon, when he was informed that one of the imperial secretaries had arrived with a message. He went aside with the envoy, who said to him roughly—speaking in the Emperor's name—'What is your object in acting contrary to my pleasure?' Ambrose replied, 'I do not know what pleasure you mean, nor do I understand what action of mine is complained of.' 'Why', asked the envoy, still speaking for his master, 'have you sent presbyters to the basilica? If you are a usurper, I wish to know it, that I may understand how to prepare myself against you.' Ambrose explained that he had sent presbyters to the New Basilica only in order to avoid the necessity of going thither himself. His action throughout the whole dispute had consistently been one of passive resistance: 'I cannot give up the basilica, but I must not fight.' How could such an attitude be construed as an attempt at usurpation? 'If the Emperor really thinks me a usurper, why does he delay to strike? By ancient right priests have conferred sovereignty, but they have never usurped it; indeed, sovereigns have coveted the priesthood more than priests have coveted sovereignty.' 'Maximus', he added, with bitter sarcasm, 'does not accuse me of usurping Valentinian's authority, though he complains that my embassy prevented him from crossing into Italy.'[1]

During the rest of the day Ambrose stayed in the Portian Basilica. He was in deep depression. The troops which had come over to his side had been withdrawn and replaced by others on whose loyalty the Government believed that it could rely. The church was now closely invested. When evening came, the Bishop found himself unable, on account of the military pickets, to return to his house; he therefore repaired to a chapel adjoining the church, and there spent the night reciting psalms with his ecclesiastics. As for the New Basilica, it was abandoned to popular disorder; children in play tore into fragments the remains of the imperial hangings which the mob had pulled down.[2]

The next day, the 10th of April, was Holy Thursday, and according to custom a portion of the Book of Jonah was read.

---

[1] Ambros. *Ep.* 20. 22 and 23. Ambrose's attitude of passive resistance without resort to violence is illustrated by his teaching, *Expos. ev. Luc.*, vii. 59; cf. ibid. v. 76, 77; vii. 27, 28; *De Jacob*, ii. 58.    [2] Ambros. *Ep.* 20. 24.

Ambrose, in the Portiana, commenced his sermon with the words, 'A book has been read, my brethren, which foretells that sinners shall come back to repentance.' As he was enlarging on this theme, the joyful news arrived that the Emperor had given orders that all the troops should be withdrawn and that the fine imposed upon the merchants should be remitted. The soldiers themselves brought the good tidings. They burst into the church, ran to the altar, and kissed it in token of peace. The entire city gave itself up to rejoicing. It seemed to the thankful people especially appropriate that they should be relieved from their distress on the day on which the Lord had delivered Him-self up for the salvation of all, and on which the Church was accustomed to grant absolution to penitents.[1]

The Court had capitulated. In view of the determined oppo-sition of the people, and, more especially, of the unexpected dis-affection of the troops, no other course was possible. The more prudent of Valentinian's councillors realized that the affair had been a blunder; they now pressed the Emperor to yield as gracefully as possible, and (in accordance with the suggestion made by the soldiers) even tried to persuade him to go in state to the cathedral on Easter Day, in token of his complete reconciliation with the Catholics. But the mortified boy was not in a mood to be conciliatory. He spoke of Ambrose with great bitterness as 'a usurper, and worse than a usurper'; and said petulantly to the Consistorians, when they begged him to visit the cathedral: 'You would give me up in chains, if Ambrose bade you.' Some of the courtiers also took their cue from the young sovereign. Calligonus, the Grand Chamberlain, sent a fierce message to Ambrose, 'Do you dare to flout Valentinian, while I am alive? I will take off your head.' To which the Bishop, who was nearly exhausted by the strain which he had undergone, replied with equal heat, 'May God grant you to do what you threaten! I shall suffer what bishops suffer, and you will act as eunuchs act.'[2]

In the summer Valentinian quitted Milan, and resided for some months in Venetia, not returning to the capital till nearly

[1] Ambros. *Ep.* 20. 25 and 26. On the reconciliation of penitents on Holy Thursday, see above, p. 117.

[2] Ibid. 20. 27 and 28. Not long afterwards Calligonus was convicted of a grave offence and decapitated (Augustin. *Contr. Jul. Pelag.* vi. 41). Ambrose refers to this man, though without naming him, in *De Joseph*, 30–5.

the end of the year. He seems to have desired to get away from Ambrose and the Catholic crowd of Milan, the sight of whom reminded him too painfully of his recent humiliation.

Thus ended Justina's first attempt at 'persecution'. The courage and resolution which Ambrose displayed cannot but excite admiration. Nevertheless it may still be asked, Was the surrender of the basilica really a matter of such crucial importance as he imagined? It seems, at first sight, not unreasonable that the Arian subjects of the Emperor should be granted one church outside the city walls for worship. Moreover, as has been pointed out, the demand for such a concession was strictly in accordance with that theory of the Sovereign's rights which (when not pressed to their own disadvantage) had been admitted unquestioningly by the Catholics. Was Ambrose, then, justified in his passionate resistance? An impartial survey of the circumstances suggests an answer in the affirmative. The danger of the concession was very real. Milan had only recently been purged of Arianism, and the formal recognition of an organized heretical congregation would have gravely imperilled the hardly recovered orthodoxy. Further, there can be no doubt that the request for the Portian Basilica was only the 'thin end of the wedge'. Had it been granted, more exacting demands would certainly have followed; and it is possible that in the end the principal Church of Northern Italy would have been recaptured by the heretics. In view of such a possibility, involving consequences of the utmost seriousness to Western Christianity, it is difficult to see how Ambrose could have acted otherwise than he did. It would have been monstrous to jeopardize the Catholic faith in Milan for the sake of obliging the Arian Empress and her Court favourites and her barbarian mercenaries.

But the struggle was not yet over.[1] During the months of absence from Milan Justina had been meditating vengeance, and on her return to the city in December she elaborated a plan. She was energetically assisted by a certain Arian bishop, named Mercurinus Auxentius, who was a disciple and biographer of the famous Ulfilas. This man had been Bishop of Dorostorum on the Lower Danube; in A.D. 383 he was still in possession of that see, but shortly afterwards was expelled therefrom by

---

[1] Ambrose himself had anticipated further trouble, *Ep.* 20. 27.

Theodosius, and at a later date—perhaps at the end of the year A.D. 385—sought a refuge in the Court of the Arian Empress at Milan. Ambrose has nothing good to say of him; but he seems to have been a talented person, and soon established himself as the leader of the Arian community.[1] Like the elder Auxentius, Ambrose's predecessor in the metropolitan see, he took his stand on the authority of the Council of Rimini[2]— which had repudiated the term 'Essence' and declared the Son to be 'like unto the Father in all things'—but he exceeded the limits observed by his more judicious namesake in that he ventured to re-baptize such Catholics as he won over to his opinions.[3]

Justina and Auxentius collaborated in a plot. An imperial law was drafted, the provisions of which were as follows. Liberty of assembling for public worship was granted to all who accepted the decisions of the Council of Rimini; similar liberty was accorded to the Catholics; but 'those who think that they are to monopolize the right of public assembly' were warned that, if they should offer opposition to the law, not merely publicly, but 'insidiously or in secret', they would be treated as movers of sedition and capitally punished.[4] The terms of this enactment should be carefully noticed. It was in form an edict of toleration. The right of assembling for public worship was not withdrawn from the Catholics, but was merely extended to those who accepted the Arian compromise of Rimini. Punishment was threatened only against persons who refused to tolerate the practice of any form of Christianity except their own. Thus, when Ambrose declaimed against the enactment as sanctioning the 'invasion of all the Churches'[5] and the ejectment of Catholic

---

[1] On Auxentius, see J. Zeiller, *Les Origines chrétiennes dans les provinces danubiennes de l'Empire romain*, pp. 338, 339; Ambros. *Serm. contr. Auxent.* 22; *Expos. ev. Luc.* vii. 52, 53. He was a Roman, not a Goth, as Ambrose suggests; we need not credit the Ambrosian story that he changed his name from Mercurinus to Auxentius when he came to Milan (*Serm. contr. Auxent.* 22). He seems to have had some skill in law, since he was capable of drawing up an edict in correct form (see below, p. 282), and he was a fluent preacher; Ambrose says that he preached 'daily' (*Serm. contr. Auxent.* 26). See also Ambrose's allusion to the Arian courtiers, *Expos. ev. Luc.* viii. 17.

[2] For Ambrose's opinion of that Council, see above, p. 187, n. 1.

[3] Ambros. *Serm. contr. Auxent.* 37.

[4] Cod. Theod. xvi. 1. 4. Cf. Ambros. *Ep.* 21. 9, 11, and 12; *Serm. contr. Auxent.* 16, 22, 24; *Expos. ev. Luc.* vii. 52, 53; Rufin. *H.E.* ii. 15; Sozomen. *H.E.* vii. 13.

[5] Ambros. *Ep.* 21. 19.

bishops;[1] when he declared that it would send 'a winged sword through all the cities'[2] and be the death-warrant of multitudes;[3] when he denounced it as a 'bloody law' expressly framed to bring destruction on all who refused to be taken in by the fallacious arguments of heretics,[4] he was, to say the least, using language of exaggeration. As a matter of fact, it is clear that, though the law was necessarily drawn in general form, there was no intention of enforcing it generally throughout the dominions of Valentinian. It was obviously directed against only one person —Ambrose; though, even in Ambrose's case, it was not meant that the penalty for disobedience should be literally carried out. The Government would never have dared to put the Bishop of Milan to death for his faith. It hoped, however, to intimidate him by the threat of capital punishment, and so force him either to acquiesce in the re-establishment of Arianism and the ministry of an Arian bishop in his own episcopal city, or else—what Justina and Auxentius most desired—to resign his see.

The rough draft of the law received the approval of the Emperor. Then Benevolus, the President of the Record Office, was ordered to put it into form for promulgation. Benevolus, however, who though only a catechumen was a devout Catholic, declined to act. He was offered promotion if he would waive his scruples; but he tore off the belt, which was the badge of his office, and flung it at the feet of the Empress, exclaiming, 'Dismiss me from my post, but leave me the integrity of my faith.' Dismissed, of course, he was, and afterwards retired to his native Brescia, where he became a light of the local Church.[5] Meanwhile the edict was formulated by Auxentius himself,[6] and published on the 23rd of January, A.D. 386.

But it was one thing to issue the edict, and quite another to enforce it. The law was unpopular from the first. The Government, by distribution of honours and preferments, might buy the support of a few people of position,[7] but it was unable to overcome the determined hostility of the masses. The citizens of Milan stood by Ambrose. Ambrose himself ignored the law, kept tight hold of all the churches, and summoned a little

---

[1] Ambros. *Serm. contr. Auxent.* 16.                    [2] Ibid. 16.
[3] Ibid. 22.                                              [4] Ibid. 24.
[5] Rufinus, *H.E.* ii. 16; Sozomen. *H.E.* vii. 13; Cassiodorus, *H.T.* ix. 20.
[6] Ambros. *Serm. contr. Auxent.* 16, 22, 24.            [7] Ibid. 21.

Council of Italian bishops to advise and support him during the crisis.[1]

The first move was made by the Government. Dalmatius, one of the secretaries of the Imperial Consistory, brought the Bishop an order to present himself in person before the Emperor and the Privy Council, and there hold argument with Auxentius on the points in dispute between them. Each of the two disputants was to choose a specified number of lay umpires, and the Emperor himself would act as supreme arbiter of the debate. Ambrose was told that, if he declined to appear in answer to this citation, he could quit Milan and go where he pleased—which meant, of course, that his see would be handed over to Auxentius.[2]

On receiving the summons, Ambrose took counsel with the assembled bishops. They were unanimous in advising him neither to go to the palace nor to leave Milan. The first alternative was inexpedient, for a discussion on matters of faith ought not to be held in the Consistory; and who could tell whether Auxentius might not choose Jews or heathen as umpires?[3] The second alternative was not to be thought of. 'It makes little difference', said the bishops, 'whether you voluntarily leave the altar of Christ or whether you betray it; for, if you leave it, you will betray it.'[4]

Fortified with this authority, Ambrose—possibly in February—addressed to the Emperor a spirited Remonstrance, wherein he bluntly declined either to take part in the proposed conference or to go into exile.[5] He reminded Valentinian of the policy of his august father, Valentinian I, who 'not only declared in words but laid it down in a law' that 'in matters of faith or ecclesiastical discipline the judges should be both qualified by office and of the same order', that is 'that bishops should judge concerning bishops'.[6] The policy of so wise and pious a sovereign ought not rashly to be abandoned. It was, indeed, an unheard-of thing that in matters pertaining to the faith bishops should be subject to the judgement of laymen. 'If a bishop is

---

[1] The Council is referred to by Ambros. *Ep.* 21. 13, 17, and 18.
[2] Ibid. 21. 1, 18, and 19.
[3] Ibid. 21. 13, 17; cf. *Serm. contr. Auxent.* 26.
[4] Ibid. 21. 18.                                          [5] *Ep.* 21.
[6] Ibid. 21. 2; cf. 5. The law quoted is not extant; but there is a law of Gratian (Cod. Theod. xvi. 2. 23), and another of Theodosius (Cod. Theod. xvi. 12. 3), to the same effect.

to be taught by a layman, what will follow? A layman will then be free to dispute on theology and the bishop will have to listen —the bishop, forsooth, will learn from the layman!'[1] Yet it was now actually proposed that the supreme arbiter of the debate should be not only a layman, but a mere boy—one, moreover, who had not even been baptized and was still ignorant of 'the sacraments of the faith'. When Valentinian was a little older he would know what to think of a bishop who would suffer the 'rights of the priesthood' to be thus trampled underfoot.[2] If a debate were to take place at all, it should be held, not in the palace but in the church, not before unknown umpires but in the presence of the instructed Christian congregation. If, in these circumstances, the people considered that Auxentius had the better of the argument, let them follow his faith; Ambrose would not be jealous![3] But the people had already given judgement on the matter when they petitioned Valentinian I to make Ambrose their bishop—Ambrose, who received from the same Valentinian a guarantee that, if he would accept the see, he should not be molested.[4] As a matter of fact, the proposed discussion in the Consistory could not be anything but a solemn farce. For how could judges deliver an unprejudiced verdict on the new law, when that law was already in force, and provided that any one who dared to criticize it should become liable to the death penalty? The very suggestion of such a discussion was, strictly speaking, illegal, and the Emperor, in making it, was guilty of breaking his own law.[5] Nay, if he really desired a conference, let him first repeal the law, and then summon a Council of bishops, before which, if Auxentius chose to appear, Ambrose, for his part, would be ready to meet him.[6] 'Be pleased, Sir, to accept my reasons for not coming to the Consistory. I have not learnt how to stand up in the Consistory except on your behalf'—that is, as Valentinian's envoy at the Court of Maximus—'and I cannot contend within the palace since I neither know nor seek to know the secrets of the palace.'[7] To this Remonstrance he appended his signature—'I, Ambrose, bishop, offer this memorial to the Most Gracious Emperor and Most Blessed Augustus, Valentinian'.

---

[1] Ambros. *Ep.* 21. 4.                         [2] Ibid. 21. 5; cf. *Serm. contr. Auxent.* 29.
[3] Id. *Ep.* 21. 6; cf. ibid. 17; *Serm. contr. Auxent.* 3.
[4] Id. *Ep.* 21.7.                                                        [5] Ibid. 21. 9–12.
[6] Ibid. 21. 15 and 16.                                          [7] Ibid. 21. 20.

Ambrose had defied the Government. But the Government, fearing a popular outbreak, for some while hesitated to take up the challenge. Instead of arresting the recalcitrant Bishop, it merely required him to hand over the Church plate. The stupid demand, as might have been expected, was refused. 'Anything that is my own', said Ambrose, '—estate or house, gold or silver —I will willingly give up; but I cannot take anything away from God's temple, or hand over that which has been entrusted to me to guard and not to surrender. I am acting thus in the Emperor's interest; for it would not be expedient either for me to make this surrender or for him to accept it. Let him listen to the warning of an independent priest—if he wishes to do what is profitable for himself let him cease to do wrong to Christ.'[1] Even after this, the Government still shrank from extreme measures. Although Ambrose daily went abroad, to pay pastoral visits or to pray at the tombs of the martyrs, and although in his walks he frequently passed the palace gates, no attempt was made to interfere with him.[2] At last, however, the situation became intolerable. Unless the Government were to lose every vestige of authority, it was bound to do something. It accordingly sent Ambrose a peremptory order to withdraw from Milan; he might go where he pleased, and any one who chose might follow him, but leave the city he must. Ambrose sent back a haughty message—'I cannot think of abandoning the Church, for I fear the Lord of the Universe more than any earthly Emperor. If the Emperor acts as sovereigns are wont to act, I am prepared to suffer what bishops are wont to suffer.'[3]

To baffle any attempt at arrest, Ambrose now remained continuously within the spacious precincts of the New Basilica, where he was watched over, day and night, by the congregation of the faithful.[4] The large church, with its adjacent buildings, was transformed into a fortress, the doors and approaches being closed and guarded.[5] Outside, the cathedral was surrounded by troops, the clash of whose arms could be distinctly heard by those within.[6] The soldiers made no attempt to force an entrance, nor did they hinder any person from entering; but those

---

[1] Ambros. *Serm. contr. Auxent.* 5.      [2] Ibid. 15.      [3] Ibid. 1, 15.
[4] Augustin. *Confess.* ix. 7.
[5] The guard, however, seems to have been careless, Ambros. *Serm. contr. Auxent.*
10.                                                                [6] Ibid. 4.

who were once inside were not permitted to pass out.[1] It is evident that the Government did not propose to resort to violence. The plan was to exhaust the enthusiasm of the people, by keeping them cooped up in a confined space; in a few days, it was thought, their spirit would be broken, and then it would be possible to lay hands on the Bishop and send him into exile.

Neither Ambrose nor his flock, however, understood the Government's intentions. Ambrose was calm, but apprehended violence.[2] The people were in a state of wild excitement. All kinds of alarming rumours passed from mouth to mouth— 'Auxentius has uttered terrible threats'; 'They have got a carriage ready to carry the Bishop into exile';[3] 'His death has been decreed, and the executioners are on the road'.[4] At one time they would fall into a panic, fancying that Ambrose, in fear for his life, was preparing to desert the Church and them; at another time, they would break into shouts of impotent rage, 'Away with Auxentius, and his law with him!'[5] All were suffering from nervous strain, which, though we know not precisely how long it lasted, was certainly kept up for several days and nights.[6]

To relieve the tension and cheer the spirits of his supporters, Ambrose encouraged them to occupy themselves with constant singing. It was apparently at this time that he made two interesting innovations in the music of the Milanese Church. First, he introduced the practice, already prevalent in the Eastern Churches, of chanting the psalms antiphonally, i.e. alternately by two choirs.[7] Secondly, he introduced the use of

---

[1] Paulinus, *Vita Ambros.* 13.

[2] Ambros. *Serm. contr. Auxent.* 4, 6, 7, 8, 14, 18, 36. Cf. also the references in *De Jacob*—sermons which appear to have been preached about this time—to the sufferings which a faithful man may be called upon to endure at the hands of persecutors, i. 27, 36, and to the heroism of those who died for the faith, ii. 43–58.

[3] Ambros. *Serm. contr. Auxent.* 15. The rumour about the carriage had some foundation; see the story related by Paulinus, *Vita Ambros.* 12; cf. Rufinus, *H.E.* ii. 15 'sacerdotem pertrahi atque in exilium agi protinus iubet'.

[4] Ambros. *Serm contr. Auxent.* 16.

[5] Ibid. 23.　　　　　　　　　　　　　　　　　　　　[6] Ibid. 7, 10.

[7] Isidor. Hispal. *De Eccl. Officiis*, i. 7: 'Antiphonas Graeci primi composuerunt, duobus choris alternatim concinentibus. . . . Apud Latinos autem primus idem beatissimus Ambrosius antiphonas constituit, Graecorum exemplum imitatus.' This mode of singing (originally Jewish) is said to have been introduced into the Christian Church by Ignatius of Antioch, after a vision of angels praising the Blessed Trinity in such manner (Socrates, *H.E.* vi. 8). Theodoret, however, states that Flavian and Diodorus were the first (among Christians) to divide the choirs into two parts, and teach them to sing the psalms alternately (*H.E.* ii. 24). In any case,

metrical hymns—a custom which was highly favoured in the
East, both among Catholics and among heretics, and which
Hilary of Poitiers had endeavoured, though with indifferent
success, to popularize in the West. The psalms and hymns
were set to simple, melodious tunes, suitable for congregational
singing.[1] These innovations are referred to by two contemporary
writers. Augustine, who was himself shut up with Ambrose in
the basilica, says—'The pious people kept watch in the church,
ready to die with their bishop. Then it was that the custom
arose of singing hymns and psalms, after the use of the Eastern
parts, lest the people should wax faint through the tediousness
of sorrow; and from that day to this the custom has been retained, many, nay, almost all, of the Christian congregations
throughout the rest of the world following herein.'[2] Paulinus,
Ambrose's biographer, after speaking of the persecution of
Justina, records that 'at this time antiphons, hymns, and vigils
first came into use in the Church of Milan; which devout usage
has continued to the present day, not only in the aforesaid
Church, but throughout almost all the provinces of the West'.[3]

Thus, at intervals during the day and through the watches
of the night, the Catholic garrison of the beleaguered church
kept up their courage and defied the Arians with the solemn
and sonorous intonation of hymns and psalms. But as time
went on, and the blockade was not relaxed, even this comforting exercise failed to soothe the agitation of the people. It was
at this point, when the tension was at its height, that the Bishop
addressed to the troubled congregation his famous *Sermon against
Auxentius*.[4]

it seems probable that this custom started at Antioch, and thence spread over the
East. Basil speaks of it as the common method of chanting in the Eastern Churches
(*Ep.* 207. 3).

[1] See the Note at the end of this chapter.          [2] Augustin. *Confess.* ix. 7.
[3] Paulinus, *Vita Ambros.* 13; on the 'vigils', see below, p. 445.
[4] Printed between the 21st and 22nd of Ambrose's *Letters*. The date on which the
discourse was delivered is uncertain. It has been conjectured that it was preached
on Palm Sunday (29 March) because St. Luke's account of the Triumphal Entry
into Jerusalem had been read (*Serm. contr. Auxent.* 8, 19). But this was not necessarily
the Gospel in the Liturgy; it seems rather to have been read 'by chance' among
other passages of Scripture, recited to occupy the attention of the people during the
siege of the church (ibid. 19). On general grounds it is probable that the struggle
with Justina took place not long after the promulgation of the law on January 23rd,
A.D. 386, and that the blockade of the church and the preaching of the sermon
should be placed in the February or March of this year.

'I perceive', he began abruptly, 'that you are unusually excited, and that your eyes are fixed upon me. What can be the reason of this? Is it that you are apprehensive lest I should desert the Church, and in fear for my life abandon you? I will never desert you of my own free will. But I cannot resist force by force. I shall have, indeed, the power of lamenting, of weeping, of groaning: against arms, soldiers, Goths, tears are my weapons; such are the defences of a priest. But in any other way I neither ought nor am able to resist. To flee, however, and desert the Church—that is not like me! You yourselves know that I am accustomed to show all deference to our rulers, but I am not accustomed to give way to them. I offer myself cheerfully to punishment, and I fear not what is prepared for me.'[1]

He explained that he would have been willing to attend the conference in the imperial palace, were it not unfitting for a bishop to do so. 'But who can deny that a question concerning the faith ought to be debated in the church? If any one has confidence in his case, let him come hither.'[2] For himself, if the need arose, he was willing to suffer martyrdom.

'Permit, I beseech you, your bishop to engage the foe. Permit, I beseech you, the contest to take place. It is for you to be spectators. Consider: if a city has an athlete or one skilled in any noble art, it is eager to put him forward for a contest. Why, then, do you refuse to do in greater matters what you invariably do in less? Yet of a surety, if the Lord has appointed me to this contest, it is in vain that you have sleeplessly kept watch and ward through so many days and nights. The will of Christ will be fulfilled. And he who loves me here cannot give a better testimony of his affection than by suffering me to become a sacrifice for Christ.'[3]

He related the beautiful story of *Quo Vadis?* St. Peter at Rome, by sowing the Divine precepts among the people and preaching chastity, roused the fury of the heathen. When they sought to kill him, the Roman Christians persuaded him to go away for a little while. He set out by night; but as he was passing through the gate, he beheld Christ coming to meet him, and entering the city. 'Lord', he cried, 'whither goest Thou?' Christ answered, 'I come to be crucified again.' The response seemed to indicate that Christ was to suffer again in the person of His servant. Peter, therefore, turned back of his own accord, and when the Chris-

---

[1] Ambros. *Serm. contr. Auxent.* 1, 2.   [2] Ibid. 3.
[3] Ibid. 4, 6, 7, 8; cf. the reference to his frustrated desire for martyrdom (*Ep.* 36. 4).

tians inquired the reason, he told them what Christ had said. Very soon afterwards he was seized and glorified the Lord Jesus by his cross.[1] 'You see, then', Ambrose commented, 'that Christ wills to suffer in His servants. And what if He saith also to me, who am His servant, "It is my will that such a one tarry, but follow thou Me"?'[2] But, whatever fate might be destined for himself, nothing would ever induce him to surrender his see to Auxentius.

'I answered those who pressed me in the Emperor's name, "God forbid that I should surrender the heritage of my fathers—the heritage of Dionysius, who died in exile for the faith, the heritage of the confessor Eustorgius, the heritage of Myrocles, and of all the faithful bishops of old time!" I answered as a bishop ought to answer; let the Emperor act as an emperor ought to act. He shall take away my life sooner than my faith.'[3]

How, indeed, could he surrender this great see to an Arian—to one who was not only an Arian, but a persecuting Arian?

'The Lord Jesus', he cried, 'drove out a few from His temple; Auxentius has left no one. Jesus casts men out of His temple with a

---

[1] Ibid. 13. The story is found in the Gnostic *Acts of Peter* (*Acta Apost. Apocrypha*, vol. i, ed. Lipsius and Bonnet)—both in the *Martyrium b. Petri Ap. a Lino ep. conscriptum* and in μαρτύριον τοῦ ἁγίου ἀποστόλου Πέτρου. In the Linus text the dialogue is longer than in Ambrose's report. 'Ut autem portam civitatis voluit egredi, vidit sibi Christum occurrere. Et adorans eum ait: Domine, quo vadis? Respondet ei Christus: Romam venio iterum crucifigi. Et ait ad eum Petrus: Domine, iterum crucifigeris? Et dixit ad eum Dominus: Etiam iterum crucifigar. Petrus autem dixit: Domine, revertar et sequar te. Et his dictis Dominus ascendit in caelum.' The story is found also in the Catholic *Acts*, where, however, it is related by Peter himself, after he has been nailed to the cross. The Latin runs: 'Dixi: Domine, quo vadis? Et dixit mihi: Sequere me, quia vado Romam iterum crucifigi. Et dum sequerer eum, redii Romam. Et dixit mihi: Noli timere, quia ego tecum sum, quousque introducam te in domum patris mei.' The legend is related by Ambrose not only in *Serm. contr. Auxent.*, but also in *De Excidio Urbis Hierosolymitanae*, iii. 2 (if Ambrose was indeed the author), where the narrative is as follows: 'Proxima nocte salutatis fratribus et celebrata oratione proficisci solus coepit. Ubi ventum est ad portam, videt sibi Christum occurrere, et adorans eum dixit: Domine, quo vadis? Dicit ei Christus: Iterum venio crucifigi. Intellexit Petrus de sua dictum passione, quod in ea Christus passurus videretur, qui patitur in singulis. . . . Et conversus in urbem redit.' Perhaps the origin of the legend may be found, partly in a reminiscence of the conversation between Christ and Peter in John xiii. 36-8 (Κύριε, ποῦ ὑπάγεις; Domine, quo vadis?) and partly in an *agraphon* preserved by Origen (*in Joan.* xx. 12), 'if any one will accept the saying recorded in the *Acts of Paul* as spoken by the Saviour, ἄνωθεν μέλλω σταυροῦσθαι.' The legend that Peter at his own request was crucified head downwards is known to Ambrose, *Expos. ps. cxviii*, 21. 21; *De Interpell. Job et David*, i. 2; *De Excidio Urb. Hieros.* iii. 2.
[2] *Serm. contr. Auxent.* 14.
[3] Ibid. 18.

scourge; Auxentius with a sword—Jesus with a scourge; Mercurinus with an axe. Our holy Lord drives out the sacrilegious with a scourge; this wretch persecutes the godly with cold steel. Those whom he cannot deceive with his arguments he thinks should be smitten with the sword. With his mouth he dictates bloody laws, with his hand he writes them, and imagines that a law can impose a creed on men.'[1]

This was the creature who had stirred up the Emperor. His constant cry was, 'Ought not the Emperor to have *one* basilica to go to? Does Ambrose aspire to be more powerful than the Emperor, so as to deny him the liberty of going to church?'[2] But there was no disloyalty in Ambrose's attitude; he was willing that the Emperor should take anything he pleased, excepting only what belonged to God.

'If the Emperor asks for tribute, we do not refuse it. The estates of the Church pay tribute. If he covets the estates, he has power to claim them: none of us will interfere. The contributions of the people will more than suffice for the poor. Let not the Arians stir up ill will against us on account of the estates; let them take them, if it be the Emperor's pleasure. I do not, indeed, give them, but I do not refuse them.'[3]

The Arians accused him of procuring the support of the people by bribery.

'Of this charge', he said, 'I have no great fear. I confess that I have stipendiaries; my stipendiaries are the poor of Christ—a treasure which I am well used to collect. May this be ever my offence, that I pay out gold to the poor! And if they accuse me of seeking to defend myself by means of them, I do not deny, nay, I even court, the charge. The poor are my defenders, but it is by their prayers; blind though they are and lame, weak and old, yet are they stronger than the stoutest warriors.'[4]

'We say, then, to those who stir up ill will against us on the Emperor's account, "We render to Caesar the things that are Caesar's, and to God the things that are God's." Tribute is due to Caesar, we deny it not; but the Church is God's and ought not therefore to be assigned to Caesar, because Caesar can have no rights over God's temple. And no one can deny that in saying this we pay due honour to the Emperor. For what can be more to the Emperor's honour

---

[1] Ambros. *Serm. contr. Auxent.* 23, 24; cf. the bitter attack on Auxentius, *Expos. ev. Luc.* vii. 49–53, and the indirect reference to him, ibid. viii. 17.

[2] Ambros. *Serm. contr. Auxent.* 30.     [3] Ibid. 33.

[4] Ibid. 33.

than to say that he is a son of the Church? In making this statement we honour him without sinning against God. For the Emperor is within the Church, not over the Church; and a good Emperor seeks the aid of the Church and does not reject it. We say this humbly, yet we assert it firmly.'[1]

Once more the Court capitulated. It was not prepared to order a direct conflict between the soldiers and the citizens. The siege of the basilica was raised, the obnoxious law was quietly dropped, and nothing more was said about the deportation of the Bishop. Auxentius, deprived of his hope of preferment to one of the greatest sees of Christendom, seems to have disappeared from Milan, and Ambrose, after his trying experience, remained master of the situation. It is evident, however, that, although he had won a notable triumph—which was followed by many conversions of pagans and heretics[2]—his position was not by any means secure. The young Emperor, jealous of his imperial rights, continued to regard him as a rebel against his authority; Justina complained—and not wholly without reason —that she had been grossly insulted by him;[3] the Court party was eager to seize any suitable opportunity of renewing the persecution, as soon as the popular enthusiasm should show signs of abating. We learn from Ambrose himself that, in the summer of A.D. 386, he was still in sore need of 'defenders'.[4]

Meanwhile, in the spring of this year, very soon after the 'persecution', a demonstration was made in Ambrose's favour in a very unexpected quarter. Away in Gaul the Emperor Maximus had been informed of the struggle between the Bishop and Justina. He saw at once that it afforded him a fine opportunity of interfering in affairs within the dominions of his young colleague; and he was not the man to miss a chance. He accordingly wrote to Valentinian, reproaching him for his pro-Arian policy, and requesting him, in vigorous terms, to cease from persecuting Catholics.

'If I were not sincerely your friend and anxious to maintain peace, I might have taken advantage of the disturbance and upheaval of Catholicism which is said to be going on in the dominions of Your

---

[1] Ambros. *Serm. contr. Auxent.* 35, 36.
[2] See *Hexaem.* iii. 3 (April, A.D. 387).
[3] Sozomen. *H.E.* vii. 13.
[4] Ambros. *Ep.* 22. 10. How skilfully he used the discovery of the relics of SS. Gervasius and Protasius in defence of the Catholic cause is related in Chap. xii.

Tranquillity. For what could one who was really your enemy more desire than that you should scheme against the Churches of God, that is, against God Himself, and set yourself to commit sin where error is inexcusable? . . . For I have heard that by Your Grace's new edicts Catholic Churches are being treated with violence, bishops are besieged in their basilicas, fines are inflicted, capital punishment is threatened, and under the name of some legal enactment the most holy law of God is overthrown. How serious all this is you will understand if you think upon the Greatness of God.'

Maximus professed himself profoundly shocked by the reprehensible attempt of the imperial boy ('Your Most Serene Youth') to change the faith which had been settled for so long, and which prevailed throughout practically the whole of the civilized West.

'All Italy and Africa hold this faith; Gaul, Aquitania, and the whole of Spain glory in it, as does venerable Rome herself, that holds the first rank in religion as in empire, because she has both known and striven to follow God. Only Illyricum—I confess it with grief—disagrees; would that there were no signal proof of its error! Would that the city of Mursa, that stronghold of Arianism, were still intact, and had not been overthrown by the judgement of God in punishment for its error! It is dangerous, believe me, to tamper with divine things.'

Did Valentinian really think that a religion which God Himself had implanted in men's minds could be uprooted by persecution? Nothing but discord, sedition, and scandal could result from such an attempt.

'The best proof that I can offer of my care for Your Grace is that I exhort you to desist from these proceedings. For I think that you will recognize that no one who was hostile to you would give you this advice. I trust that you will perceive that I have said all this in love. I hope that you will believe it. It is but right that you should refrain from violating what is dedicated to God; that you should restore to all Italy and to venerable Rome and to the rest of the provinces their own churches and their own bishops, and not interpose in these matters any more. For it is obviously more becoming that those who have deserted the Catholic Church for Arianism should return to the true faith, than that they should instil their wickedness into the minds of those who now think rightly.'[1]

The threat conveyed in this cunningly worded letter, though

---

[1] Labbe, *Concil.* ii. 1031; cf. Rufinus, *H.E.* ii. 16; Theodoret. *H.E.* v. 14.

not explicit, was unmistakable.[1] It was evident that, if the remonstrance were disregarded, this Catholic Maximus would speedily come himself, in the character of Defender of the Faith, to demand an explanation. Hence the Government of Valentinian, which dreaded an invasion above all things, was compelled to take notice. The Catholics of Milan were left more or less in peace; and in due course another embassy was sent to Trier, an account of which will be given in a later chapter.[2]

## NOTE

### The Services of Ambrose to Church Music

IT appears that Ambrose rendered valuable service to the music of the Western Church in two respects.

1. First, he improved the song itself. Hitherto the chanting had been the function of carefully trained and practised soloists, who recited the musical parts of the service in a kind of 'musical speech' or 'half-song', the congregation merely taking up the last modulations of the chant. To Ambrose belongs the credit of having introduced a more lively, varied, and melodious song, now rendered, not by the skilled precentor alone, but by the whole congregation, singing alternately in two choirs. No doubt, as compared with the Church music of modern times, the Ambrosian music was simple and austere; yet Augustine, accustomed only to the old 'musical speech', was affected even to tears by the strange sweetness of the new melodies. 'How I wept', he writes, 'at Thy hymns and canticles, touched to the quick by the voices of Thy melodious Church. The voices flowed into my ears, and the truth distilled into my heart, and thence there streamed forth a devout emotion, and my tears ran down, and I found relief therein. Only a little while ago the Church of Milan had begun to make use of this kind of consolation and exhortation— the voices and hearts of brethren singing together with great devotion.'[3] Afterwards he had doubts whether this new song did not tempt the worshipper to give greater attention to the sound than to the sense of what was sung; and was even disposed to banish such melody from the Churches, and observe instead the method used in the Church of Alexandria by the command of Athanasius, 'who made the reader of the psalm to intone it with so slight an inflexion of the voice that it bordered on reading rather than singing.' 'Nevertheless',

---

[1] Theodoret. *H.E.* v. 14 states that Maximus threatened war if his suggestions were not heeded; but the letter, though menacing in tone, does not contain an explicit threat.

[2] Chapter xiv.

[3] Augustin. *Confess.* ix. 6 and 7.

he confesses, 'when I remember the tears I shed at the songs of Thy Church, when first I recovered my faith, and how I am now touched, not merely by the singing, but by the things sung, when they are sung with clear voice and suitable modulation, I acknowledge again the great usefulness of the practice.'[1]

Ambrose himself speaks with enthusiasm of the beautiful and salutary effects produced by congregational psalm-singing in the new style. All take their part, he says, in this 'tuneful confession of faith'—old men, youths, women (whom the Apostle bids keep silence in church, but who sing the psalms so well), young girls and even little children, who by this exercise are taught lessons which they are not of age to learn in any other way. While they sing, there is no opportunity for that unseemly chatter by which the reading of the lessons is too often interrupted. While they sing, they forget their quarrels; for who can bear enmity against one with whom he has lifted up his voice to God? All take pleasure in the singing, and the sacred words, vocalized and listened to with such enjoyment, sink deeply into all hearts. Such a singing congregation is like a many-stringed instrument of music from which the Holy Spirit extracts the sweetest harmonies—harmonies by which even the most stony hearts are softened.[2] Again, the Church is compared with the sea: 'from the singing of men, women, virgins, and children, there results a harmonious volume of sound, like that produced by the waves of the ocean'.[3] Ambrose finds a justification of such singing in the Scriptures, where music is represented as a means of driving out demons, of procuring an infusion of spiritual grace, and of delighting the faithful, as they banquet in their Father's house; 'sweet, therefore, is the song which does not enervate the body, but strengthens the mind and soul.'[4] Referring to the melodious rendering of his own hymns by the Catholic congregation in the besieged basilica, he writes: 'The Arians assert that the people have been beguiled by the strain of my hymns. I certainly do not deny it. It is a sublime strain, than which nothing is more powerful. For what is more powerful than the confession of the Trinity, which is daily celebrated in song by the mouth of the whole people? All alternatively vie with one another in making their profession of faith; all know how to proclaim in verses the Father, the Son, and the Holy Ghost. So all have become teachers, who were scarcely able to be learners.'[5]

2. Secondly, Ambrose not only improved the singing, but also supplied new matter—hymns of his own composition—to be sung.[6]

---

[1] Augustin. *Confess*. x. 33.  [2] Ambros. *In ps. 1 enarr*. 9–11.
[3] Id. *Hexaem*. iii. 23.  [4] Id. *Expos. ps. cxviii* 7, 26.
[5] Id. *Serm. contr. Auxent*. 34.
[6] The Benedictines print 12 hymns (which they regard as genuine) in their

It is true, indeed, that Hilary of Poitiers was the first Latin hymn-writer and composer of a hymn-book;[1] yet his effort to introduce the use of his hymns in the public services of the Church does not appear to have been crowned with success. His fellow countrymen in Gaul could not be taught to sing these compositions[2]—which, indeed (if we may judge from the surviving fragments of three of them) were tedious, prosaic, obscurely phrased, and very ill-adapted for congregational purposes.[3] With propriety, therefore, may Ambrose be reckoned as the Father and Founder of Latin Hymnody. He was the first Western hymnographer of real poetic genius, the founder of a school of Western hymn-writers, and the true introducer of the custom of hymn-singing in the public worship of the Western Church. His simple, vigorous, and dignified hymns, written expressly for congregational rendering, established themselves immediately as a permanent element in the worship of the Church of Milan, and very soon (notwithstanding some sporadic opposition at first) in that of other Western Churches. Their immense popularity encouraged imitation. Many hymns were composed in the same metre and manner, and these, by the time of Benedict, were known by the common title of 'Ambrosian' hymns, while the *iambic dimeter*—the metre originally used by Ambrose—was designated the 'Ambrosian' metre.

It is difficult to distinguish the genuine hymns of Ambrose from the host of 'Ambrosian' imitations. Recent investigators, on various grounds—attribution to Ambrose by early writers, use in the Milanese Liturgy, similarity in style and phraseology to Ambrose's genuine compositions, and the like—are inclined to assign some fourteen or eighteen hymns to the great Bishop of Milan. But in the case of many of these poems the evidence of authorship is far from convincing. Indeed it seems possible to attribute to Ambrose only four hymns with certainty, and two, or perhaps three, others with probability. The four of which there can be no question are (i) *Aeterne rerum*

---

edition of Ambrose's Works, and 82 others in the Appendix. On Ambrose's hymns, see L. Biraghi, *Inni sinceri e carmi di Sant' Ambrogio*; G. M. Dreves, *Aurelius Ambrosius*, *der Vater des Kirchengesangs*; A. Steier, 'Untersuchungen über die Echtheit der Hymnen des Ambrosius', in *Jahrbücher für klassische Philologie*, xxviii, 1903, pp. 549 ff.; N. Ermoni, 'Saint Ambroise, hymnographe', in *Dict. d'Archéologie chrétienne et de Liturgie* (col. 1347–52); A. S. Walpole, 'Notes on the Text of the Hymns of S. Ambrose', in *Journal of Theological Studies*, ix (1908), pp. 428 ff.; also J. Kayser, *Beiträge zur Geschichte und Erklärung der ältesten Kirchenhymnen.*

[1] Isidor. Hispal. *De Eccl. Officiis*, i. 6; Hieron. *De Viris Illustr.* 100.

[2] Hieron. *Comm. in Galat.* ii, Praef.

[3] It is now generally held that the beautiful morning song *Lucis largitor splendide*, and the vesper hymn *Ad caeli clara non sum dignus sidera*, formerly ascribed to Hilary, are not his work.

*conditor*[1] (tr. 'Framer of the earth and sky,' J. H. Newman), (ii) *Deus creator omnium*[2] ('Maker of all things, God most high,' J. D. Chambers), (iii) *Jam surgit hora tertia*,[3] and (iv) *Veni redemptor gentium*[4] ('O come, Redeemer of mankind, appear,' D. T. Morgan). The authorship of these four hymns is authenticated by Augustine; that of the last is further vouched for by Pope Celestine, Faustus of Riez, and Cassiodorus. In addition to these unquestioned four, Ambrose should probably be credited with two compositions attributed to him by Cassiodorus—the Epiphany hymn, *Illuminans altissimus*,[5] and the fragment *Orabo mente Dominum*[6]—and possibly with the noble morning hymn, *Splendor paternae gloriae* ('From the Father's glory shining', W. J. Copeland) ascribed to him by Bede.[7] Of the rest the authorship must be regarded as highly uncertain.[8] I wish that I were able to follow Dreves in including, at any rate, the fine (? fifth-century) hymn for martyrs, *Aeterna Christi munera* ('The eternal gifts of Christ the King,' J. M. Neale) among the genuine Ambrosian productions.

The metre used by Ambrose was, as has been said, the *iambic dimeter*. The poems are arranged in stanzas, each consisting of four eight-syllable lines. The metre is strictly correct and the laws of quantity scrupulously observed.[9] Occasionally (as, for instance, in the first two stanzas of *Veni redemptor gentium*) rhyme is found; but its presence seems to be due to accident.

The hymns of Ambrose, deeply religious in thought and feeling,

---

[1] Augustin. *Retract*. i. 21. A passage in Ambros. *Hexaem.* v. 88 is clearly based on some lines of this hymn.

[2] Augustin. *Confess*. ix. 12; x. 34; cf. *De Musica*, vi. 23.

[3] Id. *De Natura et Gratia*, 74.

[4] Id. *Serm.* 372. 3; cf. Caelestin. ap. Amobius, *Conflict. cum Serapione*, ii. 13; Faustus Rhegiens. *Ep.* 6; Cassiod. *Expos. ps. viii.* Concl. (Migne, *P.L.* lxx. 79). The original hymn began *Veni redemptor gentium*; but in some of the later manuscripts there is prefixed a stanza, composed simply of phrases from the Vulgate of Psalm 80, commencing *Intende qui regis Israel*. The hymn was translated into German by Luther.

[5] Cassiod. *Expos. ps. lxxiv*, 8 (Migne, *P.L.* lxx. 539).

[6] Cassiod. *Expos. ps. ci*, 1; *Expos. ps. cxviii*, 164 (Migne, *P.L.* lxx. 707, 895).

[7] Beda, *De Arte Metrica*, 21.

[8] I am inclined, however, to think that the hymn for SS. Gervasius and Protasius, *Grates tibi, Jesu, novas*, exhibits intrinsic evidence of the authorship of Ambrose; the writer calls himself *repertor* of their bodies.

[9] F. J. E. Raby, *History of Christian-Latin Poetry*, p. 36. 'Wilhelm Meyer has pointed out that although the verses are strictly quantitative, their structure follows the rules of the new rhythmical poetry. After the second line in each strophe there is usually a "sense pause", and, indeed, in the manuscripts the strophes are written as though composed of two long lines. There is, of course, a more emphatic pause at the end of each strophe, but, most important of all, after each two strophes there is a sense pause which can only be explained by the fact that the hymns were composed to be sung by alternate choirs.'

are severely simple in style. The poet expresses himself clearly, tersely, directly, and with scrupulous precision in the use of theological terms. There is neither pomp of language nor rapturous outpouring of emotion; yet the restrained utterance of sober reflection on the sublime truths of religion—which is the characteristic of these poems—is extraordinarily impressive. 'It is felt', writes Archbishop Trench, 'as though there were a certain coldness in his hymns, an aloofness of the author from his subject, a refusal to blend and fuse himself with it. . . . Only after a while does one learn to feel the grandeur of this unadorned metre, and the profound, though it may have been more instinctive than conscious, wisdom of the poet in choosing it; or to appreciate that confidence in the surpassing interest of his theme, which has rendered him indifferent to any but its simplest setting forth. . . . The great objects of faith in their simplest expression are felt by him so sufficient to stir all the deepest affections of the heart, that any attempt to dress them up, to array them in moving language, were merely superfluous. The passion is there, but it is latent and repressed, a fire burning inwardly, the glow of an austere enthusiasm, which reveals itself indeed, but not to every careless beholder. Nor do we fail presently to observe how truly these poems belonged to their time, and to the circumstances under which they were produced—how suitably the faith which was in actual conflict with, and was just triumphing over, the powers of this world, found its utterance in hymns such as these, wherein is no softness, perhaps little tenderness, but in place of these a rock-like firmness, the old Roman stoicism transmuted and glorified into that nobler Christian courage, which encountered and at length overcame the world.'[1]

[1] R. C. Trench, *Sacred Latin Poetry*, pp. 87, 88.

## CHAPTER XII

## THE DISCOVERY OF THE RELICS OF SS. GERVASIUS AND PROTASIUS[1]

IN the summer of this same year, A.D. 386, Ambrose completed a basilica which he had been building[2]—the original of that famous church of Sant' Ambrogio, which for centuries held so prominent a place in Milanese history. This magnificent church, in which the powerful archbishops of Milan were accustomed to hold their synods, in which in A.D. 961 Otho the Great was crowned with the Iron Crown, in which during the factious age of liberty the popular party was wont to gather, in which from the beginning of the fourteenth century the ceremony of knighting was performed, and which, in the sixteenth century, was the goal of daily penitential processions from the Duomo during the visitations of the plague and the persecutions of the Spaniards— this church, with its crowding memories of remarkable events, takes rank for the historian, no less than for the student of architecture, as 'queen of the churches of Lombardy'. Of course, the old Ambrosian building has long ago disappeared. In the ninth century the church was completely rebuilt by the two archbishops Angilberto and Ansperto; and it seems to have undergone fresh reconstruction in the eleventh or early twelfth century. The existing church, however, with its noble forecourt surrounded on three sides by arcades, its great central nave with aisles, its lofty cupola illuminating the richly ornamented canopy beneath which stands the altar with the magnificent golden frontal (the work of Volvinio) presented by Archbishop Angilberto, is certainly a worthy successor of the fourth-century basilica, on the planning of which Ambrose expended so much care, which he dedicated with relics of his own discovery, and wherein he himself was eventually laid to rest.[3]

The church being finished, Ambrose proceeded to dedicate it

---

[1] On this event, see Ambros. *Ep.* 22; Augustin. *Confess.* ix. 7; *Serm.* 286. 5. 4; *De Civitate Dei*, xxii. 8; *De cura gerenda pro mortuis*, 21; Paulinus, *Vita Ambros.* 14–17.

[2] Ambros. *De Excessu Sat.* i. 20.

[3] On this church see L. Beltrami, *La Basilica Ambrosiana primitiva*; C. Romussi, *Sant' Ambrogio, i tempi, l'uomo, la basilica*, pp. 61–139; G. Landriani, *La Basilica Ambrosiana*.

in the simple manner of earlier times—that is, by the celebration
of the Holy Mysteries with a sermon and special prayers.[1] This
ceremony, however, did not please the people, and many
remonstrated with him, saying, 'Consecrate this as you did the
Roman basilica'.[2] Now the Roman Basilica—the cruciform
Church of the Apostles (now called S. Nazaro Grande)—had
been dedicated with relics of St. Peter and St. Paul.[3] The
people, therefore, wished that the new church should be dedicated, after the fashion which at this time was coming into
vogue, by the deposition of relics.[4] Ambrose was not unwilling.
'I will do so', he answered, 'if I find relics of martyrs.' 'And
immediately', he said afterwards, when telling the story to his
sister, 'my heart burned within me as if with a sort of presentiment.'[5]

Acting on this impulse, and disregarding the scruples of some
of his clergy, he ordered excavations to be made in the Church
of SS. Felix and Nabor, in front of the railing or screen which

[1] R. W. Muncey, *History of the Consecration of Churches and Churchyards*, c. 2. For
such a dedicatory prayer see Ambros. *Exhort. Virginitatis*, 94 (at the dedication of
Juliana's church in Florence): 'I beseech Thee now, O Lord, let Thine eye be
continually upon this house, upon this altar, which is now dedicated unto Thee;
upon these spiritual stones, in each of which a sensible temple is consecrated unto
Thee. Let the prayers of Thy servants, which are poured out in this place, be
always accepted by Thy Divine Mercy. Let every sacrifice which is offered in this
place with pure faith and pious zeal be unto Thee a sweet-smelling savour of sanctification. And when Thou lookest upon that sacrifice of salvation which taketh
away the sins of the world, look also upon these sacrifices of chastity, and defend
them by Thy continual help, that they may be sweet and acceptable sacrifices unto
Thee, and pleasing unto Christ the Lord. Vouchsafe to keep their whole spirit and
soul and body without blame unto the day of Thy Son Jesus Christ our Lord.'
[2] Ambros. *Ep.* 22. 1.
[3] Paulinus, *Vita Ambros.* 33.
[4] An early instance of this fashion of dedication is supplied by an African inscription of the year A.D. 359, referring to a memorial chapel wherein had been deposited
relics of SS. Peter and Paul and certain local martyrs, wood of the Cross, and earth
from the Holy Land (Audollent in *Mélanges de l'École de Rome*, vol. x, p. 441).
Ambrose dedicated the Ambrosian Basilica at Florence with relics of SS. Agricola
and Vitalis (*Exhort. Virginitatis*, 1–10). Rufinus, in A.D. 394, received relics of SS.
Peter and Paul for the dedication of his Church of the Apostles near Chalcedon
(Sozomen. *H.E.* viii. 17). Paulinus of Nola deposited relics of the Apostles beneath
the altar of his new church at Nola (Paulin. Nolan. *Ep.* 32. 10; cf. *Poem.* xxvii.
395 ff.); and Gaudentius of Brescia dedicated the church named Concilium Sanctorum with relics of the Forty Martyrs and of SS. John the Baptist, Andrew, Thomas,
Luke, Gervasius, Protasius, Nazarius, Sisinnius, Alexander, and Martyrius
(Gaudent. Brix. *Serm.* xvii).
[5] Ambros. *Ep.* 22. 1. Augustine in this connexion speaks mistakenly of a dream
which came to Ambrose, *De Civ. Dei*, xxii. 8; *Confess.* ix. 7.

protected the tomb of the martyrs. Here he found 'appropriate signs'—whatever that phrase may mean. He then caused to be brought thither certain possessed persons, one of whom, a woman, was seized by an evil spirit and flung prostrate on the ground. At the spot where she fell Ambrose continued his excavations, and soon unearthed two skeletons, 'of extraordinary stature, such as ancient times produced'. All the bones were intact, but the heads had been severed from the trunks. There were also traces of some substance that resembled blood.[1] The probable date of the discovery is the 17th of June.[2]

The bones were lifted from the sepulchre and arranged in order upon biers. During this day and the following, they were visited by great crowds of people. When the evening of the second day (the 18th of June) approached, they were carried, amid an immense concourse, to the Basilica Faustae—a small church close to the new Ambrosian Basilica—where a vigil was kept throughout the night.[3] The relics were now identified as those of two martyrs named Gervasius and Protasius, who were believed to have suffered under Nero. Some old men 'recollected' that they had formerly heard the names of these martyrs and had even read the inscription on their tomb.[4]

On the following day, the 19th of June, the relics were borne in solemn procession to the Ambrosian Basilica. During the transportation a very strange incident occurred. There was at Milan a blind man, named Severus, well known in the city, who had formerly been a butcher, but, owing to the loss of his eyesight, had been compelled to abandon his trade and subsisted on charity. This man, hearing the joyful acclamations of the

---

[1] Ambros. *Ep.* 22. 2 and 12; Paulinus, *Vita Ambros.* 14. Augustine incorrectly speaks of 'uncorrupted' bodies (*Confess.* ix. 7).

[2] The traditional date of the translation of the relics to the Ambrosian Basilica is 19 June. There seems to be no reason to question this. But if the date of the translation was 19 June, the date of the invention, which was two days earlier (see text), must be 17 June. It may be noted that Ambrose in *Expos. ps. cxviii.* 6. 16 implies that the discovery took place in summer. The letter to Marcellina, in which the events connected with the invention and translation are narrated (*Ep.* 22), must have been written soon after 19 June of this year.

[3] Id. *Ep.* 22. 2. Satyrus was buried in the Basilica Faustae; see above, p. 183.

[4] Ibid. 22. 12. On the legend of Gervasius and Protasius see Tillemont, *Mém.* ii. 78 ff., 498 ff.; P. F. Savio, *Nuovo bull. di archeol. crist.* 1898, p. 153; A. Ratti, *Il più antico ritratto di S. Ambrogio*, pp. 51 ff. (in *Ambrosiana*, Milan, 1897). On the pseudo-Ambrosian letter on the two martyrs, see the Note at the end of this chapter.

people, and being informed of the occasion, sprang up and demanded to be led to the biers on which the remains of the martyrs rested. He was allowed to touch the fringe of the pall which covered the relics, or (according to Augustine's account) to touch the bier with a handkerchief which he forthwith applied to his blinded eyes. Immediately his sight was restored, and he was able to return without the assistance of a guide. In gratitude for his cure, he devoted himself for the rest of his life to service in the Ambrosian Basilica, where the bones of the martyrs were buried.[1]

The translation of the relics was attended by other marvels. Possessed persons were delivered, and many who were sick were healed of their ailments—some by touching the pall with their hands, some by the mere 'shadow of the holy bodies', as they were carried by. Handkerchiefs and articles of attire were cast upon the relics, and after contact therewith became endowed with curative properties.[2] Ambrose himself is the authority for these statements. He made them publicly, and called the people to witness that they were true.

When the Ambrosian Basilica was reached, Ambrose at first felt too overcome to preach—so vast was the throng which packed the building, and so astounding had been 'the gifts of Divine grace, which had shone forth in the holy martyrs'. During the reading of the lessons, however, he regained his self-possession.[3] Taking his stand between the biers,[4] he solemnly gave thanks to Christ that, through the recovery of Gervasius and Protasius, 'heretofore long unknown', the Church of Milan, once 'barren of martyrs', had become *a joyful mother of children*[5]— had, moreover, obtained 'defenders' in an hour when, owing to the persistent hostility of the Arians, she was in special need of succour.

'Thanks be to Thee, Lord Jesus, that at this time when Thy Church needs greater protection than ever, Thou hast raised up for us the spirits of the holy martyrs. Let all understand what kind of champions I desire—such as are able to defend, but are not wont to attack. These, holy people, I have gained for you; champions who will help all and injure no one. Such are the defenders that I desire; such are

---

[1] Ambros. *Ep.* 22. 2 and 17; Augustin. *Confess.* ix. 7; *De Civitate Dei*, xxii. 8; *Serm.* 286. 5. 4; *Retract.* i. 13. 7; Paulinus, *Vita Ambros.* 14.
[2] Ambros. *Ep.* 22. 9.                                          [3] Ibid. 22. 3.
[4] Ibid. 22. 4.                                                   [5] Ibid. 22. 7.

the soldiers that I have—not soldiers of the world, but soldiers of Christ. On account of these I fear no ill-will: their patronage is as safe as it is powerful.'[1]

After referring to the Bible story, which had just been read as the Prophetic Lesson, of the unseen hosts which had encompassed Elisha at Dothan, he continued:

'Even so were our own eyes closed, so long as the bodies of the saints lay hidden in their sepulchres. But the Lord has opened our eyes, and we have seen the helpers who so often have defended us. Formerly, although we had them, we saw them not. And so, as though the Lord had said to our trembling hearts, "See what great martyrs I have given you", we with opened eyes behold the glory of the Lord, which is past indeed in the passion of the martyrs, but is still present in their working. We have escaped, brethren, no inconsiderable burden of shame: we had patrons, and we knew it not. This one thing we have found, wherein we may seem to excel our ancestors— the knowledge of the holy martyrs, which they lost, we have regained.'[2]

In conclusion, he announced his intention of depositing the relics underneath the altar.

'Let us bring these victorious victims to the spot where Christ is the Sacrifice. But He, who suffered for all, upon the altar; they, who have been redeemed by His Passion, under the altar.[3] It is the place

---

[1] Ambros. *Ep.* 22. 10. Ambrose's words, *Tales ego ambio defensores*, were inscribed by St. Charles Borromeo on a banner of SS. Gervasius and Protasius, which was carried in procession through the streets of Milan at the time of the great plague.

[2] Ibid. 22. 11. The use of the words *patroni, patrocinium* with reference to apostles and martyrs seems to be first found in the writings of Ambrose (*Ep.* 22. 10 and 11; *Expos. ev. Luc.* x. 12; *De Excessu Sat.* i. 29; *De Viduis*, 55). But the usage soon became common. Paulinus of Nola frequently applies the term 'patron' to St. Felix (*Poem.* xiii. 27; xiv. 105; xviii. 5; xxiii. 99, 202, 214, 318; xxvi. 232; xxvii. 147, 198; xxxii. 1; cf. xxxi. 1); and the expression is adopted by Augustine (*De cura gerend. pro mort.* 6, 22) and Prudentius (*Peristeph.* i. 12; ii. 579; vi. 145; xiii. 106). In addition to the general patronage of pious devotees, martyrs were believed to take special interest in, and make special exertions to help, those places, with their inhabitants, where their bodily remains rested. Thus, SS. Peter and Paul were special patrons of Rome (Leo M. *Serm.* 82. 7), Gervasius and Protasius of Milan (Ambros. *Ep.* 22. 11), Fructuosus and his deacons of Tarragona (Prudent. *Peristeph.* vi. 145), Genesius of Arles (*Passio S. Genes. Arelat.* 1, 6; Migne, *P.L.* lxi, 418–20). So far, however, there is no evidence of the medieval custom of assigning special callings or professions to the patronage of special saints.

[3] At this time relics were not placed on the altar, but in a hollow beneath the altar (Ambros. *Exhort. Virginitatis*, 10; Hieron. *Contr. Vigilant.* 8; Paulinus Nolan. *Ep.* 32. 10; Prudent. *Peristeph.* iii. 212; v. 518). From the sixth century onwards relics were often placed temporarily on the altar before their deposition or removal elsewhere (Gregor. Turon. *Hist. Franc.* ix. 6; *Glor. Confess.* 39); but not before the ninth century were they allowed to remain there permanently.

which I had destined for myself; since it is fitting that the priest should rest where he has been wont to offer. But I yield the right-hand side to the sacred victims; that place is due to the martyrs. Let us, then, inter the hallowed relics, placing them in a worthy house, and let us observe the whole day with faithful devotion.'[1]

It is clear that Ambrose purposed to bury the relics immediately. The people, however—perhaps with the idea of making the ceremony the occasion of an orthodox demonstration against the Arians—besought him to defer the deposition till the following Sunday. This seemed to him inexpedient; but he agreed to postpone the final proceedings to the next day.[2] During the remainder of this day and throughout the night the crowd continued in the basilica, praying and singing psalms;[3] and many energumens were exorcized amid frantic excitement, the demons crying out that they were tormented by the martyrs.[4] Meanwhile the Arians in the palace, whether from malice or because they were honestly sceptical, ridiculed the whole affair. They denied that the bones discovered by Ambrose were really those of martyrs, denied that Severus had really been blind before his alleged restoration to sight, denied that demoniacs had really been cured. Venal persons, they declared, had been bribed by the Bishop to counterfeit demoniacal possession; the business from first to last was an imposture.[5]

[1] Ambros. *Ep.* 22. 13.    [2] Ibid. 22. 14 and 23.    [3] Ibid. 22. 15.
[4] Ibid. 22. 16, 21, and 22; Paulinus, *Vita Ambros.* 14, 16. The frenzies, wild cries, and 'confessions' of possessed persons were common phenomena in connexion with the relics and tombs of martyrs; cf. Ambros. *Exhort. Virginitatis*, 9; Paulinus, *Vita Ambros.* 29, 33; Augustin. *De cura gerend. pro mort.* 21; Hieron. *Contr. Vigilant.* 5; Prudent. *Peristeph.* i. 97–111. 'Our adversary and his legions are daily tormented by the virtue of the martyrs' (Ambros. *De Obitu Theod.* 10).
[5] Ambros. *Ep.* 22. 16–18, 22; Paulinus, *Vita Ambros.* 15. In modern times Dr. Rendel Harris (*The Dioscuri in the Christian Legends*, c. 3) appears to consider that Ambrose played off a trick on the Arians. He endeavours to establish a connexion between Gervasius and Protasius and the Dioscuri. He lays stress on the assertion in the Pseudo-Ambrosian Epistle (see Note at end of this chapter) that the martyrs were twins; urges that Ambrose refers to their extraordinary stature in terms similar to those used by Dionysius of Halicarnassus (vi. 13) and Plutarch (*Aemilius Paullus*, 25) in describing Castor and Pollux; points out that the expressions applied to them by Ambrose—'champions', 'soldiers', 'defenders'—recall the twin champions at the Battle of Lake Regillus; and maintains that Ambrose's application to the martyrs of the 19th Psalm, especially the expression 'bonae noctes, noctes lucidae, quae habent stellas' (*Ep.* 22. 8), suggests the Greek myth that Zeus placed the twin brothers among the stars. On these grounds, supplemented by an extremely fanciful argument based on names and dates of festivals in the Eastern and Western calendars, Dr. Harris concludes that Ambrose 'had the Dioscuri in mind when he

In his sermon on the following day Ambrose refuted these Arian calumnies. He appealed to the evidence of facts, which the people themselves had actually witnessed. They had seen the healings wrought in connexion with the relics. Surely the genuineness of the latter was attested by their manifest efficacy.[1] Again, they knew all about Severus. That he had been really blind was not only affirmed by the man himself and by charitable persons who had formerly supported him, but was a fact well known in the city, where the blind butcher was a familiar figure.[2] As for the allegation of fraud in respect of the cures of the possessed, the people had beheld the frightful convulsions of the energumens and had heard their frenzied cries when hands were laid upon them, and must know that it would be impossible to sham such agonies.[3] Why, then, did the Arians deny the working of the martyrs? It could hardly be that they doubted that martyrs had power of helping men. To question that would be equivalent to disbelieving the promise of Christ, *And greater works than these shall ye do.* No; the true reason was that they did not wish to acknowledge that mighty works were performed by those whose faith was different from their own. 'They would not envy them their works if they did not realize that the martyrs had a faith which they themselves have not—the faith established by the tradition of our fathers, which the demons themselves cannot deny, though the Arians do.'[4]

The holy remains, so opportunely discovered, were then deposited in the cavity beneath the altar; all the lamps in the church were lighted and the Eucharist was celebrated. Henceforth the day of the invention of the relics was annually celebrated in the Church of Milan.[5] The cult of Gervasius and Protasius spread rapidly over Western Europe, and was introduced into Africa by Augustine. Relics of the two saints were widely distributed. Ambrose himself, on his second embassy to Maximus in this very summer, may have carried some into Gaul.

recovered the martyrs and put them in the forefront in the battle with the Arians' (op. cit., p. 45). 'The Arians were like the Latin forces at the battle of the Lake Regillus; they suddenly found opposed to them two men in white who were leading the Roman line of advance. And Ambrose who put them in the front of the battle knew that he was parading the Dioscuri in a Christian dress' (ibid., p. 46).

[1] Ambrose. *Ep.* 22. 16.
[2] Ibid. 22. 17 and 18; cf. Augustine's strong words, *De Civitate Dei*, xxii. 8.
[3] Ambros. *Ep.* 22. 22.
[4] Ibid. 22. 19 and 20.          [5] Id. *Expos. ps. cxviii*, 6. 16.

Here in the sixth century they were so numerous that Gregory of Tours felt it necessary to offer an explanation. He tells a fantastic story, which he had heard, but had not found in documents relating to the martyrs. During the Mass (so he says) which was celebrated after the translation of the relics to the Ambrosian Basilica, a panel fell from the vaulting and grazed the martyrs' heads, from which streams of blood began to flow: linen cloths were brought and soaked in the fluid, and fragments of these were distributed among the cities of Italy and Gaul.[1]

Meanwhile Ambrose took full advantage of his fortunate discovery. Claiming the martyrs as 'defenders' of the persecuted Catholics, he set them, in all the glory of their miraculous powers, in the forefront of the battle against the Arians. The new 'champions' won for him a decisive and lasting victory. Justina and her courtiers might scoff at the business and denounce it as an impudent fraud; but no mockery could shake the popular faith in the newly found saints and in their miraculous operations. Under the conviction that Heaven itself had sent them supernatural succours, the Catholics were fired with incredible enthusiasm to defend their faith against every attack. In such circumstances it would have been madness to renew the attempt at 'persecution'. Although the Arian party at Milan continued in existence up to the time of the invasion of Maximus and the flight of Valentinian and Justina in September, A.D. 387, Ambrose and his Catholic flock were not seriously molested.[2]

In this strange story there are certain points which seem to require elucidation. They are: (a) How did Ambrose come to make the discovery? (b) What exactly did he discover? (c) What view should be taken of the alleged miracles?

(a) As regards the first point, we may ignore the statement made by Augustine, Paulinus, and the author of the pseudo-Ambrosian letter on the invention of the martyrs, that Ambrose

---

[1] Gregor. Turon. De Glor. Martyrum, 47. Gregory refers to relics of these martyrs at Tours, Hist. Franc. x. 31. 5 and 12.

[2] Paulinus (Vita Ambros. 17) relates that, about this time, one of the most violent of the Arians, while listening to Ambrose preaching in the church, saw an angel whispering into the Bishop's ear, so that he seemed to be reporting the angel's message to the people. By this vision the man was converted, and began to defend the faith of which he had formerly been a most obstinate opponent. A representation of Ambrose preaching, inspired by an angel, adorns one of the panels of the altar of Sant' Ambrogio.

was led to the discovery by a vision or revelation.[1] Had he really received such direct guidance, he would certainly have mentioned it in the detailed account of the affair which he wrote for his sister Marcellina. In this document, however, he says only that he felt a 'presentiment' that relics would be found.[2] Perhaps we may reconstruct what happened as follows. Desiring to find relics, and considering where to look for them, Ambrose remembered that the Church of SS. Felix and Nabor was built in an ancient Christian cemetery,[3] where it was likely enough that martyrs lay entombed. This was the 'presentiment', or happy thought, that came to him. Acting thereon, he caused excavations to be made, and found two skeletons with severed heads and exhibiting traces of something resembling blood. Such remains in such a place would naturally be taken to be remains of martyrs.[4] This point being settled, the only thing left to do was to identify the skeletons. Then old men taxed their memories and began to 'recollect' that they had heard of two martyrs named Gervasius and Protasius, and, as boys, had even seen these names inscribed on this very tomb. In an uncritical age such evidence was sufficient.

(b) But what did Ambrose actually discover? It is certainly possible that the skeletons, buried long ago in a Christian cemetery, were really those of martyrs. On the other hand, the huge stature of the bodies and the appearance of blood require explanation. On this point an interesting hypothesis has been put forward by Salomon Reinach. Speaking of prehistoric burial customs, he writes:

'Certain graves, dating from the quaternary period and many others of a later age, have been found to contain skeletons, which before burial were exposed to the air till the flesh dropped off, the bones being then painted over with a layer of red ochre. Evidences

---

[1] Augustin. *Confess.* ix. 7; *De Civitate Dei*, xxii. 8; Paulinus, *Vita Ambros.* 14; and Note at end of this chapter. Gaudentius of Brescia likewise affirms that the martyrs 'deigned to reveal themselves a few years ago to the holy bishop Ambrose in the city of Milan' (*Serm.* xvii; Migne, *P.L.* xx. 963).

[2] Ambros. *Ep.* 22. 1.

[3] De Rossi, *Bullett.* 1864, p. 29.

[4] In the fourth century men were disposed to regard any human remains accidentally discovered—especially in or near a church—as remains of martyrs. See the curious story told by Sulpicius of an altar erected near Tours over the grave of a robber on the strength of a popular tradition that a martyr was buried there (*Vita S. Martini*, 11).

of this custom are to be found from Spain to Russia; its existence in Oceania and in South America has also been established. It has certainly some connexion with a religious idea, red being the colour of life, as opposed to the pale hue of death. Bodies have also been found with the head severed from the trunk, perhaps for fear of the "vampire". This seems to be the explanation of the singular discovery made at Milan in A.D. 386, of a grave containing two great decapitated skeletons painted red. St. Ambrose, then Bishop of Milan, believed and made others believe that they were the bones of Christian martyrs of the time of Nero, Gervasius and Protasius, still red with the blood shed at their execution. As if organic matter like blood could have retained its colour for three centuries!'[1]

This theory has the merit of affording an explanation of the 'blood', of the severed heads, and of the peculiar phrase of Ambrose, 'of extraordinary stature, such as ancient times produced.' It is, at any rate, conceivable that Ambrose, excavating in a locality where he had reason to expect that bodies of martyrs might be found, came upon some primitive sepulchre containing remains such as Reinach describes. The decapitated skeletons stained with red ochre would inevitably be taken for martyrs, and the 'miraculous' occurrences which followed the discovery would seem to establish that conclusion.

(c) But what view should be taken of these 'miracles'? We may leave out of account the healings of energumens, which may be explained without recourse to any theory of supernatural agency. We may also leave out of account the cures effected on sick persons to which Ambrose refers in general terms, but of which he furnishes no details. There remains, however, the case of the blind butcher Severus. As to this, it may be noted, first, that the cure was wrought in public, on a person well known, who continued to live in Milan after his restoration, and who showed his own belief in, and gratitude for, his healing by devoting himself thenceforward to the service of the martyrs; secondly, that the cure is attested by three reputable witnesses—Ambrose, Augustine, and Paulinus—of whom the first two were certainly on the spot when the mysterious event took place; thirdly, that Ambrose publicly called attention to the incident in a sermon preached to a great congregation on the day after its occurrence, and challenged critics to make full

[1] S. Reinach, *Orpheus*, pp. 111, 112; cf. *L'Anthropologie*, p. 718.

investigation and expose the fraud, if there were one; and
fourthly, that the Arians, though they obstinately denied that
Severus had really been blind before his alleged cure, were
manifestly unable to produce a scrap of evidence in support of
their contention. From all this it seems certain that a real cure
was indeed effected, that Severus had really been blind and did
in some manner really recover his sight. It does not necessarily
follow, of course, that the cure was 'miraculous' in the sense
that it was incapable of being effected by natural causes. The
man was not born blind; he suffered from an ocular disease,
of the nature of which we know nothing.[1] In the absence of
medical evidence, it is conceivable that his case ought to be
classed among those strange, but not supernatural, 'faith-cures',
of which so many instances are encountered in Christian history.
But the point is not of consequence. The man's eyesight was
restored; and to the people of the period, so extraordinary an
event, taking place under such remarkable circumstances, could
hardly have failed to appear other than miraculous.

In this connexion some brief observations may be made on
the cult of martyrs and their relics, which became so prominent
a feature of popular Christianity towards the close of the fourth
century,[2] and on the contribution made by Ambrose towards
the encouragement and promotion thereof.

# I

It was the common belief that *martyrs interceded with God on
behalf of those who invoked their help*. This doctrine of intercession
was clearly taught by Ambrose. 'You too', he said to a widow,
'have kindred to entreat for you. You have the apostles as
kindred; you have the martyrs as kindred, if, for your part,
you share the martyrs' devotion and draw near to them in
works of mercy. Cherish, therefore, kinship with Peter, affinity
with Andrew, that they may pray for you; for now they are
able to obtain blessings for us and for all. It is clear that one
who is guilty of great sin is not fit to pray for herself, still less to
obtain her petitions. Let her therefore procure others to pray

---

[1] Ambros. *Ep.* 22. 17.

[2] For general treatment of the whole subject, see especially H. Siebert, *Beiträge zur
vorreformatorischen Heiligen- und Reliquienverehrung*; J. Hahn-Hahn, *Die Märtyrer*;
E. Lucius, *Die Anfänge des Heiligenkults in der christlichen Kirche*; F. Pfister, *Der
Reliquienkult im Altertum*; and J. A. S. C. de Plancy, *Dictionnaire critique des reliques*.

to the Physician on her behalf. For, just as the sick cannot themselves invoke the assistance of a doctor, but have to request his attendance through others, so, when the flesh is weak and the soul is sick with sin, we cannot direct our feeble steps to the throne of the Great Physician. Hence the angels, who have been given us as guardians, must be entreated for us; the martyrs must be entreated, whose patronage we claim by the pledge of their bodily remains. They can pray for our sins, who washed their own sins, if they had any, in their own blood. Let us not be ashamed to call them in as intercessors for our weakness.'[1] Such teaching represents the views that were prevalent at this time. Thus Jerome writes, 'If the apostles and martyrs, while still in the body can pray for others, when they ought still to be anxious for themselves, how much more must they do so when they have won their crowns, overcome and triumphed.'[2] Augustine maintains that, if we are unworthy to ask and receive blessings from God Himself, we may yet ask for them 'through His friends'—'let them pray for us, that He also may grant to us';[3] and Prudentius speaks of the martyrs of Calahorra as 'patrons of the world', who never disappoint those who offer right petitions, but 'hear their prayers, and immediately carry them to the ear of the Eternal King'.[4]

By means of their intercessions (so it was thought), *martyrs had power to dispense blessings, both spiritual and temporal.* On the one hand, they could quicken the spiritual life of their suppliants. 'May Peter quicken you, my daughters', writes Ambrose; 'may Paul quicken you, who enjoined that virgins should be honoured . . . may John quicken you.'[5] They could further purge away impurities,[6] and procure forgiveness of sins. So Prudentius calls on St. Lawrence to 'hear a rustic poet, confessing the sins of his heart and laying bare his misdeeds. Well do I know that I am unworthy to be heard by Christ Himself, but by the patronage

---

[1] Ambros. *De Viduis*, 54, 55. Ambrose held that not only martyrs and great saints but noble spirits departed might effectually intercede for those on earth; see *De Excessu Sat.* ii. 135; *De Obitu Val.* 41 (cf. 54, 71, 76); *De Obitu Theod.* 16.

[2] Hieron. *Contr. Vigilant.* 6.

[3] Augustin. *Serm.* 332. 3. Prayer for the martyrs themselves was considered unbecoming; 'pro martyribus non orat [ecclesia], sed eorum potius orationibus se commendat' (ibid. 284. 5; cf. ibid. 159. 1; 285. 5).

[4] Prudentius, *Peristeph.* i. 11–18; cf. ibid. ii. 577–80; vi. 84; x. 1136–40.

[5] Ambros. *De Virginitate*, 130.

[6] Prudentius, *Peristeph.* xiv. 124–33.

of the martyrs I may obtain healing.'[1] Finally, they had ability to protect their votaries on the Day of Judgement.[2] On the other hand, the martyrs could confer all kinds of temporal favours. Satyrus, when sick in Sicily, made a vow to St. Lawrence, and was consequently enabled to live long enough to return to Milan;[3] Juliana of Florence obtained, through the same saint, the gift of a son;[4] Prudentius owed a safe return to Spain to the good offices of St. Hippolytus, 'to whom Christ our God has given the power of granting whatever men ask of him';[5] Florentius, a poor old cobbler of Hippo, by means of prayer to the Twenty Martyrs, received the wherewithal to purchase a new cloak;[6] a countryman of Nola recovered two stolen oxen by the grace of St. Felix.[7] It was believed that great saints were specially active in assisting their protégés against their enemies. In A.D. 394 St. John and St. Philip appeared in a dream to Theodosius, and announced that they had been sent to fight for him against Eugenius.[8] In A.D. 406, when Florence was besieged by Radagaisus, Ambrose, who had been dead for some years, presented himself in a vision to a citizen of the place, and promised that the city should be saved.[9] In A.D. 410 the Romans refused to fortify a weak part of the city wall against the Goths, 'affirming that the Apostle Peter had promised them that the guardianship of that place should be his care'.[10]

In what manner exactly the martyrs heard and helped those who invoked them was a point in dispute among theologians. Augustine was doubtful whether they actually heard the prayers addressed to them, and whether they were actually present in person to render aid.[11] Jerome, on the contrary, contended that they were virtually ubiquitous, and therefore both heard and helped directly. '*They follow the Lamb whithersoever he goeth.*

---

[1] Prudentius, *Peristeph.* ii. 573–80; cf. ibid. iv. 189–96; v. 545–68.
[2] Ibid. iv. 5 ff.; vi. 157–62; x. 1136–40.
[3] Ambros. *De Excessu Sat.* i. 17.          [4] Id. *Exhort. Virginitatis,* 15.
[5] Prudentius, *Peristeph.* xi. 177–82.
[6] Augustin. *De Civitate Dei,* xxii. 8.
[7] Paulin. Nolan. *Poem.* xviii. 220–448.
[8] Theodoret. *H.E.* v. 24. Theodosius had prepared for this struggle by visiting the tombs of the martyrs and invoking their help, Rufinus, *H.E.* ii. 33.
[9] Paulinus, *Vita Ambros.* 50; cf. the appearance of Felix of Nola in similar circumstances, Augustin. *De cura gerend. pro mort.* 19.
[10] Procopius, *De Bell. Goth.* i. 23.
[11] Augustin. *De cura gerend. pro mort.* 18–21; *De Civitate Dei,* xxii. 9.

If the Lamb is present everywhere, the same must be believed of those who are with the Lamb.'[1] Similarly Ambrose described the martyrs as 'beholders of our life and actions';[2] and Prudentius declared of St. Cyprian that 'though he possesses the realm of the sky, he nevertheless flies over all lands and does not desert this world'.[3]

The general belief was that *martyrs were present in a special manner at their tombs*, and there specially exhibited their miraculous activities. This popular conception—which was criticized by Vigilantius, when he sarcastically asked, 'Is it the case that the souls of the martyrs love their ashes, and hover round them, and are always present, lest haply, if any one came to pray and they were absent, they could not hear?'[4]—is well illustrated in a fifth-century sermon preached at Verona on St. Zeno's day by Petronius of Bologna. Speaking of the miracles wrought at St. Zeno's tomb, the preacher says, 'Healings of many kinds proceed from that burial; and he who has his place in that sepulchre gives fresh life therefrom to the dying and heals the sick, while from a never-failing spring a joyous stream gushes forth, cleanses sinners, and communicates to them the delights of salvation. And whenever his tomb, wet with tears, has received the prayers of suppliants, then on every occasion he lavishes the help desired with many and varied additions. And so the powers which the blessed seer was able to exert while he was in the body, he makes use of in fullness to-day when in his tomb. For the Spirit of God works in his living ashes.'[5] The widespread belief in the presence and activity of martyrs at their sepulchres accounts for the devotion with which such tombs were honoured. More famous tombs, such as those of the Apostles Peter and Paul, St. Hippolytus and St. Felix of Nola, were visited by crowds of pilgrims.[6] Kisses were imprinted on them,[7]

[1] Hieron. *Contr. Vigilant*. 6.
[2] Ambros. *De Viduis*, 55.
[3] See the whole passage, Prudentius, *Peristeph*. xiii. 99–106.
[4] Hieron. *Contr. Vigilant*. 8.
[5] G. Morin, *Revue Bénédict*. xiv, 1897, pp. 3 ff. See also the statement of Paulinus of Nola, *Poem*. xxvii. 440–8; and cf. Prudentius' account of the miracles wrought at the tomb of the martyrs of Calahorra (*Peristeph*. i. 97–120) and Paulinus' references to the marvels at the tomb of St. Felix (Paulin. Nolan. *Poem*. xviii, xxvi).
[6] Prudentius, *Peristeph*. xii; ibid. xi. 189 ff.; Paulin. Nolan. *Poem*. xiv.
[7] Prudentius, *Peristeph*. ix. 100; xi. 193; Hieron. *Ep*. 46. 8; Gregor. Turon. *De Glor. Mort*. 44.

perfumes were sprinkled over them,[1] and lights were kept burning before them.[2]

Being credited with such tremendous powers, *martyrs were naturally regarded with extreme veneration.* It is true that theologians definitely repudiated the notion that they either were or ought to be worshipped.[3] Yet the distinction drawn by the experts, between 'honour' paid to the martyrs and 'adoration' due to God alone, was hardly appreciated by the masses; and, in common practice, at any rate, the cult of the martyrs came perilously near to creature-worship. The following passages, taken from Prudentius, reflect the sentiments which appear to have been generally entertained with regard to these exalted and wellnigh deified beings. 'Tell the saint', is the injunction to Prudentius in St. Cassian's shrine at Imola, 'if you have any just and amiable desire, if you have any hope, if you have any trouble in your heart. Believe me, the martyr with the greatest kindness hears all prayers, and those which he approves he grants.' 'I took the advice', the poet continues; 'I embraced the tomb and sprinkled it with my tears: I made the altar warm with my kisses, the cold stone with the pressure of my breast. Then I reckoned up all the things which were secretly troubling me; I whispered what I desired and what I feared. My words were heard. I went to Rome, and prospered there, and returned safe home, and now I sing the praise of Cassian.'[4] 'Be present now', cries the poet to St. Vincent, 'and receive the beseeching voice of thy suppliants, thou who dost efficaciously intercede for our guilt before the Father's throne. By thyself, we pray thee, by thy prison, whereby thy glory was increased, by the chains, the flames, the various instruments of torture, by that iron bed which we men of later days kiss tremblingly, have pity on our prayers, that Christ may be appeased and bend a gracious ear and impute not to us all our offences. If duly we venerate with voice and heart thy solemn day, if we lie prostrate beneath the joy of thy footsteps, come hither a little while, bringing down with thee the favour of Christ, that our burdened senses may feel the relief of pardon.'[5]

[1] Prudentius, *Peristeph.* xi. 194; Paulin. Nolan. *Poem.* xviii. 38, 39.
[2] Hieron. *Ep.* 109. 1; *Contr. Vigilant.* 7.
[3] Augustin. *De Civitate Dei,* viii. 27; xxii. 10; *De Vera Rel.* 108; *Contr. Faustum,* xx. 21; Hieron. *Contr. Vigilant.* 5; *Ep.* 109. 1.
[4] Prudentius, *Peristeph.* ix. 95–106.          [5] Ibid. v. 545–68.

'O blessed and glorious virgin, illustrious dweller in the highest heaven'—the invocation this time is to St. Agnes—'turn thy face crowned with the twofold crown on my impurities. To thee alone the Almighty hath granted power to make the very brothel pure. I shall be purged by the radiance of thy gracious countenance, if thou fill my heart. Nothing is unchaste which thou, in thy chastity, deignest to look upon or to touch with thy gentle foot.'[1]

Veneration of the martyrs involved *veneration of their relics*. Their bodily remains were sought and treasured.[2] At this period, however—though relics were not infrequently translated from their original resting-place[3]—it was not considered seemly to dismember holy bodies or to separate bones or ashes which had been collected in one tomb.[4] Hence, in order to preserve the remains intact, and at the same time to satisfy the popular passion for the acquisition of relics, a fiction was invented that the body of a martyr could be represented by some object which had been associated therewith—a piece of linen saturated with his blood, a fragment of some instrument of his martyrdom, a handkerchief which had touched his sarcophagus, or a little oil from the lamps which burned before it. Possession of such an object was deemed equivalent to possession of the body of the martyr, and through it, men believed, the martyr's supernatural powers were manifested no less than through his actual remains.[5]

[1] Prudentius, *Peristeph*. xiv. 124–33.

[2] Sometimes they were surreptitiously stolen; see, e.g., Hieron. *Vita S. Hilarion.* 46.

[3] Theodosius, indeed, in A.D. 386, forbade the translation of bodies from one place to another, and also the sale of such bodies, Cod. Theod. ix. 17. 7. Spurious relics were hawked about the provinces by vagabond monks in Augustine's time, Augustin. *De Op. Monach.* 36.

[4] In the *Acts* of the martyrdom of Fructuosus of Tarragona it is stated that, after he and his companions had suffered death by burning, the brethren gathered up the relics and divided them among themselves; but the martyr appeared in a vision to several of them, and admonished them to restore the relics and bury all together in one place, which was accordingly done (Ruinart, *Acta Sincera*, p. 221; Prudentius, *Peristeph*, vi. 130–41). So Prudentius describes how the fragments of the body of St. Hippolytus were collected with pious care and deposited together in one tomb (*Peristeph*. xi. 135–52).

[5] In the sixth century Gregory the Great, after dwelling on the danger of meddling with the bodies of saints, explains how relics could still be multiplied. 'When the Romans give relics of the saints, they do not venture to touch any part of the body; but a cloth is enclosed in a box, which is then placed near the saints' most sacred bodies. This is afterwards taken up and deposited in the church which

Belief in the miraculous efficacy of relics was almost universal. Ambrose's account of the cure of Severus through contact with the relics of Gervasius and Protasius has already been noticed. A few years later, according to the testimony of Paulinus, another blind man, a native of Dalmatia, was restored to sight at Milan, by touching a chest containing relics of the martyrs of Anaunia.[1] Particularly striking is Augustine's relation of the miracles wrought in connexion with the relics of St. Stephen at various places in Africa, where there were *memoriae* of the proto-martyr. Among these we read of cures vouchsafed to a woman who was blind, to a bishop who had a fistula, to a priest suffering from the stone, to two persons tormented by gout, to a brother and sister afflicted with palsy, and to a child crushed by an ox-wagon. It is even alleged that dead persons were restored to life. Augustine says that accounts of many similar marvels were written down, and that it was the custom to read them publicly to the people.[2]

Among the more famous relics were the bodies of St. Peter and St. Paul at Rome, those of St. Andrew, St. Luke, and St. Timothy at Constantinople,[3] that of St. Stephen (discovered at Kaphar-Gamala in A.D. 415) at Jerusalem,[4] the head of John the Baptist,[5] the chair of St. James,[6] the chains of St. Paul,[7] and the column to which our Lord was bound when He suffered scourging.[8] Most sacred of all was the Cross of Christ, discovered by Helena in A.D. 326. The story of the discovery is related by Ambrose, who differs from other historians in stating that the Cross was recognized because the *titulus* was still attached to it. He speaks of the adoration of the Cross by Helena, but takes care to guard against misconception. 'It was the King that she

is to be dedicated, and the miracles wrought by it are as great as if the very bodies of the saints had been brought there. Whence it came to pass that in the time of Pope Leo of blessed memory, when certain Greeks doubted the efficacy of such relics, the pontiff, according to the tradition handed down by our ancestors, took a pair of scissors and cut the cloth, and as he cut it blood flowed out' (*Epp.* iv. 30, ed. Ewald and Hartmann in *Mon. Germ. Hist.*).

[1] Paulinus, *Vita Ambros.* 52.                    [2] Augustin. *De Civitate Dei*, xxii. 8.
[3] Hieron. *Contr. Vigilant.* 5; Philostorgius, iii. 2.
[4] See the documents printed in Migne, *P.L.* xli. 805 ff.
[5] Sozomen. *H.E.* vii. 21.                    [6] Eusebius, *H.E.* vii. 19.
[7] Chrysostom, *Hom. viii in Ep. ad Ephes.* 2. The chains of St. Peter are mentioned for the first time in the correspondence of Gregory the Great (F. Homes Dudden, *Gregory the Great*, i, pp. 278, 279).
[8] Hieron. *Ep.* 108. 9.

adored, not the wood.' He further states that, in addition to the Cross, Helena discovered the nails with which our Lord was fastened thereto; one of these (in fulfilment of the prophecy of Zechariah xiv. 20) she caused to be fashioned into a bit for Constantine's horse, another was wrought into his diadem.[1]

The martyr cult must be regarded as a Christian development of pagan custom. In heathendom deceased heroes were deified and worshipped. They were held to be capable of protecting and assisting the living; their tombs and relics were preserved with reverence; votive offerings were made to them, and miracles were believed to be wrought at their shrines. When, after the conversion of Constantine, multitudes of pagans flocked into the Church, they brought with them the ideas and practices of the traditional hero-worship; only now, instead of the hero, the martyr became the object of popular veneration. Hence it was not entirely without reason that Faustus maintained that the Christians of his period had not abandoned pagan usage, but had merely substituted martyrs for idols, and memorial feasts for sacrifices;[2] or that the presbyter Vigilantius denounced the cult as 'virtually a heathen observance introduced into the Churches under the cloak of religion', and boldly stigmatized those who practised it as 'idolaters'.[3]

This Vigilantius, a native of Aquitaine, published early in the fifth century a strong protest against various superstitious observances connected with the veneration of martyrs and their relics. In particular, he denounced the carrying round of relics in costly vessels or silken wrappings, to be kissed and adored by the faithful;[4] the prayers in which the intercession of the martyrs was invoked;[5] the building of churches in their honour[6] and the late watchings in such churches;[7] the burning of tapers at their shrines,[8] and the importance attached to the miracles

[1] Ambros. *De Obitu Theod.* 41–8. On the story of the invention of the Cross, see Rufinus, *H.E.* i. 7, 8; Sulpicius, *Chron.* ii. 34; Paulin. Nolan. *Ep.* 31; Socrates, *H.E.* i. 17; Sozomen. *H.E.* ii. 1; Theodoret. *H.E.* i. 18. Jerome ridicules the application of the words in Zechariah (*Comm. in Zech.* xiv. 20). On the passage in Ambrose, see C. Favez, 'L'Épisode de l'Invention de la Croix dans l'Oraison funèbre de Théodose par saint Ambroise' (*Revue des études latines*, 1932, pp. 423–9).

[2] Augustin. *Contr. Faust.* xx. 21.

[3] Hieron. *Contr. Vigilant.* 4; *Ep.* 109. 1. On Vigilantius, see W. S. Gilly, *Vigilantius and his Times*; W. Schmidt, *Vigilantius, sein Verhältnis zum heiligen Hieronymus.*

[4] Hieron. *Contr. Vigilant.* 4, 5.     [5] Ibid. 6.     [6] Ibid. 8.

[7] Ibid. 9.     [8] Ibid. 4, 7.

which were said to be wrought there.[1] The protest was not made rashly, but after mature deliberation; and the criticism of prevalent practices, though certainly scathing, was not unjust. The bishop of the diocese, Exuperius of Toulouse, was attracted by the reformer's views,[2] and some other bishops favoured them.[3] Then Jerome precipitated himself into the fray. In the course of a single night[4] he scribbled off a pamphlet *Against Vigilantius* —a veritable masterpiece of scurrilous abuse, which the literary world, no doubt, found very racy and amusing. Yet the indelicate treatise voiced the views, not only of the lay multitudes, but also of the majority of the clergy, and was therefore received with almost unanimous approval. Vigilantius was henceforth extinguished, and the protest against the popular martyrolatry came to nothing.[5]

## II

In the promotion of the cult of the martyrs Ambrose himself played a prominent part. Convinced as he was of the powers of help and healing which were, or might be, exercised by the departed saints, he did all he could to stimulate popular veneration of their relics. In the very beginning of his episcopate he arranged for the translation of the body of his saintly predecessor, Dionysius, to Milan. In A.D. 386 he further enriched the city with the bones, discovered by himself, of SS. Gervasius and Protasius. In A.D. 393 he 'discovered' the remains of SS. Agricola and Vitalis at Bologna, and in A.D. 395 those of SS. Nazarius and Celsus at Milan. The story of his operations on the last two occasions throws interesting light on the value set on relics, and on the treatment accorded to them, at this period.

(*a*) In the autumn of A.D. 393 Ambrose visited Bologna. Here, according to the narrative of Paulinus, it was revealed either to him or to the local bishop—the reading of the passage is uncertain—that, unknown to the Christian inhabitants of the city, the remains of two martyrs, named Agricola and Vitalis,

---

[1] Hieron. *Contr. Vigilant.* 10.        [2] Id. *Ep.* 109. 2.
[3] Id. *Contr. Vigilant.* 2.        [4] Ibid. 3, 17.
[5] Gennadius, *De Eccl. Dogmatibus*, 73, states that no Christians, but only the followers of Vigilantius and Eunomius, rejected the veneration of the relics of martyrs, and the devout pilgrimage to churches called by their names and built in their honour.

lay buried in the Jewish cemetery. Search was accordingly made, and, in the presence of a great concourse of Jews and Christians, two bodies were discovered. They found also the wood of the cross on which Agricola had suffered, a great quantity of nails—'so many', says Ambrose, 'that the martyr's wounds must have been more in number than his limbs'—and a substance that was thought to be blood. The bodies were taken from the cemetery and reinterred beneath the altar of the cathedral amid the joyous acclamations of the people and the cries of tormented spirits confessing, through the mouths of the persons whom they possessed, the merits of the martyrs.[1]

Early in A.D. 394 Ambrose went to Florence to dedicate the new basilica which had recently been built there by Juliana.[2] Thither he carried with him some of the newly discovered relics —fragments of the cross, nails, and particles of the 'blood', which he had collected with his own hands from the grave at Bologna. The dedication of the church was celebrated with the deposition of these objects beneath the altar.[3]

In his dedicatory sermon Ambrose referred to the precious gifts which he had brought.

'Those who are invited to a great banquet are wont to carry presents away with them. I was invited to a banquet at Bologna, where the translation of a holy martyr was celebrated, and I have kept for you certain presents full of holiness and grace. Presents also are distributed on the occasion of the triumph of an emperor, and these gifts which I bring are triumphal presents; for the palms of the martyrs are the triumphs of our Emperor, Christ. I did not intend to come to Florence; but, since I have been invited by you, I felt bound to bring with me gifts which I had designed for others; that, when I came, I might not disappoint your hopes, or rather that your hopes, if disappointed in me, might be more than fulfilled in the martyr.'[4]

He gave a few details concerning the passion of Agricola and Vitalis. The latter was one of Agricola's slaves, and was executed first in order to intimidate his master. Refusing to deny Christ, he was horribly tortured, so that no portion of his body was left without a wound; as he died, he prayed, 'Lord Jesus

---

[1] Ambros. *Exhort. Virginitatis*, 1–10; Paulinus, *Vita Ambros.* 29.
[2] Ambros. *Exhort. Virginitatis*, 10. The basilica was afterwards known as the Ambrosian Basilica (Paulinus, *Vita Ambros.* 50).
[3] Ambros. *Exhort. Virginitatis*, 9, 10.      [4] Ibid. 1.

Christ, my Saviour and my God, command that my spirit be
received, for now do I long to receive the crown which Thy holy
angel hath shown to me.' Next came the turn of Agricola. He
was a man of very gentle disposition, and was beloved even by
his persecutors. But since he firmly refused to abjure his faith,
he was put to death by crucifixion.[1]

(b) In the year A.D. 395 Ambrose made yet another discovery.
He himself does not refer to it in any of his writings; but an
account is given by Paulinus, who was present on the occasion.[2]
In a garden outside Milan was found the body of the martyr
Nazarius. 'We saw', writes Paulinus, 'in the sepulchre where
the body of the martyr lay—when he suffered we have been
unable to ascertain up to the present time—the martyr's blood,
as fresh as if it had been shed the same day, and his head, which
had been cut off by the wicked persecutors, so entire and uncorrupted with the hair and beard, that it looked as if it had been
just washed and arranged at the time when it was taken from
the tomb.' The body was placed on a bier and carried to the
Basilica of the Apostles, near the Roman Gate. This done,
Ambrose, accompanied by Paulinus and the clergy, immediately
returned to the same garden to pray. On this Paulinus makes
a curious remark. 'We know that he had never before prayed
in that spot; but it was a sign of the discovery of the body of
a martyr if the holy Bishop went to pray at a place where he
had never been before.' 'We learnt', he continues, 'from the
keepers of the place that their ancestors had left them injunctions never to leave it, so long as any of their family remained,
because great treasures were deposited there.' The treasure

[1] Ambros. *Exhort. Virginitatis*, 2–5; see further Paulin. Nolan. *Poem.* xxvii. 428–
35; Gregor. Turon. *Hist. Franc.* ii. 16; *De Glor. Mart.* 44. In the Appendix to
Ambrose's Works (Opp. iv. 747–9) the Benedictine editors print a letter (*Ep.* 3)
purporting to have been written by Ambrose to the bishops and faithful of Italy,
and describing the passion of the martyrs and the discovery of their relics. The
document, which is certainly by a later hand, is based on *Exhort. Virginitatis*, 1–10,
and contains no new statement of importance, except that the martyrs suffered
during the persecution of Diocletian and Maximian (*Ep.* 3. 2 and 10). It may be
noted, however, that the author says distinctly that the revelation which led to
the discovery of the bodies at Bologna was made to Ambrose himself (ibid. 2), thus
supporting the reading 'sacerdoti ipsi revelassent' in Paulinus, *Vita Ambros.* 29. He
also relates that, at the translation of the relics, not only were evil spirits cast out,
but many sick persons were healed 'sanctorum tangentes sudaria' (ibid. 4).

[2] Paulinus, *Vita Ambros.* 32, 33. Paulinus places the event at the beginning of the
'three years' following the death of Theodosius.

exhumed this time was the body of St. Celsus, which was also conveyed to the Basilica of the Apostles. Here the remains of the two martyrs were solemnly reinterred. During the ceremony, while Ambrose was preaching, a possessed person made a disturbance, but the demon was rebuked and reduced to silence by the Bishop. Such is the account of Paulinus, who is the earliest authority for these martyrs. Later on—perhaps in the early part of the fifth century—a legend of SS. Nazarius and Celsus was elaborated, but it seems to be destitute of historical value.[1]

## NOTE

*On the pseudo-Ambrosian letter 'de inventione sanctorum Gervasii et Protasii'*

In the Appendix to their edition of Ambrose's Works (iv. 743–7) the Benedictines have inserted a letter *de inventione sanctorum Gervasii et Protasii*, which purports to have been written to the bishops of Italy by Ambrose himself. The document is unquestionably a later composition, though written before the time of John Damascene, who cites a passage from it. It gives the legend of the martyrs, as it was eventually developed. First the circumstances which led to their discovery are recounted. Ambrose had a vision. During the Lenten fast he saw with his eyes open *duos iuvenes ephebos vestibus candidissimis, id est, colobio et pallio indutos, caligulis calceatos, manibus extensis orantes,* but he found himself unable to address them (Pseudo-Ambros. *Ep.* 2. 2). He prayed that, if the vision were a true one, and not merely a delusion of demons, it might appear to him again 'more fully'. He increased his fast; and the next night, about cock-crow, he saw the youths a second time (ibid. 3). The third night they appeared once more, together with another personage who *similis erat beato Paulo apostolo, cuius me vultum pictura docuerat.* St. Paul told Ambrose that his companions were martyrs of Milan, whose bodies were buried in a coffer twelve feet below the ground *in eodem loco in quo stas et oras,* and whose names and history were recorded in a *libellus* which would be found near their heads (ibid. 4). Ambrose immediately convoked his suffragans, and with their approval and in their presence commenced excavations. The coffer was found containing the bodies of the saints *quasi in ipsa hora positos, miro odore flagrantes* (ibid. 5). By their heads was a document, written by a Christian named Philip, who, with the help of his son, had stolen the bodies of the martyrs by night, and had buried them in the precincts of his own house, *credens*

---

[1] See F. Savio, *La Leggenda dei SS. Nazario e Celso (Ambrosiana,* 1897); *Acta SS.* Boll. Jul. vi. 503–34. A sermon on the natal day of SS. Nazarius and Celsus, wrongly attributed to Ambrose, is printed in the Appendix to his Works (Opp. iv. 715–19; *Serm.* 55).

*me orationibus eorum consequi misericordiam Domini nostri Jesu Christi* (ibid.
18). In this document it was stated that the bodies were those of
Gervasius and Protasius, twin sons of Vitalis and Valeria of the city of
Milan (ibid. 6: it may be noted that neither Ambrose, nor Augustine,
nor Paulinus describes the martyrs as twins). The *libellus* went on to
give a brief history of the saints. Their father, Vitalis, was a soldier,
who, refusing to sacrifice to the gods, was buried alive by order of
the anti-Christian governor Paulinus, at Ravenna, in a place called
Ad Palmam (ibid. 7–10). Their mother, Valeria, having been forbidden in a vision to remove the body of her husband (ibid. 11), was
returning to Milan, when she encountered a party of pagans, who so
ill-treated her that she died within three days (ibid. 12). Gervasius
and Protasius, thus bereft of their parents, sold their property, gave
the proceeds to the poor, and for ten years lived together in a garret,
devoting themselves to reading and prayer (ibid. 13). In the
eleventh year, Count Astasius, at the instigation of pagan enemies
of the brothers, ordered them to offer sacrifice for the success of his
expedition against the Marcomanni; and, on their refusal, caused
Gervasius to be beaten to death and Protasius to be decapitated
(ibid. 14–18). No reliance, however, can be placed on this relation.
In those parts where it can be checked it is seriously inaccurate; as
for the rest, we have the explicit testimony of Ambrose and others
that, at the time of the discovery of the relics, the memory of these
two martyrs had died out in Milan (Ambros. *Ep.* 22. 11 and 12;
Paulinus, *Vit. Ambros.* 14; Augustin. *De Civ. Dei,* xxii. 8).

## CHAPTER XIII

# THE EARLY DEVELOPMENT, CONVERSION, AND. BAPTISM OF AUGUSTINE[1]

THE conflict between Ambrose and Justina, terminating in the triumph of the former, had been watched with intense interest by one spectator—a brilliant young man named Aurelius Augustinus, who at that time held a professorship of rhetoric at Milan.

Augustine was born on the 13th of November, A.D. 354, in the small Numidian town of Thagaste (now Suk Arras in Algeria). His parents belonged to the upper class of townspeople, but were in straitened circumstances.[2] Patricius, his father, a lively, quick-tempered, but not unkindly man, of coarse manners and easy morals,[3] was still a pagan;[4] but his mother, Monnica, was an ardent Christian.[5] She was determined that her son should be brought up in her own religion. Accordingly, at his birth he was made a catechumen with salt and the sign of the cross; he was not, however, baptized. When he was still quite a child, he fell dangerously ill, and expressed a wish to receive baptism; but, as he suddenly grew better, the rite was deferred 'because, if I lived, I should inevitably get defiled again, and

---

[1] The original authorities for this chapter are the first nine books of the *Confessions*, the early works *Contra Academicos*, *De Vita Beata*, *De Ordine*, and *Soliloquia* (cf. D. Ohlmann, *De S. Augustini dialogis in Cassiciaco scriptis*, Strassburg, 1897), and Possidius, *Vita Augustini*, 1. Of the innumerable modern publications bearing on the subject, the following may be consulted with advantage: J. J. F. Poujoulat, *Histoire de S. Augustin*; J. B. M. Flottes, *Études sur S. Augustin: son génie, son âme, sa philosophie*; Fr. Wörter, *Die Geistesentwicklung des hl. Aurelius Augustinus bis zu seiner Taufe*; H. A. Naville, *S. Augustin: Étude sur le développement de sa pensée jusqu'à l'époque de son ordination*; T. Bret, *La Conversion de S. Augustin*; P. Alfaric, *L'Évolution intellectuelle de S. Augustin*; L. Gourdon, *Essai sur la conversion de S. Augustin*; and J. McCabe, *St. Augustine and his Age*.

[2] Possidius, *Vita Augustini*, 1; Augustin. *Confess*. ii. 3.

[3] Augustin. *Confess*. ix. 9.

[4] Ibid. i. 11. He was converted shortly before his death, ibid. ix. 9.

[5] Id. *De Ordine*, ii. 1 'in res divinas inflammatum animum'. Ambrose admired her for her piety (*Confess*. vi. 2), which was tinged with mysticism (ibid. vi. 13). Some interesting details of her early life are given, ibid. ix. 8, 9. See also E. Bougaud, *Hist. de S. Monique*; A. Vivoli, *Vita di S. Monica*. Besides Augustine she had another son, Navigius, and a daughter whose name is not known.

sin after baptism is of a deeper dye and fraught with greater danger to the soul than sin before it'.[1]

From an early age the boy gave tokens of extraordinary ability, and his parents, who were intensely proud of him, took care that he should have the advantage of a good education. First he was sent to an elementary school at Thagaste, and afterwards to a higher-grade academy in the neighbouring town of Madaura. He was enthralled by the charm of Virgil, but failed to appreciate the Greek classics, since 'the difficulty of learning a foreign language dashed with gall all the sweetness of Greek fable'.[2] At the age of sixteen he returned—a sparkling, high-spirited, not over-steady lad—to his home for a year, while his father raised funds for sending him to the University of Carthage.[3] Unfortunately, at this critical juncture, his father died, and Augustine's prospects were in serious jeopardy. But a wealthy fellow townsman, named Romanian, generously supplied him with the means of completing his education.[4]

To Carthage Augustine went—and he could hardly have gone to a worse place. The city itself was one of the finest in the world.[5] In the midst of it rose the Byrsa or citadel-hill, crowned with the glittering marble Temple of Aesculapius and with the Praetorium of the Proconsul of Africa. At the foot of the Byrsa, and connected therewith by three narrow streets lined with tall six-storied houses, lay the Forum, with the Senate-House and the richly ornamented Temple of Apollo: and beyond the Forum was the port, consisting of an outer harbour and an inner artificial basin, called the Mandracium, bordered all round by colonnades. The rest of the urban area was covered with streets laid out in regular pattern and pleasantly shaded by rows of trees, and with magnificent palaces, temples, and public buildings. Away to the north lay the walled suburb of Megara, renowned for its luxuriant gardens watered by canals. Yet this spacious and beautiful city—'the Rome of Africa'—bore the worst possible reputation.[6] Its inhabitants are described as cruel, treacherous, greedy, drunken, dishonest, and quite immeasurably salacious. Prostitution of both sexes was practised

---

[1] Augustin. *Confess.* i. 11; cf. v. 9.                      [2] Ibid. i. 13, 14.
[3] Ibid. ii. 3. For the story of the robbery of the pear-tree, ibid. ii. 4, 8.
[4] Id. *Contr. Academ.* ii. 3.                      [5] Ausonius, *Clarae Urbes*, ii.
[6] See Salvian's description, *De Gubern. Dei*, vii. 67 ff.

to an extent unparalleled elsewhere. Houses of ill fame abounded in every street. Except among the clergy, chastity was unknown.[1] 'I came to Carthage', writes Augustine, 'and everywhere around me roared the furnace of lust.'[2]

Augustine became a member of the University. Here the discipline was extremely lax. The students 'ragged' in their lecture-rooms and rioted in the streets, often committing offences punishable by law. But such turbulence of undergraduates was a sort of custom, and seldom was notice taken of it by the authorities.[3] The rowdiest set, who called themselves *Eversores*, used to racket about the town at night, insulting women and bullying strangers, much as the Mohocks did in London in the reign of Queen Anne. To this set Augustine belonged, though he privately disapproved of their disorderly doings.[4] He frequented the theatre, and did not deny himself sexual pleasures.[5] Yet he was never grossly vicious. Though he kept a mistress— by whom, in A.D. 372, a son, Adeodatus, was born to him[6]—he remained faithful to her for years;[7] and, in the prevailing state of morals, such a connexion was comparatively inoffensive. Moreover, even in his worst period, he did not utterly discard the moral ideal of Christianity which he had learnt in childhood from his mother. He used to pray, 'Give me chastity—but not now!'[8]

Meanwhile he devoted himself to the study of rhetoric, and in a little while became head scholar in the Rhetoric School.[9] His ambition awoke. A rhetorician of such promise might reasonably hope for rapid promotion—first, perhaps, to a professorial chair, and then to a lucrative post in the Imperial Civil Service. There was no knowing where his career might end. Suddenly, however, his interest was diverted in a new direction. He was reading Cicero—'whose eloquence almost all admire, not so his heart'—and among the writings of this author he came upon the *Hortensius*, a dialogue in praise of philosophy, of which only fragments are now extant. The book made a strange impression upon him. Rhetoric lost its charm, and the prospect of worldly preferment ceased, for a time at least, to fascinate him. He now

---

[1] Salvian. *De Gubern. Dei*, vii. 62–83.     [2] Augustin. *Confess.* iii. 1.
[3] Ibid. v. 8.          [4] Ibid. iii. 3.          [5] Ibid. iii, 1, 2.
[6] Ibid. ix. 6.                                   [7] Ibid. iv. 2.
[8] Ibid. viii. 7. The name of Jesus, which he had heard so often on his mother's lips, haunted his memory strangely, so that he was never thoroughly satisfied with any philosophical books, wherein it was not found, ibid. iii. 4.     [9] Ibid. iii. 3.

began 'with an incredibly earnest desire' to long for wisdom, which seemed to him to be the only worthy object of human ambition.[1] It was a kind of first conversion—a conversion, not indeed to religion, but to philosophy. It took place when Augustine was nineteen years of age, that is, in the year A.D. 373.[2]

Inflamed with the passion for wisdom, Augustine began to study the Holy Scriptures, wherein he had been told that true wisdom was to be found. But the Scriptures disappointed him. He could not understand them. Moreover the ruggedness of the style—accentuated in the barbarous African version—offended his literary taste. He thought them 'unworthy to be compared with the stateliness of Tully'.[3] Being thus dissatisfied with the writings recommended by the Church, and doubtful whither next he should turn for enlightenment, he fell into the hands of the Manichaeans.[4] These 'great talkers' who were always prating of 'the Truth, the Truth',[5] who appealed with confidence to the human reason and were ever ready to defend by philosophic argument even the doctrines which (as they claimed) were originally given by Divine revelation,[6] seemed to offer just what he was seeking. Their coherent and artistic system, based on the essential contrast between good and evil, light and darkness, and pretending to furnish solutions of the profoundest problems—the being and nature of God, the origin and destiny of the universe, the constitution and duty of man—strongly excited his curiosity. Behind the bizarre mythological forms, derived mainly from the old Babylonian religion, he hoped to discover a religious philosophy more satisfying than any which he had hitherto encountered. He was further attracted by the Manichaean 'higher criticism' of those Scriptures which he himself had found so difficult and

---

[1] Augustin. Confess. iii. 4; cf. De Beata Vita, 4.
[2] Id. Confess. viii. 7.     [3] Ibid. iii. 5.
[4] On the Manichaeans see F. C. Burkitt, The Religion of the Manichees; also A. Brückner, Faustus von Mileve; ein Beitrag zur Geschichte des abendländischen Manichäismus. In Augustine's time Proconsular Africa was one of the chief Manichaean regions. The sect was here well organized, having numerous communities and energetic leaders (e.g. Faustus of Mileve, whose polemic against the Catholic Church was answered by Augustine in his Contra Faustum; and Felix, with whom Augustine later held a public disputation at Hippo). Augustine himself was a professed Manichaean for nine years, and after his conversion to Catholic Christianity wrote several works against Manichaeism; unfortunately, however—probably because he was never fully initiated—he furnishes far less detailed information concerning the doctrines and practices of the sect than might have been expected.
[5] Augustin. Confess. iii. 6.     [6] Id. De Utilitate Credendi, 2.

repellent; and perhaps also by the austere discipline elaborated by the Manichaeans for the suppression of sensual tendencies, such as he experienced in his own nature but was unable to control. He accordingly joined the sect, and for a period of nine years (A.D. 373–82) remained firmly attached to it as a 'hearer', though he was never initiated into the inner circle of the 'elect'.[1]

At the conclusion of his University course Augustine returned to Thagaste. His Manichaean sympathies deeply shocked and distressed his mother, who mourned over him more than if she had seen him dead, and even doubted whether she ought to receive him beneath her roof. She was comforted, however, by a dream wherein she was assured that 'where she was, there should her son be also'.[2] Thereafter, with renewed hope, she earnestly sought to effect his conversion. She begged a Catholic bishop, skilled in dealing with souls, to reason with him and confute his errors. But the bishop realized that interference at this stage would be premature. 'Let him alone', he said, 'and be content with praying for him; presently he himself, by reading, will discover his error and impiety.' When the weeping mother still urged her request, he answered, 'Go, I beg you; it is impossible that the son of those tears should perish.'[3]

Meanwhile Augustine taught rhetoric at Thagaste, and in his leisure hours continued his studies. He was still fascinated by Manichaeism, and zealously propagated Manichaean doctrines among his friends and pupils. One of these friends, an old school-fellow, whose faith he had perverted, fell seriously ill of a fever and, his life being despaired of, was baptized in a state of unconsciousness. He rallied, however, and was visited by Augustine, who ventured to utter an unseemly jest upon the

---

[1] Augustin. *Confess.* iv. 1. The Manichaean community was divided into (*a*) ordinary adherents or 'hearers', and (*b*) adepts or 'elect'. The latter class consisted of four grades—'sons of mildness', 'sons of knowledge', 'sons of understanding', and 'sons of secrecy'. The adepts alone participated in the secret Manichaean sacraments. They had fuller understanding of the deeper meaning of the Manichaean doctrines, and abstained ascetically from many things which were permitted to the uninitiated, e.g. flesh and wine, marriage, and the acquisition of private property (cf. the forbidden things classified under 'the three seals'—'signaculum oris', 'signaculum manuum', 'signaculum sinus', Augustin. *De Mor. Eccl. Cath. et de Mor. Manich.* ii. 19). The adepts were deeply reverenced by the 'hearers', who ministered to their physical needs and invoked their help as redeemers or saviour-saints (id. *Confess.* iv. 1).

[2] Ibid. iii. 11. For Monnica's visions, see also ibid. vi. 1, 13.

[3] Ibid. iii. 12.

sacred rite. The sick man heard him with horror, and bade him, if he wished to retain his friendship, never speak to him again thus flippantly. A few days afterwards he expired.[1] Augustine was passionately afflicted by his death. He determined to leave Thagaste, with its melancholy associations, and try his fortune as a teacher of rhetoric at Carthage.[2]

At Carthage his intellectual development went on apace. He read everything—'whatever was written concerning Rhetoric, or Logic, or Geometry, or Music, or Arithmetic';[3] he published an aesthetic treatise, now lost, *On the Fair and Fitting*;[4] he won the prize in a public poetical competition;[5] he threw himself (not withstanding the advice of a wise old physician, the Proconsul Vindician) into the study of astrology;[6] and he acquired a reputation as a first-rate lecturer and tutor in 'the art of victorious speaking'.[7] As his knowledge increased, he grew more and more discontented with Manichaeism. He discovered that the 'interminable fables' concerning the heavens and the heavenly bodies, which the Manichaeans propounded as Divine revelations, were not in accord with the established conclusions of Greek science, and was thus led to doubt the validity of the whole Manichaean system.[8] The Manichaeans of Carthage, whom he consulted, were unable to resolve his difficulties. They told him, however, that one of their great doctors, Faustus of Mileve, was about to visit the city, and that, when he came, he would answer all his questions and remove his doubts. Towards the end of A.D. 382 Faustus arrived. He was a comely and charming person, whose fluent and graceful oratory excited universal admiration; but he proved surprisingly superficial. He had, indeed, read nothing except some orations of Cicero, a very few of Seneca's works, some selections of the poets, and such of the sacred books of the Manichaeans as had been translated into Latin. He was honest and sensible, however; and when Augustine began to question him on matters relating to astronomical science, he confessed with engaging candour his total ignorance of the subject.[9] The effect of Faustus's visit was to 'loosen the snare' in which Augustine was entangled. He did not, indeed,

---

[1] Augustin. *Confess.* iv. 4.    [2] Ibid. iv. 7.    [3] Ibid. iv. 16.
[4] Ibid. iv. 13. The work was dedicated to the Syrian orator, Hierius, ibid. iv. 14.
[5] Ibid. iv. 1, 2, 3.    [6] Ibid. iv. 3; cf. ibid. vii. 6.    [7] Ibid. iv. 2.
[8] Ibid. v. 3, 5.    [9] Ibid. v. 6, 7.

immediately detach himself from the Manichaeans; but he now realized that he was not likely to discover truth within a sect whose most revered and authoritative teacher was so conspicuously incompetent.[1]

Not long after this Augustine accepted an offer of a professorship in Rome. His object in removing to this new sphere was not so much to attain a better position and larger emoluments, as to escape from the Carthaginian students, whose intolerable rudeness and wildness had got on his nerves. At Rome, he was informed, 'the young men studied more peacefully, and were restrained and kept quiet by more regular discipline'.[2] On his arrival in the Eternal City, he took up his abode in the house of a Manichaean, and associated on intimate terms with the Roman members of that sect, both 'hearers' and 'elect'. But he had ceased to have any belief in the Manichaean books and tenets. Rather he inclined towards a general scepticism— such as was commonly, though incorrectly, attributed to the Academic philosophers.[3]

His sojourn in Rome was not happy. Almost immediately on his arrival he fell dangerously ill of a fever;[4] afterwards, when he recovered and began to give lectures on rhetoric, he was greatly disappointed by the behaviour of his pupils. It was true that they were better mannered than the students of Carthage; but they had an embarrassing custom of their own—they would attend the course with commendable assiduity, but when the time came for paying the professor's fees, they suddenly transferred themselves *en masse*, without discharging their obligations, to another master.[5] In a few months Augustine was heartily sick of Rome. Fortunately just at this time the citizens of Milan happened to be in want of a professor of rhetoric for their University, and requested Symmachus, the renowned orator and critic, who was then in office as Urban Praefect, to select one for them. Augustine was recommended to Symmachus by some Manichaean friends, and, after giving proof of his ability by declaiming on a set subject, received the appointment.[6] He went to Milan in the autumn of A.D. 384.[7]

The gifted young teacher now came under the influence of

---

[1] Augustin. *Confess*. v. 7.    [2] Ibid. v. 8.    [3] Ibid. v. 10; cf. v. 14.
[4] Ibid. v. 9.    [5] Ibid. v. 12.    [6] Ibid. v. 13.
[7] On the date see G. Rauschen, op. cit. p. 186.

Ambrose, who received him, though still professedly a Manichaean, with fatherly kindness. He, for his part, was impressed
by the benign personality of the Bishop, and often went to hear
him preach—not, indeed, with a hope of receiving intellectual
enlightenment from his discourses, but because, as a rhetorician,
he was interested in his oratorical style, which he found less
vivacious and insinuating, but more erudite, than that of
Faustus.[1] Yet, though at first he paid no attention to the matter
of the sermons, he was unconsciously affected by it: 'while I
opened my heart to admit "how eloquently he spoke", there
entered also by degrees a conviction "how truly he spoke".' At
length he came to two conclusions, of signal importance for his
spiritual development. First, he convinced himself of the fundamental unsoundness of the Manichaean system, and definitely
severed his connexion with that body. Secondly, under the influence of Ambrose's preaching, he began to realize that Catholic
Christianity was intellectually far more defensible than he had
imagined. He found, for example, that many of the Scriptural
difficulties, on which the Manichaeans laid such stress, could be
solved by the method of allegorical interpretation, of which
Ambrose himself was a distinguished exponent.[2] Yet, though he
recognized that there was more to be said for the Catholic faith
than he had suspected, he was not at this stage prepared to
embrace it. He was in a state of profound uncertainty in respect of almost all matters relating to religion, and 'kept his heart
from assenting to anything'.[3] He would have liked to discuss
his perplexities with Ambrose; but the great Bishop was always occupied, and he modestly shrank from intruding on him.[4]
Possibly, however, this was not altogether a misfortune; for Ambrose, able though he was, was by no means Augustine's equal in
intellect, and his arguments might well have proved disappointing
to the inquirer, and so might have hindered, rather than hastened, his gradual approach to the orthodox position.

Another influence, gentle and unobtrusive but persistent,
which must be reckoned among the factors in Augustine's
ultimate conversion, was that of his mother. For Monnica,
braving the perils of the long journey by sea and land, had
followed her son to Milan. She was serenely assured that her

[1] Augustin. *Confess*. v. 13.          [2] Ibid. v. 14; vi. 4.
[3] Ibid. vi. 4.                          [4] Ibid. vi. 3.

prayers for him would be availing. When she heard that he was no longer a Manichaean, though he could not yet accept the truths taught by the Church, she said quietly and confidently, 'I believe in Christ that, before I depart this life, I shall see you a loyal Catholic.'[1] It was not easy for Augustine to preserve a detached, agnostic attitude in such an atmosphere of faith and prayer.

Besides Monnica, two intimate friends joined Augustine at Milan—Alypius, a young man of good family and sterling character, who had studied under his direction at Thagaste and Carthage, and subsequently at Rome had been assessor in the Court of the Italian Treasury;[2] and Nebridius, who had left a fine estate near Carthage that he might devote himself to 'a most ardent search after truth and wisdom' in Augustine's company.[3] Other friends also gathered round the rising genius; and a plan was mooted that the whole party, numbering about ten persons, should live together in a community, two being chosen annually to manage the catering and other business, and the rest being free to concentrate without distraction on research. But the circumstance that some members of the circle were already married while others had matrimony in contemplation prevented the execution of this project.[4]

Meanwhile Augustine was restless and miserable. His mind was ceaselessly tormented by the great problems of religion, which he could neither solve nor let alone. The enigma of the origin of evil specially troubled him; for, having rejected the dualistic theory of the Manichaeans, he was unable to evolve any alternative explanation.[5] His brain was in perpetual ferment. At the same time he was painfully agitated by ambition and passion. The seductive idea of a splendid career once more attracted him, while the cravings of his sensual nature became

---

[1] Augustin. *Confess.* vi. 1. Monnica was devoted to Ambrose, whom she knew to be responsible for Augustine's reclamation from Manichaean errors. She 'loved him as an angel of God' (ibid.), and cheerfully relinquished even her cherished practice of entertaining the poor at the memorials of the martyrs, when she learnt that he had condemned the custom (ibid. vi. 2). Ambrose, on his side, greatly admired her 'very religious way of life', and used often to congratulate Augustine on having such a mother (ibid.).

[2] Ibid. vi. 7–10. He became Bishop of Thagaste in A.D. 394, and survived Augustine.

[3] Ibid. vi. 10. On Nebridius see also ibid. vii. 2, 6; viii. 6; ix. 3, 4.

[4] Ibid. vi. 14.  [5] Ibid. vii. 3, 5, 7.

more violent than ever. He could not decide what he really wanted. At one moment he was for letting all material interests go, and dedicating himself unreservedly to the quest after wisdom. At another, he was bent on winning some of the prizes of the world—a provincial governorship, a wealthy marriage. Conflicting desires agonized him.[1] His mother took advantage of his ambitious mood, and persuaded him to dismiss his concubine, who had come to him from Africa, and contract an honourable engagement. But the affair did not turn out well. The girl chosen for him was too young for marriage; and, though Augustine was willing to wait for her, he was not prepared to surrender his accustomed pleasures for her sake. He took another mistress.[2]

But the end of his intellectual, though not of his moral, struggle was in sight. By incessant and concentrated labour of thought, Augustine was gradually working his way towards conviction of the Catholic truths. While he was tending in this direction, he happened to read certain 'books of the Platonists'—including, it seems, the *Enneads* of Plotinus—in the Latin translation of Victorinus.[3] The perusal kindled in him 'an incredible fire'.[4] He seemed on the very verge of discovering that elusive wisdom which he had so long been seeking. As he read and re-read the books, his perplexities were resolved, and the fundamental verities of religion and philosophy grew more and more clear.[5] He noticed with keen interest the affinity between Neoplatonism and Christianity—the very Christianity which through Monnica had touched his feelings, and which through Ambrose had appealed, not wholly in vain, to his reason. He therefore addressed himself once more to the study of the Scriptures, in particular of the Pauline Epistles. They seemed to confirm what was true in the Neoplatonist writings, to correct what was false, and to supplement what was defective.[6] He became in the end a Christian

---

[1] Augustin. *Confess.* vi. 11; cf. *De Utilit. Credendi*, 3; *De Beata Vita*, 4. Yet he realized that ambition does not bring happiness, when, being entrusted with the honourable duty of pronouncing a panegyric on the Consul Bauto (1 Jan. A.D. 385), he was tormented with such nervousness that he envied the felicity of a drunken beggar in the street (*Contr. Litt. Petil.* iii. 30; *Confess.* vi. 6).    [2] Ibid. vi. 13, 15.

[3] Ibid. vii. 9; viii. 2. Augustine's early writings show intimate knowledge of Plotinus, and reminiscences of the *Enneads* may be detected in some of the most famous passages in the *Confessions*. On his relation to Neoplatonism, see L. Grandgeorge, *Saint Augustin et le Néoplatonisme* (Paris, 1896).

[4] Augustin. *Contr. Academ.* ii. 5.

[5] Id. *Confess.* vii. 10–20.    [6] Ibid. vii. 21.

believer. Henceforward, though he was subject to occasional spasms of scepticism, he never entirely lost his grip on the essentials of the Catholic faith.

Augustine's intellectual conversion was achieved. So far, however, it was a conversion only of the intellect. His mind perceived the truth, but his will refused to conform to it. He had acquired right views, but not right habits. His rational decision in favour of the Christian scheme of thought was definitely made; his moral decision in favour of the Christian way of life had still to be taken.[1]

Towards his final and complete conversion he was specially assisted by two interviews. The first of these was with Simplician, 'the father of Ambrose in grace, whom Ambrose loved truly as a father'. Augustine called on him, and was encouraged to unfold his spiritual history. The great scholar warmly congratulated him on having fallen in with the Neoplatonist works which contained so much Divine truth, and then communicated to him some particulars concerning their translator, Victorinus. He told how that famous pagan rhetorician and philosopher, skilled in all the liberal sciences, who for his services to learning had been honoured with a statue in Rome, had in advanced age become a convert to Christianity; how, for a while, through fear of giving offence to his pagan friends, he had kept his belief secret and declined to show himself in church, saying jestingly in reply to Simplician's remonstrances, 'Do walls, then, make Christians?'; how, by reading and meditation, he had gradually acquired firmness, until one day he cried suddenly, 'Let us go to the church; I wish to be made a Christian;' how he had 'given in his name that he might be regenerated by baptism, Rome wondering, the Church rejoicing'; how, though offered an opportunity of professing his faith privately, he had insisted on complying with the usage of the Roman Church, which prescribed that candidates for baptism should repeat the creed publicly from an elevated place in the presence of the congregation; and how finally he had resigned his professorial chair, when Julian's law forced Christian teachers to make their choice between renouncing their faith and quitting their schools.[2] Augustine

---

[1] Augustin. *Confess.* vii. 17; viii. 1, 5.

[2] Ibid. viii. 1, 2, 5. See also R. Schmid, *Marius Viktorinus Rhetor und seine Beziehungen zu Augustin* (Kiel, 1895).

was profoundly moved by this recital. He compared himself with Victorinus, and longed for strength to imitate his edifying example. But the 'two wills' contended within him, and though he desired what was holy and right, he could not bring himself to the point of surrendering what was pleasant.[1]

The impression thus made was deepened by another interview. One day, when Augustine was at home with Alypius, he received a visit from an African acquaintance, named Pontitian, who occupied a high position at the Imperial Court. The visitor noticed a book lying on the chess-table, and was surprised to find that it was a copy of the Epistles of St. Paul. Being a Christian, he commended Augustine for his choice of so excellent an author for study, and went on to talk of a book which he had himself been reading—Evagrius' Latin translation of the *Life of Antony* by Athanasius. He gave his hearers, who had never heard of Antony, a short account of the famous hermit, and further related how he had come to make acquaintance with the biography. Some while before he had been at Trier, and, having an afternoon off duty, while the Emperor was watching the games in the Circus, he had gone out with three friends to walk in the gardens near the city walls. Two of his companions, wandering away by themselves, had entered a cottage inhabited by some monks, and had found there the *Life of Antony*, which they read. So stirred were they by its contents, that they there and then decided to remain in the humble monastery and devote themselves to the practice of Antonian asceticism. They were both officers in the Secret Service and engaged to be married; but they abandoned everything for the religious life, and the two girls to whom they were affianced likewise dedicated themselves to virginity.[2] This conversation also had a powerful effect upon Augustine. He felt that his own half-hearted acceptance of Christianity was inexcusable, and was filled with shame and self-reproach.[3] But, although he had by this time conquered his ambitious desire for riches and worldly honours, the propensity to sensuality, which he had inherited from his father, and which by long indulgence had become ingrained in his very nature, seemed incapable of being subdued.[4]

---

[1] Augustin. *Confess*. viii. 5 (a very striking chapter). On the 'two wills', see further, ibid. viii. 9, 10.    [2] Ibid. viii. 6.

[3] Ibid. viii. 7.    [4] Ibid. viii. 1; cf. vi. 12.

The last struggle was perhaps more protracted than it is represented in the *Confessions*. Not immediately after the interview with Pontitian, but rather (as seems likely) after a tempestuous interval, occurred the incident in the garden, when Augustine, wellnigh distraught with the fury of the battle between flesh and spirit, flung himself prostrate under a fig-tree, crying, 'How long shall I say, "To-morrow and to-morrow"? Why not now?'; and heard from a neighbouring house a child's voice chanting, 'Take and read; take and read'; and (recollecting how the casual hearing of a passage of the Gospel had been the turning-point in the life of Antony) snatched up the volume of St. Paul, and opening it at random read the words, *Not in rioting and drunkenness, not in chambering and wantonness, not in strife and envying; but put ye on the Lord Jesus Christ, and make not provision for the flesh to fulfil the lusts thereof*. But whether the struggle which culminated in this strange event was brief or long, the event itself was conclusive. Suddenly the interior conflict ended. The spiritual element in the man triumphantly, decisively, and for good and all asserted itself, and his heart was filled with perfect peace.[1] This final and full conversion, so tremendously important in the history of the Christian Church, took place early in August,[2] A.D. 386.

Augustine had now to make plans for the future. He determined to be baptized and adopt the ascetic life. First, however, it was necessary to resign his professorship. This he was able to do without exciting comment, since, partly through over-work and partly as a consequence of the mental strain he had undergone, he had developed symptoms of lung-trouble—shortness of breath and pains in the chest—which would in any case have obliged him to take a lengthy holiday.[3] At the commencement of the Vintage-vacation, therefore, he quitted his lecture-room for ever, and retired for six months to a villa, lent him by one of his brother professors, at Cassiciacum (Casciago), some forty-seven miles from Milan.[4] Here he proposed to rest and prepare himself for baptism at Easter in the following year.

The villa at Cassiciacum was a charming country-house, delightfully situated on the top of a little hill, rising out of a fruitful valley and surrounded by mountains. Adjacent to it was a meadow well shaded by trees; and not far off a little stream

---

[1] Augustin. *Confess*. viii. 8, 11, 12; ix. 1.    [2] G. Rauschen, op. cit. p. 247,
[3] Augustin. *Confess*. ix. 2, 5.    [4] Ibid. ix. 3; *De Ordine*, i. 5.

rippled in cascades over the rocks, with a pleasant murmur which was audible to the occupants of the house in the stillness of the autumn nights.[1]  The house-party included, in addition to Augustine, his mother, who managed the domestic arrangements, his brother Navigius, his son Adeodatus, his friend Alypius, who had agreed to be baptized with him, two of his cousins, and two lively young pupils, named Trygetius and Licentius.  All the members of this company were on the best of terms and in the gayest spirits.  Their life was simple, but very agreeable.  They rose early, and spent the morning in reading, talking, or walking; at midday they dined—though frugally, so as not to depress their mental vivacity;[2] in the afternoon they would assemble under a great tree in the meadow, or (if the weather were unfavourable) in the covered bath-room, to hold leisurely discussions on philosophical or religious topics.  Some of the party brought tablets with them and took shorthand notes of what was said.[3]  Often the conversations were prolonged into the twilight, when a servant would carry a torch to the big tree or a lamp into the bath-hall, that the shorthand-writers might not be interrupted in their labours.  Every evening after supper Augustine explained half a book of Virgil to Trygetius and Licentius.  The two boys, who slept in their teacher's chamber,[4] were the life of the little society.  Licentius was specially harum-scarum, and sometimes got into trouble with Monnica on account of his thoughtless ways.[5]  He fancied himself a poet, and would even leave his dinner to scribble verses on the loves of Pyramus and Thisbe.[6]  He and Trygetius ('a little man, but a great eater') were perpetually sparring at one another.  Sometimes they became too boisterous, and Augustine, though secretly amused by their romps, would feel it his duty to give them a scolding.  But his rebukes were not very severe.  'If you like to call me your master', he said to the culprits on one occasion, 'then pay me my fee by being good fellows.'[7]

---

[1] Augustin. *De Ordine*, i. 6.    [2] Id. *De Beata Vita*, 6; cf. *Contr. Academ.* ii. 14.
[3] Id. *Contr. Academ.* i. 4; cf. *De Ordine*, i. 29, 30; *De Beata Vita*, 15.
[4] Id. *De Ordine*, i. 6.                                              [5] Ibid. i. 22.
[6] Id. *Contr. Academ.* iii. 7; cf. ibid. ii. 10; iii. 1; *De Ordine*, i. 5, 8, 21. At a later date his love of the world and of classical literature caused him virtually to abandon Christianity; see Augustin. *Ep.* 26; Paulin. Nolan. *Ep.* 8. An ambitious, but tasteless and uninteresting, poem of his composition is preserved (Augustin. *Ep.* 26).
[7] Id. *De Ordine*, i. 29.

Augustine had written to Ambrose to inform him of his conversion and desire for baptism, and to ask advice about his
reading. Ambrose recommended, rather oddly, the Book of
Isaiah. Augustine began the book, but, finding it unintelligible,
gave it up till he should have become more experienced in the
Scriptures.[1] Meanwhile he was regular in his devotional exercises. Part of every night he spent in meditation;[2] on rising in
the morning he prayed long and with tears;[3] he used also to
recite the psalms and was deeply affected by them.[4] Most of his
time, however, was devoted, not to Biblical or theological study,
but to those discursive philosophical discussions and self-
communings, the substance of which is recorded in the treatises
composed at this period—*Against the Academicians*, *On Order*, *On
the Happy Life*, and *Soliloquies*. These writings are extremely
interesting on account of the light which they throw on Augustine's state of mind during the months which followed his conversion.[5] Strangely enough, they contain little that is specifically
Christian. The subjects dealt with are philosophical rather than
religious—the possibility of ascertaining truth, the place of
apparent disorder in the great universal order, the nature of
happiness, the immortality of the soul—and they are handled
throughout in the manner of the Philosophical School. Augustine, it is clear, was still preoccupied with Cicero and the Neoplatonists. Although he acknowledged Christ as the supreme
authority from whom it was not permissible to deviate,[6] yet his
mind was working in the sphere of pagan speculation rather
than in that of Christian revelation. Even during the weeks
of Lent which immediately preceded his baptism he was deeply
immersed in philosophical and literary labours, composing a
treatise *On the Immortality of the Soul* and planning a series on
*The Liberal Sciences*.[7]

So the months of rest passed pleasantly. Only one incident
occurred to mar Augustine's happiness. He was seized with a
toothache so excruciating that he was unable even to speak.
But at his request, made in writing, they prayed for him to 'the
God of all kinds of health', and presently the pain departed.[8]

[1] Augustin. *Confess.* ix. 5.                [2] Id. *De Ordine*, i. 6.
[3] Ibid. i. 22.                               [4] Id. *Confess.* ix. 4.
[5] For Augustine's own criticisms on these books see *Retract.* i, cc. 1–4.
[6] Id. *Contra Academ.* iii. 43.
[7] Id. *Retract.* i, cc. 5, 6.                [8] Id. *Confess.* ix. 4.

In the spring of A.D. 387, when the season of Lent drew near, the party returned to Milan, and Augustine, Alypius, and Adeodatus 'gave in their names' as candidates for baptism at Easter.[1]

Concerning the customary preparation for, and the manner of administering, the baptismal rite in the Church of Milan, exceptionally valuable information is supplied by Ambrose.[2] Catechumens were divided into two classes—'hearers'[3] (so called because they were admitted to hear the lessons and sermon at Mass, but were dismissed before the Eucharist proper commenced) and 'competents'[4] or 'elect'.[5] Persons were received into the first class with a signing of the cross on the forehead and the administration of salt.[6] They were then recognized as Christians; but were not, of course, full members of the Christian Church. They could remain in this probationary stage as long as they chose. If, however, they desired to proceed farther, they 'gave in their names' to the bishop as candidates for baptism,[7] and so passed into the class of competents.

Public baptism was ordinarily administered on the night between Easter Eve and Easter Day.[8] The candidates, who at this epoch were normally adults, entered their names at the beginning of Lent, and devoted themselves, during the whole of this season, to elaborate preparation for the holy rite. They were regarded as athletes about to engage in a contest with the devil, and were expected to practise athletic discipline.[9] Thus they subdued their bodies by rigorous fasting,[10] abstained from the

---

[1] Augustin. *Confess.* ix. 6.

[2] See especially his *De Mysteriis*, and cf. the anonymous *De Sacramentis*. On both treatises, see below, Chapter xxii.    [3] Tertullian. *De Poenit.* 6.

[4] Ambros. *Ep.* 20. 4; Augustin. *De Fide et Opp.* 9; *De cura gerend. pro mort.* 15.

[5] Ambros. *De Elia*, 34.

[6] Augustin. *Confess.* i. 11; cf. Ambros. *De Mysteriis*, 20 (the sign of the cross), and *Expos. ev. Luc.* x. 48 (the salt).

[7] Id. *De Abraham*, i. 23 'qui ad gratiam baptismatis nomen dederunt'; *Expos. ev. Luc.* iv. 76; *De Elia*, 79. Cf. Augustin. *Serm.* 229 'nomina vestra dedistis'; *De Fide et Opp.* 8; *Confess.* viii. 2; ix. 6; *De Sacramentis*, iii. 12. It was Ambrose's custom during the season of Epiphany publicly to invite catechumens to give in their names (*Expos. ev. Luc.* iv. 76).

[8] Ambros. *De Elia*, 34 'venit iam dies resurrectionis, baptizantur electi'; *Hexaem.* i. 14. To those who were unable to present themselves at Easter, the sacrament might be administered during the period between Easter and Whitsunday (Tertullian. *De Baptismo*, 19) and also at other times (ibid. 5). The sick could be privately baptized at any time (Ambrosiast. *Comm. in Ephes.* iv. 11, 12).

[9] Ambros. *De Elia*, 79.

[10] Ibid. 79, 81; cf. Tertullian. *De Baptismo*, 20; Augustin. *Serm.* 227 'sic et vos ante

use of marriage,[1] and voluntarily mortified themselves in various ways.[2] The more formal preparation consisted partly of special services of instruction, and partly of 'scrutinies' with exorcisms. (a) In the Church of Milan, on all week-days in Lent, except Saturdays, at the third and ninth hours, special services (*missae catechumenorum*), consisting of lessons, psalms, and sermon, were held,[3] whereat the candidates received instruction on Christian morals and on the elements of the Christian religion. The moral teaching was based on the books of Genesis and Proverbs which were read as the lessons at these services during the Lenten weeks preceding Holy Week;[4] the dogmatic teaching consisted of simple exposition of the fundamental Christian verities.[5] The 'delivery of the Creed' took place on Palm Sunday, when the bishop recited and briefly explained it clause by clause.[6] Instruction concerning the sacraments was reserved till Easter week, after the baptism was over, since it was not thought proper to explain the sacred mysteries to those who were not fully initiated.[7] In the Churches of Northern Italy the exposition of the Lord's Prayer was also deferred till Easter week.[8] (b) In addition to the services of instruction, three 'scrutinies' appear to have been held on Saturdays in Lent. At the 'scrutinies' the candidates were exorcized (that they might be thoroughly purged of all influence of evil spirits) and examined to test their fitness for baptism.[9] No mention, however, of these 'scrutinies' is made by Ambrose.[10]

(baptisma) ieiunii humiliatione et exorcismi sacramento quas molebamini': id. *Serm.* 229 'coepistis moli ieiuniis et exorcismis'.

[1] Ambros. *De Elia*, 79; Augustin. *De Fide et Opp.* 8.

[2] Alypius, for example, mortified himself by going barefoot during the frosty weeks preceding his baptism, Augustin. *Confess.* ix. 6.

[3] T. Thompson and J. H. Srawley, *St. Ambrose on the Mysteries*, p. xii.

[4] Ambros. *De Mysteriis*, 1. The first book of Ambrose's *De Abraham* composed of addresses to competents (i. 23, 25, 59, 89) affords a good example of the kind of teaching given. [5] Id. *Expos. ev. Luc.* vi. 107.

[6] Id. *Ep.* 20. 4; cf. *De Mysteriis*, 6 'quid tradiderit considera'.

[7] Id. *De Mysteriis*, 2. On the *disciplina arcani*, see below, p. 453, with note 5.

[8] So the author of *De Sacramentis* expounds the Lord's Prayer, along with the doctrine of the Sacraments, to the newly baptized in the week following Easter (v. 18–30; vi. 24). Secrecy was observed with regard to this prayer, Ambros. *De Instit. Virginis*, 10 'dominica oratio quam vulgare non opus est'; *De Cain*, i. 37 'cave ne incaute symboli vel dominicae orationis divulges mysteria' (cf. ibid. i. 35).

[9] Cf. Augustin. *De Fide et Opp.* 9 'catechizantur, exorcizantur, scrutantur'.

[10] On the later scrutinies in the Church of Milan, see T. Thompson, *The Offices of Baptism and Confirmation*, pp. 133, 134.

Late on Easter Eve the solemn baptism, for which such careful preparation had been made, took place. The order and contents of the rite, as it was celebrated at Milan in Ambrose's time, may be summarized as follows.

First, the ceremony of the Effeta, or 'the mystery of the opening', was performed. The bishop touched the ears and nostrils of each candidate; no mention, however, is made in this connexion of the use of oil or saliva. The action had reference to the healing of the deaf-mute by our Lord (Mark vii. 34), and symbolized the opening of the faculties to the fruitful reception of the sacraments. The nostrils were touched instead of the mouth, because it was not considered seemly to touch the mouths of women.[1]

Next, the candidates stripped naked;[2] and—if the author of *De Sacramentis* can be accepted as a witness to Milanese usage— were anointed with oil on the whole body by the presbyters and deacons, in token that they were Christ's athletes, 'about to wrestle in the contest of this world'.[3] But since this pre-baptismal unction is neither referred to by Ambrose nor found in the later Milanese forms, it seems more probable that it did not belong to the Milanese rite, but was rather a feature which the Church of the author of *De Sacramentis* had derived from Rome.

The twofold renunciation followed. The bishop asked the candidate, 'Dost thou renounce the devil and his works?', 'Dost thou renounce the world and its pleasures?' To each question the candidate responded 'I renounce'.[4] The renunciation of the devil was apparently accompanied by the dramatic ceremony of 'spitting in his face', as a sign of contempt.[5]

[1] Ambros. *De Mysteriis*, 3, 4; *De Sacramentis*, i. 2, 3.

[2] Ambros. *In ps. 61 enarr.* 32; cf. the anonymous *De singularitate clericorum*, 14 (Hartel's *Cyprian*, Appendix, p. 189). In the larger baptisteries the male and female candidates perhaps undressed in separate chapels; or else decency was safeguarded by an arrangement of curtains. At Milan there may have been two baptisteries, one for men and the other for women (Ambros. *Ep.* 20. 4 where the majority of manuscripts read 'in baptisteriis . . . basilicae' as against 'in baptisterii . . . basilica').

[3] *De Sacramentis*, i. 4.

[4] Ambros. *De Mysteriis*, 5, 8; *De Sacramentis*, i. 5 (where the questions are apparently put by the presbyter). After the twofold renunciation *De Sacramentis* has an admonition—'Be mindful of thy words, and never let the contents of thy bond pass from thy memory'—which reappears in substance as a formula in the later Milanese books; but the admonition is not given in *De Mysteriis*.

[5] Ambros. *De Mysteriis*, 7, where the text should read 'cui renuntiando in os sputares', according to the emendation of Dom Morin (*Revue bénédictine*, xvi (1899), pp. 414–18). There are parallels, though of later date, for the spitting in the Greek and Armenian rites.

After the renunciation, the bishop proceeded to consecrate the water, which he signed with the cross.[1] As to the form of consecration, no clear indications are afforded by Ambrose; but the author of *De Sacramentis* speaks of 'an exorcism over the element of water' and 'an invocation and prayer, that the font may be hallowed and the presence of the eternal Trinity may come upon it'.[2] An exorcism is found in the later Milanese and Gallican forms; but there is no parallel in these forms to the invocation of the presence of the Holy Trinity to which this writer refers.

The moment of baptism had now arrived. In the midst of the baptistery was the baptismal basin, usually between two and four feet deep and surrounded by a low wall. The water was warmed by a stove below. Into this basin the candidate descended. Then followed a threefold interrogation and immersion. 'Dost thou believe in God the Father Almighty?' 'Dost thou believe in our Lord Jesus Christ and in His Cross?' 'Dost thou believe also in the Holy Spirit?'[3] To each question the candidate, facing towards the east,[4] responded, 'I believe'; and after each response he was immersed. This does not mean that he was totally submerged under the water, which would have involved a lying down in the shallow basin, but that, as he stood in the font, water was so poured over him that the whole of his body was completely wetted.[5] The formula, 'I baptize thee in the name of the Father, and of the Son, and of the Holy Ghost' was, of course, pronounced; but in what manner the pronouncement was combined with the three interrogations and immersions is not clear.[6]

After the baptism the neophyte was assisted from the font and dried with linen cloths. He was then led to the bishop, who anointed him on the head (the seat of intelligence) with chrism.

---

[1] Ambros. *De Mysteriis*, 8, 14, 20.

[2] *De Sacramentis*, i. 18; ii. 14.

[3] Ibid. ii. 20; cf. Ambros. *De Mysteriis*, 21, 28. The form of the second interrogation ('and in His Cross'; supported by *De Myst.* 28) is not found elsewhere, and in the later Milanese rite was replaced by the Roman form ('who was born and suffered').

[4] Ambros. *De Mysteriis*, 7.

[5] See T. Thompson, *The Offices of Baptism and Confirmation*, pp. 200 ff.

[6] Neither Ambrose nor the author of *De Sacramentis* expressly mentions the baptismal formula or gives any hint when it was said; but of course it was not omitted (cf. *De Myst.* 20 'unless he is baptized *in the name of the Father, and of the Son, and of the Holy Ghost*, he cannot receive the remission of sins nor imbibe the gift of spiritual grace'; *De Sacram.* ii. 22; vi. 5).

The prayer assigned to this action in *De Sacramentis* runs, 'God the Father Almighty, who hath regenerated thee by water and the Holy Ghost, and hath forgiven thee thy sins, Himself anoint thee unto eternal life'.[1] According to Ambrose, the post-baptismal unction signified the consecration of the newly baptized to the priesthood possessed by the whole body of the Christian Church, 'for we are all anointed with spiritual grace unto the kingdom of God and the priesthood'; by the author of *De Sacramentis* it is interpreted as the enrichment of man's faculties by Divine grace, 'for wisdom is lifeless without grace, but when wisdom has received grace, then its work begins to be perfect'.[2] This unction on the head with chrism by the bishop should probably be regarded as the beginning of the early Milanese rite of Confirmation, which was completed by the subsequent signing or 'seal'.

Next came the 'foot-washing'[3]—a ceremony at this time practised in Northern Italy and Gaul, and also in Africa (though sporadically and with considerable varieties of usage),[4] but not at Rome.[5] The bishop washed the feet of a few of the newly baptized, and the presbyters did the same for the rest. At the time of the washing the Gospel lesson, John xiii. 4 ff., was read.[6] As regards the significance of the action, Ambrose appears to teach that, while personal or actual sin is removed by baptism, transmitted or original sin is removed by the 'foot-washing'; thus of Peter he says that 'his foot is washed that hereditary sins may be removed, for our own sins are loosed through baptism'.[7] The author of *De Sacramentis* silently corrects this doctrine by affirming with emphasis that all sins are washed away in baptism; he explains the ceremony, partly as a lesson in humility, and partly as a means of special sanctification at that point where

---

[1] Ambros. *De Mysteriis*, 29, 30 (cf. the veiled allusion, id. *De Elia*, 36); *De Sacramentis*, ii. 24; iii. 1. The bishop's prayer given in *De Sacramentis*, ii. 24 is substantially the same as that found in the Gelasian Sacramentary in connexion with the post-baptismal unction at Rome.

[2] Ambros. *De Mysteriis*, 30; *De Sacramentis*, iii. 1.

[3] Ambros. *De Mysteriis*, 31–3; *De Sacramentis*, iii. 4–7.

[4] Augustin. *Ep.* 55 (*ad Januar.*), 33.

[5] *De Sacramentis*, iii. 5.

[6] Ambros. *De Mysteriis*, 31; *De Sacramentis*, iii. 4.

[7] Ambros. *De Mysteriis*, 32; cf. id. *In ps. 48 enarr.* 8, 9; *De Spiritu*, i. 16, and a passage from Ambrose's lost commentary on Isaiah quoted by Augustine, *Contr. duas epistolas Pelag.* iv. 11. See further below, chapter xxi, section 8 (end).

Adam was poisoned and tripped up by the serpent.[1] Augustine also regards the action as a lesson in humility, but not as an essential part of the sacrament of baptism.[2]

After the 'foot-washing', the newly baptized were vested in white garments, emblematic of innocence and joy, which they continued to wear throughout Easter week.[3] Thus arrayed, they were brought to the bishop to receive 'the spiritual seal'. This rite (called also 'the perfecting' in De Sacramentis) appears to have been the completion of that Confirmation which was begun with the post-baptismal unction with chrism. It consisted of a signing of the neophytes by the bishop (on what part or parts of the body is not stated), which signing was perhaps the equivalent of the primitive imposition of hands. It is probable, though not certain, that the signing was accompanied by a prayer for the sevenfold gift of the Spirit.[4]

The baptismal rite was now concluded. The bishop, the clergy, and the newly baptized, who were accompanied by their sponsors[5] and carried lights,[6] quitted the baptistery and re-entered the crowded and brilliantly illuminated cathedral. The bishop then commenced the Easter Mass. Psalms 43 and 23 (to which Ambrose refers in this connexion) may have been sung as introductory chants.[7] The newly baptized made their first communion; but at Milan they did not take part in the people's offering of bread and wine before the octave of Easter.[8]

The later Milanese custom, whereby special Masses—distinct from those attended by the general body of the faithful—were provided during Easter week for the newly baptized, is of great antiquity and may have been observed in the time of Ambrose. Certainly during this week instructions were given on the

---

[1] De Sacramentis, iii. 7.
[2] Augustin. Ep. 55 (ad Januar.), 33.
[3] Ambros. De Mysteriis, 34; cf. De Sacramentis, v. 14 'familiam candidatam'.
[4] Ambros. De Mysteriis, 42; De Spiritu, i. 79; De Sacramentis, iii. 8–10; vi. 6–8; see also Thompson and Srawley, op. cit. xxv, xxvi.
[5] Paulinus, Vita Ambros. 48.
[6] [Niceta Remes.] De Lapsu Virginis, 19.
[7] Ambros. De Mysteriis, 43; cf. De Sacramentis, iii. 11, 15; iv. 5, 7, 8.
[8] Ambros. Expos. ps. cxviii, Prol. 2 'Licet in baptismate plena sit statim purgatio, tamen quia ablutionis ipsius sacrificiique rationem baptizatus debet cognoscere, non offert sacrificium nisi octavum ingrediatur diem; ut informatus agnitione sacramentorum coelestium non quasi rudis, sed quasi rationis capax, tunc demum suum munus altaribus sacris offerat, cum coeperit esse instructior, ne offerentis inscitia contaminet oblationis mysterium.'

sacraments and the Lord's Prayer. The six addresses contained in *De Sacramentis* began on Easter Tuesday and concluded on the following Sunday.[1]

After this manner Augustine was baptized by Ambrose on Easter Eve, the 24th of April, A.D. 387. There is a picturesque legend, which can be traced back to the closing years of the eighth century, that on this occasion the two great men, carried away by inspiration, alternately extemporized the *Te Deum*.[2]

When Easter had passed, Augustine, having no further reason for lingering at Milan, decided to return to Africa. Accompanied by his mother, his son, his brother, Alypius, and another friend named Evodius, he travelled as far as Ostia. Here, at a window overlooking the garden of their lodging-house, occurred the memorable conversation between Monnica and Augustine on the nature of the beatitude of the saints in heaven, which is described in one of the finest chapters of the *Confessions*. As they were discoursing, Monnica said, 'My son, for my part, I no longer take delight in anything in this life. I know not why I am still here, now that my hope in this world is accomplished.

---

[1] Thompson and Srawley, op. cit. xx.

[2] The tradition is referred to in the famous Golden Psalter at Vienna (Cod. Vindob. 1861), which was written in Gaul *c.* A.D. 795. From the ninth century onwards it was widely current. Hinomar of Rheims in his treatise *De Praedestinatione*, 29 (*c.* A.D. 856) writes with reference to the *Te Deum* 'quia ut a maioribus nostris audivimus, tempore baptismatis sancti Augustini hunc hymnum beatus Ambrosius fecit, et idem Augustinus cum eo confecit' (Migne, *P.L.* cxxv. p. 290). In the eleventh century Landulphus Senior in the Chronicle of Milan (*Historia Mediolanensis*, i. 9), after mentioning the place of Augustine's baptism, continues 'in quibus fontibus, prout Spiritus Sanctus dabat eloqui eis, *Te deum laudamus* decantantes, cunctis qui aderant audientibus et videntibus simulque mirantibus, in posteris ediderunt quod ab universa ecclesia catholica usque hodie tenetur et religiose decantatur' (Migne, *P.L.* cxlvii. p. 833). The erroneous attribution of this part of the chronicle to Datius, Bishop of Milan (sixth century) gave at one time a quite undeserved importance to this authority. Allusion to the tradition is found in titles prefixed to the hymn in some manuscripts. Thus the Vienna Psalter, mentioned above, prefixes the title 'hymnus quem S. Ambrosius et S. Augustinus invicem condiderunt'; the Irish Book of Hymns has 'haec est laus sanctae Trinitatis quam Augustinus sanctus et Ambrosius composuit' (Trin. Coll. Dublin. E. 42, tenth century). It may be noted, however, that none of the manuscripts which preserve the tradition in the title of the *Te Deum* have any connexion with Milan, where we should expect such a tradition to be cherished, and where in fact a distinct version of the text lasted till the eleventh century. In the printed Breviaries a reference to Ambrose and Augustine is general in some form or other. But the tradition can hardly be taken seriously. There is much to be said for ascribing the authorship of the hymn to Niceta of Remesiana; see Dom. Morin, *Revue bénédictine*, 1894, xi. 49 ff., 337 ff.; A. E. Burn, *Niceta of Remesiana*, pp. xcvii ff.

I wished to live for one thing, that I might see you a Catholic
Christian before I died. My God has granted me this, and more
—even that I should see you despising earthly happiness and
devoted to His service. What do I longer here?'[1] Five days
afterwards she sickened of a fever, and realized that her end was
near. 'Lay this body anywhere', she said to her sons; 'let not
care for it give you the slightest anxiety. This only I ask of you,
to remember me at the Lord's altar, wherever you may be.' Her
long-cherished desire to be buried in her native land in the same
tomb with her husband, Patricius, was gone. 'Nothing is far
from God; there is no fear that, at the end of the world, He will
not know whence to raise me up.' On the ninth day of her illness
her 'religious and holy soul was freed from the body'.[2]

It is unnecessary to follow Augustine's history farther. How,
after staying for a year in Rome, he returned to Africa in the
summer of A.D. 388; how he proceeded to Thagaste, sold the bulk
of his inheritance for the benefit of the poor, and settled down
to a life of contemplative and literary retirement in a villa in the
environs; how, early in A.D. 391, happening to go on business
to the little Numidian sea-port town of Hippo Regius (just south
of the modern Bona), he was forcibly ordained presbyter in
response to a popular demand; how he founded a monastery
(apparently the first in Africa) in the gardens adjoining the local
church, and acquired a great reputation as a preacher and
disputer against Manichaeans and Donatists; how, shortly before
Christmas in A.D. 395, he was irregularly consecrated coadjutor-
bishop of Hippo; how, within a few months, on the death of
Bishop Valerius, he became sole bishop; and how from this
insignificant place he guided the thought of Western Christendom until his death on the 28th of August, A.D. 430—all this falls
outside the limits of the present chapter. Augustine's connexion
with Ambrose, which is the only reason for the introduction of
an account of his early career, apparently ended with his baptism
in A.D. 387.

It may possibly seem strange that Ambrose does not appear to
have appreciated the 'stupendous genius'[3] of the tall, dark-

---

[1] Augustin. *Confess*. ix. 10.

[2] Ibid. ix. 11. In 1430 her remains were removed from Ostia by Pope Martin V
and buried in the Church of St. Augustine at Rome.

[3] Leibnitz speaks of Augustine as 'virum sane magnum et ingenii stupendi'

skinned, narrow-chested young professor, with thin face and stooping shoulders, who used to listen to his sermons, and at last applied to him for baptism, or to have attached any special importance to his conversion. But the two men were never intimate.[1] The Bishop was deeply immersed in many weighty affairs of Church and State, and Augustine refrained from obtruding himself on his attention. Hence it is not, after all, surprising that Ambrose failed to recognize in his convert that extraordinary force of mind which was destined to influence the thought and history of the Christian Church through all succeeding centuries. He seems to have made no effort to maintain communication with him after his departure from Milan in A.D. 387. Yet Augustine, on his side, ever cherished warm feelings of gratitude and affection for 'the excellent steward of God, whom I venerate as a father, for in Jesus Christ he begat me through the Gospel, and through his ministry I received the washing of regeneration—the blessed Ambrose, whose grace, constancy, labours, perils for the Catholic Faith, whether in words or works, I have myself experienced, and the whole Roman world unhesitatingly proclaims with me'.[2]

(Praefat. ad Theodic. 34). Harnack regards him as incomparably the greatest man whom 'between Paul the Apostle and Luther the Reformer, the Christian Church has possessed' (*Monasticism and the Confessions of Augustine*, p. 123).

[1] For some reasons for Ambrose's lack of cordiality in his relations with Augustine, see G. Papini, *Saint Augustine*, pp. 92–8.

[2] Augustin. *Contr. Julian. Pelagian.* i. 10.

## CHAPTER XIV

# THE FALL OF MAXIMUS
# THE SEDITION AT ANTIOCH

IT was probably in the summer or autumn of A.D. 386 that
Ambrose, for the second time, went as ambassador into
Gaul.[1] The Emperor Maximus, irritated by the failure of his
ingenious scheme for bringing his young colleague under his
own control at Trier, was becoming dangerous. His ambition,
as has been said, was to govern the entire West, as Gratian had
done before him. He had hoped to manage this by peaceful
means—that is, by keeping Valentinian in a condition of subservience at Trier. But since Valentinian obstinately declined
to accept the invitation to enter the lion's den, he began to
meditate the possibility of acquiring by force the extended
sovereignty which he desired. For an invasion of Italy several
pretexts might be put forward. Maximus might complain—as
indeed he did—that he had been tricked by false promises made
by Ambrose and Bauto with regard to the coming of Valentinian
to Trier, and might urge that, since the condition on which he
had laid such stress had been neglected, he was no longer bound
to observe the peace. Or he might claim that Justina's recent
'persecution' of the Italian Catholics necessitated, or at any
rate justified, the intervention of an orthodox authority in
Italian affairs. Or he might even allege that the peace had been
broken by Valentinian himself. For in the previous year an
awkward incident had occurred. The Alemannic tribe of

---

[1] On the second embassy of Ambrose see Ambros. *Ep.* 24; *De Obitu Val.* 28;
Paulinus, *Vita Ambros.* 19. It must have taken place subsequently to the Arian
crisis of A.D. 385 (in *Ep.* 20. 23 only one embassy is mentioned) and also after the
letter of Maximus in A.D. 386, who would certainly not have written in such terms
after the break with Ambrose. Paulinus places it after the Arian persecution and
immediately before the downfall of Maximus. As the occasion of the mission
appears to have been Maximus' letter of protest against the Arian persecution, I
am inclined to refer it to the summer or autumn of A.D. 386 rather than as Tillemont
(and the older authorities) to the spring of A.D. 387. G. Rauschen (*Jahrbücher der
christlichen Kirche*, p. 487) argues for the winter of A.D. 384–5, partly on the ground
that Ambrose would not have been appointed ambassador after the Arian crisis,
when the relations between himself and the Court were strained; on this point,
however, see what I have written in the text.

Juthungi—instigated, according to Ambrose, by Maximus—had broken into Rhaetia. To get rid of them, Bauto had invited Huns and Alans to raid the Alemannic settlements. These barbarians had acted with alacrity on the hint, but unfortunately had extended their incursion to the very confines of the territory of Maximus. An angry complaint had been made by the latter, and Valentinian, fearful of furnishing him with an excuse for reprisals, had purchased the retreat of his savage allies with a considerable subsidy.[1]

The letter of protest against the persecution of the Catholics which Maximus had dispatched to Valentinian in the spring of A.D. 386[2] seemed to threaten war. The Court of Milan, in alarm, decided to send an ambassador to persuade him to maintain the peace. The ambassador selected was Ambrose.

In view of the strained relations between the Bishop and the Court, the appointment of Ambrose for this mission may, at first sight, appear surprising. But the Court had reasons for its choice. Maximus complained that he had been gulled by the false promises of Ambrose; Ambrose, therefore, was the fittest person to offer him an explanation. Maximus put himself forward as the defender of the Italian Catholics; who could assure him more authoritatively than the greatest Catholic of Northern Italy that there was no need for his intervention? These reasons were good enough. But in sending Ambrose to Gaul, the Court had another and more sinister object in view. If the negotiations at Trier broke down, it intended to discredit Ambrose and ruin his prestige in Italy by representing that his failure was deliberate —that is, that he had disloyally conspired with Maximus for the overthrow of Valentinian. Thus in any event the Court would gain something. If Ambrose succeeded, war would be averted; if he failed, then at any rate his reputation could be shattered by the charge of treacherous collusion with the enemy of his country.

Ambrose, for his part, saw the snare which had been laid for him; but he could not refuse to undertake the mission. On one point, however, he was quite determined. Even at the risk of precipitating war, he would afford his Arian enemies no excuse for charging him with collusion with Maximus. War would not necessarily be a disaster; it would at any rate distract the attention of Valentinian's Government from the affairs of the Church.

---

[1] Ambros. *Ep.* 24. 8.          [2] See above, pp. 291–3.

But the accusation of treachery, if generally believed, would irretrievably damage, not only his own good name, but also the Catholic cause in Northern Italy of which he was the acknowledged champion. He went, therefore, to Trier in obedience to the orders which he had received, but with the fixed intention of defeating the malicious intrigue of the Court by making it evident, at any cost, that there could not possibly be any alliance or collaboration between himself and Maximus. On this supposition only can we account for his extraordinary and provocative attitude towards the sovereign whom he was sent to appease.

The terms of his commission were, first and chiefly, to secure the maintenance of peace, and, secondly, to ask for the restoration to Milan of the remains of the Emperor Gratian which the usurper had hitherto retained in Gaul.[1] The day after his arrival at Trier he presented himself at the palace. He was received by the Grand Chamberlain, who, in reply to his request for an audience, inquired whether he had brought with him a letter from Valentinian. He answered that he had. He was then informed that he would be heard publicly in the Consistory. Instead of acquiescing in this arrangement, as he had done on his first embassy, he stood on his dignity, insisting angrily that a bishop, coming to confer with the Emperor on grave matters, ought to be received in private. The Grand Chamberlain withdrew to consult his master; he brought back a message that the audience would be in the Consistory. There was some further wrangling; but in the end Ambrose consented, though not with a good grace, to waive the point of etiquette.[2]

When Maximus had taken his seat in the council-room, the Bishop was introduced. The Emperor rose to give him the customary kiss of salutation; but Ambrose, instead of approaching the throne, stood stiffly among the councillors. Some of them whispered to him to go up, and the Emperor himself called him. But Ambrose said, 'Why do you offer me a kiss, when you do not acknowledge me as a bishop? For, if you did acknowledge me, you would not receive me in this place.' 'You are upset, Bishop', said the Emperor. 'I am not upset by the insult', replied Ambrose, 'but I am ashamed at being forced to appear in a

---

[1] Ambros. *De Obitu Val.* 28.
[2] Id. *Ep.* 24. 2. Valentinian's 'rescriptum' may have been the reply to the letter of protest written by Maximus (above, pp. 291–3) in the spring.

place which is not proper for me.' 'But on your first embassy ,
retorted Maximus, 'you appeared in the Consistory.' 'That was
no fault of mine', said Ambrose. 'He who summoned me was to
blame for that, not I who came in answer to the summons.'
'Why did you come?' asked the Emperor. 'Because then I was
asking for peace on behalf of one who was your inferior, whereas
now I am asking it on behalf of one who is your equal.' 'By
whose favour, pray', sneered Maximus, 'is he my equal?' 'By
the favour of Almighty God', Ambrose thundered, 'who has
reserved for Valentinian the kingdom which He bestowed
on him.' Maximus was incensed by the insolent attitude of the
Bishop. 'It was you who tricked me', he cried, 'you and that
miscreant Bauto, who keeps the boy as a figurehead but wants
the kingdom for himself, yes, and who sent barbarians against
me. As if I also had not those whom I could bring! Why,
thousands of barbarians are in my pay. If I had not been withheld at the time when you first came, who could have resisted
me and my power?' 'You need not get into a passion', Ambrose
replied; 'there is no reason for being in a passion; listen with
patience while I answer your reproaches.'[1] He proceeded to
deal in a rhetorical and evasive fashion with the charge of
'trickery' brought against himself and Bauto, boasting that he
had been the means of saving Valentinian but at the same time
denying that any promise had been given in A.D. 383 concerning
a visit of the young sovereign to Gaul. He, on his side, accused
Maximus of causing the Juthungi to invade Rhaetia, and con-
trasted his treacherous conduct with that of Valentinian, who,
so far from instigating the Huns and Alans to attack his colleague, had actually paid them to withdraw from his frontiers.[2]
Then, pointing to the usurper's brother, Marcellinus, who was
standing on the right of the throne, he reminded Maximus of
Valentinian's magnanimity in sending him back to Gaul when
he had him in his power, and insisted that it was his duty to
make a suitable return and restore Gratian's dead body.[3] The
reason alleged for refusing this request—that the sight of the
remains might inflame the troops—was futile, for it was not to
be supposed that the soldiers would trouble themselves to avenge
in death one whom they had deserted in life. Moreover the
assertion of Maximus that he was innocent of Gratian's murder

---

[1] Ambros. *Ep.* 24. 3–5.          [2] Ibid. 24. 6–8.          [3] Ibid. 24. 9.

could hardly be believed, so long as he continued to deny him
decent burial. 'Let Valentinian have at least the remains of his
brother as a pledge of your peaceful intentions.'[1] Ambrose
added that he had heard that it was considered a grievance that
the adherents of the murdered Emperor were flocking to the
Court of Theodosius; 'but what else could you expect', he cried,
'when you threatened the fugitives with punishment, and killed
those who were taken, while Theodosius loaded them with gifts
and honours?' 'Whom have I killed?' Maximus interrupted.
'Vallio', said Ambrose. 'And what a man, what a soldier he
was! Did he deserve to be put to death for being loyal to his
master?' 'I did not order him to be killed,' Maximus protested.
'I have heard that such an order was given,' Ambrose replied.
'Well', Maximus owned, 'if he had not destroyed himself, I
had ordered him to be taken to Châlons and burnt alive there.'
'Exactly', cried Ambrose; 'and that is why it was believed that
you had him killed. And could any one suppose that he himself would be spared, when a valiant warrior, a loyal soldier, and
a true comrade was thus slain?'[2]

The tone taken by Ambrose at this interview is astonishing,
and can hardly be explained except on the assumption that
he deliberately sought a rupture with Maximus. He was resolved to make it quite impossible for any one hereafter to
suspect him of complicity with the usurper. He even took the
extreme step of excluding the latter from communion. The
ground of this action was not (as Paulinus asserts[3]) the murder
of Gratian; for Maximus had denied that he was responsible for
this crime, and it had never been formally proved against him.
Ambrose took a less direct, but not less effectual, way. He
refused to communicate with the Ithacian bishops who were
guilty of persecuting the Priscillianists to the death;[4] and in this
excommunication Maximus, who supported and communicated
with these bishops, was implicitly included. The Emperor,
vehemently enraged, used threatening language to Ambrose[5]
and at last ordered him to leave Trier without delay.[6] On his
homeward journey, in the autumn, A.D. 386, the Bishop wrote
to Valentinian a formal report of his mission. It ended with the

---

[1] Ambros. *Ep.* 24. 10.      [2] Ibid. 24. 11. On Vallio see above, pp. 220, 221.
[3] Paulinus, *Vita Ambros.* 19.                    [4] Ambros. *Ep.* 24. 12.
[5] Id. *De Obitu Valent.* 39.                      [6] Id. *Ep.* 24. 12.

words, 'Farewell, Sir; be well on your guard against a man who
is hiding war under the cloak of peace.'[1]

After this unfortunate embassy there was a pause. Maximus,
as Ambrose had rightly conjectured, was making secret preparations for war; the Court of Milan, undecided what it ought next
to do, did nothing; Ambrose, in order that there should be no
mistake about his breach with the usurper, published early in
A.D. 387 a commentary on Psalm 62 containing a violent attack
on the murderers of Gratian, whose punishment was prophesied.[2]
Later in the same year, however, Valentinian's Government
bestirred itself to make another effort for the preservation of the
peace. It sent as ambassador to Trier a Syrian named Domninus
—an honourable and loyal but extremely stupid statesman, who
had the confidence of the Empress Mother.[3] Unfortunately
Maximus realized the fatuity of the man, and resolved to use him
as an instrument for the transportation of his own army through
the carefully guarded Alpine passes into the plains of Italy. He
accordingly received the envoy with flattering cordiality, loaded
him with presents, and effusively welcomed all his proposals,
assuring him that there was nothing that he more ardently
desired than to be on terms of alliance and friendship with his
well-beloved young colleague. Soon the simple ambassador was
convinced that Ambrose had misunderstood or misrepresented
the situation, and that Valentinian had in reality no truer,
kinder, or more faithful friend than Magnus Maximus. Then
the Emperor made a proposal. As a proof of his goodwill, he
offered to send into Italy, along with Domninus, a body of
troops to assist Valentinian against the barbarians who were
threatening Pannonia. The gracious suggestion was received
with enthusiasm; and the delighted ambassador, who had now
no doubt whatever that his mission had been an immense success,
started happily for Italy with his military escort. Close behind
him, though taking care to keep well out of observation, Maximus, with the pick of his army, followed. In the wake of the
envoy, and therefore unsuspected by the troops which held the
passes, he crossed the Cottian Alps,[4] and traversed the difficult

---

[1] Ambros. *Ep.* 24. 13.

[2] *In ps. 61 enarr.* 16–26. On this work see Chapter xxii. For another attack on
Maximus see *Apol. David*, 27 (perhaps to be dated Whitsuntide, A.D. 387).

[3] On the embassy of Domninus, see Zosimus, iv. 42.    [4] Pacatus, *Panegyr.* 30.

marshy land which lay at their foot; then, having no further reason
for concealment, he openly marched his forces in the direction
of Milan. This took place in the autumn of A.D. 387.

Warned of the enemy's approach, Valentinian, with his
mother and his sister Galla, quitted the capital in September,
and fled (*via* Aquileia) to Thessalonica. Thence he sent to Theodosius, imploring him to come immediately to his help. The
Emperor of the East was astounded by the news of what had
occurred, and hurried away to Thessalonica, carrying with him
some of the leading members of the Constantinopolitan Senate.
On his arrival a council was held, and all present expressed the
opinion that Maximus ought to be punished.[1]

Maximus meanwhile had made himself master of Italy. The
change of rulers appears to have been effected with little disturbance. It is possible, indeed, that some cities offered resistance to the invader, and were consequently given up to pillage;
but the evidence for violence on any considerable scale is inconclusive.[2] The inhabitants of Italy were not disposed to
undertake a bloody war on behalf of their runaway Emperor
and his heretical mother; and Maximus, on his side, seems to
have behaved with moderation. Indeed, the only offence alleged
against him, after his advent on Italian soil, is the issue of an
order for the rebuilding of a synagogue in Rome which had
been burnt in a popular tumult. The Christians shook their
heads over this concession to unbelievers. 'No good will come
to this man,' they said. 'The Emperor has turned Jew!'[3]

Theodosius still hesitated to declare war, and at one time
seemed even inclined to make a bargain with the usurper.
Zosimus attributes this conduct to constitutional indolence;[4]
but we can understand that there may well have been sounder

---

[1] Zosimus, iv. 43.

[2] Ambrose (*Ep.* 39. 3) refers to the ruinous condition of various Italian cities—
Bologna, Modena, Reggio, Brescello, Piacenza, and others—and Baronius finds
here an allusion to the consequences of an ineffectual effort to resist the arms of
Maximus. But the passage (which is modelled on Cic. *ad fam.* iv. 5) seems to suggest
a desolation caused, not by human instrumentality (e.g. an invading army),
but by some natural cataclysm such as an earthquake. Perhaps the reference
is to the earthquakes mentioned by Marcellinus as having occurred in the autumn
of 394 (cf. Ambros. *De Obitu Theodos.* 1 'motus terrarum graves'). If this view
be adopted, *Ep.* 39 must have been written towards the end of A.D. 394, and
contains no allusion to the invasion of Maximus.

[3] Id. *Ep.* 40. 23.                              [4] Zosimus, iv. 44.

reasons for his attitude. War is always a risky game, and, in view of the conditions which prevailed in the Eastern Empire and of the ever-present barbarian menace on the frontiers, it could not be undertaken rashly. Moreover, so ultra-orthodox a prince as Theodosius must have found it embarrassing to champion the cause of a persecuting Arian, against a Catholic who publicly proclaimed that he had entered Italy with the express object of defending the faith of Nicaea.[1] A woman's cleverness, however, put an end to his vacillation. Since the death of his saintly wife, Flaccilla,[2] in A.D. 385, the Emperor had remained a widower; but he was a man of amorous temperament, extremely susceptible to feminine charms. Knowing this, the cunning Justina introduced into his presence her lovely daughter Galla, who joined with her mother in imploring him, with tears, to take up Valentinian's cause. Theodosius, though he did not immediately accede to the request, was moved by the touching spectacle of beauty in distress; presently his tender interest became an infatuation; at last he demanded the damsel's hand in marriage. Justina accorded her consent on one condition—that he should forthwith declare war on Maximus, avenge the murder of Gratian, and restore Valentinian to his kingdom.[3]

Before commencing hostilities, Theodosius deemed it expedient to reconcile Valentinian with the offended Catholics. He accordingly insisted that he should adopt the Nicene faith. The technical arguments presented by Court theologians were reinforced by the admonitions of the Emperor himself, who bluntly told his protégé that he ought not to be surprised either at his own recent misfortunes or at his enemy's successes; 'for you', said he, 'have been fighting against religion and Maximus on its side'.[4] Having reformed Valentinian's opinions to his own

---

[1] Sozomen. *H.E.* vii. 13; Theodoret. *H.E.* v. 14.

[2] Ambrose describes Flaccilla as 'fidelis anima Deo' (*De Obitu Theod.* 40), and Theodoret gives a glowing account of her piety and charity (*H.E.* v. 19). See also the *Oratio Funebris de Flaccilla* by Gregory Nyssen (Migne, *P.G.*, vol. iii of his works, pp. 877–92). She was the mother of Arcadius and Honorius, and of a daughter, Pulcheria, who predeceased her.

[3] Zosimus, iv. 44. On the other hand, the marriage of Theodosius with Galla is placed by some authorities as early as A.D. 385 (*Chron. Pasch*) or A.D. 386 (Marcellinus). I am inclined, however, to accept the account of Zosimus. Galla died in child-birth in A.D. 394 (Zos. iv. 57).

[4] See the letter which Theodosius had written to Valentinian, before the latter arrived at Thessalonica, Theodoret. *H.E.* v. 15; cf. Ambros. *Ep.* 53. 2.

and the bishops' satisfaction, Theodosius devoted himself, during the early months of A.D. 388, to completing his military prepara- tions.[1] He also sent messengers to John of Egypt—a very cele- brated anchorite who dwelt on the top of a mountain near Lycopolis in the Thebaid, and was held in high estimation on account of his prophecies and miracles—to make inquiry as to the issue of the approaching campaign. John predicted that he would be victorious.[2]

In June, A.D. 388, Theodosius marched towards the West.[3] He reached Stobi on June the 14th and Scupi (Uskub) on June the 21st; thence he pressed on by forced marches to Siscia (the modern Siszek) on the river Save, where the main body of the enemy was awaiting him. His panting and dust-covered troops spurred their horses into the stream, swam across to the farther bank, and charged their opponents with such fury that they almost immediately broke and fled.[4] About the same time, one of the three divisions of the Theodosian army, which had apparently moved up the valley of the Drave, won a second victory at Pettau, where some Western forces, under the com- mand of the usurper's brother Marcellinus, made for a while a stubborn stand, but at last, after suffering appalling losses, surrendered.[5]

From Siscia Theodosius swept on to Aemona (Laibach), which had been undergoing a long siege and now joyfully opened her gates to the deliverer. The people, led by priests in purple and white-robed civic dignitaries, crowded out to bid him welcome; the gates were crowned with garlands, the streets were hung with carpets and brilliantly illuminated.[6] Without pausing, how- ever, to enjoy the festivities, Theodosius pushed forward with incredible speed over the spurs of the Julian Alps, and in an amazingly short space of time arrived in the neighbourhood of Aquileia, whither Maximus, now stricken with panic, had pre- cipitately retreated.[7]

[1] For details see Pacatus, *Panegyr.* 32, 33; Zosimus, iv. 45.
[2] Augustin. *De Civitate Dei*, v. 26; *De cura gerend. pro mortuis*, 21.
[3] Materials for the history of the campaign against Maximus are supplied by Pacatus (*Panegyr.* 34–45), Zosimus (iv. 45–7), Orosius (vii. 35), and Ambrose (*Ep.* 40. 22 and 23). Consult generally H. Richter, *Das weströmische Reich besonders unter den Kaisern Gratianus, Valentinianus II und Maximus*; A. Güldenpenning and J. Ifland, *Der Kaiser Theodosius der Grosse*; H. Schiller, *Geschichte der römischen Kaiserzeit*, ii.
[4] Pacatus, *Panegyr.* 34.     [5] Ibid. 35, 36; Ambros. *Ep.* 40. 23.
[6] Pacatus, *Panegyr.* 37.     [7] Ibid. 38, 39.

The fates were against Maximus. An inopportune invasion of Franks and Saxons had disappointed his expectation of receiving reinforcements from Gaul.[1] He appears also to have made an unfortunate miscalculation. He had imagined that Theodosius would make his attack by sea, and had dispatched his best general, Andragathius—the murderer of Gratian—with the flower of his troops, in a fleet of swift cruisers to intercept him in the Adriatic. Owing to the same mistaken notion, he had neglected to secure the passes of the Alps; and the extraordinary rapidity of Theodosius's advance allowed him no opportunity of repairing the blunder.[2] Indeed, when the Eastern army descended into the plain of Italy, he had barely time to shut himself up, with a small body of Moorish mercenaries,[3] in the strong fortress of Aquileia.

Theodosius advanced to a spot three miles from the city, and thence sent forward a detachment of his troops to storm the walls. The garrison was too small to make an effective resistance. With little opposition, the attacking party forced an entrance, and swarmed through the streets in search of the usurper. They found him still alive—for, though he realized that all was lost, he lacked the resolution to put an end to his existence—sitting in state upon his throne, and distributing his treasure among his soldiers. In a moment they had struck the imperial diadem from his head and torn from his person the purple robe and scarlet shoes; then, binding his hands behind his back, they dragged him, like a runaway slave, to Theodosius' tribunal. The Eastern Emperor asked him sternly whether it was true, as he had given out, that he had usurped the throne with his approval? 'No', confessed Maximus, 'it is not true; but, if I had not pretended to have your approval, I could not have induced the troops to join in the rebellion.' Theodosius briefly upbraided him for his crime against the State; yet seemed half-inclined to show mercy to his former comrade. He did not interfere, however, when the soldiers laid violent hands on him and carried him off to execution.[4]

---

[1] Details are given in a fragment of Sulpicius Alexander preserved in Gregory of Tours, *Hist. Franc.* ii. 9. There is an allusion to the invasion in Ambrose, *Ep.* 40. 23.

[2] Zosimus, iv. 46; Orosius, vii. 35; Ambros. *Ep.* 40. 22.

[3] Pacatus, *Panegyr.* 45.

[4] Zosimus, iv. 46; Pacatus, *Panegyr.* 41–4. Idatius and Prosper mention that Maximus was killed three miles from Aquileia. Philostorgius states that he was beheaded (x. 8). Another account of his end is given by Sozomen, who alleges that

Thus Maximus paid the penalty of his extravagant ambition on the 28th of July, A.D. 388.[1] The orator of Bordeaux, Latinus Pacatus Drepanius, has exhausted the resources of rhetoric in a malignant attack on his reputation. But the view taken of his character, both as a man and as a sovereign, by less prejudiced authorities is not unfavourable. Personally, though greedy of power and not scrupulous as to the means which he used to obtain it, he was by no means deficient in praiseworthy qualities; and he appears to have been (notwithstanding his drastic financial policy)[2] a vigorous, just, and conscientious ruler. Two grave mistakes, however—the murder of Gratian and the execution of the Priscillianists—have left a dark stain upon his memory.

In less than two months, and with comparatively trifling loss to himself,[3] Theodosius had finished the war. By superior strategy, and especially by that lightning rapidity of movement which left his adversary no time to revise his plans or to recover from reverses, he had completely shattered the land-power of Maximus. A naval victory in the neighbourhood of Sicily[4] destroyed what remained of the latter's strength at sea.[5] In gratitude for his quick success, the conqueror was disposed to act with clemency. It is true that the son of Maximus, Flavius Victor, who had been left as regent in Gaul, was put to death by Count Arbogast, who was sent thither for this purpose;[6] but the daughters of Maximus were not only spared, but suitably provided for, and his mother was pensioned.[7] The adherents of the usurper (excepting a few of the leaders and the Moorish guards, who were massacred) were granted a free pardon.[8]

---

he was slain by the treachery of his own soldiers (*H.E.* vii. 14). Ausonius congratulates Aquileia on having been the scene of the tyrant's execution (*Clarae Urbes*, vii).

[1] So Idatius, probably correctly; Socrates, however, gives 27 August as the date of the execution (*H.E.* v. 14). See G. Rauschen, op. cit., p. 283.

[2] Pacatus, *Panegyr.* 25, 26.

[3] Ambros. *Ep.* 40. 22 'intra ipsum Alpium vallum victoriam tibi contuli, ut sine damno vinceres'. The point is emphasized, and probably exaggerated, by Orosius, vii. 35.                                                                 [4] Ambros. *Ep.* 40. 23.

[5] Andragathius, having been informed of the defeat and death of Maximus, threw himself into the sea and was drowned, Orosius, vii. 35; Zosimus, iv. 47; Claudian, *De IV Cons. Honor.* 91, 92. Pacatus, however, seems to say that he was drowned in the river Save, *Panegyr.* 34; cf. Socrates, *H.E.* v. 14; Sozomen. *H.E.* vii. 14.

[6] Zosimus, iv. 47; cf. G. Rauschen, op. cit., p. 283.       [7] Ambros. *Ep.* 40. 32.

[8] Pacatus, *Panegyr.* 45; Ambros. *Ep.* 40. 25. Ambrose affirms that the pardon was granted at his own request—'me petente'.

Even Symmachus, who had publicly recited a panegyric on the tyrant, and who, in fear for his life, had fled for sanctuary to a Christian church, was forgiven, at the intercession of the bishop of the Novatianist sect in Rome.[1]

Meanwhile Valentinian proceeded by sea to Rome;[2] thence, after a short stay at Milan, he went to reside in Gaul, the administration of which was assigned to him by Theodosius. Either before his departure for Gaul, or during some subsequent visit to Italy, he became reconciled with Ambrose. He seems, indeed, to have developed a real affection for the great Bishop, 'so that he loved him whom he had formerly persecuted, and esteemed as a father him whom he had formerly repulsed as an enemy.'[3] Ambrose, on his side, was willing to forgive the past, and received the returning prodigal with generous charity.[4] As for Justina, obdurate in heresy to the end, she seems to have died in this year, shortly before or shortly after her son's restoration.[5]

Theodosius, with a magnificent gesture, not only reinstated Valentinian in his kingdom,[6] but also added to his dominions the territories once ruled by Gratian.[7] But this was no more than a gesture. The youth of seventeen, who had always been under the control of somebody—first of Gratian, and then of Justina and her ministers—was incapable of ruling. Although he was sovereign in name, and although he was graciously allowed to exercise some of the prerogatives of a sovereign, he was in fact completely dependent on the virile Theodosius—the sole actual and absolute master of both the East and the West.

It is necessary now to go back a year, and take account of an event which throws an interesting light on the character of Theodosius, on the relationship between the Emperor and the Church in the East, and on the social, political, and religious life of the time. This event is the notorious sedition at Antioch.[8]

---

[1] Socrates, *H.E.* v. 14.  [2] Zosimus, iv. 45.

[3] Ambros. *Ep.* 53. 2.

[4] Id. *De Obitu Val.* 79. There may be a reference to Valentinian's deliverance at this time, both from external perils and heretical errors, in *Expos. ev. Luc.* ix. 32.

[5] Rufinus, *H.E.* ii. 17; Sozomen, *H.E.* vii. 14. But Zosimus (iv. 47) states that after the restoration she resided with her son, assisting his inexperience with her prudent counsels.

[6] Augustin. *De Civitate Dei*, v. 26.  [7] Zosimus, iv. 47.

[8] On the sedition see Chrysostom's series of Homilies, *Ad populum Antiochenum de Statuis* (Migne, *P.G.* xlix); Libanius, *Orat.* xix–xxii, xxx, xxxiv; Zosimus, iv. 41;

In the beginning of A.D. 387 the Emperor, being in need of money, determined to levy an extraordinary tax. It happened to be the fifth year of the reign of his son Arcadius and the ninth of his own;[1] and to celebrate the double festival—the Quinquennalia of Arcadius and his own Decennalia, kept a year too early—he directed that a substantial subsidy should be collected from the opulent Eastern cities. The magnitude of the sum demanded excited general indignation. At Alexandria meetings of protest were held and seditious outcries were raised in the theatre.[2] At Antioch there was a serious riot.

Antioch was pre-eminently the pleasure-city of the East. Its genial climate, its charming situation on the plain between Mount Cassius and the Orontes, only a few miles from the sea, its long, sheltered ambulatories glittering at night with thousands of lamps, its well-stocked bazaars, its laurel and cypress groves, its countless rivulets and fountains ministering perennial streams of exquisitely pure water—all these attractions drew to it a cosmopolitan population of about 200,000 people, devoted for the most part to the chase after enjoyment. Here life was a perpetual festival. Every sort and kind of amusement, reputable and disreputable, was available. The city teemed with singers, dancers, acrobats,[3] venal women, charioteers. The theatres advertised performances daily. The sumptuous baths were open to all comers at all hours. Horse-races—here, as in Rome, the chief delight of the proletariat—were held at frequent intervals. Olympic games, instituted in the time of Caracalla, were annually celebrated in the Grove of Daphne, and furnished the people of Antioch with a special means of recreation. It has been said that in no city of antiquity was pleasure so much the

Sozomen. *H.E.* vii. 23; Theodoret. *H.E.* v. 20. Consult especially A. Hug, 'Antiochia und der Aufstand des Jahres 387 n. Chr.', in *Studien aus dem klassischen Altertum*, i, pp. 133 ff.; also G. R. Sievers, *Das Leben des Libanius*, pp. 172 ff.; and G. Rauschen, op. cit., pp. 259–66, 512–20.

[1] Arcadius was created Augustus on 16 January, A.D. 383, Theodosius on 19 January, A.D. 379. Thus the fifth year of Arcadius commenced on 16 January, A.D. 387, and the ninth of Theodosius on 19 January of the same year. On such festivals as the fifth and tenth anniversaries of the sovereign's accession considerable public expenditure was incurred, and the troops expected a liberal donative; hence Theodosius's decision to combine the celebration of his own Decennalia (not strictly due for another year) with that of his son's Quinquennalia may have been taken from motives of economy.                                                    [2] Libanius, *Orat.* xix.

[3] Chrysostom gives an interesting description of some of their performances, *Hom. de Stat.* xix. 4.

main object of life, and duty so incidental. Of the inhabitants
of this gay place about 100,000 were nominally Christian,
though in their habits and behaviour they seem to have been
hardly distinguishable from their pagan neighbours. The upper
class was luxurious, effeminate, and dissipated. The mob, which
was noted for its scurrilous wit and its aptitude for the invention
of nicknames, was superlatively sensual and idle.[1] It was often
outrageously disrespectful to the authorities, but unlike the
Alexandrine mob, which loved risings and rebellions more than
anything in the world, it seldom indulged in acts of violence.[2]

The riot took place on the 4th of March, A.D. 387. The edict
imposing the levy was proclaimed by a herald in the presence
of a great concourse. Some of the leading citizens, on whom
the burden of the exaction fell, uttered petulant exclamations—
'Our life is not worth living; the city will be ruined; no one can
stand this crushing burden'[3]—but they were accustomed to
being bled, and had no thought of active resistance. The
excitable mob, however, which had nothing whatever to lose,
worked itself up into a frenzy. It went in search of Bishop
Flavian—a diplomatic prelate, who was known to be a
favourite at Court—with the intention of persuading him to
make representations to the Emperor; but unfortunately the
Bishop was not to be found.[4] Then the crowd became tumultuous. Egged on, it is said, by some rascally foreign adventurers,[5]
it rushed into one of the public baths, and smashed the great
brazen lamps which hung suspended from the ceiling. From the
bath it passed on to the Praetorium, the official residence of
the Count of the East. The great judgement-hall was empty,
for the inmates of the palace had fled; only the painted wooden
statues of the imperial family, ranged above the judicial chair,
silently confronted the invaders. Some mischievous street-boys
had stones in their hands, and they started to throw them at
the 'sacred' effigies. The rest joined in, and in a few moments
every statue was battered to pieces. Next the rioters turned

---

[1] When Juvenal denounced the moral degradation of Rome, the most scathing
reproach he could frame was that 'the Syrian Orontes has flowed into the Tiber'
(*Sat.* iii. 62).

[2] Chrysostom insists on the good character of the city in this respect; never before
had it been guilty of active sedition, *Hom. de Stat.* iii. 1.

[3] Ibid. v. 3.                                                [4] Libanius, *Or.* xix.

[5] Chrysostom, *Hom. de Stat.* ii. 3; iii. 1; vi. 1.

their attention to the brazen representations of Imperial Majesty which adorned the colonnades and open spaces of the city. The statues of Theodosius, of his gentle wife Flaccilla, of their children, and of the elder Theodosius, father of the Emperor, were dislodged from their pedestals, shockingly mutilated, and dragged, with ribald jests and roars of laughter, through the streets. The people by this time were utterly reckless. Bringing torches they set fire to the house of a principal citizen, and were preparing to burn the imperial palace. Suddenly, however, the commander of the garrison, with a company of archers, appeared upon the scene. Many of the rioters were taken into custody; the rest dispersed. By noon the streets of Antioch were quiet and empty. The tumult, which had lasted for about three hours, was over.[1]

When the citizens had time to reflect on the monstrous insult which had been offered to the Majesty of the Emperor,[2] and on the frightful consequences which might result therefrom, they were overcome with terror. They knew the temper of Theodosius, and realized that in his white-hot fury he was capable of anything—even of ordering a general massacre and the demolition of the city.[3] In panic they hastened to Flavian and implored him to go at once in person to Constantinople and plead with the Emperor for their forgiveness. The Bishop was an old man and in feeble health; his only sister was apparently at the point of death and needed his ministrations; moreover the season of the year was extremely unfavourable for undertaking a long and arduous journey of nearly eight hundred Roman miles. But he could not refuse the entreaties of his people.

---

[1] Libanius, *Or.* xix, xx, xxii; Zosimus, iv. 41; Sozomen. *H.E.* vii. 23.

[2] The statue represented the Imperial Majesty and to injure it deliberately was high treason. 'Whoever contemns the Emperor's statue is deemed to have injured the Emperor himself' (Ambros. *Expos. ps. cxviii*, 10. 25). The busts and statues of reigning emperors were crowned with flowers (ibid.) and saluted with profound respect (*Hexaem.* vi. 57). On the other hand, the fall of an emperor was signalized by the overthrow of his statues; see the accounts of the destruction of the statues of Domitian (Plin. *Panegyr.* 52. 4–5) and Commodus (Lamprid. 18. 12). Ambrose refers to the overthrow of the images of tyrants (*De Interpell. Job.* iv. 24; cf. *In ps. 38 enarr.* 27; *De Officiis,* i. 244).

[3] Chrysostom, *Hom. de Stat.* xvii. 1 'We had expected innumerable woes: that our property would be plundered, that the houses would be burned together with the inmates, that the city would be plucked up from the midst of the world, that its very fragments would be utterly destroyed, that its soil would be placed under the plough.' Cf. ibid. xii. 1.

Disregarding his age, his infirmities, the inclemency of the season, the difficulties of the journey, and even the claims of his sister in her extremity, he started for the Court on the 6th of March.[1] He travelled with all possible speed; for he hoped to overtake the Government couriers, who, bearing news of the sedition, had left Antioch two days before, but who had been delayed on their journey, perhaps by snowdrifts in the passes of Taurus.[2]

Meanwhile the authorities at Antioch endeavoured to atone for past neglect by punishing the arrested rioters with merciless severity. No excuses were admitted, nor was any allowance made for youth. Even children, who under ordinary circumstances would have been let off with a light reprimand, were condemned to be beheaded or buried alive or thrown to the beasts. As they were led away to 'the pit', armed soldiers guarding them on either side, their distracted mothers followed at a distance; but even they dared not approach them or lament aloud their piteous fate.[3]

The gay and noisy city, 'where once the multitudes of people swarmed like bees about their hive', became suddenly and strangely silent.

'There is a silence big with horror, and loneliness everywhere; the pleasant hum of the crowd is stifled; the city is stricken with speechlessness, like a city of the dead; all are silent under the calamity just as though they were turned to stone—profoundly silent, as though enemies had come upon them and had consumed them all at once by fire and sword.'[4]

Many of the inhabitants, abandoning their possessions, fled precipitately with their wives and families into the desert or to the mountains, where not a few died from exposure or were devoured by wild beasts;[5] it was remarked that the Cynic philosophers—'those long-bearded, cloak-wearing, staff-bearing fellows'—were among the first to run away.[6] Such citizens as remained barricaded themselves in their houses, as though they

---

[1] Chrysostom, *Hom. de Stat.* iii. 1; xxi. 1. Zosimus, iv. 41, wrongly states that Libanius was sent as delegate to the Emperor.

[2] Chrysostom, *Hom. de Stat.* vi. 2. Flavian did not overtake the couriers, for on his journey to Constantinople he met the Commissioners, whom the Emperor, having been informed of the riot, had ordered to proceed to Antioch, ibid. xxi. 2.

[3] Ibid. iii. 6.                                              [4] Ibid. ii. 2.

[5] Ibid. ii. 1; xi. 1; xiii. 1; xxi. 3: Libanius, *Or.* xxxiv.

[6] Chrysostom, *Hom. de Stat.* xvii. 2. On the cowardly philosophers see also ibid. xix. 1.

were in a state of siege. They were aware that the magistrates, having disposed of most of the criminals who had been caught red-handed, were looking for fresh victims, and they feared that, if they ventured to show themselves abroad, they would be noticed and summarily arrested. Cowering behind their bolted doors, surrounded by their trembling households, they had only one subject of thought and talk—'Who has been taken to-day? Who has been executed? How was it done?' If any one, braver than the rest, dared to sally out into the Forum —heretofore the liveliest, busiest, and most populous locality in the city—the dismal spectacle of two or three drooping and melancholy fellow creatures, creeping stealthily about like ghosts in the midst of the enormous solitude, speedily drove him within doors again.[1]

During this period of dreadful suspense, when 'the very souls of the people were shaken with terror, as the foundations of the city used to be shaken by earthquakes', John Chrysostom— that 'great clerk and godly preacher'—played the part of a true pastor to the Christian flock. Day after day the pallid little presbyter, with his bald pate, dome-like forehead, deep-set eyes, and 'spidery' frame, took his place in the ambo of the Golden Church, and, with unrivalled eloquence,[2] strove to tranquillize the frightened people. He took advantage of the opportunity to castigate some of their vices and follies—the ostentatious luxury of the rich,[3] the prevalence of slander and malicious gossip,[4] the artful devices for lessening the inconvenience of the Lenten fast,[5] the shocking irreverence of their behaviour in church,[6] and, above all, the objectionable habit of profane swearing, which appears to have been peculiarly rife among the Antiochenes.[7] Certainly he had a unique chance of producing a salutary

---

[1] Chrysostom, *Hom. de Stat.* ii. 2; for the deserted Forum, see ibid. xiii. 1.

[2] His eloquence was much admired by Libanius, who declared on his death-bed that he would have chosen John as his own successor, if the Christians had not stolen him (Sozomen. *H.E.* viii. 2).

[3] Chrysostom, *Hom. de Stat.* ii. 5–9.

[4] Ibid. iii. 5.

[5] Ibid. xv. 1. In xviii. 1 Chrysostom reproves those who rejoiced that Len was half over, as though they had gained a great victory.

[6] Ibid. xx. 2.

[7] On the universality of this bad habit, see especially ibid. xiv. 1. Chrysostom suggested a practical remedy. 'When you detect your wife or any of your household yielding to this evil habit, order them supperless to bed; and if you yourself are guilty, impose the same penalty on yourself' (ibid. v. 7). He threatened to exclude

3 A

impression. In these days of intense anxiety, when the hippo-drome and the theatres and even the workshops were closed,[1] the church was always thronged—just as a harbour, says Chry-sostom, gets crowded with shipping in foul weather.[2] It even became the fashion for people to attend service after dinner.[3] They listened to the homilies, long though they were, with rapt attention,[4] and not infrequently demonstrated their approval of a striking passage by applause.[5]

The great question which absorbed all minds was, What will the Emperor do to the city?[6] The wildest rumours flew about.[7] One day there was a panic, owing to the spread of a report that soldiers were coming to perpetrate an indiscriminate massacre. To calm the agitation, the Praetorian Praefect of the East (although he happened to be a pagan) went in person to the church, and spoke some soothing words. Chrysostom was grateful to the Praefect for his considerate act; but he was not a little mortified that, after so many of his own sermons, the Christian congregation should have needed a pagan's assurances to restore it to calmness.[8]

Thus three weeks passed away. About the middle of Lent, on Monday the 29th of March, two Imperial Commissioners arrived at Antioch—Hellebichus, the Commander-in-chief of the army quartered in the neighbourhood of Constantinople, and Caesarius, Master of the Offices. They brought with them a decree of punishment, which was to the following effect—the theatres, hippodrome, and other places of amusement, which were already closed, were not to be reopened; the baths also were to be closed; the grain-largesses were to cease; and Antioch itself, 'the beautiful Queen of the Orient',[9] was to be degraded from her rank and privileges as capital, the metropolitan honours being transferred to the petty coast-town of Laodicea.[10] The Commissioners were instructed to institute a drastic inquiry into the recent outrages. Their attention was directed more

swearers from the Holy Mysteries, until they should be reformed (ibid. xx. 9). For his exhortations on the subject, see ibid. i. 12; iv. 5; v. 7; vi. 6, 7; vii. 5; viii. 4; ix. 5; xi. 4; xii. 6; xiv. 1–6; xv. 5; xvi. 2; xix. 4; xx. 8, 9.

[1] Chrysostom, *Hom. de Stat.* xv. 1.                    [2] Ibid. iv. 1.
[3] Ibid. x. 1; cf. ix. 1.                                       [4] Ibid. ii. 3; iv. 1.
[5] Ibid. ii. 4; v. 2, 7; vii. 5; xvi. 2.                       [6] Ibid. vi. 7.
[7] Ibid. xi. 1.                                                    [8] Ibid. xvi. 1.
[9] Ammian. xxii. 9. 14, 'Orientis apex pulcher'.
[10] Chrysostom, *Hom. de Stat.* xvii; Theodoret. *H.E.* v. 20.

particularly to the conduct of the civic dignitaries and wealthy burghers, who, though they had not, of course, participated actively in the riot, had nevertheless—whether through cowardice or through disloyalty—made no effort to prevent or repress it.[1]

On the 29th of March Hellebichus and Caesarius entered the city in state. They were humane men and Christians, and Hellebichus, at any rate, had many friends among the citizens; but their business now was to terrorize them into abject penitence and submission, and they were determined to do the work thoroughly. On Tuesday, the day after their arrival, they held a preliminary inquiry at their lodgings. On Wednesday, the 31st of March, they took their seats before dawn in the Praetorium, and the judicial proceedings commenced.

It was long before the memory of that Black Wednesday died out in Antioch. Among the accused were many of the richest and most important citizens—men who lived in splendid houses[2] and kept studs of horses,[3] who had discharged with distinction civic offices, and who had exhibited games for the people at their own expense. They were now dragged to the tribunal like the lowest malefactors, and (with no advocates to plead for them) were immediately subjected to ruthless interrogation, being scourged till the torment wrung from them confessions or statements incriminating others. The doors of the Court were closed and guarded by soldiers, armed with swords and clubs; but the strokes of the scourges, the shrieks and moans of the tortured, and the harsh voices of the inquisitors could be heard in the ante-room beyond. This outer hall was filled with women—mothers and wives and daughters of the persons undergoing examination. Clad in deep mourning and unattended by friends or servants, they waited in agony, hour after hour, to get intelligence of the fate of their relatives. Some wept and prayed;

---

[1] Chrysostom, *Hom. de Stat.* ii. 4: 'We are dreading lest the wrath of the Emperor shall descend on all; for it is not sufficient for us to plead in defence, "I was not present; I was not an accomplice or sharer in these acts." "For this very reason", he may reply, "you shall be punished and pay the extreme penalty—because you were not present, and did not check or restrain the rioters, and did not run any risk for the honour of the Emperor. You say that you did not participate in those audacious deeds. I commend and approve that. But neither did you prohibit the doing of those things. This is a cause of accusation." '

[2] On the large and splendid houses of the wealthy citizens, see ibid. ii. 5.

[3] Ibid. xiii. 2; xviii. 1; cf. iii. 4.

some frantically implored the help of any one who was seen
passing into the Court; some, in the abandonment of despair,
flung themselves prostrate on the pavement in front of the closed
doors, grovelling almost under the feet of the rough soldiers who
kept order. Outside the Praetorium the terrified remnant of the
people gathered. They stood in unbroken silence, gazing fur-
tively on one another but not daring to speak, for each man suspected that his neighbour might be an informer. Only they
stretched out supplicating hands to Heaven, praying inwardly
that the hearts of the judges might be softened.

All day long the trials went on. Towards evening the orator
Libanius—who had remained honourably at his post and done
invaluable work in comforting and encouraging his afflicted
fellow citizens—stole timidly into the Court. Caesarius, to whom
he was known, observed him, and, pitying his anxiety, assured
him in a whisper that he and his colleague would pass no death
sentence. And indeed, though very many persons were found
guilty, none were condemned to suffer the extreme penalty, the
decision as to their punishment being reserved for the Emperor.
At the close of the day the convicted criminals, loaded with
irons, were led through the Forum to the jail. All their
properties were for the time confiscated, and the Government
seals were affixed to their doors. Their unhappy wives, accustomed to live in the greatest luxury, with troops of waiting-
maids and eunuchs to minister to their slightest whims, were
turned out homeless into the streets. It was with difficulty that
they obtained any shelter even for a night; for every man feared
that, by harbouring relatives of the condemned, he might bring
himself under suspicion.[1]

On the following day, Thursday, the 1st of April, as the Commissioners were riding from their lodgings to the Hall of Justice,
they encountered a throng of unwashed, unshorn, wild-looking
beings, clad in tattered and filthy sheepskins. They were hermits
from the mountains in the vicinity of Antioch, who, of their own
accord and uninvited, had left the caves and huts wherein for
years they had been immured, and come down 'like angels from
heaven' to comfort and help the stricken city. One of these, a
little ragged old man, ran forward, and, laying hold of the

---

[1] For a description of the scenes on the day of the trials, see Chrysostom, *Hom.
de Stat.* xiii. 1, 2 (cf. xx. 3); Libanius, *Or.* xxii.

military cloak of Hellebichus, imperiously ordered him and his companion to dismount. The indignant General repulsed him roughly. He was informed, however, that this was the revered solitary, Macedonius the Barley-eater—'a man totally ignorant of all learning, whether sacred or profane, who passed his days and nights on a mountain-top, offering pure prayers to the Saviour of mankind'. Immediately the two Commissioners alighted, and, clasping the knees of the uncouth saint, apologized for their rudeness. 'My friends', said the hermit, 'go to the Emperor and say, "You are an emperor, but also a man, and you rule over beings of like nature with yourself. Now man was made in the image of God; do not then command God's image to be destroyed, and anger the Maker thereof. You are making all this stir about statues of bronze; but how far does a living creature surpass in value a lifeless image! It is easy to replace the statues; but if you put men to death, not one hair of their heads can be re-made." ' Others of the hermits clamoured for a general pardon of all the criminals. When the judges explained that this could be granted only by the Emperor, they pleaded that they themselves might be sent as intercessors to the Court. 'Our sovereign', they cried, 'is a religious man, faithful and pious; we shall assuredly appease him. We will not let you stain the sword with the blood of these people; if they die, we are resolved to die with them. Great indeed are the crimes which have been committed, but the Emperor's clemency is greater still.' The Commissioners were not prepared to send these strange petitioners to Constantinople. They agreed, however, that Caesarius should proceed thither immediately, carrying with him a plea for mercy drawn up in writing at the dictation of the hermits; and that until the will of the Emperor, after the receipt of this appeal, was known, the judicial proceedings in the Praetorium should be suspended.[1]

On the same day, the 1st of April, Caesarius left Antioch, amid the blessings of the people, and, travelling day and night, reached Constantinople in less than a week.[2] He found Theodosius

---

[1] Theodoret. *H.E.* v. 20; Chrysostom, *Hom. de Stat.* xvii (cf. xviii. 4). Chrysostom says that the appeal of the hermits was zealously seconded by the bishops of the neighbouring towns and by the local clergy, who intercepted the Commissioners on their way to the Court, embracing their knees and kissing their hands, and would not suffer them to proceed until they had extorted from them satisfactory assurances.

[2] Libanius, *Or.* xxi. Libanius attributes the pardon to the good offices of

already mollified by the prayers and tears of Flavian. There can be little doubt that the Bishop had had several interviews with the Emperor, though Chrysostom, dramatically summarizing what had occurred, speaks as though there had been only one.[1] The account which he gives is briefly as follows. Being introduced into the imperial presence, Flavian at first had said no word, but with bowed head and covered face, had stood at a distance weeping, as though he himself had been responsible for his city's crimes. Even the choleric Emperor was touched by his distress. Advancing towards him, he complained, but without harshness, of the ingratitude of the city, which he had always treated generously, and which he had long desired to visit; even if the people had grounds for reproach against himself, they might at least have refrained from insult to his wife and father— 'the dead who had never done them any wrong'.[2] The Bishop, in his reply, did not attempt to make excuses. The crime was enormous, and deserved the severest chastisement. It could only be supposed that demons, jealous of the imperial favours to the city, had seduced the people from their allegiance—demons, who would triumph, if the Emperor determined on revenge.[3] If, on the other hand, he forgave the insult offered to him, he would discomfit the demons, and win for himself a crown of virtue more honourable and splendid even than the imperial diadem. What if his statues had been thrown down? By a free pardon he could set up in the hearts of his thankful subjects an image of himself far more enduring and far more glorious than the gilded effigies that had been demolished. Years ago the Emperor Constantine, when the head of one of his statues had been damaged by the mob with stones, had refused to notice the affront, and said smiling, as he passed his hand over his face and head, 'I do not find any injury here'—a saying which had won

Caesarius, Chrysostom to those of Flavian; but the two accounts are not inconsistent.

[1] Chrysostom, *Hom. de Stat.* xxi. Chrysostom obtained his information from an eyewitness, but not from Flavian himself, who modestly declined to give any account of his successful negotiations with the Emperor.

[2] Ibid. xxi. 2.

[3] For the attribution of the riot to the instigation of demons, cf. ibid. iii. 6. Libanius tells of an old man among the rioters, who changed under their eyes to a youth, then to a boy, and finally vanished (*Or.* xix). Sozomen also has a story of a gigantic female figure, terrible of aspect, who paraded the streets of the city, brandishing a scourge, on the night before the riot (*H.E.* vii. 23).

him more fame than all his victories. And only recently Theodosius himself, when he issued letters for a general release of prisoners at Easter, had written, 'Would to God that I could also recall the dead to life!' That aspiration might now be realized. Antioch, dead with remorse and fear, might be miraculously restored to life by the Emperor's gracious word. Such clemency would not only strengthen the imperial throne; it would advance the cause of Christianity. For Jews and heathen, even barbarians, were watching to see what Theodosius would do; if he showed mercy, they would cry, 'Heavens! how wonderful is the power of the Christian religion, which has restrained the wrath of a monarch who has not his equal upon earth, and taught him to exhibit a degree of philosophy of which even a private person is seldom capable! Great indeed must be the God of the Christians, who makes men into angels and raises them above the limitations of human nature.' Let the Emperor, then, refrain from further punishment of a city which, in its agonies and terrors, had already suffered perhaps more than enough. Let him rather listen favourably to the words of one aged priest, who came into his presence not merely as the delegate of the poor, panic-stricken people of Antioch, but also as the ambassador of the 'common Lord of angels and men', to remind him that to forgive is the condition of receiving forgiveness. 'Remember, then, that Day when we shall all give an account of our actions. Reflect that, if you have sins, you will be able to wash them away, without difficulty and without toil, by a merciful sentence. I am come before Your Majesty with the holy laws, and exhort you to imitate your Lord, who though daily offended by us, unceasingly ministers His blessings to all,'[1]

By such arguments Theodosius became gradually appeased; and when Caesarius presented the hermits' petition, backing it with a strong recommendation of his own, the last vestiges of his anger vanished. He consented to rescind the decree which had deprived Antioch of her privileges and to grant a free pardon to the inhabitants. 'If the Master of the world', said he, 'prayed for forgiveness for those who crucified Him, what wonder is it

---

[1] Chrysostom, *Hom. de Stat.* xxi. 3. According to Chrysostom, Flavian ended his appeal with the curious threat that, if the Emperor refused to pardon Antioch, he himself would not return thither or acknowledge it as his city: 'for God forbid that I should ever belong to a country which you, the most mild and merciful of all men, refuse to admit to peace and reconciliation!'

that a man should forgive his fellow men?' He was now as
intent on showing kindness as he had lately been on taking
vengeance. When Flavian, as a mark of his gratitude, offered to
remain a little longer in Constantinople and celebrate Easter with
his sovereign, he considerately declined the proposal. 'I know',
he said, 'that your people are in great affliction; go and comfort
them. When they see the steersman again at the helm, they will
forget the storm which has passed away.' Flavian ventured to
suggest that, in token of his complete reconciliation, he should
send his son Arcadius to Antioch; but this petition was not
granted. 'Pray', said the Emperor, 'that the present obstacles
may be removed and these wars brought to an end, and then I
will certainly come myself.' Even after the Bishop had crossed
the Bosphorus on his homeward way, Theodosius sent after him
messengers to expedite his journey, lest the joy of his people in
the Easter celebration should be marred by their pastor's absence. Flavian, for his part, lost no time; but in order to relieve
the anxiety of the city at the earliest possible moment, he
generously determined to forgo the great pleasure of bringing
the tidings of pardon himself, and dispatched a courier to deliver
the imperial letters to Hellebichus.[1]

Meanwhile at Antioch the situation had become less tense.
The delirious terror of the people had subsided, and been replaced by a fairly confident hope that the appeals to the Emperor's clemency would be effectual.[2] But, though relieved from
the dread of destruction by the sword, the citizens were far from
happy. They were deeply mortified by the degradation of their
city from its metropolitan rank,[3] and the compulsory closing of
all places of amusement depressed their spirits. They were
specially affected by their exclusion from the baths, which, for
dwellers in a hot climate, were almost indispensable for health
as well as for comfort.[4] Deprived of this much-needed luxury,
the dirty, perspiring rabble, both men and women, flocked to
the bank of the Orontes, and, with unseemly merriment and

---

[1] Chrysostom, *Hom. de Stat.* xxi. 4.

[2] Ibid. xi. 1; xii. 1; xiii. 1; xvii. 1.

[3] Ibid. xvii. 2. 'It is complained that the Emperor has taken away the dignity
of the city, and has no more permitted it to be called a metropolis. . . . I have heard
many in the Forum saying, "Alas for thee, Antioch! What has become of thee?
How art thou dishonoured!" '

[4] Ibid. xiv. 6.

frank disregard of decency, promiscuously sought refreshment in the cooling waters.[1] Moreover, though the common people had got off lightly, and seemed to be now secure from danger, this was not by any means the case with the more aristocratic citizens.[2] Herded together in a jail which was so overcrowded that they hardly had room to stretch themselves for sleep, fed on scandalously bad and insufficient rations, faced with the prospect of a cruel and ignominious death at the hands of the executioner, these once-prosperous senators and civic functionaries were in pitiable plight. Hellebichus himself was moved by their sufferings, and, by piercing the wall between the congested prison and the Senate-House, provided the captives with more adequate shelter and accommodation.[3]

But at last the long-drawn agony ended. On Thursday in Holy Week, the 22nd of April, the courier sent forward by Flavian with the letters of pardon entered Antioch. The people abandoned themselves to rejoicings. The Forum was hung with garlands, the streets and porticoes were illuminated, and couches were spread in front of the workshops for a public feast.[4] Hellebichus showed himself, and received a tremendous ovation. On Holy Saturday, the 24th of April, Bishop Flavian drove through the Northern Gate, just in time to keep the Easter festival with his people. Finally, on the morning of Easter Day, John Chrysostom related to a vast congregation in the Great Church the story of the Bishop's intercession with the Emperor, and exhorted his hearers to give hearty thanks to God, not only for delivering them from the peril of destruction, but also for having visited them with so wholesome a chastisement, the salutary effects of which—so, at least, he hoped—would last for many generations.[5]

To the historian this affair at Antioch is in many respects instructive. Not least among the points of interest is the illustration which it furnishes of the attitude of the Eastern episcopate,

---

[1] Chrysostom, *Hom. de Stat.* xviii. 4.

[2] Chrysostom contrasts their miserable situation with the freedom from peril enjoyed by the mob, ibid. xviii. 1.

[3] Libanius, *Or.* xxii.          [4] Chrysostom, *Hom. de Stat.* xxi. 4.

[5] Ibid. One happy result of these troubles was the conversion of many of the pagan inhabitants of Antioch to Christianity. Chrysostom elsewhere mentions the labour imposed on him, after Flavian's return, of instructing those who, in consequence of the events related, had 'deserted from Gentile error' (*Hom. de Anna,* i. 1).

represented by Flavian, towards the Emperor. The Bishop of
Antioch was a God-fearing, public-spirited, and courageous
man; nevertheless, in the Emperor's presence, he showed an
exaggerated deference, even a servility of demeanour, such as
the typical Oriental is accustomed to exhibit when face to face
with an absolute potentate. He wept, he apologized, he pleaded;
he used every device for convincing the reason and touching the
feelings: the one thing which he never so much as thought of
doing was to command. Even when he reminded his august
hearer of the Divine law of forgiveness, he spoke with the discreet adroitness of a courtier rather than with the authority of a
bishop, seeming to suggest a desirable course rather than enjoin
an imperative duty. All this is characteristic of the attitude of
the Eastern hierarchy towards that immeasurably exalted
personage whom Chrysostom with awe describes as 'without
peer upon earth, for he is the Head and Crown of everything in
the world'.[1] Very different was the behaviour of Ambrose—true
representative, as he was, of that strong and defiant Western
Church which again and again in the course of its history has
forced sovereigns to bow before it. When Theodosius moved
away from the East and the flattering subservience of Eastern
prelates, and encountered the Churchmanship of the West
embodied in the robust and dominating personality of the
Bishop of Milan, he must have experienced a shock. But an
account of the relations between Ambrose and the Augustus had
better be reserved for a separate chapter.

[1] Chrysostom, *Hom. de Stat.* ii. 2. Yet Chrysostom did not hesitate to maintain
that a bishop, a prince of the Church, was even greater in dignity than the Emperor:
'for the sacred laws take and place under his hands even the royal head; and
when there is need of any good thing from above, the Emperor resorts to the priest,
not the priest to the Emperor' (ibid. iii. 2).

PRINTED IN
GREAT BRITAIN
AT THE
UNIVERSITY PRESS
OXFORD
BY
JOHN JOHNSON
PRINTER
TO THE
UNIVERSITY

# Date Due

DEMCO-293

| | | | |
|---|---|---|---|
| JUL 21 1960 | | | |
| AUG 4 1960 | | | |
| DEC 13 1960 | | | |
| JAN 1 7 1961 | | | |
| FEB 9 1965 | | | |
| APR 1 1965 | | | |
| MAR 1 9 1971 | | | |
| FEB 1 5 1973 | | | |
| AUG 2 4 1996 | | | |
| | | | |
| | | | |
| | | | |
| SEP 0 5 1997 | | | |
| | | | |
| | | | |
| | | | |